AUTOMOTIVE ENGINES
THEORY AND SERVICING

SIXTH EDITION

James D. Halderman

PEARSON

Prentice
Hall

Upper Saddle River, New Jersey
Columbus, Ohio

Library of Congress Cataloging-in-Publication Data

Halderman, James D.
  Automotive engines : theory and servicing / James D. Halderman. 6th ed.
     p. cm.
  Includes index.
  ISBN 978-0-13-503689-1
  1. Automobiles—Motors. 2. Automobiles—Motors—Maintenance and repair. I. Title.
  TL210.H29 2009
  629.25'040288--dc22

                                    2008024507

Editor in Chief: Vernon Anthony
Acquisitions Editor: Wyatt Morris
Editorial Assistant: Christopher Reed
Production Coordination: Kelli Jauron, S4Carlisle Publishing Services
Project Manager: Holly Shufeldt
Operations Specialist: Laura Weaver
Art Director: Candace Rowley
Cover and Interior Design: Candace Rowley
Director of Marketing: David Gesell
Marketing Assistant: Les Roberts

This book was set in Weidemann by S4Carlisle Publishing Services and was printed and bound by Edwards Brothers. The cover was printed by Phoenix Color Corp.

Pearson Education Ltd., London
Pearson Education Singapore Pte. Ltd.
Pearson Education Canada, Inc.
Pearson Education—Japan

Pearson Education Australia Pty. Limited
Pearson Education North Asia Ltd., Hong Kong
Pearson Educación de Mexico, S.A. de C.V.
Pearson Education Malaysia Pte. Ltd.

10 9 8 7 6 5 4 3 2 1
ISBN-13: 978-0-13-503689-1
ISBN-10:   0-13-503689-5

PREFACE

PROFESSIONAL TECHNICIAN SERIES

Part of Prentice Hall Automotive's Professional Technician Series, the sixth edition of *Automotive Engines: Theory and Servicing* presents students and instructors with a practical, real-world approach to automotive technology and service. The series includes textbooks that cover all eight ASE certification test areas of automotive service: Engine Repair (A1), Automotive Transmissions/Transaxles (A2), Manual Drive Trains and Axles (A3), Suspension and Steering (A4), Brakes (A5), Electrical/Electronic Systems (A6), Heating and Air Conditioning (A7), and Engine Performance (A8).

Current revisions are written by the experienced author and peer reviewed by automotive instructors and experts in the field to ensure technical accuracy.

UPDATES TO THE SIXTH EDITION

The sixth edition has been updated throughout and now has 31 chapters compared to 24 chapters in the fifth edition.

- An expanded chapter on shop safety includes how to safely de-power hybrid electric vehicles (Chapter 1).
- Information on hand tools (Chapter 4) and power tools/shop equipment (Chapter 5) has been expanded and now each is covered in a separate chapter.
- Service information (Chapter 8) and vehicle identification information (Chapter 9) are now in separate chapters to make learning and teaching this material easier.
- Updated chapters on the cooling system (Chapter 13) and the lubrication system (Chapter 14) include many changes in the industry and systems.
- Expanded coverage on automotive fuels now includes all alternative fuels (Chapter 11).
- Expanded coverage on diesel engines includes the new after-treatment devices needed for diesel engines to meet the latest emissions standards (Chapter 12).

- A new chapter on preparation for assembly (Chapter 29) details all of the steps and procedures that are needed to successfully blueprint and assemble an engine.
- There is expanded coverage on variable valve timing and variable displacement engines (Chapter 10).

ASE AND NATEF CORRELATED

NATEF-certified programs need to demonstrate that they use course materials that cover NATEF and ASE tasks. This textbook has been correlated to the ASE and NATEF task lists and offers comprehensive coverage of all tasks. A NATEF TASK CORRELATION CHART and an ASE TEST CORRELATION CHART are located in the appendices to the book.

A COMPLETE INSTRUCTOR AND STUDENT SUPPLEMENTS PACKAGE

This textbook is accompanied by a full package of instructor and student supplements. See page vi for a detailed list of all supplements available with this book.

A FOCUS ON DIAGNOSIS AND PROBLEM SOLVING

The Professional Technician series has been developed to satisfy the need for a greater emphasis on problem diagnosis. Automotive instructors and service managers agree that students and beginning technicians need more training in diagnostic procedures and skill development. To meet this need and demonstrate how real-world problems are solved, the "Real World Fix" features are included throughout and highlight how real-life problems are diagnosed and repaired.

The following pages highlight the unique core features that set the Professional Technician series apart from other automotive textbooks.

IN-TEXT FEATURES

OBJECTIVES and **KEY TERMS** appear at the beginning of each chapter to help students and instructors focus on the most important material in each chapter. The chapter objectives are based on specific ASE and NATEF tasks.

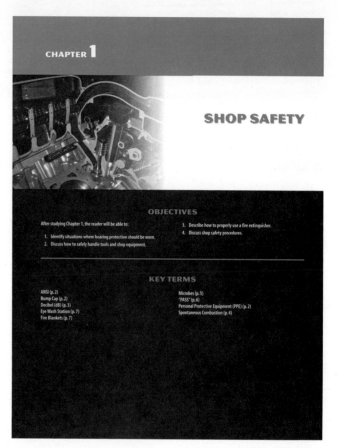

CHAPTER 1

SHOP SAFETY

OBJECTIVES

After studying Chapter 1, the reader will be able to:

3. Describe how to properly use a fire extinguisher.
4. Discuss shop safety procedures.

1. Identify situations where hearing protection should be worn.
2. Discuss how to safely handle tools and shop equipment.

KEY TERMS

ANSI (p. 2)
Bump Cap (p. 2)
Decibel (dB) (p. 3)
Eye Wash Station (p. 7)
Fire Blankets (p. 7)

Microbes (p. 5)
"PASS" (p. 6)
Personal Protective Equipment (PPE) (p. 2)
Spontaneous Combustion (p. 4)

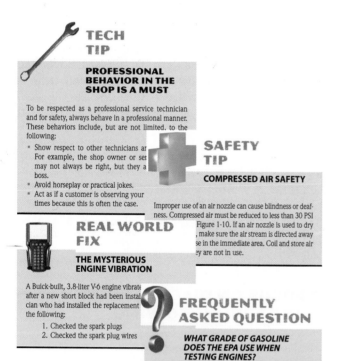

TECH TIP

PROFESSIONAL BEHAVIOR IN THE SHOP IS A MUST

To be respected as a professional service technician and for safety, always behave in a professional manner. These behaviors include, but are not limited. to the following:

- Show respect to other technicians ar For example, the shop owner or ser may not always be right, but they a boss.
- Avoid horseplay or practical jokes.
- Act as if a customer is observing your times because this is often the case.

SAFETY TIP

COMPRESSED AIR SAFETY

Improper use of an air nozzle can cause blindness or deafness. Compressed air must be reduced to less than 30 PSI Figure 1-10. If an air nozzle is used to dry , make sure the air stream is directed away se in the immediate area. Coil and store air ey are not in use.

REAL WORLD FIX

THE MYSTERIOUS ENGINE VIBRATION

A Buick-built, 3.8-liter V-6 engine vibrate after a new short block had been instal cian who had installed the replacement the following:

1. Checked the spark plugs
2. Checked the spark plug wires

FREQUENTLY ASKED QUESTION

WHAT GRADE OF GASOLINE DOES THE EPA USE WHEN TESTING ENGINES?

Due to the various grades and additives used in commercial fuel, the government (EPA) uses a liquid called indolene. Indolene has a research octane number of 96.5 and a motor method octane rating of 88, which results in an R + M ÷ 2 rating of 92.25.

TECH TIPS feature real-world advice and "tricks of the trade" from ASE-certified master technicians.

SAFETY TIPS alert students to possible hazards on the job and how to avoid them.

REAL WORLD FIXES present students with actual automotive service scenarios and show how these common (and sometimes uncommon) problems were diagnosed and repaired.

FREQUENTLY ASKED QUESTIONS are based on the author's own experience and provide answers to many of the most common questions asked by students and beginning service technicians.

NOTES provide students with additional technical information to give them a greater understanding of a specific task or procedure.

CAUTIONS alert students about potential *damage to the vehicle* that can occur during a specific task or service procedure.

WARNINGS alert students to potential *harm to the technician* that could occur during a specific task or service procedure.

NOTE: The release of only 1 gallon of used oil (a typical oil change) can make a million gallons of fresh water undrinkable.

CAUTION: Never use compressed air to blow brake dust. The fine, talc-like brake dust can create a health hazard even if asbestos is not present or is present in dust rather than fiber form.

WARNING: Hazardous waste disposal laws include serious penalties for anyone responsible for breaking these laws.

STEP-BY-STEP photo sequences show in detail the steps involved in performing a specific task or service procedure.

HEATING METAL Step-by-Step

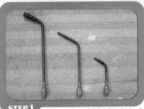

STEP 1 Heating attachments include ordinary heating tips (middle and right) and a "rosebud" (left). Ordinary heating tips work fine for most purposes, but occasionally the rosebud is utilized when a great deal of heat is needed.

STEP 2 Note that while acetylene bottle pressures are relatively low, the oxygen bottle can be filled to over 2000 psi. This can represent a serious hazard if precautions are not taken. Be absolutely certain that the bottles are chained properly to the cart before attempting to move it!

STEP 3 Any time heating or cutting operations are being performed, be sure that any flammables have been removed from the immediate area. A fire blanket may be placed over floor drains or other objects to prevent fires. A fire extinguisher should be on hand in case of an emergency.

STEP 4 Be sure to wear appropriate personal protective equipment during heating and cutting operations.

STEP 5 Note that heating operations should be performed over steel or firebrick. Never heat or cut steel close to concrete, as it could cause the concrete to explode.

STEP 6 When heating steel, move the torch in a circular pattern to prevent melting of the metal. Don't hold the torch too close to the work as this will cause a "snapping" or "backfire" that can extinguish the flame.

The **SUMMARY, REVIEW QUESTIONS, AND CHAPTER QUIZ** at the end of each chapter help students review the material presented in the chapter and test their mastery of the material.

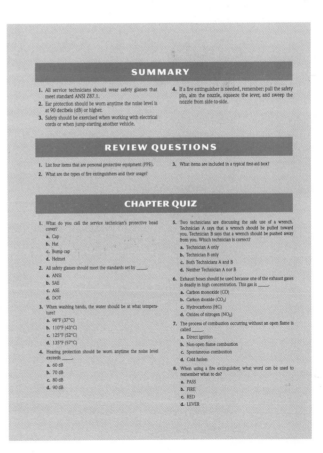

SUMMARY

1. All service technicians should wear safety glasses that meet standard ANSI Z87.1.
2. Ear protection should be worn anytime the noise level is at 90 decibels (dB) or higher.
3. Safety should be exercised when working with electrical cords or when jump-starting another vehicle.
4. If a fire extinguisher is needed, remember: pull the safety pin, aim the nozzle, squeeze the lever, and sweep the nozzle from side-to-side.

REVIEW QUESTIONS

1. List four items that are personal protective equipment (PPE).
2. What are the types of fire extinguishers and their usage?
3. What items are included in a typical first-aid box?

CHAPTER QUIZ

1. What do you call the service technician's protective head cover?
   a. Cap
   b. Hat
   c. Bump cap
   d. Helmet
2. All safety glasses should meet the standards set by _____.
   a. ANSI
   b. SAE
   c. ASE
   d. DOT
3. When washing hands, the water should be at what temperature?
   a. 98°F (37°C)
   b. 110°F (43°C)
   c. 125°F (52°C)
   d. 135°F (57°C)
4. Hearing protection should be worn anytime the noise level exceeds _____.
   a. 60 dB
   b. 70 dB
   c. 80 dB
   d. 90 dB
5. Two technicians are discussing the safe use of a wrench. Technician A says that a wrench should be pulled toward you. Technician B says that a wrench should be pushed away from you. Which technician is correct?
   a. Technician A only
   b. Technician B only
   c. Both Technicians A and B
   d. Neither Technician A nor B
6. Exhaust hoses should be used because one of the exhaust gases is deadly in high concentration. This gas is _____.
   a. Carbon monoxide (CO)
   b. Carbon dioxide (CO$_2$)
   c. Hydrocarbons (HC)
   d. Oxides of nitrogen (NO$_x$)
7. The process of combustion occurring without an open flame is called _____.
   a. Direct ignition
   b. Non-open flame combustion
   c. Spontaneous combustion
   d. Cold fusion
8. When using a fire extinguisher, what word can be used to remember what to do?
   a. PASS
   b. FIRE
   c. RED
   d. LEVER

SUPPLEMENTS

The comprehensive **INSTRUCTOR'S MANUAL** includes chapter outlines, answers to all questions from the book, teaching tips, and additional exercises.

An **INSTRUCTOR'S RESOURCE CD-ROM** features:

- A complete text-specific **TEST BANK WITH TEST CREATION SOFTWARE**
- A comprehensive, text-specific **POWERPOINT PRESENTATION** featuring much of the art from the text as well as video clips and animations
- An **IMAGE LIBRARY** featuring additional images to use for class presentations
- Additional student activities including **CROSSWORD PUZZLES, WORD SEARCHES,** and other worksheets
- A **SAMPLE ASE TEST** as well as the complete **ASE TASK LIST**

To access supplmentary materials online, instructors need to request an instructor access code. Go to **www.pearson-highered.com/irc,** where you can register for an instructor access code. Within 48 hours after registering, you will receive a confirming e-mail, including an instructor access code. Once you have received your code, go to the site and log on for full instructions on downloading the materials you wish to use.

Available to be packaged with the book, the **STUDENT WORKTEXT** (NATEF CORRELATED TASK SHEETS), includes 100% of the job sheets tied to specific (A1) Engine Repair NATEF tasks. Contact your local Prentice Hall representative for information on ordering the textbook packaged with the student worktext.

Included with every copy of the book, access to the following website: www.pearsoned.com/autostudent. This resource contains powerpoint presentations, crosswood puzzles, word searches, a NATEF task checklist, a sample ASE test, and the complete ASE task list.

ACKNOWLEDGMENTS

A large number of people and organizations have cooperated in providing the reference material and technical information used in this text. The author wishes to express sincere thanks to the following organizations for their special contributions:

Auto Parts Distributors
Automotion, Inc.
Automotive Engine Rebuilders Association
B-H-J Products, Inc.
Camwerks Corporation
Castrol Incorporated
Champion Spark Plug Company
Chrysler Corporation
Clayton Manufacturing Company
Curtiss Wright Corporation
Dana Corporation
Defiance Engine Rebuilders Incorporated
Dow Chemical Company
Fel-Pro Incorporated
Ford Motor Company
General Motors Corporation, Service and Parts
    Operations
George Olcott Company
Goodson Auto Machine Shop Tools and Supplies
Greenlee Brothers and Company
Jasper Engines and Transmissions
K-Line
Linder Technical Services
Modine Manufacturing Company
Neway
Parsons and Meyers Racing Engines
Prestolite Company
Rottler Manufacturing
Sealed Power Corporation
Society of Automotive Engineers
Stanadyne Corporation
Sunnen Products Company
TRW, Michigan Division

Technical and Content Reviewers

The following people reviewed the manuscript before production and checked it for technical accuracy and clarity of presentation. Their suggestions and recommendations were included in the final draft of the manuscript. Their input helped make this textbook clear and technically accurate while maintaining the easy-to-read style that has made other books from the same author so popular.

Jim Anderson
Greenville High School

Victor Bridges
Umpqua Community College

John Bronisz
Albuquerque Technical-Vocational Institute

Dr. Roger Donovan
Illinois Central College

A. C. Durdin
Moraine Park Technical College

Herbert Ellinger
Western Michigan University

Al Engledahl
College of Dupage

Gary Gage
Ferris State

James M. Gore
Albuquerque Technical-Vocational Institute

Larry Hagelberger
Upper Valley Joint Vocational School

Oldrick Hajzler
Red River College

Betsy Hoffman
Vermont Technical College

Joseph Kidd
Morrisville State College

Steven T. Lee
Lincoln Technical Institute

Carlton H. Mabe, Sr.
Virginia Western Community College

Roy Marks
Owens Community College

Kerry Meier
San Juan College

Fritz Peacock
Indiana Vocational Technical College

Dennis Peter
NAIT (Canada)

Kenneth Redick
Hudson Valley Community College

Mark Spisak
Central Piedmont Community College

Mitchell Walker
St. Louis Community College at Forest Park

Jennifer Wise
Sinclair Community College

Photo Sequences

I wish to thank Chuck Taylor, Mike Garblik, and Blaine Heeter, of Sinclair Community College, Dayton, Ohio, who helped with many of the photos.

Special thanks to Richard Reaves and Tony Martin from the University of Alaska Southeast for all their help. Most of all, I wish to thank Michelle Halderman for her assistance in all phases of manuscript preparation.

James D. Halderman

BRIEF CONTENTS

CONTENTS

CHAPTER **1**

SHOP SAFETY

OBJECTIVES

After studying Chapter 1, the reader will be able to:

1. Identify situations where hearing protection should be worn.
2. Discuss how to safely handle tools and shop equipment.
3. Describe how to properly use a fire extinguisher.
4. Discuss shop safety procedures.

KEY TERMS

ANSI (p. 2)
Bump Cap (p. 2)
Decibel (dB) (p. 3)
Eye Wash Station (p. 7)
Fire Blankets (p. 7)

Microbes (p. 5)
"PASS" (p. 6)
Personal Protective Equipment (PPE) (p. 2)
Spontaneous Combustion (p. 4)

PERSONAL PROTECTIVE EQUIPMENT

Safety is not just a buzzword on a poster in the work area. Safe work habits can reduce accidents and injuries, ease the workload, and keep employees pain free.

Safety Glasses

The most important **personal protective equipment (PPE)** a technician should wear all the time are safety glasses, which meet standard **ANSI** Z87.1. See Figure 1-1.

Steel-Toed Shoes

Steel-toed safety shoes are also a good investment. See Figure 1-2. If safety shoes are not available, then leather-topped shoes offer more protection than canvas or cloth.

Gloves

Wear gloves to protect your hands from rough or sharp surfaces. Thin rubber gloves are recommended when working around automotive liquids such as engine oil, antifreeze, transmission fluid, or any other liquids that may be hazardous. Several types of gloves and their characteristics include:

- **Latex surgical gloves.** These gloves are relatively inexpensive, but tend to stretch, swell, and weaken when exposed to gas, oil, or solvents.
- **Vinyl gloves.** These gloves are also inexpensive and are not affected by gas, oil, or solvents.
- **Polyurethane gloves.** These gloves are more expensive, yet very strong. Even though these gloves are also not affected by gas, oil, or solvents, they do tend to be slippery.
- **Nitrile gloves.** These gloves are exactly like latex gloves, but are not affected by gas, oil, or solvents, yet they tend to be expensive.

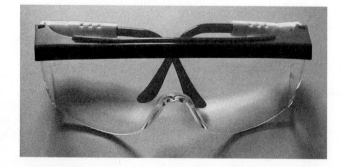

FIGURE 1-1   Safety glasses should be worn at all times when working on or around any vehicle or servicing any component.

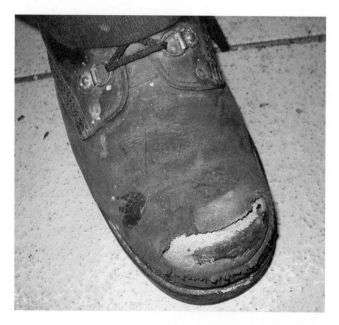

FIGURE 1-2   Steel-toed shoes are a worthwhile investment to help prevent foot injury due to falling objects. Even these well-worn shoes can protect the feet of this service technician.

FIGURE 1-3   Protective gloves such as these vinyl gloves are available in several sizes. Select the size that allows the gloves to fit snugly. Vinyl gloves last a long time and often can be worn all day to help protect your hands from dirt and possible hazardous materials.

- **Mechanic's gloves.** These gloves are usually made of synthetic leather and spandex and provide thermo protection, as well as protection from dirt and grime. See Figure 1-3.

Bump Cap

Service technicians working under a vehicle should wear a **bump cap** to protect the head against under-vehicle objects and the pads of the lift. See Figure 1-4.

FIGURE 1-4   One version of a bump cap is this padded plastic insert that is worn inside a regular cloth cap.

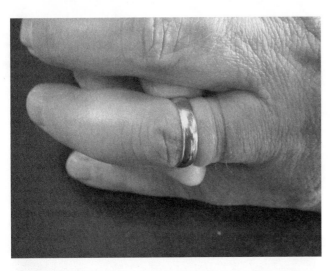

FIGURE 1-5   Remove all jewelry before performing service work on any vehicle.

Hands, Jewelry, and Clothing

Remove jewelry that may get caught on something or act as a conductor to an exposed electrical circuit. See Figure 1-5.

Take care of your hands. Keep your hands clean by washing with soap and hot water that is at least 110°F (43°C). Avoid loose or dangling clothing. Also, ear protection should be worn if the sound around you requires that you raise your voice (sound level higher than 90 **decibels [dB]**).

NOTE: A typical lawnmower produces noise at a level of about 110 dB. This means that everyone who uses a lawnmower or other lawn or garden equipment should wear ear protection.

TECH TIP

PROFESSIONAL BEHAVIOR IN THE SHOP IS A MUST

To be respected as a professional service technician and for safety, always behave in a professional manner. These behaviors include, but are not limited, to the following:

- Show respect to other technicians and employees. For example, the shop owner or service manager may not always be right, but they are always the boss.
- Avoid horseplay or practical jokes.
- Act as if a customer is observing your behavior at all times because this is often the case.

SAFETY TIPS FOR TECHNICIANS

- When lifting any object, get a secure grip with solid footing. Keep the load close to your body to minimize the strain. Lift with your legs and arms, not your back.
- Do not twist your body when carrying a load. Instead, pivot your feet to help prevent strain on the spine.
- Ask for help when moving or lifting heavy objects.
- Push a heavy object rather than pull it. (This is opposite to the way you should work with tools—never push a wrench! If you do and a bolt or nut loosens, your entire weight is used to propel your hand(s) forward. This usually results in cuts, bruises, or other painful injury.)
- Always connect an exhaust hose to the tailpipe of any running vehicle to help prevent the buildup of carbon monoxide inside a closed garage space. See Figure 1-6.
- When standing, keep objects, parts, and tools with which you are working between chest height and waist height. If seated, work at tasks that are at elbow height.
- Always be sure the hood is securely held open. See Figure 1-7.

CLEANING METHODS AND PROCESSES

There are four basic types of cleaning methods and processes used in vehicle service, including:

FIGURE 1-6   Always connect an exhaust hose to the tailpipe of the engine of a vehicle to be run inside a building.

(a)

FIGURE 1-7a   A crude but effective method is to use locking pliers on the chrome-plated shaft of a hood strut. Locking pliers should only be used on defective struts because the jaws of the pliers can damage the strut shaft.

Power Washing

Power washing uses an electric or gasoline powered compressor to increase the pressure of water and force it out of a nozzle. The pressure of the water itself is usually enough to remove dirt, grease, and grime from vehicle components. Sometimes

(b)

FIGURE 1-7b   A commercially available hood clamp. This tool uses a bright orange tag to help remind the technician to remove the clamp before attempting to close the hood. The hood could be bent if force is used to close the hood with the clamp in place.

SHOP CLOTH DISPOSAL

Always dispose of oily shop cloths in an enclosed container to prevent a fire. See Figure 1-8. Whenever oily cloths are thrown together on the floor or workbench, a chemical reaction can occur which can ignite the cloth even without an open flame. This process of ignition without an open flame is called **spontaneous combustion.**

a chemical cleaner, such as a detergent, is added to the water to help with cleaning.

Safe Use of Power Washers.   Because water is being sprayed at high pressure, a face shield should be worn when using a power washer to protect not only the eyes but to also protect the face in the event of the spray being splashed back toward the technician. Also use a pressure washer in an area

FIGURE 1-8   All oily shop cloths should be stored in a metal container equipped with a lid to help prevent spontaneous combustion.

TECH TIP

POUND WITH SOMETHING SOFTER

If you must pound on something, be sure to use a tool that is softer than what you are about to pound on to avoid damage. Examples are given in the following table.

The Material Being Pounded	What to Pound With
Steel or cast iron	Brass or aluminum hammer or punch
Aluminum	Plastic or rawhide mallet or plastic-covered dead-blow hammer
Plastic	Rawhide mallet or plastic dead-blow hammer

where the runoff from the cleaning will not contaminate local groundwater or cause harm to plants or animals.

Chemical/Microbe Cleaning

Chemical cleaning involves one of several cleaning solutions, including detergent, solvents, or small, living microorganisms

called **microbes** that eat oil and grease. The microbes live in water and eat the hydrocarbons that are the basis of grease and oil.

Safe Use of Chemical Cleaning.   A face shield should be worn when cleaning parts using a chemical cleaner. Avoid spilling the cleaner on the floor to help prevent slipping accidents. Clean and replace the chemical cleaner regularly.

Abrasive Cleaning

Abrasive cleaning is usually used to clean disassembled parts, such as engine blocks. The abrasives used include steel shot, ground walnut shells, or in the case of cleaning paint from a vehicle body, baking soda can be used.

Safe Use of Abrasive Cleaners.   Always wear a protective face shield and protective clothing, including gloves, long sleeves, and long pants.

Thermal Ovens

Thermal cleaning uses heat to bake off grease and dirt with special high-temperature ovens. This method of cleaning does require the use of expensive equipment but does not use any hazardous chemicals and is environmentally safe.

Safe Use of Thermal Ovens.   Because thermal ovens operate at high temperatures, often exceeding 600°F (315°C), the oven should be turned off and allowed to cool overnight before removing the parts from the oven to avoid being exposed to the high temperature.

ELECTRICAL CORD SAFETY

Use correctly grounded three-prong sockets and extension cords to operate power tools. Some tools use only two-prong plugs. Make sure these are double insulated and repair or replace any electrical cords that are cut or damaged to prevent the possibility of an electrical shock. When not in use, keep electrical cords off the floor to prevent tripping over them. Tape the cords down if they are placed in high foot traffic areas.

JUMP-STARTING AND BATTERY SAFETY

To jump-start another vehicle with a dead battery, connect good-quality copper jumper cables as indicated in Figure 1-9 or use a jump box. The last connection made should always be on the engine block or an engine bracket as far from the battery as possible. It is normal for a spark to be created when the jumper cables finally complete the jumping circuit, and

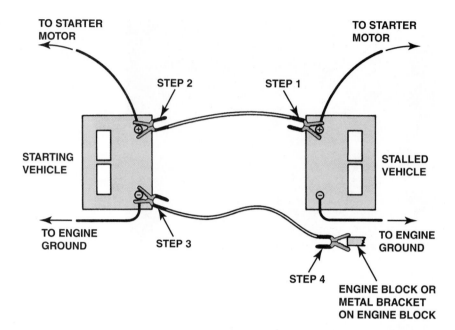

FIGURE 1-9 Jumper cable usage guide.

SAFETY TIP

COMPRESSED AIR SAFETY

Improper use of an air nozzle can cause blindness or deafness. Compressed air must be reduced to less than 30 PSI (206 kPa). See Figure 1-10. If an air nozzle is used to dry and clean parts, make sure the air stream is directed away from anyone else in the immediate area. Coil and store air hoses when they are not in use.

FIGURE 1-10 The air pressure going to the nozzle should be reduced to 30 PSI or less.

this spark could cause an explosion of the gases around the battery. Many newer vehicles have special ground connections built away from the battery just for the purpose of jump-starting. Check the owner's manual or service information for the exact location.

Batteries contain acid and should be handled with care to avoid tipping them greater than a 45-degree angle. Always remove jewelry when working around a battery to avoid the possibility of electrical shock or burns, which can occur when the metal comes in contact with a 12-volt circuit and ground, such as the body of the vehicle.

FIRE EXTINGUISHERS

There are four classes of fire extinguishers. Each class should be used on specific fires only:

- *Class A* is designed for use on general combustibles, such as cloth, paper, and wood.
- *Class B* is designed for use on flammable liquids and greases, including gasoline, oil, thinners, and solvents.
- *Class C* is used only on electrical fires.
- *Class D* is effective only on combustible metals such as powdered aluminum, sodium, or magnesium.

The class rating is clearly marked on the side of every fire extinguisher. Many extinguishers are good for multiple types of fires. See Figure 1-11.

When using a fire extinguisher, remember the word **"PASS."**

P = Pull the safety pin.
A = Aim the nozzle of the extinguisher at the base of the fire.

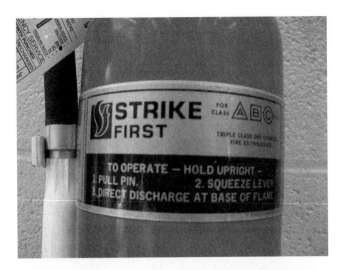

FIGURE 1-11   A typical fire extinguisher designed to be used on class A, B, or C fires.

FIGURE 1-12   A CO_2 fire extinguisher being used on a fire set in an open steel drum during a demonstration at a fire department training center.

S = Squeeze the lever to actuate the extinguisher.
S = Sweep the nozzle from side-to-side.

See Figure 1-12.

Types of Fire Extinguishers

Types of fire extinguishers include the following:

- **Water.** A water fire extinguisher, usually in a pressurized container, is good to use on Class A fires by reducing the temperature to the point where a fire cannot be sustained.
- **Carbon dioxide (CO_2).** A carbon dioxide fire extinguisher is good for almost any type of fire, especially Class B or Class C materials. A CO_2 fire extinguisher works by removing the oxygen from the fire and the cold CO_2 also helps reduce the temperature of the fire.
- **Dry chemical (yellow).** A dry chemical fire extinguisher is good for Class A, B, or C fires by coating the flammable materials, which eliminates the oxygen from the fire. A dry chemical fire extinguisher tends to be very corrosive and will cause damage to electronic devices.

FIRE BLANKETS

Fire blankets are required to be available in the shop areas. If a person is on fire, a fire blanket should be removed from its storage bag and thrown over and around the victim to smother the fire. See Figure 1-13 showing a typical fire blanket.

FIRST AID AND EYE WASH STATIONS

All shop areas must be equipped with a first-aid kit and an eye wash station centrally located and kept stocked with emergency supplies.

First-Aid Kit

A first-aid kit should include:

- Bandages (variety)
- Gauze pads
- Roll gauze
- Iodine swab sticks
- Antibiotic ointment
- Hydrocortisone cream
- Burn gel packets
- Eye wash solution
- Scissors
- Tweezers
- Gloves
- First-aid guide

See Figure 1-14. Every shop should have a person trained in first aid. If there is an accident, call for help immediately.

Eye Wash Station

An **eye wash station** should be centrally located and used whenever any liquid or chemical gets into the eyes. If such an emergency does occur, keep eyes in a constant stream of water and call for professional assistance. See Figure 1-15.

TECH TIP

MARK OFF THE SERVICE AREA

Some shops rope off the service bay area to help keep traffic and distractions to a minimum, which could prevent personal injury. See Figure 1-16.

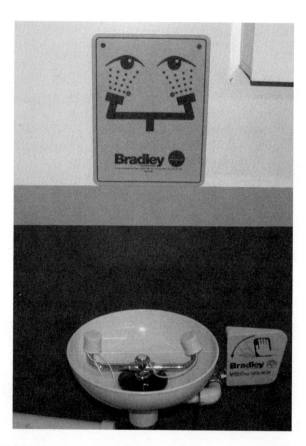

FIGURE 1-15   A typical eye wash station. Often a thorough flushing of the eyes with water is the best treatment in the event of eye contamination.

FIGURE 1-13   A treated wool blanket is kept in this easy-to-open wall-mounted holder and should be placed in a centralized location in the shop.

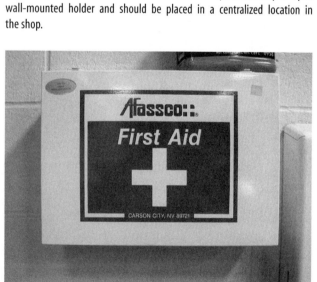

FIGURE 1-14   A first-aid box should be centrally located in the shop and kept stocked with the recommended supplies.

FIGURE 1-16   This area has been blocked off to help keep visitors from the dangerous work area.

SUMMARY

1. All service technicians should wear safety glasses that meet standard ANSI Z87.1.
2. Ear protection should be worn anytime the noise level is at 90 decibels (dB) or higher.
3. Safety should be exercised when working with electrical cords or when jump-starting another vehicle.
4. If a fire extinguisher is needed, remember: pull the safety pin, aim the nozzle, squeeze the lever, and sweep the nozzle from side-to-side.

REVIEW QUESTIONS

1. List four items that are personal protective equipment (PPE).
2. What are the types of fire extinguishers and their usage?
3. What items are included in a typical first-aid box?

CHAPTER QUIZ

1. What do you call the service technician's protective head cover?
   a. Cap
   b. Hat
   c. Bump cap
   d. Helmet

2. All safety glasses should meet the standards set by _____.
   a. ANSI
   b. SAE
   c. ASE
   d. DOT

3. When washing hands, the water should be at what temperature?
   a. 98°F (37°C)
   b. 110°F (43°C)
   c. 125°F (52°C)
   d. 135°F (57°C)

4. Hearing protection should be worn anytime the noise level exceeds _____.
   a. 60 dB
   b. 70 dB
   c. 80 dB
   d. 90 dB

5. Two technicians are discussing the safe use of a wrench. Technician A says that a wrench should be pulled toward you. Technician B says that a wrench should be pushed away from you. Which technician is correct?
   a. Technician A only
   b. Technician B only
   c. Both Technicians A and B
   d. Neither Technician A nor B

6. Exhaust hoses should be used because one of the exhaust gases is deadly in high concentration. This gas is _____.
   a. Carbon monoxide (CO)
   b. Carbon dioxide (CO_2)
   c. Hydrocarbons (HC)
   d. Oxides of nitrogen (NO_X)

7. The process of combustion occurring without an open flame is called _____.
   a. Direct ignition
   b. Non-open flame combustion
   c. Spontaneous combustion
   d. Cold fusion

8. When using a fire extinguisher, what word can be used to remember what to do?
   a. PASS
   b. FIRE
   c. RED
   d. LEVER

9. Which type of fire extinguisher is usable for most types of fires?
   a. CO_2
   b. Dry chemical
   c. Water
   d. CO

10. Which item is usually *not* included in a first-aid kit?
    a. Eye wash solution
    b. Antibiotic cream
    c. Fire blanket
    d. Bandages

CHAPTER 2

ENVIRONMENTAL AND HAZARDOUS MATERIALS

OBJECTIVES

After studying Chapter 2, the reader will be able to:

1. Prepare for the ASE assumed knowledge content required by all service technicians to adhere to environmentally appropriate actions and behavior.
2. Define the Occupational Safety and Health Act (OSHA).
3. Explain the term Material Safety Data Sheet (MSDS).
4. Identify hazardous waste materials in accordance with state and federal regulations and follow proper safety precautions while handling hazardous waste materials.
5. Define the steps required to safely handle and store automotive chemicals and waste.

KEY TERMS

AGST (p. 15)
Asbestosis (p. 13)
BCI (p. 19)
CAA (p. 13)
CFR (p. 12)
EPA (p. 12)
HEPA Vacuum (p. 14)
Mercury (p. 20)

MSDSs (p. 13)
OSHA (p. 13)
RCRA (p. 12)
Right-to-Know Laws (p. 13)
Solvent (p. 16)
Used Oil (p. 15)
UST (p. 15)
WHMIS (p. 13)

Safety and the handling of hazardous waste material are extremely important in the automotive shop. The improper handling of hazardous material affects us all, not just those in the shop. Shop personnel must be familiar with their rights and responsibilities regarding hazardous waste disposal. Right-to-know laws explain these rights. Shop personnel must also be familiar with hazardous materials in the automotive shop, and the proper way to dispose of these materials according to state and federal regulations.

OCCUPATIONAL SAFETY AND HEALTH ACT

The U.S Congress passed the Occupational Safety and Health Act in 1970. This legislation was designed to assist and encourage the citizens of the United States in their efforts to assure safe and healthful working conditions by providing research, information, education, and training in the field of occupational safety and health, as well as to assure safe and healthful working conditions for working men and women by authorizing enforcement of the standards developed under the act. Since approximately 25% of workers are exposed to health and safety hazards on the job, the standards are necessary to monitor, control, and educate workers regarding health and safety in the workplace.

HAZARDOUS WASTE

CAUTION: When handling hazardous waste material, one must always wear the proper protective clothing and equipment detailed in the right-to-know laws. This includes respirator equipment. All recommended procedures must be followed accurately. Personal injury may result from improper clothing, equipment, and procedures when handling hazardous materials.

Hazardous waste materials are chemicals, or components, that the shop no longer needs that pose a danger to the environment and people if they are disposed of in ordinary garbage cans or sewers. However, one should note that no material is considered hazardous waste until the shop has finished using it and is ready to dispose of it. The **Environmental Protection Agency (EPA)** publishes a list of hazardous materials that is included in the **Code of Federal Regulations (CFR).** The EPA considers waste hazardous if it is included on the EPA list of hazardous materials, or it has one or more of the following characteristics.

Reactive

Any material which reacts violently with water or other chemicals is considered hazardous.

Corrosive

If a material burns the skin, or dissolves metals and other materials, a technician should consider it hazardous. A pH scale is used, with the number 7 indicating neutral. Pure water has a pH of 7. Lower numbers indicate an acidic solution and higher numbers indicate a caustic solution. If a material releases cyanide gas, hydrogen sulfide gas, or similar gases when exposed to low-pH acid solutions, it is considered hazardous.

Toxic

Materials are hazardous if they leak one or more of eight different heavy metals in concentrations greater than 100 times the primary drinking water standard.

Ignitable

A liquid is hazardous if it has a flash point below 140°F (60°C), and a solid is hazardous if it ignites spontaneously.

Radioactive

Any substance that emits measurable levels of radiation is radioactive. When individuals bring containers of a highly radioactive substance into the shop environment, qualified personnel with the appropriate equipment must test them.

WARNING: Hazardous waste disposal laws include serious penalties for anyone responsible for breaking these laws.

RESOURCE CONSERVATION AND RECOVERY ACT (RCRA)

Federal and state laws control the disposal of hazardous waste materials. Every shop employee must be familiar with these laws. Hazardous waste disposal laws include the **Resource Conservation and Recovery Act (RCRA).** This law states that hazardous material users are responsible for hazardous materials from the time they become a waste until the proper waste disposal is completed. Many shops hire an independent hazardous waste hauler to dispose of hazardous waste material. The shop owner, or manager, should have a written contract with the hazardous waste hauler. Rather than have hazardous waste material hauled to an approved hazardous waste disposal site, a shop may choose to recycle the material in the shop. Therefore, the user must store hazardous waste material properly and safely, and be responsible for the transportation of this material until it arrives at an approved hazardous waste disposal site, where it can be processed according to the law. The RCRA controls these types of automotive waste:

- Paint and body repair products waste
- Solvents for parts and equipment cleaning
- Batteries and battery acid
- Mild acids used for metal cleaning and preparation
- Waste oil, and engine coolants or antifreeze
- Air-conditioning refrigerants and oils
- Engine oil filters

The **right-to-know laws** state that employees have a right to know when the materials they use at work are hazardous. The right-to-know laws started with the Hazard Communication Standard published by the **Occupational Safety and Health Administration (OSHA)** in 1983. Originally, this document was intended for chemical companies and manufacturers that required employees to handle hazardous materials in their work situation. Meanwhile, the federal courts have decided to apply these laws to all companies, including automotive service shops. Under the right-to-know laws, the employer has responsibilities regarding the handling of hazardous materials by their employees. All employees must be trained about the types of hazardous materials they will encounter in the workplace. The employees must be informed about their rights under legislation regarding the handling of hazardous materials.

CLEAN AIR ACT

Air-conditioning (A/C) systems and refrigerant are regulated by the **Clean Air Act (CAA)**, Title VI, Section 609. Technician certification and service equipment is also regulated. Any technician working on automotive A/C systems must be certified. A/C refrigerants must not be released or vented into the atmosphere, and used refrigerants must be recovered.

MATERIAL SAFETY DATA SHEETS (MSDSs)

All hazardous materials must be properly labeled, and information about each hazardous material must be posted on **Material Safety Data Sheets (MSDSs)** available from the manufacturer. See Figure 2-1. In Canada, MSDSs are called **Workplace Hazardous Materials Information Systems (WHMIS).**

The employer has a responsibility to place MSDSs where they are easily accessible by all employees. The MSDSs provide the following information about the hazardous material: chemical name, physical characteristics, protective handling equipment, explosion/fire hazards, incompatible materials,

FIGURE 2-1 Material Safety Data Sheets (MSDSs) should be readily available for use by anyone in the area who may come into contact with hazardous materials.

health hazards, medical conditions aggravated by exposure, emergency and first-aid procedures, safe handling, and spill/leak procedures.

The employer also has a responsibility to make sure that all hazardous materials are properly labeled. The label information must include health, fire, and reactivity hazards posed by the material, as well as the protective equipment necessary to handle the material. The manufacturer must supply all warning and precautionary information about hazardous materials. This information must be read and understood by the employee before handling the material.

THE DANGERS OF EXPOSURE TO ASBESTOS

Friction materials such as brake and clutch linings often contain asbestos. While asbestos has been eliminated from most original-equipment friction materials, the automotive service technician cannot know whether or not the vehicle being serviced is or is not equipped with friction materials containing asbestos. It is important that all friction materials be handled as if they do contain asbestos.

Asbestos exposure can cause scar tissue to form in the lungs. This condition is called **asbestosis.** It gradually causes increasing shortness of breath, and the scarring to the lungs is permanent.

Even low exposures to asbestos can cause mesothelioma, a type of fatal cancer of the lining of the chest or abdominal cavity. Asbestos exposure can also increase the risk of lung cancer as well as cancer of the voice box, stomach, and large intestine. It usually takes 15 to 30 years or more for cancer or asbestos lung scarring to show up after exposure. (Scientists call this the latency period.)

Government agencies recommend that asbestos exposure should be eliminated or controlled to the lowest level possible. These agencies have developed recommendations and standards that the automotive service technician and equipment manufacturer should follow. These U.S. federal agencies include the National Institute for Occupational Safety and Health (NIOSH), Occupational Safety and Health Administration (OSHA), and Environmental Protection Agency (EPA).

ASBESTOS OSHA STANDARDS

The Occupational Safety and Health Administration (OSHA) has established three levels of asbestos exposure. Any vehicle service establishment that does either brake or clutch work must limit employee exposure to asbestos to less than 0.2 fibers per cubic centimeter (cc) as determined by an air sample.

If the level of exposure to employees is greater than specified, corrective measures must be performed and a large fine may be imposed.

NOTE: Research has found that worn asbestos fibers such as those from automotive brakes or clutches may not be as hazardous as first believed. Worn asbestos fibers do not have sharp, flared ends that can latch onto tissue, but rather are worn down to a dust form that resembles talc. Grinding or sawing operations on unworn brake shoes or clutch discs *will* contain harmful asbestos fibers. To limit health damage, always use proper handling procedures while working around any component that may contain asbestos.

ASBESTOS EPA REGULATIONS

The federal Environmental Protection Agency (EPA) has established procedures for the removal and disposal of asbestos. The EPA procedures require that products containing asbestos be "wetted" to prevent the asbestos fibers from becoming airborne. According to the EPA, asbestos-containing materials can be disposed of as regular waste. Only when asbestos becomes airborne is it considered to be hazardous.

ASBESTOS HANDLING GUIDELINES

The air in the shop area can be tested by a testing laboratory, but this can be expensive. Tests have determined that asbestos levels can easily be kept below the recommended levels by using a solvent or a special vacuum.

NOTE: Even though asbestos is being removed from brake and clutch lining materials, the service technician cannot tell whether or not the old brake pads, shoes, or clutch disc contain asbestos. Therefore, to be safe, the technician should assume that all brake pads, shoes, or clutch discs contain asbestos.

HEPA Vacuum

A special **high-efficiency particulate air (HEPA) vacuum** system has been proven to be effective in keeping asbestos exposure levels below 0.1 fibers per cubic centimeter.

Solvent Spray

Many technicians use an aerosol can of brake cleaning solvent to wet the brake dust and prevent it from becoming airborne. Commercial brake cleaners are available that use a concentrated cleaner that is mixed with water. See Figure 2-2.

The waste liquid is filtered, and, when dry, the filter can be disposed of as solid waste.

FIGURE 2-2   All brakes should be moistened with water or solvent to help prevent brake dust from becoming airborne.

CAUTION: Never use compressed air to blow brake dust. The fine, talc-like brake dust can create a health hazard even if asbestos is not present or is present in dust rather than fiber form.

Disposal of Brake Dust and Brake Shoes

The hazard of asbestos occurs when asbestos fibers are airborne. Once the asbestos has been wetted down, it is then considered to be solid waste, rather than hazardous waste. Old brake shoes and pads should be enclosed, preferably in a plastic bag, to help prevent any of the brake material from becoming airborne. *Always follow current federal and local laws concerning disposal of all waste.*

USED BRAKE FLUID

Most brake fluid is made from polyglycol, is water soluble, and can be considered hazardous if it has absorbed metals from the brake system.

- Collect brake fluid in containers clearly marked to indicate that they are dedicated for that purpose.
- If your waste brake fluid is hazardous, manage it appropriately and use only an authorized waste receiver for its disposal.
- If your waste brake fluid is nonhazardous (such as old, but unused), determine from your local solid waste collection provider what should be done for its proper disposal.
- Do not mix brake fluid with used engine oil.
- Do not pour brake fluid down drains or onto the ground.
- Recycle brake fluid through a registered recycler.

USED OIL

Used oil is any petroleum-based or synthetic oil that has been used. During normal use, impurities such as dirt, metal scrapings, water, or chemicals can get mixed in with the oil. Eventually, this used oil must be replaced with virgin or re-refined oil. The EPA's used oil management standards include a three-pronged approach to determine if a substance meets the definition of used oil. To meet the EPA's definition of used oil, a substance must meet each of the following three criteria:

- **Origin.** The first criterion for identifying used oil is based on the oil's origin. Used oil must have been refined from crude oil or made from synthetic materials. Animal and vegetable oils are excluded from the EPA's definition of used oil.

- **Use.** The second criterion is based on whether and how the oil is used. Oils used as lubricants, hydraulic fluids, heat-transfer fluids, and for other similar purposes are considered used oil. Unused oil, such as bottom clean-out waste from virgin fuel oil storage tanks or virgin fuel oil recovered from a spill, does not meet the EPA's definition of used oil because these oils have never been "used." The EPA's definition also excludes products used as cleaning agents, as well as certain petroleum-derived products such as antifreeze and kerosene.
- **Contaminants.** The third criterion is based on whether or not the oil is contaminated with either physical or chemical impurities. In other words, to meet the EPA's definition, used oil must become contaminated as a result of being used. This aspect of the EPA's definition includes residues and contaminants generated from handling, storing, and processing used oil.

NOTE: The release of only 1 gallon of used oil (a typical oil change) can make a million gallons of fresh water undrinkable.

If used oil is dumped down the drain and enters a sewage treatment plant, concentrations as small as 50 to 100 PPM (parts per million) in the waste water can foul sewage treatment processes. Never mix a listed hazardous waste, gasoline, waste water, halogenated solvent, antifreeze, or an unknown waste material with used oil. Adding any of these substances will cause the used oil to become contaminated, which classifies it as hazardous waste.

DISPOSAL OF USED OIL

Once oil has been used, it can be collected, recycled, and used over and over again. An estimated 380 million gallons of used oil are recycled each year. Recycled used oil can sometimes be used again for the same job or can take on a completely different task. For example, used engine oil can be re-refined and sold at the store as engine oil or processed for furnace fuel oil. After collecting used oil in an appropriate container (e.g., a 55-gallon steel drum), the material must be disposed of in one of two ways:

- Shipped offsite for recycling
- Burned in an onsite or offsite EPA-approved heater for energy recovery

USED OIL STORAGE

Used oil must be stored in compliance with an existing **underground storage tank (UST)** or an **aboveground storage tank (AGST)** standard, or kept in separate containers.

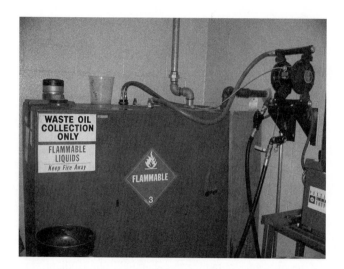

FIGURE 2-3   A typical aboveground oil storage tank.

See Figure 2-3. Containers are portable receptacles, such as a 55-gallon steel drum.

Keep Used Oil Storage Drums in Good Condition

This means that they should be covered, secured from vandals, properly labeled, and maintained in compliance with local fire codes. Frequent inspections for leaks, corrosion, and spillage are an essential part of container maintenance.

Never Store Used Oil in Anything Other Than Tanks and Storage Containers

Used oil may also be stored in units that are permitted to store regulated hazardous waste.

Used Oil Filter Disposal Regulations

Used oil filters contain used engine oil that may be hazardous. Before an oil filter is placed into the trash or sent to be recycled, it must be drained using one of the following hot-draining methods approved by the EPA:

- Puncturing the filter anti-drainback valve or filter dome end and hot draining for at least 12 hours
- Hot draining and crushing
- Dismantling and hot draining
- Any other hot draining method that will remove all the used oil from the filter

After the oil has been drained from the oil filter, the filter housing can be disposed of in any of the following ways:

- Sent for recycling
- Pickup by a service contract company
- Disposed of in regular trash

SOLVENTS

The major sources of chemical danger are liquid and aerosol brake cleaning fluids that contain chlorinated hydrocarbon **solvents.** Several other chemicals that do not deplete the ozone, such as heptane, hexane, and xylene, are now being used in nonchlorinated brake cleaning solvents. Some manufacturers are also producing solvents they describe as environmentally responsible, which are biodegradable and noncarcinogenic.

Sources of Chemical Poisoning

The health hazards presented by brake cleaning solvents occur from three different forms of exposure: ingestion, inhalation, and physical contact. It should be obvious that swallowing brake cleaning solvent is harmful, and such occurrences are not common. Still, brake cleaning solvents should always be handled and stored properly, and kept out of the reach of children. The dangers of inhalation are perhaps the most serious problem, as even very low levels of solvent vapors are hazardous.

Allowing brake cleaning solvents to come in contact with the skin presents a danger because these solvents strip natural oils from the skin and cause irritation of the tissues, plus they can be absorbed through the skin directly into the bloodstream. The transfer begins immediately upon contact, and continues until the liquid is wiped or washed away.

There is no specific standard for physical contact with chlorinated hydrocarbon solvents or the chemicals replacing them. All contact should be avoided whenever possible. The law requires an employer to provide appropriate protective equipment and ensure proper work practices by an employee handling these chemicals.

Effects of Chemical Poisoning

The effects of exposure to chlorinated hydrocarbon and other types of solvents can take many forms. Short-term exposure at low levels can cause headache, nausea, drowsiness, dizziness, lack of coordination, or unconsciousness. It may also cause irritation of the eyes, nose, and throat, and flushing of the face and neck. Short-term exposure to higher concentrations can cause liver damage with symptoms such as yellow jaundice or dark urine. Liver damage may not become evident until several weeks after the exposure.

Health Care Rights

The OSHA regulations concerning on-the-job safety place certain responsibilities on the employer, and give employees specific rights. Any person who feels there might be unsafe conditions where he or she works, whether asbestos exposure, chemical poisoning, or any other problem, should discuss the issue with fellow workers, union representatives (where applicable), and his or her supervisor or employer. If no action is taken and there is reason to believe the employer is not complying with OSHA standards, a complaint can be filed with OSHA and it will investigated.

The law forbids employers from taking action against employees who file a complaint concerning a health or safety hazard. However, if workers fear reprisal as the result of a complaint, they may request that OSHA withhold their names from the employer.

SAFETY TIP

HAND SAFETY

Service technicians should wash their hands with soap and water after handling engine oil or differential or transmission fluids, or wear protective rubber gloves. Another safety hint is that the service technician should not wear watches, rings, or other jewelry that could come in contact with electrical or moving parts of a vehicle. See Figure 2-4.

FIGURE 2-4 Washing hands and removing jewelry are two important safety habits all service technicians should practice.

SOLVENT HAZARDOUS AND REGULATORY STATUS

Most solvents are classified as hazardous wastes. Other characteristics of solvents include the following:

- Solvents with flash points below 140°F (60°C) are considered flammable and, like gasoline, are federally regulated by the Department of Transportation (DOT).
- Solvents and oils with flash points above 140°F (60°C) are considered combustible and, like engine oil, are also regulated by the DOT. See Figure 2-5.

It is the responsibility of the repair shop to determine if its spent solvent is hazardous waste. Waste solvents that are considered hazardous waste have a flash point below 140°F (60°C). Hot water or aqueous parts cleaners may be used to avoid disposing of spent solvent as hazardous waste. Solvent-type parts cleaners with filters are available to greatly extend solvent life and reduce spent-solvent disposal costs. Solvent reclaimers are available that clean and restore the solvent so that it lasts indefinitely.

USED SOLVENTS

Used or spent solvents are liquid materials that have been generated as waste and may contain xylene, methanol, ethyl ether, and methyl isobutyl ketone (MIBK). These materials must be stored in OSHA-approved safety containers with the lids or caps closed tightly. These storage receptacles must show no signs of leaks or significant damage due to dents or rust. In addition, the

FIGURE 2-5 Typical fireproof flammable storage cabinet.

FIGURE 2-6 All solvents and other hazardous waste should be disposed of properly.

FIGURE 2-7 Used antifreeze coolant should be kept separate and stored in a leakproof container until it can be recycled or disposed of according to federal, state, and local laws. Note that the storage barrel is placed inside another container to catch any coolant that may spill out of the inside barrel.

containers must be stored in a protected area equipped with secondary containment or a spill protector, such as a spill pallet. Additional requirements include the following:

- Containers should be clearly labeled "Hazardous Waste" and the date the material was first placed into the storage receptacle should be noted.
- Labeling is not required for solvents being used in a parts washer.
- Used solvents will not be counted toward a facility's monthly output of hazardous waste if the vendor under contract removes the material.
- Used solvents may be disposed of by recycling with a local vendor, such as *SafetyKleen,* to have the used solvent removed according to specific terms in the vendor agreement. See Figure 2-6.
- Use aqueous-based (nonsolvent) cleaning systems to help avoid the problems associated with chemical solvents.

COOLANT DISPOSAL

Coolant is a mixture of antifreeze and water. New antifreeze is not considered to be hazardous even though it can cause death if ingested. Used antifreeze may be hazardous due to dissolved metals from the engine and other components of the cooling system. These metals can include iron, steel, aluminum, copper, brass, and lead (from older radiators and heater cores).

1. Coolant should be recycled either onsite or offsite.
2. Used coolant should be stored in a sealed and labeled container. See Figure 2-7.
3. Used coolant can often be disposed of into municipal sewers with a permit. Check with local authorities and obtain a permit before discharging used coolant into sanitary sewers.

LEAD–ACID BATTERY WASTE

About 70 million spent lead–acid batteries are generated each year in the United States alone. Lead is classified as a toxic metal and the acid used in lead–acid batteries is highly corrosive. The vast majority (95% to 98%) of these batteries are recycled through lead reclamation operations and secondary lead smelters for use in the manufacture of new batteries.

BATTERY HAZARDOUS AND REGULATORY STATUS

Used lead–acid batteries must be reclaimed or recycled in order to be exempt from hazardous waste regulations. Leaking batteries must be stored and transported as hazardous waste. Some states have more strict regulations, which require special handling procedures and transportation. According to the

Battery Council International (BCI), battery laws usually include the following rules:

- Lead–acid battery disposal is prohibited in landfills or incinerators. Batteries are required to be delivered to a battery retailer, wholesaler, recycling center, or lead smelter.
- All retailers of automotive batteries are required to post a sign that displays the universal recycling symbol and indicates the retailer's specific requirements for accepting used batteries.

CAUTION: Battery electrolyte contains sulfuric acid, which is a very corrosive substance capable of causing serious personal injury, such as skin burns and eye damage. In addition, the battery plates contain lead, which is highly poisonous. For this reason, disposing of batteries improperly can cause environmental contamination and lead to severe health problems.

BATTERY HANDLING AND STORAGE

Batteries, whether new or used, should be kept indoors if possible. The storage location should be an area specifically designated for battery storage and must be well ventilated (to the outside). If outdoor storage is the only alternative, a sheltered and secured area with acid-resistant secondary containment is strongly recommended. It is also advisable that acid-resistant secondary containment be used for indoor storage. In addition, batteries should be placed on acid-resistant pallets and never stacked!

FUEL SAFETY AND STORAGE

Gasoline is a very explosive liquid. The expanding vapors that come from gasoline are extremely dangerous. These vapors are present even in cold temperatures. Vapors formed in gasoline tanks on many vehicles are controlled, but vapors from gasoline storage may escape from the can, resulting in a hazardous situation. Therefore, place gasoline storage containers in a well-ventilated space. Although diesel fuel is not as volatile as gasoline, the same basic rules apply to diesel fuel and gasoline storage. These rules include the following:

- Approved gasoline storage cans have a flash-arresting screen at the outlet. These screens prevent external ignition sources from igniting the gasoline within the can when someone pours the gasoline or diesel fuel.
- Technicians must always use red approved gasoline containers to allow for proper hazardous substance identification. See Figure 2-8.
- Do not fill gasoline containers completely full. Always leave the level of gasoline at least 1 inch from the top of the container. This action allows expansion of the gasoline

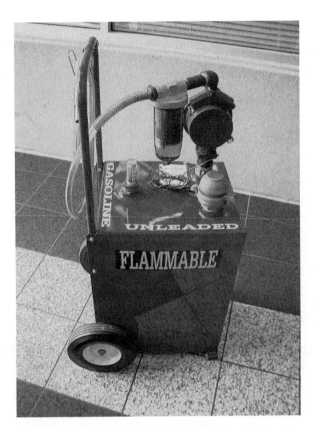

FIGURE 2-8   This red gasoline container holds about 30 gallons of gasoline and is used to fill vehicles used for training.

at higher temperatures. If gasoline containers are completely full, the gasoline will expand when the temperature increases. This expansion forces gasoline from the can and creates a dangerous spill. If gasoline or diesel fuel containers must be stored, place them in a designated storage locker or facility.

- Never leave gasoline containers open, except while filling or pouring gasoline from the container.
- Never use gasoline as a cleaning agent.
- Always connect a ground strap to containers when filling or transferring fuel or other flammable products from one container to another to prevent static electricity that could result in explosion and fire. These ground wires prevent the buildup of a static electric charge, which could result in a spark and disastrous explosion.

AIRBAG HANDLING

Airbag modules are pyrotechnic devices that can be ignited if exposed to an electrical charge or if the body of the vehicle is subjected to a shock. Airbag safety should include the following precautions:

1. Disarm the airbag(s) if you will be working in the area where a discharged bag could make contact with any

part of your body. Consult service information for the exact procedure to follow for the vehicle being serviced. The usual procedure is to deploy the airbag using a 12-volt power supply, such as a jump-start box, using long wires to connect to the module to ensure a safe deployment.

2. Do not expose an airbag to extreme heat or fire.
3. Always carry an airbag pointing away from your body.
4. Place an airbag module facing upward.
5. Always follow the manufacturer's recommended procedure for airbag disposal or recycling, including the proper packaging to use during shipment.
6. Always wash your hands or body well if exposed to a deployed airbag. The chemicals involved can cause skin irritation and possible rash development.
7. Wear protective gloves if handling a deployed airbag.

USED TIRE DISPOSAL

Used tires are an environmental concern for several reasons, including the following:

1. In a landfill, they tend to "float" up through the other trash and rise to the surface.
2. The inside of tires traps and holds rainwater, which is a breeding ground for mosquitoes. Mosquito-borne diseases include encephalitis and dengue fever.
3. Used tires present a fire hazard and, when burned, create a large amount of black smoke that contaminates the air.

Used tires should be disposed of in one of the following ways:

1. Used tires can be reused until the end of their useful life.
2. Tires can be retreaded.
3. Tires can be recycled or shredded for use in asphalt.
4. Derimmed tires can be sent to a landfill (most landfill operators will shred the tires because it is illegal in many states to landfill whole tires).
5. Tires can be burned in cement kilns or other power plants where the smoke can be controlled.
6. A registered scrap tire handler should be used to transport tires for disposal or recycling.

AIR-CONDITIONING REFRIGERANT OIL DISPOSAL

Air-conditioning refrigerant oil contains dissolved refrigerant and is therefore considered to be hazardous waste. This oil must be kept separate from other waste oil or the entire amount of oil must be treated as hazardous. Used refrigerant oil must be sent to a licensed hazardous waste disposal company for recycling or disposal. See Figure 2-9.

FIGURE 2-9   Air-conditioning refrigerant oil must be kept separate from other oils because it contains traces of refrigerant and must be treated as hazardous waste.

TECH TIP

REMOVE COMPONENTS THAT CONTAIN MERCURY

Some vehicles have a placard near the driver's side door that lists the components that contain **mercury,** a heavy metal. See Figure 2-10.

These components should be removed from the vehicle before the rest of the body is sent to be recycled to help prevent the release of mercury into the environment.

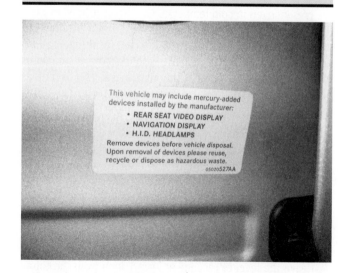

FIGURE 2-10   Placard near driver's door listing the devices in the vehicle that contain mercury.

TECH TIP

WHAT EVERY TECHNICIAN SHOULD KNOW

The Hazardous Material Identification Guide (HMIG) is the standard labeling for all materials. The service technician should be aware of the meaning of the label. See Figure 2-11.

Waste Chart

All automotive service facilities create some waste and while most of it is handled properly, it is important that all hazardous and nonhazardous waste be accounted for and properly disposed. See the chart for a list of typical wastes generated at automotive shops, plus a checklist for keeping track of how these wastes are handled.

Hazardous Materials Identification Guide (HMIG)

TYPE HAZARD		DEGREE	
○	HEALTH	4 - Extreme
○	FLAMMABILITY	3 - Serious
○	REACTIVITY	2 - Moderate
○	PROTECTIVE EQUIPMENT	1 - Slight
		0 - Minimal

HAZARD RATING AND PROTECTIVE EQUIPMENT

Health		Flammable		Reactive	
Type of Possible Injury		Susceptibility of materials to burn		Susceptibility of materials to release energy	
4	Highly Toxic. May be fatal on short term exposure. Special protective equipment required.	4	Extremely flammable gas or liquid. Flash Point below 73F.	4	Extreme. Explosive at room temperature.
3	Toxic. Avoid inhalation or skin contact.	3	Flammable. Flash Point 73F to 100F.	3	Serious. May explode if shocked, heated under confinement or mixed w/ water.
2	Moderately Toxic. May be harmful if inhaled or absorbed.	2	Combustible. Requires moderate heating to ignite. Flash Point 100F to 200F.	2	Moderate. Unstable, may react with water.
1	Slightly Toxic. May cause slight irritation.	1	Slightly Combustible. Requires strong heating to ignite.	1	Slight. May react if heated or mixed with water.
0	Minimal. All chemicals have a slight degree of toxicity.	0	Minimal. Will not burn under normal conditions.	0	Minimal. Normally stable, does not react with water.

Protective Equipment

A	Safety Glasses	E	Safety Glasses + Gloves + Dust Respirator	I	Safety Glasses + Gloves + Combination Dust & Vapor Respirator
B	Safety Glasses + Gloves	F	Safety Glasses + Gloves + Apron + Dust Respirator	J	Chemical Goggles + Gloves + Apron + Combination Dust & Vapor Respirator
C	Safety Glasses + Gloves + Apron	G	Safety Glasses + Gloves + Vapor Respirator	K	Apron + Gloves + Full Protection Suit + Boots
D	Faceshield + Gloves + Apron	H	Chemical Goggles + Gloves + Apron + Vapor Respirator	X	Ask your supervisor for guidance.

FIGURE 2-11   The Environmental Protection Agency (EPA) Hazardous Materials Identification Guide is a standardized listing of the hazards and the protective equipment needed.

Typical Wastes Generated at Auto Repair Shops and Typical Category (Hazardous or Nonhazardous) by Disposal Method

Waste Stream	Typical Category if Not Mixed with Other Hazardous Waste	If Disposed in Landfill and Not Mixed with a Hazardous Waste	If Recycled
Used oil	Used oil	Hazardous waste	Used oil
Used oil filters	Nonhazardous solid waste, if completely drained	Nonhazardous solid waste, if completely drained	Used oil, if not drained
Used transmission fluid	Used oil	Hazardous waste	Used oil
Used brake fluid	Used oil	Hazardous waste	Used oil
Used antifreeze	Depends on characterization	Depends on characterization	Depends on characterization
Used solvents	Hazardous waste	Hazardous waste	Hazardous waste
Used citric solvents	Nonhazardous solid waste	Nonhazardous solid waste	Hazardous waste
Lead–acid automotive batteries	Not a solid waste if returned to supplier	Hazardous waste	Hazardous waste
Shop rags used for oil	Used oil	Depends on used oil characterization	Used oil
Shop rags used for solvent or gasoline spills	Hazardous waste	Hazardous waste	Hazardous waste
Oil spill absorbent material	Used oil	Depends on used oil characterization	Used oil
Spill material for solvent and gasoline	Hazardous waste	Hazardous waste	Hazardous waste
Catalytic converter	Not a solid waste if returned to supplier	Nonhazardous solid waste	Nonhazardous solid waste
Spilled or unused fuels	Hazardous waste	Hazardous waste	Hazardous waste
Spilled or unusable paints and thinners	Hazardous waste	Hazardous waste	Hazardous waste
Used tires	Nonhazardous solid waste	Nonhazardous solid waste	Nonhazardous solid waste

Consolidated Screening Checklist for Automotive Repair Facilities

1. Waste Management		
Waste Management	Has the facility determined which wastes are hazardous wastes?	yes/no
	Does the facility generate more than 100 kg (220 lbs.) of hazardous waste per month?	yes/no
	If yes, does the facility have a U.S. EPA hazardous waste generator I.D. number?	yes/no
Used Oil	Are used oil containers and piping leak free, segregated, and labeled "used oil"?	yes/no
	Are hazardous waste fluids mixed with used oil?	yes/no
	Is used oil collected and sent offsite for recycling, or burned in an onsite heater?	recycle/onsite heater/burned offsite/other
	Does the facility accept household used oil?	yes/no
	If yes, is it tested for hazardous waste (solvent/gasoline) contamination?	yes/no
Used Oil Filters	Are used oil filters completely drained before disposal?	yes/no
	How are used oil filters disposed of?	scrap metal/service/trash/other
Used Antifreeze	Is used antifreeze properly contained, segregated, and labeled?	yes/no
	Does the facility generate any antifreeze that is a hazardous waste (>5 PPM lead)?	yes/no/do not know
	If yes, is it recycled onsite in a closed-loop system?	yes/no
	If no, is it counted toward facility generator status?	yes/no
	If used antifreeze is not recycled onsite, how is it disposed of?	recycled offsite/mixed with other fluids/landfill/other
Used Solvents	Are used solvents stored in proper containers and properly labeled?	yes/no/N/A
	How are used solvents disposed of?	service/mixed with other fluids/other
	Does the facility have hazardous waste manifests for shipping papers on file?	yes/no/N/A
Batteries	Does the facility return used batteries to new battery suppliers?	yes/no/N/A
	If not, how are used automotive batteries disposed of?	recycle/hazardous waste landfill/other
	Are used batteries contained and covered prior to disposal?	yes/no
Rags	How are used rags and towels disposed of?	laundry service/burned for heat/trash
	How are used rags stored while onsite?	separate container/shop trash can/floor
Tires	How are used tires disposed of?	resale/retreading/landfill/customer/N/A/other

(Continued)

Consolidated Screening Checklist for Automotive Repair Facilities *(Continued)*

Absorbents	Does the facility use sawdust or other absorbents for spills or leaks?	yes/no
	Does the facility determine whether used absorbents are considered hazardous before disposal?	yes/no
	How are absorbents used for oil spills disposed of?	N/A/burned for energy/disposed of as hazardous waste/characterized as nonhazardous and landfilled
2. Wastewater Management		
Floor Drains and Wastewater Management	How does the facility clean shop floor and surrounding area?	uses dry cleanup/uses water
	Are fluids (oil, antifreeze, solvent) allowed to enter floor drains for disposal?	yes/no/no floor drains onsite
	How are fluids disposed of?	municipal sanitary sewer/storm sewer/street/other
	If floor drains discharge to municipal sanitary sewer, to storm sewer system, or the street, has the facility notified Publicly Owned Treatment Works (POTW) about potential contamination in wash water?	yes/no
	If drains discharge directly to surface waters or to an underground injection well, does the facility have a National Pollutant Discharge Elimination System (NPDES) (surface) or UIC (underground) permit?	yes/no/N/A
Stormwater	Does the facility store parts, fluids, and/or other materials outside?	yes/no
	Are materials protected from rain/snow in sealed containers or under tarp or roof?	yes/no/N/A
3. Air Pollution Control		
Parts Cleaners	If the facility uses parts-cleaning sinks with halogenated solvents, has the facility submitted a notification report to the EPA?	yes/no/N/A
	Are sinks kept closed and sealed except when actually used for cleaning parts?	yes/no
	Does the facility follow required work and operational practices?	yes/no
Motor Vehicle Air Conditioning (CFCs)	Are Mobile Vehicle Air Conditioning MVAC technicians trained and certified by an accredited program?	yes/no/N/A
	If yes, are certificates on file?	yes/no
	Is CFC recovery and/or recycling equipment EPA approved?	yes/no/N/A
	Is equipment recovery/recycling or recovery only? (circle one)	recovery/recycling/recovery only/N/A
	If recovery only, is refrigerant reclaimed by an EPA-approved reclaimer?	yes/no

Catalytic Converters (CCs)	Does the facility replace CCs that are the correct type based on vehicle requirements?	yes/no/N/A
	Does the facility replace CCs on vehicles covered under original manufacturer's warranty?	yes/no
	If yes, was original CC missing, or is replacement due to state/local inspection program requirement?	yes/no
	Does facility properly mark and keep replaced CCs onsite for at least 15 days?	yes/no
	Does facility completely fill out customer paperwork and maintain onsite for at least 6 months?	yes/no
Fuels	Is Stage I vapor recovery equipment operated properly during unloading of gasoline?	yes/no/N/A
	Is Stage II vapor recovery equipment installed and working at pumps?	yes/no/N/A
	Do fuel delivery records indicate compliance with appropriate fuel requirements?	yes/no/records not available
	Are pumps clearly labeled with the product they contain?	yes/no
	Do gasoline pump nozzles comply with the 10-gallon-per-minute flow rate?	yes/no/don't know
	Is dyed, high-sulfur diesel/kerosene available for sale to motor vehicles?	yes/no
Paints and Thinners	Are paints and thinners properly contained and marked when not in use?	yes/no/N/A
	Does the facility use low-VOC (Volatile Organic Compounds) paints?	yes/no/N/A
	Does the facility determine whether paints are considered hazardous before disposal?	yes/no
	How are used paints, thinners, and solvents disposed of?	reuse/recycle/mix w/other fluids/landfill
	Does the facility mix paint amounts according to need?	yes/no
	Does the facility use newer, "high transfer efficiency" spray applications?	yes/no
	If hazardous paints are used, are spray paint booth air filters disposed of properly as hazardous waste?	yes/no
	If filters are not hazardous, how are they disposed of?	recycled/landfill

(Continued)

Consolidated Screening Checklist for Automotive Repair Facilities *(Continued)*

4. UST/SPCC/Emergency Spill Procedures		
Underground Storage Tanks	Has the state UST program been notified of any USTs located onsite?	yes/no/N/A
	Does the facility conduct leak detection for tank and piping of all onsite UST systems?	yes/no/N/A
	Do USTs at the facility meet requirements for spill, overfill, and corrosion protection?	yes/no/N/A
	Are records and documentation readily available (as applicable) for installation, leak detection, corrosion protection, spill/overfill protection, corrective action, financial responsibility, and closure?	yes/no/N/A
Spill and Emergency Response	Does the facility have a gasoline, fuel oil, or lubricating oil storage capacity total greater than 1,320 gallons (or greater than 660 gallons in any one tank) in aboveground tanks or total underground tank storage capacity greater than 42,000 gallons?	yes/no
	If yes, could spilled gasoline fuel oil or lubricating oil conceivably reach navigable waters?	yes/no
	If yes, does the facility have an SPCC (Spill Prevention Control and Countermeasure plan) signed by a professional engineer?	yes/no
	Are phone numbers of the national, station, and local emergency contact available onsite for immediate reporting of oil or chemical spills?	yes/no

SUMMARY

1. Hazardous materials include common automotive chemicals, liquids, and lubricants, especially those whose ingredients contain *chlor* or *fluor* in their name.
2. Right-to-know laws require that all workers have access to Material Safety Data Sheets (MSDSs).
3. Asbestos fibers should be avoided and removed according to current laws and regulations.
4. Used engine oil contains metals worn from parts and should be handled and disposed of properly.
5. Solvents represent a serious health risk and should be avoided as much as possible.
6. Coolant should be recycled.
7. Batteries are considered to be hazardous waste and should be discarded to a recycling facility.

REVIEW QUESTIONS

1. List five common automotive chemicals or products that may be considered hazardous materials.
2. List five precautions to which every technician should adhere when working with automotive products and chemicals.

CHAPTER QUIZ

1. Hazardous materials include all of the following, *except* _____.
   a. Engine oil
   b. Asbestos
   c. Water
   d. Brake cleaner

2. To determine if a product or substance being used is hazardous, consult _____.
   a. A dictionary
   b. An MSDS
   c. SAE standards
   d. EPA guidelines

3. Exposure to asbestos dust can cause which of the following conditions?
   a. Asbestosis
   b. Mesothelioma
   c. Lung cancer
   d. All of the above are possible

4. Wetted asbestos dust is considered to be _____.
   a. Solid waste
   b. Hazardous waste
   c. Toxic
   d. Poisonous

5. An oil filter should be hot drained for how long before disposing of the filter?
   a. 30 to 60 minutes
   b. 4 hours
   c. 8 hours
   d. 12 hours

6. Used engine oil should be disposed of by all of the following methods, *except* _____.
   a. Disposed of in regular trash
   b. Shipped offsite for recycling
   c. Burned onsite in a waste-oil-approved heater
   d. Burned offsite in a waste-oil-approved heater

7. All of the following are the proper ways to dispose of a drained oil filter, *except* _____.
   a. Sent for recycling
   b. Picked up by a service contract company
   c. Disposed of in regular trash
   d. Considered to be hazardous waste and disposed of accordingly

8. Which is *not* considered to be a hazardous solvent?
   a. Nonchlorinated hydrocarbon solvent
   b. Tetrachloroethylene
   c. MIBK
   d. Chlorinated hydrocarbon solvent

9. Gasoline should be stored in approved containers that include what color(s)?
   a. A red container with yellow lettering
   b. A red container
   c. A yellow container
   d. A yellow container with red lettering

10. What automotive devices may contain mercury?
    a. Rear seat video displays
    b. Navigation displays
    c. HID headlights
    d. All of the above

CHAPTER 3

FASTENERS AND THREAD REPAIR

OBJECTIVES

After studying Chapter 3, the reader will be able to:

1. Explain the terms used to identify bolts and other threaded fasteners.
2. Explain the strength ratings of threaded fasteners.
3. Describe the proper use of nonthreaded fasteners.
4. Discuss how snap rings are used.

KEY TERMS

Bolts (p. 29)
Cap Screws (p. 29)
Capillary Action (p. 37)
Christmas Tree Clips (p. 35)
Cotter Pins (p. 36)
Crest (p. 29)
Die (p. 32)
Grade (p. 30)
Helical Insert (p. 38)
Helicoil® (p. 38)
Jam Nut (p. 36)
Metric Bolts (p. 29)
Pal Nut (p. 36)

Penetrating Oil (p. 37)
Pitch (p. 29)
Pop Rivet (p. 36)
Prevailing Torque Nuts (p. 32)
Self-Tapping Screw (p. 34)
Snap Ring (p. 35)
Stud (p. 29)
Tap (p. 32)
Tensile Strength (p. 31)
Threaded Insert (p. 39)
UNC (Unified National Coarse) (p. 29)
UNF (Unified National Fine) (p. 29)
Washers (p. 34)

THREADED FASTENERS

Most of the threaded fasteners used on vehicles are cap screws. They are called **cap screws** when they are threaded into a casting. Automotive service technicians usually refer to these fasteners as **bolts,** regardless of how they are used. In this chapter, they are called bolts. Sometimes, studs are used for threaded fasteners. A **stud** is a short rod with threads on both ends. Often, a stud will have coarse threads on one end and fine threads on the other end. The end of the stud with coarse threads is screwed into the casting. A nut is used on the opposite end to hold the parts together.

The fastener threads *must* match the threads in the casting or nut. The threads may be measured either in fractions of an inch (called fractional) or in metric units. The size is measured across the outside of the threads, called the **crest** of the thread. See Figure 3-1.

Fractional threads are either coarse or fine. The coarse threads are called **Unified National Coarse (UNC),** and the fine threads are called **Unified National Fine (UNF).** Standard combinations of sizes and number of threads per inch (called **pitch**) are used. Pitch can be measured with a thread pitch gauge as shown in Figure 3-2.

Bolts are identified by their diameter and length as measured from below the head, and not by the size of the head or

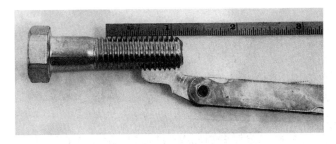

FIGURE 3-2   Thread pitch gauge used to measure the pitch of the thread. This bolt has 13 threads to the inch.

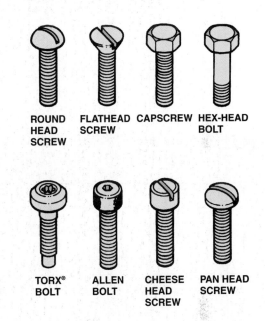

FIGURE 3-3   Bolts and screws have many different heads which determine what tool must be used.

the size of the wrench used to remove or install the bolt. Bolts and screws have many different-shaped heads. See Figure 3-3.

Fractional thread sizes are specified by the diameter in fractions of an inch and the number of threads per inch. Typical UNC thread sizes would be 5/16–18 and 1/2–13. Similar UNF thread sizes would be 5/16–24 and 1/2–20. See Figure 3-4.

METRIC BOLTS

The size of a **metric bolt** is specified by the letter *M* followed by the diameter in millimeters (mm) across the outside (crest) of the threads. Typical metric sizes would be M8 and M12. Fine metric threads are specified by the thread diameter followed by *X* and the distance between the threads measured in millimeters (M8 × 1.5). See Figure 3-5.

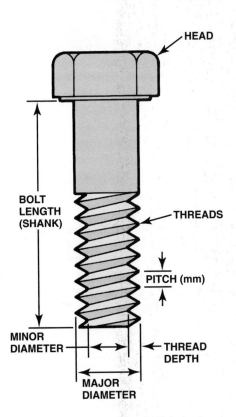

FIGURE 3-1   The dimensions of a typical bolt showing where sizes are measured.

Size	Threads per inch		Outside Diameter Inches
	NC UNC	NF UNF	
0	. .	80	0.0600
1	64	. .	0.0730
1	. .	72	0.0730
2	56	. .	0.0860
2	. .	64	0.0860
3	48	. .	0.0990
3	. .	56	0.0990
4	40	. .	0.1120
4	. .	48	0.1120
5	40	. .	0.1250
5	. .	44	0.1250
6	32	. .	0.1380
6	. .	40	0.1380
8	32	. .	0.1640
8	. .	36	0.1640
10	24	. .	0.1900
10	. .	32	0.1900
12	24	. .	0.2160
12	. .	28	0.2160
1/4	20	. .	0.2500
1/4	. .	28	0.2500
5/16	18	. .	0.3125
5/16	. .	24	0.3125
3/8	16	. .	0.3750
3/8	. .	24	0.3750
7/16	14	. .	0.4375
7/16	. .	20	0.4375
1/2	13	. .	0.5000
1/2	. .	20	0.5000
9/16	12	. .	0.5625
9/16	. .	18	0.5625
5/8	11	. .	0.6250
5/8	. .	18	0.6250
3/4	10	. .	0.7500
3/4	. .	16	0.7500
7/8	9	. .	0.8750
7/8	. .	14	0.8750
1	8	. .	1.0000
1	. .	12	1.0000
1 1/8	7	. .	1.1250
1 1/8	. .	12	1.1250
1 1/4	7	. .	1.2500
1 1/4	. .	12	1.2500
1 3/8	6	. .	1.3750
1 3/8	. .	12	1.3750
1 1/2	6	. .	1.5000
1 1/2	. .	12	1.5000
1 3/4	5	. .	1.7500
2	4 1/2	. .	2.0000
2 1/4	4 1/2	. .	2.2500
2 1/2	4	. .	2.5000
2 3/4	4	. .	2.7500
3	4	. .	3.0000
3 1/4	4	. .	3.2500
3 1/2	4	. .	3.5000
3 3/4	4	. .	3.7500
4	4	. .	4.0000

FIGURE 3-4 The American National System is one method of sizing fasteners.

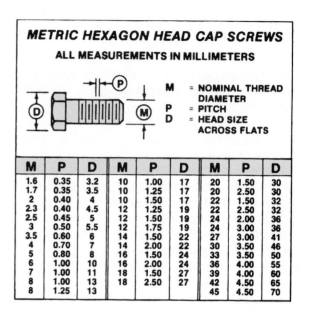

FIGURE 3-5 The metric system specifies fasteners by diameter, length, and pitch.

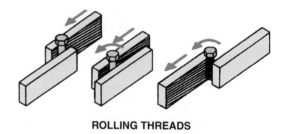

ROLLING THREADS

FIGURE 3-6 Stronger threads are created by cold-rolling a heat-treated bolt blank instead of cutting the threads using a die.

GRADES OF BOLTS

Bolts are made from many different types of steel, and for this reason some are stronger than others. The strength or classification of a bolt is called the **grade.** The bolt heads are marked to indicate their grade strength. Graded bolts are commonly used in the suspension parts of the vehicle but can be used almost anywhere in the vehicle.

The actual grade of bolts is two more than the number of lines on the bolt head. Metric bolts have a decimal number to indicate the grade. More lines or a higher grade number indicate a stronger bolt. Higher grade bolts usually have threads that are rolled rather than cut, which also makes them stronger. See Figure 3-6. In some cases, nuts and machine screws have similar grade markings.

CAUTION: *Never* use hardware store (nongraded) bolts, studs, or nuts on any vehicle steering, suspension, or brake component. Always use the exact size and grade of hardware that is specified and used by the vehicle manufacturer.

TENSILE STRENGTH

Graded fasteners have a higher tensile strength than non-graded fasteners. **Tensile strength** is the maximum stress used under tension (lengthwise force) without causing failure of the fastener. Tensile strength is specified in pounds per square inch (PSI). See the following chart that shows the grade and specified tensile strength.

The strength and type of steel used in a bolt is supposed to be indicated by a raised mark on the head of the bolt. The type of mark depends on the standard to which the bolt was manufactured. Most often, bolts used in machinery are made to SAE Standard J429.

Metric bolt tensile strength property class is shown on the head of the bolt as a number, such as 4.6, 8.8, 9.8, and 10.9; the higher the number, the stronger the bolt. See Figure 3-7.

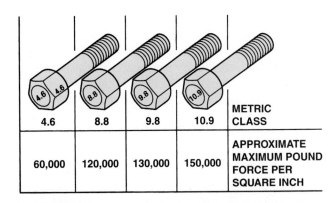

4.6	8.8	9.8	10.9	METRIC CLASS
60,000	120,000	130,000	150,000	APPROXIMATE MAXIMUM POUND FORCE PER SQUARE INCH

FIGURE 3-7   Metric bolt (cap screw) grade markings and approximate tensile strength.

NUTS

Most nuts used on cap screws have the same hex size as the cap screw head. Some inexpensive nuts use a hex size larger

SAE Bolt Designations

SAE Grade No.	Size range	Tensile strength, PSI	Material	Head marking
1	1/4 through 1-1/2	60,000	Low or medium carbon steel	
2	1/4 through 3/4 7/8 through 1-1/2	74,000 60,000		
5	1/4 through 1 1-1/8 through 1-1/2	120,000 105,000	Medium carbon steel, quenched & tempered	
5.2	1/4 through 1	120,000	Low carbon martensite steel*, quenched & tempered	
7	1/4 through 1-1/2	133,000	Medium carbon alloy steel, quenched & tempered	
8	1/4 through 1-1/2	150,000	Medium carbon alloy steel, quenched & tempered	
8.2	1/4 through 1	150,000	Low carbon martensite steel*, quenched & tempered	

*Martensite steel is steel that has been cooled rapidly, thereby increasing its hardness. It is named after a German metallurgist, Adolf Martens.

than the cap screw head. Metric nuts are often marked with dimples to show their strength. More dimples indicate stronger nuts. Some nuts and cap screws use interference fit threads to keep them from accidentally loosening. This means that the shape of the nut is slightly distorted or that a section of the threads is deformed. Nuts can also be kept from loosening with a nylon washer fastened in the nut or with a nylon patch or strip on the threads. See Figure 3-8.

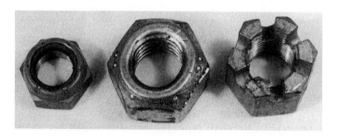

FIGURE 3-8 Types of lock nuts. On the left, a nylon ring; in the center, a distorted shape; and on the right, a castle for use with a cotter key.

TECH TIP

A 1/2-INCH WRENCH DOES NOT FIT A 1/2-INCH BOLT

A common mistake made by persons new to the automotive field is to think that the size of a bolt or nut is the size of the head. The size of the bolt or nut (outside diameter of the threads) is usually smaller than the size of the wrench or socket that fits the head of the bolt or nut. Examples are given in the following table:

Wrench Size	Thread Size
7/16 in.	1/4 in.
1/2 in.	5/16 in.
9/16 in.	3/8 in.
5/8 in.	7/16 in.
3/4 in.	1/2 in.
10 mm	6 mm
12 mm or 13 mm*	8 mm
14 mm or 17 mm*	10 mm

*European (Système International d'Unités-SI) metric.

Hint: An open-end wrench can be used to gauge bolt sizes. A 3/8-in. wrench will fit the threads of a 3/8-in. bolt.

NOTE: Most of these "locking nuts" are grouped together and are commonly referred to as **prevailing torque nuts.** This means that the nut will hold its tightness or torque and not loosen with movement or vibration. Most prevailing torque nuts should be replaced whenever removed to ensure that the nut will not loosen during service. Always follow the manufacturer's recommendations. Anaerobic sealers, such as Loctite®, are used on the threads where the nut or cap screw must be both locked and sealed.

TAPS AND DIES

Taps and dies are used to cut threads. **Taps** are used to cut threads in holes drilled to an exact size depending on the size of the tap. A **die** is used to cut threads on round rods or studs. Most taps and dies come as a complete set for the most commonly used fractional and metric threads.

Taps

There are two commonly used types of taps, including:

- Tapered tap. This is the most commonly used tap and is designed to cut threads by gradually enlarging the threaded hole.
- Bottoming tap. This tap has a flat bottom instead of a tapered tip to allow it to cut threads to the bottom of a drilled hole. See Figure 3-9.

All taps must be used in the proper size hole called a "tap drill size." This information is often stamped on the tap itself or in a chart that is included with a tap and die tool set. See Figure 3-10.

Dies

A die is a hardened steel round cutter with teeth on the inside of the center hole. See Figure 3-11. A die is rotated using a die handler over a rod to create threads.

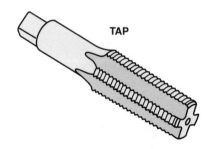

TAP

FIGURE 3-9 A typical bottoming tap used to create threads in holes that are not open, but stop in a casting, such as an engine block.

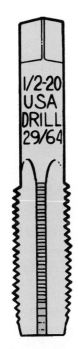

FIGURE 3-10   Many taps, especially larger ones, have the tap drill size printed on the top.

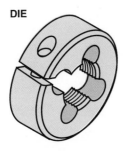

DIE

FIGURE 3-11   A die is used to cut threads on a metal rod.

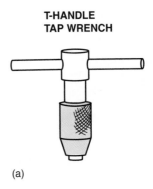

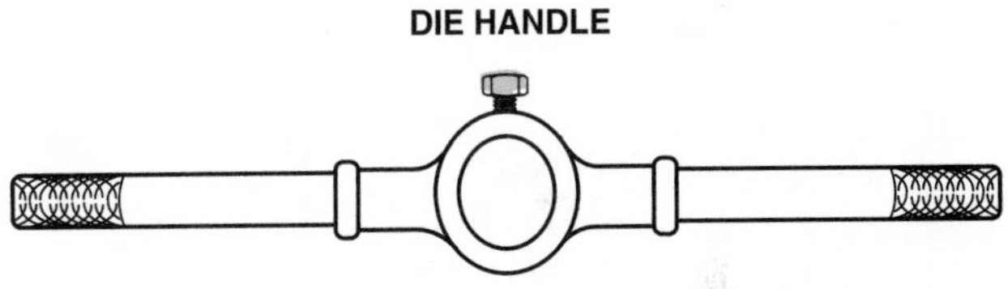

T-HANDLE
TAP WRENCH

(a)

FIGURE 3-12a   A T-handle is used to hold and rotate small taps.

HAND TAP WRENCH

(b)

FIGURE 3-12b   A tap wrench is used to hold and drive larger taps.

DIE HANDLE

FIGURE 3-13   A die handle used to rotate a die while cutting threads on a metal rod.

Proper Use of Taps and Dies

Taps and dies are used to cut threads on roll stock in the case of a die or in a hole for a tap. A small tap can be held using a T-handle but for larger taps a tap handle is needed to apply the needed force to cut threads. See Figures 3-12a and 3-12b.

Tap Usage.   Be sure that the hole is the correct size for the tap and start by inserting the tap straight into the hole. Lubricate the tap using tapping lubricant. Rotate the tap about one full turn clockwise, then reverse the direction of the tap one-half turn to break the chip that was created. Repeat the procedure until the hole is completely threaded.

Die Usage.   A die should be used on the specified diameter rod for the size of the thread. Install the die securely into the die handle. See Figure 3-13.

Lubricate the die and the rod and place the die onto the end of the rod to be threaded. Rotate the die handle one full turn clockwise, then reverse the direction and rotate the die handle about a half turn counterclockwise to break the chip that was created. Repeat the process until the threaded portion has been completed.

THREAD PITCH GAUGE

A thread pitch gauge is a hand tool that has the outline of various thread sizes machined on stamped blades. To determine the thread pitch size of a fastener, the technician matches the thread of the thread pitch gauge to the threads of the fastener. See Figure 3-14.

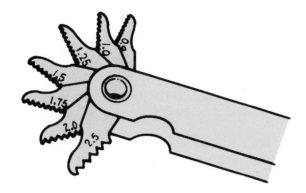

FIGURE 3-14   A typical thread pitch gauge.

FREQUENTLY ASKED QUESTION

WHAT IS THE DIFFERENCE BETWEEN A TAP AND A THREAD CHASER?

A tap is a cutting tool and is designed to cut new threads. A thread chaser has more rounded threads and is designed to clean dirty threads without removing metal. Therefore, when cleaning threads, it is best to use a thread chaser rather than a tap to prevent the possibility of removing metal, which would affect the fit of the bolt being installed. See Figure 3-15.

FIGURE 3-15   A thread chaser is shown at the top compared to a tap on the bottom. A thread chaser is used to clean threads without removing metal.

SHEET METAL SCREWS

Sheet metal screws are fully threaded screws with a point for use in sheet metal. Also called **self-tapping screws,** they are used in many places on the vehicle, including fenders, trim, and door panels. See Figure 3-16.

These screws are used in unthreaded holes and the sharp threads cut threads as they are installed. This makes for a quick and easy installation when installing new parts, but the sheet metal screw can easily strip out the threads when used on the same part over and over, so care is needed.

When reinstalling self-tapping screws, first turn the screw lightly backwards until you feel the thread drop into the existing thread in the screw hole. Then, turn the screw in; if it threads in easily, continue to tighten the screw. If the screw seems to turn hard, stop and turn it backwards about another half turn to locate the existing thread and try again. This technique can help prevent stripped holes in sheet metal and plastic parts.

Sheet metal screws are sized according to their major thread diameter.

Size	Diameter Decimal (inch)	Diameter Nearest Fraction (inch)
	0.11	7/64
	0.14	9/64
	0.17	11/64
0	0.19	3/16
2	0.22	7/32
4	0.25	1/4

WASHERS

Washers are often used under cap screw heads and under nuts. See Figure 3-17.

Plain flat washers are used to provide an even clamping load around the fastener. Lock washers are added to prevent accidental loosening. In some accessories, the washers are locked onto the nut to provide easy assembly.

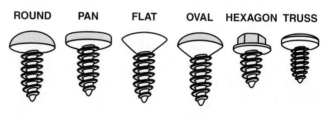

FIGURE 3-16   Sheet metal screws come with many head types.

HEX NUT   JAM NUT   NYLON LOCK NUT   CASTLE NUT   ACORN NUT

FLAT WASHER   LOCK WASHER   STAR WASHER   STAR WASHER

FIGURE 3-17 Various types of nuts (top) and washers (bottom) serve different purposes and all are used to secure bolts or cap screws.

SNAP RINGS AND CLIPS

Snap Rings

Snap rings are not threaded fasteners, but instead attach with a springlike action. Snap rings are constructed of spring steel and are used to attach parts without using a threaded fastener. There are several different types of snap rings and most require the use of a special pair of pliers, called snap-ring pliers, to release or install. The types of snap rings include:

- Expanding (internal)
- Contracting (external)
- E-clip
- C-clip
- Holeless snap rings in both expanding and contracting styles

See Figure 3-18.

Door Panel Clips

Interior door panels and other trim pieces are usually held in place with plastic clips. Due to the tapered and fluted shape, these clips are often called **Christmas tree clips.** See Figure 3-19.

A special tool is often used to remove interior door panels without causing any harm. See Figure 3-20.

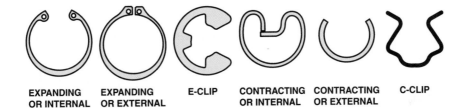

EXPANDING OR INTERNAL   EXPANDING OR EXTERNAL   E-CLIP   CONTRACTING OR INTERNAL   CONTRACTING OR EXTERNAL   C-CLIP

FIGURE 3-18 Some different types of snap rings. An internal snap ring fits inside of a housing or bore, into a groove. An external snap ring fits into a groove on the outside of a shaft or axle. An E-clip fits into a groove in the outside of a shaft. A C-clip shown is used to retain a window regulator handle on its shaft.

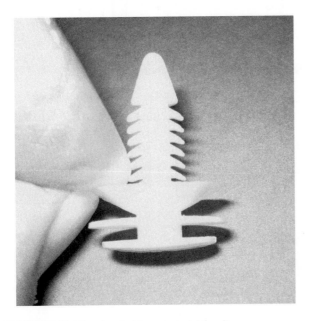

FIGURE 3-19 A typical door panel retaining clip.

FIGURE 3-20 Plastic or metal trim tools are available to help the technician remove interior door panels and other trim without causing harm.

CAUTION: Use extreme care when removing panels that use plastic or nylon clips. It is very easy to damage the door panel or clip during removal.

Pins

Cotter pins, also called a cotter key, are used to keep linkage or a threaded nut in place or to keep it retained. The word *cotter* is an Old English verb meaning "to close or fasten." There are many other types of pins used in vehicles, including clevis pins, roll pins, and hair pins. See Figure 3-21.

Pins are used to hold together shafts and linkages, such as shift linkages and cable linkages. The clevis pin is held in place with a cotter pin, while the taper and roll pins are driven in and held by friction. The hair pin snaps into a groove on a shaft.

Rivets

Rivets are used in many locations to retain components, such as window mechanisms, that do not require routine removal and/or do not have access to the back side for a nut. A drill is usually used to remove a rivet and a rivet gun is needed to properly install a rivet. Some rivets are plastic and are used to hold some body trim pieces. The most common type of rivet is called a **pop rivet** because as the rivet tool applies a force to

the shaft of the pop rivet, it causes the rivet to expand and tighten the two pieces together. When the shaft of the rivet, which looks like a nail, is pulled to its maximum, the shaft breaks, causing a "pop" sound.

Rivets may be used in areas of the vehicle where a semipermanent attachment is needed and in places where there is no access to the back side of the workpiece. They are installed using a rivet gun or by peening with a ball-peen hammer. See Figure 3-22.

Both types of blind rivets require the use of a rivet gun to install. The straight rivet is placed through the workpieces and then peened over with a ball-peen hammer or an air-operated tool. The plastic rivet is used with a rivet gun to install some body trim parts.

Locking Nuts

Some nuts, called jam nuts, are used to keep bolts and screws from loosening. **Jam nuts** screw on top of a regular nut and jam against the regular nut to prevent loosening. A jam nut is so called because of its intended use, rather than a special design. Some jam nuts are thinner than a standard nut. Jam nuts are also called **pal nuts.** See Figure 3-23.

CLEVIS   TAPER   ROLL   HAIR PIN   COTTER

FIGURE 3-21   Pins come in various types.

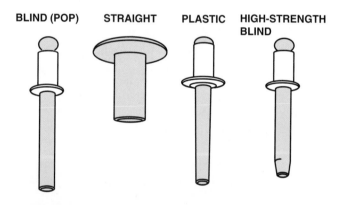

BLIND (POP)   STRAIGHT   PLASTIC   HIGH-STRENGTH BLIND

FIGURE 3-22   Various types of rivets.

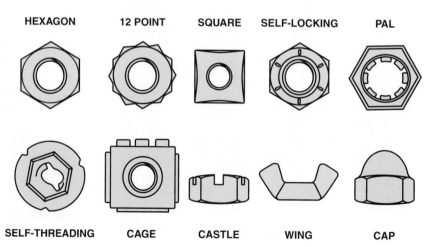

HEXAGON   12 POINT   SQUARE   SELF-LOCKING   PAL

SELF-THREADING   CAGE   CASTLE   WING   CAP

FIGURE 3-23   All of the nuts shown are used by themselves except for the pal nut, which is used to lock another nut to a threaded fastener so they will not be loosened by vibration.

There are also self-locking nuts of various types. Some have threads that are bent inward to grip the threads of the bolt. Some are oval-shaped at one end to fit tightly on a bolt. Fiber lock nuts have a fiber insert near the top of the nut or inside it; this type of nut is also made with a plastic or nylon insert. When the bolt turns through the nut, it cuts threads in the fiber or plastic. This puts a drag on the threads that prevents the bolt from loosening.

One of the oldest types of retaining nuts is the castle nut. It looks like a small castle, with slots for a cotter pin. A castellated nut is used on a bolt that has a hole for the cotter pin. See Figure 3-24.

Flat washers are placed underneath a nut to spread the load over a wide area and prevent gouging of the material. However, flat washers do not prevent a nut from loosening.

Lock washers are designed to prevent a nut from loosening. Spring-type lock washers resemble a loop out of a coil spring. As the nut or bolt is tightened, the washer is compressed. The tension of the compressed washer holds the fastener firmly against the threads to prevent it from loosening. Lock washers should not be used on soft metal such as aluminum. The sharp ends of the steel washers would gouge the aluminum badly, especially if they are removed and replaced often.

Another type of locking washer is the star washer. The teeth on a star washer can be external or internal, and they bite into the metal because they are twisted to expose their edges. Star washers are used often on sheet metal or body parts. They are seldom used on engines. The spring steel lock washer also uses the tension of the compressed washer to prevent the fastener from loosening. The waves in this washer make it look like a distorted flat washer.

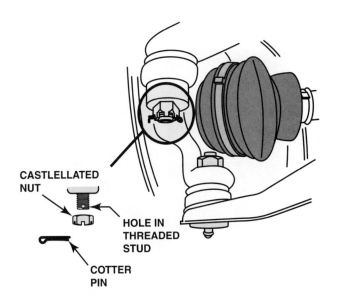

CASTLELLATED
NUT

HOLE IN
THREADED
STUD

COTTER
PIN

FIGURE 3-24   A castellated nut is locked in place with a cotter pin.

HOW TO AVOID BROKEN FASTENERS

Try not to break, strip, or round off fasteners in the first place. There are several ways that you can minimize the number of fasteners you damage. First, never force fasteners loose during disassembly. Taking a few precautionary steps will often prevent damage. If a bolt or nut will not come loose with normal force, try tightening it in slightly and then backing it out. Sometimes turning the fastener the other way will break corrosion loose, and the fastener will then come out easily. Another method that works well is to rest a punch on the head of a stubborn bolt and strike it a sharp blow with a hammer. Often this method will break the corrosion loose.

Left-Handed Threads

Although rare, left-handed fasteners are occasionally found on engine assemblies. These fasteners will loosen when you turn them clockwise, and tighten when you turn them counterclockwise. Left-handed fasteners are used to fasten parts to the ends of rotating assemblies that turn counterclockwise, such as crankshafts and camshafts. Most automobile engines do not use left-handed threads; however, they will be found on many older motorcycle engines. Some left-handed fasteners are marked for easy identification, others are not. Left-handed threads are also found inside some transaxles.

Penetrating Oil

Penetrating oil is a lightweight lubricant similar to kerosene, which soaks into small crevices in the threads, called **capillary action.** The chemical action of penetrating oils helps to break up and dissolve rust and corrosion. The oil forms a layer of boundary lubrication on the threads to reduce friction and make the fastener easier to turn.

For best results, allow the oil time to soak in before removing the nuts and bolts. To increase the effectiveness of penetrating oil, tap on the bolt head or nut with a hammer, or alternately work the fastener back and forth with a wrench. This movement weakens the bond of the corrosion and lets more of the lubricant work down into the threads.

Proper Tightening

Proper tightening of bolts and nuts is critical for proper clamping force, as well as to prevent breakage. All fasteners should be tightened using a torque wrench. A torque wrench allows the technician to exert a known amount of torque to the fasteners. However, rotating torque on a fastener does not mean clamping force because up to 80% of the torque used to rotate a bolt or nut is absorbed by friction by the threads. Therefore, for accurate tightening, two things must be performed:

- The threads must be clean and lubricated if service information specifies that they be lubricated.
- Always use a torque wrench to not only ensure proper clamping force, but also to ensure that all fasteners are tightened the same.

THREAD REPAIR INSERTS

Thread repair inserts are used to replace the original threaded hole when it has become damaged beyond use. The original threaded hole is enlarged and a threaded insert is installed to restore the threads to the original size.

Helical Inserts

A **helical insert** looks like a small, stainless-steel spring. See Figure 3-25.

To install a helical insert, a hole must be drilled to a specified oversize, and then it is tapped with a special tap designed for the thread inserts. The insert is then screwed into the hole. See Figure 3-26.

FIGURE 3-25 Helical inserts look like small, coiled springs. The outside is a thread to hold the coil in the hole, and the inside is threaded to fit the desired fastener.

FIGURE 3-26 The insert provides new, stock-size threads inside an oversize hole so that the original fastener can be used.

The insert stays in the casting as a permanent repair and bolts can be removed and replaced without disturbing the insert. One advantage of a helical insert is that the original bolt can be used because the internal threads are the same size. When correctly installed, an insert is often stronger than the original threads, especially in aluminum castings. Some vehicle manufacturers such as BMW specify that the threads be renewed using an insert if the cylinder head has to be removed and reinstalled. Plus many high-performance engine rebuilders install inserts in blocks, manifolds, and cylinder heads as a precaution.

One of the best known of the helical fasteners is the **Helicoil®**, manufactured by Helicoil® Products. To install Helicoil® inserts, you will need to have a thread repair kit. The kit includes a drill bit, tap, installation mandrel, and inserts. Repair kits are available for a wide variety of diameters and pitch to fit both American Standard and metric threads. A simple kit contains the tooling for one specific thread size. Master kits that cover a range of sizes are also available. Installing an insert is similar to tapping new threads. A summary of the procedures includes:

1. Select the Helicoil® kit designed for the specific diameter and thread pitch of the hole to be repaired. See Figure 3-27.
2. Use the drill bit supplied with the kit. The drill size is also specified on the Helicoil® tap, to open up the hole to the necessary diameter and depth.
3. Tap the hole with the Helicoil® tap, being sure to lubricate the tap. Turn it in slowly and rotate counterclockwise occasionally to break the chip that is formed.
4. Thread an insert onto the installation mandrel until it seats firmly. Apply a light coating of the recommended thread locking compound to the external threads of the insert.
5. Use the mandrel to screw the insert into the tapped hole. Once started, spring tension prevents the insert from

FIGURE 3-27 Helicoil® kits, available in a wide variety of sizes, contain everything needed to repair a damaged hole back to its original size.

unscrewing. Stop when the top of the insert is 1/4 to 1/2 turn below the surface.

6. Remove the mandrel by unscrewing it from the insert, and then use a small punch or needle-nose pliers to break off the tang at the base of the insert. Never leave the tang in the bore. The finished thread is ready for use immediately.

Threaded Inserts

Threaded inserts are tubular, case-hardened, solid steel wall pieces that are threaded inside and outside. The inner thread of the insert is sized to fit the original fastener of the hole to be repaired. The outer thread design will vary. These may be self-tapping threads that are installed in a blank hole, or machine threads that require the hole to be tapped. Threaded inserts return a damaged hole to original size by replacing part of the surrounding casting so drilling is required. Most inserts fit into three categories:

- Self-tapping
- Solid-bushing
- Key-locking

Self-Tapping Inserts

The external threads of a self-tapping insert are designed to cut their own way into a casting. This eliminates the need of running a tap down the hole. To install a typical self-tapping insert, follow this procedure:

1. Drill out the damaged threads to open the hole to the proper size, using the specified size drill bit.
2. Select the proper insert and mandrel. As with Helicoils®, the drill bit, inserts, and mandrel are usually available as a kit.
3. Thread the insert onto the mandrel. Use a tap handle or wrench to drive the insert into the hole. Because the insert will cut its own path into the hole, it may require a considerable amount of force to drive the insert in.
4. Thread the insert in until the nut or flange at the bottom of the mandrel touches the surface of the workpiece. This is the depth stop to indicate the insert is seated.
5. Hold the nut or flange with a wrench, and turn the mandrel out of the insert. The threads are ready for immediate use.

Solid-Bushing Inserts

The external threads of solid-bushing inserts are ground to a specific thread pitch, so you will have to run a tap into the hole. See Figure 3-28.

Some inserts use a machine thread so a standard tap can be used; others have a unique thread and you have to use a special tap. The thread inserts come with a matching installation kit. See Figure 3-29.

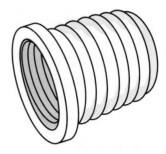

FIGURE 3-28   This solid-bushing insert is threaded on the outside, to grip the workpiece. The inner threads match the desired bolt size.

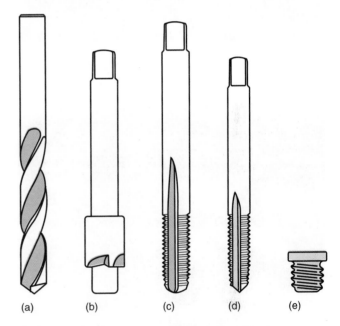

(a)   (b)   (c)   (d)   (e)

FIGURE 3-29   A Timesert® kit includes the drill (a), the recess cutter (b), a special tap (c), the installer (d), and the Timesert® threaded bushing (e).

To install threaded inserts, follow this procedure:

1. Drill out the damaged threads to open the hole to the proper size. The drill bit supplied with the kit must be the one used because it is properly sized to the tap. See Figure 3-30.
2. Cut the recess in the top of the hole with the special tool, then clean the hole with a brush or compressed air.
3. Use the previously detailed tapping procedures to thread the hole. See Figure 3-31. Be sure to tap deep enough; the top of the insert must be flush with the casting surface.
4. Thread the insert onto the installation driver, using the driver to screw the insert into the hole. Some inserts require that a thread-locking compound be applied; others go in dry.
5. Remove the installation driver, and the new threads are ready for service with the original fastener.

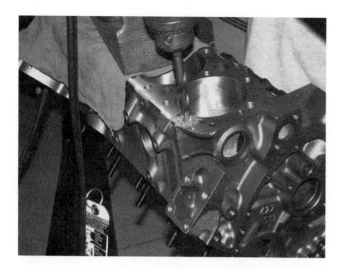

FIGURE 3-30   Drill out the damaged threads with the correct bit.

FIGURE 3-31   Use a special tap for the insert.

FIGURE 3-32   Put some thread-locking compound on the insert.

Key-Locking Inserts

Key-locking inserts are similar to solid-bushing inserts, but are held in place by small keys. After the insert has been installed, the keys are driven into place—perpendicular to the threads—to keep the insert from turning out. A typical installation procedure includes the following steps:

1. Drill out the damaged thread with the specified drill size.
2. Tap the drilled hole with the specified tap.
3. After putting thread-locking compound on the insert, use the mandrel to screw the insert into the tapped hole until it is slightly below the surface. See Figure 3-32. The keys act as a depth stop and prevent the insert from turning.
4. Drive the keys down using the driver supplied with the insert kit. Be sure the keys are flush with the top of the insert. See Figures 3-33 and 3-34.

FIGURE 3-33   Use the driver to drive the keys down flush with the surface of the workpiece.

FIGURE 3-34   The insert and insert locks should be below the surface of the workpiece.

SUMMARY

1. The most common type of fastener is a threaded one often referred to as a bolt. A nut or thread hole is used at the end of a bolt to fasten two parts together.

2. The size of threaded fasteners includes the diameter, length, and pitch of the threads, as well as the shape of the head of the bolt.

3. Metric bolts are labeled with an "M," and the diameter across the threads is in millimeters followed by the distance between the threads measured in millimeters, such as M8 × 1.5.

4. Graded bolts are hardened and are capable of providing more holding force than nongraded bolts.

5. Many nuts are capable of remaining attached to the bolt regardless of vibration. These types of nuts are often called prevailing torque nuts.

6. Other commonly used fasteners in the automotive service industry include sheet metal screws, snap rings and clips, door panel clips, cotter pins, and rivets.

7. Threads can be repaired using a Helicoil® or threaded insert.

REVIEW QUESTIONS

1. What is the difference between a bolt and a stud?

2. How is the size of a metric bolt expressed?

3. What is meant by the grade of a threaded fastener?

4. How do prevailing torque nuts work?

5. How are threaded inserts installed?

CHAPTER QUIZ

1. The thread pitch of a bolt is measured in what units?
   a. Millimeters
   b. Threads per inch
   c. Fractions of an inch
   d. Both a and b can be correct

2. Technician A says that the diameter of a bolt is the same as the wrench size used to remove or install the fastener. Technician B says that the length is measured from the top of the head of the bolt to the end of the bolt. Which technician is correct?
   a. Technician A only
   b. Technician B only
   c. Both Technicians A and B
   d. Neither Technician A nor B

3. The grade of a fastener, such as a bolt, is a measure of its ____.
   a. Tensile strength
   b. Hardness
   c. Finish
   d. Color

4. Which of the following is a metric bolt?
   a. 5/16 – 18
   b. 1/2 – 20
   c. M12 × 1.5
   d. 8 mm

5. A bolt that is threaded into a casting is often called a ____.
   a. Stud
   b. Cap screw
   c. Block bolt
   d. Crest bolt

6. The marks (lines) on the heads of bolts indicate ____.
   a. Size
   b. Grade
   c. Tensile strength
   d. Both b and c

7. A bolt that requires a 1/2-inch wrench to rotate is usually what size when measured across the threads?
   a. 1/2 inch
   b. 5/16 inch
   c. 3/8 inch
   d. 7/16 inch

8. A screw that can make its own threads when installed is called a _____ screw.
   a. Sheet metal
   b. Tapered
   c. Self-tapping
   d. Blunt-end

9. All of the following are types of clips *except* _____.
   a. E-clip
   b. Cotter
   c. C-clip
   d. Internal

10. What type of fastener is commonly used to retain interior door panels?
    a. Christmas tree clips
    b. E-clips
    c. External clips
    d. Internal clips

CHAPTER 4

HAND TOOLS

OBJECTIVES

After studying Chapter 4, the reader will be able to:

1. Describe what tool is the best to use for each job.
2. Discuss how to safely use hand tools.

3. Explain the difference between the brand name (trade name) and the proper name for tools.
4. Explain how to maintain hand tools.

KEY TERMS

WRENCHES

Wrenches are the most used hand tool by service technicians. Most wrenches are constructed of forged alloy steel, usually chrome-vanadium steel. See Figure 4-1.

After the wrench is formed, the wrench is hardened, then tempered to reduce brittleness, and then chrome plated. There are several types of wrenches.

Open-End Wrench

An **open-end wrench** is usually used to loosen or tighten bolts or nuts that do not require a lot of torque. An open-end wrench can be easily placed on a bolt or nut with an angle of 15 degrees, which allows the wrench to be flipped over and used again to continue to rotate the fastener. The major disadvantage of an open-end wrench is the lack of torque that can be applied

FIGURE 4-1 A forged wrench after it has been forged but before the flashing; extra material around the wrench has been removed.

due to the fact that the open jaws of the wrench only contact two flat surfaces of the fastener. An open-end wrench has two different sizes; one at each end. See Figure 4-2.

Box-End Wrench

A **box-end wrench** is placed over the top of the fastener and grips the points of the fastener. A box-end wrench is angled 15 degrees to allow it to clear nearby objects. See Figure 4-3.

Therefore, a box-end wrench should be used to loosen or to tighten fasteners. A box-end wrench is also called a **close-end**

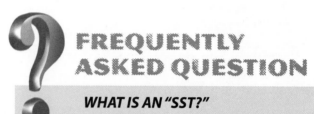

FREQUENTLY ASKED QUESTION

WHAT IS AN "SST?"

Vehicle manufacturers often specify a **special service tool (SST)** to properly disassemble and assemble components, such as transmissions and other components. These tools are also called special tools and are available from the vehicle manufacturer or their tool supplier, such as Kent-Moore and Miller tools. Many service technicians do not have access to special service tools so they use generic versions that are available from after-market sources.

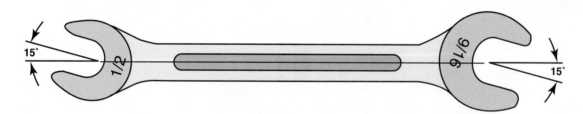

FIGURE 4-2 A typical open-end wrench. The size is different on each end. Notice that the head is angled 15 degrees at each end.

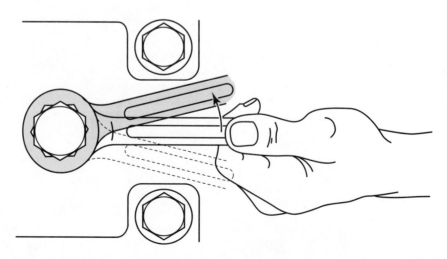

FIGURE 4-3 A typical box-end wrench is able to grip the bolt or nut at points completely around the fastener. Each end is a different size.

wrench. A box-end wrench has two different sizes; one at each end. See Figure 4-4.

Most service technicians purchase **combination wrenches,** which have the open end at one end and the same size box end on the other end. See Figure 4-5.

A combination wrench allows the technician to loosen or tighten a fastener using the box end of the wrench, turn it

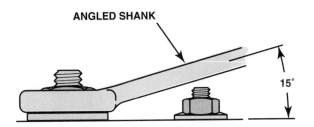

FIGURE 4-4 The end of a box-end wrench is angled 15 degrees to allow clearance for nearby objects or other fasteners.

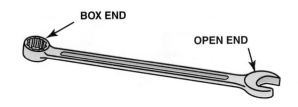

FIGURE 4-5 A combination wrench has an open end at one end and a box end at the other end.

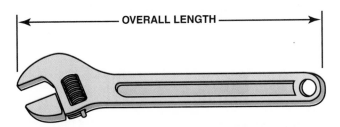

FIGURE 4-6 An adjustable wrench. Adjustable wrenches are sized by the overall length of the wrench and not by how far the jaws open. Common sizes of adjustable wrenches include 8, 10, and 12 inch.

FIGURE 4-7 The end of a typical line wrench, which shows that it is capable of grasping most of the head of the fitting.

around, and use the open end to increase the speed of rotating the fastener.

Adjustable Wrench

An **adjustable wrench** is often used where the exact size wrench is not available or when a large nut, such as a wheel spindle nut, needs to be rotated but not tightened. An adjustable wrench should not be used to loosen or tighten fasteners because the torque applied to the wrench can cause the movable jaws to loosen their grip on the fastener, causing it to become rounded. See Figure 4-6.

Line Wrenches

Line wrenches are also called **flare-nut wrenches, fitting wrenches,** or **tube-nut wrenches** and are designed to grip almost all the way around a nut used to retain a fuel or refrigerant line, and yet, be able to be installed over the line. See Figure 4-7.

Safe Use of Wrenches Wrenches should be inspected before use to be sure they are not cracked, bent, or damaged. All wrenches should be cleaned after use before being returned to the toolbox. Always use the correct size of wrench for the fastener being loosened or tightened to help prevent the rounding of the flats of the fastener. When attempting to loosen a fastener, pull a wrench—do not push a wrench. If a wrench is pushed, your knuckles can be hurt when forced into another object if the fastener breaks loose.

RATCHETS, SOCKETS, AND EXTENSIONS

A **socket** fits over the fastener and grips the points and/or flats of the bolt or nut. The socket is rotated (driven) using either a long bar called a **breaker bar (flex handle)** or a **ratchet.** See Figures 4-8 and 4-9.

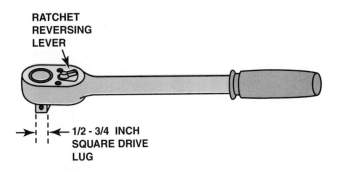

FIGURE 4-8 A typical ratchet used to rotate a socket. A ratchet makes a ratcheting noise when it is being rotated in the opposite direction from loosening or tightening. A knob or lever on the ratchet allows the user to switch directions.

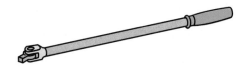

FIGURE 4-9   A typical flex handle used to rotate a socket, also called a breaker bar because it usually has a longer handle than a ratchet and, therefore, can be used to apply more torque to a fastener than a ratchet.

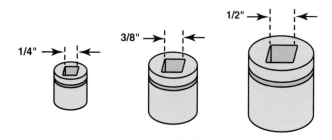

FIGURE 4-10   The most commonly used socket drive sizes include 1/4-inch, 3/8-inch, and 1/2-inch drive.

TECH TIP

RIGHT TO TIGHTEN

It is sometimes confusing which way to rotate a wrench or screwdriver, especially when the head of the fastener is pointing away from you. To help visualize while looking at the fastener, say "righty tighty, lefty loosey."

A ratchet turns the socket in only one direction and allows the rotating of the ratchet handle back and forth in a narrow space. Socket **extensions** and **universal joints** are also used with sockets to allow access to fasteners in restricted locations.

Sockets are available in various **drive sizes,** including 1/4-inch, 3/8-inch, and 1/2-inch sizes for most automotive use. See Figures 4-10 and 4-11.

Many heavy-duty truck and/or industrial applications use 3/4-inch and 1-inch sizes. The drive size is the distance of each side of the square drive. Sockets and ratchets of the same size are designed to work together.

Crowfoot Sockets

A **crowfoot socket** is a socket that is an open-end or line wrench to allow access to fasteners that cannot be reached using a conventional wrench. See Figure 4-12.

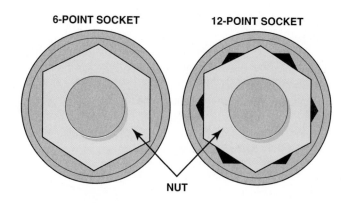

FIGURE 4-11   A 6-point socket fits the head of the bolt or nut on all sides. A 12-point socket can round off the head of a bolt or nut if a lot of force is applied.

FIGURE 4-12   A crowfoot socket is designed to reach fasteners using a ratchet or breaker bar with an extension.

Crowfoot sockets are available in the following categories:

- Fractional inch open-end wrench
- Metric open-end wrench
- Fractional line wrench
- Metric line wrench

Torque Wrenches

Torque wrenches are socket turning handles that are designed to apply a known amount of force to the fastener. There are two basic types of torque wrenches including:

1. **Clicker type.** A **clicker-type torque wrench** is first set to the specified torque and then it "clicks" when the set torque value has been reached. When force is removed from the torque wrench handle, another click is heard. The setting on a clicker-type torque wrench should be set back to zero after use and checked for proper calibration regularly. See Figure 4-13.
2. **Beam type.** A **beam-type torque wrench** is used to measure torque, but instead of presetting the value, the actual torque is displayed on the dial of the wrench as the fastener is being tightened. Beam-type torque wrenches are available in 1/4-inch, 3/8-inch, and 1/2-inch drives and both English and metric units. See Figure 4-14.

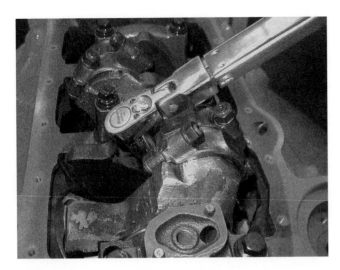

FIGURE 4-13 Using a torque wrench to tighten connecting rod nuts on an engine.

FIGURE 4-14 A beam-type torque wrench that displays the torque reading on the face of the dial. The beam display is read as the beam defects, which is in proportion to the amount of torque applied to the fastener.

FIGURE 4-15 Torque wrench calibration checker.

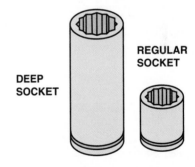

FIGURE 4-16 Deep sockets allow access to the nut that has a stud plus other locations needing great depth, such as spark plugs.

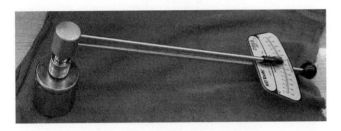

TECH TIP

CHECK TORQUE WRENCH CALIBRATION REGULARLY

Torque wrenches should be checked regularly. For example, Honda has a torque wrench calibration setup at each of their training centers. It is expected that a torque wrench be checked for accuracy before every use. Most experts recommend that torque wrenches be checked and adjusted as needed at least every year and more often if possible. See Figure 4-15.

Safe Use of Sockets and Ratchets. Always use the proper size socket that correctly fits the bolt or nut. All sockets and ratchets should be cleaned after use before being placed back into the toolbox. Sockets are available in short and deep well designs. See Figure 4-16.

Also select the appropriate drive size. For example, for small work, such as on the dash, select a 1/4-inch drive. For most general service work, use a 3/8-inch drive and for suspension and steering and other large fasteners, select a 1/2-inch drive. When loosening a fastener, always pull the ratchet toward you rather than push it outward.

FREQUENTLY ASKED QUESTION

IS IT LB-FT OR FT-LB OF TORQUE?

The unit for torque is expressed as a force times the distance (leverage) from the object. Therefore, the official unit for torque is lb-ft (pound-feet) or Newton-meters (a force times a distance). However, it is commonly expressed in ft-lbs and even some torque wrenches are labeled with this unit.

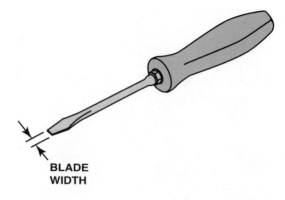

FIGURE 4-17 A flat-tip (straight blade) screwdriver. The width of the blade should match the width of the slot in the fastener being loosened or tightened.

TECH TIP

DOUBLE-CHECK THE SPECIFICATIONS

Misreading torque specifications is easy to do but can have serious damaging results. Specifications for fasteners are commonly expressed lb-ft. Many smaller fasteners are tightened to specifications expressed in lb-in.

1 lb-ft = 12 lb-in.

Therefore, if a fastener were to be accidentally tightened to 24 lb-ft instead of 24 lb-in., the actual torque applied to the fastener will be 288 lb-in. instead of the specified 24 lb-in.

This extra torque will likely break the fastener, but it could also warp or distort the part being tightened. Always double-check the torque specifications.

TECH TIP

USE SOCKET ADAPTERS WITH CAUTION

Socket adapters are available and can be used for different drive size sockets on a ratchet. Combinations include:

1/4-inch drive—3/8-inch sockets
3/8-inch drive—1/4-inch sockets
3/8-inch drive—1/2-inch sockets
1/2-inch drive—3/8-inch sockets

Using a larger drive ratchet or breaker bar on a smaller size socket can cause the application of too much force to the socket, which could crack or shatter. Using a smaller size drive tool on a larger socket will usually not cause any harm, but would greatly reduce the amount of torque that can be applied to the bolt or nut.

CAUTION: Do not use a screwdriver as a pry tool or as a chisel. Always use the proper tool for each application.

SCREWDRIVERS

Many smaller fasteners are removed and installed by using a **screwdriver.** Screwdrivers are available in many sizes and tip shapes. The most commonly used screwdriver is called a **flat tip** or **straight blade.**

Flat-tip screwdrivers are sized by the width of the blade and this width should match the width of the slot in the screw. See Figure 4-17.

Another type of commonly used screwdriver is called a Phillips screwdriver, named for Henry F. Phillips, who invented the crosshead screw in 1934. Due to the shape of the crosshead screw and screwdriver, a Phillips screw can be driven with more torque than can be achieved with a slotted screw.

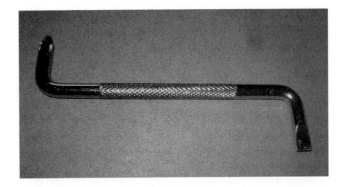

FIGURE 4-19   An offset screwdriver is used to install or remove fasteners that do not have enough space above to use a conventional screwdriver.

TECH TIP

AVOID USING "CHEATER BARS"

Whenever a fastener is difficult to remove, some technicians will insert the handle of a ratchet or a breaker bar into a length of steel pipe. The extra length of the pipe allows the technician to exert more torque than can be applied using the drive handle alone. However, the extra torque can easily overload the socket and ratchet, causing them to break or shatter, which could cause personal injury.

FIGURE 4-20   An impact screwdriver used to remove slotted or Phillips head fasteners that cannot be broken loose using a standard screwdriver.

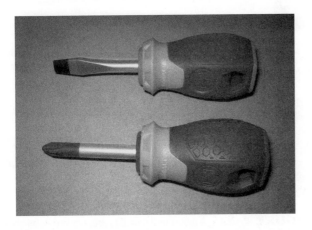

FIGURE 4-18   Two stubby screwdrivers that are used to access screws that have limited space above. A straight blade is on top and a #2 Phillips screwdriver is on the bottom.

have a straight blade at one end and a Phillips end at the opposite end. See Figure 4-19.

Impact Screwdriver

An impact screwdriver is used to break loose or tighten a screw. A hammer is used to strike the end after the screwdriver holder is placed in the head of the screw and rotated in the desired direction. The force from the hammer blow does two things: it applies a force downward holding the tip of the screwdriver in the slot and then applies a twisting force to loosen (or tighten) the screw. See Figure 4-20.

Safe Use of Screwdrivers.   Always use the proper type and size screwdriver that matches the fastener. Try to avoid pressing down on a screwdriver because if it slips, the screwdriver tip could go into your hand, causing serious personal injury. All screwdrivers should be cleaned after use. Do not use a screwdriver as a pry bar; always use the correct tool for the job.

A Phillips head screwdriver is specified by the length of the handle and the size of the point at the tip. A #1 tip has a sharp point, a #2 tip is the most commonly used, and a #3 tip is blunt and is only used for larger sizes of Phillips head fasteners. For example, a #2 × 3-inch Phillips screwdriver would typically measure 6 inches from the tip of the blade to the end of the handle (3-inch-long handle and 3-inch-long blade) with a #2 tip.

Both straight blade and Phillips screwdrivers are available with a short blade and handle for access to fasteners with limited room. See Figure 4-18.

Offset Screwdrivers

Offset screwdrivers are used in places where a conventional screwdriver cannot fit. An offset screwdriver is bent at the ends and is used similar to a wrench. Most offset screwdrivers

FREQUENTLY ASKED QUESTION

WHAT IS A ROBERTSON SCREWDRIVER?

A Canadian named P. L. Robertson invented the Robertson screw and screwdriver in 1908, which uses a square-shaped tip with a slight taper. The Robertson screwdriver uses color-coded handles because different size screws require different tip sizes. The color and sizes include:

Orange (#00)—Number 1 and 2 screws
Yellow (#0)—Number 3 and 4 screws
Green (#1)—Number 5, 6, and 7 screws
Red (#2)—Number 8, 9, and 10 screws
Black (#3)—Number 12 and larger screws

The Robertson screws are rarely found in the United States but are common in Canada.

HAMMERS AND MALLETS

Hammers

Hammers and mallets are used to force objects together or apart. The shape of the back part of the hammer head (called the **peen**) usually determines the name. For example, a ball-peen hammer has a rounded end like a ball and it is used to straighten oil pans and valve covers, using the hammer head, and for shaping metal, using the ball peen. See Figure 4-21.

NOTE: A claw hammer has a claw used to remove nails and is not used for automotive service.

A hammer is usually sized by the weight of the head of the hammer and the length of the handle. For example, a commonly used ball-peen hammer has an 8-ounce head with an 11-inch handle.

Mallets

Mallets are a type of hammer with a large striking surface, which allows the technician to exert force over a larger area than a hammer, so as not to harm the part or component. Mallets are made from a variety of materials including rubber, plastic, or wood. See Figure 4-22.

A shot-filled plastic hammer is called a **dead-blow hammer.** The small lead balls (shot) inside a plastic head prevent the hammer from bouncing off of the object when struck. See Figure 4-23.

Safe Use of Hammers and Mallets.   All mallets and hammers should be cleaned after use and not exposed to extreme temperatures. Never use a hammer or mallet that is damaged in any way and always use caution to avoid doing damage to the components and the surrounding area. Always follow the hammer manufacturer's recommended procedures and practices.

FIGURE 4-21   A typical ball-peen hammer.

FIGURE 4-22   A rubber mallet used to deliver a force to an object without harming the surface.

FIGURE 4-23   A dead-blow hammer that was left outside in freezing weather. The plastic covering was damaged, which destroyed this hammer. The lead shot is encased in the metal housing and then covered.

PLIERS

Slip-Joint Pliers

Pliers are capable of holding, twisting, bending, and cutting objects and are an extremely useful classification of tools. The common household type of pliers is called the **slip-joint pliers.** There are two different positions where the junction of the handles meets to achieve a wide range of sizes of objects that can be gripped. See Figure 4-24.

Multigroove Adjustable Pliers

For gripping larger objects, a set of **multigroove adjustable pliers** is a commonly used tool of choice by many service technicians. Originally designed to remove the various size

nuts holding rope seals used in water pumps, the name **water pump pliers** is also used. See Figure 4-25.

Linesman's Pliers

Linesman's pliers are specifically designed for cutting, bending, and twisting wire. While commonly used by construction workers and electricians, linesman's pliers are very useful tools for the service technician who deals with wiring. The center parts of the jaws are designed to grasp round objects such as pipe or tubing without slipping. See Figure 4-26.

Diagonal Pliers

Diagonal pliers are designed for cutting only. The cutting jaws are set at an angle to make it easier to cut wires. Diagonal

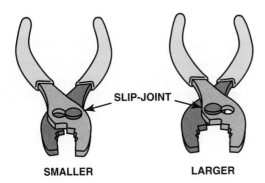

SLIP-JOINT

SMALLER   **LARGER**

FIGURE 4-24   Typical slip-joint pliers, which are also common household pliers. The slip joint allows the jaws to be opened to two different settings.

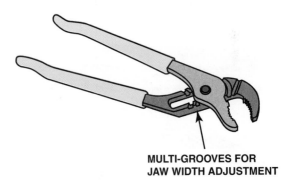

MULTI-GROOVES FOR JAW WIDTH ADJUSTMENT

FIGURE 4-25   Multigroove adjustable pliers are known by many names, including the trade name "Channel Locks."

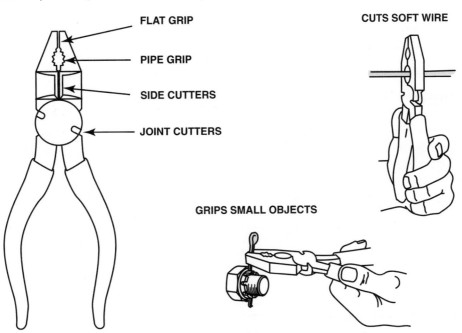

FLAT GRIP

PIPE GRIP

SIDE CUTTERS

JOINT CUTTERS

CUTS SOFT WIRE

GRIPS SMALL OBJECTS

FIGURE 4-26   A linesman's pliers are very useful because they can help perform many automotive service jobs.

CUTTING WIRES CLOSE TO TERMINALS

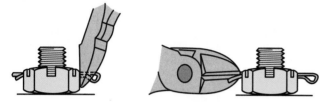

PULLING OUT AND SPREADING COTTER PIN

FIGURE 4-27   Diagonal-cut pliers are another common tool that has many names.

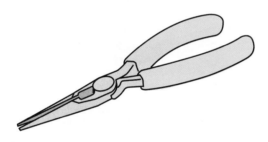

FIGURE 4-28   Needle-nose pliers are used where there is limited access to a wire or pin that needs to be installed or removed.

pliers are also called **side cut** or **dike.** These pliers are constructed of hardened steel and they are used mostly for cutting wire. See Figure 4-27.

Needle-Nose Pliers

Needle-nose pliers are designed to grip small objects or objects in tight locations. Needle-nose pliers have long, pointed jaws, which allow the tips to reach into narrow openings or groups of small objects. See Figure 4-28.

Most needle-nose pliers have a wire cutter located at the base of the jaws near the pivot. There are several variations of needle-nose pliers, including right angle jaws or slightly angled to allow access to certain cramped areas.

Locking Pliers

Locking pliers are adjustable pliers that can be locked to hold objects from moving. Most locking pliers also have wire cutters built into the jaws near the pivot point. Locking

FIGURE 4-29   Locking pliers are best known by their trade name Vise Grips®.

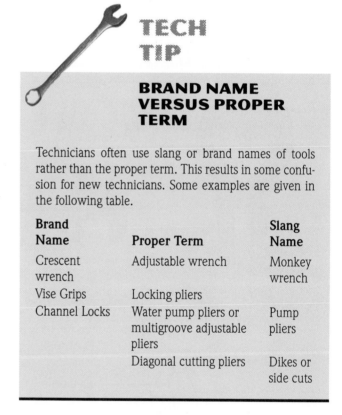

TECH TIP

BRAND NAME VERSUS PROPER TERM

Technicians often use slang or brand names of tools rather than the proper term. This results in some confusion for new technicians. Some examples are given in the following table.

Brand Name	Proper Term	Slang Name
Crescent wrench	Adjustable wrench	Monkey wrench
Vise Grips	Locking pliers	
Channel Locks	Water pump pliers or multigroove adjustable pliers	Pump pliers
	Diagonal cutting pliers	Dikes or side cuts

pliers come in a variety of styles and sizes and are commonly referred to by their trade name **VISE GRIPS®.** The size is the length of the pliers, not how far the jaws open. See Figure 4-29.

Safe Use of Pliers.   Pliers should not be used to remove any bolt or other fastener. Pliers should only be used when specified for use by the vehicle manufacturer.

Snap-Ring Pliers

Snap-ring pliers are used to remove and install snap rings. Many snap-ring pliers are designed to be able to remove and install inward, as well as outward, expanding snap rings.

Snap-ring pliers can be equipped with serrated-tipped jaws for grasping the opening in the snap ring, while others are equipped with points, which are inserted into the holes in the snap ring. See Figure 4-30.

Files

Files are used to smooth metal and are constructed of hardened steel with diagonal rows of teeth. Files are available with

a single row of teeth called a **single-cut file,** as well as two rows of teeth cut at an opposite angle called a **double-cut file.** Files are available in a variety of shapes and sizes from small flat files, half-round files, and triangular files. See Figure 4-31.

Safe Use of Files.   Always use a file with a handle. Because files only cut when moved forward, a handle must be attached to prevent possible personal injury. After making a forward strike, lift the file and return the file to the starting position; avoid dragging the file backward.

CUTTERS

Snips

Service technicians are often asked to fabricate sheet metal brackets or heat shields and need to use one or more types of cutters available. The simplest is called **tin snips,** which are designed to make straight cuts in a variety of materials, such as sheet steel, aluminum, or even fabric. A variation of the tin snips is called **aviation tin snips.** There are three designs of aviation snips including one designed to cut straight (called a **straight cut aviation snip**), one designed to cut left (called an **offset left aviation snip**), and one designed to cut right (called an **offset right aviation snip**). See Figure 4-32.

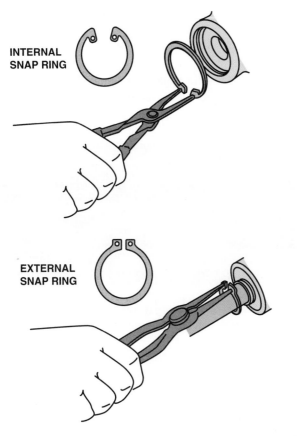

INTERNAL SNAP RING

EXTERNAL SNAP RING

FIGURE 4-30   Snap-ring pliers are also called lock-ring pliers and are designed to remove internal and external snap rings (lock rings).

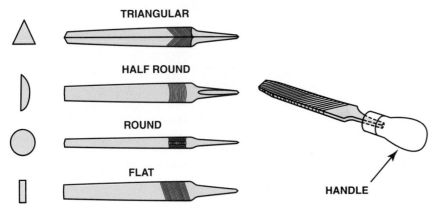

TRIANGULAR

HALF ROUND

ROUND

FLAT

HANDLE

FIGURE 4-31   Files come in many different shapes and sizes. Never use a file without a handle.

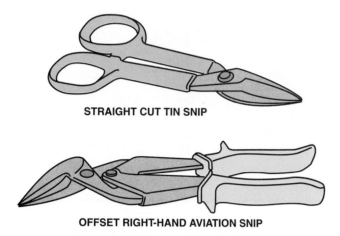

STRAIGHT CUT TIN SNIP

OFFSET RIGHT-HAND AVIATION SNIP

FIGURE 4-32   Tin snips are used to cut thin sheets of metal or carpet.

FIGURE 4-33   A utility knife uses replaceable blades and is used to cut carpet and other materials.

Utility Knife

A **utility knife** uses a replaceable blade and is used to cut a variety of materials such as carpet, plastic, wood, and paper products, such as cardboard. See Figure 4-33.

Safe Use of Cutters.   Whenever using cutters, always wear eye protection or a face shield to guard against the possibility of metal pieces being ejected during the cut. Always follow recommended procedures.

PUNCHES AND CHISELS

Punches

A **punch** is a small diameter steel rod that has a smaller diameter ground at one end. A punch is used to drive a pin out that is used to retain two components. Punches come in a variety of sizes, which are measured across the diameter of the machined end. Sizes include 1/16 inch, 1/8 inch, 3/16 inch, and 1/4 inch. See Figure 4-34.

PIN

FIGURE 4-34   A punch used to drive pins from assembled components. This type of punch is also called a pin punch.

WEAR SAFETY GOGGLES

FIGURE 4-35   Warning stamped in the side of a punch warning that goggles should be worn when using this tool. Always follow safety warnings.

Chisels

A **chisel** has a straight, sharp cutting end that is used for cutting off rivets or to separate two pieces of an assembly. The most common design of chisel used for automotive service work is called a **cold chisel.**

Safe Use of Punches and Chisels.   Always wear eye protection when using a punch or a chisel because the hardened steel is brittle and parts of the punch could fly off and cause serious personal injury. See the warning stamped on the side of this automotive punch in Figure 4-35.

Punches and chisels can also have the top rounded off, which is called "mushroomed." This material must be ground off to help avoid the possibility that the overhanging material is loosened and becomes airborne during use. See Figure 4-36.

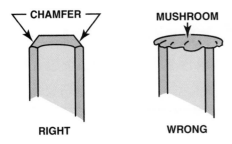

FIGURE 4-36 Use a grinder or a file to remove the mushroom material on the end of a punch or chisel.

REMOVERS

Removers are tools used to remove damaged fasteners. A remover tool is not normally needed during routine service unless the fastener is corroded or has been broken or damaged by a previous attempt to remove the bolt or nut.

To help prevent the need for a remover tool, all rusted and corroded fasteners should be sprayed with penetrating oil. Penetrating oil is a low viscosity oil that is designed to flow in between the threads of a fastener or other small separation between two parts. Commonly used penetrating oils include WD-40, Kroil, and CRC 5-56.

CAUTION: Do not use penetrating oil as a lubricating oil because it is volatile and will evaporate soon after usage leaving little lubricant behind for protection.

Removers are a classification of tool used to remove stuck or broken fasteners. Over time, rust and corrosion can cause the threads of the fastener to be attached to the nut or the casting making it very difficult to remove. There are several special tools that can be used to remove damaged fasteners. Which one to use depends on the type of damage.

Damaged Heads

If the bolt head or a nut becomes damaged or rounded, there are two special tools that can be used, including:

- Stud remover. A **stud removal tool** grips the part of the stud above the surface and uses a cam or wedge to grip the stud as it is being rotated by a ratchet or breaker bar. See Figure 4-37.
- Nut splitter. A **nut splitter** is used to remove the nut by splitting it from the bolt. A nut splitter is used by inserting the cutter against a flat of the nut and tightening the threaded bolt of the splitter. The nut will be split away from the bolt and can then be removed. See Figure 4-38.

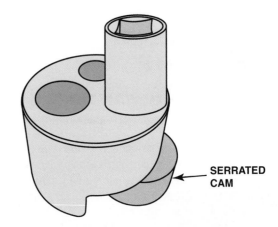

FIGURE 4-37 A stud remover uses an offset serrated wheel to grasp the stud so it will be rotated when a ratchet or breaker bar is used to rotate the assembly.

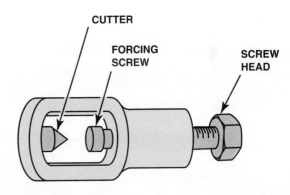

FIGURE 4-38 A nut splitter is used to split a nut that cannot be removed. After the nut has been split, a chisel is then used to remove the nut.

CAUTION: Do not rotate the entire nut splitter or damage to the cutting wedge will occur.

Broken Bolts, Studs, or Screws

Often, bolts, studs, or screws break even with, or below, the surface, making stud removal tools impossible to use. Bolt extractors are commonly called **"easy outs."** An easy out is constructed of hardened steel with flutes or edges ground into the side in an opposite direction of most threads. See Figure 4-39.

NOTE: Always select the largest extractor that can be used to help avoid the possibility of breaking the extractor while attempting to remove the bolt.

A hole is drilled into the center of a broken bolt. Then, the extractor (easy out) is inserted into the hole and rotated

TECH TIP

THE WAX TRICK

Many times rusted fasteners can be removed by using heat to expand the metal and break the rust bond between the fastener and the nut or casting. Many technicians heat the fastener using a torch and then apply paraffin wax or a candle to the heated fastener. See Figure 4-40. The wax will melt and, as the part cools, will draw the liquid wax down between the threads. After allowing the part to cool, attempt to remove the fastener. It will often be removed without any trouble.

FIGURE 4-39   A set of bolt extractors, commonly called easy outs.

FIGURE 4-40   Removing plugs or bolts is easier if the plug is first heated to cherry red color, using a torch, and then applying wax. During cooling, the wax flows in between the threads, making it easier to remove.

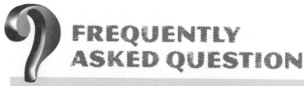

FREQUENTLY ASKED QUESTION

I BROKE OFF AN EASY OUT—NOW WHAT?

An extractor (easy out) is hardened steel and removing this and the broken bolt is now a job for a professional machine shop. The part, which could be as large as an engine block, needs to be removed from the vehicle and taken to a machine shop that is equipped to handle this type of job. One method involves using an electrical discharge machine (EDM). An EDM uses a high amperage electrical current to produce thousands of arcs between the electrode and the broken tool. The part is submerged in a nonconducting liquid and each tiny spark vaporizes a small piece of the broken tool.

counterclockwise using a wrench. As the extractor rotates, the grooves grip tighter into the wall of the hole drilled in the broken bolt. As a result, most extractors are capable of removing most broken bolts.

HACKSAWS

A **hacksaw** is used to cut metals, such as steel, aluminum, brass, or copper. The cutting blade of a hacksaw is replaceable and the sharpness and number of teeth can be varied to meet the needs of the job. Use 14 or 18 teeth per inch (tpi) for cutting plaster or soft metals, such as aluminum and copper. Use 24 or 32 teeth per inch for steel or pipe. Hacksaw blades should be installed with the teeth pointing away from the handle. This means that a hacksaw cuts while the blade is pushed in the forward direction, and then pressure should be released as the blade is pulled rearward before repeating the cutting operation. See Figure 4-41.

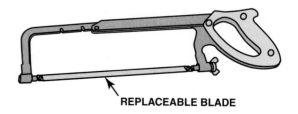

REPLACEABLE BLADE

FIGURE 4-41   A typical hacksaw that is used to cut metal. If cutting sheet metal or thin objects, a blade with more teeth should be used.

Safe Use of Hacksaws. Check that the hacksaw is equipped with the correct blade for the job and that the teeth are pointed away from the handle. When using a hacksaw, move the hacksaw slowly away from you, then lift slightly and return for another cut.

BASIC HAND TOOL LIST

Hand tools are used to turn fasteners (bolts, nuts, and screws). The following is a list of hand tools every automotive technician should possess. Specialty tools are not included.

Safety glasses
Tool chest
1/4-inch drive socket set (1/4 to 9/16 in. standard and deep sockets; 6 to 15 mm standard and deep sockets)
1/4-inch drive ratchet
1/4-inch drive 2-inch extension
1/4-inch drive 6-inch extension
1/4-inch drive handle
3/8-inch drive socket set (3/8 to 7/8 in. standard and deep sockets;10 to 19 mm standard and deep sockets)
3/8-inch drive Torx set (T40, T45, T50, and T55)
3/8-inch drive 13/16-inch plug socket
3/8-inch drive 5/8-inch plug socket
3/8-inch drive ratchet
3/8-inch drive 1 1/2-inch extension
3/8-inch drive 3-inch extension
3/8-inch drive 6-inch extension
3/8-inch drive 18-inch extension
3/8-inch drive universal
1/2-inch drive socket set (1/2 to 1 in. standard and deep sockets)
1/2-inch drive ratchet
1/2-inch drive breaker bar
1/2-inch drive 5-inch extension
1/2-inch drive 10-inch extension
3/8-inch to 1/4-inch adapter
1/2-inch to 3/8-inch adapter
3/8-inch to 1/2-inch adapter
Crowfoot set (fractional inch)
Crowfoot set (metric)
3/8- through 1-inch combination wrench set
10 millimeters through 19 millimeters combination wrench set
1/16-inch through 1/4-inch hex wrench set
2 millimeters through 12 millimeters hex wrench set
3/8-inch hex socket
13 millimeters to 14 millimeters flare nut wrench
15 millimeters to 17 millimeters flare nut wrench
5/16-inch to 3/8-inch flare nut wrench
7/16-inch to 1/2-inch flare nut wrench
1/2-inch to 9/16-inch flare nut wrench

Diagonal pliers
Needle pliers
Adjustable-jaw pliers
Locking pliers
Snap-ring pliers
Stripping or crimping pliers
Ball-peen hammer
Rubber hammer
Dead-blow hammer
Five-piece standard screwdriver set
Four-piece Phillips screwdriver set
#15 Torx screwdriver
#20 Torx screwdriver
File
Center punch
Pin punches (assorted sizes)
Chisel
Utility knife
Valve core tool
Filter wrench (large filters)
Filter wrench (smaller filters)
Test light
Feeler gauge
Scraper
Magnet

TOOL SETS AND ACCESSORIES

A beginning service technician may wish to start with a small set of tools before spending a lot of money on an expensive, extensive tool box. See Figures 4-42 and 4-43.

TECH TIP

HIDE THOSE FROM THE BOSS

An apprentice technician started working for a dealership and put his top tool box on a workbench. Another technician observed that, along with a complete set of good-quality tools, the box contained several adjustable wrenches. The more experienced technician said, "Hide those from the boss." If any adjustable wrench is used on a bolt or nut, the movable jaw often moves or loosens and starts to round the head of the fastener. If the head of the bolt or nut becomes rounded, it becomes that much more difficult to remove.

FIGURE 4-42 A typical beginning technician tool set that includes the basic tools to get started.

FIGURE 4-43 A typical large tool box, showing just one of many drawers.

TECH TIP

NEED TO BORROW A TOOL MORE THAN TWICE? BUY IT!

Most service technicians agree that it is okay for a beginning technician to borrow a tool occasionally. However, if a tool has to be borrowed more than twice, then be sure to purchase it as soon as possible. Also, whenever a tool is borrowed, be sure that you clean the tool and let the technician you borrowed the tool from know that you are returning the tool. These actions will help in any future dealings with other technicians.

TECH TIP

THE VALVE GRINDING COMPOUND TRICK

Apply a small amount of valve grinding compound to a Phillips or Torx screw or bolt head. The gritty valve grinding compound "grips" the screwdriver or tool bit and prevents the tool from slipping up and out of the screw head. Valve grinding compound is available in a tube from most automotive parts stores.

SEAL DRIVERS AND PULLERS

Seal Pullers

Grease seals are located on many automotive components, including brake rotors, transmission housings, and differentials. A **seal puller** is used to properly remove grease seals, as shown in Figure 4-44.

Seal Drivers

A **seal driver** can be either plastic or metal, usually aluminum, and is used to seat the outer lip of a grease seal into the grease seal pocket. A seal is usually driven into position using a

FIGURE 4-44 A seal puller being used to remove a seal from a rear axle.

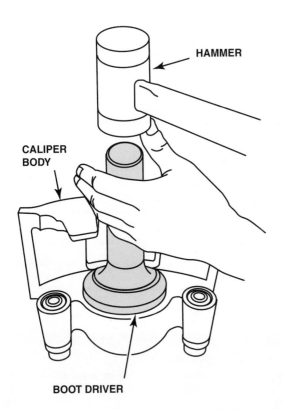

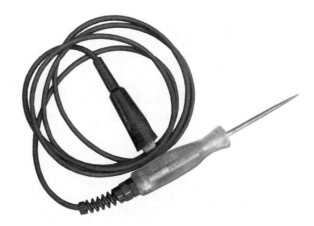

FIGURE 4-46   A typical 12-volt test light.

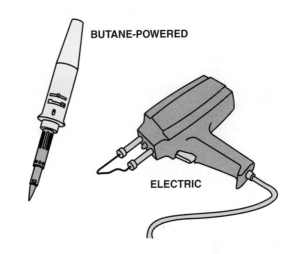

FIGURE 4-45   A seal driver or installer is usually plastic and is designed to seat the seal.

plastic mallet and a seal driver that is the same size as the outside diameter of the grease seal retainer. See Figure 4-45.

ELECTRICAL HAND TOOLS

Test Lights

A test light is used to test for electricity. A typical automotive test light consists of a clear plastic screwdriver-like handle that contains a light bulb. A wire is attached to one terminal of the bulb, which the technician connects to a clean metal part of the vehicle. The other end of the bulb is attached to a point that can be used to test for electricity at a connector or wire. When there is power at the point and a good connection at the other end, the light bulb lights. See Figure 4-46.

Soldering Guns

- **Electric soldering gun.** This type of soldering gun is usually powered by 110-volt AC and often has two power settings expressed in watts. A typical electric soldering gun will produce from 85 to 300 watts of heat at the tip, which is more than adequate for soldering. See Figure 4-47.
- **Electric soldering pencil.** This type of soldering iron is less expensive and creates less heat than an electric soldering

FIGURE 4-47   An electric soldering gun used to make electrical repairs. Soldering guns are sold by the wattage rating. The higher the wattage, the greater amount of heat created. Most solder guns used for automotive electrical work usually fall within the 60- to 160-watt range.

gun. A typical electric soldering pencil (iron) creates 30 to 60 watts of heat and is suitable for soldering smaller wires and connections.
- **Butane-powered soldering iron.** A butane-powered soldering iron is portable and very useful for automotive service work because an electrical cord is not needed. Most butane-powered soldering irons produce about 60 watts of heat, which is enough for most automotive soldering.

In addition to a soldering iron, most service technicians who do electrical-related work should have the following:

- Wire cutters
- Wire strippers
- Wire crimpers
- Heat gun

A digital meter is a necessary tool for any electrical diagnosis and troubleshooting. A digital multimeter, abbreviated

TECH TIP

IT JUST TAKES A SECOND

Whenever removing any automotive component, it is wise to screw the bolts back into the holes a couple of threads by hand. This ensures that the right bolt will be used in its original location when the component or part is put back on the vehicle. Often, the same diameter of fastener is used on a component, but the length of the bolt may vary. Spending just a couple of seconds to put the bolts and nuts back where they belong when the part is removed can save a lot of time when the part is being reinstalled. Besides making certain that the right fastener is being installed in the right place, this method helps prevent bolts and nuts from getting lost or kicked away. How much time have you wasted looking for that lost bolt or nut?

DMM, is usually capable of measuring the following units of electricity:

- DC volts
- AC volts
- Ohms
- Amperes

SAFETY TIPS FOR USING HAND TOOLS

The following safety tips should be kept in mind whenever you are working with hand tools:

- Always *pull* a wrench toward you for best control and safety. Never push a wrench.
- Keep wrenches and all hand tools clean to help prevent rust and to allow for a better, firmer grip.
- Always use a 6-point socket or a box-end wrench to break loose a tight bolt or nut.
- Use a box-end wrench for torque and an open-end wrench for speed.
- Never use a pipe extension or other type of **"cheater bar"** on a wrench or ratchet handle. If more force is required, use a larger tool or use penetrating oil and/or heat on the frozen fastener. (If heat is used on a bolt or nut to remove it, always replace it with a new part.)

TECH TIP

USE A BINDER CLIP

A binder clip (size 1 1/4 inches wide) is used by wise technicians to help keep fender covers in place. See Figure 4-48. Binder clips are found at office supply stores.

FIGURE 4-48 A binder clip being used to keep a fender cover from falling.

- Always use the proper tool for the job. If a specialized tool is required, use the proper tool and do not try to use another tool improperly.
- Never expose any tool to excessive heat. High temperatures can reduce the strength ("draw the temper") of metal tools.
- Never use a hammer on any wrench or socket handle unless you are using a special "staking face" wrench designed to be used with a hammer.
- Replace any tools that are damaged or worn.

HAND TOOL MAINTENANCE

Most hand tools are constructed of rust-resistant metals but they can still rust or corrode if not properly maintained. For best results and long tool life, the following steps should be taken:

- Clean each tool before placing it back into the tool box.
- Keep tools separated. Moisture on metal tools will start to rust more readily if the tools are in contact with another metal tool.

- Line the drawers of the tool box with a material that will prevent the tools from moving as the drawers are opened and closed. This helps to quickly locate the proper tool and size.

- Release the tension on all "clicker-type" torque wrenches.
- Keep the tool box secure.

SUMMARY

1. Wrenches are available in open end, box end, and combination open and box end.
2. An adjustable wrench should only be used where the proper size is not available.
3. Line wrenches are also called flare-nut wrenches, fitting wrenches, or tube-nut wrenches and are used to remove fuel or refrigerant lines.
4. Sockets are rotated by a ratchet or breaker bar, also called a flex handle.
5. Torque wrenches measure the amount of torque applied to a fastener.
6. Screwdriver types include straight blade (flat tip) and Phillips.
7. Hammers and mallets come in a variety of sizes and weights.
8. Pliers are a useful tool and are available in many different types, including slip-joint, multigroove, linesman's, diagonal, needle-nose, and locking pliers.
9. Other common hand tools include snap-ring pliers, files, cutters, punches, chisels, and hacksaws.

REVIEW QUESTIONS

1. Why are wrenches offset 15 degrees?
2. What are the other names for a line wrench?
3. What are the standard automotive drive sizes for sockets?
4. Which type of screwdriver requires the use of a hammer or mallet?
5. What is inside a dead-blow hammer?
6. What type of cutter is available in left and right cutters?

CHAPTER QUIZ

1. When working with hand tools, always _____.
   a. Push the wrench—don't pull toward you
   b. Pull a wrench—don't push a wrench
2. The proper term for Channel Locks is _____.
   a. Vise Grips
   b. Crescent wrench
   c. Locking pliers
   d. Multigroove adjustable pliers
3. The proper term for Vise Grips is _____.
   a. Locking pliers
   b. Slip-joint pliers
   c. Side cuts
   d. Multigroove adjustable pliers
4. Which tool listed is a brand name?
   a. Locking pliers
   b. Monkey wrench
   c. Side cutters
   d. Vise Grips
5. Two technicians are discussing torque wrenches. Technician A says that a torque wrench is capable of tightening a fastener with more torque than a conventional breaker bar or ratchet. Technician B says that a torque wrench should be calibrated regularly for the most accurate results. Which technician is correct?
   a. Technician A only
   b. Technician B only
   c. Both Technicians A and B
   d. Neither Technician A nor B

6. What type of screwdriver should be used if there is very limited space above the head of the fastener?

   a. Offset screwdriver

   b. Stubby screwdriver

   c. Impact screwdriver

   d. Robertson screwdriver

7. Where is the "peen" of the hammer?

   a. The striking face

   b. The handle

   c. The back part opposite the striking face

   d. The part that connects to the handle

8. What type of hammer is plastic coated, has a metal casing inside, and is filled with small lead balls?

   a. Dead-blow hammer

   b. Soft-blow hammer

   c. Sledge hammer

   d. Plastic hammer

9. Which type of pliers is capable of fitting over a large object?

   a. Slip-joint pliers

   b. Linesman's pliers

   c. Locking pliers

   d. Multigroove adjustable pliers

10. Which tool has a replaceable cutting edge?

    a. Side-cut pliers

    b. Tin snips

    c. Utility knife

    d. Aviation snips

CHAPTER 5

POWER TOOLS AND SHOP EQUIPMENT

OBJECTIVES

After studying Chapter 5, the reader will be able to:

1. Identify commonly used power tools.
2. Identify commonly used shop equipment.

3. Discuss the proper use of power tools and shop equipment.
4. Describe the safety procedures that should be followed when working with power tools and shop equipment.

KEY TERMS

Air-Blow Gun (p. 66)
Air Compressor (p. 64)
Air Drill (p. 65)
Air Ratchet (p. 65)
Bearing Splitter (p. 68)
Bench Grinder (p. 67)
Bench Vise (p. 67)
Die Grinder (p. 65)
Engine Stand (p. 69)

Hydraulic Press (p. 68)
Impact Wrench (p. 64)
Incandescent Light (p. 66)
Light Emitting Diode (LED) (p. 67)
Portable Crane (p. 68)
Stone Wheel (p. 67)
Trouble Light (p. 66)
Wire Brush Wheel (p. 67)
Work Light (p. 66)

AIR COMPRESSOR

A shop air compressor is usually located in a separate room or an area away from the customer area of a shop. An **air compressor** is powered by a 220-V AC electric motor and includes a storage tank and the compressor itself, as well as the pressure switches, which are used to maintain a certain minimum level of air pressure in the system. The larger the storage tank, expressed in gallons, the longer an air tool can be operated in the shop without having the compressor start operating. See Figure 5-1.

FIGURE 5-1   A typical shop compressor. It is usually placed out of the way, yet accessible to provide for maintenance to the unit.

FIGURE 5-2   A typical air nozzle. Always use an air nozzle that is OSHA approved.

REAL WORLD FIX

THE CASE OF THE RUSTY AIR IMPACT WRENCHES

In one busy shop, it was noticed by several technicians that water was being pumped through the air compressor lines and out of the vents of air impact wrenches whenever they were used. It is normal for moisture in the air to condense in the air storage tank of an air compressor. One of the routine service procedures is to drain the water from the air compressor. The water had been drained regularly from the air compressor at the rear of the shop, but the problem continued. Then someone remembered that there was a second air compressor mounted over the parts department. No one could remember ever draining the tank from that compressor. After that tank was drained, the problem of water in the lines was solved. The service manager assigned a person to drain the water from both compressors every day and to check the oil level. The oil in the compressor is changed every six months to help ensure long life of the expensive compressors.

Safe Use of Compressed Air

Air under pressure can create dangerous situations. For example, an object, such as a small piece of dirt, could be forced out of an air hose blow gun with enough force to cause serious personal injury. All OSHA approved air nozzles have air vents drilled around the outside of the main discharge hole to help reduce the force of the air blast. Also, the air pressure used by an air nozzle (blow gun) must be kept to 30 PSI (207 kPa) or less. See Figure 5-2.

AIR AND ELECTRICALLY OPERATED TOOLS

Impact Wrench

An **impact wrench,** either air (pneumatic) or electrically powered, is a tool that is used to remove and install fasteners. The air-operated 1/2-inch drive impact wrench is the most commonly used unit. See Figure 5-3.

The direction of rotation is controlled by a switch. See Figure 5-4.

Electrically powered impact wrenches commonly include:

- Battery-powered units. See Figure 5-5.

FIGURE 5-3   A typical 1/2-inch drive impact wrench.

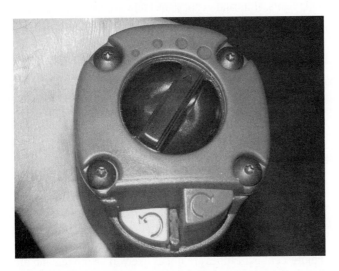

FIGURE 5-4   This impact wrench features a variable torque setting using a rotary knob. The diameter of rotation can be changed by pressing the button at the bottom.

FIGURE 5-5   A typical battery-powered 3/8-inch drive impact wrench.

- 110-volt AC-powered units. This type of impact wrench is very useful, especially if compressed air is not readily available.

CAUTION: Always use impact sockets with impact wrenches, and be sure to wear eye protection in case the socket or fastener shatters. Impact sockets are thicker walled and constructed with premium alloy steel. They are hardened with a black oxide finish to help prevent corrosion and distinguish them from regular sockets. See Figure 5-6.

Air Ratchet

An **air ratchet** is used to remove and install fasteners that would normally be removed or installed using a ratchet and a socket. An air ratchet is much faster, yet has an air hose attached, which reduces accessibility to certain places. See Figure 5-7.

Die Grinder

A **die grinder** is a commonly used air-powered tool, which can also be used to sand or remove gaskets and rust. See Figure 5-8.

Air Drill

An **air drill** is a drill that rotates faster than electric drills (up to 1800 RPM). Air drills are commonly used in auto body work when many holes need to be drilled for plug welding.

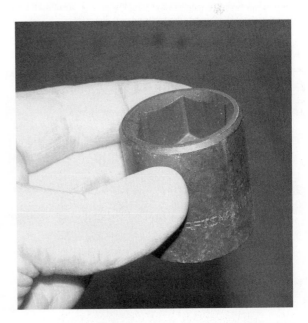

FIGURE 5-6   A black impact socket. Always use impact-type sockets whenever using an impact wrench to avoid the possibility of shattering the socket, which can cause personal injury.

Air-Blow Gun

An **air-blow gun** is used to clean equipment and other purposes where a stream of air would be needed. Automotive air-blow guns should meet OSHA requirements and include passages to allow air to escape outward at the nozzle, thereby relieving pressure if the nozzle were to become blocked.

Air-Operated Grease Gun

An air-operated grease gun uses shop air to operate a plunger, which then applies a force to grease a grease cartridge. Most air-operated grease guns use a 1/4-inch air inlet and operate on 90 PSI of air pressure.

FIGURE 5-7 An air ratchet is a very useful tool that allows fast removal and installation of fasteners, especially in areas that are difficult to reach or do not have room enough to move a hand ratchet wrench.

FIGURE 5-8 This typical die grinder surface preparation kit includes the air-operated die grinder, as well as a variety of sanding discs for smoothing surfaces or removing rust.

Battery-Powered Grease Gun

Battery-powered grease guns are more expensive than air-operated grease guns but offer the convenience of not having an air hose attached, making use easier. Many use rechargeable 14- to 18-volt batteries and use standard grease cartridges.

TROUBLE LIGHTS

Incandescent

Incandescent lights use a filament that produces light when electric current flows through the bulb. This was the standard **trouble light,** also called a **work light** for many years until safety issues caused most shops to switch to safer fluorescent or LED lights. If incandescent light bulbs are used, try to locate bulbs that are rated "rough service," which is designed to withstand shock and vibration more than conventional light bulbs.

WARNING: Do not use incandescent trouble lights around gasoline or other flammable liquids. The liquids can cause the bulb to break and the hot filament can ignite the flammable liquid.

Fluorescent

A trouble light is an essential piece of shop equipment, and for safety, should be fluorescent rather than incandescent. Incandescent light bulbs can scatter or break if gasoline were to be splashed onto the bulb creating a serious fire hazard. Fluorescent light tubes are not as likely to be broken and are usually protected by a clear plastic enclosure. Trouble lights

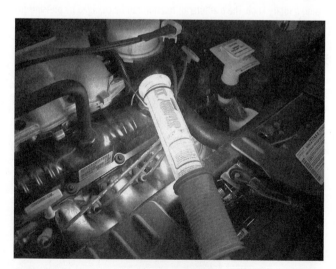

FIGURE 5-9 A fluorescent trouble light operates cooler and is safer to use in the shop because it is protected against accidental breakage where gasoline or other flammable liquids would happen to come in contact with the light.

are usually attached to a retractor, which can hold 20 to 50 feet of electrical cord. See Figure 5-9.

LED Trouble Light

Light emitting diode (LED) trouble lights are excellent to use because they are shock resistant, long lasting, and do not represent a fire hazard. Some trouble lights are battery powered and therefore can be used in places where an attached electrical cord could present problems.

BENCH/PEDESTAL GRINDER

A grinder can be mounted on a workbench or on a stand-alone pedestal.

Bench- or Pedestal-Mounted Grinder

These high-powered grinders can be equipped with a wire brush wheel and/or a stone wheel.

- A **wire brush wheel** is used to clean threads of bolts as well as to remove gaskets from sheet metal engine parts.
- A **stone wheel** is used to grind metal or to remove the mushroom from the top of punches or chisels. See Figure 5-10.

CAUTION: Always wear a face shield when using a wire wheel or a grinder. Also keep the part support ledge (table) close to the stone.

Most **bench grinders** are equipped with a grinder wheel (stone) on one end or the other of a wire brush. A bench grinder is a very useful piece of shop equipment and the wire wheel end can be used for the following:

- Cleaning threads of bolts
- Cleaning gaskets from sheet metal parts, such as steel valve covers

---

CAUTION: Only use a steel wire brush on steel or iron components. If a steel wire brush is used on aluminum or copper-based metal parts, it can remove metal from the part.

The grinding stone end of the bench grinder can be used for the following:

- Sharpening blades and drill bits
- Grinding off the heads of rivets or parts
- Sharpening sheet metal parts for custom fitting
- Cleaning threads using the wire brush wheel

BENCH VISE

A **bench vise** is used to hold components so that work can be performed on the unit. The size of a vise is determined by the length of the jaws. Two common sizes of vises are 4-inch and 6-inch models. The jaws of most vises are serrated and can cause damage to some components unless protected. Many types of protection can be used, including aluminum jaw covers or by simply placing wood between the vise jaws and the component being held. See Figure 5-11.

FIGURE 5-10   A typical pedestal grinder with a wire wheel on the left side and a stone wheel on the right side. Even though this machine is equipped with guards, safety glasses or a face shield should always be worn when using a grinder or wire wheel.

FIGURE 5-11   A typical vise mounted to a workbench.

Safe Use of Vises

The jaws of vises can cause damage to the part or component being held. Use pieces of wood or other soft material between the steel jaws and the workpiece to help avoid causing damage. Many vises are sold with optional aluminum jaw covers. When finished using a vise, be sure to close the jaws and place the handle straight up and down to help avoid personal injury to anyone walking near the vise.

HYDRAULIC PRESSES

Hydraulic presses are hand-operated hydraulic cylinders mounted to a stand and designed to press bearings on or off of shafts, as well as other components. To press off a bearing, a unit called a **bearing splitter** is often required to apply force to the inner race of a bearing. Hydraulic presses use a pressure gauge to show the pressure being applied. Always follow the operating instructions supplied by the manufacturer of the hydraulic press. See Figure 5-12.

PORTABLE CRANE AND CHAIN HOIST

A **portable crane** is used to remove and install engines and other heavy vehicle components. Most portable cranes use a hand-operated hydraulic cylinder to raise and lower a boom that is equipped with a nylon strap or steel chain. At the end of the strap or chain is a steel hook that is used to attach around a bracket or auxiliary lifting device. See Figure 5-13.

Safe Use of Portable Cranes

Always be sure to attach the hook(s) of the portable crane to a secure location on the unit being lifted. The hook should also be attached to the center of the weight of the object so it can be lifted straight up without tilting.

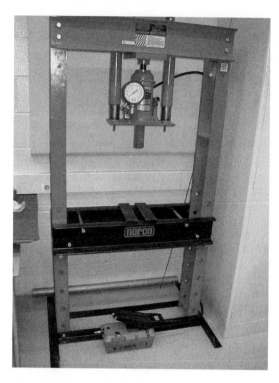

FIGURE 5-12   A hydraulic press is usually used to press bearings on and off on rear axles and transmissions.

TECH TIP

COVER WORK WHILE PRESSING

Whenever pressing on a bearing or other component, use an old brake drum over the shaft and the bearing. In the event the bearing shatters during the pressing operation, the brake drum will prevent the parts of the bearing from flying outward where they could cause serious personal injury.

FIGURE 5-13   A typical portable crane used to lift and move heavy assemblies, such as engines and transmissions.

CAUTION: Always keep feet and other body parts out from underneath the engine or unit being lifted. Always work around a portable crane as if the chain or strap could break at any time.

ENGINE STANDS

An **engine stand** is designed to safely hold an engine and to allow it to be rotated. This allows the technician to easily remove, install, and perform service work to the engine. See Figure 5-14.

Most engine stands are constructed of steel and supported by four casters to allow easy movement. There are two basic places where an engine stand attaches to the engine depending on the size of the engine. For most engines and stands, the retaining bolts attach to the same location as the bell housing at the rear of the engine.

On larger engines, such as the 5.9 Cummins inline six-cylinder diesel engine, the engine mounts to the stand using the engine mounting holes in the block. See Figure 5-15.

Safe Operation of an Engine Stand

When mounting an engine to an engine stand, be sure that the engine is being supported by a portable crane. Be sure

the attaching bolts are grade 5 or 8 and the same thread size as the threaded holes in the block. Be sure that all attaching bolts are securely tightened before releasing the weight of the engine from the crane. Use caution when loosening the rotation retaining bolts because the engine could rotate rapidly, causing personal injury.

CARE AND MAINTENANCE OF SHOP EQUIPMENT

All shop equipment should be maintained in safe working order. Maintenance of shop equipment usually includes the following operations or procedures:

- **Keep equipment clean.** Dirt and grime can attract and hold moisture, which can lead to rust and corrosion. Oil or grease can attract dirt.
- **Keep equipment lubricated.** While many bearings are sealed and do not require lubrication, always check the instructions for the use of the equipment for suggested lubrication and other service procedures.

CAUTION: Always follow the instructions from the equipment manufacturer regarding proper use and care of the equipment.

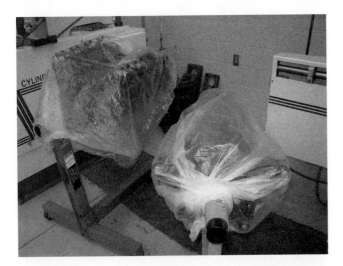

FIGURE 5-14   Two engines on engine stands. The plastic bags over the engines help keep dirt from getting onto these engines and engine parts.

FIGURE 5-15   An engine stand that grasps the engine from the sides rather than the end.

SETUP AND LIGHTING A TORCH   Step-by-Step

STEP 1 Inspect the cart and make sure the bottles are chained properly before moving it to the work location.

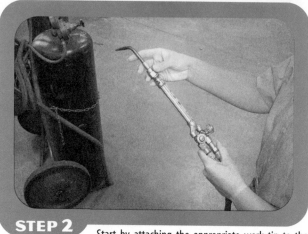

STEP 2 Start by attaching the appropriate work tip to the torch handle. The fitting should only be tightened hand tight.

STEP 3 The high pressure gauge shows bottle pressure, and the low pressure gauge indicates working pressure.

STEP 4 Open the oxygen bottle valve fully open, and open the acetylene bottle valve 1/2 turn.

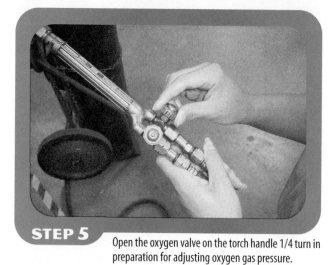

STEP 5 Open the oxygen valve on the torch handle 1/4 turn in preparation for adjusting oxygen gas pressure.

STEP 6 Turn the oxygen regulator valve clockwise and adjust oxygen gas pressure to 20 PSI.

SETUP AND LIGHTING A TORCH continued

STEP 7 Open the acetylene valve on the torch handle 1/4 turn and adjust acetylene gas pressure to 7 PSI. Close the acetylene valve on the torch handle.

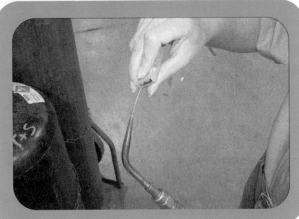

STEP 8 Open the oxygen valve on the torch handle 1/4 turn and use an appropriate size tip cleaner to clean the tip orifice. Finish by closing the oxygen valve.

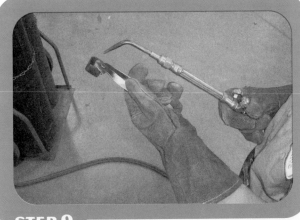

STEP 9 Put on leather gloves and open the acetylene valve on the torch handle 1/4 turn. Use a flint striker to ignite the acetylene gas exiting the torch tip.

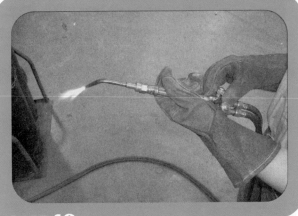

STEP 10 Slowly open the oxygen valve on the torch handle and adjust for a neutral flame (blue cone is well-defined).

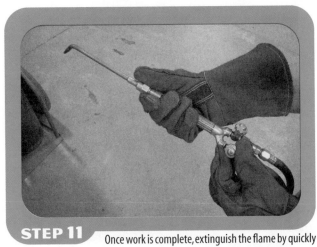

STEP 11 Once work is complete, extinguish the flame by quickly closing the acetylene valve on the torch handle.

STEP 12 Close the valves on both bottles and turn the regulator handles CCW until they no longer contact the internal springs.

HEATING METAL Step-by-Step

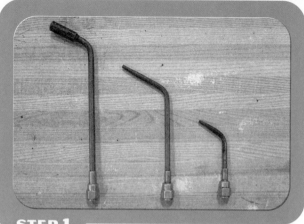

STEP 1
Heating attachments include ordinary heating tips (middle and right) and a "rosebud" (left). Ordinary heating tips work fine for most purposes.

STEP 2
Note that while acetylene bottle pressures are relatively low, the oxygen bottle can be filled to over 2000 PSI. Be absolutely certain that the bottles are chained properly to the cart before attempting to move it!

STEP 3
A fire blanket may be placed over floor drains or other objects to prevent fires. A fire extinguisher should be on hand in case of an emergency.

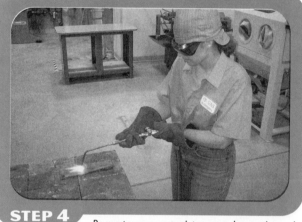

STEP 4
Be sure to wear appropriate personal protective equipment during heating and cutting operations.

STEP 5
Note that heating operations should be performed over steel or firebrick. Never heat or cut steel close to concrete, as it could cause the concrete to explode.

STEP 6
When heating steel, move the torch in a circular pattern to prevent melting of the metal.

CUTTING METAL   Step-by-Step

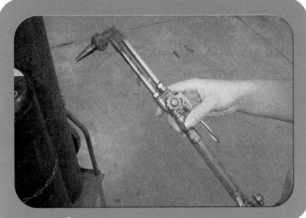

STEP 1
Affix the cutting attachment to the torch handle. Note that the cutting attachment has a cutting handle and a separate oxygen valve.

STEP 2
Fully open the oxygen valve on the torch handle. Oxygen flow will now be controlled with the valve on the cutting attachment.

STEP 3
Oxygen gas pressure should be adjusted to 30 PSI whenever using the cutting attachment. Acetylene pressure is kept at 7 PSI.

STEP 4
Open the acetylene valve on the torch handle 1/4 turn and light the torch. Slowly open the oxygen valve on the cutting attachment and adjust the flame until the blue cone is well-defined.

STEP 5
Direct the flame onto a thin spot or sharp edge of the metal to be cut. This will build the heat quicker in order to get the cut started.

STEP 6
When the metal glows red, depress the cutting handle and move the torch to advance the cut.

SUMMARY

1. Most shops are equipped with a large air compressor that supplies pressurized air to all stalls for use by the technician.

2. An air impact wrench is the most commonly used power tool in the shop. It is used mostly to remove fasteners. Caution should be exercised not to overtighten a fastener, using an air impact wrench.

3. Other air-operated tools include an air ratchet and a die grinder.

4. A bench or pedestal grinder usually has both a grinding stone and a wire brush wheel.

5. Trouble lights should be fluorescent or LED for maximum safety in the shop.

6. A hydraulic press is used to remove bearings from shafts and other similar operations.

7. A portable crane is used to remove and install engines or engine/transmission assemblies from vehicles.

8. Engine stands are designed to allow the technician to rotate the engine to get access to the various parts and components.

REVIEW QUESTIONS

1. List the tools used by service technicians that use compressed air.

2. Which trouble light design(s) is (are) the recommended type for maximum safety?

3. What safety precautions should be adhered to when working with a vise?

4. When using a blow gun, what precautions need to be taken?

CHAPTER QUIZ

1. When using compressed air and a blow gun, what is the maximum allowable air pressure?
   a. 10 PSI
   b. 20 PSI
   c. 30 PSI
   d. 40 PSI

2. Which air impact drive size is the most commonly used?
   a. 1/4 inch
   b. 3/8 inch
   c. 1/2 inch
   d. 3/4 inch

3. For safe use of compressed air using a blow gun, the pressure should not exceed _____.
   a. 10 PSI
   b. 20 PSI
   c. 30 PSI
   d. 40 PSI

4. What can be used to cover the jaws of a vise to help protect the object being held?
   a. Aluminum
   b. Wood
   c. Plastic
   d. All of the above

5. Technician A says that impact sockets have thicker walls than conventional sockets. Technician B says that impact sockets have a black oxide finish. Which technician is correct?
   a. Technician A only
   b. Technician B only
   c. Both Technicians A and B
   d. Neither Technician A nor B

6. Two technicians are discussing the use of a typical bench/pedestal-mounted grinder. Technician A says that a wire brush wheel can be used to clean threads. Technician B says that the grinding stone can be used to clean threads. Which technician is correct?

   a. Technician A only

   b. Technician B only

   c. Both Technicians A and B

   d. Neither Technician A nor B

7. A hydraulic press is being used to separate a bearing from a shaft. What should be used to cover the bearing during the pressing operation?

   a. A shop cloth

   b. A brake drum

   c. A fender cover

   d. A paper towel

8. Which type of trouble light is recommended for use in the shop?

   a. Incandescent

   b. Fluorescent

   c. LED

   d. Either b or c

9. When mounting an engine to an engine stand, what grade of bolt should be used?

   a. 5 or 8

   b. 4 or 7

   c. 3 or 5

   d. 1 or 4

10. Proper care of shop equipment includes _____.

    a. Tuning up every 6 months

    b. Keeping equipment clean

    c. Keeping equipment lubricated

    d. Both b and c

CHAPTER **6**

VEHICLE LIFTING AND HOISTING

OBJECTIVES

After studying Chapter 6, the reader will be able to:

1. Identify vehicle hoisting and lifting equipment.

2. Discuss safety procedures related to hoisting or lifting a vehicle.

3. Describe the proper methods to follow to safely hoist a vehicle.

KEY TERMS

Creeper (p. 77)
Floor Jack (p. 77)

Jack Stands (p. 77)
Safety Stands (p. 77)

FLOOR JACK

A **floor jack** is a hand-operated hydraulic device that is used to lift vehicles or components, such as engines, transmissions, and rear axle assemblies. Most floor jacks use four casters, which allow the jack to be easily moved around the shop. See Figure 6-1.

Safe Use of Floor Jacks

Floor jacks are used to lift a vehicle or major vehicle component, but they are not designed to hold a load. Therefore **safety stands,** also called **jack stands,** should always be used to support the vehicle. After the floor jack has lifted the vehicle, safety stands should be placed under the vehicle, and then, using the floor jack, lowered onto the safety stands. The floor jack can be lifted in position as another safety device but the load should be removed from the floor jack. If a load is retained on the floor jack, hydraulic fluid can leak past seals in the hydraulic cylinders, which would lower the vehicle, possibly causing personal injury. See Figure 6-2.

CREEPERS

When working underneath a vehicle, most service technicians use a **creeper,** which consists of a flat or concaved surface equipped with low-profile casters. A creeper allows the technician to maneuver under the vehicle easily.

FIGURE 6-1   A hydraulic hand-operated floor jack.

FIGURE 6-2   Safety stands are being used to support the rear of this vehicle. Notice a creeper also.

Safe Use of Creepers

Creepers can create a fall hazard if left on the floor. When a creeper is not being used, it should be picked up and placed vertically against a wall or tool box to help prevent accidental falls.

VEHICLE HOISTS

Vehicle hoists include older in-ground pneumatic/hydraulic (air pressure over hydraulic) and aboveground units. Most of the vehicle hoists used today use an electric motor to pressurize hydraulic fluid, which lifts the vehicle using hydraulic cylinders. Hoists are rated by the maximum weight that they can safely lift, such as 7,000 lbs to 12,000 lbs or more. Hoists can also have equal length arms or can be equipped with different length arms allowing the vehicle to be set so the doors can be opened and not hit the center support column. Many chassis and underbody service procedures require that the vehicle be hoisted or lifted off the ground. The simplest methods involve the use of drive-on ramps or a floor jack and safety (jack) stands, whereas in-ground or surface-mounted lifts provide greater access.

Setting the Pads Is a Critical Part of This Procedure

All automobile and light-truck service manuals include recommended locations to be used when hoisting (lifting) a vehicle. Newer vehicles have a triangle decal on the driver's door indicating the recommended lift points. The recommended standards for the lift points and lifting procedures are found in SAE Standard JRP-2184. See Figure 6-3.

These recommendations typically include the following points:

1. The vehicle should be centered on the lift or hoist so as not to overload one side or put too much force either forward or rearward. See Figure 6-4.

2. The pads of the lift should be spread as far apart as possible to provide a stable platform.

3. Each pad should be placed under a portion of the vehicle that is strong and capable of supporting the weight of the vehicle.

   a. Pinch welds at the bottom edge of the body are generally considered to be strong.

CAUTION: Even though pinch weld seams are the recommended location for hoisting many vehicles with unitized bodies (unit-body), care should be taken not to place the pad(s) too far forward or rearward. Incorrect placement of the vehicle on the lift could cause the vehicle to be imbalanced, and the vehicle could fall. This is exactly what happened to the vehicle in Figure 6-5.

---

   b. Boxed areas of the body are the best places to position the pads on a vehicle without a frame. Be careful to note whether the arms of the lift might come into contact with other parts of the vehicle before the pad touches the intended location. Commonly damaged areas include the following:

     1. Rocker panel moldings
     2. Exhaust system (including catalytic converter)
     3. Tires or body panels. (See Figures 6-6 and 6-7.)

4. The vehicle should be raised about a foot (30 centimeters [cm]) off the floor, then stopped and shaken to check for stability. If the vehicle seems to be stable when checked at a short distance from the floor, continue raising the vehicle and continue to view the vehicle until it has reached the desired height. The hoist should be lowered onto the mechanical locks, and then raised off of the locks before lowering.

CAUTION: Do not look away from the vehicle while it is being raised (or lowered) on a hoist. Often one side or one end of the hoist can stop or fail, resulting in the vehicle being slanted enough to slip or fall, creating physical damage not only to the vehicle and/or hoist but also to the technician or others who may be nearby.

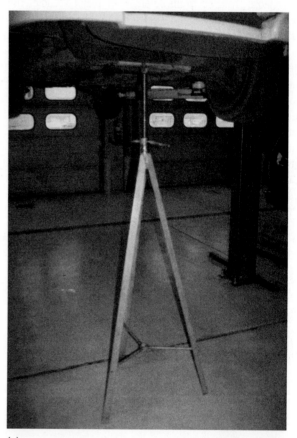

(a)

(b)

FIGURE 6-4 (a) Tall safety stands can be used to provide additional support for a vehicle while on a hoist. (b) A block of wood should be used to avoid the possibility of doing damage to components supported by the stand.

LIFT POINT LOCATION SYMBOL

FIGURE 6-3 Most newer vehicles have a triangle symbol indicating the recommended hoisting lift points.

FIGURE 6-5   This vehicle fell from the hoist because the pads were not set correctly. No one was hurt, but the vehicle was a total loss.

(a)

(b)

(a)

(b)

FIGURE 6-7   (a) In this photo the pad arm is just contacting the rocker panel of the vehicle. (b) This photo shows what can occur if the technician places the pad too far inward underneath the vehicle. The arm of the hoist has dented in the rocket panel.

(b)

FIGURE 6-6   (a) An assortment of hoist pad adapters that are often necessary to safely hoist many pickup trucks, vans, and sport utility vehicles. (b) A view from underneath a Chevrolet pickup truck showing how the pad extensions are used to attach the hoist lifting pad to contact the frame.

NOTE: Most hoists can be safely placed at any desired height as long as it is high enough for the safety latches to engage. For ease while working, the area in which you are working should be at chest level. When working on brakes or suspension components, it is not necessary to work on them down near the floor or over your head. Raise the hoist so that the components are at chest level.

5. Before lowering the hoist, the safety latch(es) must be released and the direction of the controls reversed. The speed downward is often adjusted to be as slow as possible for additional safety.

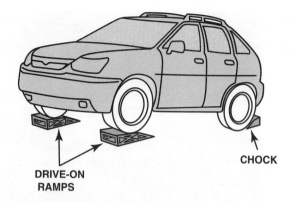

**DRIVE-ON
RAMPS**

CHOCK

FIGURE 6-8 Drive-on-type ramps. The wheels on the ground level *must* be chocked (blocked) to prevent accidental movement down the ramp.

DRIVE-ON RAMPS

Ramps are an inexpensive way to raise the front or rear of a vehicle. See Figure 6-8. Ramps are easy to store, but they can be dangerous because they can "kick out" when driving the vehicle onto the ramps.

CAUTION: Professional repair shops do not use ramps because they are dangerous to use. Use only with extreme care.

HOISTING THE VEHICLE   Step-by-Step

STEP 1 The first step in hoisting a vehicle is to properly align the vehicle in the center of the stall.

STEP 2 Most vehicles will be correctly positioned when the left front tire is centered on the tire pad.

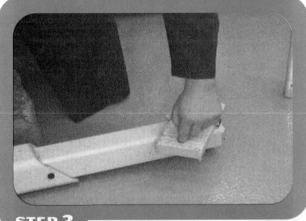

STEP 3 Most pads at the end of the hoist arms can be rotated to allow for many different types of vehicle construction.

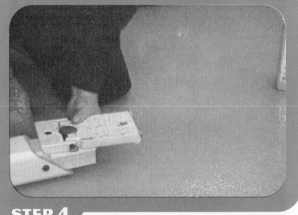

STEP 4 The arms of the lifts can be retracted or extended to accommodate vehicles of many different lengths.

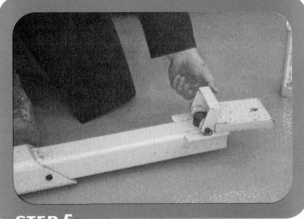

STEP 5 Most lifts are equipped with short pad extensions that are often necessary to use to allow the pad to contact the frame of a vehicle without causing the arm of the lift to hit and damage parts of the body.

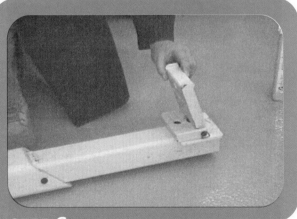

STEP 6 Tall pad extensions can also be used to gain access to the frame of a vehicle. This position is needed to safely hoist many pickup trucks, vans, and sport utility vehicles.

(continued)

HOISTING THE VEHICLE   continued

STEP 7
An additional extension may be necessary to hoist a truck or van equipped with running boards to give the necessary clearance.

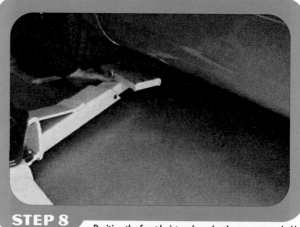

STEP 8
Position the front hoist pads under the recommended locations as specified in the owner's manual and for service information for the vehicle being serviced.

STEP 9
Position the rear pads under the vehicle under the recommended locations.

STEP 10
This photo shows an asymmetrical lift where the front arms are shorter than the rear arms. This design is best used for passenger cars and allows the driver to exit the vehicle easier because the door can be opened wide without it hitting the vertical support column.

STEP 11
After being sure all pads are correctly positioned, use the electromechanical controls to raise the vehicle.

STEP 12
Raise the vehicle about 1 foot (30 cm) and stop to double-check that all pads contact the body or frame in the correct positions.

HOISTING THE VEHICLE   continued

STEP 13   With the vehicle raised about 1 foot off the ground, push down on the vehicle to check to see if it is stable on the pads. If the vehicle rocks, lower the vehicle and reset the pads. Be sure the safety is engaged before working on or under the vehicle.

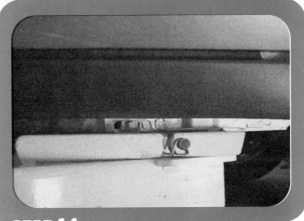

STEP 14   This photo shows the pads set flat and contacting the pinch welds of the body.

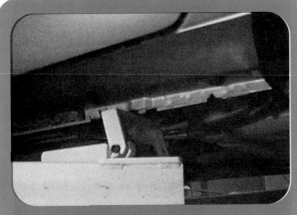

STEP 15   Where additional clearance is necessary for the arms to clear the rest of the body, the pads can be raised and placed under the pinch weld area as shown.

STEP 16   When the service work is completed, the hoist should be raised slightly and the safety released before using the hydraulic lever to lower the vehicle.

STEP 17   After lowering the vehicle, be sure all arms of the lift are moved out of the way before driving the vehicle out of the work stall.

STEP 18   Notice that all of the lift arms have been neatly moved out of the way to provide clearance so that the tires will not contact the arms when the vehicle is driven out of the stall.

SUMMARY

1. Whenever a vehicle is raised off the ground, it must be supported using safety stands.
2. Creepers should be stored vertically to prevent the possibility of stepping on it, which could cause a fall and personal injury.
3. Always adhere to the specified hoisting locations as found in service information.
4. Adapters or extensions are often needed when hoisting pickup trucks or vans.

REVIEW QUESTIONS

1. Why must safety stands be used after lifting a vehicle with a floor jack?
2. What precautions should be adhered to when storing a creeper?
3. What precautions should be adhered to when hoisting a vehicle?

CHAPTER QUIZ

1. A safety stand is also called a _____.
   a. Jack
   b. Jack stand
   c. Bottle jack
   d. Safety stool

2. A creeper should be stored _____.
   a. Vertically
   b. Under a vehicle
   c. Flat on the floor
   d. Upside down on the floor

3. The SAE standard for hoist location is _____.
   a. J-1980
   b. SAE-2009
   c. JRP-2184
   d. J-14302

4. Tall safety stands would be used to _____.
   a. Support an engine while the vehicle is hoisted
   b. Lift a vehicle
   c. Lift a component such as an engine high off the ground
   d. Both b and c

5. Commonly damaged areas of a vehicle during hoisting include _____.
   a. Rocker panels
   b. Exhaust systems
   c. Tires or body panels
   d. All of the above

6. Pad extensions may be needed when hoisting what type of vehicle?
   a. Small cars
   b. Pickup trucks
   c. Vans
   d. Either b or c

7. Technician A says that a hoist can be stopped at any level as long as the safety latch engages. Technician B says that the vehicle should be hoisted to the top of the hoist travel for safety. Which technician is correct?
   a. Technician A only
   b. Technician B only
   c. Both Technicians A and B
   d. Neither Technician A nor B

8. Before lowering the vehicle, what should the technician do?

   a. Be sure nothing is underneath the vehicle

   b. Raise the vehicle enough to release the safety latch

   c. Be sure no one will be walking under or near the vehicle

   d. All of the above

9. Technician A says that a creeper should be stored vertically. Technician B says that a creeper should be stored on its casters. Which technician is correct?

   a. Technician A only

   b. Technician B only

   c. Both Technicians A and B

   d. Neither Technician A nor B

10. When checking for proper pad placement, how high should the vehicle be raised?

    a. About 2 inches (5 cm)

    b. About 6 inches (15 cm)

    c. About 1 foot (30 cm)

    d. About 3 feet (91 cm)

MEASURING SYSTEMS AND TOOLS

OBJECTIVES

After studying Chapter 7, the reader will be able to:

1. Describe how to read a ruler.

2. Explain how to use a micrometer and vernier dial caliper.

3. Describe how to use a telescopic gauge and a micrometer to measure cylinder and lifter bores.

4. Discuss how to measure valve guides using a small-hole gauge.

5. Calculate engine displacement and compression ratios.

KEY TERMS

Barrel (p. 88)
Feeler Gauge (p. 91)
Small-Hole Gauge (p. 91)
Spindle (p. 88)

Split-Ball Gauge (p. 91)
Straightedge (p. 91)
Thickness Gauge (p. 91)
Thimble (p. 88)

ENGLISH CUSTOMARY MEASURING SYSTEM

The English customary measuring system was established about A.D. 1100 in England during the reign of Henry I. The foot was determined to be 12 inches and was taken from the length of a typical foot. The yard (36 inches) was determined to be the length from King Henry's nose to the end of his outstretched hand. The mile came from Roman days and was originally defined as the distance traveled by a soldier in 1,000 paces or steps. Other English units, such as the pound (weight) and gallon (volume), evolved over the years from Roman and English measurements.

The Fahrenheit temperature scale was created by Gabriel Fahrenheit (1686–1736) and he used 100°F as the temperature of the human body, which he missed by 1.4 degrees (98.6°F is considered now to be normal temperature). On the Fahrenheit scale, water freezes at 32°F and water boils at 212°F.

METRIC SYSTEM OF MEASURE

Most of the world uses the metric system of measure. The metric system was created in the late 1700s in France and used the physical world for the basis of the measurements. For example, the meter was defined as being 1/40,000,000 of the circumference of the earth (the distance around the earth at the poles). The Celsius temperature scale developed by Anders Celsius (1701–1744) used the freezing point of water as 0°C (32°F) and the boiling point of water as 100°C (212°F). Other units include a liter of water, which was then used as a standard of weight where 1 liter of water (about 1 quart) weighs 1 kilogram (1,000 grams). Units of measure are then divided or multiplied by 10, 100, and 1,000 to arrive at usable measurements. For example, a kilometer is 1,000 meters and is the most commonly used metric measurement for distance for travel. Other prefixes include:

m = milli = 1/1,000
k = kilo = 1,000
M = mega = 1,000,000

Linear Metric Measurements

1 kilometer = 0.62 miles
1 meter = 39.37 inches
1 centimeter (1/100 meter) = 0.39 inch
1 millimeter (1/1,000 meter) = 0.039 inch

Volume Measurement

1 cc (cubic centimeter) = 0.06 cubic inches
1 liter = 0.26 U.S. gallons (about 1 quart)

FREQUENTLY ASKED QUESTION

WHAT WEIGHS A GRAM?

To better understand the metric system measurements, it is often helpful to visualize a certain object and relate it to a metric unit of measure. For example, the following objects weigh about one gram:

- A dollar bill
- A small paper clip

Weight Measurement

1 gram = 0.035 ounces
1 kilogram (1,000 grams) = 2.2 pounds

Pressure Measurements

1 kilopascal (kPa) = 0.14 pounds per square inch (6.9 kPa = 1 PSI)
1 bar = 14.5 pounds per square inch

Derived Units

All units of measure, except for the base units, are a combination of units that are referred to as derived units of measure. Some examples of derived units include:

Torque
Velocity
Density
Energy
Power

LINEAR MEASUREMENTS (TAPE MEASURE/RULE)

A tape measure or machinist rule divides inches into smaller units. Each smaller unit is drawn with a line shorter than the longer unit. The units of measure starting with the largest include:

1 inch
1/2 inch
1/4 inch
1/8 inch
1/16 inch

See Figure 7-1.

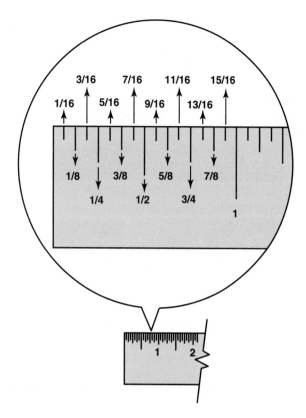

FIGURE 7-1 A rule showing that the larger the division, the longer the line .

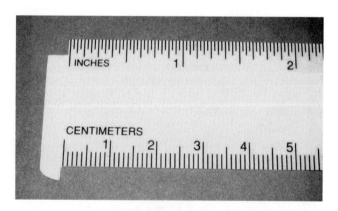

FIGURE 7-2 A plastic rule that has both inches and centimeters. Each line between the numbers on the centimeters represents one millimeter because there are 10 millimeters in 1 centimeter.

A metric scale is also included on many tape measures and machinists rules. See Figure 7-2.

MICROMETER

A micrometer is the most used measuring instrument in engine service and repair. See Figure 7-3.

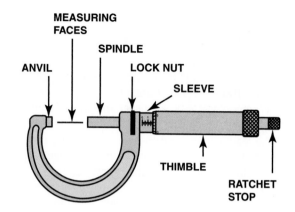

FIGURE 7-3 A typical micrometer showing the names of the parts .

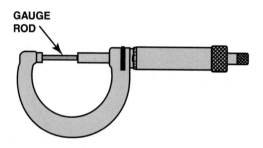

FIGURE 7-4 All micrometers should be checked and calibrated as needed using a gauge rod.

The **thimble** rotates over the **barrel** on a screw that has 40 threads per inch. Every revolution of the thimble moves the **spindle** 0.025 inch. The thimble is graduated into 25 equally spaced lines; therefore, each line represents 0.001 inch. Every micrometer should be checked for calibration on a regular basis. See Figures 7-4 through 7-6.

Crankshaft Measurement

Even though the connecting rod journals and the main bearing journals are usually different sizes, they both can and should be measured for out-of-round and taper. See Figure 7-7 on page 90.

Out-of-Round.   A journal should be measured in at least two positions across the diameter and every 120 degrees around the journal, as shown in Figure 7-8, for an example of the six readings. Calculate the out-of-round measurement by subtracting the lowest reading from the highest reading for both A and B positions.

Position A: $2.000 - 1.9995 = 0.0005$ inch
Position B: $2.000 - 1.9989 = 0.0011$ inch

The maximum out-of-round measurement occurs in position B (0.0011 inch), which is the measurement that should

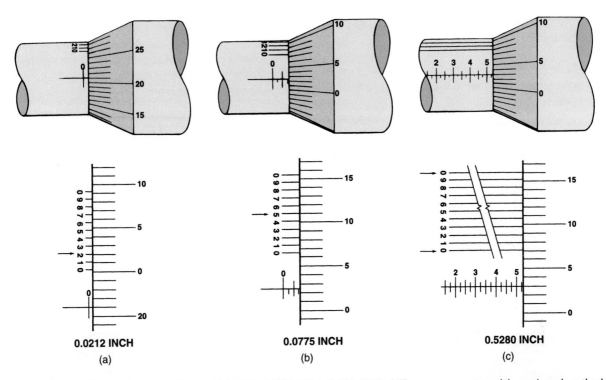

0.0212 INCH

(a)

0.0775 INCH

(b)

0.5280 INCH

(c)

FIGURE 7-5 The three micrometer readings are (a) 0.0212 inch; (b) 0.0775 inch; (c) 0.5280 inch. These measurements used the vernier scale on the sleeve to arrive at the ten-thousandth measurement. The number that is aligned represents the digit in the ten-thousandth place.

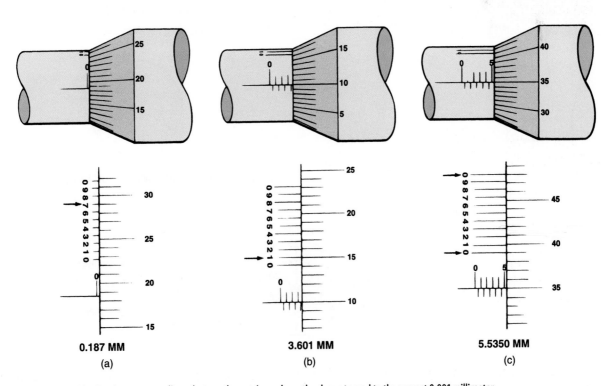

0.187 MM

(a)

3.601 MM

(b)

5.5350 MM

(c)

FIGURE 7-6 Metric micrometer readings that use the vernier scale on the sleeve to read to the nearest 0.001 millimeter.

be used to compare against factory specifications to determine if any machining will be necessary.

Taper.   To determine the taper of the journal, compare the readings in the same place between A and B positions and subtract the lower reading from the higher reading.
For example:

Position A		Position B	
2.0000	–	2.0000	= 0.0000
1.9999	–	1.9999	= 0.0000
1.9995	–	1.9989	= 0.0006

Use 0.0006 inch as the taper for the journal and compare with factory specifications.

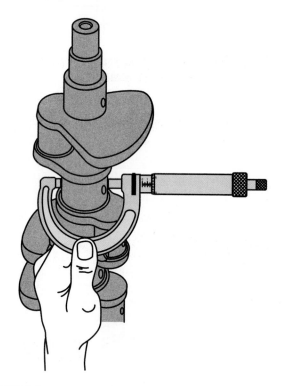

FIGURE 7-7   Using a micrometer to measure the connecting rod journal for out-of-round and taper.

Camshaft Measurement

The journal of the camshaft(s) can also be measured using a micrometer and compared with factory specifications for taper and out-of-round. See Figure 7-9.

NOTE: On overhead valve (pushrod) engines, the camshaft journal diameter often decreases slightly toward the rear of the engine. Overhead camshaft engines usually have the same journal diameter.

The lift can also be measured with a micrometer and compared with factory specifications, as shown in Figure 7-10.

TELESCOPIC GAUGE

A telescopic gauge is used with a micrometer to measure the inside diameter of a hole or bore.

The cylinder bore can be measured by inserting a telescopic gauge into the bore and rotating the handle lock to allow the arms of the gauge to contact the inside bore of the cylinder. Tighten the handle lock and remove the gauge from the cylinder. Use a micrometer to measure the telescopic gauge. See Figure 7-11.

A telescopic gauge can also be used to measure the following:

- Camshaft bearing (see Figure 7-12 on page 92)
- Main bearing bore (housing bore) measurement
- Connecting rod bore measurement

FIGURE 7-9   Camshaft journals should be measured in three locations, 120 degrees apart, to check for out-of-round.

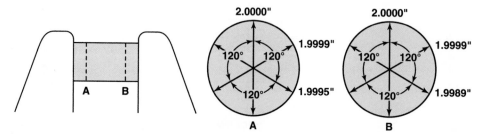

FIGURE 7-8   Crankshaft journal measurements. Each journal should be measured in at least six locations, but also in position A and position B and at 120-degree intervals around the journal.

(a)

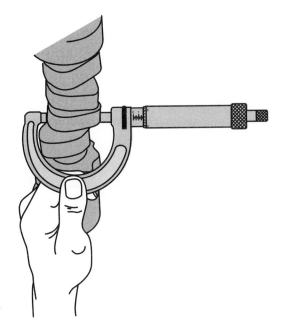

FIGURE 7-10   Checking a camshaft for wear by measuring the lobe height with a micrometer.

SMALL-HOLE GAUGE

A **small-hole gauge** (also called a **split-ball gauge**) is used with a micrometer to measure the inside diameter of small holes such as a valve guide in a cylinder head. See Figures 7-13 and 7-14.

VERNIER DIAL CALIPER

A vernier dial caliper is normally used to measure the outside diameter or length of a component such as a piston diameter or crankshaft and camshaft bearing journal diameter. See Figure 7-15 on page 93.

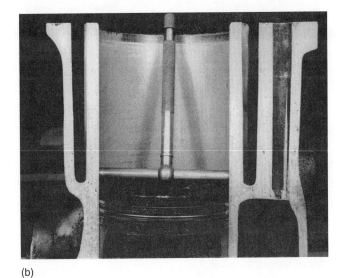

(b)

FIGURE 7-11   When the head is first removed, the cylinder taper and out-of-round should be checked below the ridge (a) and above the piston when it is at the bottom of the stroke (b) .

FEELER GAUGE

A **feeler gauge** (also known as a **thickness gauge**) is an accurately manufactured strip of metal that is used to determine the gap or clearance between two components. See Figure 7-16 on page 93.

A feeler gauge can be used to check the following:

- Piston ring gap (see Figure 7-17 on page 93)
- Piston ring side clearance
- Connecting rod side clearance

STRAIGHTEDGE

A **straightedge** is a precision ground metal measuring gauge that is used to check the flatness of engine components when used with a feeler gauge. A straightedge is used to check the flatness of the following:

- Cylinder heads (see Figure 7-18 on page 94)
- Cylinder block deck
- Straightness of the main bearing bores (saddles)

(a)

(b)

FIGURE 7-12 (a) A telescopic gauge being used to measure the inside diameter (ID) of a camshaft bearing. (b) An outside micrometer used to measure the telescopic gauge.

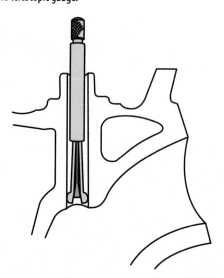

FIGURE 7-13 Cutaway of a valve guide with a hole gauge adjusted to the hole diameter.

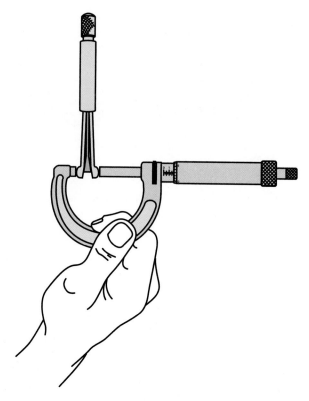

FIGURE 7-14 The outside of a hole gauge being measured with a micrometer.

 FREQUENTLY ASKED QUESTION

 WHAT IS THE DIFFERENCE BETWEEN THE WORD GAGE AND GAUGE?

The word *gauge* means "measurement or dimension to a standard of reference." The word *gauge* can also be spelled *gage*. Therefore, in most cases, the words mean the same.

NOTE: One vehicle manufacturing representative told me that *gage* was used rather than *gauge* because even though it is the second acceptable spelling of the word, it is correct and it saved the company a lot of money in printing costs because the word *gage* has one less letter! One letter multiplied by millions of vehicles with gauges on the dash and the word *gauge* used in service manuals adds up to a big savings to the manufacturer.

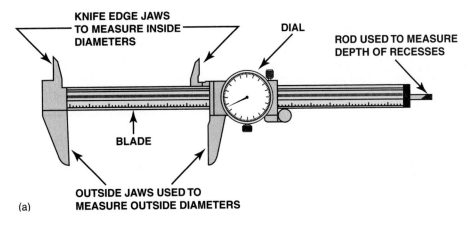

KNIFE EDGE JAWS
TO MESURE INSIDE
DIAMETERS

DIAL

ROD USED TO MEASURE
DEPTH OF RECESSES

BLADE

OUTSIDE JAWS USED TO
MEASURE OUTSIDE DIAMETERS

(a)

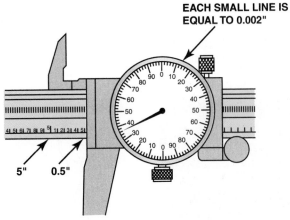

EACH SMALL LINE IS
EQUAL TO 0.002"

5"   0.5"

ADD READING ON BLADE (5.5")
TO READING ON DIAL (0.036") TO
GET FINAL TOTAL MEASUREMENT (5.536")

(b)

FIGURE 7-15   (a) A typical vernier dial caliper. This is a very useful measuring tool for automotive engine work because it is capable of measuring inside and outside measurements. (b) To read a vernier dial caliper, simply add the reading on the blade to the reading on the dial.

FIGURE 7-16   A group of feeler gauges (also known as thickness gauges), used to measure between two parts. The long gauges on the bottom are used to measure the piston-to-cylinder wall clearance.

FEELER GAUGE

PISTON RING

FIGURE 7-17   A feeler gauge, also called a thickness gauge, is used to measure the small clearances such as the end gap of a piston ring.

DIAL INDICATOR

A dial indicator is a precision measuring instrument used to measure crankshaft end play, crankshaft runout, and valve guide wear. A dial indicator can be mounted three ways, including:

- **Magnetic mount.** This is a very useful method because a dial indicator can be attached to any steel or cast iron part.
- **Clamp mount.** A clamp-mounted dial indicator is used in many places where a mount could be clamped.
- **Threaded rod.** Using a threaded rod allows the dial indicator to be securely mounted, such as shown in Figure 7-19.

DIAL BORE GAUGE

A dial bore gauge is an expensive, but important, gauge used to measure cylinder taper and out-of-round as well as main

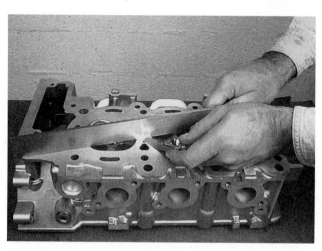

FIGURE 7-18 A straightedge is used with a feeler gauge to determine if a cylinder head is warped or twisted.

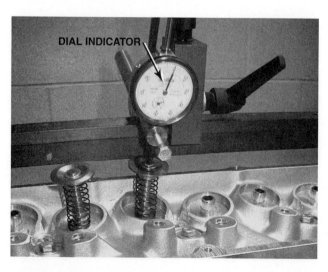

FIGURE 7-19 A dial indicator is used to measure valve lift during flow testing of a high performance cylinder head.

bearing (block housing) bore for taper and out-of-round. See Figure 7-20. A dial bore gauge has to be adjusted to a dimension, such as the factory specifications. The reading on the dial bore gauge then indicates plus (+) or minus (−) readings from the predetermined dimension. This is why a dial bore is best used to measure taper and out-of-round because it shows the difference in cylinder or bore rather than an actual measurement.

DEPTH MICROMETER

A depth micrometer is similar to a conventional micrometer except that it is designed to measure the depth from a flat surface. See Figure 7-21.

FIGURE 7-20 A dial bore gauge is used to measure cylinders and other engine parts for out-of-round and taper conditions.

FIGURE 7-21 A depth micrometer being used to measure the height of the rotor of an oil pump from the surface of the housing.

SUMMARY

1. A tape measure or machinist rule can be used to measure linear distances.

2. A micrometer can measure 0.001 inch by using a thimble that has 40 threads per inch. Each rotation of the thimble moves the thimble 0.025 inch. The circumference of the thimble is graduated into 25 marks, each representing 0.001 inch.

3. A micrometer is used to check the diameter of a crankshaft journal as well as the taper and out-of-round.

4. A camshaft bearing and lobe can be measured using a micrometer.

5. A telescopic gauge is used with a micrometer to measure the inside of a hole or bore, such as the big end of a connecting rod or a cylinder bore.

6. A small-hole gauge (also called a split-ball gauge) is used with a micrometer to measure small holes such as the inside diameter of a valve guide in a cylinder head.

7. A vernier dial caliper is used to measure the outside diameter of components such as pistons or crankshaft bearing journals.

8. A feeler gauge (also called a thickness gauge) is used to measure the gap or clearance between two components such as piston ring gap, piston ring side clearance, and connecting rod side clearance. A feeler gauge is also used with a precision straightedge to measure the flatness of blocks and cylinder heads.

9. A dial indicator and dial bore gauge are used to measure differences in a component such as crankshaft end play (dial indicator) or cylinder taper (dial bore gauge).

REVIEW QUESTIONS

1. Explain how a micrometer is read.

2. Describe how to check a crankshaft journal for out-of-round and taper.

3. List engine components that can be measured with the help of a telescopic gauge.

4. List the gaps or clearances that can be measured using a feeler (thickness) gauge.

5. Explain why a dial bore gauge has to be set to a dimension before using.

CHAPTER QUIZ

1. The threaded movable part that rotates on a micrometer is called the _____.
   a. Barrel
   b. Thimble
   c. Spindle
   d. Anvil

2. To check a crankshaft journal for taper, the journal should be measured in at least how many locations?
   a. One
   b. Two
   c. Four
   d. Six

3. To check a crankshaft journal for out-of-round, the journal should be measured in at least how many locations?
   a. Two
   b. Four
   c. Six
   d. Eight

4. A telescopic gauge can be used to measure a cylinder bore if what other measuring device is used to measure the telescopic gauge?
   a. Micrometer
   b. Feeler gauge
   c. Straightedge
   d. Dial indicator

5. To directly measure the diameter of a valve guide in a cylinder head, use a micrometer and a _____.
   a. Telescopic gauge
   b. Feeler gauge
   c. Small-hole gauge
   d. Dial indicator

6. Which of the following *cannot* be measured using a feeler gauge?
   a. Valve guide clearance
   b. Piston ring gap
   c. Piston ring side clearance
   d. Connecting rod side clearance

7. Which of the following *cannot* be measured using a straight-edge and a feeler gauge?
   a. Cylinder head flatness
   b. Block deck flatness
   c. Straightness of the main bearing bores
   d. Straightness of the cylinder bore

8. Which measuring gauge needs to be set up (adjusted) to a fixed dimension before use?
   a. Dial indicator
   b. Dial bore gauge
   c. Vernier dial gauge
   d. Micrometer

9. The freezing point of water is _____.
   a. 0°C
   b. 32°F
   c. 0°F
   d. Both a and b

10. Which metric unit of measure is used for volume measurement?
    a. Meter
    b. cc
    c. Centimeter
    d. Millimeter

CHAPTER 8

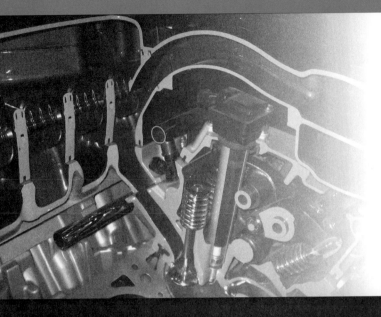

SERVICE INFORMATION

OBJECTIVES

After studying Chapter 8, the reader will be able to:

1. Discuss the importance of vehicle history.
2. Retrieve vehicle service information.

3. Read and interpret service manuals and electronic service information.
4. Describe the use of the vehicle owner's manual.

KEY TERMS

Julian Date (JD) (p. 105)
Service Information (p. 98)

Technical Service Bulletin (TSB) (p. 103)

VEHICLE SERVICE HISTORY RECORDS

Whenever service work is performed, the record of what was done is usually kept on file by the shop or service department for a number of years. The wise service technician will check the vehicle service history if working on a vehicle with an unusual problem. Often, a previous repair may indicate the reason for the current problem or it could be related to the same circuit or components.

OWNER'S MANUALS

It has been said by many automotive professional technicians and service advisors that the owner's manual is not read by many vehicle owners. Most owner's manuals contain all or most of the following information:

1. How to reset the maintenance reminder light
2. Specifications, including viscosity of oil needed and number of quarts (liters)
3. Tire pressures and standard and optional tire sizes
4. Maintenance schedule for all fluids, including coolant, brake fluid, automatic transmission fluid, and differential fluid
5. How to program the remote control as well as the power windows and door locks
6. How to reset the tire pressure monitoring system after a tire rotation

LUBRICATION GUIDES

Lubrication guides, such as those published by Chek-Chart and Chilton, include all specifications for lubrication-related service including:

- Hoisting location
- Lubrication points
- Grease and oil specifications
- Capacities for engine oil, transmission fluid, coolant for cooling systems, and differential fluid

SERVICE MANUALS

Factory and aftermarket service manuals contain specifications and service procedures. While factory service manuals cover just one year and one or more models of the same vehicle, most aftermarket service manuals cover multiple years and/or models in one manual. See Figure 8-1.

Included in most service manuals are the following:

- Capacities and recommended specifications for all fluids
- Specifications including engine and routine maintenance items

- Testing procedures
- Service procedures including the use of special tools when needed

While some factory service manuals are printed in one volume, most factory **service information** is printed in several

REAL WORLD FIX

OWNER'S MANUAL IS THE KEY TO PROPER OPERATION

A customer purchased a used Pontiac Vibe and complained to a shop that the cruise control would disengage and had to be reset if driven below 25 mph (40 km/h). The service technician was able to verify that in fact this occurred, but did not know if this feature was normal or not. The technician checked the owner's manual and discovered that this vehicle was designed to operate this way. Unlike other cruise control systems, those systems on Toyota-based vehicles are designed to shut off below 25 mph, requiring the driver to reset the desired speed. The customer was informed that nothing could be done to correct this concern and the technician also learned something. Vehicles that use the Toyota cruise control system include all Toyotas, plus Lexus, Pontiac Vibe, and Chevrolet Prism.

NOTE: Many vehicle manufacturers offer owner's manuals on their website for a free download.

FIGURE 8-1   Many service manuals include diagnostic information as well as specifications and repair procedures.

volumes due to the amount and depth of information presented. The typical factory service manual is divided into sections.

General Information

General information includes topics such as:

- Warnings and cautions
- VIN identification numbers on engine, transmission/transaxle, and body parts
- Lock cylinder coding
- Fastener information
- Decimal and metric equivalents
- Abbreviations and standard nomenclature used
- Service parts identification label and process code information

Maintenance and Lubrication Information

Maintenance and lubrication information includes topics such as:

- Schedule for "normal" as well as "severe" usage time and mileage charts
- Specified oil and other lubricant specifications
- Chassis lubrication points
- Tire rotation methods
- Periodic vehicle inspection services (items to check and time/mileage intervals)
- Maintenance item part numbers, such as oil and air filter numbers, and specifications, such as oil capacity and tire pressures

Engines

- Engine electrical diagnosis (battery, charging, cranking, ignition, and wiring)
- Engine mechanical diagnosis
- Specific engine information for each engine that may be used in the vehicle(s) covered by the service manual, including:
  - Engine identification
  - On-vehicle service procedures
  - Description of the engine and the operation of the lubrication system
  - Exploded views showing all parts of the engine
  - Disassembly procedures
  - Inspection procedures and specifications of the parts and subsystems
  - Assembly procedures
  - Torque specifications for all fasteners, including the torque sequence

EXPLODED VIEWS

Exploded views of components such as engines and transmissions are available in shop manuals and electronic service information, as well as in parts and labor time guides. These views, showing all of the parts as if the assembly was blown apart, give the service technician a clear view of the various parts and their relationship to other parts in the assembly. See Figure 8-2.

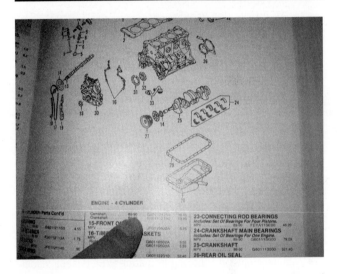

FIGURE 8-2   An exploded view of an engine as shown in a time and parts guide.

Automatic Transmission/Transaxle

- General information (identification and specifications)
- Diagnosis procedures, including preliminary checks and fluid level procedures
- General service, including leak detection and correction
- Cooler flushing procedures
- Unit removal procedures
- Unit disassembly procedures and precautions
- Unit assembly procedures and torque specifications

Electrical Systems

- Symbols used
- Troubleshooting procedures
- Repair procedures (wire repair, connectors, and terminals)
- Power distribution
- Ground distribution

- Component location views
- Harness routing views
- Individual electrical circuits, including circuit operation and schematics

Heating, Ventilation, and Air Conditioning

- Heater system
  - General description
  - Heater control assembly
  - Diagnosis, including heater electrical wiring and vacuum system
  - Blower motor and fan assembly diagnosis and servicing procedures
  - Air distribution values
  - Fastener torque specifications
- Air-conditioning system
  - General description and system components
  - Air-conditioning system diagnosis, including leak detection
  - Air-conditioning and heater function tests
  - Air-conditioning service procedures
  - Refrigerant recovery, recycling, adding oil, evacuating procedures, and charging procedures
  - Troubleshooting guide

Engine Performance (Driveability and Emissions)

- Vehicle emission control information (VECI) label, visual/physical under-hood inspection
- On-board diagnostic system

PRINT IT OUT

It is often a benefit to have the written instructions or wiring diagrams at the vehicle while diagnosing or performing a repair. One advantage of a hard copy service manual is that it can be taken to the vehicle and used as needed. However, dirty hands can often cause pages to become unreadable. The advantage of electronic format service information is that the material can be printed out and taken to the vehicle for easy access. This also allows the service technician to write or draw on the printed copy, which can be a big help when performing tests such as electrical system measurements. These notes can then be used to document the test results on the work order.

- Scan tool values
- Wiring harness service
- Symptom charts

ADVANTAGES OF HARD COPY VERSUS ELECTRONIC SERVICE INFORMATION

All forms of service information have some advantages, including:

Hard Copy	Electronic Service Information
- Easy to use—no hardware or expensive computers needed	- Information can be printed out and taken to the vehicle
- Can be taken to the vehicle for reference	- Has a search function for information
- Can view several pages easily for reference	- Internet or network access allows use at several locations in the shop

DISADVANTAGES OF HARD COPY VERSUS ELECTRONIC SERVICE INFORMATION

All forms of service information have some disadvantages, including:

Hard Copy	Electronic Service Information
- Can be lost or left in the vehicle	- Requires a computer and printer
- Cost is high for each manual	- Internet or network access can be a challenge
- Can get dirty and unreadable	- Cost can be high

LOOK FOR SEVERE SERVICE TIMES

Many time guides provide additional time for vehicles that may be excessively rusted due to climate conditions or have been subjected to abuse. Be sure to quote the higher rate if any of these conditions are present on the customer's vehicle. See Figure 8-3.

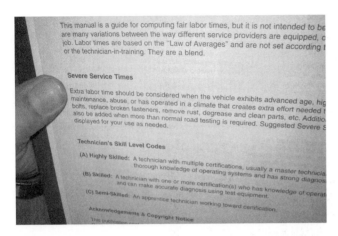

This manual is a guide for computing fair labor times, but it is not intended to be ___ are many variations between the way different service providers are equipped, ___ job. Labor times are based on the "Law of Averages" and are not set according ___ or the technician-in-training. They are a blend.

Severe Service Times

Extra labor time should be considered when the vehicle exhibits advanced age, hig___ maintenance, abuse, or has operated in a climate that creates extra effort needed ___ bolts, replace broken fasteners, remove rust, degrease and clean parts, etc. Additio___ also be added when more than normal road testing is required. Suggested Severe S___ displayed for your use as needed.

Technician's Skill Level Codes

(A) Highly Skilled: A technician with multiple certifications, usually a master technicia___ thorough knowledge of operating systems and has strong diagnos___

(B) Skilled: A technician with one or more certification(s) who has knowledge of operat___ and can make accurate diagnosis using test equipment.

(C) Semi-Skilled: An apprentice technician working toward certification.

Acknowledgements & Copyright Notice

This publication ___

FIGURE 8-3   Extra time should be added if work is being performed on a vehicle that has excessive rust or other factors as stated in the time guide.

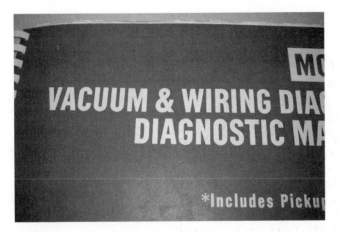

FIGURE 8-4   Often wiring diagrams and vacuum diagrams are combined into one manual.

TYPES OF SERVICE INFORMATION

Various hard copy manuals are available, including:

- Wiring diagrams—see Figure 8-4.
- Vacuum hose diagrams—see Figure 8-5.
- Electrical troubleshooting and/or schematic manuals—see Figures 8-6 and Figure 8-7.
- Electrical component location guide—see Figures 8-8 and 8-9.

LABOR GUIDE MANUALS

Labor guides, also called flat-rate manuals, list vehicle service procedures and the time it should take an average technician to complete the task. This flat-rate time is then the basis for estimates and for pay for technicians. Some manuals also include

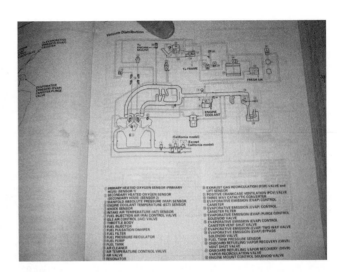

FIGURE 8-5   Typical vacuum diagram as shown in a factory service manual.

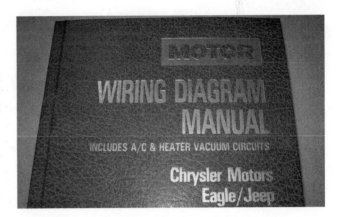

FIGURE 8-6   A typical electrical wiring diagram manual.

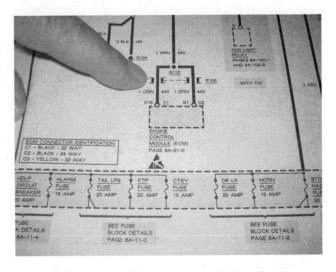

FIGURE 8-7   Typical factory service manual wiring schematic.

FIGURE 8-8   A component locator manual is a helpful manual to have, especially if work is being performed on a vehicle with which you are not familiar.

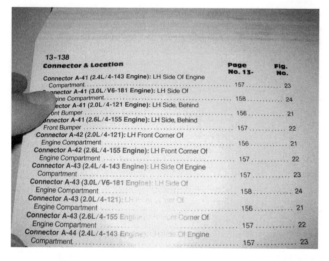

FIGURE 8-9   A component location guide typically shows the location of components in words and in figures.

FIGURE 8-10   Some guides include labor information only.

a parts list, including the price of the part to help service advisors create complete estimates for both labor and parts. These manuals are usually called "parts and time guides." Some guides include labor time only. See Figure 8-10.

See Figure 8-11 for an example of a time guide showing both standard and severe service times.

HOW TO USE HARD COPY MANUALS

The most efficient way to find information in a manual is to look at the table of contents in the front of the book first. See Figure 8-12.

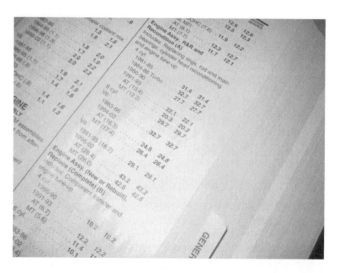

FIGURE 8-11   A typical time guide showing the times specified for the replacement or reconditioning of components.

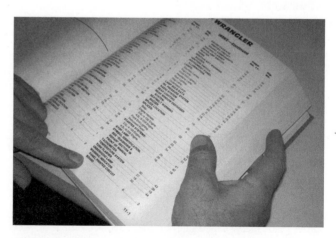

FIGURE 8-12   The wise service technician starts to look for service information at the front of the manual in the table of contents.

Next, go to the page (or pages) where the desired information is located. See Figure 8-13.

If bulb information or location of a component is needed, check the table of contents for the location of this information. See Figure 8-14.

Service information and testing procedures should be closely followed including any symptom charts or flow charts. A sample of a symptom information chart is shown in Table 8-1.

ELECTRONIC SERVICE INFORMATION

There are many programs available that will provide service information for the automotive industry. Sometimes the vehicle makers make information available online. However, many shops choose to purchase software from an aftermarket supplier. ALL Data and Mitchell On-Demand are commonly used software programs that include service information for many vehicles.

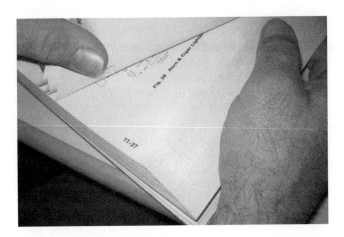

FIGURE 8-13   Many pages are numbered with the section, as in this case 11, followed by the page number 27 in that section.

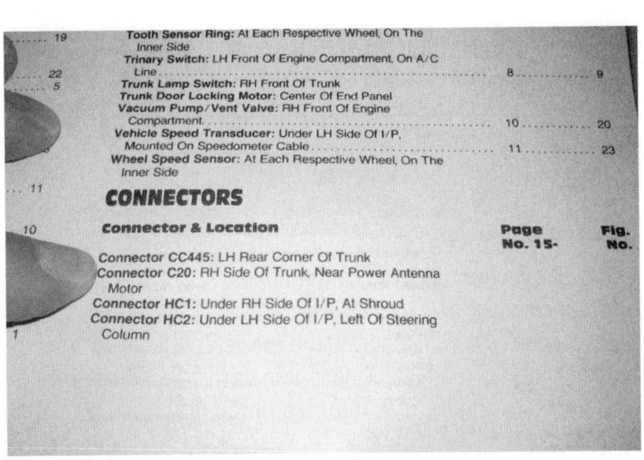

FIGURE 8-14   The component location section of a service manual is very helpful, especially when working on an unfamiliar vehicle.

Home Screen

The Home screen is the first screen displayed when you start. It displays buttons that represent the major sections of the program. Access to the Home screen is available from anywhere within the program by clicking the Home button on the toolbar.

Toolbars

A main toolbar is displayed on most screens, providing quick access to certain functions. This toolbar varies somewhat, depending upon what information is being accessed.

Electronic Service Information

Electronic service information is available mostly by subscription and provides access to an Internet site where service manual–type information is available. Most vehicle manufacturers also offer electronic service information to their dealers and to most schools and colleges that offer corporate training programs.

Technical Service Bulletins

Technical service bulletins, often abbreviated **TSBs,** are issued by the vehicle manufacturer to notify service technicians of a problem and include the necessary corrective action. Technical service bulletins are designed for dealership technicians but are republished by aftermarket companies and made available along with other service information to shops and vehicle repair facilities.

Internet

The Internet has opened the field for information exchange and access to technical advice. One of the most useful websites is the International Automotive Technician's network at www.iatn.net. This is a free site but service technicians need to register to join. For a small monthly sponsor fee, the shop or service technician can gain access to the archives, which include thousands of successful repairs in the searchable database.

Recalls and Campaigns

A recall or campaign is issued by a vehicle manufacturer and a notice is sent to all owners in the event of a safety- or emission-related fault or concern. While these faults may be repaired by independent shops, it is generally handled by a local dealer. Items that have created recalls in the past have included potential fuel system leakage problems, exhaust leakage, or electrical malfunctions that could cause a possible fire or the engine to stall. Unlike technical service bulletins whose cost is only covered when the

TABLE 8-1   Hesitation

Possible Cause	Reason
Throttle-position (TP) sensor	▪ The TP sensor should be within the specified range at idle. If too high or too low, the computer may not provide a strong enough extra pulse to prevent a hesitation. ▪ An open or short in the TP sensor can result in hesitation because the computer would not be receiving correct information regarding the position of the throttle.
Throttle-plate deposit buildup (port fuel-injected engines)	An airflow restriction at the throttle plates creates not only less air reaching the engine but also swirling air due to the deposits. This swirling or uneven airflow can cause an uneven air–fuel mixture being supplied to the engine, causing poor idle quality and a sag or hesitation during acceleration.
Manifold absolute pressure (MAP) sensor fault	The MAP sensor detects changes in engine load and signals to the computer to increase the amount of fuel needed for proper operation. Check the vacuum hose and the sensor itself for proper operation.
Check the throttle linkage for binding	A kinked throttle cable or cruise (speed) control cable can cause the accelerator pedal to bind.
Contaminated fuel	Fuel contaminated with excessive amounts of alcohol or water can cause a hesitation or sag during acceleration. *HINT:* To easily check for the presence of alcohol in gasoline, simply get a sample of the fuel and place it in a clean container. Add some water and shake. If no alcohol is in the gasoline, the water will settle to the bottom and be clear. If there is alcohol in the gasoline, the alcohol will absorb the water. The alcohol-water combination will settle to the bottom of the container, but will be cloudy rather than clear.
Clogged, shorted, or leaking fuel injectors	Any injector problem that results in less than an ideal amount of fuel being delivered to the cylinders can result in a hesitation, a sag, or stumble during acceleration.
Spark plugs or spark plug wires	Any fault in the ignition system such as a defective spark plug wire or cracked spark plug can cause hesitation, a sag, or stumble during acceleration. At higher engine speeds, a defective spark plug wire is not as noticeable as it is at lower speeds, especially in vehicles equipped with a V-8 engine.
EGR valve operation	Hesitation, a sag, or stumble can occur if the EGR valve opens too soon or is stuck partially open.
False air	A loose or cracked intake hose between the mass airflow (MAF) sensor and the throttle plate can be the cause.

vehicle is within the warranty period, a recall or campaign is always done at no cost to the vehicle owner.

HOTLINE SERVICES

A hotline service provider is a subscription-based helpline to assist service technicians solve technical problems. While services vary, most charge a monthly fee for a certain amount of time each month to talk to an experienced service technician who has

a large amount of resource materials available for reference. Often, the technician hired by the hotline services specializes in one vehicle make and is familiar with many of the pattern failures that are seen by other technicians in the field. Hotline services are an efficient way to get information on an as-needed basis.

Some examples of hotline automotive service providers include:

▪ Identifix
▪ Autohotlineusa

- Taylor Automotive Tech-Line
- Aspire

FREQUENTLY ASKED QUESTION

JULIAN DATE

The **Julian date** (abbreviated **JD**) is the number of the day of the year. January 1 is day 001. The Julian date is named for Julius Caesar, who developed the current calendar.

TECH TIP

USE A BLUETOOTH HANDS-FREE TELEPHONE

When talking to a hotline service provider, it is wise to be looking at the vehicle during the call to be able to provide information about the vehicle and perform the suggested tests. This makes the job of troubleshooting easier and faster for both the technician and the service provider, resulting in shorter length calls. Using a Bluetooth hands-free telephone should help shorten the length of calls, which means the cost will be less for the help service.

SPECIALTY REPAIR MANUALS

Examples of specialty repair manuals include unit repair for assembled components, such as automatic transmission/transaxle, manual transmission/transaxle, differentials, and engines. Some specialty repair manuals cover older or antique vehicles, which may include unit repair sections.

AFTERMARKET SUPPLIER'S GUIDES AND CATALOGS

Aftermarket supplier's guides and catalogs often include expanded views of assembled parts along with helpful hints and advice. Sometimes the only place where this information is available is at trade shows associated with automotive training conferences and expos. Go to the following websites for examples of training conferences with trade shows:

- *www.lindertech.com*
- *www.avtechexpo.com*
- *www.visionkc.com (Vision Expo)*

SUMMARY

1. Vehicle history records are sometimes very helpful in determining problems that may be related to a previous fault or repair.
2. The vehicle owner's manual is very helpful to the service technician because it includes the procedures for resetting the maintenance reminder light (oil change light), as well as how to reset the tire pressure monitoring system after a tire rotation, and other important settings and specifications.
3. Lubrication guides provide information on the specified oil and lubricants needed along with the capacities and the location of lubrication points.
4. Factory service manuals or electronic services include information that is vehicle and year specific and very detailed.
5. Other types of service information are labor and parts guides, vacuum hose and wiring diagrams, component locator manuals, specialty manuals, and aftermarket supplies guides and catalogs.
6. Hotline services are subscription based and allow a technician to talk to an experienced technician who has many resources.

REVIEW QUESTIONS

1. What is included in the vehicle owner's manual that could be helpful for a service technician?

2. Lubrication service guides include what type of information?

3. Explain why factory service manuals or factory electronic service information is the most detailed of all service information.

4. Explain how flat-rate and parts guides are useful to customers.

5. List additional types of service manuals that are available.

6. Describe how hotline services and Internet sites assist service technicians.

CHAPTER QUIZ

1. What type of information is commonly included in the owner's manual that would be a benefit to service technicians?
   a. Maintenance reminder light reset procedures
   b. Tire pressure monitoring system reset procedures
   c. Maintenance items specifications
   d. All of the above

2. Two technicians are discussing the need for the history of the vehicle. Technician A says that an accident could cause faults to occur after the repair due to hidden damage. Technician B says that some faults could be related to a previous repair. Which technician is correct?
   a. Technician A only
   b. Technician B only
   c. Both Technicians A and B
   d. Neither Technician A nor B

3. The viscosity of engine oil is found where?
   a. Owner's manual
   b. Factory service manual or service information
   c. Lubrication guide
   d. All of the above

4. Wiring diagrams are usually found where?
   a. Owner's manuals
   b. Factory service manuals
   c. Unit repair manuals
   d. Lubrication guides

5. What type of manual includes time needed to perform service procedures?
   a. Flat-rate manuals
   b. Owner's manuals
   c. Factory service manuals
   d. Parts guide

6. Component location can be found in _____.
   a. Factory service manuals
   b. Owner's manuals
   c. Component location manuals
   d. Both a and c

7. Aftermarket service information is available in what format?
   a. Manuals
   b. CDs or DVDs
   c. Internet
   d. All of the above are possible source formats

8. Hotline services are _____.
   a. Free
   b. Available for a service fee
   c. Available on CD or DVD format
   d. Accessed by the Internet

9. Aftermarket parts catalogs can be a useful source of information and they are usually _____.
   a. Free
   b. Available by paid subscription
   c. Available on CD or DVD
   d. Available for a fee on a secured Internet site

10. Which type of manual or service information includes the flat-rate time and the cost of parts?
    a. Parts and time guides
    b. Factory service manuals
    c. Component location guides
    d. Free Internet site

VEHICLE IDENTIFICATION AND EMISSION RATINGS

OBJECTIVES

After studying Chapter 9, the reader will be able to:

1. Identify a vehicle.
2. Interpret vehicle identification numbers and placard information.
3. Interpret vehicle emissions and emission control information.
4. Read and interpret casting numbers.
5. Locate calibration codes.

KEY TERMS

Bin Number (p. 111)
Calendar Year (CY) (p. 108)
Calibration Codes (p. 111)
California Air Resources Board (CARB) (p. 109)
Casting Numbers (p. 111)
Country of Origin (p. 108)
Environmental Protection Agency (EPA) (p. 109)

Gross Axle Weight Rating (GAWR) (p. 109)
Gross Vehicle Weight Rating (GVWR) (p. 109)
Model Year (MY) (p. 108)
Tier 1 (p. 109)
Tier 2 (p. 109)
Vehicle Emissions Control Information (VECI) (p. 109)
Vehicle Identification Number (VIN) (p. 108)

PARTS OF A VEHICLE

The names of the parts of a vehicle are based on the location and purpose of the component.

Left Side of the Vehicle— Right Side of the Vehicle

Both of these terms refer to the left and right as if the driver is sitting behind the steering wheel. Therefore, the left side (including components under the hood) is on the driver's side.

Front and Rear

The proper term for the back portion of any vehicle is rear (for example, left rear tire).

FRONT-WHEEL DRIVE VERSUS REAR-WHEEL DRIVE

Front-wheel drive (FWD) means that the front wheels are being driven by the engine, as well as turned by the steering wheel. Rear-wheel drive (RWD) means that the rear wheels are driven by the engine. If the engine is in the front, it can be either front- or rear-wheel drive. In many cases, a front engine vehicle can also drive all four wheels called four-wheel drive (4WD) or all-wheel drive (AWD). If the engine is located at the rear of the vehicle, it can be rear-wheel drive or four-wheel (4WD) drive.

VEHICLE IDENTIFICATION

All service work requires that the vehicle, including the engine and accessories, be properly identified. The most common identification is the make, model, and year of the vehicle.

> Make: e.g., Chevrolet
> Model: e.g., Trailblazer
> Year: e.g., 2007

The year of the vehicle is often difficult to determine exactly. A model may be introduced as the next year's model as soon as January of the previous year. Typically, a new **model year** (abbreviated **MY**) starts in September or October of the year prior to the actual new year, but not always. This is why the **vehicle identification number,** usually abbreviated **VIN,** is so important. See Figure 9-1.

Since 1981 all vehicle manufacturers have used a VIN that is 17 characters long. Although every vehicle manufacturer assigns various letters or numbers within these 17 characters, there are some constants, including:

FIGURE 9-1 Typical vehicle identification number (VIN) as viewed through the windshield.

- The first number or letter designates the **country of origin.**
- The model of the vehicle is commonly the fourth and/or fifth character.

1 = United States	6 = Australia	L = China	V = France
2 = Canada	8 = Argentina	R = Taiwan	W = Germany
3 = Mexico	9 = Brazil	S = England	X = Russia
4 = United States	J = Japan	T = Czechoslovakia	Y = Sweden
5 = United States	K = Korea	U = Romania	Z = Italy

- The eighth character is often the engine code. (Some engines cannot be determined by the VIN number.)
- The tenth character represents the **calendar year** (abbreviated **CY**) on all vehicles. See the following chart.

VIN Year Chart *(The pattern repeats every 30 years)*

A = 1980/2010	J = 1988/2018	T = 1996/2026	4 = 2004/2034
B = 1981/2011	K = 1989/2019	V = 1997/2027	5 = 2005/2035
C = 1982/2012	L = 1990/2020	W = 1998/2028	6 = 2006/2036
D = 1983/2013	M = 1991/2021	X = 1999/2029	7 = 2007/2037
E = 1984/2014	N = 1992/2022	Y = 2000/2030	8 = 2008/2038
F = 1985/2015	P = 1993/2023	1 = 2001/2031	9 = 2009/2039
G = 1986/2016	R = 1994/2024	2 = 2002/2032	
H = 1987/2017	S = 1995/2025	3 = 2003/2033	

VEHICLE SAFETY CERTIFICATION LABEL

A vehicle safety certification label is attached to the left side pillar post on the rearward-facing section of the left front door. This label indicates the month and year of manufacture as well as the **gross vehicle weight rating (GVWR),** the **gross axle weight rating (GAWR),** and the vehicle identification number (VIN).

VECI LABEL

The **vehicle emissions control information (VECI)** label under the hood of the vehicle shows informative settings and emission hose routing information. See Figure 9-2.

The VECI label (sticker) can be located on the bottom side of the hood, the radiator fan shroud, the radiator core support, or the strut towers. The VECI label usually includes the following information:

- Engine identification
- Emissions standard that the vehicle meets
- Vacuum hose routing diagram
- Base ignition timing (if adjustable)
- Spark plug type and gap
- Valve lash
- Emission calibration code

EMISSION STANDARDS IN THE UNITED STATES

In the United States, emissions standards are managed by the **Environmental Protection Agency (EPA)** as well as some U.S. state governments. Some of the strictest standards in the world are formulated in California by the **California Air Resources Board (CARB).**

Tier 1 and Tier 2

Federal emission standards are set by the Clean Air Act Amendments (CAAA) of 1990 grouped by *tier.* All vehicles sold in the United States must meet **Tier 1** standards that went into effect in 1994 and are the least stringent. Additional **Tier 2** standards have been optional since 2001, and are currently being phased in to be fully adopted by 2009. The current Tier 1 standards are different between automobiles and light trucks (SUVs, pickup trucks, and minivans), but Tier 2 standards are the same for both types.

There are several ratings that can be given to vehicles, and a certain percentage of a manufacturer's vehicles must meet different levels in order for the company to sell its products in affected regions. Beyond Tier 1, and in order by stringency, are the following levels:

- TLEV—Transitional Low-Emission Vehicle. More stringent for HC than Tier 1.
- LEV—(also known as LEV I)—Low-Emission Vehicle. An intermediate California standard about twice as stringent as Tier 1 for HC and NO_X.
- ULEV (also known as ULEV I)—Ultra-Low-Emission Vehicle. A stronger California standard emphasizing very low HC emissions.
- ULEV II—Ultra-Low-Emission Vehicle. A cleaner-than-average vehicle certified under the Phase II LEV standard. Hydrocarbon and carbon monoxide emissions levels are nearly 50% lower than those of a LEV II-certified vehicle. See Figure 9-3.

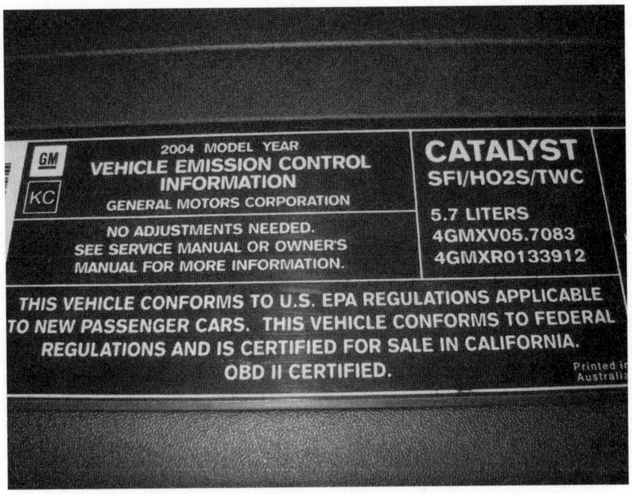

FIGURE 9-2   A VECI label on a 2004 Pontiac GTO.

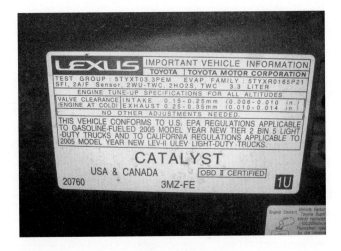

FIGURE 9-3   The underhood decal showing that this Lexus RX-330 meets both national (Tier 2; BIN 5) and California LEV-II (ULEV) regulation standards.

- SULEV—Super-Ultra-Low-Emission Vehicle. A California standard even tighter than ULEV, including much lower HC and NO$_x$ emissions; roughly equivalent to Tier 2 Bin 2 vehicles.
- ZEV—Zero-Emission Vehicle. A California standard prohibiting any tailpipe emissions. The ZEV category is largely restricted to electric vehicles and hydrogen-fueled vehicles. In these cases, any emissions that are created are produced at another site, such as a power plant or hydrogen reforming center, unless such sites run on renewable energy.

NOTE: A battery-powered electric vehicle charged from the power grid will still be up to 10 times cleaner than even the cleanest gasoline vehicles over their respective lifetimes.

The current California ZEV regulation allows manufacturers a choice of two options for meeting the ZEV requirements:

1. Vehicle manufacturers can meet the ZEV obligations by meeting standards that are similar to the ZEV rule as it existed in 2001. This means using a formula allowing a vehicle mix of 2% pure ZEVs, 2% AT-PZEVs (vehicles earning advanced technology partial ZEV credits), and 6% PZEVs (extremely clean conventional vehicles). The ZEV obligation is based on the number of passenger cars and small trucks a manufacturer sells in California.

2. Manufacturers may also choose a new alternative ZEV compliance strategy of meeting part of the ZEV requirement by producing the sales-weighted market share of

approximately 250 fuel-cell vehicles by 2008. The remainder of the ZEV requirements could be achieved by producing 4% AT-PZEVs and 6% PZEVs. The required number of fuel-cell vehicles will increase to 2,500 from 2009 to 2011, 25,000 from 2012 through 2020, and 50,000 from 2015 through 2017. Manufacturers can substitute battery electric vehicles for up to 50% of the fuel-cell vehicle requirements.

- PZEV—Partial-Zero-Emission Vehicle—Compliant with the SULEV standard; additionally has near-zero evaporative emissions and a 15-year/150,000-mile warranty on its emission control equipment.

Tier 2 standards are even more stringent. Tier 2 variations are appended with "II," such as LEV II or SULEV II. Other categories have also been created:

- ILEV—Inherently Low-Emission Vehicle
- AT-PZEV—Advanced Technology Partial-Zero-Emission Vehicle. If a vehicle meets the PZEV standards and is using high-technology features, such as an electric motor or high-pressure gaseous fuel tanks for compressed natural gas, it qualifies as an AT-PZEV. Hybrid electric vehicles such as the Toyota Prius can qualify, as can internal combustion engine vehicles that run on natural gas (CNG), such as the Honda Civic GX. These vehicles are classified as "partial" ZEV because they receive partial credit for the number of ZEV vehicles that automakers would otherwise be required to sell in California.
- NLEV—National Low-Emission Vehicle. All vehicles nationwide must meet this standard, which started in 2001. See Tables 9-1 and 9-2.

TABLE 9-1   LEV Standard Categories

		NMOG Grams (Mile)	CO Grams (Mile)	NO$_x$ Grams (Mile)
LEV I (Cars)	TLEV	0.125 (0.156)	3.4 (4.2)	0.4 (0.6)
	LEV	0.075 (0.090)	3.4 (4.2)	0.2 (0.3)
	ULEV	0.040 (0.055)	1.7 (2.1)	0.2 (0.3)
LEV II (Cars and Trucks < 8,500 lbs)	LEV	0.075 (0.090)	3.4 (4.2)	0.05 (0.07)
	ULEV	0.040 (0.055)	1.7 (2.1)	0.05 (0.07)
	SULEV	–(0.010)	–(1.0)	–(0.02)

Note: Numbers in parentheses are 100,000-mile standards for LEV I, and 120,000-mile standards for LEV II. NMOG means non-methane organic gases, which includes alcohol. CO means carbon monoxide. NO$_x$ means oxides of nitrogen. Data compiled from California Environmental Protection Agency—Air Resource Board (CARB) documents.

TABLE 9-2 California LEV II 120,000-Mile Tailpipe Emissions Limits

Certification Level	NMOG (g/mi)	CO (g/mi)	NOₓ (g/mi)
LEV-II	0.090	4.2	0.07
ULEV-II	0.055	2.1	0.07
SULEV-II	0.010	1.0	0.02

Note: Numbers in parentheses are 100,000-mile standards for LEV I, and 120,000-mile standards for LEV II. NMOG means non-methane organic gases, which includes alcohol. CO means carbon monoxide. NOₓ means oxides of nitrogen. The specification is in grams per mile (g/mi). Data compiled from California Environmental Protection Agency—Air Resources Board (CARB) documents.

TABLE 9-3 EPA Tier 2—120,000-Mile Tailpipe Emission Limits

Certification Level	NMOG (g/mi)	CO (g/mi)	NOₓ (g/mi)
Bin 1	0.0	0.0	0.0
Bin 2	0.010	2.1	0.02
Bin 3	0.055	2.1	0.03
Bin 4	0.070	2.1	0.04
Bin 5	0.090	4.2	0.07
Bin 6	0.090	4.2	0.10
Bin 7	0.090	4.2	0.15
Bin 8a	0.125	4.2	0.20
Bin 8b	0.156	4.2	0.20
Bin 9a	0.090	4.2	0.30
Bin 9b	0.130	4.2	0.30
Bin 9c	0.180	4.2	0.30
Bin 10a	0.156	4.2	0.60
Bin 10b	0.230	6.4	0.60
Bin 10c	0.230	6.4	0.60
Bin 11	0.230	7.3	0.90

Note: The bin number is determined by the type and weight of the vehicle. The highest bin allowed for vehicles built after January 1, 2007, is Bin 8. Data compiled from the Environmental Protection Agency (EPA).

Federal EPA Bin Number

The higher the tier number, the newer the regulation; the lower the **bin number,** the cleaner the vehicle. The 2004 Toyota Prius is a very clean Bin 3, while the Hummer H2 is a dirty Bin 11. Examples include:

- Tier 1: The former federal standard; carried over to model year 2004 for those vehicles not yet subject to the phase-in.
- Tier 2, Bin 1: The cleanest federal Tier 2 standard; a zero-emission vehicle (ZEV).
- Tier 2, Bins 2–4: Cleaner than the average standard.
- Tier 2, Bin 5: "Average" of new Tier 2 standards, roughly equivalent to a LEV II vehicle.
- Tier 2, Bins 6–9: Not as clean as the average requirement for a Tier 2 vehicle.
- Tier 2, Bin 10: Least-clean Tier 2 bin applicable to passenger vehicles. See Tables 9-3 and 9-4.

CALIBRATION CODES

Calibration codes are usually located on power train control modules (PCMs) or other controllers. Some calibration codes are only accessible with a scan tool. Whenever diagnosing an engine operating fault, it is often necessary to know the calibration code to be sure that the vehicle is the subject of a technical service bulletin or other service procedure. See Figure 9-4.

CASTING NUMBERS

Whenever an engine part such as a block is cast, a number is put into the mold to identify the casting. See Figure 9-5. These **casting numbers** can be used to check dimensions such as the cubic inch displacement and other information. Sometimes changes are made to the mold, yet the casting number is not changed. Most often the casting number is the best piece of identifying information that the service technician can use for identifying an engine.

TABLE 9-4   Air Pollution Score

U.S. EPA Vehicle Information Program (The Higher the Score, the Lower the Emissions)	
Selected Emissions Standards	Score
Bin 1 and ZEV	10
PZEV	9.5
Bin 2	9
Bin 3	8
Bin 4	7
Bin 5 and LEV II cars	6
Bin 6	5
Bin 7	4
Bin 8	3
Bin 9a and LEV I cars	2
Bin 9b	2
Bin 10a	1
Bin 10b and Tier 1 cars	1
Bin 11	0

Courtesy of the Environmental Protection Agency (EPA).

FIGURE 9-4   A typical computer calibration sticker on the case of the controller. The information on the sticker is often needed when ordering parts or a replacement controller.

FIGURE 9-5   Engine block identification number cast into the block is used for identification.

SUMMARY

1. The front, rear, left, and right side of a vehicle are as viewed from the driver's seat.

2. The vehicle identification number (VIN) is very important as it includes when the vehicle was built, as well as the engine code and many other details about the vehicle.

3. The VECI label under the hood often needs to be checked by the technician to properly service the vehicle.

4. Other vehicle information that the technician may need for a service or repair include calibration codes, casting numbers, and emissions rating.

REVIEW QUESTIONS

1. From what position are the terms left and right determined?

2. What are the major pieces of information that are included in the vehicle identification number (VIN)?

3. What information is included on the VECI label under the hood?

4. What does Tier 2 Bin 5 mean?

CHAPTER QUIZ

1. The passenger side is called the _____ .
   a. Right side
   b. Left side
   c. Either right or left side, depending on how the vehicle is viewed
   d. Both a and b

2. A vehicle with the engine in the front can be _____ .
   a. Front-wheel drive
   b. Rear-wheel drive
   c. Four-wheel drive
   d. Any of the above

3. The vehicle identification number (VIN) is how many characters long?
   a. 10
   b. 12
   c. 17
   d. 21

4. The tenth character represents the year of the vehicle. If the tenth character is a "Y," what year is the vehicle?
   a. 1998
   b. 2000
   c. 2002
   d. 2004

5. The first character of the vehicle identification number is the country of origin. Where was the vehicle built that has a "5" as the first character?
   a. United States
   b. Canada
   c. Mexico
   d. Japan

6. The VECI label includes all *except* _____ .
   a. Engine identification
   b. Horsepower and torque rating of the engine
   c. Spark plug type and gap
   d. Valve lash

7. The vehicle safety certification label includes all *except* _____ .
   a. VIN
   b. GVWR
   c. Tire pressure recommendation
   d. GAWR

8. What are the characters that are embedded in most engine blocks and are used for identification?
   a. VIN
   b. Calibration codes
   c. Bin number
   d. Casting number

9. If the first number of the VIN is an "S," where was the vehicle made?
   a. United States
   b. Mexico
   c. Canada
   d. England

10. Technician A says that the lower the Bin number is, the cleaner. Technician B says that SULEV has cleaner standards than ULEV. Which technician is correct?
    a. Technician A only
    b. Technician B only
    c. Both Technicians A and B
    d. Neither Technician A nor B

CHAPTER 10

GASOLINE ENGINE OPERATION, PARTS, AND SPECIFICATIONS

OBJECTIVES

After studying Chapter 10, the reader will be able to:

1. Prepare for Engine Repair (A1) ASE certification test content area "A" (General Engine Diagnosis).
2. Explain how a four-stroke cycle gasoline engine operates.
3. List the various characteristics by which vehicle engines are classified.
4. Discuss how a compression ratio is calculated.
5. Explain how engine size is determined.
6. Describe how turbocharging or supercharging increases engine power.

KEY TERMS

ENERGY AND POWER

Energy is used to produce power. The chemical energy in fuel is converted to heat by the burning of the fuel at a controlled rate. This process is called **combustion.** If engine combustion occurs within the power chamber, the engine is called an **internal combustion engine.**

NOTE: An **external combustion engine** is an engine that burns fuel outside of the engine itself, such as a steam engine.

Engines used in automobiles are internal combustion heat engines. They convert the chemical energy of the gasoline into heat within a power chamber that is called a **combustion chamber.** Heat energy released in the combustion chamber raises the temperature of the combustion gases within the chamber. The increase in gas temperature causes the pressure of the gases to increase. The pressure developed within the combustion chamber is applied to the head of a piston or to a turbine wheel to produce a usable **mechanical force,** which is then converted into useful **mechanical power.**

ENGINE CONSTRUCTION OVERVIEW

Block

All automotive and truck engines are constructed using a solid frame, called a **block.** A block is constructed of cast iron or aluminum and provides the foundation for most of the engine components and systems. The block is cast and then machined to very close tolerances to allow other parts to be installed.

Rotating Assembly

Pistons are installed in the block and move up and down during engine operation. Pistons are connected to *connecting rods*, which connect the pistons to the crankshaft. The crankshaft converts the up-and-down motion of the piston to rotary motion, which is then transmitted to the drive wheels and propels the vehicle. See Figure 10-1.

Cylinder Heads

All engines use a cylinder head to seal the top of the cylinders, which are in the engine block. The cylinder head also contains valves that allow air and fuel into the cylinder, called intake valves and exhaust valves, which open after combustion to allow the hot gases left over to escape from the engine. Cylinder heads are constructed of cast iron or aluminum and are then machined for the valves and other valve-related components.

Cooling passages are formed during the casting process and coolant is circulated around the combustion chamber to keep temperatures controlled. See Figure 10-2.

Intake and Exhaust Manifolds

Air and fuel enters the engine through an intake manifold and exits the engine through the exhaust manifold. Intake manifolds operate cooler than exhaust manifolds and are therefore constructed of nylon reinforced plastic or aluminum. Exhaust manifolds must be able to withstand hot exhaust gases and therefore most are constructed from cast iron.

Cooling System

All engines must have a cooling system to control engine temperatures. While some older engines were air cooled, all current production passenger vehicle engines are cooled by circulating

FIGURE 10-1   The rotating assembly for a V-8 engine that has eight pistons and connecting rods and one crankshaft.

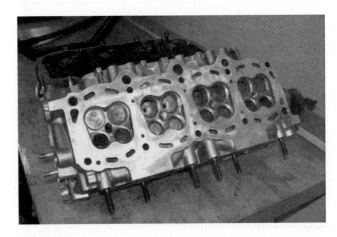

FIGURE 10-2   A cylinder head with four valves per cylinder, two intake valves (larger) and two exhaust valves (smaller).

antifreeze coolant through passages in the block and cylinder head. The coolant picks up the heat from the engine and after the thermostat opens, the water pump circulates the coolant through the radiator where the excess heat is released to the outside air, cooling the coolant. The coolant is continuously circulated through the cooling system and the temperature is controlled by the thermostat. See Figure 10-3.

Lubrication System

All engines contain moving and sliding parts that must be kept lubricated to reduce wear and friction. The oil pan, bolted to the bottom of the engine block, holds 4 to 7 quarts (liters) of oil. An oil pump, which is driven by the engine, forces the oil through the oil filter and then into passages in the crankshaft and block. These passages are called **oil galleries.** The oil is also forced up to the valves and then falls down through openings in the cylinder head and block back into the oil pan. See Figure 10-4.

FIGURE 10-3   The coolant temperature is controlled by the thermostat which opens and allows coolant to flow to the radiator when the temperature reaches the rating temperature of the thermostat.

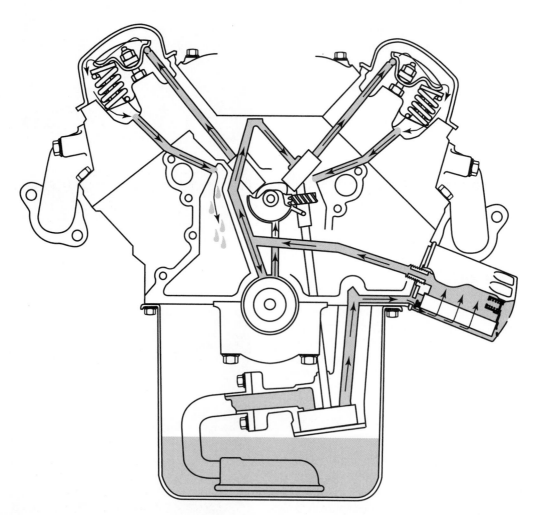

FIGURE 10-4   A typical lubrication system, showing the oil pan, oil pump, oil filter, and oil passages.

Fuel System and Ignition System

All engines require fuel and an ignition system to ignite the fuel–air mixture in the cylinders. The fuel system includes the following components:

- Fuel tank where fuel is stored
- Fuel filter and lines
- Fuel injectors, which spray fuel into the intake manifold or directly into the cylinder, depending on the type of system used

The ignition system is designed to take 12 volts from the battery and convert it to 5,000 to 40,000 volts needed to jump the gap of a spark plug. Spark plugs are threaded into the cylinder head of each cylinder, and when the spark occurs, it ignites the air–fuel mixture in the cylinder creating pressure and forcing the piston down in the cylinder. The components included on the ignition system include:

- Spark plugs
- Ignition coils
- Ignition control module (ICM)
- Associated wiring

FOUR-STROKE CYCLE OPERATION

Most automotive engines use the four-stroke cycle of events, begun by the starter motor which rotates the engine. The four-stroke cycle is repeated for each cylinder of the engine. See Figure 10-5.

- **Intake stroke.**   The **intake valve** is open and the piston inside the cylinder travels downward, drawing a mixture of air and fuel into the cylinder.
- **Compression stroke.**   As the engine continues to rotate, the intake valve closes and the piston moves upward in the cylinder, compressing the air–fuel mixture.
- **Power stroke.**   When the piston gets near the top of the cylinder (called **top dead center [TDC]**), the spark at the spark plug ignites the air–fuel mixture, which forces the piston downward.
- **Exhaust stroke.**   The engine continues to rotate, and the piston again moves upward in the cylinder. The exhaust valve opens, and the piston forces the residual burned gases out of the **exhaust valve** and into the exhaust manifold and exhaust system.

This sequence repeats as the engine rotates. To stop the engine, the electricity to the ignition system is shut off by the ignition switch.

A piston that moves up and down, or reciprocates, in a **cylinder** can be seen in this illustration. The piston is attached to a **crankshaft** with a **connecting rod.** This arrangement allows the piston to reciprocate (move up and down) in the cylinder as the crankshaft rotates. See Figure 10-6 on page 119.

The combustion pressure developed in the combustion chamber at the correct time will push the piston downward to rotate the crankshaft.

THE 720° CYCLE

Each cycle of events requires that the engine crankshaft make two complete revolutions or 720° (360° × 2 = 720°). The greater the number of cylinders, the closer together the power strokes occur. To find the angle between cylinders of an engine, divide the number of cylinders into 720°.

Angle with three cylinders = 720°/3 = 240°
Angle with four cylinders = 720°/4 = 180°
Angle with five cylinders = 720°/5 = 144°
Angle with six cylinders = 720°/6 = 120°
Angle with eight cylinders = 720°/8 = 90°
Angle with ten cylinders = 720°/10 = 72°

This means that in a four-cylinder engine, a power stroke occurs at every 180° of the crankshaft rotation (every 1/2 rotation). A V-8 is a much smoother operating engine because a power stroke occurs twice as often (every 90° of crankshaft rotation).

Engine cycles are identified by the number of piston strokes required to complete the cycle. A **piston stroke** is a one-way piston movement between the top and bottom of the cylinder. During one stroke, the crankshaft revolves 180° (1/2 revolution). A **cycle** is a complete series of events that continually repeat. Most automobile engines use a **four-stroke cycle.**

ENGINE CLASSIFICATION AND CONSTRUCTION

Engines are classified by several characteristics including:

- **Number of strokes.** Most automotive engines use the four-stroke cycle.
- **Cylinder arrangement.** An engine with more cylinders is smoother operating because the power pulses produced by the power strokes are more closely spaced. An inline engine places all cylinders in a straight line. Four-, five-, and six-cylinder engines are commonly manufactured inline engines. A V-type engine, such as a V-6 or V-8, has the number of cylinders split and built into a V-shape. See Figure 10-7 on page 119. Horizontally opposed four- and

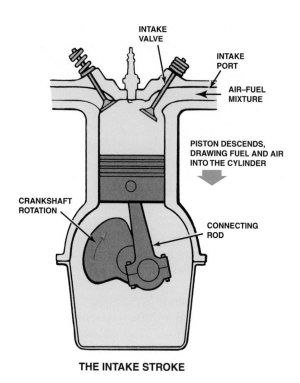

THE INTAKE STROKE

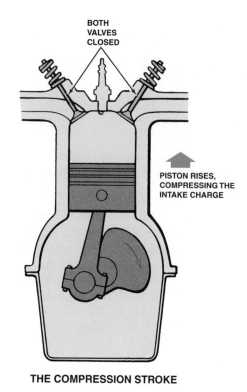

THE COMPRESSION STROKE

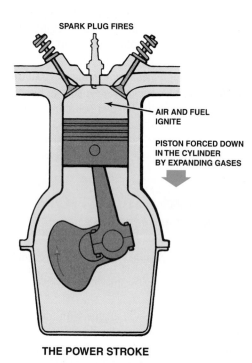

THE POWER STROKE

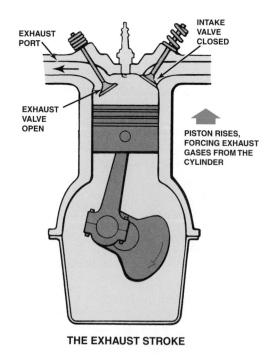

THE EXHAUST STROKE

FIGURE 10-5 The downward movement of the piston draws the air–fuel mixture into the cylinder through the intake valve on the intake stroke. On the compression stroke, the mixture is compressed by the upward movement of the piston with both valves closed. Ignition occurs at the beginning of the power stroke, and combustion drives the piston downward to produce power. On the exhaust stroke, the upward-moving piston forces the burned gases out the open exhaust valve.

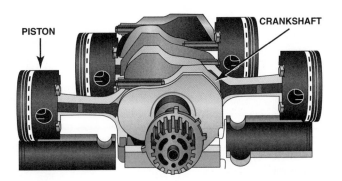

FIGURE 10-8   A horizontally opposed engine design helps to lower the vehicle's center of gravity.

FIGURE 10-6   Cutaway of an engine showing the cylinder, piston, connecting rod, and crankshaft.

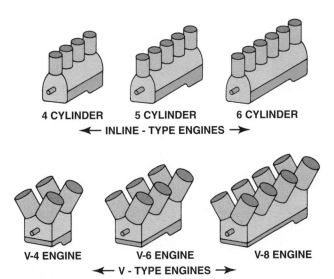

4 CYLINDER   5 CYLINDER   6 CYLINDER

← **INLINE - TYPE ENGINES** →

V-4 ENGINE   V-6 ENGINE   V-8 ENGINE

← **V - TYPE ENGINES** →

FIGURE 10-7   Automotive engine cylinder arrangements.

six-cylinder engines have two banks of cylinders that are horizontal, resulting in a low engine. This style of engine is used in Porsche and Subaru engines and is often called the **boxer** or **pancake** engine design. See Figure 10-8.

- **Longitudinal or transverse mounting.** Engines may be mounted either parallel with the length of the vehicle

(longitudinally) or crosswise (transversely). See Figures 10-9 and 10-10. The same engine may be mounted in various vehicles in either direction.

NOTE: Although it might be possible to mount an engine in different vehicles both longitudinally and transversely, the engine component parts may not be interchangeable. Differences can include different engine blocks and crankshafts, as well as different water pumps.

- **Valve and camshaft number and location.** The number of valves and the number and location of camshafts are a major factor in engine operation. A typical older-model engine uses one intake valve and one exhaust valve per cylinder. Many newer engines use two intake and two exhaust valves per cylinder. The valves are opened by a **camshaft.** For high-speed engine operation, the camshaft should be overhead (over the valves). Some engines use one camshaft for the intake valves and a separate camshaft for the exhaust valves. When the camshaft is located in the block, the valves are operated by lifters, pushrods, and rocker arms. See Figure 10-11. This type of engine is called a **pushrod engine** or **cam-in-block design.** An overhead camshaft engine has the camshaft above the valves in the cylinder head. When one overhead camshaft is used, the design is called a **single overhead camshaft (SOHC)** design. When two overhead camshafts are used, the design is called a **double overhead camshaft (DOHC)** design. See Figures 10-12 and 10-13 on page 121.

NOTE: A V-type engine uses two banks or rows of cylinders. An SOHC design therefore uses two camshafts, but only one camshaft per bank (row) of cylinders. A DOHC V-6, therefore, has four camshafts, two for each bank.

- **Type of fuel.** Most engines operate on gasoline, whereas some engines are designed to operate on methanol, natural gas, propane, or diesel fuel.

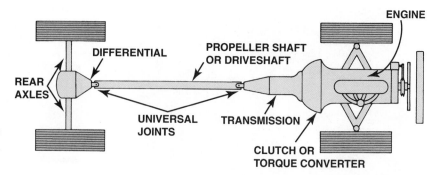

FIGURE 10-9 A longitudinally mounted engine drives the rear wheels through a transmission, driveshaft, and differential assembly.

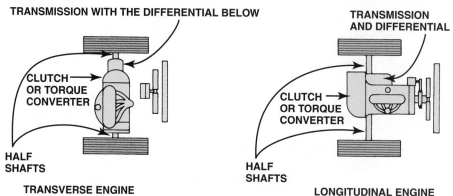

FIGURE 10-10 Two types of front-engine, front-wheel drive.

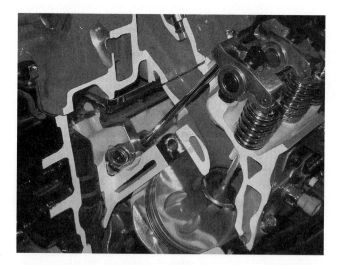

FIGURE 10-11 Cutaway of a V-8 engine showing the lifters, pushrods, roller rocker arms, and valves.

- **Cooling method.** Most engines are liquid cooled, but some older models were air cooled.
- **Type of induction pressure.** If atmospheric air pressure is used to force the air–fuel mixture into the cylinders, the engine is called **naturally aspirated.** Some engines use a **turbocharger** or **supercharger** to force the air–fuel mixture into the cylinder for even greater power.

FREQUENTLY ASKED QUESTION

WHAT IS A ROTARY ENGINE?

A successful alternative engine design is the **rotary engine,** also called the **Wankel engine** after its inventor. The Mazda RX-7 and RX-8 represents the only long-term use of the rotary engine. The rotating combustion chamber engine runs very smoothly, and it produces high power for its size and weight.

The basic rotating combustion chamber engine has a triangular-shaped rotor turning in a housing. The housing is in the shape of a geometric figure called a two-lobed epitrochoid. A seal on each corner, or apex, of the rotor is in constant contact with the housing, so the rotor must turn with an eccentric motion. This means that the center of the rotor moves around the center of the engine. The eccentric motion can be seen in Figure 10-14 on page 122.

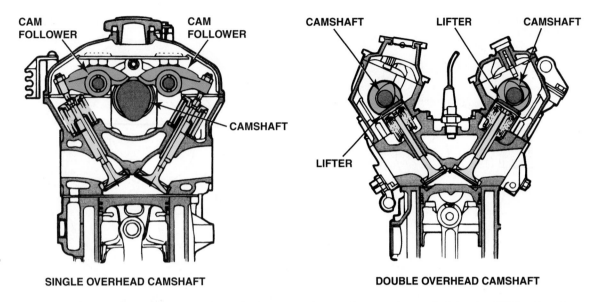

SINGLE OVERHEAD CAMSHAFT   DOUBLE OVERHEAD CAMSHAFT

FIGURE 10-12   SOHC engines usually require additional components such as a rocker arm to operate all of the valves. DOHC engines often operate the valves directly.

FIGURE 10-13   A dual overhead camshaft (DOHC) V-8 engine with part of the cam cover cut away.

ENGINE ROTATION DIRECTION

The SAE standard for automotive engine rotation is counterclockwise (CCW) as viewed from the flywheel end (clockwise as viewed from the front of the engine). The flywheel end of the engine is the end to which the power is applied to drive the vehicle. This is called the **principal end** of the engine. The **nonprincipal end** of the engine is opposite the principal end and is generally referred to as the *front* of the engine, where the accessory belts are used. See Figure 10-15 on page 123.

In most rear-wheel-drive vehicles, therefore, the engine is mounted longitudinally with the principal end at the rear of the engine. Most transversely mounted engines also adhere to the

FREQUENTLY ASKED QUESTION

WHERE DOES AN ENGINE STOP?

When the ignition system is turned off, the firing of the spark plugs stops and the engine will rotate until it stops due to the inertia of the rotating parts. The greatest resistance that occurs in the engine happens during the compression stroke. It has been determined that an engine usually stops when one of the cylinders is about 70 degrees before top dead center (BTDC) on the compression stroke with a variation of plus or minus 10 degrees.

This explains why technicians discover that the starter ring gear is worn at two locations on a four-cylinder engine. The engine stops at one of the two possible places depending on which cylinder is on the compression stroke.

same standard for direction of rotation. Many Honda engines and some marine applications may differ from this standard.

BORE

The diameter of a cylinder is called the **bore.** The larger the bore, the greater the area on which the gases have to work. Pressure is measured in units, such as pounds per square inch (PSI). The greater the area (in square inches), the higher the

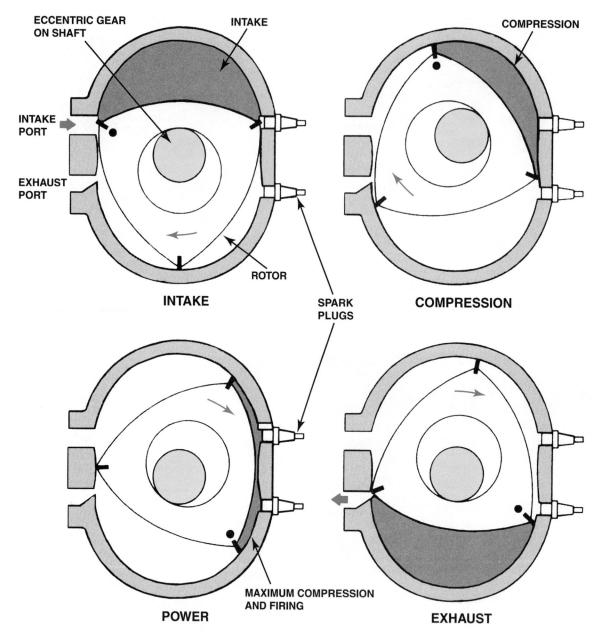

FIGURE 10-14 Rotary engine operates on the four-stroke cycle but uses a rotor instead of a piston and crankshaft to achieve intake, compression, power, and exhaust stroke.

force exerted by the pistons to rotate the crankshaft. See Figure 10-16.

STROKE

The distance the piston travels down in the cylinder is called the **stroke.** The longer this distance is, the greater the amount of air–fuel mixture that can be drawn into the cylinder. The more air–fuel mixture inside the cylinder, the more force will result when the mixture is ignited.

ENGINE DISPLACEMENT

Engine size is described as displacement. **Displacement** is the cubic inch (cu. in.) or cubic centimeter (cc) volume displaced or swept by all of the pistons. A liter (L) is equal to 1,000 cubic centimeters; therefore, most engines today are identified by their displacement in liters.

1 L = 1,000 cc
1 L = 61 cu. in.
1 cu. in. = 16.4 cc

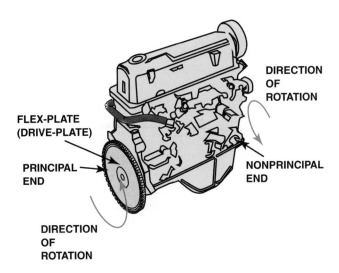

FIGURE 10-15 Inline four-cylinder engine showing principal and nonprincipal ends. Normal direction of rotation is clockwise (CW) as viewed from the front or accessory belt end (nonprincipal end).

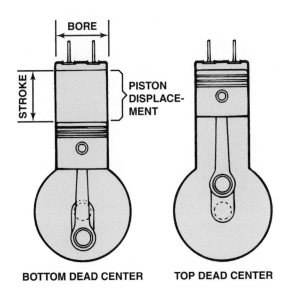

FIGURE 10-16 The bore and stroke of pistons are used to calculate an engine's displacement.

The formula to calculate the displacement of an engine is basically the formula for determining the volume of a cylinder multiplied by the number of cylinders. However, because the formula has been publicized in many different forms, it seems somewhat confusing. Regardless of the method used, the results will be the same. The easiest and most commonly used formula is

Bore × bore × stroke × 0.7854 × number of cylinders

For example, take a 6-cylinder engine where, bore = 4.000 in., stroke = 3.000 in. Applying the formula,

4.000 in. × 4.000 in. ×3.000 in. ×0.7854 × 6 = 226 cu. in.

Engine Size Conversion Chart Liters to Cubic Inches

Liters	Cubic Inches	Liters	Cubic Inches
1.0	61	4.2	255/258
1.3	79	4.3	260/262/265
1.4	85	4.4	267
1.5	91	4.5	273
1.6	97/98	4.6	280/281
1.7	105	4.8	292
1.8	107/110/112	4.9	300/301
1.9	116	5.0	302/304/305/307
2.0	121/122	5.2	318
2.1	128	5.3	327
2.2	132/133/134/135	5.4	330
2.3	138/140	5.7	350
2.4	149	5.8	351
2.5	150/153	6.0	366/368
2.6	156/159	6.1	370
2.8	171/173	6.2	381
2.9	177	6.4	389/390/391
3.0	181/182/183	6.5	396
3.1	191	6.6	400
3.2	196	6.9	420
3.3	200/201	7.0	425/427/428/429
3.4	204	7.2	440
3.5	215	7.3	445
3.7	225	7.4	454
3.8	229/231/232	7.5	460
3.9	239/240	7.8	475/477
4.0	241/244	8.0	488
4.1	250/252	8.8	534

Because 1 cubic inch equals 16.4 cubic centimeters, this engine displacement equals 3,706 cubic centimeters or, rounded to 3,700 cubic centimeters, 3.7 liters.

How to convert cubic inches to liters: 61.02 cubic inches = 1 liter

Example

From liter to cubic inch—5.0 L × 61.02 = 305 CID
From cubic inch to liter—305 ÷ 61.02 = 5.0 L

Engine Size versus Horsepower

The larger the engine, the more power the engine is capable of producing. Several sayings are often quoted about engine size:

"There is no substitute for cubic inches."
"There is no replacement for displacement."

Although a large engine generally uses more fuel, making an engine larger is often the easiest way to increase power.

COMPRESSION RATIO

The compression ratio of an engine is an important consideration when rebuilding or repairing an engine. **Compression ratio (CR)** is the ratio of the volume in the cylinder above the piston when the piston is at the bottom of the stroke to the volume in the cylinder above the piston when the piston is at the top of the stroke. See Figure 10-17.

If Compression Is Lower	If Compression Is Higher
Lower power	Higher power possible
Poorer fuel economy	Better fuel economy
Easier engine cranking	Harder to crank engine, especially when hot
More advanced ignition timing possible without spark knock (detonation)	Less ignition timing required to prevent spark knock (detonation)

$$CR = \frac{\text{Volume in cylinder with piston at bottom of cylinder}}{\text{Volume in cylinder with piston at top center}}$$

See Figure 10-18.

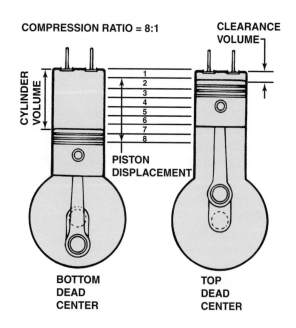

COMPRESSION RATIO = 8:1

CLEARANCE VOLUME

CYLINDER VOLUME

1 2 3 4 5 6 7 8

PISTON DISPLACEMENT

BOTTOM DEAD CENTER

TOP DEAD CENTER

FIGURE 10-17 Compression ratio is the ratio of the total cylinder volume (when the piston is at the bottom of its stroke) to the clearance volume (when the piston is at the top of its stroke).

TECH TIP

ALL 3.8-LITER ENGINES ARE NOT THE SAME!

Most engine sizes are currently identified by displacement in liters. However, not all 3.8-liter engines are the same. See, for example, the following table:

Engine	Displacement
Chevrolet-built 3.8-L, V-6	229 cu. in.
Buick-built 3.8-L, V-6 (also called 3,800 cc)	231 cu. in.
Ford-built 3.8-L, V-6	232 cu. in.

The exact conversion from liters (or cubic centimeters) to cubic inches is 231.9 cubic inches. However, due to rounding of exact cubic-inch displacement and rounding of the exact cubic-centimeter volume, several entirely different engines can be marketed with the exact same liter designation. To reduce confusion and reduce the possibility of ordering incorrect parts, the vehicle identification number (VIN) should be noted for the vehicle being serviced. The VIN should be visible through the windshield on all vehicles. Since 1980, the *engine* identification number or letter is usually the eighth digit or letter from the left.

Smaller, 4-cylinder engines can also cause confusion because many vehicle manufacturers use engines from both overseas and domestic manufacturers. Always refer to service manual information to be assured of correct engine identification.

For example: What is the compression ratio of an engine with 50.3-cu. in. displacement in one cylinder and a combustion chamber volume of 6.7 cu. in.?

$$CR = \frac{50.3 + 6.7 \text{ cu. in.} = 57.0}{6.7 \text{ cu. in.}} = 8.5$$

THE CRANKSHAFT DETERMINES THE STROKE

The stroke of an engine is the distance the piston travels from top dead center (TDC) to bottom dead center (BDC). This distance is determined by the throw of the crankshaft. The throw is the distance from the centerline of the crankshaft to the centerline of the crankshaft rod journal. The throw is one-half of the stroke. See Figure 10-19 for an example of a crankshaft as installed in a GM V-6 engine.

If the crankshaft is replaced with one with a greater stroke, the pistons will be pushed up over the height of the top of the block (deck). The solution to this problem is to install replacement pistons with the piston pin relocated higher on the piston. Another alternative is to replace the connecting rod with a shorter one to prevent the piston from traveling too far up in the cylinder. Changing the connecting rod length does *not* change the stroke of an engine. Changing the connecting rod only changes the position of the piston in the cylinder.

TORQUE

Torque is the term used to describe a rotating force that may or may not result in motion. Torque is measured as the amount of force multiplied by the length of the lever through which it acts. If a one-foot-long wrench is used to apply 10 pounds of force to the end of the wrench to turn a bolt, then you are exerting 10 pound-feet of torque. See Figure 10-20.

The metric unit for torque is Newton-meters because Newton is the metric unit for force and the distance is expressed in meters.

one pound-foot = 1.3558 Newton-meters
one Newton-meter = 0.7376 pound-foot

POWER

The term power means the rate of doing work. Power equals work divided by time. Work is achieved when a certain amount of mass (weight) is moved a certain distance by a force. If the object is moved in 10 seconds or 10 minutes does not make a difference in the amount of work accomplished, but it does affect the amount of power needed. Power is expressed in units of foot-pounds per minute.

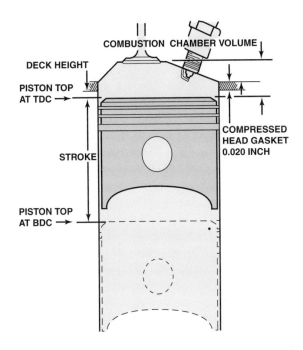

FIGURE 10-18   Combustion chamber volume is the volume above the piston with the piston at top dead center.

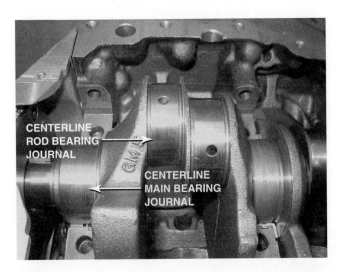

FIGURE 10-19   The distance between the centerline of the main bearing journal and the centerline of the connecting rod journal determines the stroke of the engine. This photo is a little unusual because this is from a V-6 with a splayed crankshaft used to even out the impulses on a 90°, V-6 engine design.

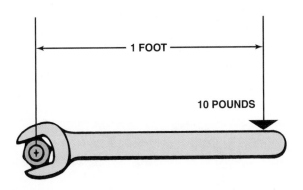

FIGURE 10-20   Torque is a twisting force equal to the distance from the pivot point times the force applied expressed in units called pound-feet (lb-ft) or Newton-meters (N-m).

QUICK-AND-EASY ENGINE EFFICIENCY CHECK

A good, efficient engine is able to produce a lot of power from little displacement. A common rule of thumb is that an engine is efficient if it can produce *1 horsepower per cubic inch* of displacement. Many engines today are capable of this feat, such as the following:

Ford	4.6 L V-8 (281 cu. in.)—305 hp
Chevrolet	3.4 L V-6 (207 cu. in.)—210 hp
Chrysler	3.5 L V-6 (214 cu. in.)—214 hp
Acura	3.2 L V-6 (195 cu. in.)—270 hp

An engine is very powerful for its size if it can produce *100 hp per liter*. This efficiency goal is harder to accomplish. Most factory stock engines that can achieve this feat are supercharged or turbocharged.

HORSEPOWER AND ALTITUDE

Because the density of the air is lower at high altitude, the power that a normal engine can develop is greatly reduced at high altitude. According to SAE conversion factors, a nonsupercharged or nonturbocharged engine loses about 3% of its power for every 1,000 feet (300 meters [m]) of altitude.

Therefore, an engine that develops 150 brake horsepower at sea level will only produce about 85 brake horsepower at the top of Pike's Peak in Colorado at 14,110 feet (4,300 meters). Supercharged and turbocharged engines are not as greatly affected by altitude as normally aspirated engines. Normally aspirated, remember, means engines that breathe air at normal atmospheric pressure.

SUMMARY

1. The four strokes of the four-stroke cycle are intake, compression, power, and exhaust.

2. Engines are classified by number and arrangement of cylinders and by number and location of valves and camshafts, as well as by type of mounting, fuel used, cooling method, and induction pressure.

3. Most engines rotate clockwise as viewed from the front (accessory) end of the engine. The SAE standard is counterclockwise as viewed from the principal (flywheel) end of the engine.

4. Engine size is called displacement and represents the volume displaced or swept by all of the pistons.

REVIEW QUESTIONS

1. Name the strokes of a four-stroke cycle.

2. If an engine at sea level produces 100 horsepower, how many horsepower would it develop at 6,000 feet of altitude?

CHAPTER QUIZ

1. All overhead valve engines _____.
   a. Use an overhead camshaft
   b. Have the overhead valves in the head
   c. Operate by the two-stroke cycle
   d. Use the camshaft to close the valves

2. An SOHC V-8 engine has how many camshafts?
   a. One
   b. Two
   c. Three
   d. Four

3. The coolant flow through the radiator is controlled by the _____.
   a. Size of the passages in the block
   b. Thermostat
   c. Cooling fan(s)
   d. Water pump

4. Torque is expressed in units of _____.
   a. Pound-feet
   b. Foot-pounds
   c. Foot-pounds per minute
   d. Pound-feet per second

5. Horsepower is expressed in units of _____.
   a. Pound-feet
   b. Foot-pounds
   c. Foot-pounds per minute
   d. Pound-feet per second

6. A normally aspirated automobile engine loses about _____ power per 1,000 feet of altitude.
   a. 1%
   b. 3%
   c. 5%
   d. 6%

7. One cylinder of an automotive four-stroke cycle engine completes a cycle every _____.
   a. 90°
   b. 180°
   c. 360°
   d. 720°

8. How many rotations of the crankshaft are required to complete each stroke of a four-stroke cycle engine?
   a. One-fourth
   b. One-half
   c. One
   d. Two

9. A rotating force is called _____.
   a. Horsepower
   b. Torque
   c. Combustion pressure
   d. Eccentric movement

10. Technician A says that a crankshaft determines the stroke of an engine. Technician B says that the length of the connecting rod determines the stroke of an engine. Which technician is correct?
    a. Technician A only
    b. Technician B only
    c. Both Technicians A and B
    d. Neither Technician A nor B

GASOLINE AND ALTERNATIVE FUELS

OBJECTIVES

After studying Chapter 11, the reader will be able to:

1. Describe how the proper grade of gasoline affects engine performance.
2. List gasoline purchasing hints.
3. Discuss how volatility affects driveability.
4. Explain how oxygenated fuels can reduce CO exhaust emissions.
5. Discuss the advantages and disadvantages of various alternative fuels.

KEY TERMS

The quality of the fuel any engine uses is important to its proper operation and long life. If the fuel is not right for the air temperature or if the tendency of the fuel to evaporate is incorrect, severe driveability problems can result. An engine burns about 15 pounds of air for every pound of gasoline.

AUTOMOTIVE FUEL REFINING

As it comes out of the ground, **petroleum** (meaning "rock oil") crude can be as thin and light colored as apple cider or as thick and black as melted tar. Thin crude oil has a high American Petroleum Institute (API) gravity, and therefore is called *high-gravity* crude, and thick crude oil is called *low-gravity* crude. High-gravity-type crude contains more natural gasoline and its lower sulfur and nitrogen content makes it easier to refine.

NOTE: Low-sulfur crude oil is also known as "sweet" crude and high-sulfur crude oil is also known as "sour crude."

Processes

Refining is a complex combination of interdependent processing units, and it all starts with the simple physical separation process called **distillation.**

Distillation

In the late 1800s, crude was separated into different products by boiling. Distillation works because crude is composed of hydrocarbons with a wide range of molecular weights, and therefore a broad range of boiling points. Each product was assigned a temperature range and the product was obtained by condensing the vapor that boiled off in this range at atmospheric pressure (atmospheric distillation). The earliest crude stills were simple pot stills consisting of a container where crude was heated and a condenser to condense the vapor. Later, distillation became a continuous process with a pump to provide crude flow, a furnace to heat the crude, and a distillation column to separate the different boiling cuts.

In a distillation column, the vapor of the lowest-boiling hydrocarbons, propane and butane, rises to the top. The straight-run gasoline (also called naphtha), kerosene, and diesel fuel cuts are drawn off at successively lower positions in the column.

Cracking

The discovery that hydrocarbons with higher boiling points could be broken down (cracked) into lower-boiling hydrocarbons by subjecting them to very high temperatures offered a way to correct the mismatch between supply and demand. This process, thermal **cracking,** was used to increase gasoline production starting in 1913. It is the nature of thermal cracking to make a lot of olefins, which have higher octane numbers but may cause engine deposits. By today's standards, the quality and performance of this early cracked gasoline was low, but it was sufficient for the engines of the day.

Eventually heat was supplemented by a catalyst, transforming thermal cracking into **catalytic cracking.** A catalyst is a material that speeds up or otherwise facilitates a chemical reaction without undergoing a permanent chemical change itself. Catalytic cracking produces gasoline of higher quality than thermal cracking.

Hydrocracking is similar to catalytic cracking in that it uses a catalyst, but the catalyst is in a hydrogen atmosphere. Hydrocracking can break down hydrocarbons that are resistant to catalytic cracking alone. It more commonly is used to produce diesel fuel rather than gasoline.

Other types of refining processes include:

- Reforming
- Alkylation
- Isomerization
- Hydrotreating
- Desulfurization

See Figure 11-1.

Shipping

The gasoline is transported to regional storage facilities by tank railway car or by pipeline. In the pipeline method, all gasoline from many refiners is often sent through the same pipeline and can become mixed. All gasoline is said to be *miscible*, meaning that it is capable of being mixed because each grade is created to specification so there is no reason to keep the different gasoline brands separated except for grade. Regular grade, midgrade, and premium grades are separated in the pipeline and the additives are added at the regional storage facilities and then shipped by truck to individual gas stations.

GASOLINE

Gasoline is a term used to describe a complex mixture of various hydrocarbons refined from crude petroleum oil for use as a fuel in spark-ignition engines. Most gasoline is "blended" to meet the needs of the local climates and altitudes.

VOLATILITY

Volatility describes how easily the gasoline evaporates (forms a vapor). The definition of volatility assumes that the vapors

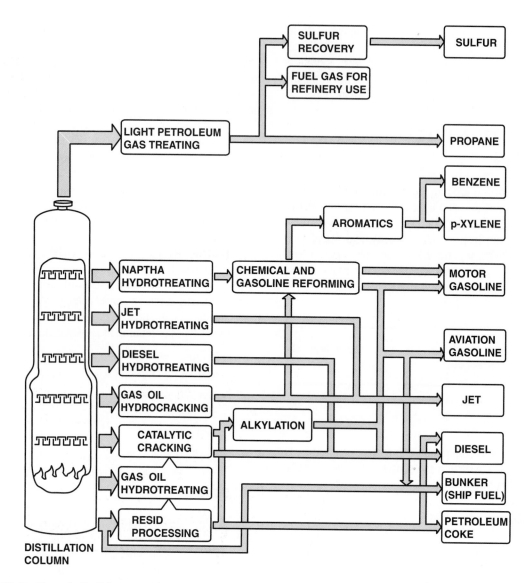

FIGURE 11-1   The crude oil refining process showing most of the major steps and processes.

will remain in the fuel tank or fuel line and will cause a certain pressure based on the temperature of the fuel.

Winter Blend

Reid vapor pressure (RVP) is the pressure of the vapor above the fuel when the fuel is at 100°F (38°C). Increased vapor pressure permits the engine to start in cold weather. Gasoline without air will not burn. Gasoline must be vaporized (mixed with air) to burn in an engine. Cold temperatures reduce the normal vaporization of gasoline; therefore, winter-blended gasoline is specially formulated to vaporize at lower temperatures for proper starting and driveability at low ambient temperatures. The **American Society for Testing and Materials (ASTM)** standards for winter-blend gasoline allow volatility of up to 15 pounds per square inch (PSI) RVP.

Summer Blend

At warm ambient temperatures, gasoline vaporizes easily. However, the fuel system (fuel pump, carburetor, fuel-injector nozzles, etc.) is designed to operate with liquid gasoline. The volatility of summer-grade gasoline should be about 7.0 PSI RVP. According to ASTM standards, the maximum RVP should be 10.5 PSI for summer-blend gasoline.

Volatility Problems

At higher temperatures, liquid gasoline can easily vaporize, which can cause **vapor lock.** Vapor lock is a *lean* condition caused by vaporized fuel in the fuel system. This vaporized fuel takes up space normally occupied by liquid fuel. Vapor

FREQUENTLY ASKED QUESTION

WHAT IS A CALIFORNIA GAS CAN?

When researching for ways to reduce hydrocarbon emissions in California, it was discovered that leakage from small gasoline containers used to refill small lawnmowers and other power equipment was a major source of unburned gasoline entering the atmosphere. As a result of this discovery, a new design for a gas can (container) was developed that is kept closed by a spring and uses O-rings to seal the opening. To use this container, the nozzle release lever is held against the side of the fuel opening and, when depressed, allows air to enter the container and fuel to flow. The flow of fuel stops automatically when the tank is full, eliminating any spillage. See Figure 11-2.

FIGURE 11-2   A gas can that meets the California Resources Board (CARB) approval uses a spring-loaded sealed nozzle that eliminates gasoline spillage and leaks into the atmosphere.

lock is caused by bubbles that form in the fuel, preventing proper operation of the fuel-injection system.

Bubbles in the fuel can be caused by heat or by sharp bends in the fuel system. Heat causes some fuel to evaporate, thereby causing bubbles. Sharp bends cause the fuel to be restricted at the bend. When the fuel flows past the bend, the fuel can expand to fill the space after the bend. This expansion drops the pressure, and bubbles form in the fuel lines. When the fuel is full of bubbles, the engine is not being supplied with enough fuel and the engine runs lean. A lean engine will stumble during acceleration, will run rough, and may stall. Warm weather and alcohol-blended fuels both tend to increase vapor lock and engine performance problems.

If winter-blend gasoline (or high-RVP fuel) is used in an engine during warm weather, the following problems may occur:

1. Rough idle
2. Stalling
3. Hesitation on acceleration
4. Surging

The RVP can be tested using the test kit shown in Figure 11-3.

DISTILLATION CURVE

Besides Reid vapor pressure, another method of classifying gasoline volatility is the **distillation curve.** A curve on a graph is created by plotting the temperature at which the various percentage of the fuel evaporates. A typical distillation curve is shown in Figure 11-4.

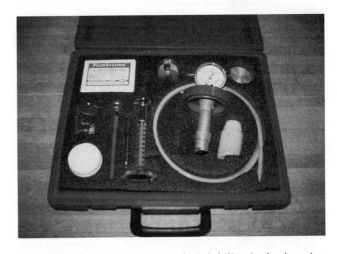

FIGURE 11-3   A gasoline testing kit. Included is an insulated container where water at 100°F is used to heat a container holding a small sample of gasoline. The reading on the pressure gauge is the Reid vapor pressure (RVP).

DRIVEABILITY INDEX

A distillation curve shows how much of a gasoline evaporates at what temperature range. To predict cold-weather driveability, an index was created called the **driveability index,** also called the **distillation index,** and abbreviated **DI.**

The DI was developed using the temperature for the evaporated percentage of 10% (labeled T10), 50% (labeled T50), and 90% (labeled T90). The formula for DI is:

$$DI = 1.5 \times T10 + 3 \times T50 + T90$$

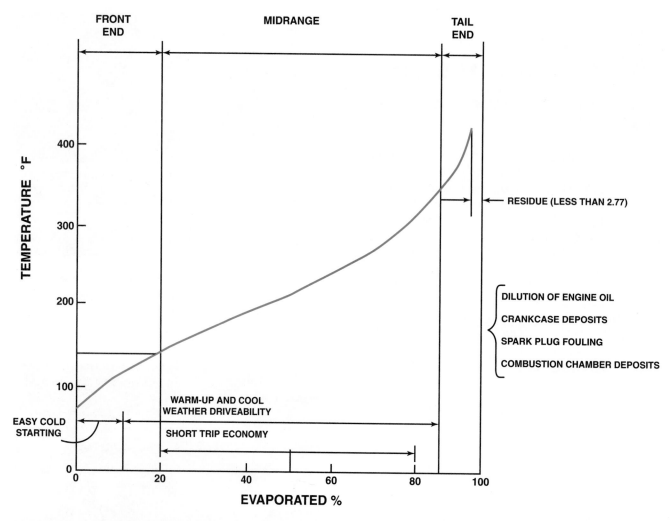

FIGURE 11-4 A typical distillation curve. Heavier molecules evaporate at higher temperatures and contain more heat energy for power, whereas the lighter molecules evaporate easier for starting.

The total DI is a temperature and usually ranges from 1,000° to 1,200°F. The lower values of DI generally result in good cold-start and warm-up performance. A high DI number is less volatile than a low DI number.

NOTE: Most premium-grade gasoline has a higher (worse) DI than regular or midgrade gasoline, which could cause poor cold-weather driveability. Vehicles designed to operate on premium-grade gasoline are programmed to handle the higher DI, but engines designed to operate on regular-grade gasoline may not be able to provide acceptable cold-weather driveability.

NORMAL AND ABNORMAL COMBUSTION

The **octane rating** of gasoline is the measure of its antiknock properties. *Engine knock* (also called **detonation, spark**

knock, or **ping**) is a metallic noise an engine makes, usually during acceleration, resulting from abnormal or uncontrolled combustion inside the cylinder.

Normal combustion occurs smoothly and progresses across the combustion chamber from the point of ignition. See Figure 11-5.

Normal flame-front combustion travels between 45 and 90 mph (72 and 145 km/h). The speed of the flame front depends on air–fuel ratio, combustion chamber design (determining amount of turbulence), and temperature.

During periods of spark knock (detonation), the combustion speed increases by up to 10 times to near the speed of sound. The increased combustion speed also causes increased temperatures and pressures, which can damage pistons, gaskets, and cylinder heads. See Figure 11-6.

One of the first additives used in gasoline was **tetraethyl lead (TEL).** TEL was added to gasoline in the early 1920s to reduce the tendency to knock. It was often called ethyl or high-test gasoline.

FREQUENTLY ASKED QUESTION

WHY DO I GET LOWER GAS MILEAGE IN THE WINTER?

Several factors cause the engine to use more fuel in the winter than in the summer, including:

- Gasoline that is blended for use in cold climates is designed for ease of starting and contains fewer heavy molecules, which contribute to fuel economy. The heat content of winter gasoline is lower than summer-blended gasoline.
- In cold temperatures, all lubricants are stiff, causing more resistance. These lubricants include the engine oil, as well as the transmission and differential gear lubricants.
- Heat from the engine is radiated into the outside air more rapidly when the temperature is cold, resulting in longer run time until the engine has reached normal operating temperature.
- Road conditions, such as ice and snow, can cause tire slippage or additional drag on the vehicle.

TECH TIP

THE SNIFF TEST

Problems can occur with stale gasoline from which the lighter parts of the gasoline have evaporated. Stale gasoline usually results in a no-start situation. If stale gasoline is suspected, sniff it. If it smells rancid, replace it with fresh gasoline.

NOTE: If storing a vehicle, boat, or lawnmower over the winter, put some gasoline stabilizer into the gasoline to reduce the evaporation and separation that can occur during storage. Gasoline stabilizer is frequently available at lawnmower repair shops or marinas.

Some experts recommend that a diesel fuel additive be used to kill bacteria and fungi growth that occurs in fuels when moisture is present. To kill algae and stop bacterial growth, use from 0.25 to 0.50 fl. oz. of additive in each 20 gallons. While algae growth is usually associated with diesel fuel when water collects at the bottom of the tank, gasoline tanks can still be a source of algae, especially when vehicles are stored for long periods of time, usually over 90 days.

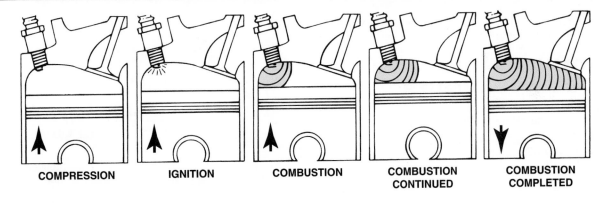

COMPRESSION   IGNITION   COMBUSTION   COMBUSTION CONTINUED   COMBUSTION COMPLETED

FIGURE 11-5   Normal combustion is a smooth, controlled burning of the air–fuel mixture.

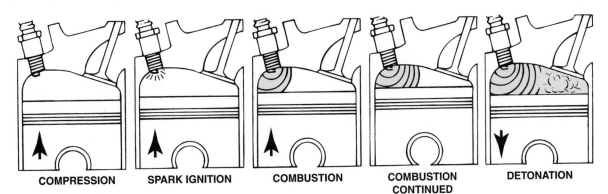

COMPRESSION   SPARK IGNITION   COMBUSTION   COMBUSTION CONTINUED   DETONATION

FIGURE 11-6   Detonation is a secondary ignition of the air–fuel mixture. It is also called spark knock or pinging.

OCTANE RATING

The antiknock standard or basis of comparison was the knock-resistant hydrocarbon isooctane, chemically called trimethylpentane (C_8H_{18}), also known as 2-2-4 trimethylpentane. If a gasoline tested had the exact same antiknock characteristics as isooctane, it was rated as 100-octane gasoline. If the gasoline tested had only 85% of the antiknock properties of isooctane, it was rated as 85 octane. Remember, octane rating is only a comparison test.

The two basic methods used to rate gasoline for antiknock properties (octane rating) are the *research method* and the *motor method*. Each uses a model of the special cooperative fuel research (CFR) single-cylinder engine. The research method and the motor method vary as to temperature of air, spark advance, and other parameters. The research method typically results in readings that are 6 to 10 points higher than those of the motor method. For example, a fuel with a research octane number (RON) of 93 might have a motor octane number (MON) of 85.

The octane rating posted on pumps in the United States is the average of the two methods and is referred to as (R + M) ÷ 2, meaning that, for the fuel used in the previous example, the rating posted on the pumps would be

$$\frac{RON + MON}{2} = \frac{93 + 85}{2} = 89$$

The pump octane is called the **antiknock index (AKI)**.

GASOLINE GRADES AND OCTANE NUMBER

The posted octane rating on gasoline pumps is the rating achieved by the average of the research and the motor methods. See Figure 11-7.

FREQUENTLY ASKED QUESTION

WHAT GRADE OF GASOLINE DOES THE EPA USE WHEN TESTING ENGINES?

Due to the various grades and additives used in commercial fuel, the government (EPA) uses a liquid called indolene. Indolene has a research octane number of 96.5 and a motor method octane rating of 88, which results in an R + M ÷ 2 rating of 92.25.

FIGURE 11-7 A typical fuel pump showing regular (87 octane), midgrade (89 octane), and premium (92 octane). These ratings can vary with brand as well as in different parts of the country, especially in high-altitude areas where the ratings are lower.

Except in high-altitude areas, the grades and octane ratings are as follows:

Grades	Octane Rating
Regular	87
Midgrade (also called Plus)	89
Premium	91 or higher

TECH TIP

HORSEPOWER AND FUEL FLOW

To produce 1 hp, the engine must be supplied with 0.50 lb of fuel per hour (lb/hr). Fuel injectors are rated in pounds per hour. For example, a V-8 engine equipped with 25 lb/hr fuel injectors could produce 50 hp per cylinder (per injector) or 400 hp. Even if the cylinder head or block is modified to produce more horsepower, the limiting factor may be the injector flow rate.

The following are flow rates and resulting horsepower for a V-8 engine:

30 lb/hr: 60 hp per cylinder or 480 hp
35 lb/hr: 70 hp per cylinder or 560 hp
40 lb/hr: 80 hp per cylinder or 640 hp

Of course, injector flow rate is only one of many variables that affect power output. Installing larger injectors without other major engine modification could decrease engine output and drastically increase exhaust emissions.

REAL WORLD FIX

THE STALLING ACURA

On a warm day in March, a customer walked into an automotive repair shop and asked for help. The car was parked on the street just outside the shop. A service technician accompanied the owner to check out the situation. The owner complained that the engine would start, then immediately stall. The engine would again start, and then stall during another attempt.

The service technician slid into the driver's seat and turned the ignition key. When the engine started, the technician depressed the accelerator slightly and the engine continued to run without any apparent problem. The car owner had never depressed the accelerator pedal and had never had any previous engine trouble.

The technician suspected winter-grade (high-RVP) gasoline was the problem. The owner replied that the present tank of fuel had been purchased during the last week in February. The technician explained that the uncommonly warm weather caused the fuel to vaporize in the fuel rail. Enough condensed fuel was available to start the engine, but the fuel injectors were designed to handle liquid fuel—not vapor—so the engine stalled.

The technician was probably lucky because by the third start enough of the remaining vapor had been drawn into the engine so that all that remained was liquid gasoline.

OCTANE IMPROVERS

When gasoline companies, under federal EPA regulations, removed tetraethyl lead from gasoline, other methods were developed to help maintain the antiknock properties of gasoline. Octane improvers (enhancers) can be grouped into three broad categories:

1. Aromatic hydrocarbons (hydrocarbons containing the benzene ring) such as xylene and toluene
2. Alcohols such as ethanol (ethyl alcohol), methanol (methyl alcohol), and tertiary butyl alcohol (TBA)
3. Metallic compounds such as methylcyclopentadienyl manganese tricarbonyl (MMT)

NOTE: MMT has been proven to be harmful to catalytic converters and can cause spark plug fouling. However, MMT is currently one of the active ingredients commonly found in octane improvers available to the public and in some gasoline sold in Canada. If an octane boost additive has been used that contains MMT, the spark plug porcelain will be rust colored around the tip.

FREQUENTLY ASKED QUESTION

CAN REGULAR-GRADE GASOLINE BE USED IF PREMIUM IS THE RECOMMENDED GRADE?

Yes. It is usually possible to use regular or midgrade (plus) grade gasoline in most newer vehicles without danger of damage to the engine. Most vehicles built since the 1990s are equipped with at least one knock sensor. If a lower octane gasoline than specified is used, the engine ignition timing setting will usually cause the engine to spark knock, also called detonation or ping. This spark knock is detected by the knock sensor(s), which sends a signal to the computer. The computer then retards the ignition timing until the spark knock stops.

NOTE: Some scan tools will show the "estimated octane rating" of the fuel being used, which is based on knock sensor activity.

As a result of this spark timing retardation, the engine torque is reduced. While this reduction in power is seldom noticed, it will reduce fuel economy, often by 4 to 5 miles per gallon. If premium gasoline is then used, the PCM will gradually permit the engine to operate at the more advanced ignition timing setting. Therefore, it may take several tanks of premium gasoline to restore normal fuel economy. For best overall performance, use the grade of gasoline recommended by the vehicle manufacturer.

Propane and butane, which are volatile by-products of the refinery process, are also often added to gasoline as octane improvers. The increase in volatility caused by the added propane and butane often leads to hot-weather driveability problems.

OXYGENATED FUELS

Oxygenated fuels contain oxygen in the molecule of the fuel itself. Examples of oxygenated fuels include methanol, ethanol, methyl tertiary butyl ether (MTBE), tertiary-amyl methyl ether (TAME), and ethyl tertiary butyl ether (ETBE).

Oxygenated fuels are commonly used in high-altitude areas to reduce carbon monoxide (CO) emissions. The extra oxygen in the fuel itself is used to convert harmful CO into carbon dioxide (CO_2). The extra oxygen in the fuel helps ensure that there is enough oxygen to convert all the CO into CO_2 during the combustion process in the engine or catalytic converter.

Methyl Tertiary Butyl Ether (MTBE)

MTBE is manufactured by means of the chemical reaction of methanol and isobutylene. Unlike methanol, MTBE does not increase the volatility of the fuel, and is not as sensitive to water as are other alcohols. The maximum allowable volume level, according to the EPA, is 15% but is currently being phased out due to health concerns, as well as MTBE contamination of drinking water if spilled from storage tanks.

Tertiary-Amyl Methyl Ether

Tertiary-amyl methyl ether **(TAME)** is an oxygenate added to gasoline and is flammable and can form explosive mixtures with air. It is slightly soluble in water, very soluble in ethers and alcohol, and soluble in most organic solvents including hydrocarbons. TAME is an ether, which contains an oxygen atom bonded to two carbon atoms.

Ethyl Tertiary Butyl Ether

ETBE is derived from ethanol. The maximum allowable volume level is 17.2%. The use of ETBE is the cause of much of the odor from the exhaust of vehicles using reformulated gasoline.

Ethanol

Ethyl alcohol is drinkable alcohol and is usually made from grain. Adding 10% ethanol (ethyl alcohol or grain alcohol) increases the $(R + M) \div 2$ octane rating by three points. The alcohol added to the base gasoline, however, also raises the volatility of the fuel about 0.5 PSI. Most automobile manufacturers permit up to 10% ethanol if driveability problems are not experienced. The oxygen content of a 10% blend of **ethanol** in gasoline, called **E10,** is 3.5% oxygen by weight. See Figure 11-8.

Methanol

Methyl alcohol is made from wood **(wood alcohol),** natural gas, or coal. Methanol is poisonous if ingested and tends to be more harmful to the materials in the fuel system and to separate when combined with gasoline unless used with a co-solvent. A co-solvent is another substance (usually another alcohol) that is soluble in both methanol and gasoline and is used to reduce the tendency of the liquids to separate.

Methanol can damage fuel system parts. Methanol is corrosive to lead (used as a coating of fuel tanks), aluminum, magnesium, and some plastics and rubber. Methanol can also cause rubber products (elastomers) to swell and soften. Methanol contains oxygen and gasoline containing 5% methanol would have an oxygen content of 2.5% by weight.

FIGURE 11-8   This fuel pump indicates that the gasoline is blended with 10% ethanol (ethyl alcohol) and can be used in any gasoline vehicle. E85 contains 85% ethanol and can only be used in vehicles specifically designed to use it.

CAUTION: All alcohols absorb water, and the alcohol–water mixture can separate from the gasoline and sink to the bottom of the fuel tank. This process is called *phase separation.* To help avoid engine performance problems, try to keep at least a quarter tank of fuel at all times, especially during seasons when there is a wide temperature span between daytime highs and nighttime lows. These conditions can cause moisture to accumulate in the fuel tank as a result of condensation of the moisture in the air. Keeping the fuel tank full reduces the amount of air and moisture in the tank. See Figure 11-9.

ALCOHOL ADDITIVES— ADVANTAGES AND DISADVANTAGES

The advantages and disadvantages of using alcohol as an additive to gasoline can be summarized as follows:

Advantages

1. Alcohol absorbs moisture in the fuel tank.
2. Ten percent alcohol added to gasoline raises the octane rating, $(R + M) \div 2$, by three points.
3. Alcohol cleans the fuel system.
4. Alcohol reduces CO emissions because it contains oxygen.

Disadvantages

1. The use of alcohol can result in the clogging of fuel filters with dirt and other debris cleaned from the fuel tank, pump, and lines.
2. Alcohol raises the volatility of fuel about 0.5 PSI; this can cause hot-weather driveability problems.

FIGURE 11-9 A container with gasoline containing alcohol. Notice the separation line where the alcohol–water mixture separated from the gasoline and sank to the bottom.

3. Alcohol reduces the heat content of the resulting fuel mixture (it has about one-half of the energy content of gasoline)—60,000 to 75,000 **British thermal units (BTUs)** per gallon for alcohol versus about 130,000 BTUs per gallon for gasoline.

4. Alcohol absorbs water and then separates from the gasoline, especially as temperature drops. Separated alcohol and water on the bottom of the tank can cause hard starting during cold weather. Alcohol does not vaporize easily at low temperatures.

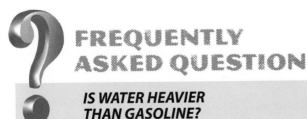

FREQUENTLY ASKED QUESTION

IS WATER HEAVIER THAN GASOLINE?

Yes. Water weighs about 7 pounds per gallon whereas gasoline weighs about 6 pounds per gallon. The density as measured by specific gravity includes:

Water = 1.000 (the baseline for specific gravity)
Gasoline = 0.730 to 0.760

This means that any water that gets into the fuel tank will sink to the bottom.

TESTING GASOLINE FOR ALCOHOL CONTENT

Take the following steps when testing gasoline for alcohol content.

1. Pour suspect gasoline into a small clean beaker or glass container.

   CAUTION: DO NOT SMOKE OR RUN THE TEST AROUND SOURCES OF IGNITION!

2. Carefully fill the graduated cylinder to the 10-mL mark.

3. Add 2 mL of water to the graduated cylinder by counting the number of drops from an eyedropper. (Before performing the test, the eyedropper must be calibrated to determine how many drops equal 2.0 mL.)

4. Put the stopper in the cylinder and shake vigorously for 1 minute. Relieve built-up pressure by occasionally removing the stopper. Alcohol dissolves in water and will drop to the bottom of the cylinder.

5. Place the cylinder on a flat surface and let it stand for 2 minutes.

6. Take a reading near the bottom of the cylinder at the boundary between the two liquids.

7. For percent of alcohol in gasoline, subtract 2 from the reading and multiply by 10. For example,

The reading is 3.1 mL: $3.1 - 2 = 1.1 \times 10 =$
11% alcohol
The reading is 2.0 mL: $2 - 2 = 0 \times 10 = 0\%$ alcohol
(no alcohol)

If the increase in volume is 0.2% or less, it may be assumed that the test gasoline contains no alcohol. Alcohol content can also be checked using an electronic tester. See the step-by-step sequence at the end of the chapter.

COMBUSTION CHEMISTRY

Internal combustion engines burn an organic fuel to produce power. The term **organic** refers to a product (gasoline) from a source that originally was alive. Because crude oil originally came from living plants and animals, all products of petroleum are considered organic fuels and are composed primarily of hydrogen (H) and carbon (C).

The combustion process involves the chemical combination of oxygen (O_2) from the air (about 21% of the atmosphere) with the hydrogen and carbon from the fuel. In a gasoline engine, a spark starts the combustion process, which takes about 3 ms (0.003 sec) to be completed inside the cylinder of an engine. The chemical reaction that takes place can be summarized as follows: hydrogen (H) plus carbon (C) plus oxygen (O_2) plus nitrogen (N) plus spark equals heat plus

FREQUENTLY ASKED QUESTION

HOW DOES ALCOHOL CONTENT IN THE GASOLINE AFFECT ENGINE OPERATION?

In most cases, the use of gasoline containing 10% or less of ethanol (ethyl alcohol) has little or no effect on engine operation. However, because the addition of 10% ethanol raises the volatility of the fuel slightly, occasional rough idle or stalling may be noticed, especially during warm weather. The rough idle and stalling may also be noticeable after the engine is started, driven, then stopped for a short time. Engine heat can vaporize the alcohol-enhanced fuel, causing bubbles to form in the fuel system. These bubbles in the fuel prevent the proper operation of the fuel injection system and result in a hesitation during acceleration, rough idle, or in severe cases repeated stalling until all the bubbles have been forced through the fuel system, replaced by cooler fuel from the fuel tank.

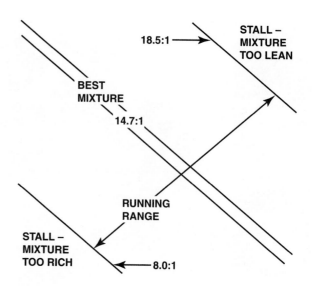

FIGURE 11-10   An engine will not run if the air–fuel mixture is either too rich or too lean.

water (H_2O) plus carbon monoxide (CO) (if incomplete combustion) plus carbon dioxide (CO_2) plus hydrocarbons (HC) plus oxides of nitrogen (NO_X) plus many other chemicals.

AIR–FUEL RATIOS

Fuel burns best when the intake system turns it into a fine spray and mixes it with air before sending it into the cylinders. In fuel-injected engines, the fuel becomes a spray and mixes with the air in the intake manifold. There is a direct relationship between engine airflow and fuel requirements; this is called the **air–fuel ratio.**

The air–fuel ratio is the proportion by weight of air and gasoline that the injection system mixes as needed for engine combustion. The mixtures, with which an engine can operate without stalling, range from 8 to 1 to 18.5 to 1. See Figure 11-10.

These ratios are usually stated by weight, such as:

- 8 parts of air by weight combined with 1 part of gasoline by weight (8:1), which is the richest mixture that an engine can tolerate and still fire reliably.
- 18.5 parts of air mixed with 1 part of gasoline (18.5:1), which is the leanest practical ratio. Richer or leaner air–fuel ratios cause the engine to misfire badly or not run at all.

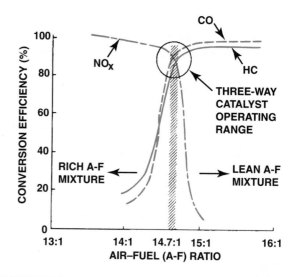

FIGURE 11-11   With a three-way catalytic converter, emission control is most efficient with an air–fuel ratio between 14.65:1 and 14.75:1.

Stoichiometric Air–Fuel Ratio

The ideal mixture or ratio at which all of the fuel combines with all of the oxygen in the air and burns completely is called the **stoichiometric** ratio, a chemically perfect combination. In theory, this ratio is an air–fuel mixture of 14.7 to 1. See Figure 11-11.

In reality, the exact ratio at which perfect mixture and combustion occurs depends on the molecular structure of gasoline, which can vary. The stoichiometric ratio is a compromise between maximum power and maximum economy.

Stoichiometric Air–Fuel Ratio for Various Fuels

If the combustion process is complete, all gasoline or HCs will be completely combined with all the available oxygen. This total combination of all components of the fuel is called *stoichiometric air–fuel ratio*. The stoichiometric quantities for gasoline are 14.7 parts air for 1 part gasoline by weight. Different fuels have different stoichiometric proportions. See the accompanying table comparing the heat and stoichiometric ratio for alcohol versus gasoline.

Fuel	Heat Energy (BTU/gal)	Stoichiometric Ratio
Gasoline	About 130,000	14.7:1
Ethyl (ethanol) alcohol	About 76,000	9.0:1
Methyl (methanol) alcohol	About 60,000	6.4:1

The heat produced by the combustion process is measured in British thermal units (BTUs). One BTU is the amount of heat required to raise one pound of water one Fahrenheit degree. The metric unit of heat is the calorie (cal). One calorie is the amount of heat required to raise the temperature of one gram (g) of water one Celsius degree.

HIGH-ALTITUDE OCTANE REQUIREMENTS

As the altitude increases, atmospheric pressure drops. The air is less dense because a pound of air takes more volume. The octane rating of fuel does not need to be as high because the engine cannot take in as much air. This process will reduce the combustion (compression) pressures inside the engine. In mountainous areas, gasoline (R + M) = 2 octane ratings are two or more numbers lower than normal (according to the SAE, about one octane number lower per 1,000 ft or 300 m in altitude). See Figure 11-12.

A secondary reason for the lowered octane requirement of engines running at higher altitudes is the normal enrichment of the air–fuel ratio and lower engine vacuum with the decreased air density. Some problems, therefore, may occur when driving out of high-altitude areas into lower-altitude areas where the octane rating must be higher. Most computerized engine control systems can compensate for changes in altitude and modify air–fuel ratio and ignition timing for best operation.

Because the combustion burn rate slows at high altitude, the ignition (spark) timing can be advanced to improve power. The amount of timing advance can be about 1 degree per 1,000 ft over 5,000 ft. Therefore, if driving at 8,000 ft of altitude, the ignition timing can be advanced 3 degrees.

FIGURE 11-12 Photo of gasoline pump taken in a high-altitude area. Note the lower-than-normal octane ratings. The "ethanol" sticker reads that all grades contain 10% ethanol from November 1 through February 28 each year to help reduce CO exhaust emissions.

High altitude also allows fuel to evaporate more easily. The volatility of fuel should be reduced at higher altitudes to prevent vapor from forming in sections of the fuel system, which can cause driveability and stalling problems. The extra heat generated in climbing to higher altitudes plus the lower atmospheric pressure at higher altitudes combine to cause vapor lock problems as the vehicle goes to higher altitudes.

REFORMULATED GASOLINE

Reformulated gasoline (RFG) is manufactured by refiners to help reduce emissions. The gasoline refiners reformulate gasoline by using additives that contain at least 2% oxygen by weight and reducing the additive benzene to a maximum of 1% by volume. Two other major changes done at the refineries are as follows:

1. **Reduce light compounds.** Refineries eliminate butane, pentane, and propane, which have a low boiling point and evaporate easily. These unburned hydrocarbons are released into the atmosphere during refueling and through the fuel tank vent system, contributing to smog formation. Therefore, reducing the light compounds from gasoline helps reduce evaporative emissions.
2. **Reduce heavy compounds.** Refineries eliminate heavy compounds with high boiling points such as aromatics and olefins. The purpose of this reduction is to reduce the amount of unburned hydrocarbons that enter the catalytic converter, which makes the converter more efficient, thereby reducing emissions.

Because many of the heavy compounds are eliminated, a drop in fuel economy of about 1 mpg has been reported in areas where reformulated gasoline is being used. Formaldehyde

FREQUENTLY ASKED QUESTION

WHAT IS "TOP-TIER" GASOLINE?

Top-tier gasoline is gasoline that has specific standards for quality, including enough detergent to keep all intake valves clean. The standards were developed by the four automobile manufacturers, including BMW, General Motors, Honda, and Toyota. Top-tier gasoline exceeds the quality standards developed by the **World Wide Fuel Charter (WWFC)** that was established in 2002 by vehicle and engine manufacturers. The gasoline companies that agreed to make fuel that matches or exceeds the standards as a top-tier fuel include Chevron Texaco and Conoco Phillips. Ford has specified that BP fuel, sold in many parts of the country, is the recommended fuel to use in Ford vehicles. See Figure 11-13.

FIGURE 11-13 The gas cap on a Ford vehicle notes that BP fuel is recommended.

is formed when RFG is burned, and the vehicle exhaust has a unique smell when reformulated gasoline is used.

GENERAL GASOLINE RECOMMENDATIONS

The fuel used by an engine is a major expense in the operation cost of the vehicle. The proper operation of the engine depends on clean fuel of the proper octane rating and vapor pressure for the atmospheric conditions.

FREQUENTLY ASKED QUESTION

WHY SHOULD I KEEP THE FUEL GAUGE ABOVE ONE-QUARTER TANK?

The fuel pickup inside the fuel tank can help keep water from being drawn into the fuel system unless water is all that is left at the bottom of the tank. Over time, moisture in the air inside the fuel tank can condense, causing liquid water to drop to the bottom of the fuel tank (water is heavier than gasoline—about 8 lb per gallon for water and about 6 lb per gallon for gasoline). If alcohol-blended gasoline is used, the alcohol can absorb the water and the alcohol–water combination can be burned inside the engine. However, when water combines with alcohol, a separation layer occurs between the gasoline at the top of the tank and the alcohol–water combination at the bottom. When the fuel level is low, the fuel pump will draw from this concentrated level of alcohol and water. Because alcohol and water do not burn as well as pure gasoline, severe driveability problems can occur such as stalling, rough idle, hard starting, and missing.

To help ensure proper engine operation and keep fuel costs to a minimum, follow these guidelines:

1. Purchase fuel from a busy station to help ensure that it is fresh and less likely to be contaminated with water or moisture.
2. Keep the fuel tank above one-quarter full, especially during seasons in which the temperature rises and falls by more than 20°F between daytime highs and nighttime lows. This helps to reduce condensed moisture in the fuel tank and could prevent gas line freeze-up in cold weather.

NOTE: Gas line freeze-up occurs when the water in the gasoline freezes and forms an ice blockage in the fuel line.

3. Do not purchase fuel with a higher octane rating than is necessary. Try using premium high-octane fuel to check for operating differences. Most newer engines are equipped with a detonation (knock) sensor that signals the vehicle computer to retard the ignition timing when spark knock occurs. Therefore, an operating difference may not be noticeable to the driver when using a low-octane fuel, except

TECH TIP

DO NOT OVERFILL THE FUEL TANK

Gasoline fuel tanks have an expansion volume area at the top. The volume of this expansion area is equal to 10% to 15% of the volume of the tank. This area is normally not filled with gasoline, but rather is designed to provide a place for the gasoline to expand into, if the vehicle is parked in the hot sun and the gasoline expands. This prevents raw gasoline from escaping from the fuel system. A small restriction is usually present to control the amount of air and vapors that can escape the tank and flow to the charcoal canister.

This volume area could be filled with gasoline if the fuel is slowly pumped into the tank. Since it can hold an extra 10% (2 gallons in a 20-gallon tank), some people deliberately try to fill the tank completely. When this expansion volume is filled, liquid fuel (rather than vapors) can be drawn into the charcoal canister. When the purge valve opens, liquid fuel can be drawn into the engine, causing an excessively rich air–fuel mixture. Not only can this liquid fuel harm vapor recovery parts, but overfilling the gas tank could also cause the vehicle to fail an exhaust emission test, particularly during an enhanced test when the tank could be purged while on the rollers.

FIGURE 11-14 Many gasoline service stations have signs posted warning customers to place plastic fuel containers on the ground while filling. If placed in a trunk or pickup truck bed equipped with a plastic liner, static electricity could build up during fueling and discharge from the container to the metal nozzle, creating a spark and possible explosion. Some service stations have warning signs not to use cell phones while fueling to help avoid the possibility of an accidental spark creating a fire hazard.

for a decrease in power and fuel economy. In other words, the engine with a knock sensor will tend to operate knock free on regular fuel, even if premium, higher-octane fuel is specified. Using premium fuel may result in more power and greater fuel economy. The increase in fuel economy, however, would have to be substantial to justify the increased cost of high-octane premium fuel. Some drivers find a good compromise by using midgrade (plus) fuel to benefit from the engine power and fuel economy gains without the cost of using premium fuel all the time.

4. Avoid using gasoline with alcohol in warm weather, even though many alcohol blends do not affect engine driveability. If warm-engine stumble, stalling, or rough idle occurs, change brands of gasoline.

5. Do not purchase fuel from a retail outlet when a tanker truck is filling the underground tanks. During the refilling procedure, dirt, rust, and water may be stirred up in the underground tanks. This undesirable material may be pumped into your vehicle's fuel tank.

6. Do not overfill the gas tank. After the nozzle clicks off, add just enough fuel to round up to the next dime. Adding additional gasoline will cause the excess to be drawn into the charcoal canister. This can lead to engine flooding and excessive exhaust emissions.

7. Be careful when filling gasoline containers. Always fill a gas can on the ground to help prevent the possibility of static electricity build-up during the refueling process. See Figure 11-14.

ALTERNATIVE FUELS

Alternative fuels include a number of fuels besides gasoline for use in passenger vehicles. See Figure 11-15.

FIGURE 11-15   Some retail stations offer a variety of fuel choices, such as this station in Ohio where biodiesel, E10, and E85 are available.

Ethanol

Ethanol is also called ethyl alcohol or **grain alcohol,** because it is usually made from grain and is the type of alcohol found in alcoholic drinks such as beer, wine, and distilled spirits like whiskey. Ethanol is composed of two carbon atoms and six hydrogen atoms with one added oxygen atom. See Figure 11-16.

Conventional ethanol and **cellulose ethanol** are the same product, but cellulose ethanol is produced using the nonfood portion of the feedstock. Conventional ethanol is derived from grains, such as corn, wheat, or soybeans. Corn, for example, is converted to ethanol in either a dry or wet milling process. In dry milling operations, liquefied cornstarch is produced by heating cornmeal with water and enzymes. A second enzyme converts the liquefied starch to sugars, which are fermented by yeast into ethanol and carbon dioxide. Wet milling operations separate the fiber, germ (oil), and protein from the starch before it is fermented into ethanol.

Cellulose ethanol can be produced from a wide variety of cellulose biomass feedstock, including agricultural plant wastes (corn stalks, cereal straws), plant wastes from industrial

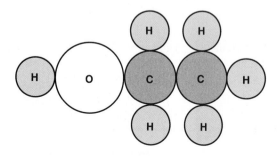

FIGURE 11-16   The ethanol molecule showing two carbon atoms, six hydrogen atoms, and one oxygen atom.

processes (sawdust, paper pulp), and energy crops grown specifically for fuel production. These nongrain products are often referred to as **cellulosic biomass.** Cellulosic biomass is composed of cellulose and lignin, with smaller amounts of proteins, lipids (fats, waxes, and oils), and ash. About two-thirds of cellulosic materials are present as cellulose, with lignin making up the bulk of the remaining dry mass.

As with grains, processing cellulose biomass strives to extract fermentable sugars from the feedstock. But the sugars in cellulose are locked in complex carbohydrates called polysaccharides (long chains of simple sugars). Separating these complex structures into fermentable sugars is needed to achieve the efficient and economic production of cellulose ethanol.

Two processing options are employed to produce fermentable sugars from cellulose biomass:

- Acid hydrolysis is used to break down the complex carbohydrates into simple sugars.
- Enzymes are employed to convert the cellulose biomass to fermentable sugars. The final step involves microbial fermentation, yielding ethanol and carbon dioxide.

NOTE: Grain-based ethanol uses fossil fuels to produce heat during the conversion process, generating substantial greenhouse gas emissions. Cellulose ethanol production substitutes biomass for fossil fuels. The greenhouse gases produced by the combustion of biomass are offset by the CO_2 absorbed by the biomass as it grows in the field.

The majority of the ethanol in the United States is made from:

- Corn
- Grain
- Sorghum
- Wheat
- Barley
- Potatoes

In Brazil, the world's largest ethanol producer, it is made from sugarcane. Ethanol can be made by the dry mill process in which the starch portion of the corn is fermented into sugar and then distilled into alcohol.

The major steps in the dry mill process include:

1. **Milling.** The feedstock passes through a hammer mill that turns it into a fine powder called meal.
2. **Liquefaction.** The meal is mixed with water and then passed through cookers where the starch is liquefied. Heat is applied at this stage to enable liquefaction. Cookers use a high-temperature stage of about 250°F to 300°F (120°C to 150°C) to reduce bacteria levels and then a lower temperature of about 200°F (95°C) for a holding period.

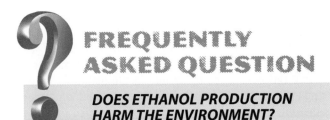

FREQUENTLY ASKED QUESTION

DOES ETHANOL PRODUCTION HARM THE ENVIRONMENT?

The production of ethanol is referred to as being *carbon neutral* because the amount of CO_2 released during production is equal to the amount of CO_2 that would be released if the corn or other products were left to decay.

3. Saccharification. The mash from the cookers is cooled and the secondary enzyme is added to convert the liquefied starch to fermentable sugars (dextrose).

4. Fermentation. Yeast is added to the mash to ferment the sugars to ethanol and carbon dioxide.

5. Distillation. The fermented mash, now called beer, contains about 10% alcohol plus all the nonfermentable solids from the corn and yeast cells. The mash is pumped to the continuous-flow, multicolumn distillation system where the alcohol is removed from the solids and the water. The alcohol leaves the top of the final column at about 96% strength, and the residue mash, called silage, is transferred from the base of the column to the co-product processing area.

6. Dehydration. The alcohol from the top of the column passes through a dehydration system where the remaining water will be removed. Most ethanol plants use a molecular sieve to capture the last bit of water in the ethanol. The alcohol product at this stage is called **anhydrous ethanol** (pure, no more than 5% water).

7. Denaturing. Ethanol that will be used for fuel must be denatured, or made unfit for human consumption, with a small amount of gasoline (2–5%), methanol, or denatonium benzoate. This is done at the ethanol plant.

E85

Vehicle manufacturers have available vehicles that are capable of operating on gasoline plus ethanol or a combination of gasoline and ethanol called **E85.** E85 is composed of 85% ethanol and 15% gasoline. Pure ethanol has an octane rating of about 113, whereas E85, which contains 35% oxygen by weight, has an octane rating of about 100 to 105 compared to a regular unleaded gasoline rating of 87.

NOTE: The octane rating of E85 depends on the exact percent of ethanol used, which can vary from 81% to 85%, as well as the octane rating of the gasoline used.

E85 has less heat energy than gasoline.

$$\text{Gasoline} = 114{,}000 \text{ BTUs per gallon}$$
$$\text{E85} = 87{,}000 \text{ BTUs per gallon}$$

This means that the fuel economy is reduced by 20% to 30% if E85 is used instead of gasoline.

For example, a Chevrolet Tahoe 5.3-liter V-8, automatic transmission has an EPA rating using gasoline of 15 mpg in the city and 20 mpg on the highway. If this same vehicle was fueled with E85, the EPA fuel economy rating drops to 11 mpg in the city and 15 mpg on the highway.

The 15% gasoline in this blend helps the engine start, especially in cold weather. Vehicles equipped with this capability are commonly referred to as **alternative-fuel vehicles (AFVs), Flex Fuels,** and **flexible fuel vehicles,** or **FFV.** See Figure 11-17. Using E85 in a flex fuel vehicle can result in a power increase of about 5%. For example, an engine rated at 200 hp using gasoline or E10 could produce 210 hp if using E85.

NOTE: E85 may test as containing less than 85% ethanol if tested because it is often blended according to outside temperature. A lower percentage of ethanol with a slightly higher percentage of gasoline helps engines start in cold climates.

These vehicles are equipped with an electronic sensor that detects the fuel temperature and percentage of ethanol and then programs the fuel injector on-time and ignition timing to match the needs of the fuel being used.

E85 contains less heat energy, and therefore will use more fuel, but the benefits include a lower cost of the fuel and

FIGURE 11-17 A vehicle emission control information (VECI) sticker on a flexible fuel vehicle indicating the percentage of ethanol with which it is able to operate.

the environmental benefit associated with using an oxygenated fuel.

General Motors, Ford, Chrysler, Mazda, and Honda are a few of the manufacturers offering E85–compatible vehicles. E85 vehicles use fuel system parts designed to withstand the additional alcohol content, modified driveability programs that adjust fuel delivery and timing to compensate for the various percentages of ethanol fuel, and a **fuel compensation sensor,** also called a **fuel composition sensor,** which measures both the percentage of ethanol blend and the temperature of the fuel. This sensor is also called a **variable fuel sensor.** See Figures 11-18 and 11-19.

Most E85 vehicles are very similar to non-E85 vehicles. Fuel system components may be redesigned to withstand the effects of higher concentrations of ethanol. In addition, since the stoichiometric point for ethanol is 9:1 instead of 14.7:1 as for gasoline, the air–fuel mixture has to be adjusted for the percentage of ethanol present in the fuel tank. In order to determine this percentage of ethanol in the fuel tank, a fuel compensation sensor is used. The fuel compensation sensor is the only additional piece of hardware required on some E85 vehicles. The fuel compensation sensor provides both the ethanol percentage and the fuel temperature to the PCM. The PCM uses this information to adjust both the ignition timing and the quantity of fuel delivered to the engine. The fuel compensation sensor uses a microprocessor to measure both the ethanol percentage and the fuel temperature. This information is sent to the PCM on the signal circuit. The compensation sensor produces a square wave frequency and pulse width signal. The normal frequency range of the fuel compensation sensor is 50 hertz, which represents 0% ethanol, and 150 hertz, which represents 100% ethanol. The pulse width of the signal varies from 1 millisecond to 5 milliseconds. One millisecond would represent a fuel temperature of −40°F (−40°C), and 5 milliseconds would represent a fuel temperature of 257°F (125°C). Since the PCM knows both the fuel temperature and the ethanol percentage of the fuel, it can adjust fuel quantity and ignition timing for optimum performance and emissions.

The benefits of E85 vehicles are less pollution, less CO_2 production, and less dependence on oil. See Figure 11-20.

Ethanol-fueled vehicles generally produce the same pollutants as gasoline vehicles; however, they produce less CO and CO_2 emissions. While CO_2 is not considered a pollutant, it is thought to lead to global warming and is called a greenhouse gas.

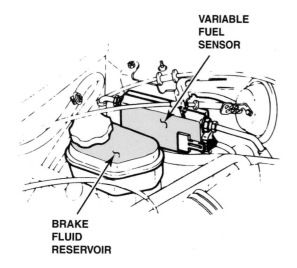

FIGURE 11-18 The location of the variable fuel sensor can vary, depending on the make and model of vehicle, but it is always in the fuel line between the fuel tank and the fuel injectors.

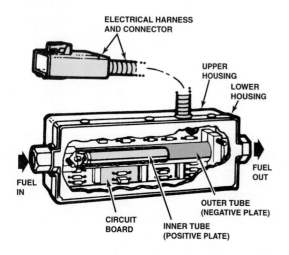

FIGURE 11-19 A cutaway view of a typical variable fuel sensor.

FREQUENTLY ASKED QUESTION

HOW DOES A SENSORLESS FLEX FUEL SYSTEM WORK?

Many General Motors flex fuel vehicles do not use a fuel compensation sensor and instead use the oxygen sensor to detect the presence of the lean mixture and the extra oxygen in the fuel.

The powertrain control module (PCM) then adjusts the injector pulse width and the ignition timing to optimize engine operation to the use of E85. This type of vehicle is called a virtual flexible fuel vehicle, abbreviated **V-FFV.** The virtual flexible fuel vehicle can operate on pure gasoline, E10, E85, or any combination.

FIGURE 11-20   A pump for E85 (85% ethanol and 15% gasoline). There are few, if any, of these pumps in many states.

FREQUENTLY ASKED QUESTION

WHAT IS SWITCHGRASS?

Switchgrass (*Panicum virgatum*) is a summer perennial grass that is native to North America. It is a natural component of the tall-grass prairie, which covered most of the Great Plains, but was also found on the prairie soils in the Black Belt of Alabama and Mississippi. Switchgrass is resistant to many pests and plant diseases, and is capable of producing high yields with very low applications of fertilizer. This means that the need for agricultural chemicals to grow switchgrass is relatively low. Switchgrass is also very tolerant of poor soils, flooding, and drought, which are widespread agricultural problems in the southeast.

There are two main types of switchgrass:

- *Upland types*—usually grow 5 to 6 feet tall
- *Low-land types*—grow up to 12 feet tall and are typically found on heavy soils in bottomland sites

Better energy efficiency is gained because less energy is used to produce ethanol from switchgrass.

TECH TIP

AVOID RESETTING FUEL COMPENSATION

Starting in 2006, General Motors vehicles designed to operate on E85 do not use a fuel compensation sensor, but instead use the oxygen sensor and refueling information to calculate the percentage of ethanol in the fuel. The PCM uses the fuel level sensor to sense that fuel has been added and starts to determine the resulting ethanol content by using the oxygen sensor. However, if a service technician were to reset fuel compensation by clearing long-term fuel trim, the PCM starts the calculation based on base fuel, which is gasoline with less than or equal to 10% ethanol (E10). If the fuel tank has E85, then the fuel compensation cannot be determined unless the tank is drained and refilled with base fuel. Therefore, avoid resetting the fuel compensation setting unless it is known that the fuel tank contains gasoline or E10 only.

Flex Fuel Vehicles

Vehicles that are flexible fuel include:

Chrysler

2004–2005
- 4.7L Dodge Ram Pickup 1500 Series
- 2.7L Dodge Stratus Sedan
- 2.7L Chrysler Sebring Sedan
- 3.3L Caravan and Grand Caravan SE

2003–2004
- 2.7L Dodge Stratus Sedan
- 2.7L Chrysler Sebring Sedan

2003
- 3.3L Dodge Cargo Minivan

2000–2003
- 3.3L Chrysler Voyager Minivan
- 3.3L Dodge Caravan Minivan
- 3.3L Chrysler Town and Country Minivan

1998–1999
- 3.3L Dodge Caravan Minivan
- 3.3L Plymouth Voyager Minivan
- 3.3L Chrysler Town & Country Minivan

Ford Motor Company

*Ford offers the flex fuel capability as an option on select vehicles—see the owner's manual.

2004–2005

- 4.0L Explorer Sport Trac
- 4.0L Explorer (4-door)
- 3.0L Taurus Sedan and Wagon

2002–2004

- 4.0L Explorer (4-door)
- 3.0L Taurus Sedan and Wagon

2002–2003

- 3.0L Supercab Ranger Pickup 2WD

2001

- 3.0L Supercab Ranger Pickup 2WD
- 3.0L Taurus LX, SE, and SES Sedan

1999–2000

- 3.0L Ranger Pickup 4WD and 2WD

General Motors

*Select vehicles only—see your owner's manual.

2005

- 5.3L Vortec-Engine Avalanche
- 5.3L Vortec-Engine Police Package Tahoe

2003–2005

- 5.3L V8 Chevy Silverado* and GMC Sierra* Half-Ton Pickups, 2WD and 4WD
- 5.3L Vortec-Engine Suburban, Tahoe, Yukon, and Yukon XL

2002

- 5.3L V8 Chevy Silverado* and GMC Sierra* Half-Ton Pickups, 2WD and 4WD
- 5.3L Vortec-Engine Suburban, Tahoe, Yukon, and Yukon XL
- 2.2L Chevy S10 Pickup 2WD
- 2.2L Sonoma GMC Pickup 2WD

2000–2001

- 2.2L Chevy S10 Pickup 2WD
- 2.2L GMC Sonoma Pickup 2WD

Isuzu

2000–2001

- 2.2L Hombre Pickup 2WD

Mazda

1999–2003

- 3.0L Selected B3000 Pickups

Mercedes-Benz

2005

- 2.6L C240 Luxury Sedan and Wagon

2003

- 3.2L C320 Sport Sedan and Wagon

Mercury

2002–2004

- 4.0L Selected Mountaineers

2000–2004

- 3.0L Selected Sables

Nissan

*Select vehicles only—see the owner's manual or VECI sticker under the hood.

2005

- 5.6L DOHC V8 Engine

How to Read a Vehicle Identification Number

The vehicle identification number (VIN) is required by federal regulation to contain specific information about the vehicle. The following chart shows the VIN number and information from Ford Motor Company, General Motors, and Chrysler on identifying flexible fuel vehicles by the character in the eighth position in the VIN.

Ford Motor Company

Vehicle	8th Character
Ford Crown Victoria	V
Ford F-150	V
Ford Explorer	K
Ford Ranger	V
Ford Taurus	2
Lincoln Town Car	V
Mercury Mountaineer	K
Mercury Sable	2
Mercury Grand Marquis	V

General Motors

Vehicle	8th Character
Chevrolet Avalanche	Z
Chevrolet Impala	K
Chevrolet Monte Carlo	K

Vehicle	8th Character
Chevrolet S-10 Pickup	5
Chevrolet Sierra	Z
Chevrolet Suburban	Z
Chevrolet Tahoe	Z
GMC Yukon and Yukon XL	Z
GMC Silverado	Z
GMC Sonoma	5

Chrysler

Vehicle	8th Character
Chrysler Sebring	T
Chrysler Town and Country	E, G, or 3
Dodge Caravan	E, G, or 3
Dodge Cargo Minivan	E, G, or 3
Dodge Durango	P
Dodge Ram	P
Dodge Stratus	T
Plymouth Voyager	E, G, or 3

Mazda

Vehicle	8th Character
B3000 Pickup	V

Nissan

Vehicle	8th Character
Titan	B

Mercedes Benz

Check owner's manual or the VECI sticker under the hood.

NOTE: For additional information on E85 and for the location of E85 stations in your area go to *www.e85fuel.com*.

Methanol

Methanol, also known as *methyl alcohol* or *wood alcohol*, is a chemical compound with a chemical formula that includes one carbon atom and four hydrogen atoms and one oxygen. See Figure 11-21.

Methanol is a light, volatile, colorless, tasteless, flammable, poisonous liquid with a very faint odor. It is used as an antifreeze,

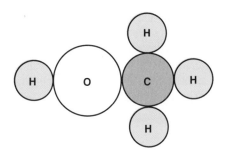

FIGURE 11-21   The molecular structure of methanol showing the one carbon atom, four hydrogen atoms, and one oxygen atom.

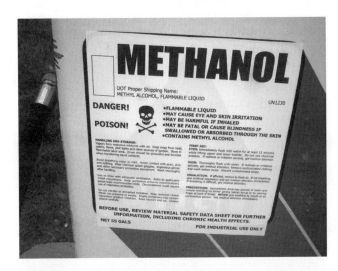

FIGURE 11-22   Sign on methanol pump shows that methyl alcohol is a poison and can cause skin irritation and other personal injury. Methanol is used in industry as well as a fuel source.

solvent, and fuel, and to denature ethanol. Methanol burns in air, forming CO_2 (carbon dioxide) and H_2O (water). A methanol flame is almost colorless. Because of its poisonous properties, methanol is also used to denature ethanol. Methanol is often called wood alcohol because it was once produced chiefly as a by-product of the destructive distillation of wood. See Figure 11-22.

The biggest source of methanol in the United States is coal. Using a simple reaction between coal and steam, a gas mixture called **syn-gas (synthesis gas)** is formed. The components of this mixture are carbon monoxide and hydrogen, which, through an additional chemical reaction, are converted to methanol.

Natural gas can also be used to create methanol and is reformed or converted to synthesis gas, which is later made into methanol.

Biomass can be converted to synthesis gas by a process called partial oxidation, and later converted to methanol. **Biomass** is organic material, such as urban wood wastes, primary mill residues, forest residues, agricultural residues, and dedicated energy crops (e.g., sugarcane and sugar beets), that can be made into fuel.

Electricity can be used to convert water into hydrogen, which is then reacted with carbon dioxide to produce methanol.

Methanol is toxic and can cause blindness and death. It can enter the body by ingestion, inhalation, or absorption through the skin. Dangerous doses will build up if a person is regularly exposed to fumes or handles liquid without skin protection. If methanol has been ingested, a doctor should be contacted immediately. The usual fatal dose is 4 fl oz (100–125 mL).

M-85

Some flexible fuel vehicles are designed to operate on 85% methanol and 15% gasoline. Methanol is very corrosive and requires that the fuel system components be constructed of stainless steel and other alcohol-resistant rubber and plastic components. The heat content of **M85** is about 60% of that of gasoline.

Propane

Propane is normally a gas but is easily compressed into a liquid and stored in inexpensive containers. When sold as a fuel, it is also known as **liquefied petroleum gas (LPG)** or LP-gas because the propane is often mixed with about 10% of other gases such as butane, propylene, butylenes, and mercaptan to give the colorless and odorless propane a smell. Propane is nontoxic, but if inhaled can cause asphyxiation through lack of oxygen. Propane is heavier than air and lays near the floor if released into the atmosphere. Propane is commonly used in forklifts and other equipment used inside warehouses and factories because the exhaust from the engine using propane is not harmful. Propane comes from a by-product of petroleum refining of natural gas. In order to liquefy the fuel, it is stored in strong tanks at about 300 PSI (2,000 kPa). The heating value of propane is less than that of gasoline; therefore, more is required, which reduces the fuel economy. See Figure 11-23.

FIGURE 11-23   Propane fuel storage tank in the trunk of a Ford taxi.

Compressed Natural Gas (CNG)

Another alternative fuel that is often used in fleet vehicles is **compressed natural gas**, or **CNG,** and vehicles using this fuel are often referred to as **natural gas vehicles (NGVs)**. Look for the blue CNG label on vehicles designed to operate on compressed natural gas. See Figure 11-24.

Natural gas has to be compressed to about 3,000 PSI (20,000 kPa) or more, so that the weight and the cost of the storage container is a major factor when it comes to preparing a vehicle to run on CNG. The tanks needed for CNG are typically constructed of 0.5-inch-thick (3 mm) aluminum reinforced with fiberglass. The octane rating of CNG is about 130 and the cost per gallon is about half of the cost of gasoline. However, the heat value of CNG is also less, and therefore more is required to produce the same power and the miles per gallon is less.

Compressed natural gas is made up of a blend of methane, propane, ethane, N-butane, carbon dioxide, and nitrogen. Once it is processed, it is at least 93% methane. Natural gas is nontoxic, odorless, and colorless in its natural state. It is odorized during processing, using ethyl mercaptan ("skunk"), to allow for easy leak detection. Natural gas is lighter than air and will rise when released into the air. Since CNG is already a vapor, it does not need heat to vaporize before it will burn, which improves cold start-up and results in lower emissions during cold operation. However, because it is already in a gaseous state, it does displace some of the air charge in the intake manifold. This leads to about a 10% reduction in engine power as compared to an engine operating on gasoline. Natural gas also burns slower than gasoline; therefore, the ignition timing must be advanced more when the vehicle operates on natural gas. Natural gas has an octane rating of about 115 octane. The stoichiometric ratio, the point at which all the air and fuel is used or burned, is 16.5:1 compared to 14.7:1 for gasoline. This means that more air is required to burn one pound of natural gas than is required to burn one pound of gasoline. See Figure 11-25.

FIGURE 11-24   The blue sticker on the rear of this vehicle indicates that it is designed to use compressed natural gas.

FIGURE 11-25 The fuel injectors used on this Honda Civic GX CNG engine are designed to flow gaseous fuel instead of liquid fuel and cannot be interchanged with any other type of injector.

FIGURE 11-26 A CNG storage tank from a Honda Civic GX shown with the fixture used to support it while it is being removed or installed in the vehicle. Honda specifies that three technicians be used to remove or install the tank through the rear door of the vehicle due to the size and weight of the tank.

The CNG engine is designed to include:

- Increased compression ratio
- Strong pistons and connecting rods
- Heat-resistant valves
- Fuel injectors designed for gaseous fuel instead of liquid fuel

When completely filled, the CNG tank has 3,600 PSI of pressure in the tank. When the ignition is turned on, the alternate fuel electronic control unit activates the high-pressure lock-off, which allows high-pressure gas to pass to the high-pressure regulator. The high-pressure regulator reduces the high-pressure CNG to approximately 170 PSI and sends it to the low-pressure lock-off. The low-pressure lock-off is also controlled by the alternate fuel electronic control unit and is activated at the same time that the high-pressure lock-off is activated. From the low-pressure lock-off, the CNG is directed to the low-pressure regulator. This is a two-stage regulator that first reduces the pressure to approximately 4 to 6 PSI in the first stage and then to 4.5 to 7 inches of water in the second stage. From here, the low-pressure gas is delivered to the gas mass sensor/mixture control valve. This valve controls the air–fuel mixture. The CNG gas distributor adapter then delivers the gas to the intake stream.

CNG vehicles are designed for fleet use that usually have their own refueling capabilities. One of the drawbacks to using CNG is the time that it takes to refuel a vehicle. The ideal method of refueling is the slow fill method. The slow filling method compresses the natural gas as the tank is being fueled. This method ensures that the tank will receive a full charge of CNG; however, this method can take three to five hours to accomplish. If more than one vehicle needs filling, the facility will need multiple CNG compressors to refuel the

vehicles. There are three commonly used CNG refilling station pressures:

P24—2,400 PSI
P30—3,000 PSI
P36—3,600 PSI

Try to find and use a station with the highest pressure to help ensure a long driving range. Filling at lower pressures will result in less compressed natural gas being installed in the storage tank, thereby reducing the driving range. See Figure 11-26.

The fast fill method uses CNG that is already compressed. However, as the CNG tank is filled rapidly, the internal temperature of the tank will rise, which causes a rise in tank pressure. Once the temperature drops in the CNG tank, the pressure in the tank also drops, resulting in an incomplete charge in the CNG tank. This refueling method may take only about five minutes; however, it will result in an incomplete charge to the CNG tank, reducing the driving range.

P-SERIES FUELS

P-series alternative fuel is patented by Princeton University and is a non-petroleum-based fuel suitable for use in flexible fuel vehicles or any vehicle designed to operate on E85 (85% ethanol, 15% gasoline). P-series fuels are blends of the following:

- Ethanol (ethyl alcohol)
- Methyltetrahydrofuron, abbreviated **MTHF**
- Natural gas liquids, such as pentanes
- Butane

The ethanol and MTHF are produced from renewable feedstocks, such as corn, waste paper, biomass, agricultural waste, and wood waste (scraps and sawdust). The components used in P-type fuel can be varied to produce regular grade, premium grade, or fuel suitable for cold climates.

Composition of P-Series Fuels (by volume)

Component	Regular Grade	Premium Grade	Cold Weather
Pentanes plus	32.5%	27.5%	16.0%
MTHF	32.5%	17.5%	26.0%
Ethanol	35.0%	55.0%	47.0%
Butane	0.0%	0.0%	11.0%

See the following comparison chart that summarizes the characteristics of the most commonly used fuels.

The advantages of P-series alternative fuels include:

- Can be used as produced without being mixed with gasoline.
- The cost is slightly less to produce than gasoline, and heat produced when used in an engine is also slightly less, making it a suitable alternative to gasoline.

FREQUENTLY ASKED QUESTION

WHAT IS A TRI-FUEL VEHICLE?

In Brazil, most vehicles are designed to operate on ethanol or gasoline or any combination of the two. In this South American country, ethanol is made from sugarcane, is commonly available, and is lower in price than gasoline. Compressed natural gas (CNG) is also being made available, so many vehicle manufacturers in Brazil, such as General Motors and Ford, are equipping vehicles to be capable of using gasoline, ethanol, or CNG. These vehicles are called tri-fuel vehicles.

The disadvantages include:

- Limited availability
- Can only be used in flexible fuel vehicles (FFV)

Alternate Fuel Comparison Chart

Characteristic	Propane	CNG	Methanol	Ethanol	Regular Unleaded Gas
Octane	104	130	100	100	87–93
BTU per gallon	91,000	N.A.	70,000	83,000	114,000–125,000
Gallon equivalent	1.15	122 cubic feet–1 gallon of gasoline	1.8	1.5	1
On-board fuel storage	Liquid	Gas	Liquid	Liquid	Liquid
Miles/gallon as compared to gas	85%	N.A.	55%	70%	100%
Relative tank size required to yield driving range equivalent to gas	Tank is 1.25 times larger	Tank is 3.5 times larger	Tank is 1.8 times larger	Tank is 1.5 times larger	
Pressure	200 PSI	3,000–3,600 PSI	N.A.	N.A.	N.A.
Cold weather capability	Good	Good	Poor	Poor	Good
Vehicle power	5–10% power loss	10–20% power loss	4% power increase	5% power increase	Standard
Toxicity	Nontoxic	Nontoxic	Highly toxic	Toxic	Toxic
Corrosiveness	Noncorrosive	Noncorrosive	Corrosive	Corrosive	Minimally corrosive
Source	Natural gas/petroleum refining	Natural gas/crude oil	Natural gas/coal	Sugar and starch crops/biomass	Crude oil

DIESEL FUEL

Diesel fuel must meet an entirely different set of standards than gasoline. The fuel in a diesel engine is not ignited with a spark, but is ignited by the heat generated by high compression. The pressure of compression (400 to 700 PSI, or 2,800 to 4,800 kilopascals) generates temperatures of 1,200° to 1,600°F (700° to 900°C), which speeds the preflame reaction to start the ignition of fuel injected into the cylinder.

All diesel fuel must be clean, be able to flow at low temperatures, and be of the proper cetane rating.

- **Cleanliness.** It is imperative that the fuel used in a diesel engine be clean and free from water. Unlike the case with gasoline engines, the fuel is the lubricant and coolant for the diesel injector pump and injectors. Good-quality diesel fuel contains additives such as oxidation inhibitors, detergents, dispersants, rust preventatives, and metal deactivators.

- **Low-temperature fluidity.** Diesel fuel must be able to flow freely at all expected ambient temperatures. One specification for diesel fuel is its "pour point," which is the temperature below which the fuel would stop flowing. Cloud point is another concern with diesel fuel at lower temperatures. Cloud point is the low-temperature point at which the waxes present in most diesel fuels tend to form crystals that clog the fuel filter. Most diesel fuel suppliers distribute fuel with the proper pour point and cloud point for the climate conditions of the area.

- **Cetane number.** The cetane number for diesel fuel is the opposite of the octane number for gasoline. The cetane number is a measure of the ease with which the fuel can be ignited. The **cetane rating** of the fuel determines, to a great extent, its ability to start the engine at low temperatures and to provide smooth warm-up and even combustion. The cetane rating of diesel fuel should be between 45 and 50. The higher the cetane rating, the more easily the fuel is ignited.

Other diesel fuel specifications include its flash point, sulfur content, and classification. The flash point is the temperature at which the vapors on the surface of the fuel will ignite if exposed to an open flame. The flash point does *not* affect diesel engine operation. However, a lower-than-normal flash point could indicate contamination of the diesel fuel with gasoline or a similar substance.

The sulfur content of diesel fuel is very important to the life of the engine. Most engine manufacturers specify that only fuel containing less than about 0.3% sulfur be used. The current limit as set by the American Society for Testing and Materials (ASTM) is 0.5% maximum. Sulfur in the fuel creates sulfuric acid during the combustion process, which can damage engine components and cause piston ring wear. Federal regulations are getting extremely tight on sulfur content. High-sulfur fuel contributes to acid rain.

ASTM also classifies diesel fuel by volatility (boiling range) into the following grades:

Grade #1.   This grade of diesel fuel has the lowest boiling point and the lowest cloud and pour points, as well as a lower BTU content—less heat per pound of fuel. As a result, grade #1 is suitable for use during low-temperature (winter) operation. Grade #1 produces less heat per pound of fuel compared to grade #2 and may be specified for use in diesel engines involved in frequent changes in load and speed, such as those found in city buses and delivery trucks.

Grade #2.   This grade has a higher boiling point, cloud point, and pour point as compared with grade #1. It is usually specified where constant speed and high loads are encountered, such as in long-haul trucking and automotive diesel applications.

Diesel Fuel Specific Gravity Testing

The density of diesel fuel should be tested whenever there is a driveability concern. The density or specific gravity of diesel fuel is measured in units of **API gravity.** (See the following API Gravity Comparison Chart.) API gravity is an arbitrary scale expressing the gravity or density of liquid petroleum products devised jointly by the American Petroleum Institute and the National Bureau of Standards. The measuring scale is calibrated in terms of degrees API. Oil with the least specific gravity has the highest API gravity. The formula for determining API gravity is as follows:

$$\text{Degree API gravity} = (141.5 \div \text{specific gravity at } 60°\text{F}) - 131.5$$

The normal API gravity for #1 diesel fuel is 39 to 44 (typically 40). The normal API gravity for #2 diesel fuel is 30 to 39 (typically 35). A hydrometer calibrated in API gravity units should be used to test diesel fuel. See Figure 11-27.

Diesel Fuel Heaters

Diesel fuel heaters, either coolant or electric, help prevent power loss and stalling in cold weather. The heater is placed in the fuel line between the tank and the primary filter. Some coolant heaters are thermostatically controlled, which allows fuel to bypass the heater once it has reached operating temperature.

Ultra-Low-Sulfur Diesel Fuel

Diesel fuel is used in diesel engines and is usually readily available throughout the United States, Canada, and Europe, where

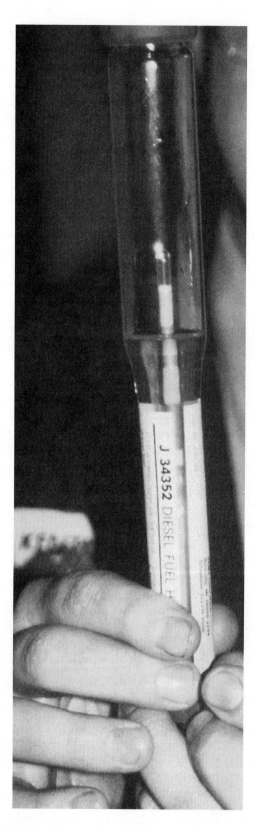

FIGURE 11-27
Testing the API viscosity of a diesel fuel sample using a hydrometer.

API Gravity Comparison Chart

API Gravity Scale	Values for API Scale Oil		
	Specific Gravity	Weight Density, lb/ft	Pounds per Gallon
0			
2			
4			
6			
8			
10	1.0000	62.36	8.337
12	0.9861	61.50	8.221
14	0.9725	60.65	8.108
16	0.9593	59.83	7.998
18	0.9465	59.03	7.891
20	0.9340	58.25	7.787
22	0.9218	57.87	7.736
24	0.9100	56.75	7.587
26	0.8984	56.03	7.490
28	0.8871	55.32	7.396
30	0.8762	54.64	7.305
32	0.8654	53.97	7.215
34	0.8550	53.32	7.128
36	0.8448	52.69	7.043
38	0.8348	51.06	6.960
40	0.8251	50.96	6.879
42	0.8155	50.86	6.799
44	0.8030	50.28	6.722
46	0.7972	49.72	6.646
48	0.7883	49.16	6.572
50	0.7796	48.62	6.499
52	0.7711	48.09	6.429
54	0.7628	47.57	6.359
56	0.7547	47.07	6.292
58	0.7467	46.57	6.225
60	0.7389	46.08	6.160
62	0.7313	45.61	6.097
64	0.7238	45.14	6.034
66	0.7165	44.68	5.973
68	0.7093	44.23	5.913
70	0.7022	43.79	5.854
72	0.6953	43.36	5.797
74	0.6886	42.94	5.741
76	0.6819	42.53	5.685
78	0.6754	41.92	5.631
80	0.6690	41.72	5.577
82	0.6628	41.33	5.526
84	0.6566	40.95	5.474
86	0.6506	40.57	5.424
88	0.6446	40.20	5.374
90	0.6388	39.84	5.326
92	0.6331	39.48	5.278
94	0.6275	39.13	5.231
96	0.6220	38.79	5.186
98	0.6116	38.45	5.141
100	0.6112	38.12	5.096

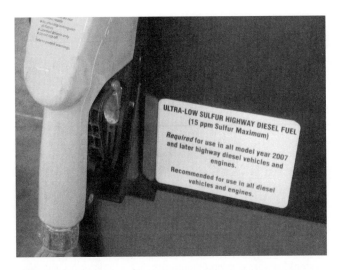

FIGURE 11-28 A pump decal indicating that the diesel fuel is ultra-low-sulfur diesel (ULSD) and must be used in 2007 and newer diesel vehicles.

FIGURE 11-29 Biodiesel is available at few locations.

FREQUENTLY ASKED QUESTION

HOW CAN YOU TELL IF GASOLINE HAS BEEN ADDED TO THE DIESEL FUEL BY MISTAKE?

If gasoline has been accidentally added to diesel fuel and is burned in a diesel engine, the result can be very damaging to the engine. The gasoline can ignite faster than diesel fuel, which would tend to increase the temperature of combustion. This high temperature can harm injectors and glow plugs, as well as pistons, head gaskets, and other major diesel engine components. If contaminated fuel is suspected, first smell the fuel at the filler neck. If the fuel smells like gasoline, then the tank should be drained and refilled with diesel fuel. If the smell test does not indicate a gasoline smell (or any rancid smell), then test a sample for proper API gravity.

NOTE: Diesel fuel designed for on-road use should be green in color. Red diesel fuel (high sulfur) should only be found in off-road or farm equipment.

many more cars are equipped with diesel engines. Diesel engines manufactured to 2007 or newer standards must use ultra-low-sulfur diesel fuel containing less than 15 parts per million (PPM) of sulfur compared to the older low-sulfur specification of 500 PPM. The purpose of the lower sulfur amount in diesel fuel is to reduce emissions of sulfur oxides (SO_x) and particulate

matter (PM) from heavy-duty highway engines and vehicles that use diesel fuel. The emission controls used on 2007 and newer diesel engines require the use of **ultra-low-sulfur diesel (ULSD)** for reliable operation. See Figure 11-28.

Ultra-low-sulfur diesel (ULSD) will eventually replace the current highway diesel fuel, low-sulfur diesel, which can have as much as 500 PPM of sulfur. ULSD is required for use in all model year 2007 and newer diesel-powered highway vehicles. These vehicles are equipped with advanced emission control systems that are incompatible with low sulfur (500 PPM) fuel. ULSD looks lighter in color and has less smell than other diesel fuel.

BIODIESEL

Biodiesel is a domestically produced, renewable fuel that can be manufactured from vegetable oils, animal fats, or recycled restaurant greases. Biodiesel is safe, biodegradable, and reduces serious air pollutants such as particulate matter (PM), carbon monoxide, and hydrocarbons. Biodiesel is defined as mono-alkyl esters of long-chain fatty acids derived from vegetable oils or animal fats that conform to ASTM D6751 specifications for use in diesel engines. Biodiesel refers to the pure fuel before blending with diesel fuel. See Figure 11-29.

Biodiesel blends are denoted as "BXX" with "XX" representing the percentage of biodiesel contained in the blend (i.e., **B20** is 20% biodiesel, 80% petroleum diesel). Blends of 20% biodiesel with 80% petroleum diesel (B20) can generally be used in unmodified diesel engines; however, users should consult their OEM and engine warranty statement. Biodiesel can also be used in its pure form (B100), but it may require certain engine modifications to avoid maintenance and performance problems and may not be suitable for wintertime use. Users should consult their engine warranty statement for more information on fuel blends of greater than 20% biodiesel.

In general, B20 costs 30 to 40 cents more per gallon than conventional diesel. Although biodiesel costs more than regular diesel fuel, often called **petrodiesel,** fleet managers can make the switch to alternative fuels without purchasing new vehicles, acquiring new spare parts inventories, rebuilding refueling stations, or hiring new service technicians. Biodiesel has the following characteristics:

1. Purchasing biodiesel in bulk quantities decreases the cost of fuel.
2. Biodiesel maintains similar horsepower, torque, and fuel economy.
3. Biodiesel has a higher cetane number than conventional diesel, which increases the engine's performance.
4. Biodiesel has a high flash point and low volatility so it does not ignite as easily as petrodiesel, which increases the margin of safety in fuel handling. In fact, it degrades four times faster than petrodiesel and is not particularly soluble in water.
5. It is nontoxic, which makes it safe to handle, transport, and store. Maintenance requirements for B20 vehicles and petrodiesel vehicles are the same. B100 does pose a few concerns, however.
6. Biodiesel acts as a lubricant and this can add to the life of the fuel system components.

E-DIESEL FUEL

E-diesel, also called **diesohol** outside of the United States, is standard No. 2 diesel fuel that contains up to 15% ethanol. While E-diesel can have up to 15% ethanol by volume, typical blend levels are from 8% to 10%.

Cetane Rating

The higher the cetane number, the shorter the delay between injection and ignition. Normal diesel fuel has a cetane number of about 50. Adding 15% ethanol lowers the cetane number. To increase the cetane number back to that of conventional diesel fuel, a cetane-enhancing additive is added to E-diesel. The additive used to increase the cetane rating of E-diesel is ethylhexylnitrate or ditertbutyl peroxide.

The flash point is the minimum temperature at which the fuel will ignite (flash). E-diesel has a lower flash point than conventional diesel fuel (50°F instead of 126°F) and therefore is less safe to handle.

FREQUENTLY ASKED QUESTION

I THOUGHT BIODIESEL WAS VEGETABLE OIL?

Biodiesel is vegetable oil with the glycerin component removed by means of reacting the vegetable oil with a catalyst. The resulting hydrocarbon esters are 16 to 18 carbon atoms in length, almost identical to the petroleum diesel fuel atoms. This allows the use of biodiesel fuel in a diesel engine with no modifications needed. Biodiesel powered vehicles do not *need* a second fuel tank, whereas vegetable-oil-powered vehicles do.

There are three main types of fuel used in diesel engines. These are:

- Petroleum diesel, a fossil hydrocarbon with a carbon chain length of about 16 carbon atoms.
- Biodiesel, a hydrocarbon with a carbon chain length of 16 to 18 carbon atoms.
- Vegetable oil is a triglyceride with a glycerin component joining three hydrocarbon chains of 16 to 18 carbon atoms each, called straight vegetable oil (SVO). Other terms used when describing vegetable oil include:
  - **Pure plant oil (PPO)**—a term most often used in Europe to describe **SVO**
  - **Waste vegetable oil (WVO)**—this oil could include animal or fish oils from cooking
  - **Used cooking oil (UCO)**—a term used when the oil may or may not be pure vegetable oil

Vegetable oil is not liquid enough at common ambient temperatures for use in a diesel engine fuel delivery system designed for the lower-viscosity petroleum diesel fuel. Vegetable oil needs to be heated to obtain a similar viscosity to biodiesel and petroleum diesel. This means that a heat source needs to be provided before the fuel can be used in a diesel engine. This is achieved by starting on petroleum diesel or biodiesel fuel until the engine heat can be used to sufficiently warm a tank containing the vegetable oil. It also requires purging the fuel system of vegetable oil with petroleum diesel or biodiesel fuel prior to stopping the engine to avoid the vegetable oil thickening and solidifying in the fuel system away from the heated tank. The use of vegetable oil in its natural state does, however, eliminate the need to remove the glycerin component.

Many vehicle and diesel engine fuel system suppliers permit the use of biodiesel fuel that is certified as meeting testing standards. None permit the use of vegetable oil in its natural state.

NOTE: For additional information on biodiesel and the locations where it can be purchased, visit *www.biodiesel.org*.

FREQUENTLY ASKED QUESTION

HOW LONG CAN OXYGENATED FUEL BE STORED BEFORE ALL OF THE OXYGEN ESCAPES?

The oxygen in oxygenated fuels, such as E10, E85, and E-diesel, is not in a gaseous state like the CO_2 in soft drinks. The oxygen is part of the molecule of ethanol or other oxygenates and does not bubble out of the fuel. Oxygenated fuels, just like any fuel, have a shelf life of about 90 days.

E-diesel has better cold-flow properties than conventional diesel. The heat content of E-diesel is about 6% less than conventional diesel, but the particulate matter (PM) emissions are reduced by as much as 40%, 20% less carbon monoxide, and a 5% reduction in oxides of nitrogen (NO_X).

Currently, E-diesel is considered to be experimental and can be used legally in off-road applications or in mass-transit buses with EPA approval. For additional information, visit *www.e-diesel.org*.

SYNTHETIC FUELS

Synthetic fuels were first developed using the Fischer-Tropsch method and have been in use since the 1920s to convert coal, natural gas, and other fossil fuel products into a fuel that is high in quality and clean-burning. The process for producing Fischer-Tropsch fuels was patented by two German scientists, Franz Fischer and Hans Tropsch, during World War I. The Fischer-Tropsch method uses carbon monoxide and hydrogen (the same synthesis gas used to produce hydrogen fuel) to convert coal and other hydrocarbons to liquid fuels in a process similar to hydrogenation, another method for hydrocarbon

conversion. The process using natural gas, also called **gas-to-liquid (GTL)** technology, uses a catalyst, usually iron or cobalt, and incorporates steam reforming to give off the by-products of carbon dioxide, hydrogen, and carbon monoxide.

Whereas traditional fuels emit environmentally harmful particulates and chemicals, namely sulfur compounds, Fischer-Tropsch fuels combust with no soot or odors and emit only low levels of toxins. Fischer-Tropsch fuels can also be blended with traditional transportation fuels with little equipment modification, as they use the same engine and equipment technology as traditional fuels.

The fuels contain a very low sulfur and aromatic content and they produce virtually no particulate emissions. Researchers also expect reductions in hydrocarbon and carbon monoxide emissions. Fischer-Tropsch fuels do not differ in fuel performance from gasoline and diesel. At present, Fischer-Tropsch fuels are very expensive to produce on a large scale, although research is under way to lower processing costs. However, some synthetic diesel fuel is currently being used in South Africa. Diesel fuel created using the **Fischer-Tropsch Diesel (FTD)** process is often called GTL diesel. GTL diesel can also be combined with petroleum diesel to produce a GTL blend. This fuel product is currently being sold in Europe, and plans are in place to introduce it in North America.

Coal to Liquid (CTL)

Coal is very abundant in the United States and coal can be converted to a liquid fuel through a process called **coal to liquid (CTL)**. The huge cost is the main obstacle to these plants. The need to invest $1.4 billion per plant before it can make any product is the reason no one has built a CTL plant yet in the United States. Investors need to be convinced that the cost of oil is going to remain high in order to get them to commit this kind of money.

A large plant might be able to produce 120,000 barrels of liquid fuel a day and would consume about 50,000 tons of coal per day. However, such a plant would create about 6,000 tons of CO_2 per day. These CO_2 emissions and the cost involved make CTL a new technology that is not likely to expand.

Two procedures can be used to convert coal-to-liquid fuel:

1. Direct—In the direct method, coal is broken down to create liquid products. First the coal is reacted with hydrogen (H_2) at high temperatures and pressure with a catalyst. This process creates a synthetic crude, called syncrude, which is then refined to produce gasoline or diesel fuel.
2. Indirect—In the indirect method, coal is first turned into a gas and the molecules are reassembled to create the desired product. This process involves turning coal into a gas called syn-gas. The syn-gas is then converted into liquid, using the Fischer-Tropsch (FT) process.

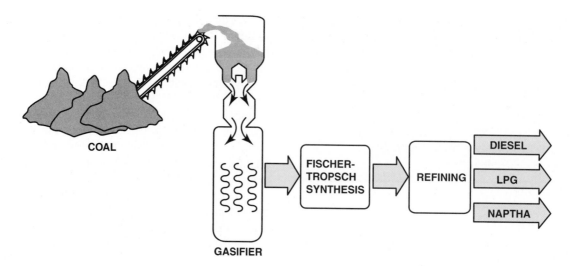

FIGURE 11-30   A typical coal-to-liquid plant.

Russia has been using CTL by injecting air into the underground coal seams. Ignition is provided and the resulting gases are trapped and converted to liquid gasoline and diesel fuel through the Fischer-Tropsch process. This underground method is called **underground coal gasification (UCG).** See Figure 11-30.

Methanol to Gasoline

Exxon Mobil has developed a process for converting methanol (methyl alcohol) into gasoline in a process called **methanol-to-gasoline (MTG).** The MTG process was discovered by accident when a gasoline additive made from methanol was being created. The process instead created olefins (alkenes), paraffins (alkenes), and aromatic compounds, which in combination are known as gasoline. The process uses a catalyst and is currently being produced in New Zealand.

Future of Synthetic Fuels

Producing gasoline and diesel fuels by other methods besides refining from crude oil has usually been more expensive. With the increasing cost of crude oil, alternative methods are now becoming economically feasible. Whether or not the diesel fuel or gasoline is created from coal, natural gas, or methanol, or created by refining crude oil, the transportation and service pumps are already in place. Compared to using compressed natural gas or other similar alternative fuels, synthetic fuels represent the lowest cost.

SAFETY PROCEDURES WHEN WORKING WITH ALTERNATIVE-FUEL VEHICLES

All fuels are flammable and many are explosive under certain conditions. Whenever working around compressed gases of any kind (CNG, LNG, propane, or LPG), always wear personal protective equipment (PPE), including at least the following items:

1. Safety glasses and/or face shield.
2. Protective gloves.
3. Long-sleeve shirt and pants to help protect bare skin from the freezing effects of gases under pressure in the event that the pressure is lost.
4. If any fuel gets on the skin, the area should be washed immediately.
5. If fuel spills on clothing, change into clean clothing as soon as possible.
6. If fuel spills on a painted surface, flush the surface with water and air dry. If simply wiped off with a dry cloth, the paint surface could be permanently damaged.
7. As with any fuel-burning vehicle, always vent the exhaust to the outside. If methanol fuel is used, the exhaust contains formaldehyde, which has a sharp odor and can cause severe burning of the eyes, nose, and throat.

WARNING: Do not smoke or have an open flame in the area when working around or refueling any vehicle.

TESTING FOR ALCOHOL CONTENT IN GASOLINE Step-by-Step

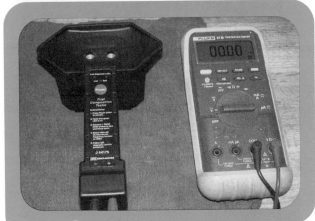

STEP 1 A fuel composition tester is the recommended tool to use to test the alcohol content of gasoline.

STEP 2 This battery-powered tester uses light-emitting diodes (LEDs), meter lead terminals, and two small openings for the fuel sample.

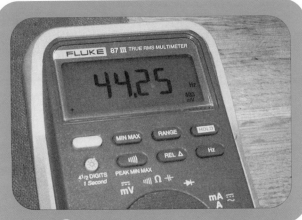

STEP 3 The first step is to verify the proper operation of the tester by measuring the air frequency by selecting AC hertz on the meter. The air frequency should be between 35 Hz and 48 Hz.

STEP 4 After verifying that the tester is capable of correctly reading the air frequency, gasoline is poured into the testing cell of the tool.

STEP 5 Record the AC frequency as shown on the meter and subtract 50 from the reading (e.g., 60.50 − 50.00 = 10.5). This number (10.5) is the percentage of alcohol in the gasoline sample.

STEP 6 Adding additional amounts of ethyl alcohol (ethanol) increases the frequency reading.

SUMMARY

1. Gasoline is a complex blend of hydrocarbons. Gasoline is blended for seasonal usage to achieve the correct volatility for easy starting and maximum fuel economy under all driving conditions.

2. Winter-blend fuel used in a vehicle during warm weather can cause a rough idle and stalling because of its higher Reid vapor pressure (RVP).

3. Abnormal combustion (also called detonation or spark knock) increases both the temperature and the pressure inside the combustion chamber.

4. Most regular-grade gasoline today, using the $(R + M) \div 2$ rating method, is 87 octane; midgrade (plus) is 89 and premium grade is 91 or higher.

5. Oxygenated fuels contain oxygen to lower CO exhaust emissions.

6. Gasoline should always be purchased from a busy station, and the tank should not be overfilled.

7. Flexible fuel vehicles are designed to operate on gasoline or gasoline-ethanol blends up to 85% ethanol.

REVIEW QUESTIONS

1. What is the difference between summer-blend and winter-blend gasoline?

2. What is Reid vapor pressure?

3. What is vapor lock?

4. What does the $(R + M) = 2$ gasoline pump octane rating indicate?

5. What are five octane improvers that may be used during the refining process?

6. What is stoichiometric?

CHAPTER QUIZ

1. Winter-blend gasoline _____.
   a. Vaporizes more easily than summer-blend gasoline
   b. Has a higher RVP
   c. Can cause engine driveability problems if used during warm weather
   d. All of the above

2. Vapor lock can occur _____.
   a. As a result of excessive heat near fuel lines
   b. If a fuel line is restricted
   c. During both a and b
   d. During neither a nor b

3. Technician A says that spark knock, ping, and detonation are different names for abnormal combustion. Technician B says that any abnormal combustion raises the temperature and pressure inside the combustion chamber and can cause severe engine damage. Which technician is correct?
   a. Technician A only
   b. Technician B only

   c. Both technicians A and B
   d. Neither technician A nor B

4. Technician A says that the research octane number is higher than the motor octane number. Technician B says that the octane rating posted on fuel pumps is an average of the two ratings. Which technician is correct?
   a. Technician A only
   b. Technician B only
   c. Both technicians A and B
   d. Neither technician A nor B

5. Technician A says that in going to high altitudes, engines produce lower power. Technician B says that most engine control systems can compensate the air–fuel mixture for changes in altitude. Which technician is correct?
   a. Technician A only
   b. Technician B only
   c. Both technicians A and B
   d. Neither technician A nor B

6. When refueling a CNG vehicle, why is it recommended that the tank be filled to a high pressure?

   a. The range of the vehicle is increased

   b. The cost of the fuel is lower

   c. Less of the fuel is lost to evaporation

   d. Both a and c

7. The use of premium high-octane gasoline in an engine designed to use regular-grade gasoline will increase engine power.

   a. True

   b. False

8. To avoid problems with the variation of gasoline, all government testing uses _____ as a fuel during testing procedures.

   a. MTBE (methyl tertiary butyl ether)

   b. Indolene

   c. Xylene

   d. TBA (tertiary butyl alcohol)

9. Avoid topping off the fuel tank because _____.

   a. It can saturate the charcoal canister

   b. The extra fuel simply spills onto the ground

   c. The extra fuel increases vehicle weight and reduces performance

   d. The extra fuel goes into the expansion area of the tank and is not used by the engine

10. Using ethanol-enhanced or reformulated gasoline can result in reduced fuel economy.

   a. True

   b. False

DIESEL ENGINE OPERATION AND DIAGNOSIS

OBJECTIVES

After studying Chapter 12, the reader will be able to:

1. Prepare for ASE Engine Performance (A8) certification test content area "C" (Fuel, Air Induction, and Exhaust Systems Diagnosis and Repair).
2. Explain how a diesel engine works.
3. Describe the difference between direct injection (DI) and indirect injection (IDI) diesel engines.
4. List the parts of the typical diesel engine fuel system.
5. Explain how glow plugs work.
6. List the advantages and disadvantages of a diesel engine.
7. Describe how diesel fuel is rated and tested.

KEY TERMS

API Gravity (p. 173)
Diesel Oxidation Catalyst (DOC) (p. 170)
Differential Pressure Sensor (DPS) (p. 171)
Direct Injection (DI) (p. 161)
Glow Plug (p. 167)
Heat of Compression (p. 161)
High-Pressure Common Rail (HPCR) (p. 164)
Hydraulic Electronic Unit Injection (HEUI) (p. 164)

Indirect Injection (IDI) (p. 161)
Injection Pump (p. 161)
Lift Pump (p. 163)
Opacity (p. 175)
Pop Tester (p. 174)
Regeneration (p. 171)
Water-Fuel Separator (p. 163)

DIESEL ENGINES

In 1892, a German engineer named Rudolf Diesel perfected the compression-ignition engine that bears his name. The diesel engine uses heat created by compression to ignite the fuel, so it requires no spark ignition system.

The diesel engine requires compression ratios of 16:1 and higher. Incoming air is compressed until its temperature reaches about 1000°F (540°C). This is called **heat of compression.** As the piston reaches the top of its compression stroke, fuel is injected into the cylinder, where it is ignited by the hot air. See Figure 12-1.

As the fuel burns, it expands and produces power. Because of the very high compression and torque output of a diesel engine, it is made heavier and stronger than the same size gasoline-powered engine.

A common diesel engine uses a fuel system precision **injection pump** and individual fuel injectors. The pump delivers fuel to the injectors at a high pressure and at timed intervals. Each injector sprays fuel into the combustion chamber at the precise moment required for efficient combustion. See Figure 12-2.

In a diesel engine, air is not controlled by a throttle as in a gasoline engine. Instead, the amount of fuel injected is varied to control power and speed. The air–fuel mixture of a diesel can vary from as lean as 85:1 at idle to as rich as 20:1 at full load. This higher air–fuel ratio and the increased compression pressures make the diesel more fuel-efficient than a gasoline engine in part because diesel engines do not suffer from throttling losses. Throttling losses involve the power needed in a gasoline engine to draw air past a closed or partially closed throttle.

In a gasoline engine, the speed and power are controlled by the throttle valve, which controls the amount of air entering the engine. Adding more fuel to the cylinders of a gasoline engine without adding more air (oxygen) will not increase the speed or power of the engine. In a diesel engine, speed and power are not controlled by the amount of air entering the cylinders because the engine air intake is always wide open. Therefore, the engine always has enough oxygen to burn the fuel in the cylinder and will increase speed (and power) when additional fuel is supplied.

Diesel engines are built in both two-stroke and four-stroke versions. The most common two-stroke diesels were the truck and industrial engines made by Detroit Diesel. In these engines, air intake is through ports in the cylinder wall. Exhaust is through poppet valves in the head. A blower pushes air into the air box surrounding liner ports to supply air for combustion and to blow the exhaust gases out of the exhaust valves.

Indirect and Direct Injection

In an **indirect injection** (abbreviated **IDI**) diesel engine, fuel is injected into a small prechamber, which is connected to the cylinder by a narrow opening. The initial combustion takes place in this prechamber. This has the effect of slowing the rate of combustion, which tends to reduce noise. See Figure 12-3.

All indirect diesel injection engines require the use of a glow plug.

In a **direct injection** (abbreviated **DI**) diesel engine, fuel is injected directly into the cylinder. The piston incorporates a depression where initial combustion takes place. Direct injection diesel engines are generally more efficient than indirect injection engines, but have a tendency to produce greater amounts of noise. See Figure 12-4.

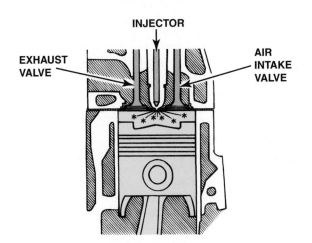

FIGURE 12-1 Diesel combustion occurs when fuel is injected into the hot, highly compressed air in the cylinder.

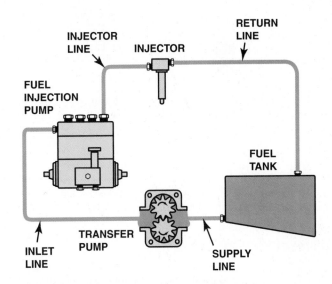

FIGURE 12-2 A typical injector-pump-type automotive diesel fuel injection system.

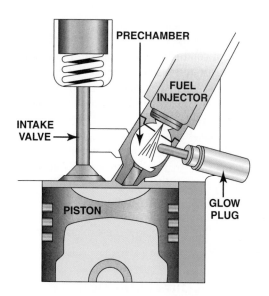

FIGURE 12-3   An indirect injection diesel engine uses a prechamber and a glow plug.

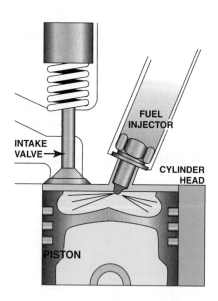

FIGURE 12-4   A direct injection diesel engine injects the fuel directly into the combustion chamber. Many designs do not use a glow plug.

While some direct injection diesel engines use glow plugs to help cold starting and to reduce emissions, many direct injection diesel engines do not use glow plugs.

Diesel Fuel Ignition

Ignition occurs in a diesel engine by injecting fuel into the air charge, which has been heated by compression to a temperature greater than the ignition point of the fuel or about 1000°F (538°C). The chemical reaction of burning the fuel liberates heat, which causes the gases to expand, forcing the piston to rotate the crankshaft. A four-stroke diesel engine requires two rotations of the crankshaft to complete one cycle. On the intake stroke, the piston passes TDC, the intake valve(s) open, the fresh air is admitted into the cylinder, and the exhaust valve is still open for a few degrees to allow all of the exhaust gases to escape. On the compression stroke, after the piston passes BDC, the intake valve closes and the piston travels up to TDC (completion of the first crankshaft rotation). On the power stroke, the piston nears TDC on the compression stroke, the diesel fuel is injected by the injectors, and the fuel starts to burn, further heating the gases in the cylinder. During this power stroke, the piston passes TDC and the expanding gases force the piston down, rotating the crankshaft. On the exhaust stroke, as the piston passes BDC, the exhaust valves open and the exhaust gases start to flow out of the cylinder. This continues as the piston travels up to TDC, pumping the spent gases out of the cylinder. At TDC, the second crankshaft rotation is complete.

THREE PHASES OF COMBUSTION

There are three distinct phases or parts to the combustion in a diesel engine.

1. **Ignition delay.** Near the end of the compression stroke, fuel injection begins, but ignition does not begin immediately. This period is called delay.
2. **Rapid combustion.** This phase of combustion occurs when the fuel first starts to burn, creating a sudden rise in cylinder pressure. It is this rise in combustion chamber pressure that causes the characteristic diesel engine knock.
3. **Controlled combustion.** After the rapid combustion occurs, the rest of the fuel in the combustion chamber begins to burn and injection continues. This is an area near the injector that contains fuel surrounded by air. This fuel burns as it mixes with the air.

DIESEL ENGINE CONSTRUCTION

Diesel engines must be constructed heavier than gasoline engines because of the tremendous pressures that are created in the cylinders during operation. The torque output of a diesel engine is often double or more than the same size gasoline powered engines. See the comparison chart.

System or Component	Diesel Engine	Gasoline Engine
Block	Cast iron and heavy See Figure 12-5.	Cast iron or aluminum and as light as possible
Cylinder head	Cast iron or aluminum	Cast iron or aluminum
Compression ratio	17:1 to 25:1	8:1 to 12:1
Peak engine speed	2,000 to 2,500 RPM	5,000 to 8,000 RPM
Pistons and connecting rods	Aluminum with combustion pockets and heavy-duty rods See Figure 12-6.	Aluminum, usually flat top or with valve relief but no combustion pockets

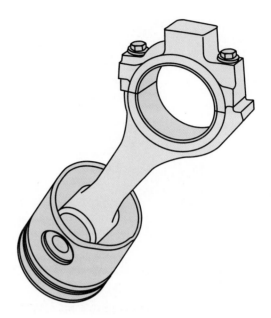

FIGURE 12-6   A rod/piston assembly from a 5.9-liter Cummins diesel engine used in a Dodge pickup truck.

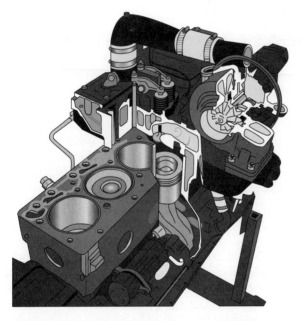

FIGURE 12-5   The common rail on a Cummins diesel engine. A high-pressure pump (up to 30,000 PSI) is used to supply diesel fuel to this common rail, which has cubes running to each injector. Note the thick cylinder walls and heavy-duty construction.

FUEL TANK AND LIFT PUMP

A fuel tank used on a vehicle equipped with a diesel engine differs from the one used with a gasoline engine in several ways, including:

- A larger filler neck for diesel fuel. Gasoline filler necks are smaller for the unleaded gasoline nozzle.
- No evaporative emission control devices or charcoal (carbon) canister. Diesel fuel is not as volatile as gasoline and,

therefore, diesel vehicles do not have evaporative emission control devices.

The diesel fuel is drawn from the fuel tank by a **lift pump** and delivers the fuel to the injection pump. Between the fuel tank and the lift pump is a **water-fuel separator.** Water is heavier than diesel fuel and sinks to the bottom of the separator. Part of normal routine maintenance on a vehicle equipped with a diesel engine is to drain the water from the water-fuel separator. A float is usually used inside the separator, which is connected to a warning light on the dash that lights if the water reaches a level where it needs to be drained.

NOTE: Water can cause corrosive damage as well as wear to diesel engine parts because water is not a good lubricant. Water cannot be atomized by a diesel fuel injector nozzle and will often "blow out" the nozzle tip.

Many diesel engines also use a fuel temperature sensor. The computer uses this information to adjust fuel delivery based on the density of the fuel. See Figure 12-7.

Injection Pump

A diesel engine injection pump is used to increase the pressure of the diesel fuel from very low values from the lift pump to the extremely high pressures needed for injection.

Injection pumps are usually driven by the camshaft at the front of the engine. As the injection pump shaft rotates, the

FIGURE 12-7   Using an ice bath to test the fuel temperature sensor.

FIGURE 12-8   A typical distributor-type diesel injection pump showing the pump, lines, and fuel filter.

diesel fuel is fed from a fill port to a high-pressure chamber. If a distributor-type injection pump is used, the fuel is forced out of the injection port to the correct injector nozzle through the high-pressure line. See Figure 12-8.

NOTE: Because of the very tight tolerances in a diesel engine, the smallest amount of dirt can cause excessive damage to the engine and to the fuel injection system.

Distributor Injection Pump

A distributor diesel injection pump is a high-pressure pump assembly with lines leading to each individual injector. The high-pressure lines between the distributor and the injectors must be the exact same length to ensure proper injection timing. The injection pump itself creates the injection advance needed for engine speeds above idle and the fuel is discharged into the lines. The high-pressure fuel causes the injectors to open. Due to the internal friction of the lines, there is a slight delay before fuel pressure opens the injector nozzle. See Figure 12-9.

NOTE: The lines expand some during an injection event. This is how timing checks are performed. The pulsing of the injector line is picked up by a probe used to detect the injection event similar to a timing light used to detect a spark on a gasoline engine.

High-Pressure Common Rail

Newer diesel engines use a fuel delivery system referred to as a **high-pressure common rail (HPCR)** design. Diesel fuel under high pressure, over 20,000 PSI (138,000 kPa), is applied to the injectors, which are opened by a solenoid controlled by the computer. Because the injectors are computer controlled, the combustion process can be precisely controlled to provide maximum engine efficiency with the lowest possible noise and exhaust emissions. See Figure 12-10 on page 166.

HEUI SYSTEM

Ford 7.3- and 6.0-liter diesels use a system Ford calls a **Hydraulic Electronic Unit Injection** system, or **HEUI** system. The components that replace the traditional mechanical injection pump include a high-pressure oil pump and reservoir, pressure regulator for the oil, and passages in the cylinder head for flow of fuel to the injectors.

Fuel is drawn from the tank by the tandem fuel pump, which circulates fuel at low pressure through the fuel filter/water separator/fuel heater bowl and then fuel is directed back to the fuel pump where fuel is pumped at high pressure into the cylinder head fuel galleries. The injectors, which are hydraulically actuated by the oil pressure from the high-pressure oil pump, are then fired by the power train control module (PCM). The control system for the fuel injectors is the PCM and the injectors are fired based on various inputs received by the PCM. See Figure 12-11 on page 166.

HEUI injectors rely on O-rings to keep fuel and oil from mixing or escaping, causing performance problems or engine damage. HEUI injectors use five O-rings. The three external O-rings should be replaced with updated O-rings if they fail. The two internal O-rings are not replaceable and if these fail,

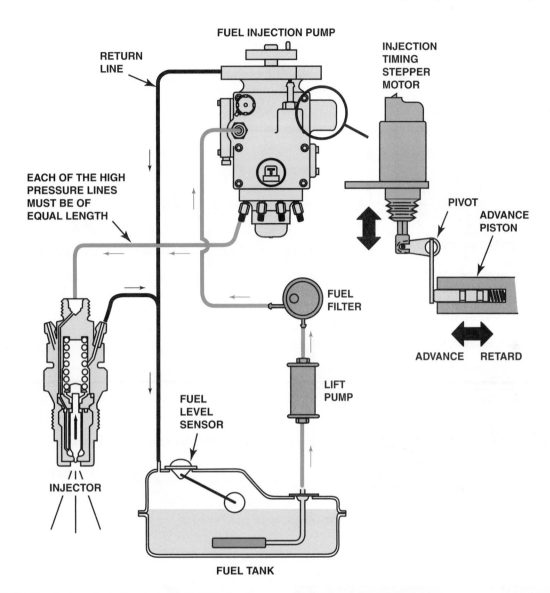

FIGURE 12-9   A schematic of a Stanadyne diesel fuel injection pump assembly showing all of the related components.

the injector or injectors must be replaced. The most common symptoms of injector O-ring trouble include:

- Oil getting in the fuel
- The fuel filter element turning black
- Long cranking times before starting
- Sluggish performance
- Reduction in power
- Increased oil consumption often accompanies O-ring problems or any fault that lets fuel in the oil

DIESEL INJECTOR NOZZLES

Diesel injector nozzles are spring-loaded closed valves that spray fuel directly into the combustion chamber or precom-

bustion chamber. Injector nozzles are threaded into the cylinder head, one for each cylinder, and are replaceable as an assembly.

The top of the injector nozzle has many holes to deliver an atomized spray of diesel fuel into the cylinder. Parts of a diesel injector nozzle include:

- **Heat shield.** This is the outer shell of the injector nozzle and has external threads where it seals in the cylinder head.
- **Injector body.** This is the inner part of the nozzle and contains the injector needle valve and spring, and threads into the outer heat shield.
- **Diesel injector needle valve.** This precision machined valve and the tip of the needle seal against the injector body when it is closed. When the valve is open, diesel fuel is sprayed into the combustion chamber. This passage is

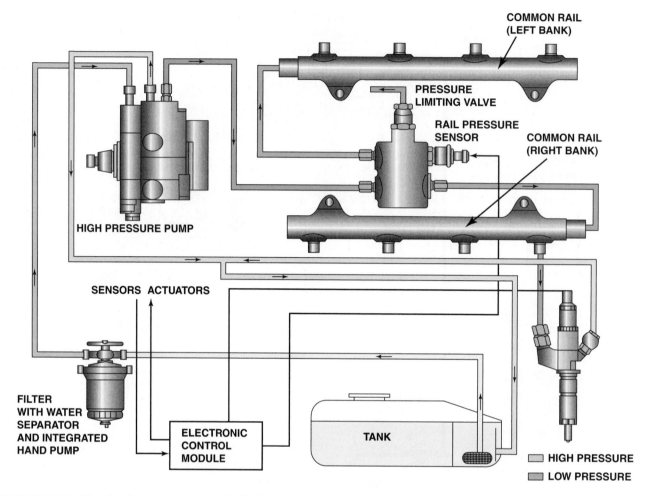

FIGURE 12-10 Overview of a computer-controlled high-pressure common rail V-8 diesel engine.

FIGURE 12-11 A HEUI injector from a Ford PowerStroke diesel engine. The grooves indicate the location of the O-rings.

TECH TIP

CHANGE OIL REGULARLY IN A FORD DIESEL ENGINE

Ford 7.3- and 6.0-liter diesel engines pump unfiltered oil from the sump to the high-pressure oil pump and then to the injectors. This means that not changing oil regularly can contribute to accumulation of dirt in the engine and will subject the fuel injectors to wear and potential damage as particles suspended in the oil get forced into the injectors.

TECH TIP

NEVER ALLOW A DIESEL ENGINE TO RUN OUT OF FUEL

If a gasoline-powered vehicle runs out of gasoline, it is an inconvenience and a possible additional expense to get some gasoline. However, if a vehicle equipped with a diesel engine runs out of fuel, it can be a major concern.

Besides adding diesel fuel to the tank, the other problem is getting all of the air out of the pump, lines, and injectors so the engine will operate correctly.

The procedure usually involves cranking the engine long enough to get liquid diesel fuel back into the system, but at the same time keeping cranking time short enough to avoid overheating the starter. Consult service information for the exact service procedure if the diesel engine is run out of fuel.

NOTE: Some diesel engines such as the General Motors Duramax V-8 are equipped with a priming pump located under the hood on top of the fuel filter. Pushing down and releasing the priming pump with a vent valve open will purge any trapped air from the system. Always follow the vehicle manufacturer's instructions.

controlled by a solenoid on diesel engines equipped with computer-controlled injection.

- **Injector pressure chamber.** The pressure chamber is a machined cavity in the injector body around the tip of the injector needle. Injection pump pressure forces fuel into this chamber, forcing the needle valve open.

DIESEL INJECTOR NOZZLE OPERATION

The electric solenoid attached to the injector nozzle is computer controlled and opens to allow fuel to flow into the injector pressure chamber. See Figure 12-12.

The diesel injector nozzle is mechanically opened by the high-pressure fuel delivered to the nozzle by the injector pump. The fuel flows down through a fuel passage in the injector body and into the pressure chamber. The high fuel pressure in the pressure chamber forces the needle valve upward, compressing the needle valve return spring and forcing the

FIGURE 12-12 Typical computer-controlled diesel engine fuel injectors.

needle valve open. When the needle valve opens, diesel fuel is discharged into the combustion chamber in a hollow cone spray pattern.

Any fuel that leaks past the needle valve returns to the fuel tank through a return passage and line.

GLOW PLUGS

Glow plugs are always used in diesel engines equipped with a precombustion chamber and may be used in direct injection diesel engines to aid starting. A **glow plug** is a heating element that uses 12 volts from the battery and aids in the starting of a cold engine. As the temperature of the glow plug increases, the resistance of the heating element inside increases, thereby reducing the current in amperes needed by the glow plugs.

Most glow plugs used in newer vehicles are controlled by the power train control module (PCM), which monitors coolant temperature and intake air temperature. The glow plugs are turned on or pulsed on or off depending on the temperature of the engine. The PCM will also keep the glow plug turned on after the engine starts to reduce white exhaust smoke (unburned fuel) and to improve idle quality after starting. See Figure 12-13.

The "wait to start" lamp will light when the engine and the outside temperature is low to allow time for the glow plugs to get hot. The "wait to start" lamp will not come on when the glow plugs are operating after the engine starts.

NOTE: The glow plugs are removed to test cylinder compression using a special high-pressure reading gauge.

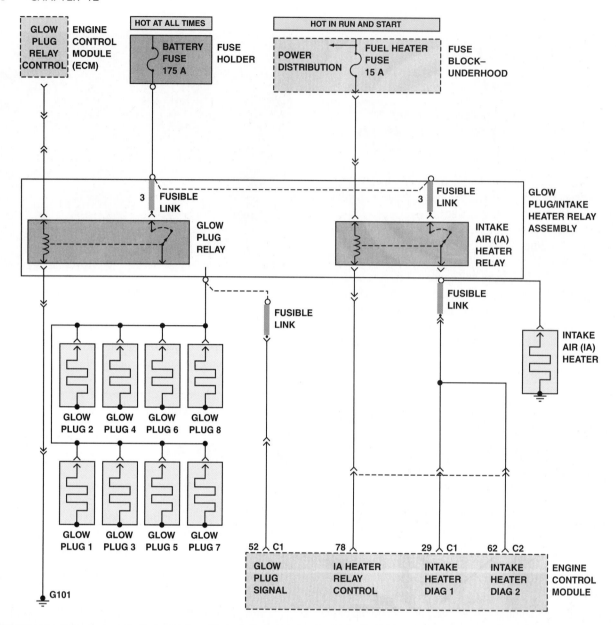

FIGURE 12-13 A schematic of a typical glow plug circuit. Notice that the relay for the glow plug and intake air heater are both computer controlled.

FREQUENTLY ASKED QUESTION

WHAT ARE DIESEL ENGINE ADVANTAGES AND DISADVANTAGES?

A diesel engine has several advantages compared to a similar size gasoline-powered engine including:

1. More torque output
2. Greater fuel economy
3. Long service life

A diesel engine has several disadvantages compared to a similar size gasoline-powered engine including:

1. Engine noise, especially when cold and/or at idle speed

2. Exhaust smell
3. Cold weather startability
4. A vacuum pump is needed to supply the vacuum needs of the heat, ventilation, and air conditioning system
5. Heavier than a gasoline engine (See Figure 12-14.)
6. Fuel availability
7. Usually turbocharged adding to the number of parts and increasing the cost of the engine. See Figure 12-15.

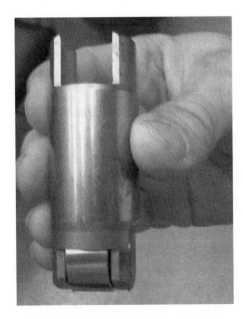

FIGURE 12-14   Roller lifter from a GM Duramax 6.6-liter V-8 diesel engine. Notice the size of this lifter compared to a roller lifter used in a gasoline engine.

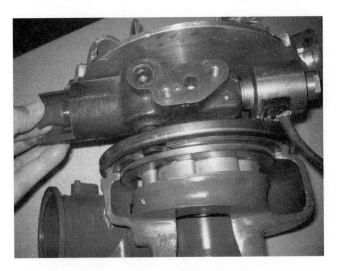

FIGURE 12-15   All light diesels built in the last ten years are turbocharged with most equipped with variable vane turbochargers.

FIGURE 12-16   A wire wound electrical heater is used to warm the intake air on some diesel engines.

FREQUENTLY ASKED QUESTION

WHAT IS THE BIG DEAL FOR THE NEED TO CONTROL VERY SMALL SOOT PARTICLES?

For many years soot or particulate matter (PM) was thought to be less of a health concern than exhaust emissions from gasoline engines. It was felt that the soot could simply fall to the ground without causing any noticeable harm to people or the environment. However, it was discovered that the small soot particulates when breathed in are not expelled from the lungs like larger particles but instead get trapped in the deep areas of the lungs where they accumulate.

ENGINE-DRIVEN VACUUM PUMP

Because a diesel engine is unthrottled, it creates very little vacuum in the intake manifold. Several engine and vehicle components operate using vacuum, such as the exhaust gas recirculation (EGR) valve and the heating and ventilation blend and air doors. Most diesels used in cars and light trucks are equipped with an engine-driven vacuum pump to supply the vacuum for these components.

HEATED INTAKE AIR

Some diesels, such as the General Motors 6.6-liter Duramax V-8, use an electrical heater wire to warm the intake air to help in cold weather starting and running. See Figure 12-16.

ACCELERATOR PEDAL POSITION SENSOR

Some light truck diesel engines are equipped with an electronic throttle to control the amount of fuel injected into the engine. Because a diesel engine does not use a throttle in the air intake, the only way to control engine speed is by controlling

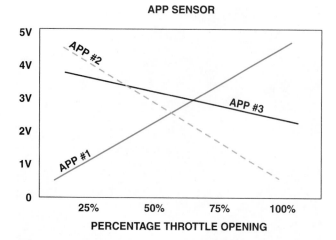

APP SENSOR

FIGURE 12-17 A typical accelerator pedal position (APP) sensor uses three different sensors in one package with each creating a different voltage as the accelerator is moved.

the amount of fuel being injected into the cylinders. Instead of a mechanical link from the accelerator pedal to the diesel injection pump, a throttle-by-wire system uses an accelerator pedal position sensor. To ensure safety, it consists of three separate sensors that change in voltage as the accelerator pedal is depressed. See Figure 12-17.

The computer checks for errors by comparing the voltage output of each of the three sensors inside the APP and compares them to what they should be if there are no faults. If an error is detected, the engine and vehicle speed are often reduced.

SOOT OR PARTICULATE MATTER

Soot particles may come directly from the exhaust tailpipe or they can also form when emissions of nitrogen oxide and various sulfur oxides chemically react with other pollutants suspended in the atmosphere. Such reactions result in the formation of ground-level ozone, commonly known as smog. Smog is the most visible form of what is generally referred to as particulate matter. Particulate matter refers to tiny particles of solid or semisolid material suspended in the atmosphere. This includes particles between 0.1 micron and 50 microns in diameter. The heavier particles, larger than 50 microns, typically tend to settle out quickly due to gravity. Particulates are generally categorized as follows:

- TSP, Total Suspended Particulate—Refers to all particles between 0.1 and 50 microns. Up until 1987, the EPA standard for particulates was based on levels of TSP.
- PM10—Particulate matter of 10 microns or less (approximately 1/6 the diameter of a human hair). EPA has a standard for particles based on levels of PM10.

- PM2.5—Particulate matter of 2.5 microns or less (approximately 1/20 the diameter of a human hair), also called "fine" particles. In July 1997, the EPA approved a standard for PM2.5.

In general, soot particles produced by diesel combustion fall into the categories of fine, that is, less than 2.5 microns and ultrafine, less than 0.1 micron. Ultrafine particles make up about 80% to 95% of soot.

DIESEL OXIDATION CATALYST (DOC)

Diesel oxidation catalyst (DOC) consists of a flow-through honeycomb-style substrate structure that is washcoated with a layer of catalyst materials, similar to those used in a gasoline engine catalytic converter. These materials include the precious metals platinum and palladium, as well as other base metals catalysts. Catalysts chemically react with exhaust gas to convert harmful nitrogen oxide into nitrogen dioxide, and to oxidize absorbed hydrocarbons. The chemical reaction acts as a combustor for the unburned fuel that is characteristic of diesel compression ignition. The main function of the DOC is to start a regeneration event by converting the fuel-rich exhaust gases to heat.

The DOC also reduces carbon monoxide, hydrocarbons, plus odor-causing compounds such as aldehydes and sulfur, and the soluble organic fraction of particulate matter. During a regeneration event, the Catalyst System Efficiency test will run. The engine control module (ECM) monitors this efficiency of the DOC by determining if the exhaust gas temperature sensor (EGT Sensor 1) reaches a predetermined temperature during a regeneration event.

DIESEL EXHAUST PARTICULATE FILTER (DPF)

The heated exhaust gas from the DOC flows into the diesel particulate filter (DPF), which captures diesel exhaust gas particulates (soot) to prevent them from being released into the atmosphere. This is done by forcing the exhaust through a porous cell which has a silicon carbide substrate with honeycomb-cell-type channels that trap the soot. The channels are washcoated with catalyst materials similar to those in the DOC filter. The main difference between the DPF and a typical catalyst filter is that the entrance to every other cell channel in the DPF substrate is blocked at one end. So instead of flowing directly through the channels, the exhaust gas is forced through the porous walls of the blocked channels and exits through the adjacent open-ended channels. This type of filter is also referred to as a "wall-flow" filter.

Soot particulates in the gas remain trapped on the DPF channel walls where, over time, the trapped particulate matter will begin to clog the filter. The filter must therefore be

FIGURE 12-18 A diesel exhaust particulate filter on a Cummins 6.7-liter diesel engine.

purged periodically to remove accumulated soot particles. The process of purging soot from the DPF is described as **regeneration.** See Figure 12-18.

Exhaust Gas Temperature Sensors

There are two exhaust gas temperature sensors that function in much the same way as engine temperature sensors. EGT Sensor 1 is positioned between the DOC and the DPF where it can measure the temperature of the exhaust gas entering the DPF. EGT Sensor 2 measures the temperature of the exhaust gas stream immediately after it exits the DPF.

The engine control module (ECM) monitors the signals from the EGT sensors as part of its calibrations to control DPF regeneration. The ECM supplies biased 5-volts to the signal circuit and a ground on the low reference circuit to EGT Sensor 1. When the EGT Sensor 1 is cold, the sensor resistance is high. As the temperature increases, the sensor resistance decreases. With high sensor resistance, the ECM detects a high voltage on the signal circuit. With lower sensor resistance, the ECM detects a lower voltage on the signal circuit. Proper exhaust gas temperatures at the inlet of the DPF are crucial for proper operation and for starting the regeneration process. Too high a temperature at the DPF will cause the DPF substrate to melt or crack. Regeneration will be terminated at temperatures above 1470°F (800°C). With too low a temperature, self-regeneration will not fully complete the soot-burning process.

DPF Differential Pressure Sensor (DPS)

The DPF **differential pressure sensor (DPS)** has two pressure sample lines:

- One line is attached before the DPF, labeled P1
- The other is located after the DPF, labeled P2

FIGURE 12-19 A differential pressure sensor showing the two hoses from the diesel exhaust particulate filter.

FREQUENTLY ASKED QUESTION

WHAT IS AN EXHAUST AIR COOLER?

An exhaust air cooler is simply a length of tubing with a narrower center section that acts as a venturi. The cooler is attached to the tailpipe with a bracket that provides a gap between the two. As hot exhaust rushes past the gap, the venturi effect draws surrounding air into the cooler and reduces the exhaust temperature. The cooler significantly lowers exhaust temperature at the tailpipe from a potential 788° to 806°F (420° to 430°C) to approximately 520°F (270°C).

The exact location of the DPS varies by vehicle model type (medium duty, pickup or van). By measuring P1 exhaust supply pressure from the DOC, and P2, post DPF pressure, the ECM can determine differential pressure, also referred to as "delta" pressure, across the DPF. Data from the DPF differential pressure sensor is used by the ECM to calibrate for controlling DPF exhaust system operation. See Figure 12-19.

Diesel Particulate Filter Regeneration

Soot particulates in the gas remain trapped on the DPF channel walls where, over time, the buildup of trapped particulate matter will begin to clog the filter. The filter must therefore be purged periodically to remove accumulated soot particles. The process of purging soot from the DPF by incineration is described as regeneration. When the temperature of the exhaust gas is increased sufficiently, the heat incinerates the soot particles trapped in the filter, leaving only residual ash from the engine's combustion of lubrication oil. The filter is effectively renewed.

The primary reason for soot removal is to prevent the buildup of exhaust back pressure. Excessive back pressure increases fuel consumption, reduces power output, and can potentially cause engine damage. There are a number of operational factors that can trigger the diesel engine control module to initiate a DPF regeneration sequence. The ECM monitors:

- Distance since last DPF regeneration
- Fuel used since last DPF regeneration
- Engine run time since last DPF regeneration
- Exhaust differential pressure across the DPF

DPF Regeneration Process

A number of engine components are required to function together for the regeneration process to be performed. ECM controls that impact DPF regeneration include late post-injections, engine speed, and adjusting fuel pressure. Adding late post-injection pulses provides the engine with additional fuel to be oxidized in the DOC which increases exhaust temperatures entering the DPF to about 900°F (500°C) and higher. The intake air valve acts as a restrictor that reduces air entry to the engine which increases engine operating temperature. The intake air heater may also be activated to warm intake air during regeneration.

The variable vane turbocharger also plays a role in achieving regeneration temperatures by reducing or increasing boost depending on engine load.

Types of DPF Regeneration

DPF regeneration can be initiated in a number of ways, depending on the vehicle application and operating circumstances. The two main regeneration types are:

- Passive
- Active

Passive Regeneration.   During normal vehicle operation when driving conditions produce sufficient load and exhaust temperatures, passive DPF regeneration may occur. This passive regeneration occurs without input from the ECM or the driver. A passive regeneration may typically occur while the vehicle is being driven at highway speed or towing a trailer.

Active Regeneration.   Active regeneration is commanded by the ECM when it determines that the DPF requires it to remove excess soot buildup and conditions for filter regeneration have been met. Active regeneration is usually not noticeable to the driver. The vehicle needs to be driven at speeds above 30 mph for approximately 20 to 30 minutes to complete a full regeneration. During regeneration, the exhaust gases reach temperatures above 1000°F (550°C). If a regeneration event is interrupted for any reason, it will continue where it left off (including the next drive cycle) when the conditions are met for regeneration. Active regeneration is for the most part transparent to the customer. There are times when regeneration is required, but the operating conditions do not meet the ECM's requirements, such as on a delivery vehicle that is driven on frequent short trips or subjected to extended idling conditions. In such cases, the ECM turns on a "regeneration required" indicator to notify the vehicle operator that the filter requires cleaning.

DPF Service Regeneration

Another active regeneration method, the "DPF Service Regeneration" is a useful tool for the dealership technician. The procedure would typically be used to clean the DPF when vehicle operating conditions did not allow the DPF to regenerate normally while the vehicle is driven. A service regeneration procedure can also be run in order to clean the DPF when there is an unknown amount of soot present. This might result from engine or engine control errors caused by a Charge Air Cooler leak or low compression. In these cases, a DTC P2463 would normally set, and the DPF would have 80 grams or less of accumulated soot. If over 100 grams of soot are present, P244B sets and a service light comes on to warn the driver.

FREQUENTLY ASKED QUESTION

WILL THE POST-INJECTION PULSES REDUCE FUEL ECONOMY?

Maybe. Due to the added fuel injection pulses and late fuel injection timing, an increase in fuel consumption may be noticed on the Driver Information Center (DIC) during the regeneration time period. A drop in overall fuel economy should not be noticeable.

Conditions for Running a DPF Service Regeneration

A service regeneration cannot be initiated if there are active diagnostic trouble codes (DTCs) present. Other conditions that the ECM checks are as follows:

- The battery voltage is greater than 10 volts.
- The engine speed is between 600 and 1,250 RPM.
- The brake pedal is in the released position.
- The accelerator pedal is in the released position.
- The transmission must be in park or neutral.
- The engine coolant temperature (ECT) is between 158°F (70°C) and 239°F (115°C).
- The vehicle's fuel tank level must be between 15% and 85% capacity. For safety, refueling should never be performed during the regeneration process.
- The exhaust gas temperature (EGT Sensors 1 and 2) must be less than 752°F (400°C).

CAUTION: To avoid extremely elevated exhaust temperatures, inspect the exhaust cooler vent located at the tailpipe and remove any debris or mud that would impede its operation.

1. DO NOT connect any shop exhaust removal hoses to the vehicle's tailpipe.
2. Park the vehicle outdoors and keep people, other vehicles, and combustible material a safe distance away from the vehicle during Service Regeneration.
3. Do not leave the vehicle unattended during Service Regeneration.

WARNING: Tailpipe outlet exhaust temperature will be greater than 572°F (300°C) during service regeneration. To help prevent personal injury or property damage from fire or burns, keep vehicle exhaust away from any object and people.

ASH LOADING

Regeneration will not burn off ash. Only the particulate matter (PM) is burned off during regeneration. Ash is a noncombustible by-product from normal oil consumption. Ash accumulation in the DPF will eventually cause a restriction in the particulate filter. To service an ash loaded DPF, the DPF will need to be removed from the vehicle and cleaned or replaced. Low ash content engine oil (API CJ-4) is required for vehicles with the DPF system. The CJ-4 rated oil is limited to 1% ash content.

DIESEL EXHAUST SMOKE DIAGNOSIS

While some exhaust smoke is considered normal operation for many diesel engines, especially older units, the cause of excessive exhaust smoke should be diagnosed and repaired.

Black Smoke

Black exhaust smoke is caused by incomplete combustion because of a lack of air or a fault in the injection system that could cause an excessive amount of fuel in the cylinders. Items that should be checked include the following:

- Check the fuel specific gravity (API gravity).
- Perform an injector balance test to locate faulty injectors using a scan tool.
- Check for proper operation of the engine coolant temperature (ECT) sensor.
- Check for proper operation of the fuel rail pressure (FRP) sensor.
- Check for restrictions in the intake or turbocharger.
- Check to see if the engine is using oil.

White Smoke

White exhaust smoke occurs most often during cold engine starts because the smoke is usually condensed fuel droplets. White exhaust smoke is also an indication of cylinder misfire on a warm engine. The most common causes of white exhaust smoke include:

- Inoperative glow plugs
- Low engine compression
- Incorrect injector spray pattern
- A coolant leak into the combustion chamber

Gray or Blue Smoke

Blue exhaust smoke is usually due to oil consumption caused by worn piston rings, scored cylinder walls, or defective valve stem seals. Gray or blue smoke can also be caused by a defective injector(s).

SCAN TOOL DIAGNOSIS

Diesel engines since the late 1980s have been computer controlled and are equipped with sensors and activators to control functions that were previously mechanically controlled. All light truck diesels since 1996 have also adhered to on-board diagnostic systems (second generation [OBD-II]). The use of a

FIGURE 12-20 A scan tool is used to retrieve diagnostic trouble codes and to perform injector balance tests.

scan tool to check for diagnostic trouble codes (DTCs) and to monitor engine operation is one of the first diagnostic steps. See Figure 12-20.

COMPRESSION TESTING

A compression test is fundamental for determining the mechanical condition of a diesel engine. Worn piston rings can cause low power and excessive exhaust smoke. A diesel engine should produce at least 300 PSI (2,068 kPa) of compression pressure and all cylinders should be within 50 PSI (345 kPa) of each other. See Figure 12-21.

GLOW PLUG RESISTANCE BALANCE TEST

Glow plugs increase in resistance as their temperature increases. All glow plugs should have about the same resistance when checked with an ohmmeter. A similar test of the resistance of the glow plugs can be used to detect a weak cylinder. This test is particularly helpful on a diesel engine that is not computer controlled. To test for even cylinder balance using glow plug resistance, perform the following on a warm engine.

1. Unplug, measure, and record the resistance of all of the glow plugs.
2. With the wires still removed from the glow plugs, start the engine.

FIGURE 12-21 A compression gauge designed for the higher compression rate of a diesel engine should be used when checking the compression.

3. Allow the engine to run for several minutes to allow the combustion inside the cylinder to warm the glow plugs.
4. Measure the plugs and record the resistance of all of the glow plugs.
5. The resistance of all of the glow plugs should be higher than at the beginning of the test. A glow plug that is in a cylinder that is not firing correctly will not increase in resistance as much as the others.
6. Another test is to measure exhaust manifold temperature at each exhaust port. Misfiring cylinders will run cold. This can be done with a contact or noncontact thermometer.

INJECTOR POP TESTING

A **pop tester** is a device used for checking a diesel injector nozzle for proper spray pattern. The handle is depressed and pop off pressure is displayed on the gauge. See Figure 12-22.

The spray pattern should be a hollow cone. This will vary depending on design. The nozzle should also be tested for leakage—dripping of the nozzle while under pressure. If the spray pattern is not correct, cleaning, repairing, or replacing of the injector nozzle may be necessary.

FIGURE 12-22   A typical pop tester used to check the spray pattern of a diesel engine injector.

TECH TIP

ALWAYS USE CARDBOARD TO CHECK FOR HIGH-PRESSURE LEAKS

If diesel fuel is found on the engine, a high-pressure leak could be present. When checking for a high-pressure leak, wear protective clothing including safety glasses and face shield plus gloves and long-sleeved shirt. Then use a piece of cardboard to locate the high-pressure leak. When a diesel is running, the pressure in the common rail and injector tubes can reach over 20,000 PSI. At these pressures the diesel fuel is atomized and cannot be seen but can penetrate the skin and cause personal injury. A leak will be shown as a dark area on the cardboard. When a leak is found, shut off the engine and locate the exact location of the leak without the engine running.

CAUTION: Sometimes a leak can actually cut through the cardboard, so use extreme care.

DIESEL EMISSION TESTING

The most commonly used diesel exhaust emission test used in state or local testing programs is called the **opacity** test. Opacity means the percentage of light that is blocked by the exhaust smoke.

- A 0% opacity means that the exhaust has no visible smoke and does not block light from a beam projected through the exhaust smoke.
- A 100% opacity means that the exhaust is so dark that it completely blocks light from a beam projected through the exhaust smoke.
- A 50% opacity means that the exhaust blocks half of the light from a beam projected through the exhaust smoke.

Snap Acceleration Test

In a snap acceleration test, the vehicle is held stationary with wheel chocks and brakes released as the engine is rapidly accelerated to high idle with the transmission in neutral while smoke emissions are measured. This test is conducted a minimum of six times and the three most consistent measurements are averaged together for a final score.

Rolling Acceleration Test

Vehicles with a manual transmission are rapidly accelerated in low gear from an idle speed to a maximum governed RPM while the smoke emissions are measured.

Stall Acceleration Test

Vehicles with automatic transmissions are held in a stationary position with the parking brake and service brakes applied while the transmission is placed in "drive." The accelerator is depressed and held momentarily while smoke emissions are measured.

The standards for diesels vary according to the type of vehicle and other factors, but usually include a 40% opacity or less.

TECH TIP

DO NOT SWITCH INJECTORS

In the past, it was common practice to switch diesel fuel injectors from one cylinder to another when diagnosing a dead cylinder problem. However, most high-pressure common rail systems used in new diesels use precisely calibrated injectors that should not be mixed up during service. Each injector has its own calibration number. See Figure 12-23.

FIGURE 12-23 The letters on the side of this injector on a Cummins 6.7-liter diesel indicate the calibration number for the injector.

SUMMARY

1. A diesel engine uses heat of compression to ignite the diesel fuel when it is injected into the compressed air in the combustion chamber.

2. There are two basic designs of combustion chambers used in diesel engines. Indirect injection (IDI) uses a pre-combustion chamber whereas a direct injection (DI) occurs directly into the combustion chamber.

3. The three phases of diesel combustion include:
   a. Ignition delay
   b. Rapid combustion
   c. Controlled combustion

4. The typical diesel engine fuel system consists of the fuel tank, lift pump, water-fuel separator, and fuel filter.

5. The engine-driven injection pump supplies high-pressure diesel fuel to the injectors.

6. The two most common types of fuel injection used in automotive diesel engines are:
   a. Distributor-type injection pump
   b. Common rail design where all of the injectors are fed from the same fuel supply from a rail under high pressure

7. Injector nozzles are either opened by the high-pressure pulse from the distributor pump or electrically by the computer on a common rail design.

8. Glow plugs are used to help start a cold diesel engine and help prevent excessive white smoke during warm-up.

9. The higher the cetane rating of diesel fuel, the more easily the fuel is ignited.

10. Most automotive diesel engines are designed to operate on grade #2 diesel fuel in moderate weather conditions.

11. The API specific gravity of diesel fuel should be 30 to 39 with a typical reading of 35 for #2 diesel fuel.

12. Diesel engines can be tested using a scan tool, as well as measuring the glow plug resistance or compression reading to determine a weak or nonfunctioning cylinder.

REVIEW QUESTIONS

1. What is the difference between direct injection and indirect injection?

2. What are the three phases of diesel ignition?

3. What are the two most commonly used types of automotive diesel injection systems?

4. Why are glow plugs kept working after the engine starts?

5. What is the advantage of using diesel fuel with a high cetane rating?

6. How is the specific gravity of diesel fuel tested?

CHAPTER QUIZ

1. How is diesel fuel ignited in a warm diesel engine?
   a. Glow plugs
   b. Heat of compression
   c. Spark plugs
   d. Distributorless ignition system

2. Which type of diesel injection produces less noise?
   a. Indirect injection (IDI)
   b. Common rail
   c. Direct injection
   d. Distributor injection

3. Which diesel injection system requires the use of a glow plug?
   a. Indirect injection (IDI)
   b. High-pressure common rail
   c. Direct injection
   d. Distributor injection

4. The three phases of diesel ignition include _____.
   a. Glow plug ignition, fast burn, slow burn
   b. Slow burn, fast burn, slow burn
   c. Ignition delay, rapid combustion, controlled combustion
   d. Glow plug ignition, ignition delay, controlled combustion

5. What fuel system component is used in a vehicle equipped with a diesel engine that is not usually used on the same vehicle when it is equipped with a gasoline engine?
   a. Fuel filter
   b. Fuel supply line
   c. Fuel return line
   d. Water-fuel separator

6. The diesel injection pump is usually driven by a _____.
   a. Gear off the camshaft
   b. Belt off the crankshaft
   c. Shaft drive off of the crankshaft
   d. Chain drive off of the camshaft

7. Which diesel system supplies high-pressure diesel fuel to all of the injectors all of the time?
   a. Distributor
   b. Inline
   c. High-pressure common rail
   d. Rotary

8. Glow plugs should have high resistance when _____ and lower resistance when _____.
   a. Cold/warm
   b. Warm/cold
   c. Wet/dry
   d. Dry/wet

9. Technician A says that glow plugs are used to help start a diesel engine and are shut off as soon as the engine starts. Technician B says that the glow plugs are turned off as soon as a flame is detected in the combustion chamber. Which technician is correct?
   a. Technician A only
   b. Technician B only
   c. Both Technicians A and B
   d. Neither Technician A nor B

10. What part should be removed to test cylinder compression on a diesel engine?
    a. An injector
    b. An intake valve rocker arm and stud
    c. An exhaust valve
    d. A glow plug

COOLING SYSTEM OPERATION AND DIAGNOSIS

OBJECTIVES

After studying Chapter 13, the reader will be able to:

1. Prepare for Engine Repair (A1) ASE certification test content area "D" (Lubrication and Cooling Systems Diagnosis and Repair).

2. Describe how coolant flows through an engine.

3. Discuss the operation of the thermostat.

4. Explain the radiator pressure cap purpose and function.

5. Describe the various types of antifreezes and how to recycle and discard used coolant.

6. Discuss how to diagnose cooling system problems.

KEY TERMS

Back Flushing (p. 202)
Bar (p. 190)
Bleed Holes (p. 194)
Bypass (p. 182)
Centrifugal Pump (p. 192)
Coolant Recovery System (p. 191)
Cooling Fins (p. 188)
Core Tubes (p. 188)
DEX-COOL (p. 185)
Embittered Coolant (p. 186)
Ethylene Glycol-Based Antifreeze (p. 184)
Hybrid Organic Additive Technology (HOAT) (p. 186)

Impeller (p. 192)
Inorganic Additive Technology (IAT) (p. 185)
Organic Additive Technology (OAT) (p. 185)
Parallel Flow System (p. 194)
Reverse Cooling (p. 192)
Scroll (p. 193)
Series Flow System (p. 194)
Series-Parallel Flow System (p. 194)
Silicone Coupling (p. 196)
Steam Slits (p. 194)
Surge Tank (p. 190)
Thermostatic Spring (p. 197)

COOLING SYSTEM PURPOSE AND FUNCTION

Satisfactory cooling system operation depends on the design and operating conditions of the system. The design is based on heat output of the engine, radiator size, type of coolant, size of water pump (coolant pump), type of fan, thermostat, and system pressure. Unfortunately, the cooling system is usually neglected until there is a problem. Proper routine maintenance can prevent problems.

The cooling system must allow the engine to warm up to the required operating temperature as rapidly as possible and then maintain that temperature. It must be able to do this when the outside air temperature is as low as $-30°F$ ($-35°C$) and as high as $110°F$ ($45°C$).

Peak combustion temperatures in the engine cycle run from $4,000°$ to $6,000°F$ ($2,200°$ to $3,300°C$). The combustion temperatures will *average* between $1,200°$ and $1,700°F$ ($650°$ and $925°C$). Continued temperatures as high as this would weaken engine parts, so heat must be removed from the engine. The cooling system keeps the head and cylinder walls at a temperature that is within the range for maximum efficiency. See Figure 13-1.

LOW-TEMPERATURE ENGINE PROBLEMS

Engine operating temperatures must be above a minimum temperature for proper engine operation. When the temperature is too low, there is not enough heat to properly vaporize

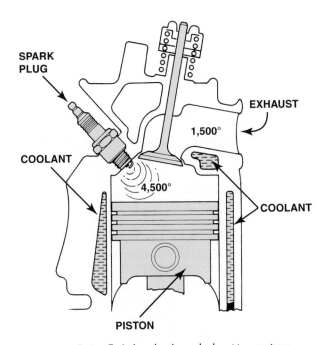

FIGURE 13-1   Typical combustion and exhaust temperatures.

TECH TIP

OVERHEATING CAN BE EXPENSIVE

A faulty cooling system seems to be a major cause of engine failure. Engine rebuilders often have nightmares about seeing their rebuilt engine placed back in service in a vehicle with a clogged radiator. Most engine technicians routinely replace the water pump and all hoses after an engine overhaul or repair. The radiator should also be checked for leaks and proper flow whenever the engine is repaired or replaced. Overheating is one of the most common causes of engine failure.

the fuel in the intake charge. As a result, extra fuel must be added to supply more volatile fuel to make a combustible mixture. The heavy, less volatile part of the gasoline does not vaporize, and so it remains as unburned liquid fuel. In addition, cool engine surfaces quench part of the combustion gases, leaving partially burned fuel as soot.

Gasoline combustion is a rapid oxidation process that releases heat as the hydrocarbon fuel chemically combines with oxygen from the air. *For each gallon of fuel used, moisture equal to a gallon of water is produced.* It is a part of this moisture that condenses and gets into the oil pan, along with unburned fuel and soot, and causes sludge formation. The condensed moisture combines with unburned hydrocarbons and additives to form carbonic acid, sulfuric acid, nitric acid, hydrobromic acid, and hydrochloric acid. These acids are responsible for engine wear by causing corrosion and rust within the engine. Rust occurs rapidly when the coolant temperature is below $130°F$ ($55°C$). Below $110°F$ ($45°C$), water from the combustion process will actually accumulate in the oil. High cylinder wall wear rates occur whenever the coolant temperature is below $150°F$ ($65°C$).

To reduce cold-engine problems and to help start engines in cold climates, most manufacturers offer block heaters as an option. These block heaters are plugged into household current (110 volts AC) and the heating element warms the coolant. See Figure 13-2.

HIGH-TEMPERATURE ENGINE PROBLEMS

Maximum temperature limits are required to protect the engine. High temperatures will oxidize the engine oil. This breaks the oil down, producing hard carbon and varnish. If high temperatures are allowed to continue, the carbon that is

(a)

(b)

FIGURE 13-2   (a) Loosening the screw that tightens the block heater element into the core plug opening in the side of the block. (b) Block heater element removed from block. The heater warms the coolant around the element, and the warm coolant rises, drawing cooler coolant up. As a result of this thermal circulation, all coolant surrounding the entire engine is warmed.

produced will plug piston rings. The varnish will cause the hydraulic valve lifter plungers to stick. High temperatures always thin the oil. Metal-to-metal contact within the engine will occur when the oil is too thin. This will cause high friction, loss of power, and rapid wear of the parts. Thinned oil will also get into the combustion chamber by going past the piston rings and through valve guides to cause excessive oil consumption.

The combustion process is very sensitive to temperature. High coolant temperatures raise the combustion temperatures to a point that may cause detonation and preignition to occur. These are common forms of abnormal combustion. If they are allowed to continue for any period of time, the engine will be damaged.

TECH TIP

ENGINE TEMPERATURE AND EXHAUST EMISSIONS

Many areas of the United States and Canada have exhaust emission testing. Hydrocarbon (HC) emissions are simply unburned gasoline. To help reduce HC emissions and be able to pass emission tests, be sure that the engine is at normal operating temperature. Vehicle manufacturers' definition of "normal operating temperature" includes the following:

1. Upper radiator hose is hot and pressurized.
2. Electric cooling fan(s) cycles twice.

Be sure that the engine is operating at normal operating temperature before testing for exhaust emissions. For best results, the vehicle should be driven about *20 miles* (32 kilometers) to be certain that the catalytic converter and engine oil, as well as the coolant, are at normal temperature. This is particularly important in cold weather. Most drivers believe that their vehicle will "warm up" if allowed to idle until heat starts flowing from the heater. The heat from the heater comes from the coolant. Most manufacturers recommend that idling be limited to a maximum of 5 minutes and that the vehicle should be warmed up by driving slowly after just a minute or two to allow the oil pressure to build.

COOLING SYSTEM DESIGN

Coolant flows through the engine, where it picks up heat. It then flows to the radiator, where the heat is given up to the outside air. The coolant continually recirculates through the cooling system, as illustrated in Figures 13-3 and 13-4. Its temperature rises as much as 15°F (8°C) as it goes through the engine; then it recools as it goes through the radiator. *The coolant flow rate may be as high as 1 gallon (4 liters) per minute for each horsepower the engine produces.*

Hot coolant comes out of the thermostat housing on the top of the engine. The engine coolant outlet is connected to the top of the radiator by the upper hose and clamps. The coolant in the radiator is cooled by air flowing through the radiator. As it cools, it moves from the top to the bottom of the radiator. Cool coolant leaves the lower radiator area through an outlet and lower hose, going into the inlet side of the water pump, where it is recirculated through the engine.

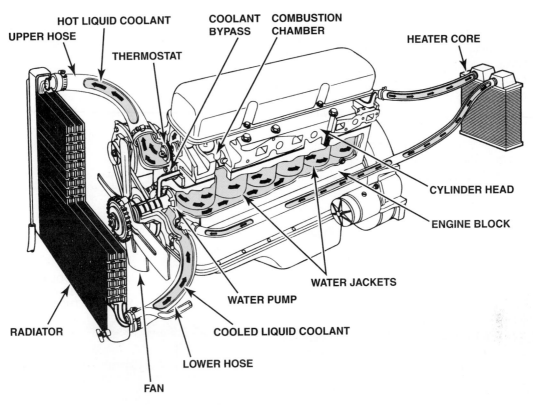

FIGURE 13-3   Coolant flow through a typical engine cooling system.

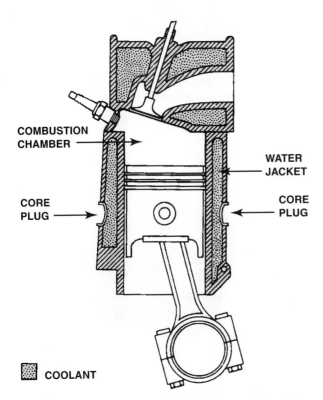

FIGURE 13-4   Coolant circulates through the water jackets in the engine block and cylinder head.

NOTE: Some newer engine designs such as Chrysler's 4.7 L V-8 and General Motors' 4.8, 5.3, 5.7, and 6.0 L V-8s place the thermostat on the inlet side of the water pump. As the cooled coolant hits the thermostat, the thermostat closes until the coolant temperature again causes it to open. Placing the thermostat in the inlet side of the water pump therefore reduces thermal cycling by reducing the rapid temperature changes that could cause stress in the engine, especially if aluminum heads are used with a cast-iron block.

Much of the cooling capacity of the cooling system is based on the functioning of the radiator. Radiators are designed for the maximum rate of heat transfer using minimum space. Cooling airflow through the radiator is aided by a belt- or electric motor-driven cooling fan.

THERMOSTAT TEMPERATURE CONTROL

There is a normal operating temperature range between low-temperature and high-temperature extremes. The thermostat controls the minimum normal temperature. The thermostat is a temperature-controlled valve placed at the engine coolant outlet. An encapsulated, wax-based, plastic-pellet heat sensor is located on the engine side of the thermostatic valve. As the engine warms, heat swells the heat sensor. See Figure 13-5.

A mechanical link, connected to the heat sensor, opens the thermostat valve. As the thermostat begins to open, it allows some coolant to flow to the radiator, where it is cooled. The remaining part of the coolant continues to flow through the bypass, thereby bypassing the thermostat and flowing back through the engine. See Figure 13-6.

The rated temperature of the thermostat indicates the temperature at which the thermostat starts to open. The thermostat is fully open at about 20°F higher than its opening temperature. See the following examples.

Thermostat Temperature Rating	Starts to Open	Fully Open
180°F (82°C)	180°F (82°C)	200°F (93°C)
195°F (91°C)	195°F (91°C)	215°F (107°C)

If the radiator, water pump, and coolant passages are functioning correctly, the engine should always be operating within the opening and fully open temperature range of the thermostat. See Figure 13-7.

NOTE: A **bypass** around the closed thermostat allows a small part of the coolant to circulate within the engine during warm-up. It is a small passage that leads from the engine side of the thermostat to the inlet side of the water pump. It allows some coolant to bypass the thermostat even when the thermostat is open. The bypass may be cast or drilled into the engine and pump parts. See Figures 13-8 and 13-9.

The bypass aids in uniform engine warm-up. Its operation eliminates hot spots and prevents the building of excessive coolant pressure in the engine when the thermostat is closed.

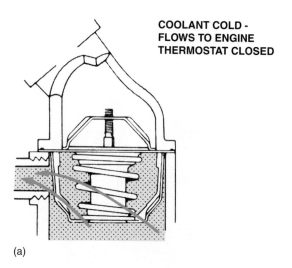

COOLANT COLD - FLOWS TO ENGINE THERMOSTAT CLOSED

(a)

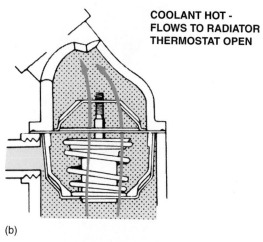

COOLANT HOT - FLOWS TO RADIATOR THERMOSTAT OPEN

(b)

FIGURE 13-6 (a) When the engine is cold, the coolant flows through the bypass. (b) When the thermostat opens, the coolant can flow to the radiator.

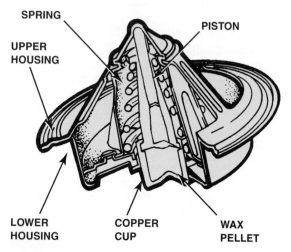

SPRING
PISTON
UPPER HOUSING
LOWER HOUSING
COPPER CUP
WAX PELLET

FIGURE 13-5 A cross-section of a typical wax-actuated thermostat showing the position of the wax pellet and spring.

FIGURE 13-7 A thermostat stuck in the open position caused the engine to operate too cold. The vehicle failed an exhaust emission test because of this defect.

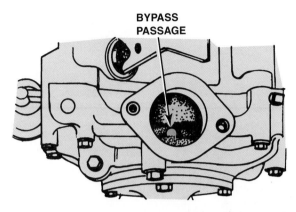

FIGURE 13-8 This internal bypass passage in the thermostat housing directs cold coolant to the water pump.

FIGURE 13-9 One type of cooling system external bypass.

TESTING THE THERMOSTAT

There are three basic methods that can be used to check the operation of the thermostat.

1. **Hot water method.** If the thermostat is removed from the vehicle and is closed, insert a 0.015-inch (0.4-millimeter) feeler gauge in the opening so that the thermostat will hang on the feeler gauge. The thermostat should then be suspended by the feeler gauge in a bath along with a thermometer. See Figure 13-10. The bath should be heated until the thermostat opens enough to release and fall from the feeler gauge. The temperature of the bath when the thermostat falls is the opening temperature of the

TECH TIP

DO NOT TAKE OUT THE THERMOSTAT!

Some vehicle owners and technicians remove the thermostat in the cooling system to "cure" an overheating problem. In some cases, removing the thermostat can *cause* overheating—not stop overheating. This is true for three reasons:

1. Without a thermostat the coolant can flow more quickly through the radiator. The thermostat adds some restriction to the coolant flow, and therefore keeps the coolant in the radiator longer. The presence of the thermostat thus ensures a greater reduction in the coolant temperature before it returns to the engine.
2. Heat transfer is greater with a greater difference between the coolant temperature and air temperature. Therefore, when coolant flow rate is increased (no thermostat), the temperature difference is reduced.
3. Without the restriction of the thermostat, much of the coolant flow often bypasses the radiator entirely and returns directly to the engine.

If overheating is a problem, removing the thermostat will usually not solve the problem. Remember, the thermostat controls the temperature of the engine coolant by opening at a certain temperature and closing when the temperature falls below the minimum rated temperature of the thermostat. If overheating occurs, two basic problems could be the cause:

1. The engine is producing too much heat for the cooling system to handle. For example, if the engine is running too lean or if the ignition timing is either excessively advanced or excessively retarded, overheating of the engine can result.
2. The cooling system has a malfunction or defect that prevents it from getting rid of its heat.

thermostat. If it is within 5°F (4°C) of the temperature stamped on the thermostat, the thermostat is satisfactory for use. If the temperature difference is greater, the thermostat should be replaced.

2. **Infrared pyrometer method.** An infrared pyrometer can be used to measure the temperature of the coolant near the thermostat. The area on the engine side of the thermostat should be at the highest temperature that

FIGURE 13-10 Setup used to check the opening temperature of a thermostat.

exists in the engine. A properly operating cooling system should cause the pyrometer to read as follows:

a. As the engine warms, the temperature reaches near thermostat opening temperature.

b. As the thermostat opens, the temperature drops just as the thermostat opens, sending coolant to the radiator.

c. As the thermostat cycles, the temperature should range between the opening temperature of the thermostat and 20°F (11°C) above the opening temperature.

> **NOTE:** If the temperature rises higher than 20°F (11°C) above the opening temperature of the thermostat, inspect the cooling system for a restriction or low coolant flow. A clogged radiator could also cause the excessive temperature rise.

3. Scan tool method. A scan tool can be used on many vehicles to read the actual temperature of the coolant as detected by the engine coolant temperature (ECT) sensor. Although the sensor or the wiring to and from the sensor may be defective, at least the scan tool can indicate what the computer "thinks" the engine coolant temperature is.

THERMOSTAT REPLACEMENT

An overheating engine may result from a faulty thermostat. An engine that does not get warm enough always indicates a faulty thermostat.

FIGURE 13-11 Some thermostats are an integral part of the housing. This thermostat and radiator hose housing is serviced as an assembly. Some thermostats simply snap into the engine radiator fill tube underneath the pressure cap.

To replace the thermostat, coolant will have to be drained from the radiator drain petcock to lower the coolant level below the thermostat. It is not necessary to completely drain the system. The upper hose should be removed from the thermostat housing neck; then the housing must be removed to expose the thermostat. See Figure 13-11.

The gasket flanges of the engine and thermostat housing should be cleaned, and the gasket surface of the housing must be flat. The thermostat should be placed in the engine with the sensing pellet *toward* the engine. Make sure that the thermostat position is correct, and install the thermostat housing with a new gasket.

> **CAUTION:** Failure to set the thermostat into the recessed groove will cause the housing to become tilted when tightened. If this happens and the housing bolts are tightened, the housing will usually crack, creating a leak.

The upper hose should then be installed and the system refilled. Install the proper size of radiator hose clamp.

ANTIFREEZE/COOLANT

Coolant is a mixture of antifreeze and water. Water is able to absorb more heat per gallon than any other liquid coolant. Under standard conditions, water boils at 212°F (100°C) and freezes at 32°F (0°C). *When water freezes, it increases in volume about 9%.* The expansion of the freezing water can easily crack engine blocks, cylinder heads, and radiators. All manufacturers recommend the use of **ethylene glycol-based antifreeze** mixtures for protection against this problem.

A curve depicting the freezing point as compared with the percentage of antifreeze mixture is shown in Figure 13-12.

It should be noted that the freezing point increases as the antifreeze concentration is increased above 60%. The normal mixture is 50% antifreeze and 50% water. Ethylene glycol antifreezes contain anticorrosion additives, rust inhibitors, and water pump lubricants.

At the maximum level of protection, an ethylene glycol concentration of 60% will absorb about 85% as much heat as will water. Ethylene glycol-based antifreeze also has a higher boiling point than water. See Figure 13-13.

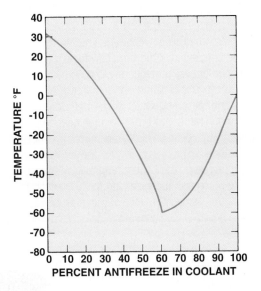

FIGURE 13-12   Graph showing the relationship of the freezing point of the coolant to the percentage of antifreeze used in the coolant.

If the coolant boils, it vaporizes and does not act as a cooling agent because it is not in liquid form and in contact with the cooling surfaces.

All coolants have rust and corrosion inhibitors to help protect the metals in the engine and cooling systems. Most conventional green antifreeze contains inorganic salts such as sodium silicate and phosphates.

TYPES OF COOLANT

Antifreeze coolant contains about 93% ethylene glycol plus water and additives. There are three basic types of coolant available today, which are grouped according to the additives used for rust and corrosion protection.

Inorganic Additive Technology (IAT)

Inorganic additive technology (IAT) is conventional coolant that has been used for over 50 years. The additives used to protect against rust and corrosion include phosphates and silicates. Silicates have been found to be the cause of erosive wear to water pump impellers. The color of IAT coolant is usually green. Phosphates in these coolants can cause deposits to form if used with water that is hard (contains minerals).

Organic Additive Technology (OAT)

Organic additive technology (OAT) antifreeze coolant contains ethylene glycol, but does not contain silicates or phosphates. This type of coolant is usually orange in color and was first developed by Havoline (called **DEX-COOL**) and used in General Motors vehicles starting in 1996. See Figure 13-14.

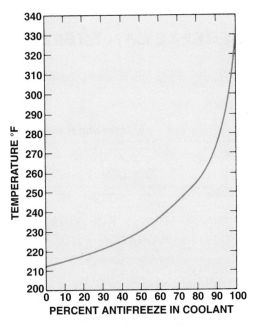

FIGURE 13-13   Graph showing how the boiling point of the coolant increases as the percentage of antifreeze in the coolant increases.

FIGURE 13-14   DEX-COOL coolant uses organic acid technology and is both silicate and phosphate free.

Hybrid Organic Additive Technology (HOAT)

A newer variation of this technology is called **hybrid organic additive technology (HOAT)** and is similar to the OAT-type antifreeze as it uses organic acid salts (carboxylates) additives that are not abrasive to water pumps, yet provide the correct pH. The pH of the coolant is usually above 11. A pH of 7 is neutral, with lower numbers indicating an acidic solution and higher numbers indicating a caustic solution. If the pH is too high, the coolant can cause scaling and reduce the heat transfer ability of the coolant. If the pH is too low, the resulting acidic solution could cause corrosion of the engine components exposed to the coolant. HOAT coolants can be green, orange, yellow, gold, pink, red, or blue.

Some samples of HOAT coolants include:

- VW/Audi pink—contains some silicates and an organic acid and is phosphate free
- Mercedes yellow—low amounts of silicate and no phosphate
- Ford yellow—low silicate, no phosphate, and dyed yellow for identification

FREQUENTLY ASKED QUESTION

WHAT IS "PET FRIENDLY" ANTIFREEZE?

Conventional ethylene glycol antifreeze, regardless of the additives used, is attractive to pets and animals because it is sweet. Ethylene glycol is fatal to any animal if swallowed and therefore, any spill should be cleaned up quickly. Another type of antifreeze coolant, called propylene glycol, is less attractive to pets and animals because it is less sweet, but is still harmful if swallowed. This type of coolant should not be mixed with ethylene glycol coolant.

NOTE: Some IAT coolant has been made bitter to deter animals and is called **embittered coolant.**

CAUTION: Some vehicle manufacturers do not recommend the use of propylene glycol coolant. Check the recommendation in the owner's manual or service information before using it in a vehicle.

REAL WORLD FIX

IF 50% IS GOOD, 100% MUST BE BETTER

A vehicle owner said that the cooling system of his vehicle would never freeze or rust. He said that he used 100% antifreeze (ethylene glycol) instead of a 50/50 mixture with water.

However, after the temperature dropped to −20°F (−29°C), the radiator froze and cracked. (Pure antifreeze freezes at about 0°F [−18°C].) After thawing, the radiator had to be repaired. The owner was lucky that the engine block did not also crack.

For best freeze protection with good heat transfer, use a 50/50 mixture of antifreeze and water. A 50/50 mixture of antifreeze and water is the best compromise between temperature protection and the heat transfer that is necessary for cooling system operation. Do not exceed 70% antifreeze (30% water). As the percentage of antifreeze increases, the boiling temperature increases, and freezing protection increases (up to 70% antifreeze), but the heat transfer performance of the mixture decreases.

- Honda blue—a special coolant that contains just one organic acid
- European blue—low silicates and no phosphates (*Glysantin* is the trade name associated with this coolant.)
- Asian red—contains no silicates but has some phosphate

ANTIFREEZE CAN FREEZE

An antifreeze and water mixture is an example wherein the freezing point differs from the freezing point of either pure antifreeze or pure water.

	Freezing Point
Pure water	32°F (0°C)
Pure antifreeze*	0°F (−18°C)
50/50 mixture	−34°F (−37°C)
70% antifreeze/30% water	−84°F (−64°C)

*Pure antifreeze is usually 95% ethylene glycol, 2% to 3% water, and 2% to 3% additives.

Depending on the exact percentage of water used, antifreeze, as sold in containers, freezes between −8°F and +8°F (−13°C and −22°C). Therefore, it is easiest just to remember that most antifreeze freezes at about 0°F (−18°C).

TECH TIP

IGNORE THE WIND-CHILL FACTOR

The wind-chill factor is a temperature that combines the actual temperature and the wind speed to determine the overall heat loss effect on exposed skin. Because it is the heat loss factor for exposed skin, the wind-chill temperature is *not* to be considered when determining antifreeze protection levels.

Although moving air does make it feel colder, the actual temperature is not changed by the wind and the engine coolant will not be affected by the wind-chill. Not convinced? Try this. Place a thermometer in a room and wait until a stable reading is obtained. Now turn on a fan and have the air blow across the thermometer. The temperature will not change.

FIGURE 13-15 Checking the freezing and boiling protection levels of the coolant using a hydrometer.

The boiling point of antifreeze and water is also a factor of mixture concentrations.

	Boiling Point at Sea Level	*Boiling Point with 15 PSI Pressure Cap*
Pure water	212°F (100°C)	257°F (125°C)
50/50 mixture	218°F (103°C)	265°F (130°C)
70/30 mixture	225°F (107°C)	276°F (136°C)

HYDROMETER TESTING

Coolant can be checked using a coolant hydrometer. The hydrometer measures the density of the coolant. The higher the density, the more concentration of antifreeze in the water. Most coolant hydrometers read the freezing point and boiling point of the coolant. See Figure 13-15.

If the engine is overheating and the hydrometer reading is near −50°F (−60°C), suspect that pure 100% antifreeze is present. For best results, the coolant should have a freezing point lower than −20°F (−29°C) and a boiling point above 234°F (112°C).

RECYCLING COOLANT

Coolant (antifreeze and water) should be recycled. Used coolant may contain heavy metals, such as lead, aluminum, and iron, which are absorbed by the coolant during its use in the engine.

Recycle machines filter out these metals and dirt and re-install the depleted additives. The recycled coolant, restored to be like new, can be reinstalled into the vehicle.

CAUTION: Most vehicle manufacturers warn that antifreeze coolant should not be reused unless it is recycled and the additives restored.

DISPOSING OF USED COOLANT

Used coolant drained from vehicles can usually be disposed of by combining it with used engine oil. The equipment used for recycling the used engine oil can easily separate the coolant from the waste oil. Check with recycling companies authorized by local or state governments for the exact method recommended for disposal in your area. See Figure 13-16.

REPLACING COOLANT

Coolant should be replaced according to the vehicle manufacturer's recommended interval. For most new vehicles using OAT or HOAT-type coolant, this interval may be every five years or 150,000 miles (241,000 km) whichever occurs first. Japanese-brand vehicles usually have a replacement interval of three years or 36,000 miles (58,000 km) whichever occurs

FIGURE 13-16   Used antifreeze coolant should be kept separate and stored in a leak-proof container until it can be recycled or disposed of according to federal, state, and local laws. Note that the storage barrel is placed inside another container to catch any coolant that may spill out of the inside barrel.

first. If the coolant is changed from long-life-type coolant to conventional IAT-type coolant, then the replacement interval needs to be changed to every two years or 24,000 miles (39,000 km), whichever occurs first. Always check service information for the exact recommended replacement interval for the vehicle being serviced.

RADIATOR

Two types of radiator cores are in common use in domestic vehicles—the serpentine fin core and the plate fin core. In each of these types the coolant flows through oval-shaped **core tubes.** Heat is transferred through the tube wall and soldered joint to **cooling fins.** The fins are exposed to airflow, which removes heat from the radiator and carries it away. See Figures 13-17 through 13-19.

Older automobile radiators were made from yellow brass. Since the 1980s, most radiators have been made from aluminum. These materials are corrosion resistant, have good heat-transferring ability, and are easily formed.

Core tubes are made from 0.0045- to 0.012-inch (0.1- to 0.3-millimeter) sheet brass or aluminum, using the thinnest possible materials for each application. The metal is rolled into round tubes and the joints are sealed with a locking seam.

The main limitation of heat transfer in a cooling system is in the transfer from the radiator to the air. Heat transfers from the water to the fins as much as seven times faster than heat transfers from the fins to the air, assuming equal surface exposure. The radiator must be capable of removing an amount of heat energy approximately equal to the heat energy of the

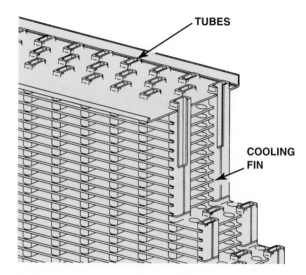

FIGURE 13-17   The tubes and fins of the radiator core.

power produced by the engine. *Each horsepower is equivalent to 42 Btu (10,800 calories) per minute.* As the engine power is increased, the heat-removing requirement of the cooling system is also increased.

With a given frontal area, radiator capacity may be increased by increasing the core thickness, packing more material into the same volume, or both. The radiator capacity may also be increased by placing a shroud around the fan so that more air will be pulled through the radiator.

NOTE: The lower air dam in the front of the vehicle is used to help direct the air through the radiator. If this air dam is broken or missing, the engine may overheat, especially during highway driving due to the reduced airflow through the radiator.

Radiator headers and tanks that close off the ends of the core were made of sheet brass 0.020 to 0.050 inch (0.5 to 1.25 millimeters) thick and now are made of molded plastic. When a transmission oil cooler is used in the radiator, it is placed in the outlet tank, where the coolant has the lowest temperature (Figure 13-20).

PRESSURE CAP

The filler neck is fitted with a pressure cap. The cap has a spring-loaded valve that closes the cooling system vent. This causes cooling pressure to build up to the pressure setting of the cap. At this point, the valve will release the excess pressure to prevent system damage. See Figure 13-21 on page 190.

Engine cooling systems are pressurized to raise the boiling temperature of the coolant. *The boiling temperature will increase by approximately 3°F (1.6°C) for each pound of increase in pressure.* At standard atmospheric pressure, water

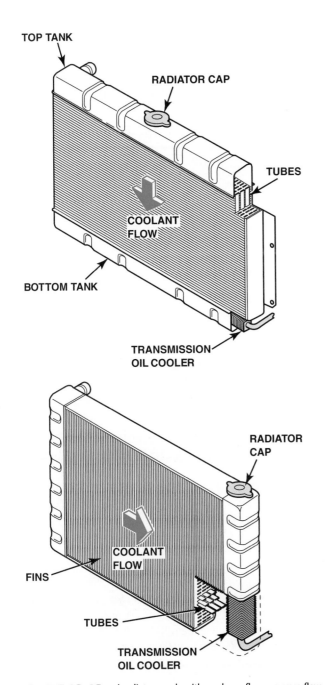

FIGURE 13-18 A radiator may be either a down-flow or a cross-flow type.

FIGURE 13-19 Cutaway of a typical radiator showing restriction of tubes. Changing antifreeze frequently helps prevent this of problem.

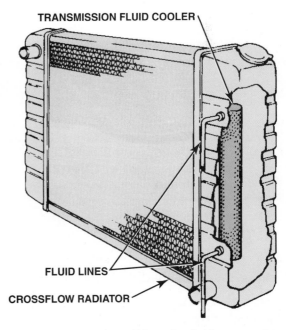

FIGURE 13-20 Many vehicles equipped with an automatic transmission use a transmission fluid cooler installed in one of the radiator tanks.

will boil at 212°F (100°C). With a 15 PSI (100 kPa) pressure cap, water will boil at 257°F (125°C), which is a maximum operating temperature for an engine.

The high coolant system temperature serves two functions.

1. It allows the engine to run at an efficient temperature, close to 200°F (93°C), with no danger of boiling the coolant.
2. The higher the coolant temperature, the more heat the cooling system can transfer. The heat transferred by the cooling system is proportional to the temperature difference between the coolant and the outside air. This

characteristic has led to the design of small, high-pressure radiators that are capable of handling large quantities of heat. For proper cooling, the system must have the right pressure cap correctly installed.

NOTE: The proper operation of the pressure cap is especially important at high altitudes. The boiling point of water is lowered by about 1°F for every 550-foot increase in altitude. Therefore in Denver, Colorado (altitude 5,280 feet), the boiling point of water is about 202°F, and at the top of Pike's Peak in Colorado (14,110 feet) water boils at 186°F.

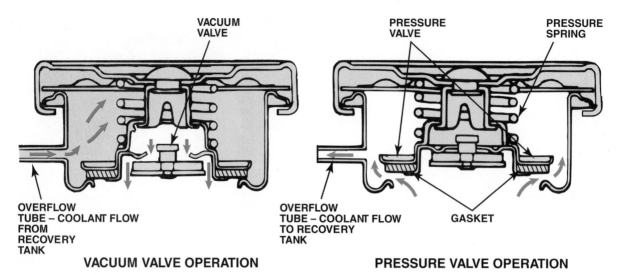

VACUUM VALVE OPERATION

PRESSURE VALVE OPERATION

FIGURE 13-21 The pressure valve maintains the system pressure and allows excess pressure to vent. The vacuum valve allows coolant to return to the system from the recovery tank.

FIGURE 13-22 Some vehicles use a surge tank, which is located at the highest level of the cooling system with a radiator cap.

TECH TIP

WORKING BETTER UNDER PRESSURE

A problem that sometimes occurs with a high-pressure cooling system involves the water pump. For the pump to function, the inlet side of the pump must have a lower pressure than its outlet side. If inlet pressure is lowered too much, the coolant at the pump inlet can boil, producing vapor. The pump will then spin the coolant vapors and not pump coolant. This condition is called *pump cavitation*. Therefore, a radiator cap could be the cause of an overheating problem. A pump will not pump enough coolant if not kept under the proper pressure for preventing vaporization of the coolant.

SURGE TANK

Some vehicles use a **surge tank,** which is located at the highest level of the cooling system and holds about 1 quart (1 liter) of coolant. A hose attaches to the bottom of the surge tank to the inlet side of the water pump. A smaller bleed hose attaches to the side of the surge tank to the highest point of the radiator. The bleed line allows some coolant circulation through the surge tank, and air in the system will rise below the radiator cap and be forced from the system if the pressure in the system exceeds the rating of the radiator cap. See Figure 13-22.

METRIC RADIATOR CAPS

According to the *SAE Handbook,* all radiator caps must indicate their nominal (normal) pressure rating. Most original equipment radiator caps are rated at about 14 to 16 PSI (97 to 110 kPa).

However, many vehicles manufactured in Japan or Europe have the radiator pressure indicated in a unit called a **bar.** One bar is the pressure of the atmosphere at sea level, or about 14.7 PSI. The following conversion can be used when replacing a radiator cap to make certain it matches the pressure rating of the original.

Bar or Atmospheres	Pounds per Square Inch (PSI)
1.1	16
1.0	15
0.9	13
0.8	12
0.7	10
0.6	9
0.5	7

NOTE: Many radiator repair shops use a 7-PSI (0.5-bar) radiator cap on a repaired radiator. A 7-PSI cap can still provide boil protection of 21°F (3°F × 7 PSI = 21°F) above the boiling point of the coolant. For example, if the boiling point of the antifreeze coolant is 223°F, 21°F is added for the pressure cap, and boilover will not occur until about 244°F (223°F + 21°F = 244°F). Even though this lower-pressure radiator cap does provide some protection and will also help protect the radiator repair, the coolant can still boil *before* the "hot" dash warning light comes on and, therefore, should not be used.

COOLANT RECOVERY SYSTEM

Excess pressure usually forces some coolant from the system through an overflow. Most cooling systems connect the overflow to a plastic reservoir to hold excess coolant while the system is hot. See Figure 13-23.

When the system cools, the pressure in the cooling system is reduced and a partial vacuum forms. This pulls the coolant from the plastic container back into the cooling system, keeping the system full. Because of this action, this system is called a **coolant recovery system.** The filler cap used on a coolant system without a coolant saver is fitted with a vacuum valve. This valve allows air to reenter the system as the system cools so that the radiator parts will not collapse under the partial vacuum.

PRESSURE TESTING

Pressure testing using a hand-operated pressure tester is a quick and easy cooling system test. The radiator cap is removed (engine cold!) and the tester is attached in the place of the radiator cap. By operating the plunger on the pump, the entire cooling system is pressurized. See Figure 13-24.

(a)

(b)

FIGURE 13-24   (a) Using a hand-operated pressure tester to pressurize the entire cooling system. (b) Notice the coolant leaking out of a hole in the radiator hose. This is the reason why the owner of this minivan noticed a "hot coolant" smell.

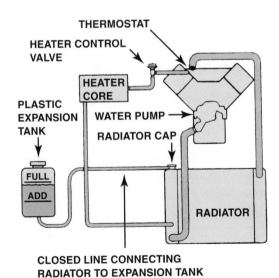

FIGURE 13-23   The level in the coolant recovery system raises and lowers with engine temperature.

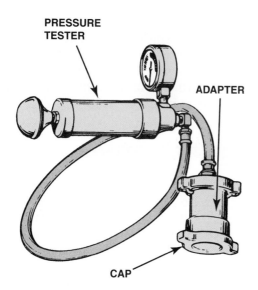

FIGURE 13-25   The pressure cap should be checked for proper operation using a pressure tester as part of the cooling system diagnosis.

CAUTION: Do not pump up the pressure beyond that specified by the vehicle manufacturer. Most systems should not be pressurized beyond 14 PSI (100 kPa). If a greater pressure is used, it may cause the water pump, radiator, heater core, or hoses to fail.

If the cooling system is free from leaks, the pressure should stay and not drop. If the pressure drops, look for evidence of leaks anywhere in the cooling system including:

1. Heater hoses
2. Radiator hoses
3. Radiator
4. Heat core
5. Cylinder head
6. Core plugs in the side of the block or cylinder head

Pressure testing should be performed whenever there is a leak or suspected leak. The pressure tester can also be used to test the radiator cap. An adapter is used to connect the pressure tester to the radiator cap. Replace any cap that will not hold pressure. See Figure 13-25.

COOLANT DYE LEAK TESTING

One of the best methods to check for a coolant leak is to use a fluorescent dye in the coolant. Use a dye designed for coolant. Operate the vehicle with the dye in the coolant until the engine reaches normal operating temperature. Use a black light to inspect all areas of the cooling system. When there is a leak, it will be easy to spot because the dye in the coolant

TECH TIP

USE DISTILLED WATER IN THE COOLING SYSTEM

Two technicians are discussing refilling the radiator after changing antifreeze. One technician says that distilled water is best to use because it does not contain minerals that can coat the passages of the cooling system. The other technician says that any water that is suitable to drink can be used in a cooling system. Both technicians are correct. If water contains minerals, however, it can leave deposits in the cooling system that could prevent proper heat transfer. Because the mineral content of most water is unknown, distilled water, which has no minerals, is better to use. Although the cost of distilled water must be considered, the amount of water required (usually about 2 gallons [8 liters] or less of water) makes the expense minor in comparison with the cost of radiator or cooling system failure.

---

will be seen as bright green. See Figure 13-26 for a cooling system inspection checklist that can be used to help locate cooling system–related problems.

WATER PUMP OPERATION

The water pump (also called a coolant pump) is driven by a belt from the crankshaft or driven by the camshaft. Coolant recirculates from the radiator to the engine and back to the radiator. Low-temperature coolant leaves the radiator by the bottom outlet. It is pumped into the warm engine block, where it picks up some heat. From the block, the warm coolant flows to the hot cylinder head, where it picks up more heat.

NOTE: Some engines use **reverse cooling**. This means that the coolant flows from the radiator to the cylinder head(s) before flowing to the engine block.

Water pumps are not positive displacement pumps. The water pump is a **centrifugal pump** that can move a large volume of coolant without increasing the pressure of the coolant. The pump pulls coolant in at the center of the **impeller.** Centrifugal force throws the coolant outward so

COOLING SYSTEM INSPECTION CHECKLIST

Drive Belts

❑ Glazing, deterioration, cracks, fraying, or other damage
❑ Age, replace every 4 years
❑ Pulley alignment
❑ Tension

Hoses

❑ Hardness, cracks, brittleness, cuts, or other damage
❑ Sponginess or interior damage
❑ Loose connections or leakage
❑ Age, replace every 4 years

Coolant Leakage

❑ Core plugs
❑ Water pump shaft seal
❑ Water pump gaskets
❑ Thermostat gasket
❑ Hose connections

Radiator

❑ Leaks or corrosion at the tank seams or on the radiator tubes
❑ Clogged or bent radiator core fins
❑ Blocked air intake paths
❑ Loose or missing mounting bolts
❑ Coolant recovery tank installation
❑ Coolant level and concentration
❑ Coolant age, replace every 2 years
❑ Rust, oil, or other coolant contamination
❑ Pressure test

Radiator Cap

❑ Secure filler neck fit
❑ Correct pressure rating
❑ Brittle or damaged seal
❑ Sufficient spring action
❑ Pressure test

Heater Assembly

❑ Rust or corrosion on the core
❑ Hose connections
❑ Hose condition
❑ Heater control valve operation, leakage, and mounting
❑ Secure core assembly mounting
❑ Coolant leakage
❑ Condition of the air ducts

Water Pump

❑ Coolant leakage at the shaft
❑ Coolant leakage at the gasket
❑ Secure hose connections
❑ Pulley and belt alignment
❑ Excessive play

Radiator Fan

❑ Bent or cracked fan blades
❑ Binding between the fan and shaft
❑ Fan clutch or electric fan operation

Fan Shrouds and Air Deflectors

❑ Location and mounting
❑ Condition
❑ Clearance

Unusual Noises

❑ Engine thump—coolant flow restriction
❑ Screeching—loose drive belt or bad water pump bearing
❑ Buzz or whistle—poor radiator cap seal or vibrating fan shroud
❑ Ringing or grinding—water pump shaft bearing, loose pulley, or tensioner bearing
❑ Gurgling radiator—plugged radiator or air in the coolant

FIGURE 13-26 Cooling system inspection checklist.

that it is discharged at the impeller tips. This can be seen in Figure 13-27.

As engine speeds increase, more heat is produced by the engine and more cooling capacity is required. The pump impeller speed increases as the engine speed increases to provide extra coolant flow at the very time it is needed.

Coolant leaving the pump impeller is fed through a **scroll.** The scroll is a smoothly curved passage that changes the fluid flow direction with minimum loss in velocity. The scroll is connected to the front of the engine so as to direct the coolant into the engine block. On V-type engines, two outlets are usually used, one for each cylinder bank. Occasionally,

SCROLL

FIGURE 13-27   Coolant flow through the impeller and scroll of a coolant pump for a V-type engine.

FREQUENTLY ASKED QUESTION

HOW MUCH COOLANT CAN A WATER PUMP PUMP?

A typical water pump can move a maximum of about 7,500 gallons (28,000 liters) of coolant per hour, or re-circulate the coolant in the engine over 20 times per minute. This means that a water pump could be used to empty a typical private swimming pool in an hour! The slower the engine speed, the less power is consumed by the water pump. However, even at 35 miles per hour (56 kilometers per hour), the typical water pump still moves about 2,000 gallons (7,500 liters) per hour or 1/2 gallon (2 liters) per second! See Figure 13-28.

FIGURE 13-28   A demonstration engine running on a stand, showing the amount of coolant flow that actually occurs through the cooling system.

diverters are necessary in the water pump scroll to equalize coolant flow between the cylinder banks of a V-type engine to equalize the cooling.

COOLANT FLOW IN THE ENGINE

Coolant flows through the engine in one of two ways—parallel or series. In the **parallel flow system,** coolant flows into the block under pressure and then crosses the gasket to the head through main coolant passages beside *each* cylinder. The gasket openings of a parallel system are shown in Figure 13-29.

In the **series flow system,** the coolant flows around all the cylinders on each bank. All the coolant flows to the *rear* of the block, where large main coolant passages allow the coolant to flow across the gasket. Figure 13-30 shows the main coolant passages.

The coolant then enters the rear of the heads. In the heads, the coolant flows forward to an outlet at the *highest point* in the engine cooling passage. This is usually located at the front of the engine. The outlet is either on the heads or in the intake manifold. Some engines use a combination of these two coolant flow systems and call it a **series-parallel flow system.** Any steam that develops will go directly to the top of the radiator. In series flow systems, **bleed holes** or **steam slits** in the gasket, block, and head perform the function of letting out the steam.

The coolant can also be directed through an oil filter adapter to help warm the engine oil when the engine is first started in cold weather as well as cool the engine oil when the oil is hot. See Figure 13-31.

WATER PUMP SERVICE

A worn impeller on a water pump can reduce the amount of coolant flow through the engine. See Figure 13-32. If the seal of the water pump fails, coolant will leak out of the hole as seen in Figure 13-33 on page 196. The hole allows coolant to escape without getting trapped and forced into the water pump bearing assembly.

If the bearing is defective, the pump will usually be noisy and will have to be replaced. Before replacing a water pump that has failed because of a loose or noisy bearing, be sure to do all of the following:

1. Check belt tension.
2. Check for bent fan.
3. Check fan for balance.

If the water pump drive belt is too tight, excessive force may be exerted against the pump bearing. If the cooling fan is

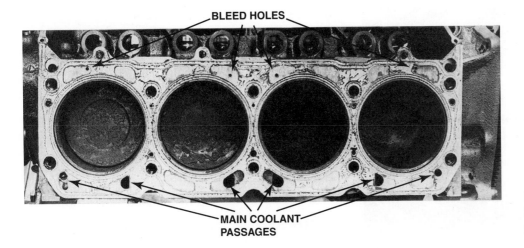

BLEED HOLES

MAIN COOLANT
PASSAGES

FIGURE 13-29
Gasket openings for a cooling system with a parallel type of flow.

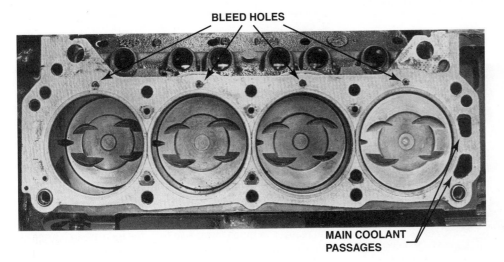

BLEED HOLES

MAIN COOLANT
PASSAGES

FIGURE 13-30
Gasket openings for a series-type cooling system.

OIL COOLER

FIGURE 13-31   An engine oil cooler. Coolant lines connect to the oil filter adapter to transfer heat from the hot engine oil to the cooling system. Because the coolant usually reaches operating temperature before the oil during cold weather, this cooler can also heat the cold engine oil so it reaches normal operating temperature quicker, thereby helping to reduce engine wear.

FIGURE 13-32   This severely corroded water pump could not circulate enough to keep the engine cool. As a result, the engine overheated and blew a head gasket.

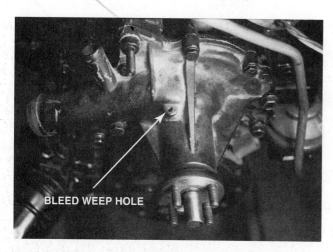

FIGURE 13-33 The bleed weep hole in the water pump allows coolant to leak out of the pump and not be forced into the bearing. If the bearing failed, more serious damage could result.

FIGURE 13-34 A cutaway of a typical water pump showing the long bearing assembly and the seal. The weep hole is located between the seal and the bearing. If the seal fails, then coolant flows out of the weep hole to prevent the coolant from damaging the bearing.

bent or out of balance, the resulting vibration can damage the water pump bearing. See Figure 13-34.

COOLING FANS

Air is forced across the radiator core by a cooling fan. On older engines used in rear-wheel-drive vehicles, it is attached to a fan hub that is pressed on the water pump shaft.

Many installations with rear-wheel drive and all transverse engines drive the fan with an electric motor. See Figure 13-35.

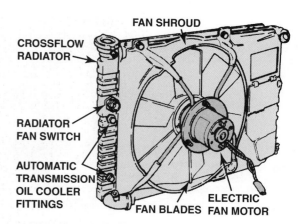

FIGURE 13-35 A typical electric cooling fan.

NOTE: Most electric cooling fans are computer controlled. To save energy, most cooling fans are turned off whenever the vehicle is traveling faster than 35 mph (55 km/h). The ram air from the vehicle's traveling at that speed should be enough to keep the radiator cool. Of course, if the computer senses that the temperature is still too high, the computer will turn on the cooling fan, to "high," if possible, in an attempt to cool the engine to avoid severe engine damage.

The fan is designed to move enough air at the lowest fan speed to cool the engine when it is at its highest coolant temperature. The fan shroud is used to increase the cooling system efficiency. The horsepower required to drive the fan increases at a much faster rate than the increase in fan speed. Higher fan speeds also increase fan noise. Fans with flexible plastic or flexible steel blades have been used. These fans have high blade angles that pull a high volume of air when turning at low speeds. As the fan speed increases, the fan blade angle flattens, reducing the horsepower required to rotate the blade at high speeds. See Figure 13-36.

THERMOSTATIC FANS

Since the early 1980s, most cooling fans have been computer-controlled electric motor units. On some rear-wheel-drive vehicles, a thermostatic cooling fan is driven by a belt from the crankshaft. It turns faster as the engine turns faster. Generally, the engine is required to produce more power at higher speeds. Therefore, the cooling system will also transfer more heat. Increased fan speed aids in the required cooling. Engine heat also becomes critical at low engine speeds in traffic where the vehicle moves slowly.

The thermal fan is designed so that it uses little power at high engine speeds and minimizes noise. The thermal fan has a **silicone coupling** fan drive mounted between the drive pulley and the fan.

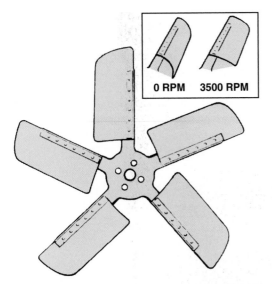

FIGURE 13-36 Flexible cooling fan blades change shape as the engine speed changes.

NOTE: Whenever diagnosing an overheating problem, look carefully at the cooling fan. If silicone is leaking, then the fan may not be able to function correctly and should be replaced.

A second type of thermal fan has a **thermostatic spring** added to the silicone coupling fan drive. The thermostatic spring operates a valve that allows the fan to freewheel when the radiator is cold. As the radiator warms to about 150°F (65°C), the air hitting the thermostatic spring will cause the spring to change its shape. The new shape of the spring opens a valve that allows the drive to operate like the silicone coupling drive. When the engine is very cold, the fan may operate at high speeds for a short time until the drive fluid warms slightly. The silicone fluid will then flow into a reservoir to let the fan speed drop to idle. See Figure 13-37.

ELECTRONICALLY CONTROLLED COOLING FAN

Many rear-wheel-drive vehicles use an electric cooling fan. For example, a typical GM engine cooling fan system consists of one cooling fan and two relays. The cooling fan has 2 windings in the motor. One winding is for low speed and the other winding is for high speed. Voltage is supplied to the relays through the 30-ampere cooling fan 1 and 30-ampere cooling fan 2 fuses. The engine control module (ECM) controls the low-speed fan operation by grounding the cool fan 1 relay control circuit. When the cooling fan 1 relay is energized, voltage is sent to the cooling fan low-speed winding. The ECM controls the high-speed fan operation by grounding the cool fan 2 relay control circuit.

TECH TIP

CAUSE AND EFFECT

A common cause of overheating is an inoperative cooling fan. Most front-wheel-drive vehicles and many rear-wheel-drive vehicles use electric motor-driven cooling fans. A fault in the cooling fan circuit often causes overheating during slow city-type driving.

Even slight overheating can soften or destroy rubber vacuum hoses and gaskets. The gaskets most prone to overheating damage are rocker cover (valve cover) and intake manifold gaskets. Gasket and/or vacuum hose failure often results in an air (vacuum) leak that leans the air–fuel mixture. The resulting lean mixture burns hotter in the cylinders and contributes to the overheating problem.

The vehicle computer can often compensate for a minor air leak (vacuum leak), but more severe leaks can lead to driveability problems; especially idle quality problems. If the leak is severe enough, a lean diagnostic trouble code (DTC) may be present. If a lean code is not set, the vehicle's computer may indicate a defective or out-of-range MAP sensor code in diagnostics.

Therefore, a typical severe engine problem can often be traced back to a simple, easily repaired, cooling system–related problem.

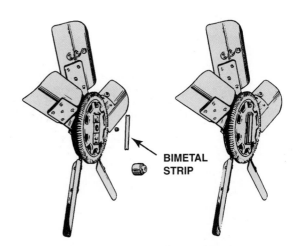

FIGURE 13-37 The bimetallic temperature sensor spring controls the amount of silicone that is allowed into the drive unit, which controls the speed of the fan.

When the cooling fan 2 relay is energized, voltage is sent to the cooling fan high-speed winding. The cooling fan motor has its own ground circuit. The ECM commands low-speed fans ON under the following conditions:

- Engine coolant temperature (ECT) exceeds approximately 223°F (106°C).
- A/C refrigerant pressure exceeds 190 PSI (1,310 kPa).

After the vehicle is shut off, the ECT at key-off is greater than 140°C (284°F) and system voltage is more than 12 volts. The fans will stay on for approximately 3 minutes. The ECM commands high-speed fans ON under the following conditions:

- ECT reaches 230°F (110°C).
- A/C refrigerant pressure exceeds 240 PSI (1,655 kPa).
- When certain diagnostic trouble codes (DTCs) set.

To prevent a fan from cycling ON and OFF excessively at idle, the fan may not turn OFF until the ignition switch is moved to the OFF position or the vehicle speed exceeds approximately 10 mph.

Electric Cooling Fan (Trailblazer)

The Chevrolet Trailblazer and similar vehicles are equipped with a cooling fan that is ECM controlled. The fan relay is supplied with a pulse width modulation (PWM) signal (12 to 14 volts) to control fan operation by controlling the fan clutch supply voltage circuit. See Figure 13-38. The power train control module (PCM) uses a PWM signal to control the speed of the cooling fan by controlling the position of the oil control valve inside the clutch. If the cooling fan RPM is too high when the PCM is commanding 0%, DTC P0495 will set.

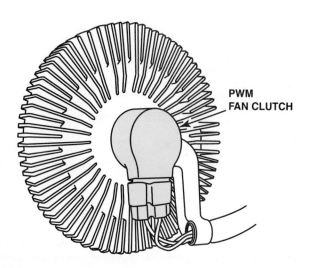

PWM FAN CLUTCH

FIGURE 13-38 A pulse-width modulated (PWM) fan clutch is used on some rear-wheel-drive vehicles, such as the Chevrolet Trailblazer.

HEATER CORE

Most of the heat absorbed from the engine by the cooling system is wasted. Some of this heat, however, is recovered by the vehicle heater. Heated coolant is passed through tubes in the small core of the heater. Air is passed across the heater fins and is then sent to the passenger compartment. In some vehicles, the heater and air conditioning work in series to maintain vehicle compartment temperature. See Figure 13-39.

HEATER PROBLEM DIAGNOSIS

When the vehicle's heater does not produce the desired amount of heat, many owners and technicians replace the thermostat before doing any other troubleshooting. It is true that a defective thermostat is the reason for the *engine* not to reach normal operating temperature. Many other causes besides a defective thermostat can result in lack of

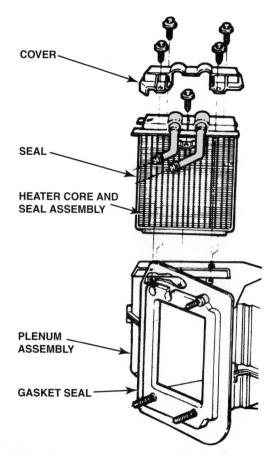

COVER

SEAL

HEATER CORE AND SEAL ASSEMBLY

PLENUM ASSEMBLY

GASKET SEAL

FIGURE 13-39 A heater core is similar to a small radiator but is mounted within the dash.

heat from the heater. To determine the exact cause, follow this procedure:

Step 1   After the engine has been operated, feel the upper radiator hose. If the engine is up to proper operating temperature, the upper radiator hose should be too hot for you to keep your hand on it. The hose should also be pressurized.

a. If the hose is not hot enough, replace the thermostat.

b. If the hose is not pressurized, test it. Replace the radiator pressure cap if it will not hold the specified pressure.

c. If okay, see step 2.

Step 2   With the engine running, feel both heater hoses. (The heater should be set to the maximum heat position.) Both hoses should be too hot to hold. If both hoses are warm (not hot) or cool, check the heater control valve for proper operation. If one hose is hot and the other (return) is just warm or cool, remove both hoses from the heater core or engine and flush the heater core with water from a garden hose.

NOTE: Heat from the heater that "comes and goes" is most likely the result of low coolant level. Usually with the engine at idle, there is enough coolant flow through the heater at higher engine speeds, however, the circulation of coolant through the heads and block prevents sufficient flow through the heater.

COOLANT TEMPERATURE WARNING LIGHT

Most vehicles are equipped with a heat sensor for the engine operating temperature. If the "hot" light comes on during driving (or the temperature gauge goes into the red danger zone), then the coolant temperature is about 250° to 258°F (120° to 126°C), which is still *below* the boiling point of the coolant (assuming a properly operating pressure cap and system). If this happens, follow these steps:

Step 1   Shut off the air conditioning and turn on the heater. The heater will help rid the engine of extra heat. Set the blower speed to high.

Step 2   If possible, shut the engine off and let it cool. (This may take over an hour.)

Step 3   Never remove the radiator cap when the engine is hot.

Step 4   Do *not* continue to drive with the hot light on, or serious damage to your engine could result.

Step 5   If the engine does not feel or smell hot, it is possible that the problem is a faulty hot light sensor or gauge. Continue to drive, but to be safe, stop occasionally and check for any evidence of overheating or coolant loss.

REAL WORLD FIX

HIGHWAY OVERHEATING

A vehicle owner complained of an overheating vehicle, but the problem occurred only while driving at highway speeds. The vehicle, equipped with a General Motors *QUAD 4*, would run in a perfectly normal manner in city-driving situations.

The technician flushed the cooling system and replaced the radiator cap and the water pump, thinking that restricted coolant flow was the cause of the problem. Further testing revealed coolant spray out of one cylinder when the engine was turned over by the starter with the spark plugs removed.

A new head gasket solved the problem. Obviously, the head gasket leak was not great enough to cause any problems until the engine speed and load created enough flow and heat to cause the coolant temperature to soar.

The technician also replaced the oxygen (O_2) sensor, because coolant contains phosphates and silicates that often contaminate the sensor. The deteriorated oxygen sensor could have contributed to the problem.

COMMON CAUSES OF OVERHEATING

Overheating can be caused by defects in the cooling system. Some common causes of overheating include:

1. Low coolant level
2. Plugged, dirty, or blocked radiator
3. Defective fan clutch or electric fan
4. Incorrect ignition timing
5. Low engine oil level
6. Broken fan belt
7. Defective radiator cap
8. Dragging brakes
9. Frozen coolant (in freezing weather)
10. Defective thermostat
11. Defective water pump (the impeller slipping on the shaft internally)

COOLING SYSTEM MAINTENANCE

The cooling system is one of the most maintenance-free systems in the engine. Normal maintenance involves an occasional check on the coolant level. It should also include a visual inspection for signs of coolant system leaks and for the condition of the coolant hoses and fan drive belts.

CAUTION: The coolant level should only be checked when the engine is cool. Removing the pressure cap from a hot engine will release the cooling system pressure while the coolant temperature is above its atmospheric boiling temperature. When the cap is removed, the pressure will instantly drop to atmospheric pressure level, causing the coolant to boil immediately. Vapors from the boiling liquid will blow coolant from the system. Coolant will be lost, and someone may be injured or burned by the high-temperature coolant that is blown out of the filler opening.

The coolant-antifreeze mixture is renewed at periodic intervals. Some vehicle manufacturers recommend that coolant system stop-leak pellets be installed whenever the coolant is changed. See Figure 13-40.

CAUTION: General Motors recommends the use of these stop-leak pellets in only certain engines. Using these pellets in some engines could cause a restriction in the cooling system and an overheating condition.

Accessory Drive Belt Tension

Drive belt condition and proper installation are important for the proper operation of the cooling system.

Belt Tension Measurement

There are four ways that vehicle manufacturers specify that the belt tension is within factory specifications.

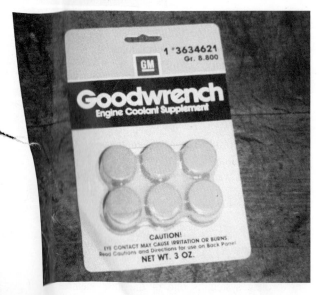

FIGURE 13-40 General Motors recommends that these stop-leak pellets be installed in the cooling system if the coolant is replaced on some engines, especially the Cadillac 4.1, 4.5, and 4.9 L, V-8s.

1. **Belt tension gauge.** A belt tension gauge is needed to achieve the specified belt tension. Install the belt and operate the engine with all of the accessories turned on to "run-in" the belt for at least 5 minutes. Adjust the tension of the accessory drive belt to factory specifications or use the table below for an example of the proper tension based on the size of the belt. Replace any serpentine belt that has more than three cracks in any one rib that appears in a 3-inch span.

Number of Ribs Used	Tension Range (lb)
3	45 to 60
4	60 to 80
5	75 to 100
6	90 to 125
7	105 to 145

TECH TIP

THE HAND CLEANER TRICK

Lower-than-normal alternator output could be the result of a loose or slipping drive belt. All belts (V and serpentine multigroove) use an interference angle between the angle of the V's of the belt and the angle of the V's on the pulley. A belt wears this interference angle off the edges of the V of the belt. As a result, the belt may start to slip and make a squealing sound even if tensioned properly.

A common trick used to determine if the noise is belt related is to use gritty hand cleaner or scouring powder. With the engine off, sprinkle some powder onto the pulley side of the belt. Start the engine. The excess powder will fly into the air, so get out from under the hood when the engine starts. If the belts are now quieter, you know that it was the glazed belt that made the noise.

NOTE: Often, belt noise sounds exactly like a noisy bearing. Therefore, before you start removing and replacing parts, try the hand cleaner trick.

Often, the grit from the hand cleaner will remove the glaze from the belt and the noise will not return. However, if the belt is worn or loose, the noise will return and the belt should be replaced. A fast alternative method to determine if the noise is from the belt is to spray water from a squirt bottle at the belt with the engine running. If the noise stops, the belt is the cause of the noise. The water quickly evaporates and therefore, unlike the gritty hand cleaner, water just finds the problem—it does not provide a short-term fix.

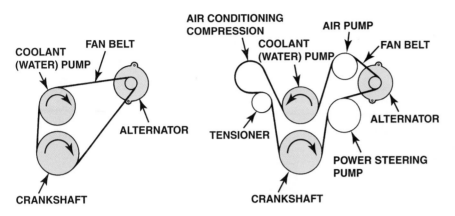

FIGURE 13-41
In the mid-1980s, many manufacturers started using serpentine belts. Older-model water pumps will bolt onto the engine, but the direction of rotation may be opposite. This could lead to overheating after the new pump is installed. If the wrong application of fan is installed, the blades of the fan will not be angled correctly to provide adequate airflow through the radiator.

FIGURE 13-42   Drive belt tension is critical for the proper operation of the water pump, as well as the generator (alternator), air-conditioning compressor, and other belt-driven accessories. A belt tension gauge should be used to make certain that accurate belt tension is achieved when replacing or retensioning any belt.

2. **Marks on a tensioner.** Many tensioners have marks that indicate the normal operating tension range for the accessory drive belt. Check service information for the location of the tensioner mark.
3. **Torque wrench reading.** Some vehicle manufacturers specify that a beam-type torque wrench be used to determine the torque needed to rotate the tensioner. If the torque reading is below specifications, the tensioner must be replaced.
4. **Deflection.** Depress the belt between the two pulleys that are the farthest apart and the flex or deflection should be 1/2 inch.

See Figures 13-41 and 13-42.

FLUSH AND REFILL

Manufacturers recommend that a cooling system be flushed and that the antifreeze be replaced at specified intervals. Draining coolant when the engine is cool eliminates the danger of being injured by hot coolant. The radiator is drained by opening a petcock in the bottom tank, and the coolant in the block is drained into a suitable container by opening plugs located in the lower part of the cooling passage.

Water should be run into the filler opening while the drains remain open. Flushing should be continued until only clear water comes from the system.

The volume of the cooling system must be determined. It is specified in the owner's handbook and in the engine service manual. The antifreeze quantity needed for the protection desired is shown on a chart that comes with the antifreeze. Open the bleeder valves and add the correct amount of the specified type of antifreeze followed by enough water to completely fill the system. See Figure 13-43.

The coolant recovery reservoir should be filled to the "level-cold" mark with the correct antifreeze mixture.

BURPING THE SYSTEM

In most systems, small air pockets can occur. The engine must be thoroughly warmed to open the thermostat. This allows full coolant flow to remove the air pockets. The heater must also be turned to full heat.

NOTE: The cooling system will not function correctly if air is not released (burped) from the system after a refill. An easy method involves replacing the radiator cap after the refill, but only to the first locked position. Drive the vehicle for several minutes and check the radiator level. Without the radiator cap tightly sealed, no pressure will build in the cooling system. Driving the vehicle helps circulate the coolant enough to force all air pockets up and out of the radiator filler. Top off the radiator after burping and replace the radiator cap to the fully locked position. Failure to burp the cooling system to remove all the air will often result in lack of heat from the heater and may result in engine overheating.

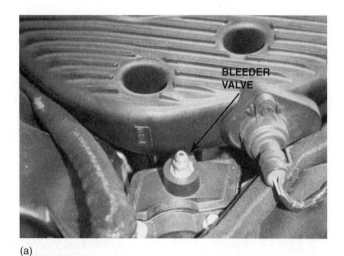

(a)

(b)

FIGURE 13-43 (a) Chrysler recommends that the bleeder valve be opened whenever refilling the cooling system. (b) Chrysler also recommends that a clear plastic hose (1/4" ID) be attached to the bleeder valve and directed into a suitable container to keep from spilling coolant onto the ground and on the engine and to allow the technician to observe the flow of coolant for any remaining oil bubbles.

HOSES

Coolant system hoses are critical to engine cooling. As the hoses get old, they become either soft or brittle and sometimes swell in diameter. Their condition depends on their material and on the engine service conditions. If a hose breaks while the engine is running, all coolant will be lost. A hose should be replaced anytime it appears to be abnormal. See Figure 13-44.

NOTE: To make hose removal easier and to avoid possible damage to the radiator, use a utility knife and slit the hose lengthwise. Then simply peel the hose off.

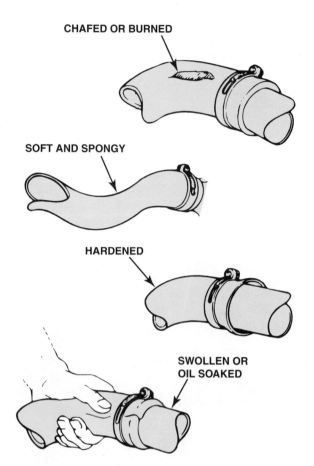

FIGURE 13-44 All cooling system hoses should be checked for wear or damage.

Care should be taken to avoid bending the soft metal hose neck on the radiator. The hose neck should be cleaned before a new hose is slipped in place. The clamp is placed on the hose; then the hose is pushed fully over the neck. The hose should be cut so that the clamp is close to the bead on the neck. This is especially important on aluminum hose necks to avoid corrosion. When the hoses are in place and the drain petcock is closed, the cooling system can be refilled with the correct coolant mixture.

BACK FLUSHING A RADIATOR

Overheating problems may be caused by deposits that restrict coolant flow. These can often be loosened by **back flushing.** Back flushing requires the use of a special gun that mixes air with water. Low-pressure air is used so that it will not damage the cooling system. See Figure 13-45.

Deposits will come out of the filler opening and out of the hose connected to the upper hose neck. If, after flushing, some deposits still plug the radiator core, then the radiator will have to be removed and sent to a radiator repair shop for cleaning.

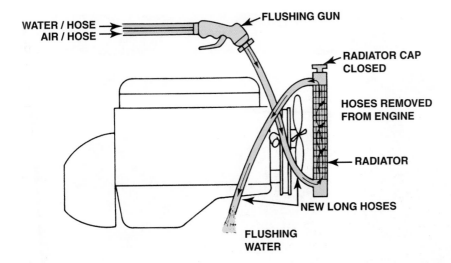

FIGURE 13-45   Setup to back flush a radiator.

TECH TIP

QUICK AND EASY COOLING SYSTEM PROBLEM DIAGNOSIS

If overheating occurs in slow stop-and-go traffic, the usual cause is low airflow through the radiator. Check for airflow blockages or cooling fan malfunction. If overheating occurs at highway speeds, the cause is usually a radiator or coolant circulation problem. Check for a restricted or clogged radiator.

CLEANING THE RADIATOR EXTERIOR

Overheating can result from exterior radiator plugging as well as internal plugging. External plugging is caused by dirt and insects. This type of plugging can be seen if you look straight through the radiator while a light is held behind it. It is most likely to occur on off-road vehicles. The plugged exterior of the radiator core can usually be cleaned with water pressure from a hose. The water is aimed at the *engine side* of the radiator. The water should flow freely through the core at all locations. If this does not clean the core, the radiator should be removed for cleaning at a radiator shop.

RADIATOR PRESSURE TEST Step-by-Step

STEP 1 This vehicle has an obvious coolant leak. The exact location or cause of the leak can be easily determined by performing a radiator pressure test.

STEP 2 After the engine has been allowed to cool, the radiator cap is removed and inspected for any obvious faults. The filler neck of the radiator and the overflow nose are also inspected visually.

STEP 3 The coolant recovery container should also be inspected. In this case the level of coolant was found to be low in the coolant recovery container but okay in the radiator.

STEP 4 An adapter is required to attach the radiator pressure tester to the radiator filler neck on this vehicle. The hand-operated pressure pump should be pumped until the pressure gauge indicates the same pressure as the rating on the pressure cap. The radiator cap was rated at 1.1 bar and because each bar is equal to 14.7 PSI the pressure tester was pumped until 16 PSI registered on the gauge.

STEP 5 The radiator cap itself can be tested by using an adapter and applying pressure to the cap using the pressure tester. In this case, the pressure cap failed to hold any pressure and was the cause for the coolant loss.

SUMMARY

1. The purpose and function of the cooling system is to maintain proper engine operating temperature.

2. The thermostat controls engine coolant temperature by opening at its rated opening temperature to allow coolant to flow through the radiator.

3. Antifreeze coolant is usually ethylene glycol-based. Other coolants include propylene glycol and phosphate-free coolants.

4. Used coolant should be recycled whenever possible.

5. Coolant fans are designed to draw air through the radiator to aid in the heat transfer process, drawing the heat from the coolant and transferring it to the outside air through the radiator.

6. The cooling system should be tested for leaks using a hand-operated pressure pump.

7. The freezing and boiling temperature of the coolant can be tested using a hydrometer.

REVIEW QUESTIONS

1. Explain why the normal operating coolant temperature is about 200° to 220°F (93° to 104°C).

2. Explain why a 50/50 mixture of antifreeze and water is commonly used as a coolant.

3. Explain the flow of coolant through the engine and radiator.

4. Why is a cooling system pressurized?

5. Describe the difference between a series and a parallel coolant flow system.

6. Explain the purpose of the coolant system bypass.

7. Describe how to perform a drain, flush, and refill procedure on a cooling system.

8. Explain the operation of a thermostatic cooling fan.

9. Describe how to diagnose a heater problem.

10. List 10 common causes of overheating.

CHAPTER QUIZ

1. Antifreeze is mostly _____.
   a. Methanol
   b. Glycerin
   c. Kerosene
   d. Ethylene glycol

2. As the percentage of antifreeze in the coolant increases, _____.
   a. The freeze point decreases (up to a point)
   b. The boiling point decreases
   c. The heat transfer increases
   d. All of the above occurs

3. Heat transfer is improved from the coolant to the air when _____.
   a. The temperature difference is great
   b. The temperature difference is small
   c. The coolant is 95% antifreeze
   d. Both a and c

4. A water pump is a positive displacement-type pump.
   a. True
   b. False

5. Water pumps _____.
   a. Only work at idle and low speeds; the pump is disengaged at higher speeds
   b. Use engine oil as a lubricant and coolant
   c. Are driven by the engine crankshaft or camshaft
   d. Disengage during freezing weather to prevent radiator failure

6. The procedure that should be used when refilling an empty cooling system includes the following _____.
   a. Determine capacity, then fill the cooling system halfway with antifreeze and the rest of the way with water
   b. Fill completely with antifreeze, but mix a 50/50 solution for the overflow bottle

c. Fill the block and one-half of the radiator with 100% pure antifreeze and fill the rest of the radiator with water

d. Fill the radiator with antifreeze, start the engine, drain the radiator, and refill with a 50/50 mixture of antifreeze and water

7. Which statement is *true* about thermostats?

a. The temperature marked on the thermostat is the temperature at which the thermostat should be fully open.

b. Thermostats often cause overheating.

c. The temperature marked on the thermostat is the temperature at which the thermostat should start to open.

d. Both a and b.

8. Technician A says that the radiator should always be inspected for leaks and proper flow before installing a rebuilt engine. Technician B says that overheating during slow city driving can only be due to a defective electric cooling fan. Which technician is correct?

a. Technician A only

b. Technician B only

c. Both Technicians A and B

d. Neither Technician A nor B

9. A customer complains that the heater works sometimes, but sometimes only cold air comes out while driving. Technician A says that the water pump is defective. Technician B says that the cooling system could be low on coolant. Which technician is correct?

a. Technician A only

b. Technician B only

c. Both Technicians A and B

d. Neither Technician A nor B

10. The normal operating temperature (coolant temperature) of an engine equipped with a 195°F thermostat is _____.

a. 175° to 195°F

b. 185° to 205°F

c. 195° to 215°F

d. 175° to 215°F

LUBRICATION SYSTEM OPERATION AND DIAGNOSIS

OBJECTIVES

After studying Chapter 14, the reader will be able to:

1. Prepare for Engine Repair (A1) ASE certification test content area "D" (Lubrication and Cooling Systems Diagnosis and Repair).

2. Explain engine oil ratings.

3. Describe how an oil pump and engine lubrication work.

4. Discuss how and when to change the oil and filter.

5. Explain how to inspect an oil pump for wear.

KEY TERMS

LUBRICATION PURPOSE AND FUNDAMENTALS

Engine oil is the lifeblood of any engine. The purposes of engine oil include the following:

1. *Lubricating* all moving parts to prevent wear.
2. Helping to *cool* the engine.
3. Helping to *seal* piston rings.
4. *Cleaning,* and holding dirt in suspension in the oil until it can be drained from the engine.
5. *Neutralizing* acids that are formed as the result of the combustion process.
6. *Reducing* friction.
7. *Preventing* rust and corrosion.

LUBRICATION PRINCIPLES

Lubrication between two moving surfaces results from an oil film that separates the surfaces and supports the load. See Figure 14-1.

Although oil does not compress, it does leak out around the oil clearance between the shaft and the bearing. In some cases, the oil film is thick enough to keep the surfaces from seizing, but can allow some contact to occur. This condition is called **boundary lubrication.** The specified oil viscosity and oil clearances must be adhered to during service to help prevent boundary lubrication and wear from occurring, which usually happens when the engine is under a heavy load and low speeds. The movement of the shaft helps prevent contact with the bearing. If oil were put on a flat surface and a heavy block were pushed across the surface, the block would slide more easily than if it were pushed across a dry surface. The reason for this is that a wedge-shaped oil film is built up between the moving block and the surface, as illustrated in Figure 14-2.

This wedging action is called **hydrodynamic lubrication** and the pressure depends on the force applied to how fast the speed between the objects and the thickness of the oil. Thickness of oil is called the **viscosity** and is defined as the ability of the oil to resist flow. High-viscosity oil is thick and low-viscosity oil is thin. The prefix *hydro-* refers to liquids, as in hydraulics, and *dynamic* refers to moving materials. Hydrodynamic lubrication occurs when a wedge-shaped film of lubricating oil develops between two surfaces that have relative motion between them. See Figure 14-3.

The engine oil pressure system feeds a continuous supply of oil into the lightly loaded part of the bearing oil clearance. Hydrodynamic lubrication takes over as the shaft rotates in the bearing to produce a wedge-shaped hydrodynamic oil film that is curved around the bearing. This film supports the bearing and reduces the turning effort to a minimum when oil of the correct viscosity is used.

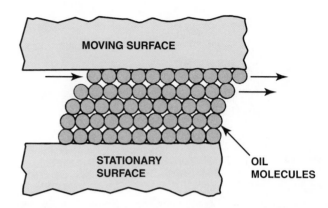

FIGURE 14-1 Oil molecules cling to metal surfaces but easily slide against each other.

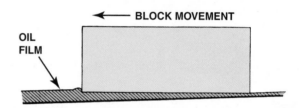

FIGURE 14-2 Wedge-shaped oil film developed below a moving block.

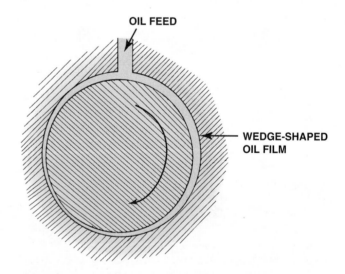

FIGURE 14-3 Wedge-shaped oil film curved around a bearing journal.

Most bearing wear occurs during the initial start-up. Wear continues until a hydrodynamic film is established.

ENGINE LUBRICATION SYSTEMS

The primary function of the engine lubrication system is to maintain a positive and continuous oil supply to the bearings.

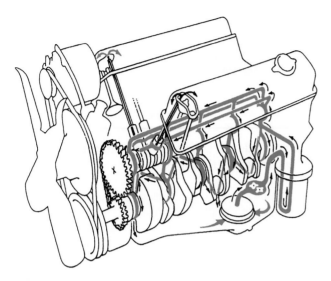

FIGURE 14-4 Typical V-8 engine lubrication system. Oil is stored in the oil pan (sump), drawn into the oil pump, and moves through the oil filter and on through the oil passages (oil galleries).

Engine oil pressure must be high enough to get the oil to the bearings with enough force to cause the oil flow that is required for proper cooling. The normal engine oil pressure range is from 10 to 60 PSI (200 to 400 kPa) (10 PSI per 1000 engine RPM). However, hydrodynamic film pressures developed in the high-pressure areas of the engine bearings may be over 1,000 PSI (6,900 kPa). The relatively low engine oil pressures obviously could not support these high bearing loads without hydrodynamic lubrication. See Figure 14-4.

PROPERTIES OF ENGINE OIL

The most important engine oil property is its thickness or viscosity. As oil cools, it thickens. As oil heats, it gets thinner. Therefore, its viscosity changes with temperature. The oil must not be too thick at low temperatures to allow the engine to start. The lowest temperature at which oil will pour is called its **pour point.** An index of the change in viscosity between the cold and hot extremes is called the **viscosity index (VI).** All oils with a high viscosity index thin less with heat than do oils with a low viscosity index. Oils must also be **miscible,** meaning they are capable of mixing with other oils (brands and viscosities, for example) without causing any problems such as sludge.

SAE RATING

Engine oils are sold with an **SAE (Society of Automotive Engineers)** grade number, which indicates the viscosity range into which the oil fits. Oils tested at 212°F (100°C) have a number with no letter following. For example, SAE 30 indicates that the oil has only been checked at 212°F (100°C). This oil's viscosity falls within the SAE 30 grade number range when the oil is hot. Oils tested at 0°F (−18°C) are rated with a number and the letter *W*, which means *winter* and indicates that the viscosity was tested at 0°F, such as SAE 20W. An SAE 5W-30 multigrade oil is one that meets the SAE 5W viscosity specification when cooled to 0°F (−18°C) and meets the SAE 30 viscosity specification when tested at 212°F (100°C).

Most vehicle manufacturers recommend the following multiviscosity engine oils:

- SAE 5W-30
- SAE 10W-30

An oil with a high viscosity has a higher resistance to flow and is thicker than lower-viscosity oil. A thick oil is not necessarily a good oil and a thin oil is not necessarily a bad oil. Generally, the following items can be considered in the selection of an engine oil within the recommended viscosity range.

- Thinner oil
  1. Improved cold-engine starting
  2. Improved fuel economy
- Thicker oil
  1. Improved protection at higher temperatures
  2. Reduced fuel economy

API RATING

The **American Petroleum Institute (API),** working with the engine manufacturers and oil companies, has established an engine oil performance classification. Oils are tested and rated in production automotive engines. The oil container is printed with the API classification of the oil. The API performance or service classification and the SAE grade marking are the only information available to help determine which oil is satisfactory for use in an engine. See Figure 14-5 for a typical API oil container "doughnut."

Gasoline Engine Rating

In gasoline engine ratings, the letter *S* means *service*, but it can be remembered as being for use in spark ignition engines. The rating system is open-ended so that newer, improved ratings can be readily added as necessary (the letter *I* is skipped to avoid confusion with the number one).

SA   Straight mineral oil (no additives), not suitable for use in any engine

SB   Nondetergent oil with additives to control wear and oil oxidation

SC   Obsolete (1964)

SD   Obsolete (1968)

FIGURE 14-5   API doughnut for a SAE 5W-30, SM engine oil. When compared to a reference oil, the "energy conserving" designation indicates a 1.1% better fuel economy for SAE 10W-30 oils and 0.5% better fuel economy for SAE 5W-30 oils.

SE	Obsolete (1972)
SF	Obsolete (1980)
SG	Obsolete (1988)
SH	Obsolete (1993–1997)
SJ	Obsolete (1997–2001)
SL	2001–2003
SM	2004+

NOTE: Older-model vehicles can use the newer, higher-rated engine oil classifications where older, now obsolete ratings were specified. Newly overhauled antique cars or engines also can use the newer, improved oils, as the appropriate SAE viscosity grade is used for the anticipated temperature range. The new oils have all the protection of the older oils, plus additional protection.

Diesel Engine Rating

Diesel classifications begin with the letter *C*, which stands for *commercial*, but can also be remembered as being for use in compression ignition or diesel engines.

CA	Obsolete
CB	Obsolete
CC	Obsolete
CD	Minimum rating for use in a diesel engine service
CE	Designed for certain turbocharged or supercharged heavy-duty diesel engine service
CF	For off-road indirect injected diesel engine service
CF-2	Two-stroke diesel engine service
CF-4	High-speed four-stroke cycle diesel engine service

CG-4	Severe-duty high-speed four-stroke diesel engine service
CI-4	Severe-duty high-speed four-stroke diesel engine service

ILSAC OIL RATING

The **International Lubricant Standardization and Approval Committee (ILSAC)** developed an oil rating that consolidates the SAE viscosity rating and the API quality rating. If an engine oil meets the standards, a "starburst" symbol is displayed on the front of the oil container. If the starburst is present, the vehicle owner and technician know that the oil is suitable for use in almost any gasoline engine. See Figure 14-6.

The original GF-1 (gasoline fueled) rating was updated to GF-2 in 1997, GF-3 in 2000, and GF-4 in 2004.

TECH TIP

THREE OIL CHANGE FACTS

The three facts needed to know when changing oil include:

1. *Recommended SAE viscosity* (thickness) for the temperature range that is anticipated before the next oil change (usually SAE 5W-30)
2. *API quality rating* as recommended by the engine or vehicle manufacturer (usually SL or SM)
3. *Recommended oil change interval* (time or mileage) (usually every 5,000 miles or every six months)

FIGURE 14-6   The International Lubricant Standardization and Approval Committee (ILSAC) starburst symbol. If this symbol is on the front of the container of oil, then it is acceptable for use in almost any gasoline engine.

FREQUENTLY ASKED QUESTION

WHY IS SAE 10W-30 RECOMMENDED INSTEAD OF SAE 10W-40?

Engine oils are manufactured in various viscosity grades. Vehicle manufacturers usually recommend that SAE 5W-30 and/or SAE 10W-30 be used. General Motors Corporation specifies that SAE 10W-40 not be used in any engine. These different viscosity grades are formulated by using a viscosity index improver, which is a polymer designed to induce thickening of a thin base oil at higher temperatures. For example, a 10W-30 oil starts as an SAE 10W oil, and viscosity index improver polymers are added to bring the high-temperature viscosity up to SAE 30 standards. These polymers react with heat to restrict the rate of flow of the oil at higher temperatures. The greater the amount of VI improver, the broader the viscosity range. For example, typical multiviscosity oils and the percentages of viscosity index improver that they use are as follows:

SAE 5W-30 7–8% VI
SAE 10W-30 6–8% VI
SAE 10W-40 12–15% VI

Even though a 10W-40 oil will resist high-temperature thinning better than a 10W-30 oil, the increased amount of VI can contribute to some problems. As oil is used in an engine, it tends to thicken. This thickening occurs because of the following:

- *Oxidation.* When oil combines with oxygen, it becomes thicker.
- *Breakdown of polymer additives.* After 1,000 to 2,000 miles, the polymer additives can shear (break down) during use, which causes the oil to become thinner. The increased oxidation causes the oil to thicken and form sludge.

EUROPEAN OIL RATINGS

The **Association des Constructeurs European d'Automobiles (ACEA)** represents most of the Western European automobile and heavy-duty truck market. The organization uses different engines for testing than those used by API and SAE, and the requirements necessary to meet the ACEA standards are different yet generally correspond with most API ratings. ACEA standards tend to specify a minimum viscosity rating and certain volatility requirements not specified by API.

Gasoline Engine Oils

ACEA A1   Low-friction, low-viscosity oil (not suitable for some engines).

ACEA A2   General-purpose oil intended for normal oil change intervals. Not suitable for some engines or extended oil drain intervals in any engine.

ACEA A3   Oil is designed for high-performance engines and/or extended oil drain intervals and under all temperature ranges.

ACEA A4   Designed to meet the requirements for gasoline direct injection (GDI) engines.

ACEA A5   A low-viscosity, low-friction oil not suitable for some engines.

Diesel Engine Oils

ACEA B1   This diesel engine oil is designed for use in a passenger vehicle diesel engine that is equipped with an indirect injection system. This low-viscosity oil is not suitable for some diesel engines.

ACEA B2   Oil meeting this designation is designed to be used in passenger vehicle diesel engines using indirect injection and using normal oil drain intervals.

ACEA B3   Oil meeting this designation is intended for use in a high-performance, indirect injected passenger vehicle diesel engine and used under extended oil drain interval conditions.

ACEA B4   Oils meeting this standard are intended to be used in direct-injected passenger vehicle diesel engines and used year-round and can be used in an indirect-injected diesel engine.

ACEA B5   A low-viscosity oil designed for extended oil drain intervals and not suitable for some engines.

ACEA C1   The ACEA C ratings are specifications for C2, C3 catalyst compatible oils, which have limits on the amount of sulfur, zinc, and other additives that could harm the catalytic converter. Starting in 2004, the ACEA began using combined ratings such as A1/B1, A3/B3, A3/B4, and A5/B5.

JAPANESE OIL RATINGS

The **Japanese Automobile Standards Organization (JASO)** also publishes oil standards. The JASO tests use small Japanese engines, and their ratings require more stringent valve train wear standards than other countries' oil ratings.

ENGINE OIL ADDITIVES

Additives are used in engine oils for three different reasons: (1) to replace some properties removed during refining, (2) to reinforce some of the oil's natural properties, and (3) to provide the oil with new properties it did not originally have. Oils from some petroleum oil fields require more and different additives than oils from other fields. Additives are usually classified according to the property they add to the oil.

- *Antioxidants* reduce the high-temperature contaminants. They prevent the formation of varnish on the parts, reduce bearing corrosion, and minimize particle formation.
- *Corrosion preventives* reduce acid formation that causes bearing corrosion.
- *Detergents* and *dispersants* prevent low-temperature sludge binders from forming and keep the sludge-forming particles finely divided. The finely divided particles will stay in suspension in the oil to be removed from the engine as the oil is removed at the next drain period.
- *Extreme pressure* and *antiwear additives* form a chemical film that prevents metal-to-metal seizure any time boundary lubrication exists.
- *Viscosity index (VI) improvers* are used to reduce viscosity change as the oil temperature changes. See Figure 14-7.
- **Pour point depressants** coat the wax crystals in the oil so that they will not stick together. The oil will then be able to flow at lower temperatures.

A number of other oil additives may be used to modify the oil to function better in the engine. These include rust preventives, metal deactivators, water repellents, emulsifiers, dyes, color stabilizers, odor control agents, and foam inhibitors.

Oil producers are careful to check the compatibility of the oil additives they use. A number of chemicals that will help each other can be used for each of the additive requirements. The balanced additives are called an **additive package.**

FIGURE 14-7 VI improver is a polymer and feels like finely ground foam rubber. When dissolved in the oil, it expands when hot to keep the oil from thinning.

OIL BRAND COMPATIBILITY

Many technicians and vehicle owners have their favorite brand of engine oil. The choice is often made as a result of marketing and advertising, as well as comments from friends, relatives, and technicians. If your brand of engine oil is not performing up to your expectations, then you may wish to change brands. For example, some owners experience lower oil pressure with a certain brand than they do with other brands with the same SAE viscosity rating.

Most experts agree that the oil changes are the most important regularly scheduled maintenance for an engine. It is also wise to check the oil level regularly and add oil when needed. According to SAE Standard J-357, all engine oils must be compatible (miscible) with all other brands of engine oil. Therefore, any brand of engine oil can be used as long as it meets the viscosity and API standards recommended by the vehicle manufacturer. Even though many people prefer a particular brand, be assured that, according to API and SAE, any *major* brand-name engine oil can be used.

FREQUENTLY ASKED QUESTION

CAN NEWER ENGINE OILS BE USED IN OLDER VEHICLES?

No. In the past using a newer standard oil in an older engine was not a concern until the mandated reduction of zinc from the oil. The zinc (commonly referred to as zinc dialkyl dithiophosphate—**ZDDP** or ZDP) can cause damage to the catalytic converter. Even though engines consume very little oil, if the oil contains zinc, the efficiency of the catalytic converter is reduced. The use of ZDDP was intended to reduce sliding friction in an engine. Sliding friction is usually found in engines that use flat-bottom lifters. Most, if not all, engines produced over the past 10 years have used roller lifters or followers, so using the new oil without ZDDP is not a concern. Even diesel oils have reduced amounts of the zinc so many camshaft manufacturers are recommending the use of an additive. Older oils had up to 0.15% ZDDP and now SM-rated oils list the zinc at just 0.08% or 800 parts per million.

If driving a vehicle with flat-bottom lifters, use engine oil specifically designed for older engines or use an additive, such as General Motors engine oil supplement (EOS), Part number 1052367 or 88862586. Check with camshaft manufacturers for their recommended oil or additive to use.

SYNTHETIC OIL

Synthetic engine oils have been available for years for military, commercial, and general public use. The term *synthetic* means that it is a manufactured product and not refined from a naturally occurring substance, as engine oil (petroleum base) is refined from crude oil. Synthetic oil is processed from several different base stocks using several different methods.

According to the American Petroleum Institute, engine oil is classified into groups as follows.

Group I. Mineral, nonsynthetic, base oil with few if any additives.
This type of oil is suitable for light lubricating needs and rust protection and is not to be used in an engine.
Group II. Mineral oils with quality additive packages.
Most of the conventional engine oils are Group II.
Group III. Hydrogenated (hydroisomerized) synthetic compounds commonly referred to as hydrowaxes or hydrocracked oil.
This is the lowest cost of synthetic engine oils. Castrol Syntec is a Group III oil.
Group IV. Synthetic oils made from mineral oil and monomolecular oil called polyalpholefin or POA.
Mobil 1 is an example of a Group IV synthetic oil. See Figure 14-8.
Group V. Nonmineral sources such as alcohol from corn called diesters or polyolesters.
Red Line synthetic oil is an example of a Group V oil.

Groups III, IV, and V are all considered to be synthetic because the molecular structure of the finished product does not occur naturally and is man-made through chemical processes. All synthetic engine oils perform better than Group II (mineral) oils, especially when tested according to the Noack Volatility Test ASTM D-5800. This test procedure measures the ability of an oil to stay in grade after it has been heated to 300°F (150°C) for one hour. The oil is then measured for percentage of weight loss. As the lighter components boil off, the oil's viscosity will increase. If you start with an SAE 5W oil, it could test as an SAE 15W or even an SAE 20W at the end of the test. It is important that the oil you buy stay in grade for the proper lubrication of your engine.

Some types of synthetic oil are not compatible with other types. Some synthetic oils are mixed with petroleum-based engine oils, but these must be labeled as a *blend*.

The major advantage of using synthetic engine oil is in its ability to remain fluid at very low temperatures. See Figure 14-9.

This characteristic of synthetic oil makes it popular in colder climates where cold-engine cranking is important. The major disadvantage is cost. The cost of synthetic engine oils can be four to five times the cost of petroleum-based engine oils.

OIL TEMPERATURE

Excessive temperatures, either too low or too high, are harmful to any engine. If the oil is too cold, it could be too thick to flow through and lubricate all engine parts. If the oil is too hot, it could become too thin to provide the film strength necessary to prevent metal-to-metal contact and wear. Estimated oil temperature can be determined with the following formula:

Estimated oil temperature = Outside air temperature + 120°F

For example,

90°F outside air temperature + 120°F = 210°F estimated oil temperature

FIGURE 14-8 Container of oil with the ILSAC starburst symbol on the front. The tri-synthetic label indicates that it contains Group IV (POA) as well as Group V (diesters) to swell seals, and some Group III (hydrocracked oil).

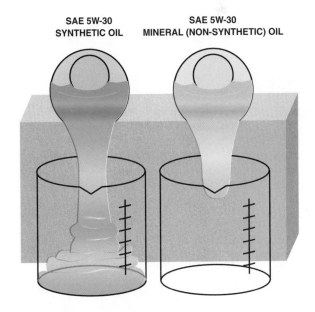

FIGURE 14-9 Both oils have been cooled to −20°F (−29°C). Notice that the synthetic oil on the left flows more freely than the mineral oil on the right even though they are both SAE 5W-30.

TECH TIP

USE SYNTHETIC ENGINE OIL IN LAWN AND GARDEN EQUIPMENT

Most 4-cycle lawn and garden equipment engines are air cooled and operate hotter than many liquid-cooled engines. Lawnmowers and other small engines are often operated near or at maximum speed and power output for hours at a time. These operating conditions are hard on any engine oil. Try using a synthetic oil. The cost is not as big a factor because most small 4-cycle lawnmower engines require only about 1/2 quart (1/2 liter) of oil. The synthetic oil is able to perform under high temperatures better than conventional mineral oils.

TECH TIP

MAKE SURE THE OIL MEETS SPECIFIC VEHICLE SPECIFICATIONS

Some oils can meet the industry specifications, such as SAE, API, and/or ILSAC ratings, but not pass the tests specified by the vehicle manufacturer. The oil used should meet those of the vehicle manufacturer, which include the following:

  BMW—Longlife 98 and Longlife-01 (abbreviated LL-01), LL-04
  General Motors—GM 6094M, GM 4718M (synthetic oil specification), GM LL-A-25 (gasoline engines), and GM LL-B-25 for GM diesels and vehicles equipped with European-built engines.
  Ford—WSS-M2C153-H, WSS-M2C929-A (low viscosity rating—SAE 5W-20), WSS-M2C930-A, WSS-M2C931-A, and WSS-M2C934-A
  Chrysler—MS-6395 (2005+ vehicles), MS-10725
  Honda—HTO-06
  Mercedes—229.3, 229.5, 229.1, 229-31, and 229.51
  Volkswagen (VW and Audi)—502.00, 505.00, 505.01, 503, 503.01, 505, 506 diesel, 506.1 diesel, and 507 diesel

TECH TIP

FOLLOW THE SEASONS

Vehicle owners often forget when they last changed the oil. This is particularly true of the person who owns or is responsible for several vehicles. A helpful method for remembering when the oil should be changed is to change the oil at the start of each season of the year.

- Fall (September 21)
- Winter (December 21)
- Spring (March 21)
- Summer (June 21)

Remembering that the oil needs to be changed on these dates helps owners budget for the expense and the time needed.

During hard acceleration (or high-power demand activities such as trailer towing), the oil temperature will quickly increase. Oil temperature should not exceed 300°F (150°C).

OIL CHANGE INTERVALS

All vehicle and engine manufacturers recommend a maximum oil change interval. The recommended intervals are almost always expressed in terms of mileage or elapsed time (or hours of operation), whichever milestone is reached first.

Most vehicle manufacturers recommend an oil change interval of 7,500 to 12,000 miles (12,000 to 19,000 kilometers) or every six months. If, however, *any one* of the conditions in the following list exists, the oil change interval recommendation drops to a more reasonable 2,000 to 3,000 miles (3,000 to 5,000 kilometers) or every three months. The important thing to remember is that these are recommended *maximum* intervals and they should be shortened substantially if any one of the following operating conditions exists.

1. Operating in dusty areas
2. Towing a trailer
3. Short-trip driving, especially during cold weather (The definition of a short trip varies among manufacturers, but it is usually defined as 4 to 15 miles [6 to 24 kilometers] each time the engine is started.)
4. Operating in temperatures below freezing (32°F, 0°C)
5. Operating at idle speed for extended periods of time (such as normally occurs in police or taxi service)

Because most vehicles driven during cold weather are driven on short trips, most technicians and automotive experts recommend changing the oil every 2,000 to 3,000 miles or every two to three months, whichever occurs first.

OIL CHANGE PROCEDURE

The oil will drain more rapidly from a warm engine than from a cold one. In addition, the contaminants are more likely to be suspended in the oil immediately after running the engine. Position a drain pan under the drain plug; then remove the plug with care to avoid contact with hot oil.

CAUTION: Used engine oil has been determined to be harmful. Rubber gloves should be worn to protect the skin. If used engine oil gets on the skin, wash thoroughly with soap and water.

Allow the oil to drain freely so that the contaminants come out with the oil. It is not critically important to get every last drop of oil from the engine oil pan, because a quantity of used oil still remains in the engine oil passages and oil pump. While the engine oil is draining, the oil plug gasket should be examined. If it appears to be damaged, it should be replaced.

NOTE: Honda/Acura recommends that the oil drain plug gasket be replaced at every oil change on many of their vehicles. The aluminum sealing gasket does not seal once it has been tightened. Always follow the vehicle manufacturer's recommendations.

When the oil stops running and starts to drip, reinstall and tighten the drain plug. Replace the oil filter if that is to be done during this oil change. Refill the engine with the proper type, grade, and quantity of oil. Restart the engine and allow the engine to idle until it develops oil pressure; then check the engine for leaks, especially at the oil filter.

(a)

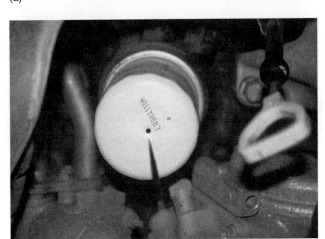
(b)

FIGURE 14-10   (a) A pick is pushed through the top of an oil filter that is positioned vertically. (b) When the pick is removed, a small hole allows air to get into the top of the filter which then allows the oil to drain out of the filter and back into the engine.

TECH TIP

THE PICK TRICK

Removing an oil filter that is installed upside down can be a real mess. When this design filter is loosened, oil flows out from around the sealing gasket. To prevent this from happening, use a pick to poke a hole in the top of the filter, as shown in Figure 14-10. This small hole allows air to get into the filter, thereby allowing the oil to drain back into the engine rather than remain in the filter. After punching the hole in the filter, be sure to wait several minutes to allow time for the trapped oil to drain down into the engine before loosening the filter.

TECH TIP

BYPASS FLOW OIL FILTER

Early engines that did have oil filters had them connected to an oil pressure gallery in parallel. This meant that the oil *could,* but did not have to, flow through the filter. Filters in the 1930s through the early 1950s did not have a bypass valve and therefore, if the filter became clogged, the flow of all oil to the engine would stop unless connected in parallel.

The first small block Chevrolet V-8 in 1955 had a bypass-type oil filter. See Figure 14-11.

FIGURE 14-11   This early Chevrolet V-8 has what was an optional oil filter, which is connected to an oil gallery and return oil flows into the oil pan.

CAUTION: Always wear protective rubber gloves when changing oil to help protect your hands.

OIL FILTERS

The oil within the engine is pumped from the oil pan through the filter before it goes into the engine lubricating system passages. The filter is made from either closely packed cloth fibers or a porous paper. Large particles are trapped by the filter. Microscopic particles will flow through the filter pores. These particles are so small that they can flow through the bearing oil film and not touch the surfaces, so they do no damage.

Many oil filters are equipped with an **antidrainback valve** that prevents oil from draining out of the filter when the engine is shut off. See Figure 14-12. This valve keeps oil in the filter and allows the engine to receive immediate lubrication as soon as the engine starts.

Either the engine or the filter is provided with a **bypass valve** that will allow the oil to go around the filter element. See Figure 14-13. The bypass allows the engine to be lubricated with dirty oil, rather than having no lubrication, if the filter becomes plugged. The oil also goes through the bypass when the oil is cold and thick. Most engine manufacturers recommend filter changes at every other oil change period. Oil filters should be crushed and/or drained of oil before discarding. See Figure 14-14.

After the oil has been drained, the filter can usually be disposed of as regular metal scrap. Always check and follow local, state, or regional oil filter disposal rules, regulations, and procedures.

FIGURE 14-12   A rubber diaphragm acts as an antidrainback valve to keep the oil in the filter when the engine is stopped and the oil pressure drops to zero.

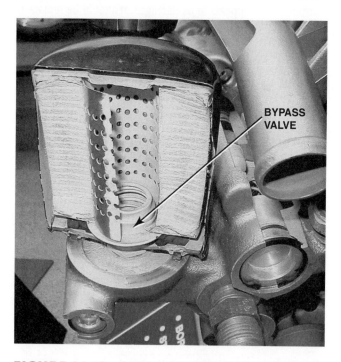

FIGURE 14-13   A cutaway of an oil filter showing the location of a typical bypass valve. When the oil filter becomes clogged, the bypass valve opens, allowing the engine to receive oil even though it is not filtered.

CHANGING OIL IN A TURBOCHARGED ENGINE

One of the most difficult jobs for engine oil is to lubricate the extremely hot bearings of a turbocharger. After a turbocharger

FIGURE 14-14   A typical oil filter crusher. The hydraulic ram forces out most of the oil from the filter. The oil is trapped underneath the crusher and is recycled.

FREQUENTLY ASKED QUESTION

WHY CHANGE OIL IF THE OIL FILTER CAN TRAP ALL THE DIRT?

Many people believe that oil filters will remove all dirt from the oil being circulated through the filtering material. Most oil filters will filter particles that are about 10 to 20 microns in size. A micron is one-millionth of a meter or 0.000039 inch. Most dirt and carbon particles that turn engine oil black are less than a micron in size. In other words, it takes about 3 million of these carbon particles to cover a pinhead. To help visualize the smallness of a micron, consider that a typical human hair is 60 microns in diameter. In fact, anything smaller than 40 microns is not visible to the human eye.

The dispersants added to engine oil prevent dirt from adhering together to form sludge. It is the same dispersant additive that prevents dirt from being filtered or removed by other means. If an oil filter could filter particles down to one micron, it would be so restrictive that the engine would not receive sufficient oil through the filter for lubrication. Oil recycling companies use special chemicals to break down the dispersants, which permit the dirt in the oil to combine into larger units that can be filtered or processed out of the oil.

has been in operation, it is always wise to let the engine idle for about a minute to allow the turbocharger to slow down before shutting off the engine. This allows the turbo to keep receiving oil from the engine while it is still revolving fast.

TECH TIP

EVERY FRIDAY?

A vehicle less than one year old came back to the dealer for some repair work. While writing the repair order, the service advisor noted that the vehicle had 88,000 miles on the odometer and was, therefore, out of warranty for the repair. Because the owner approved the repair anyway, the service advisor asked how he had accumulated so many miles in such a short time. The owner said that he was a traveling salesperson with a territory of "east of the Mississippi River."

Because the vehicle looked to be in new condition, the technician asked the salesperson how often he had the oil changed. The salesperson smiled and said proudly, "Every Friday."

Many fleet vehicles put on over 2,000 miles per week. How about changing their oil every week instead of by mileage?

However, just as with any engine, the greatest amount of wear occurs during start-up, especially following an oil change when the oil has been drained from the engine. Some technicians fill the new oil filter with new oil prior to installation to help the engine receive oil as rapidly as possible after starting.

A number of vehicle manufacturers also suggest that turbo-equipped engines be "primed" before starting. This means that the engine should be rotated without ignition so that it does not start, to allow the oil pump to pump oil to the bearings of the turbocharger before the engine starts.

On older vehicles, it is a simple process to disconnect the ignition coil wire from the distributor cap and ground it to prevent coil damage. After the ignition has been disconnected in this manner, simply crank the engine for 15 seconds. Some manufacturers recommend repeating the 15 seconds of cranking after a 30-second period to allow the starter motor to cool.

There is one simple method that works on many fuel-injected vehicles. If the accelerator pedal is held down to the floor during cranking, then the engine computer senses the throttle position and reduces the amount of fuel injected into the engine. This mode of operation is often called the *clear-flood mode,* and during it, the computer limits the fuel delivery to such an extent that the engine should not start.

Therefore, to prime most late-model turbocharged engines, simply depress the accelerator to the floor and crank for 15 seconds. To start the engine, simply return the accelerator pedal to the idle position and crank the engine.

? FREQUENTLY ASKED QUESTION

HOW DOES THE OIL LIFE MONITOR WORK?

Most vehicles built since 1990 have had some sort of oil change or maintenance reminder system. These systems vary greatly and can be grouped according to the following types:

1. **Mileage Only Method.** The maintenance reminder light comes on or flashes at a predetermined mileage interval, usually every 3,000 miles to 7,500 miles depending on the vehicle.
2. **Algorithm Method.** Used by General Motors, this method uses mathematical formulas that use engine coolant temperature, engine run time, speed, and load to calculate how harmful each is to the oil and deducts a percentage from 100 until the oil life monitor reaches 10%, and then it turns on a change oil light.
3. **Capacitance Method.** A capacitor consists of two metal plates with an insulator called a dielectric in the center. The oil is the dielectric and the physical qualities of the oil affect the ability of the capacitor to charge and discharge. Changes to the oil that change the dielectric include water, acids, coolant, and wear metals.

After an oil change, the oil life monitor should be reset. See service information for details.

OIL PUMPS

All production automobile engines have a full-pressure oil system. The pressure is maintained by an oil pump. The oil is forced into the lubrication system under pressure. In most engines that use a distributor, the distributor drive gear meshes with a gear on the camshaft, as shown in Figure 14-15.

The oil pump is driven from the end of the distributor shaft, often with a hexagon-shaped shaft. Some engines have a short shaft gear that meshes with the cam gear to drive both the distributor and oil pump. With these drive methods, the pump turns at one-half engine speed. In other engines, the oil pump is driven by the front of the crankshaft, in a setup similar to that of an automatic transmission pump, so that it turns at the same speed as the crankshaft. Examples of a crankshaft-driven oil pump are shown in Figures 14-16 and 14-17.

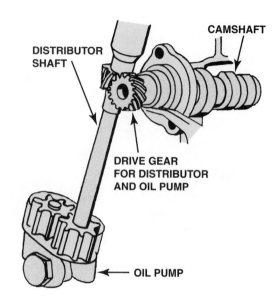

FIGURE 14-15 An oil pump driven by the camshaft.

FIGURE 14-16 A typical oil pump mounted in the front cover of the engine that is driven by the crankshaft.

Most automotive engines use one of two types of oil pumps: **gear** or **rotor.** All oil pumps are called **positive displacement pumps,** and each rotation of the pump delivers the same volume of oil; thus, everything that enters must exit. The gear-type oil pump consists of two spur gears in a close-fitting housing—one gear is driven while the other idles. As the gear teeth come out of mesh, they tend to leave a space, which is filled by oil drawn through the pump inlet. When the pump is pumping, oil is carried around the *outside* of each gear in the space between the gear teeth and the housing, as shown in Figure 14-18.

As the teeth mesh in the center, oil is forced from the teeth into an oil passage, thus producing oil pressure. The rotor-type

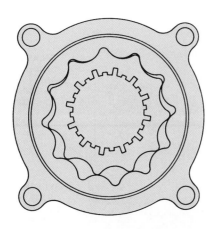

FIGURE 14-17   Geroter-type oil pump driven by the crankshaft.

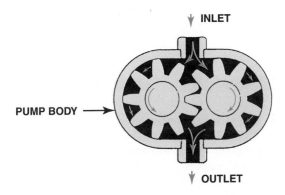

FIGURE 14-18   In a gear-type oil pump, the oil flows through the pump around the outside of each gear. This is an example of a positive displacement pump, wherein everything entering the pump must leave the pump.

oil pump consists essentially of a special lobe-shape gear meshing with the inside of a lobed rotor. The center lobed section is driven and the outer section idles. As the lobes separate, oil is drawn in just as it is drawn into gear-type pumps. As the pump rotates, it carries oil around and between the lobes. As the lobes mesh, they force the oil out from between them under pressure in the same manner as the gear-type pump. The pump is sized so that it will maintain a pressure of at least 10 PSI (70 kPa) in the oil gallery when the engine is hot and idling. Pressure will increase by about 10 PSI for each 1000 RPM as the engine speed increases, because the engine-driven pump also rotates faster.

OIL PRESSURE REGULATION

In engines with a full-pressure lubricating system, maximum pressure is limited with a pressure relief valve. The relief valve (sometimes called the **pressure regulating valve**) is located at the outlet of the pump. The relief valve controls maximum pressure by bleeding off oil to the inlet side of the pump. See Figure 14-19.

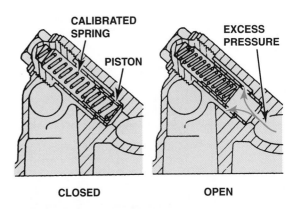

FIGURE 14-19   Oil pressure relief valves are spring loaded. The stronger the spring tension, the higher the oil pressure.

The relief valve spring tension determines the maximum oil pressure. If a pressure relief valve is not used, the engine oil pressure will continue to increase as the engine speed increases. Maximum pressure is usually limited to the lowest pressure that will deliver enough lubricating oil to all engine parts that need to be lubricated. *Between 3 to 6 gallons per minute are required to lubricate the engine.* See Figure 14-20.

The oil pump is made so that it is large enough to provide pressure at low engine speeds and small enough that it will not cavitate at high speed. **Cavitation** occurs when the pump tries to pull oil faster than it can flow from the pan to the pickup. When it cannot get enough oil, it will pull air. This puts air pockets or cavities in the oil stream. A pump is cavitating when it is pulling air or vapors.

NOTE: The reason for sheet-metal covers over the pickup screen is to prevent cavitation. Oil is trapped under the cover, which helps prevent the oil pump from drawing in air, especially during sudden stops or during rapid acceleration.

After the oil leaves the pump, it is delivered to the moving parts through drilled oil passages. See Figure 14-21 on page 221. It needs no pressure after it reaches the parts that are to be lubricated. The oil film between the parts is developed and maintained by hydrodynamic lubrication. Excessive oil pressure requires more horsepower and provides no better lubrication than the minimum effective pressure.

FACTORS AFFECTING OIL PRESSURE

Oil pressure can only be produced when the oil pump has a capacity larger than all the "leaks" in the engine. The leaks are the clearances at end points of the lubrication system. The end points are at the edges of bearings, the rocker arms, the connecting rod

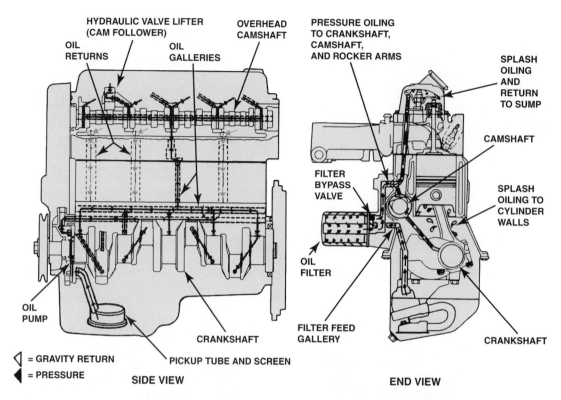

HYDRAULIC VALVE LIFTER (CAM FOLLOWER)
OVERHEAD CAMSHAFT
OIL RETURNS
OIL GALLERIES
PRESSURE OILING TO CRANKSHAFT, CAMSHAFT, AND ROCKER ARMS
SPLASH OILING AND RETURN TO SUMP
CAMSHAFT
FILTER BYPASS VALVE
SPLASH OILING TO CYLINDER WALLS
OIL FILTER
OIL PUMP
CRANKSHAFT
PICKUP TUBE AND SCREEN
FILTER FEED GALLERY
CRANKSHAFT
◁ = GRAVITY RETURN
◀ = PRESSURE
SIDE VIEW
END VIEW

FIGURE 14-20 A typical engine design that uses both pressure and splash lubrication. Oil travels under pressure through the galleries (passages) to reach the top of the engine. Other parts are lubricated as the oil flows back down into the oil pan or is splashed onto parts.

spit holes, and so on. These clearances are designed into the engine and are necessary for its proper operation. As the engine parts wear and clearance becomes greater, more oil will leak out. The oil pump *capacity* must be great enough to supply extra oil for these leaks. The capacity of the oil pump results from its size, rotating speed, and physical condition. If the pump is rotating slowly as the engine is idling, oil pump capacity is low. *If the leaks are greater than the pump capacity, engine oil pressure is low.* As the engine speed increases, the pump capacity increases and the pump tries to force more oil out of the leaks. This causes the pressure to rise until it reaches the regulated maximum pressure.

The viscosity of the engine oil affects both the pump capacity and the oil leakage. Thin oil or oil of very low viscosity slips past the edges of the pump and flows freely from the leaks. Hot oil has a low viscosity, and therefore, a hot engine often has low oil pressure. Cold oil is more viscous (thicker) than hot oil. This results in higher pressures, even with the cold engine idling. High oil pressure occurs with a cold engine, because the oil relief valve must open further to release excess oil than is necessary with a hot engine. This larger opening increases the spring compression force, which in turn increases the oil pressure. Putting higher-viscosity oil in an engine will raise the engine oil pressure to the regulated setting of the relief valve at a lower engine speed.

OIL PUMP CHECKS

The cover is removed to check the condition of the oil pump. The gears and housing are examined for scoring. If the gears and housing are heavily scored, the entire pump should be replaced. If they are lightly scored, the clearances in the pump should be measured. These clearances include the space between the gears and housing, the space between the teeth of the two gears, and the space between the side of the gear and the pump cover. A feeler gauge is often used to make these measurements. Gauging plastic can be used to measure the space between the side of the gears and the cover. The oil pump should be replaced when excessive clearance or scoring is found. See Figure 14-22 on page 222.

On most engines, the oil pump should be replaced as part of any engine work, especially if the cause for the repair is lack of lubrication.

NOTE: The oil pump is the "garbage pit" of the entire engine. Any and all debris is often forced through the gears and housing of an oil pump. See Figure 14-23 on page 222.

See Figures 14-24 and 14-25 on page 223 for examples of oil pump clearance checks.

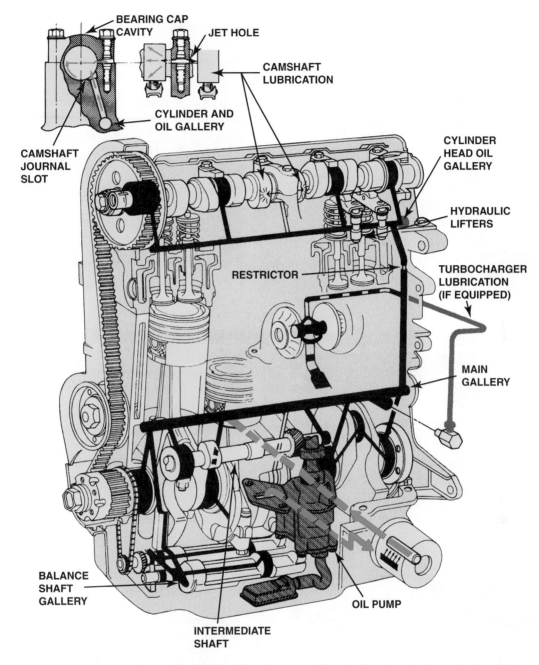

FIGURE 14-21   An intermediate shaft drives the oil pump on this overhead camshaft engine. Note the main gallery and other drilled passages in the block and cylinder head.

Always refer to the manufacturer's specifications when checking the oil pump for wear. Typical oil pump clearances include the following:

1. End plate clearance: 0.0015 inch (0.04 millimeter)
2. Side (rotor) clearance: 0.012 inch (0.30 millimeter)
3. Rotor tip clearance: 0.010 inch (0.25 millimeter)
4. Gear end play clearance: 0.004 inch (0.10 millimeter)

All parts should also be inspected closely for wear. Check the relief valve for scoring and check the condition of the spring. When installing the oil pump, coat the sealing surfaces with engine assembly lubricant. This lubricant helps draw oil from the oil pan on initial start-up.

OIL PASSAGES IN THE BLOCK

From the filter, oil goes through a drilled hole that intersects with a drilled main oil **gallery** or longitudinal header. This

(a)

(b)

FIGURE 14-22 (a) A visual inspection indicated that this pump cover was worn. (b) An embedded particle of something was found on one of the gears, making this pump worthless except for scrap metal.

is a long hole drilled from the front of the block to the back. Inline engines use one oil gallery; V-type engines may use two or three galleries. Passages drilled through the block bulkheads allow the oil to go from the main oil gallery to the main and cam bearings. See Figure 14-26 on page 224. In some engines, oil goes to the cam bearings first, and then to the main bearings.

(a)

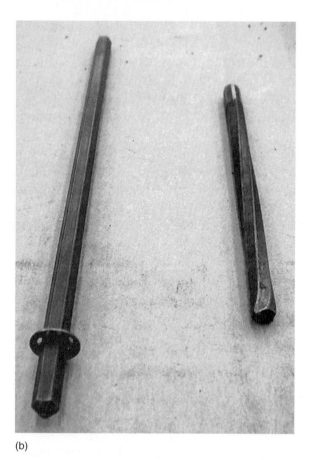

(b)

FIGURE 14-23 (a) The oil pump is the only part in an engine that gets unfiltered engine oil. The oil is drawn up from the bottom of the oil pan and is pressurized before flowing to the oil filter. (b) If debris gets into an oil pump, the drive or distributor shaft can twist and/or break. When this occurs the engine will lose all oil pressure.

FIGURE 14-24   Gear-type oil pump being checked for tooth clearance in the housing.

FIGURE 14-25   Measuring the gear-to-cover clearance of an oil pump.

It is important that the oil holes in the bearings match with the drilled passages in the bearing saddles so that the bearing can be properly lubricated. Over a long period of use, bearings will wear. This wear causes excess clearance. The excess clearance will allow too much oil to leak from the side of the bearing. When this happens, there will be little or no oil left for bearings located farther downstream in the lubricating system. This is a major cause of bearing failure. If a new bearing were installed in place of the oil-starved bearing, it, too,

would fail unless the bearing having the excess clearance was also replaced.

VALVE TRAIN LUBRICATION

The oil gallery may intersect or have drilled passages to the valve lifter bores to lubricate the lifters. When hydraulic lifters are used, the oil pressure in the gallery keeps refilling them. On some engines, oil from the lifters goes up the center of a hollow pushrod to lubricate the pushrod ends, the rocker arm pivot, and the valve stem tip. In other engines, an oil passage is drilled from either the gallery or a cam bearing to the block deck, where it matches with a gasket hole and a hole drilled in the head to carry the oil to a rocker arm shaft. Some engines use an enlarged bolt hole to carry lubrication oil around the rocker shaft cap screw to the rocker arm shaft. This design is shown by a line drawing in Figure 14-27 on page 225.

Holes in the bottom of the rocker arm shaft allow lubrication of the rocker arm pivot. Mechanical loads on the valve train hold the rocker arm against the passage in the rocker arm shaft, as shown in Figure 14-28 on page 225. This prevents excessive oil leakage from the rocker arm shaft. Often, holes are drilled in cast rocker arms to carry oil to the pushrod end and to the valve tip. Rocker arm assemblies need only a surface coating of oil, so the oil flow to the rocker assembly is minimized using restrictions or metered openings. The restriction or metering disk is in the lifter when the rocker assembly is lubricated through the pushrod. Cam journal holes that line up with oil passages are often used to meter oil to the rocker shafts.

Oil that seeps from the rocker assemblies is returned to the oil pan through drain holes. These oil drain holes are often placed so that the oil drains on the camshaft or cam drive gears to lubricate them.

Some engines have means of directing a positive oil flow to the cam drive gears or chain. This may be a nozzle or a chamfer on a bearing parting surface that allows oil to spray on the loaded portion of the cam drive mechanism.

OIL PANS

As the vehicle accelerates, brakes, or turns rapidly, the oil tends to move around in the pan. Pan baffles and oil pan shapes are often used to keep the oil inlet under the oil at all times. As the crankshaft rotates, it acts like a fan and causes air within the crankcase to rotate with it. This can cause a strong draft on the oil, churning it so that air bubbles enter the oil, which then causes oil foaming. Oil with air will not lubricate like liquid oil, so oil foaming can cause bearings to fail. A baffle or **windage tray** is sometimes installed in engines to eliminate the oil churning problem. This may be an added part, as shown in Figure 14-29 on page 225, or it may be a part of the oil pan.

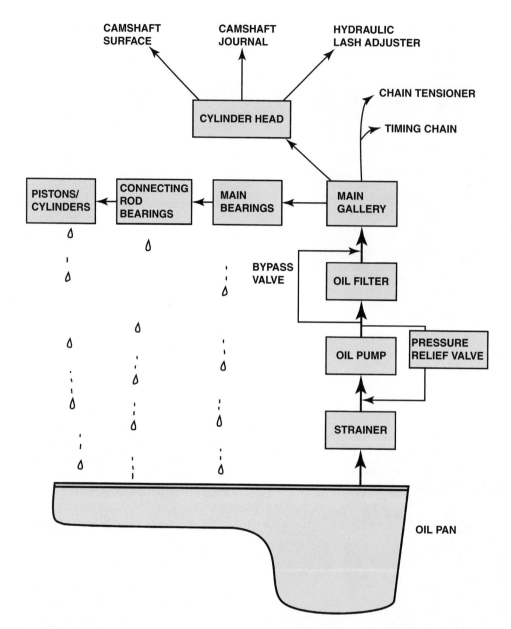

FIGURE 14-26   Oil flow through an engine starts at the oil pump pickup and eventually ends up with the oil dropping back into the oil pan.

Windage trays have the good side effect of reducing the amount of air disturbed by the crankshaft, so that less power is drained from the engine at high crankshaft speeds.

DRY SUMP SYSTEM

Construction and Operation

The term *sump* is used to describe a location where oil is stored or held. Another name for a sump is the oil pan. In most engines, oil is held in the oil pan and the oil pump drains the oil from the bottom. This type of system is called a **wet sump** oil system. In a **dry sump** system, the oil pan is shallow and

the oil is pumped into a remote reservoir. In this reservoir, the oil is cooled and any trapped air is allowed to escape before being pumped back to the engine.

Advantages

The advantages of a dry sump system include:

1. A shallow oil pan, which allows the engine to be mounted lower in the vehicle to improve cornering.
2. The oil capacity can be greatly expanded because the size of the reservoir is not limited. A larger quantity of oil means that the oil temperature can be controlled.

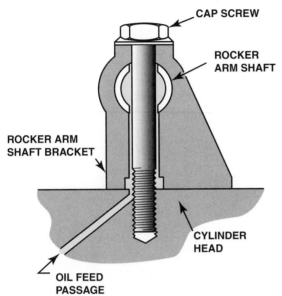

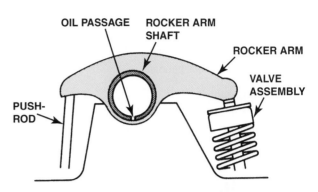

FIGURE 14-28 The rocker arm pivot is lubricated through the oil passage in the bottom of the rocker shaft. Other rocker arm styles are usually lubricated through a hollow pushrod.

FIGURE 14-27 Clearance around the rocker shaft bracket cap screw makes a passage for oil to get into the rocker shaft. (*Courtesy of Dana Corporation*)

FIGURE 14-29 Windage tray attached between the crankshaft and the oil pan.

3. A dry sump system allows the vehicle to corner and brake for long periods, which is not able to be done with a wet sump system due to the oil being thrown to one side and away from the oil pickup.

4. A dry sump system also allows the engine to develop more power as the oil is kept away from the moving crankshaft.

Disadvantages

A dry sump system does have some disadvantages including:

1. A dry sump system is expensive as it requires components and plumbing not needed in a wet sump system.

2. A dry sump system is complex because the plumbing and connections, plus the extra components, result in more places where oil leaks can occur and change the way routine maintenance is handled.

A dry sump oil system is used in most motor sport vehicles and is standard on some high-performance production vehicles, such as some models of the Chevrolet Corvette, Porsche, and BMW. See Figure 14-30.

OIL COOLERS

Oil temperature must also be controlled on many high-performance or turbocharged engines. See Figure 14-31 for an example of an engine oil cooler used on a production high-performance engine.

A larger-capacity oil pan also helps to control oil temperature. Coolant flows through the oil cooler to help warm the oil when the engine is cold and cool the oil when the engine is hot. Oil temperature should be above 212°F (100°C) to boil off any accumulated moisture, but it should not exceed about 280° to 300°F (138° to 148°C).

FREQUENTLY ASKED QUESTION

WHY IS IT CALLED A WINDAGE TRAY?

A windage tray is a plate or baffle installed under the crankshaft and is used to help prevent aeration of the oil. Where does the wind come from? Pistons push air down into the crankcase as they move from top dead center to bottom dead center. The pistons also draw air and oil upward when moving from bottom dead center to top dead center. At high engine speeds, this causes a great deal of airflow, which can easily aerate the oil. Therefore, a windage tray is used to help prevent this movement of air (wind) from affecting the oil in the pan. Try this: take an oil pan and add a few quarts (liters) of oil. Then take an electric hair dryer and use it to blow air into the oil pan. Oil will be thrown everywhere, which really helps illustrate why windage trays are used in all newer engines.

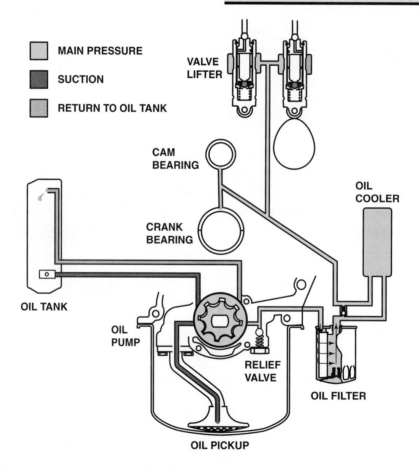

FIGURE 14-30   A dry sump system that is used on the Chevrolet Corvette.

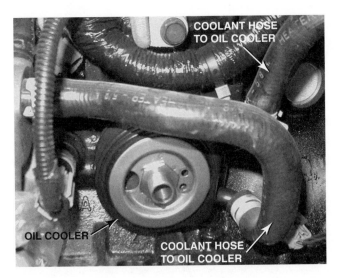

FIGURE 14-31 Typical engine oil cooler. Engine oil is cooled by passing coolant from the radiator through the auxiliary housing. The oil filter screws to the cooler.

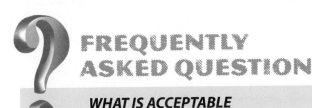

FREQUENTLY ASKED QUESTION

WHAT IS ACCEPTABLE OIL CONSUMPTION?

There are a number of opinions regarding what is acceptable oil consumption. Most vehicle owners do not want their engine to use *any* oil between oil changes even if they do not change it more often than every 7,500 miles (12,000 kilometers)! Engineers have improved machining operations and piston ring designs to help eliminate oil consumption.

Many stationary or industrial engines are not driven on the road; therefore, they do not accumulate miles, yet they still may consume excessive oil.

A general rule for "acceptable" oil consumption is that it should be about 0.002 to 0.004 pounds per horsepower per hour. To figure, use the following:

$$\frac{1.82 \times \text{quarts used}}{\text{Operating hp} \times \text{total hours}} = \text{lb/hp/hr}$$

Therefore, oil consumption is based on the amount of work an engine performs. Although the formula may not be usable for vehicle engines used for daily transportation, it may be usable by the marine or industrial engine builder. Generally, oil consumption that is greater than 1 quart for every 600 miles (1,000 kilometers per liter) is considered to be excessive with a motor vehicle.

OIL PRESSURE WARNING LAMP

All vehicles are equipped with an oil pressure gauge or a warning lamp. The warning lamp comes on whenever the engine oil pressure has dropped to 3 to 7 PSI. Normal oil pressure is considered to be 10 PSI per 1000 RPM. An electrical switch is used to convert the ground circuit of the oil pressure warning lamp if the oil pressure is below the rating of the sending unit. See Figures 14-32 and 14-33.

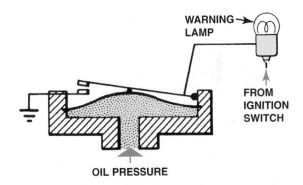

FIGURE 14-32 The oil pressure switch is connected to a warning lamp that alerts the driver of low oil pressure.

FIGURE 14-33 A typical oil pressure sending unit on a Ford V-8.

SUMMARY

1. Viscosity is the oil's thickness or resistance to flow.
2. Normal engine oil pump pressure ranges from 10 to 60 PSI (200 to 400 kPa) or 10 PSI for every 1000 engine RPM.
3. Hydrodynamic oil pressure around engine bearings is usually over 1,000 PSI (6,900 kPa).
4. Most vehicle manufacturers recommend use of SAE 5W-30 or SAE 10W-30 engine oil.
5. Most vehicle manufacturers recommend changing the engine oil every six months or every 7,500 miles (12,000 kilometers), whichever comes first. Most experts recommend changing the engine oil every 3,000 miles (5,000 kilometers), or every three months, to help ensure long engine life.
6. The oil pump is driven directly by the crankshaft or by a gear or shaft from the camshaft.

REVIEW QUESTIONS

1. What causes a wedge-shaped film to form in the oil?
2. What is hydrodynamic lubrication?
3. What is meant by the label "Energy Conserving"?
4. Explain why the oil filter is bypassed when the engine oil is cold and thick.
5. Explain why internal engine leakage affects oil pressure.
6. Explain the operation of the bypass valve located in the oil filter or oil filter adapter.
7. Describe how the oil flows from the oil pump, through the filter and main engine bearings, to the valve train.
8. What is the purpose of a windage tray?

CHAPTER QUIZ

1. Normal oil pump pressure in an engine is _____.
   a. 3 to 7 PSI
   b. 10 to 60 PSI
   c. 100 to 150 PSI
   d. 180 to 210 PSI

2. Oil change intervals as specified by the vehicle manufacturer _____.
   a. Are *maximum* time and mileage intervals
   b. Are *minimum* time and mileage intervals
   c. Only include miles driven between oil changes
   d. Generally only include time between oil changes

3. An SAE 10W-30 engine oil is _____.
   a. An SAE oil 10 with VI additives
   b. An SAE oil 20 with VI additives
   c. An SAE oil 30 with VI additives
   d. An SAE oil 30 with detergent additives

4. As engine oil is used in an engine _____.
   a. It becomes thinner as a result of chemical breakdown that occurs with age
   b. It becomes thicker because of oxidation, wear metals, and combustion by-products
   c. It becomes thicker because of temperature changes
   d. It becomes thinner because of oxidation, wear metals, and combustion by-products

5. Technician A says that the engine oil used should meet the vehicle manufacturer's standards. Technician B says that any engine oil of the correct API, SAE, and ILSAC ratings can be used. Which technician is correct?
   a. Technician A only
   b. Technician B only
   c. Both Technicians A and B
   d. Neither Technician A nor B

6. Technician A says that some vehicle manufacturers recommend an ACEA grade be used in the engine. Technician B says that an oil with the specified API rating *and* SAE viscosity rating should be used in an engine. Which technician is correct?
   a. Technician A only
   b. Technician B only
   c. Both Technicians A and B
   d. Neither Technician A nor B

7. Two technicians are discussing oil filters. Technician A says that the oil will remain perfectly clean if just the oil filter is changed regularly. Technician B says that oil filters can filter particles smaller than the human eye can see. Which technician is correct?

   a. Technician A only

   b. Technician B only

   c. Both Technicians A and B

   d. Neither Technician A nor B

8. Turbocharged engines have special engine oil needs, such as _____.

   a. Strict oil change intervals should be observed

   b. Oil of the proper API and SAE ratings should be used

   c. The turbocharger should be primed by cranking the engine before starting

   d. All of the above

9. A typical oil pump can pump how many gallons per minute?

   a. 3 to 6 gallons

   b. 6 to 10 gallons

   c. 10 to 60 gallons

   d. 50 to 100 gallons

10. In typical engine lubrication systems, what components are the last to receive oil and the first to suffer from a lack of oil or oil pressure?

    a. Main bearings

    b. Rod bearings

    c. Valve trains

    d. Oil filters

CHAPTER 15

STARTING AND CHARGING SYSTEM OPERATION AND DIAGNOSIS

OBJECTIVES

After studying Chapter 15, the reader will be able to:

1. Prepare for Engine Repair (A1) ASE certification test content area "E" (Fuel, Electrical, Ignition, and Exhaust Systems Inspections and Service).
2. List the precautions necessary whenever working with batteries.
3. Describe how to test a battery.
4. Explain how to safely charge a battery.
5. Describe how the cranking circuit works.
6. Describe how to perform cranking system testing procedures.
7. Discuss the various AC generator test procedures.

KEY TERMS

Alternator (p. 241)
Ampere Hour (p. 234)
Ampere-Hour Rating (p. 236)
Cold-Cranking Amperes (CCA) (p. 234)
Cranking Amperes (CA) (p. 234)

Load Test (p. 235)
Open-Circuit Battery Voltage Test (p. 235)
Reserve Capacity (p. 234)
Sealed Lead Acid (SLA) (p. 233)
Specific Gravity (p. 232)

For any engine to start, it must be rotated. It is the purpose and function of the cranking circuit to create the necessary power and transfer it from the battery to the starter motor that rotates the engine.

Everything electrical in a vehicle is supplied with current from the battery. The battery is one of the most important parts of a vehicle.

All vehicles operate electrical components by taking current from the battery. It is the purpose and function of the charging system to keep the battery fully charged. The SAE standardized name for an alternator is the generator.

All electrical generators use the principle of electromagnetic induction to generate electrical power from mechanical power. Electromagnetic induction involves the generation of an electrical current in a conductor when the conductor is moved through a magnetic field.

PURPOSE OF A BATTERY

The primary purpose of an automotive battery is to provide a source of electrical power for starting and for electrical demands that exceed generator output. The battery also acts as a stabilizer to the voltage for the entire electrical system. The battery is a voltage stabilizer because it acts as a reservoir where large amounts of current (amperes) can be removed quickly during starting and replaced gradually by the alternator during charging. The battery *must* be in good (serviceable) condition before the charging system and the cranking system can be tested.

HOW A BATTERY WORKS

A fully charged lead–acid battery has a positive plate of lead dioxide (peroxide) and a negative plate of lead surrounded by a sulfuric acid solution (electrolyte). The difference in potential (voltage) between lead peroxide and lead in acid is approximately 2.1 volts in each cell. See Figure 15-1.

During Discharging

The positive-plate lead dioxide (PbO_2) combines with the SO_4 from the electrolyte and releases its O_2 into the electrolyte, forming H_2O. The negative plate also combines with the SO_4 from the electrolyte and becomes lead sulfate ($PbSO_4$). See Figure 15-2.

The Fully Discharged State

When the battery is fully discharged, both the positive and the negative plates are $PbSO_4$ (lead sulfate) and the electrolyte has become water (H_2O). It is usually impossible for a

FIGURE 15-1   Photo of a cutaway battery showing the connection of the cells to each other through the partition.

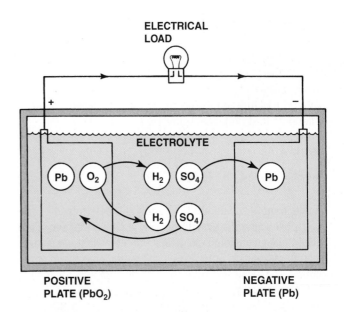

FIGURE 15-2   Chemical reaction for a lead–acid battery that is fully *charged* being discharged by the attached electrical load.

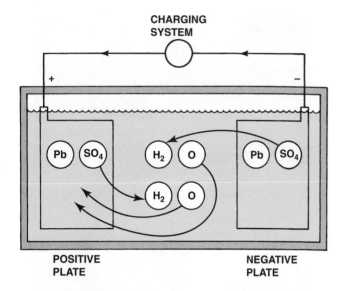

FIGURE 15-3 Chemical reaction for a lead–acid battery that is fully *discharged* being charged by the attached generator.

battery to become 100% discharged; however, as the battery is being discharged, the plates and electrolyte approach the completely dead situation.

CAUTION: There is danger of freezing when a battery is discharged, because the electrolyte is mostly water.

During Charging

During charging, the sulfate (acid) leaves both the positive and the negative plates and returns to the electrolyte, where it becomes normal-strength sulfuric acid solution. The positive plate returns to lead dioxide (PbO_2) and the negative plate is again pure lead (Pb). See Figure 15-3.

SPECIFIC GRAVITY

The amount of sulfate in the electrolyte is determined by the electrolyte's **specific gravity.** Specific gravity is the ratio of the weight of a given volume of a liquid to the weight of an equal volume of water. In other words, the more dense the material (liquid), the higher is its specific gravity. Pure water is the basis for this measurement and has a specific gravity of 1.000 at 80°F. Pure sulfuric acid has a specific gravity of 1.835. The *correct* concentration of water and sulfuric acid (called *electrolyte*—64% water, 36% acid) is 1.260 to 1.280 at 80°F.

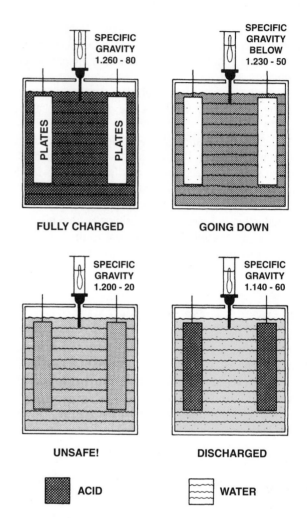

FIGURE 15-4 As the battery becomes discharged, the specific gravity of the battery acid decreases.

The higher the battery's specific gravity, the more fully it is charged. See Figure 15-4.

Charge Indicators

Some batteries are equipped with a built-in state-of-charge indicator. This indicator is simply a small ball-type hydrometer that is installed in one cell. This hydrometer uses a plastic ball that floats if the electrolyte is dense enough (when the battery is about 65% charged). When the ball floats, it appears in the hydrometer's sight glass, changing its color. See Figures 15-5 and 15-6. Because the hydrometer is only testing one cell (out of six on a 12-volt battery), and because the hydrometer ball can easily stick in one position, it should not be trusted to give accurate information about a battery's state of charge.

Specific Gravity versus State of Charge and Battery Voltage

Values for specific gravity, state of charge, and battery voltage at 80°F (27°C) are given in the following table.

Specific Gravity	State of Charge	Battery Voltage (V)
1.265	Fully charged	12.6 or higher
1.225	75% charged	12.4
1.190	50% charged	12.2
1.155	25% charged	12.0
Lower than 1.120	Discharged	11.9 or lower

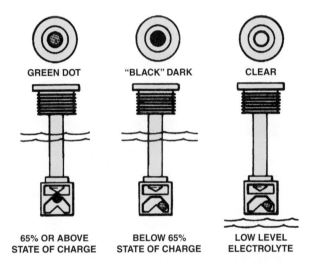

GREEN DOT — 65% OR ABOVE STATE OF CHARGE

"BLACK" DARK — BELOW 65% STATE OF CHARGE

CLEAR — LOW LEVEL ELECTROLYTE

FIGURE 15-5 Typical battery charge indicator. If the specific gravity is low (battery discharged), the ball drops away from the reflective prism. When the battery is charged enough, the ball floats and reflects the color of the ball (usually green) back up through the sight glass and the sight glass is dark.

FIGURE 15-6 Cutaway of the battery showing the charge indicator. If the electrolyte level drops below the bottom of the prism, the sight glass shows clear (light). Most battery manufacturers warn that if the electrolyte level is low on a sealed battery, the battery must be replaced. Attempting to charge a battery that has a low electrolyte level can cause a buildup of gases and possibly an explosion.

Battery Hold-Downs

All batteries must be attached securely to the vehicle to prevent battery damage. Normal vehicle vibrations can cause the active materials inside the battery to shed. Battery hold-down clamps or brackets help reduce vibration, which can greatly reduce the capacity and life of any battery.

ABSORBED GLASS MAT (AGM) BATTERY

Absorbed glass mat (AGM) batteries are sealed batteries where the electrolyte is absorbed into spongelike glass mats between the plates. The expected life is longer than the regular (called *flooded-type*), and AGM batteries can be installed in any position, even upside down. An AGM battery with a broken seal will quickly lose capacity if the plates are exposed to outside air. AGM batteries (also referred to as **sealed lead acid [SLA]** batteries) convert the released hydrogen and oxygen back into water instead of escaping as gasses. AGM batteries are able to better withstand vibration and last longer than conventional batteries that contain liquid electrolyte. See Figure 15-7.

BATTERY RATINGS

Batteries are rated according to the amount of current they can produce under specific conditions.

FIGURE 15-7 An example of an AGM battery. An AGM battery requires a special charger that allow the battery to be charged at a high current (ampere) rate but not over 15 volts. Conventional chargers often exceed 16 volts.

Cold-Cranking Amperes

Every automotive battery must be able to supply electrical power to crank the engine in cold weather and still provide voltage high enough to operate the ignition system for starting. The cold-cranking power of a battery is the number of amperes that can be supplied by a battery at 0°F (−18°C) for 30 seconds while the battery still maintains a voltage of 1.2 volts per cell or higher. This means that the battery voltage would be 7.2 volts for a 12-volt battery and 3.6 volts for a 6-volt battery. The cold-cranking performance rating is called **cold-cranking amperes (CCA).** Try to purchase a battery with the highest CCA for the money. See vehicle manufacturers' specifications for recommended battery capacity.

Cranking Amperes

Cranking amperes (CA) are not the same as CCA, but are often advertised and labeled on batteries. The designation CA refers to the number of amperes that can be supplied by the battery at 32°F (0°C). This rating results in a higher number than the more stringent rating of CCA. See Figure 15-8.

Marine Amperes

Similar to cranking amperes, this rating also tests the battery at 32°F (0°C).

Reserve Capacity

The **reserve capacity** rating for batteries is *the number of minutes* for which the battery can produce 25 amperes and still have a battery voltage of 1.75 volts per cell (10.5 volts for a 12-volt battery). This rating is actually a measurement of the time for which a vehicle can be driven in the event of a charging system failure.

Ampere Hour

Ampere hour is an older battery rating system that measures how many amperes of current the battery can produce over a period of time. For example, a battery that has a 50-amp-hour (A-H) rating can deliver 50 amperes for one hour or 1 ampere for 50 hours or any combination that equals 50 amp-hours.

BATTERY SERVICE

Safety Considerations

Batteries contain acid and release explosive gases (hydrogen and oxygen) during normal charging and discharging cycles. To help prevent physical injury or damage to the vehicle, always adhere to the following safety procedures:

1. When working on any electrical component of a vehicle, disconnect the negative battery cable from the battery. When the negative cable is disconnected, all electrical circuits in the vehicle will be open, which will prevent accidental electrical contact between an electrical component and ground. Any electrical spark has the potential to cause explosion and personal injury.
2. Wear eye protection when working around any battery.
3. Wear protective clothing to avoid skin contact with battery acid.
4. Always adhere to all safety precautions as stated in the service procedures for the equipment used in battery service and testing.
5. Never smoke or use an open flame around any battery.

Battery Maintenance

Battery maintenance includes making certain that the battery case is clean and adding clean water, if necessary. Distilled water is recommended by all battery manufacturers, but if distilled water is not available, clean ordinary drinking water, low in mineral content, can be used. Because water is the only thing in a battery that is consumed, acid should never be added to a battery. Some of the water in the electrolyte escapes during the normal operation of charging and discharging, but the acid content of the electrolyte remains in the battery. Do not overfill a battery, because normal bubbling (gassing) of the electrolyte will cause the electrolyte to escape and start corrosion on the battery terminals, hold-down brackets, and battery tray. Fill batteries to the indicator that is approximately 1 1/2 inches (3.8 centimeters) from the top of the filler tube.

FIGURE 15-8   This battery has a cranking amperes (CA) rating of 1000, which means that this battery is capable of supplying 1000 amperes to crank an engine for 30 seconds at a temperature of 32°F (0°C) at a minimum of 1.2 volts per cell (7.2 volts for a 12-volt battery).

FIGURE 15-9   A corroded battery terminal.

FIGURE 15-10   This battery cable was found to be corroded underneath. The corrosion had eaten through the insulation yet was not noticeable until it was carefully inspected. This cable should be replaced.

FIGURE 15-11   Carefully inspect all battery terminals for corrosion. This vehicle uses two positive battery cables connected at the battery using a long bolt. This is a common source of corrosion that can cause a starting (cranking) problem.

Battery cable connections should be checked and cleaned to prevent voltage drop at the connections. One common reason for an engine not starting is loose or corroded battery cable connections. See Figures 15-9 through 15-11.

Battery Voltage Testing

Testing the battery voltage with a voltmeter is a simple method for determining the state of charge of any battery. The voltage of a battery does not necessarily indicate whether the battery can perform satisfactorily, but it does indicate to the technician more about the battery's condition than a simple visual inspection. A battery that "looks good" may not be good. This test is commonly called an **open-circuit battery voltage test,** because it is conducted with an open circuit—with no current flowing and no load applied to the battery.

1. If the battery has just been charged or the vehicle has recently been driven, it is necessary to remove the surface charge from the battery before testing. A surface charge is a charge of higher-than-normal voltage that is only on the surface of the battery plates. The surface charge is quickly removed when the battery is loaded and therefore does not accurately represent the true state of charge of the battery.
2. To remove the surface charge, turn the headlights on high beam (brights) for 1 minute, then turn the headlights off and wait 2 minutes.
3. With the engine and all electrical accessories off, and the doors shut (to turn off the interior lights), connect a voltmeter to the battery posts. Connect the red positive lead to the positive post and the black negative lead to the negative post.

NOTE: If the meter reads negative, the battery has been reverse charged (has reversed polarity) and should be replaced, or the meter has been connected incorrectly.

4. Read the voltmeter and compare the results with the following state-of-charge chart. The voltages shown are for a battery at or near room temperature (70° to 80°F) or (21° to 27°C). See Figure 15-12.

Battery Voltage (V)	State of Charge
12.6 or higher	100% charged
12.4	75% charged
12.2	50% charged
12.0	25% charged
11.9 or lower	Discharged

Battery Load Testing

One of the most accurate tests to determine the condition of any battery is the **load test.** Most automotive starting and charging

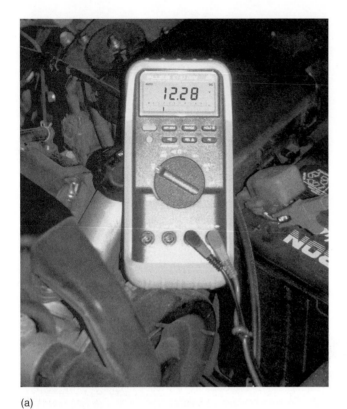

(a)

(b)

FIGURE 15-12   (a) Voltmeter showing the battery voltage after the headlights were on (engine off) for 1 minute. (b) Headlights were turned off and the battery voltage quickly recovered to indicate 12.6 volts.

testers use a carbon pile to create an electrical load on the battery. The amount of the load is determined by the original capacity of the battery being tested. The capacity is measured in cold-cranking amperes, which is the number of amperes that a battery can supply at 0°F (−18°C) for 30 seconds. *The proper electrical load to be used to test a battery is one-half the CCA rating or three times the ampere-hour rating, with a minimum 250-ampere load.* After the battery has been tested to be at least 75% charged by observing the built-in hydrometer or by performing an open-circuit voltage test, a load test can be performed. Apply the load for a full 15 seconds and observe the voltmeter at the end of the 15-second period while the battery is still under load. A good battery should indicate above 9.6 V. Many battery manufacturers recommend performing the load test twice, using the first load period to remove the surface charge on the battery and the second test to provide a truer indication of the condition of the battery. Wait 30 seconds between tests to allow time for the battery to recover. See Figure 15-13.

If the battery fails the load test, recharge the battery and retest. If a second failure occurs, replace the battery.

NOTE: Some battery testers measure the capacitance of the battery to determine the state of charge and battery condition. Always follow the test equipment manufacturer's recommended test procedure.

Electronic Battery Testers

Electronic (non-load testing) testers use the conductance of the battery to determine capacity and condition. Conductance is a measurement of the battery's ability to produce

FIGURE 15-13   A Bear Automotive starting and charging tester. This tester automatically loads the battery for 15 seconds to remove the surface charge, then waits 30 seconds to allow the battery to recover, then again loads the battery. The display indicates the status of the battery.

current. To measure conductance, the tester creates a small signal that is sent through the battery and then measures a portion of the AC current response. Conductance is a measure of the plate surface available in the battery, which determines how much power the battery can supply. As a battery ages, the plate surface can sulfate or shed active material, which adversely affects its ability to perform. In addition, conductance can be used to detect cell defects, shorts, and open circuits, which will reduce the ability of the battery to deliver current. To operate the tester, use the keys and follow the directions on the display. The tester will test the battery and display the results. See Figure 15-14.

NOTE: Good connections to the battery are critical for the proper operation of the electronic battery tester.

Battery Charging

If the state of charge of a battery is low, it must be recharged. It is best to slow-charge any battery to prevent possible overheating damage to the battery. See Figure 15-15 for the recommended charging rate. *Remember, it may take 8 hours or more to charge a fully discharged battery.* The initial charge rate should be about 35 amperes for 30 minutes to help start the charging process. Fast-charging a battery increases the temperature of the battery and can cause warping of the plates inside the battery. Fast-charging also increases the amount of gassing (release of hydrogen and oxygen), which can create a health and fire hazard. The battery temperature should not exceed 125°F (hot to the touch). *Most batteries should be charged at a rate equal to 1% of the battery's CCA rating.*

Fast charge: 15 amperes maximum
Slow charge: 5 amperes maximum

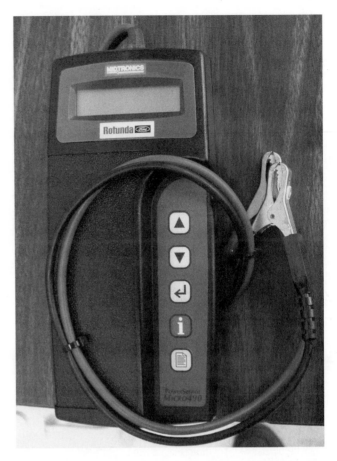

FIGURE 15-14   A typical electronic battery tester which, depending on the model, can also be used to test the starting and the charging systems.

Charging Time

The time needed to charge a battery depends on the state-of-charge and the battery reserve capacity. See the following chart.

State of Charge	75%		50%		25%		0%	
Charge Rate (Amps)	5	10	5	10	5	10	5	10
50 RC	75	35	150	75	225	130	300	150
60 RC	90	45	180	90	270	135	360	180
70 RC	105	50	210	105	315	155	420	210
80 RC	120	60	240	120	360	180	480	240
90 RC	135	65	270	135	405	200	540	270
100 RC	150	75	300	150	450	225	600	300
110 RC	165	80	330	165	495	240	660	330
120 RC	180	90	360	180	540	270	720	360

Battery Reserve (RC)
Capacity Rating in Minutes   Charge Time in Minutes

FIGURE 15-15 This battery charger is charging the battery at a 10-ampere rate. A slow rate such as this is easier on the battery than a fast charge that may overheat the battery and cause warpage of the plates inside the battery.

TECH TIP

IT COULD HAPPEN TO YOU!

The owner of a Toyota replaced the battery. After replacing the battery, the owner noted that the "airbag" amber warning lamp was lit and the radio was locked out. The owner had purchased the vehicle used from a dealer and did not know the four-digit security code needed to unlock the radio. Determined to fix it, the owner tried three four-digit numbers, hoping that one of them would work. However, after three tries, the radio became permanently disabled.

Frustrated, the owner went to a dealer. It cost over $300 to fix the problem. A special tool was required to reset the airbag lamp. The radio had to be removed and sent out of state to an authorized radio service center and then reinstalled into the vehicle.

Therefore, before disconnecting the battery, please check with the owner to be certain that the owner has the security code for a security-type radio. A "memory saver" may be needed to keep the radio powered when the battery is being disconnected. See Figure 15-16.

JUMP STARTING

To jump start another vehicle with a dead battery, connect good-quality copper jumper cables as indicated in Figure 15-17. The last connection made should always be on the engine block or an engine bracket as far from the battery as possible.

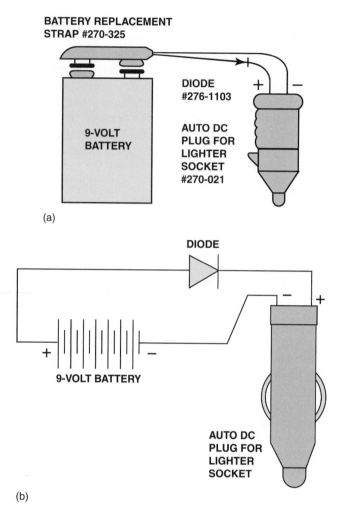

FIGURE 15-16 (a) Memory saver. The part numbers represent components from Radio Shack™. (b) A schematic drawing of the same memory saver.

It is normal for a spark to be created when the jumper cables finally complete the jumping circuit, and this spark could cause an explosion of the gases around the battery. Many newer vehicles have special ground connections built away from the battery just for the purpose of jump starting. Check the owner's manual or service manual for the exact location.

CRANKING CIRCUIT

The cranking circuit includes those mechanical and electrical components required to crank the engine for starting. In the early 1900s, the cranking force was the driver's arm. Modern cranking circuits include the following:

1. **Starter motor.** The starter is normally a 0.5 to 2.6-horsepower (0.4 to 2.0-kilowatt) electric motor. See Figure 15-18 on page 240.
2. **Battery.** The battery must be of the correct capacity and be at least 75% charged to provide the necessary current and voltage for correct operation of the starter.

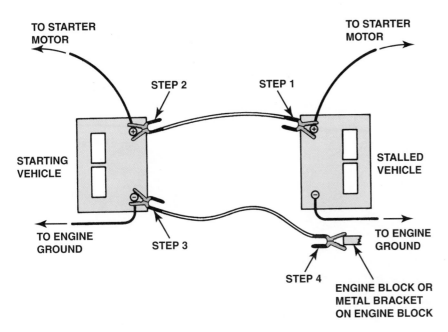

FIGURE 15-17 Jumper cable usage guide. Notice that the last electrical connection is made to the engine block or an engine bracket away from the battery to help prevent a spark that could occur, causing harm to the disabled vehicle or to the person performing the jump starting.

3. **Starter solenoid or relay.** The high current required by the starter must be able to be turned on and off. A large switch would be required if the current were controlled by the driver directly. Instead, a small current switch (ignition switch) operates a solenoid or relay that controls the high starter current.

4. **Starter drive.** The starter drive uses a small gear that contacts the engine flywheel gear and transmits starter motor power to rotate the engine.
5. **Ignition switch.** The ignition switch and safety control switches control the starter motor operation.
6. **Neutral safety (clutch switch).** This switch prevents the operation of the starter unless the gear selector is in park or neutral or the clutch pedal is depressed. See Figure 15-19.

FREQUENTLY ASKED QUESTION

SHOULD BATTERIES BE KEPT OFF CONCRETE FLOORS?

All batteries should be stored in a cool, dry place when not in use. Many technicians have been warned not to store or place a battery on concrete. According to battery experts, it is the temperature difference between the top and the bottom of the battery that causes a difference in the voltage potential between the top (warmer section) and the bottom (colder section). This difference in temperature causes self-discharge to occur. In fact, submarines cycle seawater around their batteries to keep all sections of the battery at the same temperature to help prevent self-discharge.

Therefore, always store or place batteries off the floor and in a location where the entire battery can be kept at the same temperature, avoiding extreme heat and freezing temperatures.

Concrete cannot drain the battery directly, because the battery case is a very good electrical insulator.

TECH TIP

WATCH THE DOME LIGHT

When diagnosing any starter-related problem, open the door of the vehicle and observe the brightness of the dome or interior light(s).

- The brightness of any electrical lamp is proportional to the voltage.
- Normal operation of the starter results in a slight dimming of the dome light.
- If the light remains bright, the problem is usually an open circuit in the control circuit.
- If the light goes out or almost goes out, the problem is usually a shorted or grounded armature of field coils inside the starter or a defective battery.

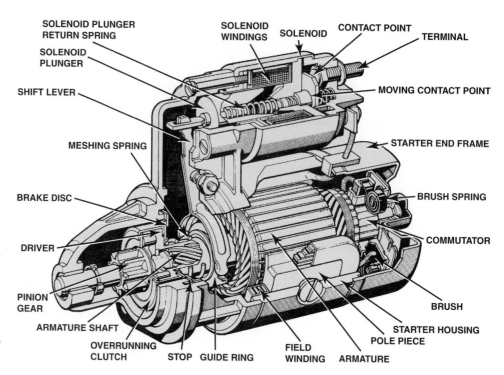

FIGURE 15-18 A cutaway view of a typical starter motor.

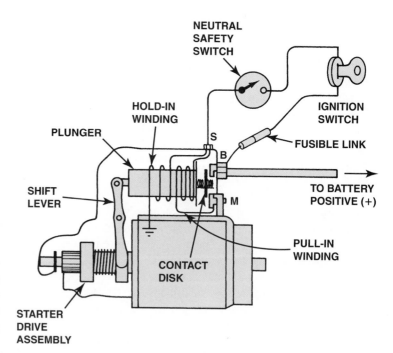

FIGURE 15-19 Wiring diagram of a typical starter solenoid. Notice that both the pull-in winding and the hold-in winding are energized when the ignition switch is first turned to the "start" position. As soon as the solenoid contact disk makes electrical contact with both the B and M terminals, the battery current is conducted to the starter motor.

STARTING SYSTEM TROUBLESHOOTING

The proper operation of the starting system depends on a good battery, good cables and connections, and a good starter motor. Because a starting problem can be caused by a defective component anywhere in the starting circuit, it is important to check for the proper operation of each part of the circuit to diagnose and repair the problem quickly.

DON'T HIT THAT STARTER!

In the past, it was common to see service technicians hitting a starter in their effort to diagnose a no-crank condition. Often the shock of the blow to the starter aligned or moved the brushes, armature, and bushings. Many times, the starter functioned after being hit—even if only for a short time.

However, most of today's starters use permanent-magnet (PM) fields, and the magnets can be easily broken if hit. A magnet that is broken becomes two weaker magnets. Some early PM starters used magnets that were glued or bonded to the field housing. If struck with a heavy tool, the magnets could be broken with parts of the magnet falling onto the armature and into the bearing pockets, making the starter impossible to repair or rebuild.

NOTE: Starter remanufacturers state that the single most common cause of starter motor failure is low battery voltage.

STARTER AMPERAGE TESTING

Before performing a starter amperage test, be certain that the battery is sufficiently charged (75% or more) and capable of supplying adequate starting current.

TOO HOT!

If a cable or connection is hot to the touch, there is electrical resistance in the cable or connection. The resistance changes electrical energy into heat energy. Therefore, if a voltmeter is not available, touch the battery cables and connections while cranking the engine. If any cable or connection is hot to the touch, it should be cleaned or replaced.

A starter amperage test should be performed when the starter fails to operate normally (is slow in cranking) or as part of a routine electrical system inspection. Some service manuals specify normal starter amperage for starter motors being tested on the vehicle; however, most service manuals only give the specifications for bench-testing a starter without a load applied. If exact specifications are not available, the following can be used as general specifications for testing a starter on the vehicle:

4-cylinder engines = 150–185 amperes
6-cylinder engines = 160–200 amperes
8-cylinder engines = 185–250 amperes

Excessive current draw may indicate one or more of the following:

1. Binding of starter armature as a result of worn bushings
2. Oil too thick (viscosity too high) for weather conditions
3. Shorted or grounded starter windings or cables
4. Tight or seized engine

Also see the starter trouble diagnostic chart in Figure 15-20.

BENCH TESTING

Every starter should be tested before it is installed in a vehicle. The usual method includes clamping the starter in a vise to prevent rotation during operation and connecting heavy-gauge jumper wires (minimum 4 gauge) to a battery known to be good, and the starter. The starter motor should rotate as fast as specifications indicate and not draw more than the free-spinning amperage permitted.

AC GENERATORS

How an AC Generator Works

A rotor inside an AC generator (also called an **alternator**) is turned by the engine through an accessory drive belt. The magnetic field of the rotor generates a current in the windings of the stator by electromagnetic induction. See Figures 15-21 and 15-22 on page 243.

Most AC generators are designed to supply between 13.5 and 15.0 volts at 2000 engine RPM. Be sure to check the vehicle manufacturer's specifications. For example, most General Motors vehicles specify a charging voltage of 14.7 volts ± 0.5 (or between 14.2 and 15.2 volts).

Charging-system voltage tests should be performed on a vehicle with a battery at least 75% charged. If the battery is discharged (or defective), the charging voltage may be below specifications. To measure charging-system voltage, follow these steps:

1. Connect the voltmeter to the positive and negative terminals of the battery.

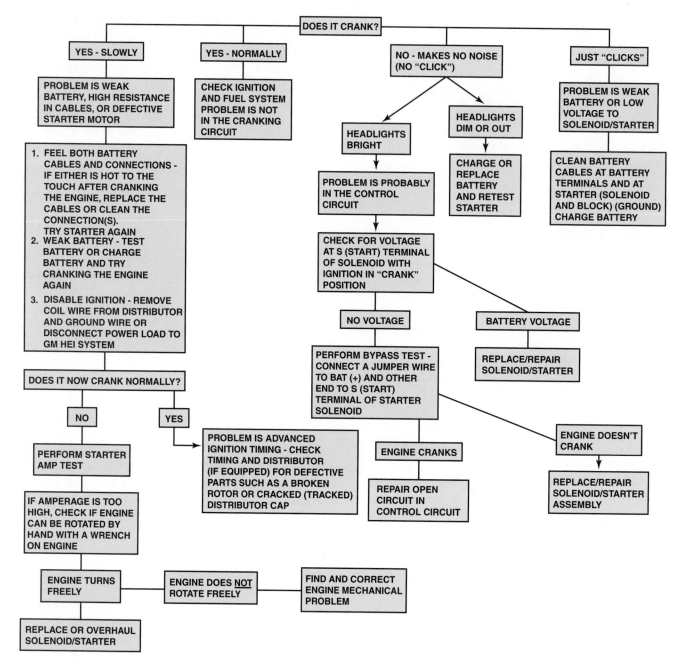

FIGURE 15-20   Starter trouble diagnostic chart.

2. Set the meter to read DC volts.
3. Start the engine and raise to a fast idle (about 2000 RPM).
4. Read the voltmeter and compare it with specifications. See Figure 15-23. If lower than specifications, charge the battery and test for excessive charging-circuit voltage drop before replacing the alternator.

NOTE: If the voltmeter reading rises then becomes lower as the engine speed is increased, the generator drive (accessory drive) belt is loose or slipping.

AC Voltage Check

A good AC generator should *not* produce any AC voltage. It is the purpose of the diodes in the AC generator to rectify all AC voltage into DC voltage. The procedure to check for AC voltage includes the following steps:

Step 1   Set the digital meter to read AC volts.
Step 2   Start the engine and operate it at 2000 RPM (fast idle).
Step 3   Connect the voltmeter leads to the positive and negative battery terminals.

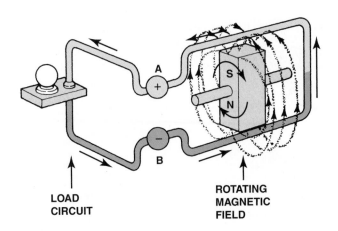

FIGURE 15-21   Magnetic lines of force cutting across a conductor induce a voltage and current in the conductor.

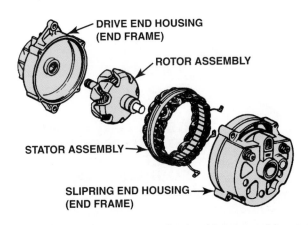

FIGURE 15-22   The aluminum housing of the generator (alternator) houses the stationary stator and the rotating rotor.

Step 4   Turn on the headlights to provide an electrical load on the AC generator.

NOTE: A higher, more accurate reading can be obtained by touching the meter lead to the output terminal of the AC generator.

The results should be interpreted as follows: If the diodes are good, the voltmeter should read *less* than 0.4 volt AC. If the reading is over 0.5 volt AC, the rectifier diodes are defective.

NOTE: This test will *not* test for a defective diode trio.

AC Generator Output Testing

A charging circuit may be able to produce correct charging-circuit voltage but not adequate amperage output. If in doubt

FIGURE 15-23   The digital multimeter should be set to read DC volts; the red lead is connected to the battery positive (+) terminal and the black meter lead is connected to the negative (−) battery terminal.

TECH TIP

THE LIGHTER PLUG TRICK

Battery voltage measurements can be read through the lighter socket. See Figure 15-24. Simply construct a test tool using a lighter plug at one end of a length of two-conductor wire and the other end connected to a double banana plug. The double banana plug will fit most meters in the common (COM) terminal and the volt terminal of the meter.

about charging-system output, first check the condition of the AC generator drive belt. With the engine off, attempt to rotate the fan of the AC generator by hand. Replace or tighten the drive belt if the AC generator fan can be rotated by hand. See Figures 15-25 and 15-26 for typical test equipment hookup.

The testing procedure for AC generator output is as follows:

1.   Connect the starting and charging test leads according to the manufacturer's instructions. Place the ammeter probe from the tester around the output cable from the back of the generator (alternator).
2.   Start the engine and operate it at 2000 RPM (fast idle). Turn the load increase control slowly to obtain the highest reading on the ammeter scale. Note the ampere reading.

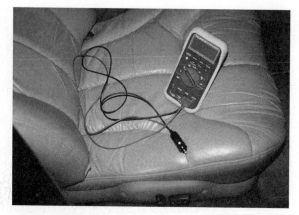

(a)

(b)

FIGURE 15-24 (a) A simple and easy-to-use tester can be made from a lighter plug and double banana plug that fits the COM and V terminals of most digital meters. (b) By plugging the lighter plug into the lighter, the charging-circuit voltage can be easily measured.

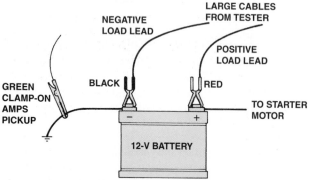

TEST LEAD CONNECTIONS FOR TESTING THE STARTING SYSTEM, CHARGING SYSTEM, VOLTAGE REGULATOR, AND DIODE STATOR.

FIGURE 15-25 Typical hookup of a starting and charging tester.

FIGURE 15-26 When connecting an inductive ammeter probe, be certain that the pickup is over *all* wires. The probe will work equally well over either all positive or all negative cables, because all current leaving a battery must return.

TECH TIP

USE A TEST LIGHT TO CHECK FOR A DEFECTIVE FUSIBLE LINK

Most AC generators (alternators) use a fusible link between the output terminal located on the slip-ring-end frame and the positive (+) terminal of the battery. If this fusible link is defective (blown), then the charging system will not operate. Many AC generators have been replaced repeatedly because of a blown fusible link that was not discovered until later. A quick and easy test to check if the fusible link is okay is to touch a test light to the output terminal. With the other end of the test light attached to a good ground, the fusible link is okay if the light lights. This test confirms that the circuit between the AC generator and the battery has continuity.

The AC generator output should be within 10% of its rated output.

NOTE: When applying a load to the battery with a carbon pile tester during an AC generator output test, do not permit the battery voltage to drop below 12 volts. Most AC generators will produce their maximum output (in amperes) above 13 volts.

ACCESSORY DRIVE BELT REPLACEMENT   Step-by-Step

STEP 1 A special tool used to remove and replace most serpentine accessory drive belts. This tool comes with various sockets that fit a variety of vehicles.

STEP 2 The tool attaches to the tensioner. The long handle provides leverage needed to remove the tension from the belt.

STEP 3 By rotating the tensioner, the tension on the belt is removed.

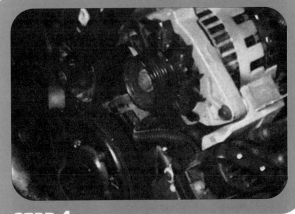

STEP 4 The belt can be easily removed after the tension has been removed.

STEP 5 Installing a new serpentine accessory drive belt requires that force be maintained on the tool while the belt is routed onto all of the accessory pulleys. Most vehicles have a placard under the hood showing the correct routing of the accessory drive belt.

STEP 6 After the belt is positioned over the pulleys, the tension can be removed from the tensioner and the tool removed. Start the engine and verify proper accessory drive belt installation.

STARTING AND CHARGING VOLTMETER TEST   Step-by-Step

STEP 1 Prepare a digital multimeter to read volts by placing the red meter lead into the "VΩ" (red) input terminal and the black meter lead into the input terminal labeled "COM" as shown.

STEP 2 Connect the red meter lead clip to the positive (+) terminal of the battery and connect the black meter lead clip to the negative (−) terminal of the battery.

STEP 3 Turn the meter on and select DC volts.

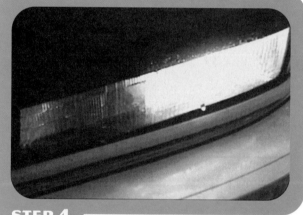

STEP 4 Turn the headlights on for about 1 minute to remove the surface charge from the battery.

STEP 5 Watch the meter display with the headlights on. A good fully charged battery will indicate a slight drop in voltage such as shown here (12.44 volts). A weak or discharged battery will usually indicate a rapidly falling voltage reading when the headlights are first turned on.

STEP 6 Turn off the headlights after about I minute or when the voltage reading stops rising.

STARTING AND CHARGING VOLTMETER TEST   continued

STEP 7 The voltage should increase after the lights are turned off. Record the voltage when the reading stops increasing. A reading of 12.6 or higher indicates a fully charged 12-volt battery.

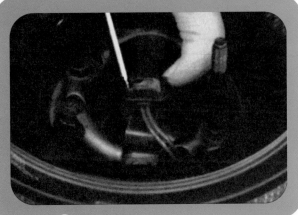

STEP 8 To prevent the engine from starting during a cranking voltage part of the test, the fuel injector can be disconnected.

STEP 9 Crank the engine using the ignition switch.

STEP 10 Observe the voltmeter while cranking. A reading of about 9.6 volts indicates that the cranking circuit is okay.

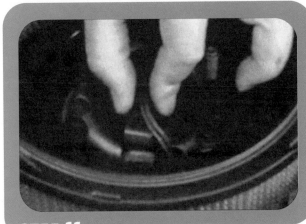

STEP 11 Reconnect the fuel injector.

STEP 12 Start and operate the engine at 2000 RPM (fast idle).

(continued)

STARTING AND CHARGING VOLTMETER TEST   continued

STEP 13 Observe the voltmeter. Acceptable charging system voltage should be between 13.5 and 15.0 volts.

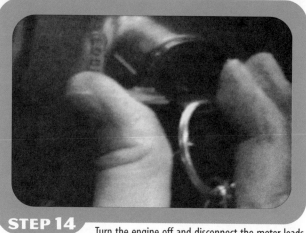

STEP 14 Turn the engine off and disconnect the meter leads. This test is complete.

BATTERY LOAD TEST   Step-by-Step

STEP 1 This type of tester uses a carbon pile to provide a connective path to load the battery, and therefore is often called a carbon-pile tester.

STEP 2 Start by connecting the large red clamp from the tester to the positive (+) terminal of the battery and the large black clamp to the negative (−) terminal of the battery.

STEP 3 Attach the inductive amp probe over the meter red tester lead wire. According to Sun Electric, the arrow on the probe should point toward the battery.

STEP 4 Zero the ammeter by turning the zero adjust knob until the needle on the meter indicates zero.

STEP 5 Determine the cold-cranking amperes (CCA) of the battery. This rating is usually on a sticker on the battery case.

STEP 6 Turn the load knob until the ammeter reading is one-half of the CCA rating of the battery. Maintain applying this load for 15 seconds. With the load still applied, observe the voltmeter reading at the end of the 15-second test. The battery voltage should be above 9.6 volts.

STARTER AMPERAGE DRAW TEST Step-by-Step

STEP 1 A Sun Electric VAT-40 is being used to measure the amount of current, in amperes, required to crank the engine.

STEP 2 Clamp the inductive ampere probe around either all of the wires from the positive terminal or over all of the wires from the negative terminal as shown.

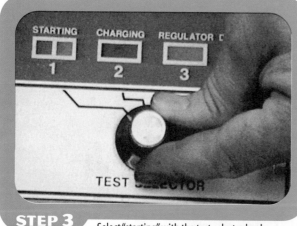

STEP 3 Select "starting" with the test selector knob.

STEP 4 Disable the ignition or the fuel system to prevent the engine from starting when the engine is being cranked.

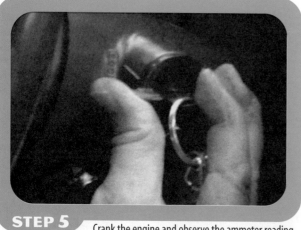

STEP 5 Crank the engine and observe the ammeter reading.

STEP 6 The starter on this vehicle equipped with a V-6 engine requires 120 amperes as displayed on the VAT-40 display. Disregard the first initial higher amperage reading.

GENERATOR (ALTERNATOR) OUTPUT TEST Step-by-Step

STEP 1 A typical Sun Electric VAT-40 (volt/amp tester model 40) used to measure the output of an AC generator (alternator).

STEP 2 Connect the large black clamp from the VAT-40 to the negative (−) terminal of the battery and the large red clamp to the positive (+) terminal of the battery.

STEP 3 Attach the ammeter inductive probe to either the negative or positive vehicle battery cable, whichever is most accessible. Be sure to clamp over *all* of the wires connecting to the battery terminal.

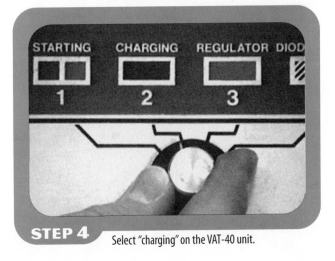

STEP 4 Select "charging" on the VAT-40 unit.

STEP 5 Start the engine. To measure the maximum output, the battery must be loaded and the engine speed increased.

STEP 6 To measure the maximum AC generator (alternator) output, increase engine speed to 2000 RPM.

(continued)

GENERATOR (ALTERNATOR) OUTPUT TEST continued

STEP 7 With the engine operating at 2000 RPM, turn the load knob until the highest ampere reading is displayed.

STEP 8 The output should be within 10% of its rated output. The specification for this vehicle was 90 amperes and output was measured at 92 amperes. This amperage should be added to the amount measured above to determine the actual maximum generator output.

STEP 9 When loading the battery during a generator output test, be sure to keep the voltage above 12 volts. Most charging systems produce the maximum output at about 13 volts, as shown here during the test.

SUMMARY

1. When a battery is being discharged, the acid (SO_4) is leaving the electrolyte and being deposited on the plates. When the battery is being charged, the acid (SO_4) is forced off the plates and back into the electrolyte.

2. Batteries are rated according to CCA, CA, ampere-hour, and reserve capacity.

3. All batteries should be securely attached to the vehicle with hold-down brackets to prevent vibration damage.

4. Batteries can be tested with a voltmeter to determine the state of charge. A battery load test loads the battery to one-half its CCA rating. A good battery should be able to maintain higher than 9.6 volts for the entire 15-second test period.

5. Proper operation of the starter motor depends on the battery being at least 75% charged and the battery cables being of the correct size (gauge) and having no more than a 0.2 voltage drop.

6. Voltage-drop testing includes cranking the engine, measuring the drop in voltage from the battery to the starter, and measuring the drop in voltage from the negative terminal of the battery to the engine block.

7. The cranking circuit should be tested for proper amperage draw.

8. Normal charging voltage (at 2000 engine RPM) is 13.5 to 15.0 volts.

9. The AC generator output is tested using a carbon pile tester connected to load the battery and measure the maximum amount of current being generated.

10. If more than 0.5 volt AC is measured at the output terminal of the battery, then the diode or stator is defective inside the AC generator.

REVIEW QUESTIONS

1. List the parts of the cranking circuit.

2. Explain why discharged batteries can freeze.

3. Identify three battery rating methods.

4. Describe the results of a voltmeter test of a battery and its state of charge.

5. List the steps for performing a battery load test.

6. Discuss how to measure the amperage output of an AC generator.

7. Explain how testing can be used to determine whether a diode or stator is defective.

CHAPTER QUIZ

1. When a battery becomes completely discharged, both positive and negative plates become _____ and the electrolyte becomes _____.
   a. H_2SO_4; Pb
   b. $PbSO_4$; H_2O
   c. PbO_2; H_2SO_4
   d. $PbSO_4$; H_2SO_4

2. A fully charged 12-volt battery should indicate _____.
   a. 12.6 volts or higher
   b. A specific gravity of 1.265 or higher
   c. 12 volts
   d. Both a and b

3. A battery measures 12.4 volts after removing the surface charge. This battery is charged at what percent?
   a. 100%
   b. 75%
   c. 50%
   d. 25%

4. Reserve capacity for batteries means _____.
   a. The number of *hours* the battery can supply 25 amperes and remain higher than 10.5 volts
   b. The number of *minutes* the battery can supply 25 amperes and remain higher than 10.5 volts
   c. The number of *minutes* the battery can supply 20 amperes and remain higher than 9.6 volts
   d. The number of *minutes* the battery can supply 10 amperes and remain higher than 9.6 volts

5. A battery high-rate discharge (load capacity) test is being performed on a 12-volt battery. Technician A says that a good battery should have a voltage reading of higher than 9.6 volts while under load at the end of the 15-second test. Technician B says that the battery should be discharged (loaded to two times its CCA rating). Which technician is correct?
   a. Technician A only
   b. Technician B only
   c. Both Technicians A and B
   d. Neither Technician A nor B

6. When charging a maintenance-free (lead-calcium) battery, _____.

   a. The initial charging rate should be about 35 amperes for 30 minutes

   b. The battery may not accept a charge for several hours, yet may still be a good (serviceable) battery

   c. The battery temperature should not exceed 125°F (hot to the touch)

   d. All of the above are correct

7. When jump starting, _____.

   a. The last connection should be the positive post of the dead battery

   b. The last connection should be the engine block of the dead vehicle

   c. The alternator must be disconnected on both vehicles

   d. Both a and c

8. Slow cranking by the starter can be caused by all *except* the following _____.

   a. A low or discharged battery

   b. Corroded or dirty battery cables

   c. Engine mechanical problems

   d. An open neutral safety switch

9. A starter motor draws more amperage than specifications. Technician A says that the battery may be discharged. Technician B says that the starter may be defective. Which technician is correct?

   a. Technician A only

   b. Technician B only

   c. Both Technicians A and B

   d. Neither Technician A nor B

10. An acceptable charging circuit voltage on a 12-volt system is _____.

   a. 13.5 to 15.0 volts

   b. 12.6 to 15.6 volts

   c. 12 to 14 volts

   d. 14.9 to 16.1 volts

CHAPTER 16

IGNITION SYSTEM OPERATION AND DIAGNOSIS

OBJECTIVES

After studying Chapter 16, the reader will be able to:

1. Prepare for Engine Repair (A1) ASE certification test content area "E" (Fuel, Electrical, Ignition, and Exhaust Systems Inspection and Service).

2. Explain how ignition coils create 40,000 volts.

3. Discuss crankshaft position sensor and pickup coil operation.

4. Describe the operation of waste-spark or coil-on-plug ignition systems.

KEY TERMS

The ignition system includes those parts and wiring required to generate and distribute a high voltage to the spark plugs. A fault anywhere in the primary (low-voltage) ignition circuit can cause a no-start condition. A fault anywhere in the secondary (high-voltage) ignition circuit can cause engine missing, hesitation, stalling, or excessive exhaust emissions.

IGNITION SYSTEM OPERATION

The ignition system includes components and wiring necessary to create and distribute a high voltage (up to 40,000 volts or more). All ignition systems apply voltage close to battery voltage to the positive side of the ignition coil and pulse the negative side to ground. When the coil negative lead is grounded, the primary (low-voltage) circuit of the coil is complete and a magnetic field is created by the coil windings. When the circuit is opened, the magnetic field collapses and induces a high-voltage spark from the secondary winding of the ignition coil. Early ignition systems used a mechanically opened set of contact points to make and break the electrical connection to ground. Electronic ignition uses a sensor such as a pickup coil or trigger to signal an electronic module that makes and breaks the primary connection of the ignition coil.

NOTE: Distributor ignition (DI) is the term specified by the Society of Automotive Engineers (SAE) for an ignition system that uses a distributor. **Electronic ignition (EI)** is the term specified by the SAE for an ignition system that does not use a distributor.

IGNITION COILS

The heart of any ignition system is the **ignition coil.** The coil creates a high-voltage spark by electromagnetic induction. Many ignition coils contain two separate but electrically connected windings of copper wire. Other coils are true transformers in which the primary and secondary windings are not electrically connected. See Figure 16-1.

The center of an ignition coil contains a core of laminated soft iron (thin strips of soft iron). This core increases the magnetic strength of the coil. Surrounding the laminated core are approximately 20,000 turns of fine wire (approximately 42 gauge). These windings are called the **secondary coil windings.** Surrounding the secondary windings are approximately 150 turns of heavy wire (approximately 21 gauge). These windings are called the **primary coil windings.** The secondary winding has about 100 times the number of turns of the primary winding, referred to as the turn ratio (approximately 100:1). In many coils, these windings are surrounded with a thin metal shield and insulating paper and placed into a metal

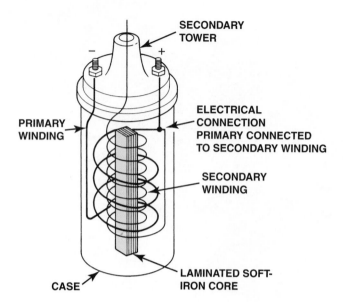

FIGURE 16-1   Internal construction of an oil-cooled ignition coil. Notice that the primary winding is electrically connected to the secondary winding. The polarity (positive or negative) of a coil is determined by the direction in which the coil is wound.

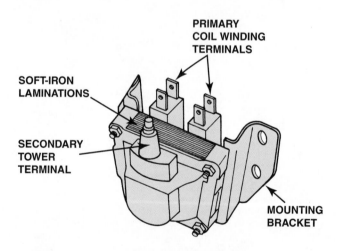

FIGURE 16-2   Typical air-cooled epoxy-filled E coil.

container. The metal container and shield help retain the magnetic field produced in the coil windings. The primary and secondary windings produce heat because of the electrical resistance in the turns of wire. Many coils contain oil to help cool the ignition coil. Other coil designs, such as those used on GM's **high energy ignition (HEI)** systems, use an air-cooled, epoxy-sealed **E coil.** The E coil is so named because the laminated, soft iron core is E shaped, with the coil wire turns wrapped around the center "finger" of the E and the primary winding wrapped inside the secondary winding. See Figures 16-2 and 16-3.

The primary windings of the coil extend through the case of the coil and are labeled as positive and negative. The positive

FIGURE 16-3   Cutaway of a General Motors Type II distributorless ignition coil. Note that the primary windings are inside of the secondary windings.

terminal of the coil attaches to the ignition switch, which supplies current from the positive battery terminal. The negative terminal is attached to an **electronic ignition module (or igniter),** which opens and closes the primary ignition circuit by opening or closing the ground return path of the circuit. When the ignition switch is on, current should be available at *both* the positive terminal and the negative terminal of the coil if the primary windings of the coil have continuity. The labeling of positive (+) and negative (−) of the coil indicates that the positive terminal is *more* positive (closer to the positive terminal of the battery) than the negative terminal of the coil. This condition is called the coil **polarity.** The polarity of the coil must be correct to ensure that electrons will flow from the hot center electrode of the spark plug. *The polarity of an ignition coil is determined by the direction of rotation of the coil windings.* The correct polarity is then indicated on the primary terminals of the coil. If the coil primary leads are reversed, the voltage required to fire the spark plugs is increased by 40%. The coil output voltage is directly proportional to the ratio of primary to secondary turns of wire used in the coil.

Self-Induction

When current starts to flow into a coil, an opposing current is created in the windings of the coil. This opposing current generation is caused by **self-induction** and is called **inductive reactance.** Inductive reactance is similar to resistance because it opposes any increase in current flow in a coil. Therefore, when an ignition coil is first energized, there is a slight delay of approximately 0.01 second before the ignition coil reaches its maximum magnetic field strength. The point at which a coil's maximum magnetic field strength is reached is called **saturation.**

Mutual Induction

In an ignition coil there are two windings, a primary and a secondary winding. When a *change* occurs in the magnetic field of one coil winding, a change also occurs in the other coil winding. Therefore, if the current is stopped from flowing (circuit is opened), the collapsing magnetic field cuts across the turns of the secondary winding and creates a high voltage in the secondary winding. This generation of an electric current in both coil windings is called **mutual induction.** The collapsing magnetic field also creates a voltage of up to 250 volts in the primary winding.

How Ignition Coils Create 40,000 Volts

All ignition systems use electromagnetic induction to produce a high-voltage spark from the ignition coil. Electromagnetic induction means that a current can be created in a conductor (coil winding) by a moving magnetic field. The magnetic field in an ignition coil is produced by current flowing through the primary windings of the coil. The current for the primary winding is supplied through the ignition switch to the positive terminal of the ignition coil. The negative terminal is connected to the ground return through an electronic ignition module (igniter).

If the primary circuit is completed, current (approximately 2 to 6 A) can flow through the primary coil windings. This flow creates a strong magnetic field inside the coil. When the primary coil winding ground return path connection is opened, the magnetic field collapses and induces a voltage of from 250 to 400 volts in the primary winding of the coil and a high-voltage (20,000 to 40,000 volts) low-amperage (20 to 80 mA) current in the secondary coil windings. This high-voltage pulse flows through the coil wire (if the vehicle is so equipped), distributor cap, rotor, and spark plug wires to the spark plugs. For each spark that occurs, the coil must be charged with a magnetic field and then discharged. The ignition components that regulate the current in the coil primary winding by turning it on and off are known collectively as the **primary ignition circuit.** The components necessary to create and distribute the high voltage produced in the secondary windings of the coil are called the **secondary ignition circuit.** See Figure 16-4. These circuits include the following components.

Primary Ignition Circuit

1. Battery
2. Ignition switch
3. Primary windings of coil
4. Pickup coil (crankshaft position sensor)
5. Ignition module (igniter)

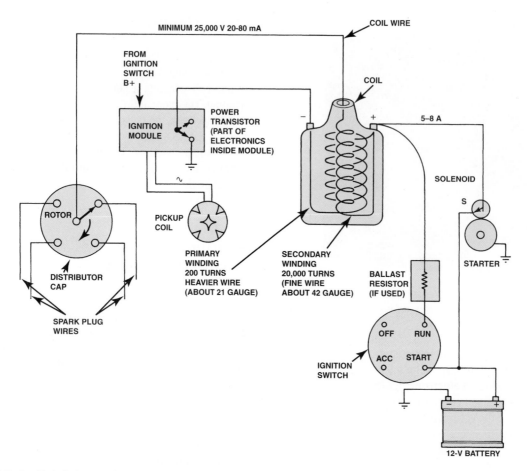

FIGURE 16-4 Typical primary and secondary electronic ignition using a ballast resistor and a distributor. To protect the ignition coil from overheating at lower engine speeds, many electronic ignitions do not use a ballast resistor, but use electronic circuits within the module.

Secondary Ignition Circuit

1. Secondary windings of coil
2. Distributor cap and rotor (if the vehicle is so equipped)
3. Spark plug wires
4. Spark plugs

Primary Circuit Operation

To get a spark out of an ignition coil, the primary coil circuit must be turned on and off. This primary circuit current is controlled by a **transistor** (electronic switch) inside the ignition module or igniter that in turn is controlled by one of several devices, including:

- Pickup coil (pulse generator)—A simple and common ignition electronic switching device is the magnetic pulse generator system used in distributor ignition systems. Most manufacturers use the rotation of the distributor shaft to time the voltage pulses. The **magnetic pulse generator** is installed in the distributor housing. The pulse generator consists of a trigger wheel (reluctor) and a pickup coil. The pickup coil consists of an iron core

wrapped with fine wire in a coil at one end, and attached to a permanent magnet at the other end. The center of the coil is called the pole piece. The pickup coil signal triggers the transistor inside the module and is also used by the computer for piston position information and engine speed (RPM). See Figures 16-5 and 16-6.

- Hall-effect switch—This switch also uses a stationary sensor and rotating trigger wheel (shutter). See Figure 16-7. Unlike the magnetic pulse generator, the Hall-effect switch requires a small input voltage to generate an output or signal voltage. Hall-effect is the ability to generate a voltage signal in semiconductor material (gallium arsenate crystal) by passing current through it in one direction and applying a magnetic field to it at a right angle to its surface. If the input current is held steady and the magnetic field fluctuates, an output voltage is produced that changes in proportion to field strength. Most Hall-effect switches in distributors have a Hall element or device, a permanent magnet, and a rotating ring of metal blades (shutters) similar to a trigger wheel (another method uses a stationary sensor with a rotating magnet). Some blades, typically found in Bosch and Chrysler systems, are designed to hang down; others, typically found

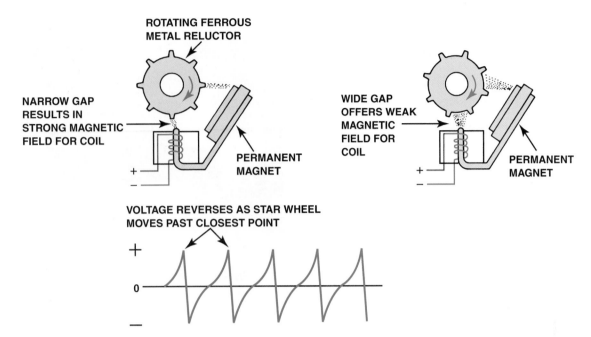

FIGURE 16-5 Operation of a typical pulse generator (pickup coil). At the bottom is a line drawing of a typical scope pattern of the output voltage of a pickup coil. The module receives this voltage from the pickup coil and opens the ground circuit to the ignition coil when the voltage starts down from its peak (just as the reluctor teeth start moving away from the pickup coil).

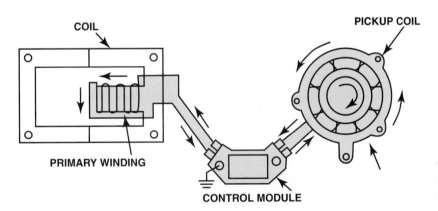

FIGURE 16-6 The varying voltage signal from the pickup coil triggers the ignition module. The ignition module grounds and ungrounds the primary winding of the ignition coil, creating a high-voltage spark.

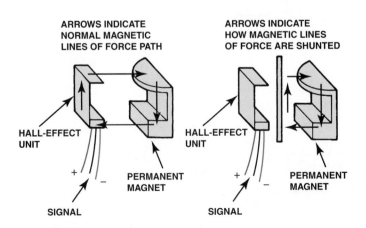

FIGURE 16-7 Hall-effect switches use metallic shutters to shunt magnetic lines of force away from a silicon chip and related circuits. All Hall-effect switches produce a square wave output for every accurate triggering.

in GM and Ford Hall-effect distributors, may be on a separate ring on the distributor shaft. When the shutter blade enters the gap between the magnet and the Hall element, it creates a magnetic shunt that changes the field strength through the Hall element, thereby creating an analog voltage signal. The Hall element contains a logic gate that converts the analog signal into a digital voltage signal, which triggers the switching transistor. The transistor transmits a digital square waveform at varying frequency to the ignition module or onboard computer. See Figure 16-8.

- **Magnetic crankshaft position sensors**—This sensor uses the changing strength of the magnetic field surrounding a coil of wire to signal the module and computer. This signal is used by the electronics in the module and computer as to piston position and engine speed (RPM). See Figure 16-9.

FIGURE 16-8 Shutter blade of a rotor as it passes between the sensing silicon chip and the permanent magnet.

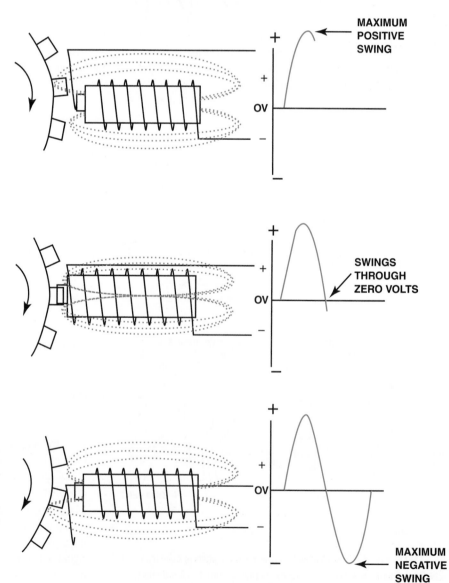

FIGURE 16-9 A magnetic sensor uses a permanent magnet surrounded by a coil of wire. The notches of the crankshaft (or camshaft) create a variable magnetic field strength around the coil. When a metallic section is close to the sensor, the magnetic field is stronger because metal is a better conductor of magnetic lines of force than air.

260

- Optical sensors—These use light from a **LED** and a phototransistor to signal the computer. An interrupter disc between the LED and the phototransistor has slits that allow the light from the LED to trigger the phototransistor on the other side of the disc. Most optical sensors (usually located inside the distributor) use two rows of slits to provide individual cylinder recognition (low-resolution) and precise distributor angle recognition (high-resolution) signals. See Figure 16-10.

DISTRIBUTOR IGNITION

General Motors HEI Electronic Ignition

As mentioned, high energy ignition (HEI) has been the standard equipment DI system on General Motors vehicles since the 1975 model year. Most V-6 and V-8 models use an ignition coil inside the distributor cap. Some V-6, inline 6-cylinder, and 4- to 6-cylinder models use an externally mounted ignition

TECH TIP

OPTICAL DISTRIBUTORS DO NOT LIKE LIGHT

Optical distributors use the light emitted from LEDs to trigger phototransistors. Most optical distributors use a shield between the distributor rotor and the optical interrupter ring. Sparks jump the gap from the rotor tip to the distributor cap inserts. This shield blocks the light from the electrical arc from interfering with the detection of the light from the LEDs.

If this shield is not replaced during service, the light signals are reduced and the engine may not operate correctly. See Figure 16-11. This can be difficult to detect because nothing looks wrong during a visual inspection. Remember that all optical distributors must be shielded between the rotor and the interrupter ring.

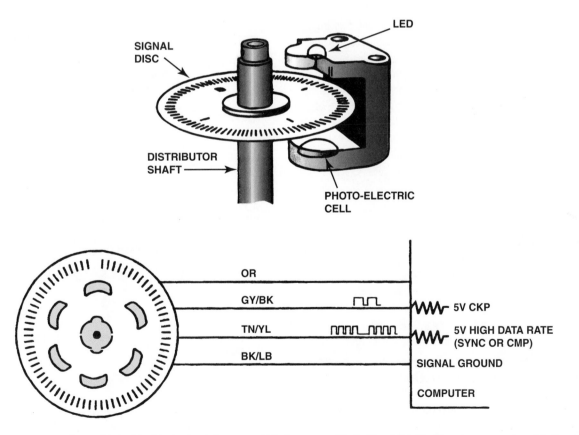

FIGURE 16-10   The small holes (slots) in the signal disc create a high-data rate used for ignition timing. The larger slots represent crankshaft position top dead center for each of the cylinders on a V-6 engine.

(a)

(b)

FIGURE 16-11   (a) An optical distributor on a Nissan 3.0 liter V-6 shown with the light shield removed. (b) A light shield being installed before the rotor is attached.

TECH TIP

THE TACHOMETER TRICK

When diagnosing a no-start or intermediate missing condition, check the operation of the tachometer. If the tachometer does not indicate engine speed (no-start condition) or drops toward zero (engine missing), then the problem is due to a defect in the *primary* ignition circuit. The tachometer gets its signal from the pulsing of the primary winding of the ignition coil. The following components in the primary circuit could cause the tachometer to not work when the engine is cranking:

- Pickup coil
- Crankshaft position sensor
- Ignition module (igniter)
- Coil primary wiring

If the vehicle is not equipped with a tachometer, connect a handheld tachometer to the negative terminal of the coil. Remember the following:

- No tachometer reading means the problem is in the primary ignition circuit.
- A tachometer reading okay means the problem is in the secondary ignition circuit or is a fuel-related problem.

coil. See Figure 16-12. The operation of both styles is similar. The large-diameter distributor cap provides additional space between the spark plug connections to help prevent crossfire. Most HEI distributors also use 8-mm-diameter spark plug wires that use female connections to the distributor cap towers. HEI coils must be replaced (if defective) with the exact replacement style. HEI

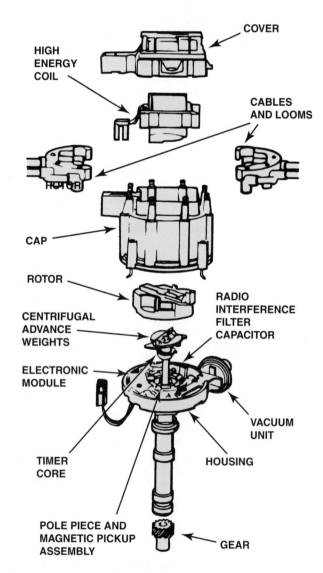

FIGURE 16-12   An HEI distributor.

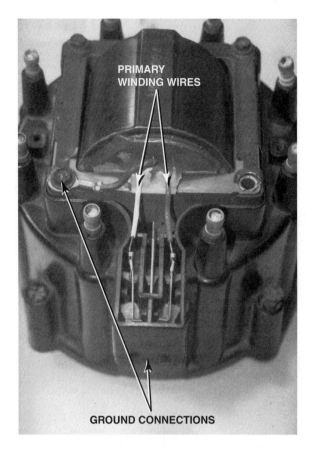

FIGURE 16-13 A typical General Motors HEI coil installed in the distributor cap. When the coil or distributor cap is replaced, check that the ground clip is transferred from the old distributor cap to the new. Without proper grounding, coil damage is likely. There are two designs of HEI coils. One uses red and white wire and the other design, which has reversed polarity, uses red and yellow wire for the primary coil.

coils differ and can be identified by the colors of the primary leads. The primary coil leads can be either white and red or yellow and red. The correct color of lead coil must be used for replacement. The colors of the leads indicate the direction in which the coil is wound, and therefore its polarity. See Figure 16-13.

Ford Electronic Ignition

Ford electronic ignition systems all function similarly, even though the name for the Ford EI system has changed many times since 1974. See Figure 16-14.

Ford Thick-Film-Integrated Ignition

The EEC IV system uses the **thick-film-integration (TFI)** ignition system. This system uses a smaller control module attached to the distributor and uses an air-cooled epoxy E coil. Thick-film integration means that all electronics are manufactured on small layers built up to form a thick film. Construction includes using pastes of different electrical resistances that are deposited on a thin, flat ceramic material by a process similar to silk-screen printing. These resistors are connected by tracks of palladium silver paste. Then the chips that form the capacitors, diodes, and integrated circuits are soldered directly to the palladium silver tracks. The thick-film manufacturing process is highly automated.

Operation of Ford Electronic Ignition

Ford EI systems function in basically the same way regardless of year and name (Duraspark, EEC, etc.). Under the distributor cap and rotor is a magnetic pickup assembly. This assembly produces a small alternating electrical pulse (approximately 1.5 volts) when the distributor armature rotates past the pickup assembly (stator). This low-voltage pulse is sent to the ignition module. The ignition module then switches (through transistors) off the primary ignition coil current. When the ignition coil primary current is stopped quickly, a high-voltage "spike" discharges from the coil secondary winding. Some Ford EI systems use a ballast resistor to help control the primary current through the ignition coil in the run mode (position); other Ford systems do not use a ballast resistor. The coil current is controlled in the module circuits by decreasing dwell (coil-charging time) depending on various factors determined by operating conditions. See Figure 16-15 on page 265.

TECH TIP

IF IT'S SOFT, THROW IT AWAY

Ford used a Hall-effect sensor in the distributor on most TFI module-equipped engines. The sensors were originally coated in a black plastic that would often become soft with age and break down electrically. The soft plastic sensor would also prevent proper connection to the TFI module, as shown in Figure 16-16 on page 266. If a no-start or rough engine operation occurs, always check the Hall-effect sensor and the connections to the module. The original Hall-effect units were black plastic and more prone to failure. Ozone formed by the high-voltage arcing in the distributor cap is highly corrosive, and it chemically attaches to the plastic. The plastic then becomes soft, pliable, and similar to tar in feel and texture. If the sensor is soft like tar, replace the Hall-effect switch assembly. Later production units use a more chemically stable white plastic material that is soft but not sticky.

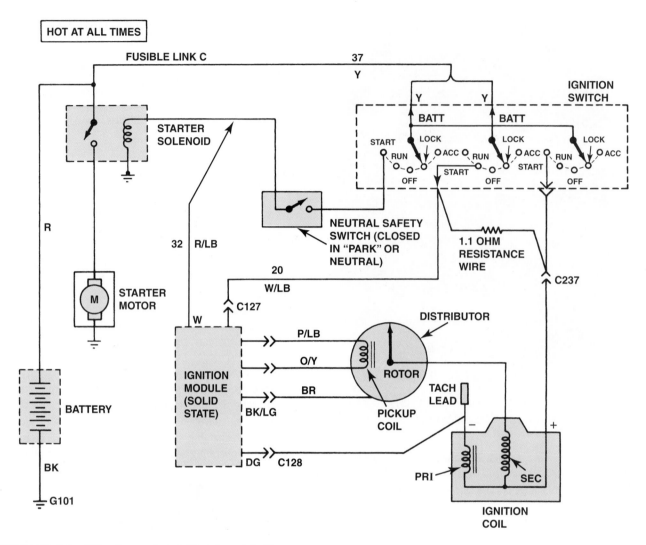

FIGURE 16-14   Wiring diagram of a typical Ford electronic ignition.

Chrysler Electronic Ignition

Chrysler was the first domestic manufacturer to produce electronic ignition as standard equipment. The Chrysler system consists of a pulse generator unit in the distributor (pickup coil and reluctor). Chrysler's name for their electronic ignition is **electronic ignition system (EIS),** and the control unit (module) is called the **electronic control unit (ECU).**

The pickup coil in the distributor (pulse generator) generates the signal to open and close the primary coil circuit. See Figure 16-17 on page 266.

WASTE-SPARK IGNITION SYSTEMS

Waste-spark ignition is another name for **distributorless ignition system (DIS)** or **electronic ignition (EI).** Waste-

spark ignition was introduced in the mid-1980s and uses the onboard computer to fire the ignition coils. These systems were first used on some Saabs and General Motors engines. Some 4-cylinder engines use four coils, but usually a 4-cylinder engine uses two ignition coils and a 6-cylinder engine uses three ignition coils. Each coil is a true transformer in which the primary winding and secondary winding are not electrically connected. Each end of the secondary winding is connected to a cylinder exactly opposite the other in the firing order. See Figure 16-18 on page 266. This means that *both* spark plugs fire at the same time! When one cylinder (for example, 6) is on the compression stroke, the other cylinder (3) is on the exhaust stroke. This spark that occurs on the exhaust stroke is called the waste spark, because it does no useful work and is only used as a ground path for the secondary winding of the ignition coil. The voltage required to jump the spark plug gap on cylinder 3 (the exhaust stroke) is only 2 to 3 kV and provides the *ground circuit* for the secondary coil

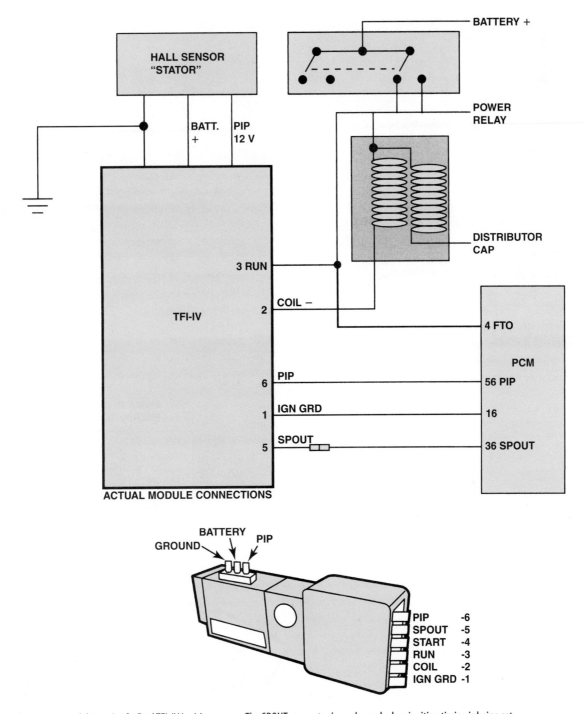

FIGURE 16-15   Schematic of a Ford TFI-IV ignition system. The SPOUT connector is unplugged when ignition timing is being set.

circuit. The remaining coil energy is used by the cylinder on the compression stroke. One spark plug of each pair fires straight polarity and the other cylinder fires reverse polarity. Spark plug life is not greatly affected by the reverse polarity. If there is only one defective spark plug wire or spark plug, two cylinders may be affected.

NOTE: With a distributor-type ignition system, the coil has two air gaps to fire: one between the rotor tip and the distributor insert (not under compression forces) and the other in the gap at the firing tip of the spark plug (under compression forces). A DIS also fires two gaps: one under compression (compression stroke plug) and one not under compression (exhaust stroke plug).

FIGURE 16-16 Thick-film-integrated type of Ford EI. Note how the module plugs into the Hall-effect switch inside the distributor. Heat-conductive silicone grease should be used between the module and the distributor mounting pad to help keep the electronic circuits inside the module cool.

FIGURE 16-17 A Chrysler electronic ignition distributor. This unit is equipped with a vacuum advance mechanism that advances the ignition timing under light engine load conditions.

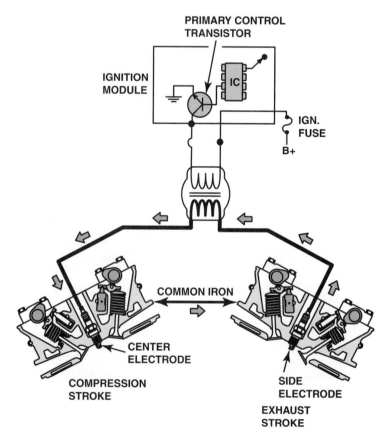

FIGURE 16-18 A waste-spark system fires one cylinder while its piston is on the compression stroke and into paired or companion cylinders while it is on the exhaust stroke. In a typical engine, it requires only about 2 to 3 kV to fire the cylinder on the exhaust strokes. The remaining coil energy is available to fire the spark plug under compression (typically about 8 to 12 kV).

Waste-spark ignitions require a sensor (usually a crankshaft sensor) to trigger the coils at the correct time. See Figure 16-19. The crankshaft sensor cannot be moved to adjust ignition timing. Ignition timing is not adjustable. The slight adjustment of the crankshaft sensor is designed to position the sensor exactly in the middle of the rotating metal disc for maximum clearance. Some engines do not use a camshaft position sensor, but rather double Hall-effect

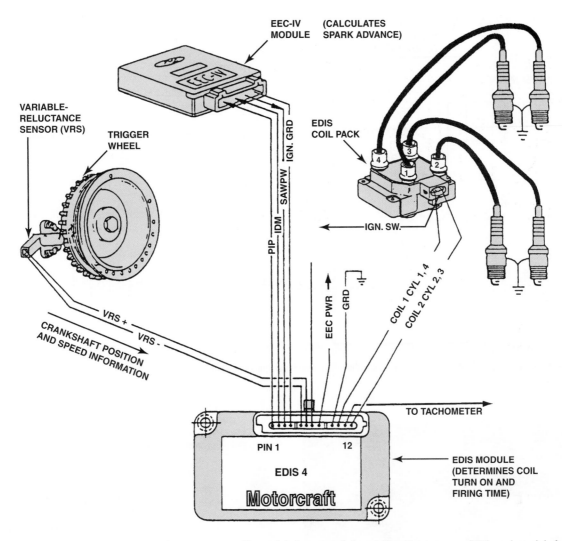

FIGURE 16-19 Typical Ford EDIS 4-cylinder ignition system. The crankshaft sensor, called a variable-reluctance sensor (VRS), sends crankshaft position and speed information to the EDIS module. A modified signal is sent to the computer as a profile ignition pickup (PIP) signal. The PIP is used by the computer to calculate ignition timing, and the computer sends a signal back to the EDIS module as to when to fire the spark plug. This return signal is called the spark angle word (SAW) signal.

crankshaft sensors and, again, ignition timing is not adjustable. See Figure 16-20.

COIL-ON-PLUG IGNITION

Coil-on-plug (COP) ignition uses one ignition for each spark plug. This system is also called **coil-by-plug, coil-near-plug,** or **coil-over-plug** ignition. The coil-on-plug system eliminates the spark plug wires which are often sources of **electromagnetic interference (EMI)** that can cause problems to some computer signals. The vehicle computer pulses the ground terminal of each coil at the proper time. Ignition timing also can be changed (retarded or advanced) on a cylinder-by-cylinder basis for maximum performance and to respond to knock sensor signals. See Figure 16-21.

General Motors vehicles use a variety of coil-on-plug-type ignition systems. Many V-8 engines use a coil-near-plug system

with individual coils and modules for each individual cylinder that are placed on the valve covers. Short secondary ignition spark plug wires are used to connect the output terminal of the ignition coil to the spark plug.

Most newer Chrysler engines use coil-over-plug-type ignition systems. Each coil is controlled by the PCM, which can vary the ignition timing separately for each cylinder based on signals the PCM receives from the knock sensor(s). For example, if the knock sensor detects that a spark knock has occurred after firing cylinder 3, then the PCM will continue to monitor cylinder 3 and retard timing on just this one cylinder if necessary to prevent engine-damaging detonation.

CHECKING FOR SPARK

In the event of a no-start condition, the first step should be to check for secondary voltage out of the ignition coil or to the

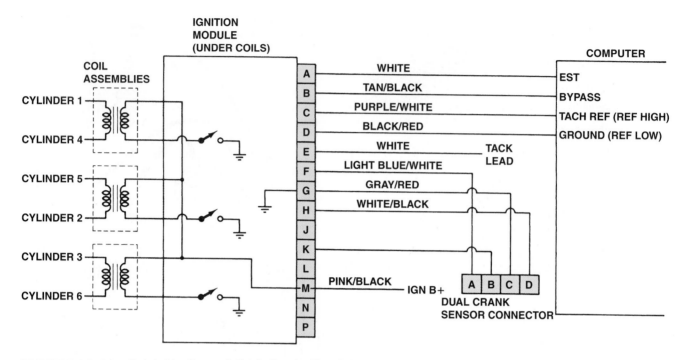

FIGURE 16-20   Typical wiring diagram of a V-6 distributorless (direct fire) ignition system.

FIGURE 16-21   Individual coils with modules shown on the General Motors 4.2 L inline 6-cylinder light truck engine. Note the aluminum cooling fins (heat sink) on top of each assembly.

spark plugs. If the engine is equipped with a separate ignition coil, remove the coil wire from the center of the distributor cap, install a **spark tester,** and crank the engine. See the Tech Tip "Always Use a Spark Tester." A good coil and ignition system should produce a blue spark at the spark tester. See Figure 16-22.

If the ignition system being tested does not have a separate ignition coil, disconnect any spark plug wire from a spark

SAFETY TIP

NEVER DISCONNECT A SPARK PLUG WIRE WHEN THE ENGINE IS RUNNING!

Ignition systems produce a high-voltage pulse necessary to ignite a lean air–fuel mixture. If you disconnect a spark plug wire when the engine is running, this high-voltage spark could cause personal injury or damage to the ignition coil and/or ignition module.

plug and, while cranking the engine, test for spark available at the spark plug wire, again using a spark tester.

NOTE: An intermittent spark should be considered a no-spark condition.

Typical causes of a no-spark (intermittent spark) condition include the following:

1. Weak ignition coil
2. Low or no voltage to the primary (positive) side of the coil
3. High resistance or open coil wire, or spark plug wire

FIGURE 16-22   Using a spark tester on an engine with direct-fire (distributorless) ignition. The spark tester is grounded to the rocker cover stud. This is the recommended type of spark tester, with the center electrode recessed into the center insulator.

4. Negative side of the coil not being pulsed by the ignition module
5. Defective pickup coil
6. Defective module

ELECTRONIC IGNITION TROUBLESHOOTING PROCEDURE

When troubleshooting any electronic ignition system for no spark, follow these steps to help pinpoint the exact cause of the problem:

1. Turn the ignition on (engine off) and, using either a voltmeter or a test light, test for battery voltage available at the positive terminal of the ignition coil. If the voltage is not available, check for an open circuit at the ignition switch or wiring. Also check the condition of the ignition fuse (if used).

NOTE: Many Chrysler products use an **automatic shutdown (ASD)** relay to power the ignition coil. The ASD relay will not supply voltage to the coil unless the engine is cranking and the computer senses a crankshaft sensor signal. This little fact has fooled many technicians.

TECH TIP

ALWAYS USE A SPARK TESTER

A spark tester looks like a spark plug without a side electrode, with a gap between the center electrode and the grounded shell. The tester commonly has an alligator clip attached to the shell so that it can be clamped on a good ground connection on the engine. A good ignition system should be able to cause a spark to jump this wide gap at atmospheric pressure. Without a spark tester, a technician might assume that the ignition system is okay, because it can spark across a normal, grounded spark plug. The voltage required to fire a standard spark plug when it is out of the engine and not under pressure is about 3,000 volts or less. An electronic ignition spark tester requires a minimum of 25,000 volts to jump the 3/4-in. gap. Therefore, never assume that the ignition system is okay because it fires a spark plug—always use a spark tester. *Remember that an intermittent spark across a spark tester should be interpreted as a no-spark condition.*

2. Connect the voltmeter or test light to the negative side of the coil and crank the engine. The voltmeter should fluctuate or the test light should blink, indicating that the primary coil current is being turned on and off. If there is no pulsing of the negative side of the coil, then the problem is a defective pickup, electronic control module, or wiring.

IGNITION COIL TESTING USING AN OHMMETER

If an ignition coil is suspected of being defective, a simple ohmmeter check can be performed to test the resistance of the primary and secondary winding inside the coil. For accurate resistance measurements, the wiring to the coil should be removed before testing. To test the primary coil winding resistance, take the following steps:

1. Set the meter to read low ohms.
2. Measure the resistance between the positive terminal and the negative terminal of the ignition coil. Most coils will give a reading between 1 and 3 ohms; however, some coils should indicate less than 1 ohm. Check the manufacturer's specifications for the exact resistance values.

To test the secondary coil winding resistance, follow these steps:

1. Set the meter to read kilohms (kΩ).
2. Measure the resistance between either primary terminal and the secondary coil tower. The normal resistance of most coils ranges between 6,000 and 30,000 ohms. Check the manufacturer's specifications for the exact resistance values.

NOTE: Many ignition coils use a screw that is inside the secondary tower of the ignition coil. If this screw is loose, an intermittent engine miss could occur. The secondary coil would also indicate high resistance if this screw was loose.

PICKUP COIL TESTING

The pickup coil, located under the distributor cap on many electronic ignition engines, can cause a no-spark condition if defective. The pickup coil must generate an AC voltage pulse to the ignition module so that the module can pulse the ignition coil.

A pickup coil contains a coil of wire, and the resistance of this coil should be within the range specified by the manufacturer. See Figure 16-23. Some common specifications include the following:

Manufacturer	Pickup Coil Resistance (ohms)
General Motors	500–1,500 (white and green leads)
Ford	400–1,000 (orange and purple leads)
Chrysler	150–900 (orange and black leads)

If the pickup coil resistance is not within the specified range, replace the pickup coil assembly.

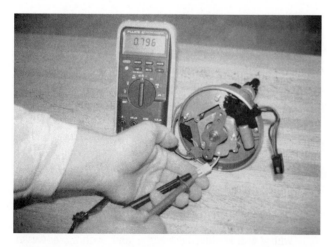

FIGURE 16-23 Measuring the resistance of an HEI pickup coil using a digital multimeter set to the ohms position. The reading on the face of the meter is 0.796 KΩ or 796 ohms right in the middle of the 500 to 1500 ohm specifications.

The pickup coil can also be tested for proper voltage output. During cranking, most pickup coils should produce a minimum of 0.25 volt AC. This can be tested with the distributor out of the vehicle by rotating the distributor drive gear by hand.

TESTING MAGNETIC SENSORS

First of all, magnetic sensors must be magnetic. If the permanent magnet inside the sensor has cracked, the result is two weak magnets.

If the sensor is removed from the engine, hold a metal (steel) object against the end of the sensor. It should exert a strong magnetic pull on the steel object. If not, replace the

TECH TIP

BAD WIRE? REPLACE THE COIL!

When performing engine testing (such as a compression test), always ground the coil wire. Never allow the coil to discharge without a path to ground for the spark. High-energy electronic ignition systems can produce 40,000 volts or more of electrical pressure. If the spark cannot spark to ground, the coil energy can (and usually does) arc inside the coil itself, creating a low-resistance path to the primary windings or the steel laminations of the coil. See Figure 16-24. This low-resistance path is called a **track** and could cause an engine miss under load even though all of the remaining component parts of the ignition system are functioning correctly. Often these tracks do not show up on any coil test, including most scopes. Because the track is a lower-resistance path to ground than normal, it requires that the ignition system be put under a load for it to be detected, and even then, the problem (engine missing) may be intermittent.

Therefore, when disabling an ignition system, perform one of the following procedures to prevent possible ignition coil damage:

1. Remove the power source wire from the ignition system to prevent any ignition operation.
2. On distributor-equipped engines, remove the secondary coil wire from the center of the distributor cap and connect a jumper wire between the disconnected coil wire and a good engine ground. This ensures that the secondary coil energy will be safely grounded and prevents high-voltage coil damage.

sensor. Second, the sensor can be tested using a digital meter set to read AC volts.

TESTING HALL-EFFECT SENSORS

As with any other sensor, the output of the Hall-effect sensor should be tested first. Using a digital voltmeter, check for the presence of an AC voltage when the engine is being cranked. The best test is to use an oscilloscope and observe the waveform.

TESTING OPTICAL SENSORS

Optical sensors will not operate if dirty or covered in oil. Perform a thorough visual inspection looking for an oil leak that could cause dirty oil to get on the LED or phototransistor. Also be sure that the light shield is securely fastened and that the seal is lightproof. An optical sensor can also be checked using an oscilloscope or a digital multimeter set to read AC volts.

IGNITION SYSTEM DIAGNOSIS USING VISUAL INSPECTION

One of the first steps in the diagnosis process is to perform a thorough visual inspection of the ignition system, including the following items:

- Check all spark plug wires for proper routing. All plug wires should be in the factory wiring separator and be clear of any metallic object that could cause damage to the insulation and cause a short-to-ground fault. See Figure 16-25.
- Check that all spark plug wires are securely attached to the spark plugs and to the distributor cap or ignition coil(s).
- Check that all spark plug wires are clean and free from excessive dirt or oil. Check that all protective covers normally covering the coil and/or distributor cap are in place and not damaged.
- Remove the distributor cap and carefully check the cap and distributor rotor for faults. See Figures 16-26 and 16-27.
- Remove the spark plugs and check for excessive wear or other visible faults. Replace if needed.

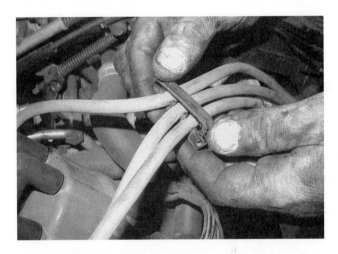

FIGURE 16-25   Always take the time to install spark plug wires back into the original holding brackets (wiring combs).

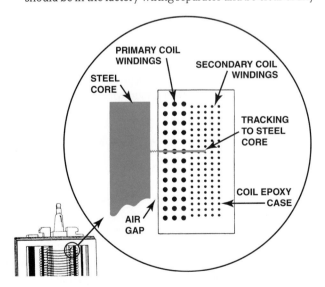

FIGURE 16-24   A track inside an ignition coil is not a short, but rather a low-resistance path or hole that has been burned through from the secondary wiring to the steel core.

FIGURE 16-26   Note where the high voltage spark jumped through the plastic rotor to arc into the distributor shaft. Always check for a defective spark plug(s) whenever a defective distributor cap or rotor is discovered. If a spark cannot jump to a spark plug, then it tries to find a ground path wherever it can.

FIGURE 16-27 This distributor cap came off a GM V-8 engine that was starting and running okay. The only problem seemed to be a "snapping" noise heard in the distributor.

NOTE: According to research conducted by General Motors, about one-fifth (20%) of all faults are detected during a *thorough visual inspection!*

TESTING FOR POOR PERFORMANCE

Many diagnostic equipment manufacturers offer methods for testing distributorless ignition systems on an oscilloscope. If using this type of equipment, follow the manufacturer's recommended procedures and interpretation of the specific test results.

A simple method of testing distributorless (waste-spark systems) ignition with the engine off involves removing the spark plug wires (or connectors) from the spark plugs (or coils or distributor cap) and installing short lengths (2 in.) of rubber vacuum hose in series.

NOTE: For best results, use rubber hose that is electrically conductive. Measure the vacuum hose with an ohmmeter. Suitable vacuum hose should give a reading of less than 10,000 ohms (10 kΩ) for a length of about 2 in. See Figure 16-28.

1. Start the engine and ground out each cylinder one at a time by touching the tip of a grounded test light to the rubber vacuum hose. Even though the computer will increase idle speed and fuel delivery to compensate for the grounded spark plug wire, a technician should watch for a change in the operation of the engine. If no change is observed or heard, the cylinder being grounded is obviously weak or defective. Check the spark plug wire or connector with an ohmmeter to be certain of continuity.

FIGURE 16-28 Using a vacuum hose and a grounded test light to ground one cylinder at a time on a DIS. This works on all types of ignition systems and provides a method for grounding out one cylinder at a time without fear of damaging any component.

2. Check all cylinders by grounding them out one at a time. If one weak cylinder is found, check the other cylinder using the same ignition coil (except on engines that use an individual coil for each cylinder). If both cylinders are affected, the problem could be an open spark plug wire, defective spark plug, or defective ignition coil.

3. To help eliminate other possible problems and determine exactly what is wrong, switch the suspected ignition coil to another position (if possible).
   - If the problem now affects the other cylinders, the ignition coil is defective and must be replaced.
   - If the problem does not "change positions," the control module affecting the suspected coil or either cylinder's spark plug or spark plug wire could be defective.

TESTING FOR A NO-START CONDITION

A no-start condition (with normal engine cranking speed) can be the result of either no spark or no fuel delivery.

Computerized engine control systems use the ignition primary pulses as a signal to inject fuel—a port or throttle-body injection (TBI) style of fuel-injection system. If there is no pulse, then there is no squirt of fuel. To determine exactly what is wrong, follow these steps:

1. Test the output signal from the crankshaft sensor. Most computerized engines with distributorless ignitions use a

crankshaft position sensor. These sensors are either the Hall-effect type or the magnetic type. The sensors must be able to produce a variable (either sine or digital) signal. A meter set on AC volts should read a voltage across the sensor leads when the engine is being cranked. If there is no AC voltage output, replace the sensor.

2. If the sensor tests okay in step 1, check for a changing AC voltage signal at the ignition module.

NOTE: Step 2 checks the wiring between the crankshaft position sensor and the ignition control module.

3. If the ignition control module is receiving a changing signal from the crankshaft position sensor, it must be capable of switching the power to the ignition coils on and off. Remove a coil or coil package, and with the ignition switched to on (run), check for voltage at the positive terminal of the coil(s).

NOTE: Several manufacturers program the current to the coils to be turned off within several seconds of the ignition being switched to on if no pulse is received by the computer. This circuit design helps prevent ignition coil damage in the event of a failure in the control circuit or driver error, by keeping the ignition switch on (run) without operating the starter (start position). Some Chrysler engines do not supply power to the positive (+) side of the coil until a crank pulse is received by the computer.

If the module is not pulsing the negative side of the coil or not supplying battery voltage to the positive side of the coil, replace the ignition control module.

NOTE: Before replacing the ignition control module, be certain that it is properly grounded (where applicable) and that the module is receiving ignition power from the ignition circuit.

CAUTION: Most distributorless (waste spark) ignition systems can produce 40,000 volts or more, with energy levels high enough to cause personal injury. Do not open the circuit of an electronic ignition secondary wire, because damage to the system (or to you) can occur.

FIRING ORDER

Firing order means the order that the spark is distributed to the correct spark plug at the right time. The firing order of an engine is determined by crankshaft and camshaft design. The firing order is determined by the location of the spark plug wires in the distributor cap of an engine equipped with a distributor. The firing order is often cast into the intake manifold for easy reference, as shown in Figure 16-29. Most service

FIGURE 16-29   The firing order is cast or stamped on the intake manifold on most engines that have a distributor ignition.

manuals also show the firing order and the direction of the distributor rotor rotation, as well as the location of the spark plug wires on the distributor cap.

CAUTION: Ford V-8s use two different firing orders depending on whether the engine is high output (HO) or standard. Using the incorrect firing order can cause the engine to backfire and could cause engine damage or personal injury. General Motors V-6s use different firing orders and different locations for cylinder 1 between the 60-degree V-6 and the 90-degree V-6. Using the incorrect firing order or cylinder number location chart could result in poor engine operation or a no start.

Firing order is also important for waste-spark-type distributorless (direct-fire) ignition systems. The spark plug wire can often be installed on the wrong coil pack that can create a no-start condition or poor engine operation.

SPARK PLUG WIRE INSPECTION

Spark plug wires should be visually inspected for cuts or defective insulation and checked for resistance with an ohmmeter. Good spark plug wires should measure less than 10,000 ohms per foot of length. See Figure 16-30. Faulty spark plug wire insulation can cause hard starting or no starting in damp weather conditions.

SPARK PLUG SERVICE

Spark plugs should be inspected when an engine performance problem occurs and should be replaced regularly to ensure proper ignition system performance. Many spark plugs have a service life of over 20,000 miles (32,000 kilometers). Platinum-tipped original equipment spark plugs have a typical service life of 60,000 to 100,000 miles (100,000 to 160,000 kilometers). Used spark plugs should *not* be cleaned and reused unless

TECH TIP

SPARK PLUG WIRE PLIERS ARE A GOOD INVESTMENT

Spark plug wires are often difficult to remove. Using good-quality spark plug wire pliers, such as shown in Figure 16-31, saves time and reduces the chance of harming the wire during removal.

absolutely necessary. The labor required to remove and replace (R & R) spark plugs is the same whether the spark plugs are replaced or cleaned. Although cleaning spark plugs often restores proper engine operation, the service life of cleaned spark plugs is definitely shorter than that of new spark plugs. *Platinum-tipped spark plugs should not be regapped!* Using a gapping tool can break the platinum after it has been used in an engine.

Be certain that the engine is cool before removing spark plugs, especially on engines with aluminum cylinder heads. To help prevent dirt from getting into the cylinder of an engine while removing a spark plug, use compressed air or a brush to remove dirt from around the spark plug before removal. See Figures 16-32 and 16-33.

Spark Plug Inspection

Spark plugs are the windows to the inside of the combustion chamber. A thorough visual inspection of the spark plugs can often lead to the root cause of an engine performance problem. Two indications and their possible root causes include the following:

1. **Carbon fouling.** If the spark plug(s) has *dry black carbon* (soot), the usual causes include:

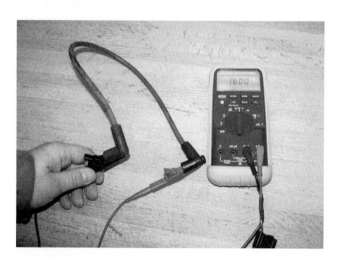

FIGURE 16-30   Measuring the resistance of a spark plug wire with a multimeter set to the ohms position. The reading of 16.03 kΩ (16,030 ohms) is okay because the wire is about 2 ft long. Maximum allowable resistance for a spark plug wire this long would be 20 kΩ (20,000 ohms).

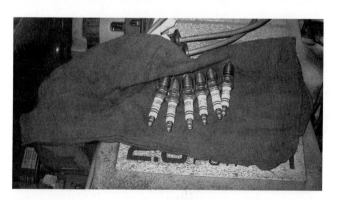

FIGURE 16-32   When removing spark plugs, it is wise to arrange them so that they can be compared and any problem be identified with a particular cylinder.

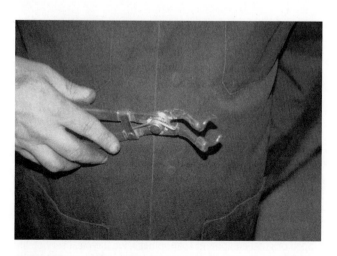

FIGURE 16-31   Spark plug wire boot pliers are a handy addition to any toolbox.

FIGURE 16-33   A spark plug thread chaser is a low-cost tool that hopefully will not be used often, but is necessary to use to clean the threads before new spark plugs are installed.

- Excessive idling
- Slow-speed driving under light loads that keeps the spark plug temperatures too low to burn off the deposits
- Overrich air–fuel mixture
- Weak ignition system output

2. **Oil fouling.** If the spark plug has *wet, oily* deposits with little electrode wear, oil may be getting into the combustion chamber from the following:
    - Worn or broken piston rings
    - Defective or missing valve stem seals

NOTE: If the deposits are heavier on the plug facing the intake valve, the cause is usually due to excessive valve stem clearance or defective intake valve stem seals.

When removing spark plugs, place them in order so that they can be inspected to check for engine problems that might affect one or more cylinders. All spark plugs should be in the same condition, and the color of the center insulator should be light tan or gray. If all the spark plugs are black or dark, the engine should be checked for conditions that could cause an overly rich air–fuel mixture or possible oil burning. If only one or a few spark plugs are black, check those cylinders for proper firing (possible defective spark plug wire) or an engine condition affecting only those particular cylinders. See Figures 16-34 and 16-35.

If all spark plugs are white, check for possible overadvanced ignition timing or a vacuum leak causing a lean air–fuel mixture. If only one or a few spark plugs are white, check for a vacuum leak affecting the fuel mixture only to those particular cylinders.

NOTE: The engine computer "senses" rich or lean air–fuel ratios by means of input from the oxygen sensor. If one cylinder is lean, the computer may make all other cylinders richer to compensate.

Inspect all spark plugs for wear by first checking the condition of the center electrode. As a spark plug wears, the center electrode becomes rounded. If the center electrode is rounded, higher ignition system voltage is required to fire the spark plug. When installing spark plugs, always use the correct tightening torque to ensure proper heat transfer from the spark plug shell to the cylinder head. See the following table.

TECH TIP

TWO-FINGER TRICK

To help prevent overtightening a spark plug when a torque wrench is not available, simply use two fingers on the ratchet handle. Even the strongest service technician cannot overtighten a spark plug by using two fingers.

FIGURE 16-34 Typical worn spark plug. Notice the rounded center electrode. The deposits indicate a possible oil usage problem.

FIGURE 16-35 New spark plug that was fouled by a too-rich air–fuel mixture. The engine from which this spark plug came had a defective (stuck partially open) injector on this one cylinder only.

	Torque with Torque Wrench (in lb-ft)		Torque without Torque Wrench (in turns)	
Spark Plug	Cast-Iron Head	Aluminum Head	Cast-Iron Head	Aluminum Head
Gasket				
14 mm	26–30	18–22	1/4	1/4
18 mm	32–38	28–34	1/4	1/4
Tapered seat				
14 mm	7–15	7–15	1/16 (snug)	1/16 (snug)
18 mm	15–20	15–20	1/16 (snug)	1/16 (snug)

TECH TIP

USE ORIGINAL EQUIPMENT MANUFACTURER'S SPARK PLUGS

A technician at an independent service center replaced the spark plugs in a Pontiac with new Champion brand spark plugs of the correct size, reach, and heat range. When the customer returned to pay the bill, he inquired as to the brand name of the replacement parts used for the tune-up. When told that Champion spark plugs were used, he stopped signing his name on the check he was writing. He said that he owned 1,000 shares of General Motors stock and he owned two General Motors vehicles and he expected to have General Motors parts used in his General Motors vehicles. The service manager had the technician replace the spark plugs with AC brand spark plugs because this brand was used in the engine when the vehicle was new. Even though most spark plug manufacturers produce spark plugs that are correct for use in almost any engine, many customers prefer that original equipment manufacturer (OEM) spark plugs be used in their engines.

NOTE: General Motors does not recommend the use of antiseize compound on the threads of spark plugs being installed in an aluminum cylinder head, because the spark plug will be overtightened. This excessive tightening torque places the threaded portion of the spark plug too far into the combustion chamber where carbon can accumulate and result in the spark plugs being difficult to remove. If antiseize compound is used on spark plug threads, reduce the tightening torque by 40%. Always follow the vehicle manufacturer's recommendations.

QUICK AND EASY SECONDARY IGNITION TESTS

Most engine running problems are caused by defective or out-of-adjustment ignition components. Many ignition problems involve the high-voltage secondary ignition circuit. Following are some quick and easy secondary ignition tests.

Test 1.   If there is a crack in a distributor cap, coil, or spark plug, or a defective spark plug wire, a spark may be visible at night. Because the highest voltage is required during partial throttle acceleration, the technician's assistant should accelerate the engine slightly with the gear selector in drive or second gear (if manual transmission) and the brake firmly applied. If any spark is visible, the location should be closely inspected and the defective parts replaced. A blue glow or "corona" around the shell of the spark plug is normal and not an indication of a defective spark plug.

Test 2.   For intermittent problems, use a spray bottle to apply a water mist to the spark plugs, distributor cap, and spark plug wires. See Figure 16-36. With the engine running, the water may cause an arc through any weak insulating materials and cause the engine to miss or stall.

NOTE: Adding a little salt or liquid soap to the water makes the water more conductive, and also makes it easier to find those hard-to-diagnose intermittent ignition faults.

Test 3.   To determine if the rough engine operation is due to secondary ignition problems, connect a 6- to 12-volt test light to the negative side (sometimes labeled "tach") of the coil. Connect the other lead of the test light to the positive lead of the coil. With the engine running, the test light should be dim and steady in brightness. If there is high resistance in the secondary circuit (such as that caused by a defective spark plug wire), the test light will pulse brightly at times. If the test light varies noticeably, this indicates that the secondary voltage cannot find ground easily and is feeding back through the primary windings of the coil. This feedback causes the test light to become brighter.

FIGURE 16-36 A water spray bottle is an excellent diagnostic tool to help find an intermittent engine miss caused by a break in a secondary ignition circuit component.

IGNITION TIMING

Ignition timing should be checked and adjusted according to the manufacturer's specifications and procedures for best fuel economy and performance, as well as lowest exhaust emissions. Generally, for testing, engines must be at idle with computer engine controls put into **base timing,** the timing of the spark before the computer advances the timing. To be assured of the proper ignition timing, follow exactly the timing procedure indicated on the underhood emission decal. See Figure 16-37 for a typical ignition timing plate and timing mark.

NOTE: Most older engines equipped with a vacuum advance must have the vacuum hose removed and plugged before it is checked for timing.

If the ignition timing is too far *advanced,* for example, if it is set at 12 degrees before top dead center (BTDC) instead of 8 degrees BTDC, the following symptoms may occur:

1. Engine ping or spark knock may be heard, especially while driving up a hill or during acceleration.
2. Cranking (starting) may be slow and jerky, especially when the engine is warm.
3. The engine may overheat if the ignition timing is too far advanced.

FIGURE 16-37 Typical timing marks. The degree numbers are on the stationary plate and the notch is on the harmonic balancer.

If the ignition timing is too far *retarded,* for example, if it is set at 4 degrees BTDC instead of 8 degrees BTDC, the following symptoms may occur:

1. The engine may lack in power and performance.
2. The engine may require a long period of starter cranking before starting.
3. Poor fuel economy may result from retarded ignition timing.
4. The engine may overheat if the ignition timing is too far retarded.

Pretiming Checks

Before the ignition timing is checked or adjusted, the following items should be checked to ensure accurate timing results:

1. The engine should be at normal operating temperature (the upper radiator hose should be hot and pressurized).
2. The engine should be at the correct timing RPM (check the specifications).
3. The vacuum hoses should be removed, and the hose from the vacuum advance unit on the distributor (if the vehicle is so equipped) should be plugged unless otherwise specified.

4. If the engine is computer equipped, check the timing procedure specified by the manufacturer. This may include disconnecting a "set timing" connector wire, grounding a diagnostic terminal, disconnecting a four-wire connector, or similar procedure.

NOTE: General Motors specifies 10 different pretiming procedures depending on the engine, type of fuel system, and type of ignition system. For example, many 4-cylinder engines use the *average* of the timing for cylinder 1 and cylinder 4! Always consult the emission decal under the hood for the exact procedure to follow.

Timing Light Connections

For checking or adjusting ignition timing, make the timing light connections as follows:

1. Connect the timing light battery leads to the vehicle battery: the red to the positive terminal and the black to the negative terminal.
2. Connect the timing light high-tension lead to spark plug cable 1.

Determining Cylinder I

The following will help in determining cylinder 1.

1. Four- or 6-cylinder engines. On all inline 4- and 6-cylinder engines, cylinder 1 is the *most forward* cylinder.

TECH TIP

"TURN THE KEY" TEST

If the ignition timing is correct, a warm engine should start immediately when the ignition key is turned to the start position. If the engine cranks a long time before starting, the ignition timing may be retarded. If the engine cranks slowly, the ignition timing may be too far advanced. However, if the engine starts immediately, the ignition timing, although it may not be exactly set according to specification, is usually adjusted fairly close to specifications. When a starting problem is experienced, check the ignition timing first, before checking the fuel system or the cranking system for a possible problem. This procedure can be used to help diagnose a possible ignition timing problem quickly without tools or equipment.

2. V-6 or V-8 engines. Most V-type engines use the left front (driver's side) cylinder as cylinder 1, except for Ford engines and some Cadillacs, which use the right front (passenger's side) cylinder.
3. Sideways (transverse) engines. Most front-wheel-drive vehicles with engines installed sideways use the cylinder to the far right (passenger's side) as cylinder 1 (plug wire closest to the drive belt[s]).

Follow this rule of thumb: If cylinder 1 is unknown for a given type of engine, it is the *most forward* cylinder as viewed from above (except in Pontiac V-8 engines). See Figure 16-38 for typical cylinder 1 locations.

NOTE: Some engines are not timed off of cylinder 1. For example, Jaguar inline 6-cylinder engines before 1988 used cylinder 6, but the cylinders were numbered from the firewall (bulkhead) forward. Therefore, cylinder 6 was the most forward cylinder. Always check for the specifications and procedures for the vehicle being tested.

NOTE: If cylinder 1 is difficult to reach, such as up against the bulkhead (firewall) or close to an exhaust manifold, simply use the opposite cylinder in the firing order (paired cylinder). The timing light will not know the difference and will indicate the correct position of the timing mark in relation to the pointer or degree mark.

Checking or Adjusting Ignition Timing

Use the following steps for checking or adjusting ignition timing:

1. Start the engine and adjust the speed to that specified for ignition timing.
2. With the timing light aimed at the stationary timing pointer, observe the position of the timing mark with the light flashing. Refer to the manufacturer's specifications on the underhood decal for the correct setting. See Figure 16-39.

NOTE: If the timing mark appears ahead of the pointer, in relation to the direction of crankshaft rotation, the timing is advanced. If the timing mark appears behind the pointer, in relation to the direction of crankshaft rotation, the timing is retarded.

3. To adjust timing, loosen the distributor locking bolt or nut and turn the distributor housing until the timing mark is in correct alignment. Turn the distributor housing

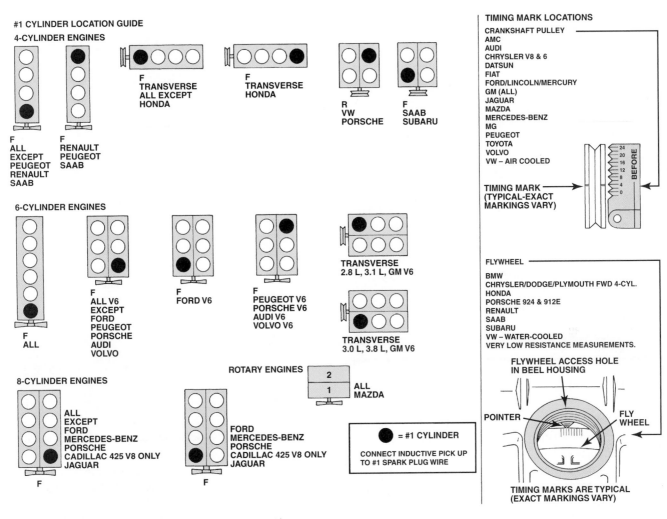

FIGURE 16-38 Cylinder 1 and timing mark location guide.

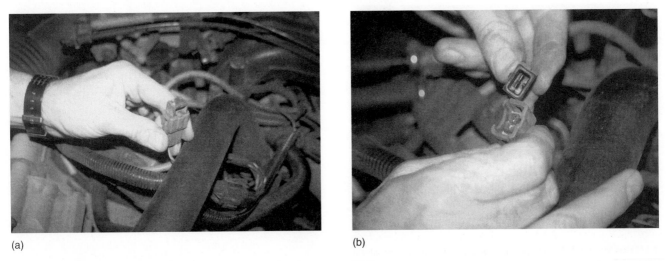

(a)

(b)

FIGURE 16-39 (a) Typical SPOUT connector as used on many Ford engines equipped with distributor ignition (DI). (b) The connector must be opened (disconnected) to check and/or adjust the ignition timing. On DIS/EDIS systems, the connector is called SPOUT/SAW (spark output/spark angle word).

TECH TIP

TWO MARKS ARE THE KEY TO SUCCESS

When a distributor is removed from an engine, always mark the direction the rotor is pointing to ensure that the distributor is reinstalled in the correct position. Because of the helical cut on the distributor drive gear, the rotor rotates as the distributor is being removed from the engine. To help reinstall a distributor without any problems, simply make another mark where the rotor is pointing just as the distributor is lifted out of the engine. Then, to reinstall, simply line up the rotor to the second mark and lower the distributor into the engine. The rotor should then line up with the original mark as a double-check. See Figure 16-40.

in the direction of rotor rotation to retard the timing and against rotor rotation to advance the timing.

4. After adjusting the timing to specifications, carefully tighten the distributor locking bolt. It is sometimes necessary to readjust the timing after the initial setting because the distributor may rotate slightly when the hold-down bolt is tightened.

IGNITION SYSTEM TROUBLESHOOTING GUIDE

The following list will assist technicians in troubleshooting ignition system problems.

Problem	Possible Causes and/or Solutions
No spark out of the coil	Possible open in the ignition switch circuit
	Possible defective ignition module (if electronic ignition coil)
	Possible defective pickup coil or Hall-effect switch (if electronic ignition)
	Possible shorted condenser
Weak spark out of the coil	Possible high-resistance coil wire or spark plug wire
	Possible poor ground between the distributor or module and the engine block
Engine missing	Possible defective (open) spark plug wire
	Possible worn or fouled spark plugs
	Possible defective pickup coil
	Possible defective module
	Possible poor electrical connections at the pickup coil and/or module

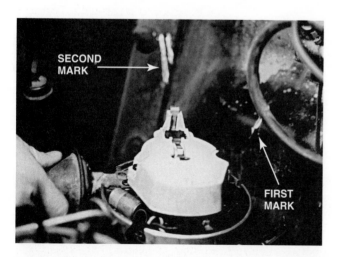

FIGURE 16-40 The first mark indicates the direction the rotor is pointing when the distributor is in the engine. The second mark indicates where the rotor is pointing just as it is pulled from the engine.

IGNITION SYSTEM DIAGNOSIS Step-by-Step

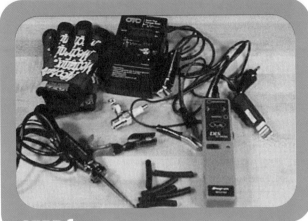

STEP 1 The tools and supplies needed to test for a fault in the secondary ignition system.

STEP 2 Using a spark plug wire boot removal tool, carefully remove the spark plug wire from the spark plug.

STEP 3 Attach a spark tester to the end of the spark plug wire and then clip the spark tester to a good engine ground. Start the engine and observe the spark tester. A spark should consistently jump the gap indicating that the system is capable of supplying at least 25,000 volts (25 kV).

STEP 4 Engine faults as well as ignition system faults can often be detected by using a tester capable of measuring spark plug firing voltage such as this unit from Snap-On tools.

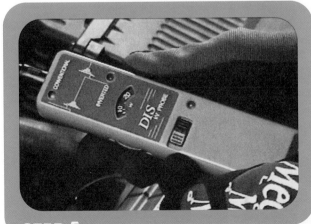

STEP 5 Start the engine and rotate the thumb wheel until the red light emitting diode (LED) just flickers off and then read the firing voltage on the display. This cylinder shows about 12–13 kV with conventional firing.

STEP 6 This cylinder is firing in the opposite polarity of the other cylinder (inverted). The firing voltage indicates a possible narrow gap or fouled spark plug.

(continued)

IGNITION SYSTEM DIAGNOSIS continued

STEP 7 Another tester that can be used is one from OTC tools. To use this tester, connect the ground clip to a good engine ground and connect the test probe around a spark plug wire.

STEP 8 This is the voltage required to fire the spark plugs; this display indicates 16.4 kV. This is higher than normal and could be due to a high-resistance spark plug wire or a wide gap spark plug.

STEP 9 Move the selector to read "burn kV." The reading indicates 1.9 kV. This is the voltage necessary to keep the spark firing after it has been started. It should be less than 2 kV for most vehicles.

STEP 10 Move the selector to "burn time." The reading is 1.2 mS (milliseconds). This is the duration of the spark and it should be between 1 and 2 mS.

STEP 11 Ground out a cylinder one at a time and observe if the engine speed or idle quality is affected. Insert 2-inch lengths of vacuum hose between the coil tower and the spark plug wires.

STEP 12 Use a grounded test light and touch the section of rubber hose with the tip. The high voltage will travel through the test light to ground and not fire the spark plug.

SUMMARY

1. All inductive ignition systems supply battery voltage to the positive side of the ignition coil and pulse the negative side of the coil on and off to ground to create a high-voltage spark.

2. If an ignition system uses a distributor, it is a distributor ignition (DI) system.

3. If an ignition system does not use a distributor, it is called an electronic ignition (EI) system.

4. A waste-spark ignition system fires two spark plugs at the same time.

5. A coil-on-plug ignition system uses an ignition coil for each spark plug.

REVIEW QUESTIONS

1. How can 12 volts from a battery be changed to 40,000 volts for ignition?

2. How does a magnetic sensor work?

3. How does a Hall-effect sensor work?

4. How does a waste spark ignition system work?

5. Why should a spark tester be used to check for spark rather than a standard spark plug?

6. What harm can occur if the engine is cranked or run with an open (defective) spark plug wire?

CHAPTER QUIZ

1. Coil polarity is determined by the _____.
   a. Direction of rotation of the coil windings
   b. Turn ratio
   c. Direction of laminations
   d. Saturation direction

2. The pulse generator _____.
   a. Fires the spark plug directly
   b. Signals the electronic control unit (module)
   c. Signals the computer that fires the spark plug directly
   d. Is used as a tachometer reference signal by the computer and has no other function

3. Two technicians are discussing distributor ignition. Technician A says that the pickup coil or optical sensor in the distributor is used to pulse the ignition module (igniter). Technician B says that some distributor ignition systems have the ignition coil inside the distributor cap. Which technician is correct?
   a. Technician A only
   b. Technician B only
   c. Both Technicians A and B
   d. Neither Technician A nor B

4. A waste-spark-type ignition system _____.
   a. Fires two spark plugs at the same time
   b. Fires one spark plug with reverse polarity
   c. Fires one spark plug with straight polarity
   d. All of the above

5. Technician A says that a defective crankshaft position sensor can cause a no-spark condition. Technician B says that a faulty ignition control module can cause a no-spark condition. Which technician is correct?
   a. Technician A only
   b. Technician B only
   c. Both Technicians A and B
   d. Neither Technician A nor B

6. Technician A says that a pickup coil (pulse generator) can be tested with an ohmmeter. Technician B says that ignition coils can be tested with an ohmmeter. Which technician is correct?
   a. Technician A only
   b. Technician B only
   c. Both Technicians A and B
   d. Neither Technician A nor B

7. Technician A says that a defective spark plug wire can cause an engine miss. Technician B says that a defective pickup coil wire can cause an engine miss. Which technician is correct?

   a. Technician A only

   b. Technician B only

   c. Both Technicians A and B

   d. Neither Technician A nor B

8. Typical primary coil resistance specifications usually range from _____ ohms.

   a. 100 to 450

   b. 500 to 1,500

   c. 1 to 3

   d. 6,000 to 30,000

9. Typical secondary coil resistance specifications usually range from _____ ohms.

   a. 100 to 450

   b. 500 to 1,500

   c. 1 to 3

   d. 6,000 to 30,000

10. Technician A says that an engine will not start and run if the ignition coil is tracked. Technician B says that one wire of any pickup coil must be grounded. Which technician is correct?

   a. Technician A only

   b. Technician B only

   c. Both Technicians A and B

   d. Neither Technician A nor B

EMISSION CONTROL DEVICES OPERATION AND DIAGNOSIS

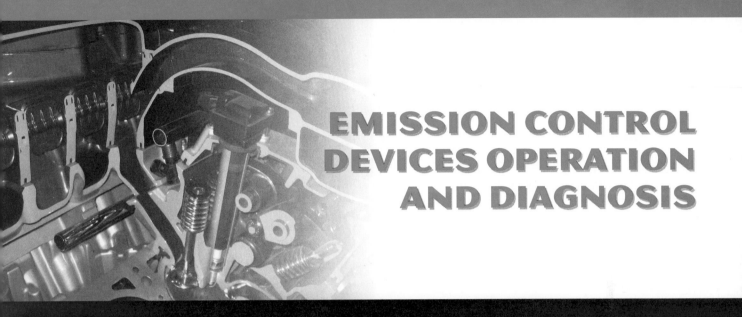

OBJECTIVES

After studying Chapter 17, the reader will be able to:

1. Prepare for the ASE Engine Performance (A8) certification test content area "D" (Emission Control Systems).

2. Describe the purpose and function of the exhaust gas recirculation system.

3. Explain methods for diagnosing and testing for faults in the exhaust gas recirculation system.

4. Describe the purpose and function of the positive crankcase ventilation and the air injection reaction system.

5. Explain methods for diagnosing and testing faults in the PCV and AIR systems.

6. Describe the purpose and function of the catalytic converter.

7. Explain the method for diagnosing and testing the catalytic converter.

KEY TERMS

AIR (p. 298)
Backpressure (p. 307)
Blowby (p. 294)
Catalyst (p. 304)
Catalytic Converter (p. 303)
Cerium (p. 309)
Check Valves (p. 299)
Digital EGR (p. 289)
DPFE (p. 291)
EGR (p. 286)
EVP (p. 288)
EVRV (p. 292)

HO2S (p. 305)
Inert (p. 286)
Infrared Pyrometer (p. 307)
Light-Off (p. 305)
Linear EGR (p. 290)
LOC (p. 305)
Mini Converter (p. 305)
Negative Backpressure (p. 288)
NO_x (p. 286)
OSC (p. 305)
Palladium (p. 304)
PCV (p. 294)

PFE (p. 288)
Platinum (p. 304)
Positive Backpressure (p. 288)
Preconverter (p. 305)
Pup Converter (p. 305)
Rhodium (p. 304)
Smog Pump (p. 298)
Tap Test (p. 306)
Thermactor Pump (p. 298)
TWC (p. 304)
Washcoat (p. 303)

EXHAUST GAS RECIRCULATION SYSTEMS

Exhaust gas recirculation (EGR) is an emission control that lowers the amount of **nitrogen oxides (NO$_X$)** formed during combustion. In the presence of sunlight, NO$_X$ reacts with hydrocarbons in the atmosphere to form ozone (O$_3$) or photochemical smog, an air pollutant.

NO$_X$ Formation

Nitrogen N$_2$ and oxygen O$_2$ molecules are separated into individual atoms of nitrogen and oxygen during the combustion process. These then bond to form NO$_X$ (NO, NO$_2$). When combustion flame front temperatures exceed 2,500°F (1,370°C), NO$_X$ formation increases dramatically.

CONTROLLING NO$_X$

The amounts of NO$_X$ formed at temperatures below 2,500°F (1,370°C) can be controlled in the exhaust by a catalyst. To handle the amounts generated above 2,500°F (1,370°C), the following are some methods that have been used to lower NO$_X$ formation:

- **Enrich the air–fuel mixture.** More fuel lowers the peak combustion temperature, but it raises hydrocarbon (HC) and carbon monoxide (CO) emissions. The reduction in fuel economy also makes this solution unattractive.
- **Lower the compression ratio.** This decreases NO$_X$ levels somewhat but also reduces combustion efficiency. When the compression ratio becomes too low, HC and CO emissions rise.
- **Dilute the air–fuel mixture.** To lower emission levels further, engineers developed a system that introduces small amounts of exhaust gas into the engine intake. This lowers combustion temperatures by displacing some of the air and absorbs heat without contributing to the combustion process. Currently, this is one of the most efficient methods to meet NO$_X$ emission level cut-points without significantly affecting engine performance, fuel economy, and other exhaust emissions. The EGR system routes small quantities, usually between 6% and 10%, of exhaust gas to the intake manifold.

Here, the exhaust gas mixes with and takes the place of some intake charge. This leaves less room for the intake charge to enter the combustion chamber. The recirculated exhaust gas is **inert** (chemically inactive) and does not enter into the combustion process. The result is a lower peak combustion temperature. As the combustion temperature is lowered, the production of oxides of nitrogen is also reduced.

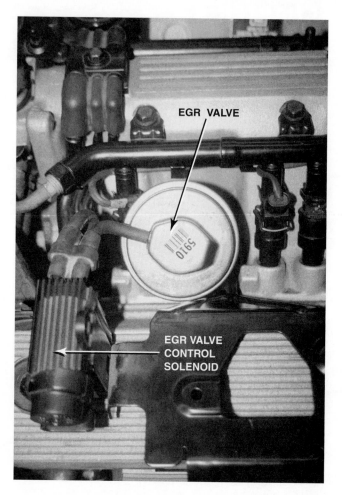

FIGURE 17-1 Typical vacuum-operated EGR valve. The operation of the valve is controlled by the computer by pulsing the EGR control solenoid on and off.

The EGR system has some means of interconnecting the exhaust and intake manifolds. See Figure 17-1. The interconnecting passage is controlled by the EGR valve. On V-type engines, the intake manifold crossover is used as a source of exhaust gas for the EGR system. A cast passage connects the exhaust crossover to the EGR valve. The gas is sent from the EGR valve to openings in the manifold. On in-line-type engines, an external tube is generally used to carry exhaust gas to the EGR valve. This tube is often designed to be long so that the exhaust gas is cooled before it enters the EGR valve.

NOTE: The amount of EGR is subtracted from the mass air flow calculations. While the EGR gases do occupy space, they do not affect the air–fuel mixture.

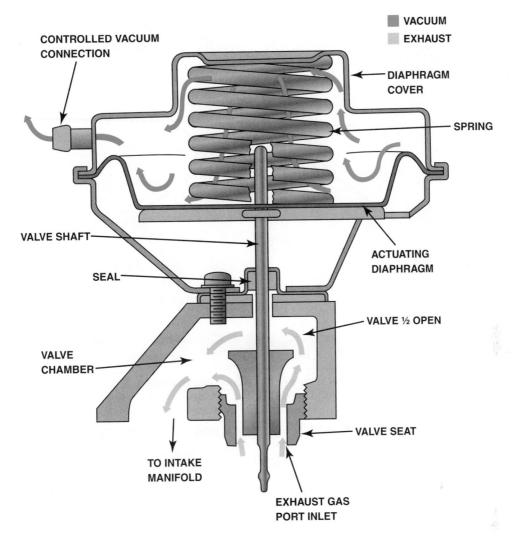

■ VACUUM
■ EXHAUST

CONTROLLED VACUUM
CONNECTION

DIAPHRAGM
COVER

SPRING

VALVE SHAFT

ACTUATING
DIAPHRAGM

SEAL

VALVE ½ OPEN

VALVE
CHAMBER

TO INTAKE
MANIFOLD

VALVE SEAT

EXHAUST GAS
PORT INLET

FIGURE 17-2   When the EGR valve opens, exhaust flows through the valve and into passages in the intake manifold.

EGR SYSTEM OPERATION

Since small amounts of exhaust are all that is needed to lower peak combustion temperatures, the orifice that the exhaust passes through is small. See Figure 17-2.

Because combustion temperatures are low, EGR is usually not required during the following conditions:

- Idle speed
- When the engine is cold
- At wide-open throttle (WOT)

The level of NO_X emission changes according to engine speed, temperature, and load. EGR is not used at wide-open throttle (WOT) because it would reduce engine performance and the engine does not operate under these conditions for a long period of time.

In addition to lowering NO_X levels, the EGR system also helps control detonation. Detonation, or ping, occurs when high pressure and heat cause the air–fuel mixture to ignite. This uncontrolled combustion can severely damage the engine.

Using the EGR system allows for greater ignition timing advance and for the advance to occur sooner without detonation problems, which increases power and efficiency.

POSITIVE AND NEGATIVE BACKPRESSURE EGR VALVES

Some EGR valves used on older engines are designed with a small valve inside that bleeds off any applied vacuum and prevents the valve from opening. These types of EGR valves

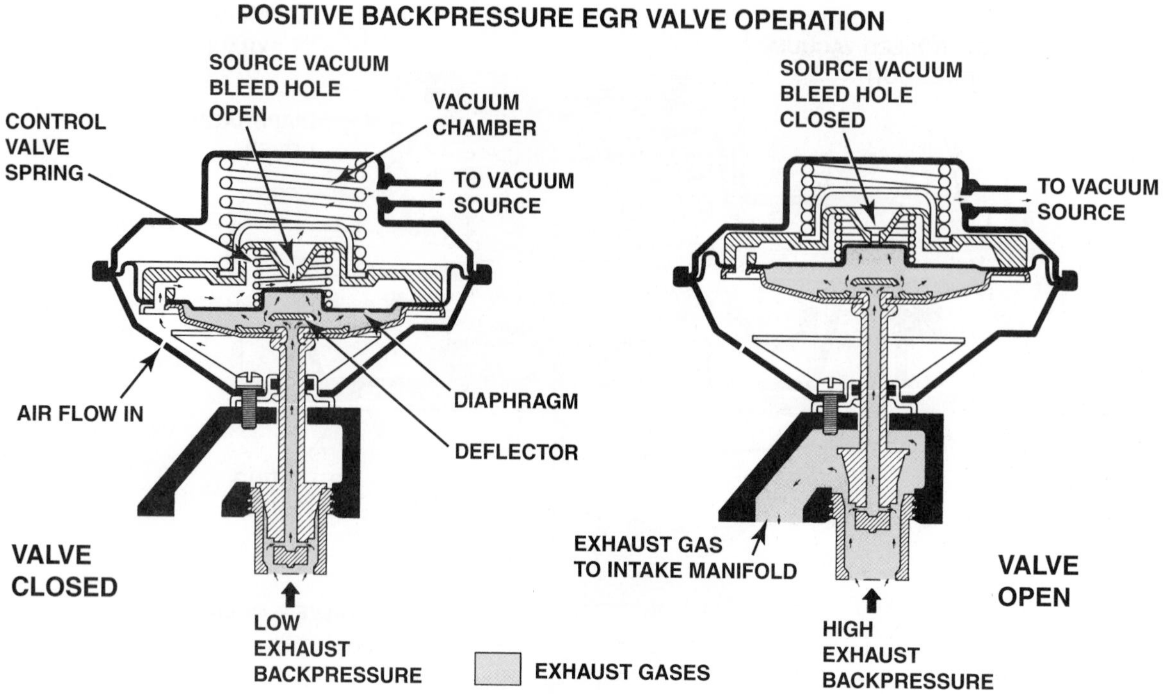

POSITIVE BACKPRESSURE EGR VALVE OPERATION

FIGURE 17-3   Backpressure in the exhaust system is used to close the control valve, thereby allowing engine vacuum to open the EGR valve.

require a positive backpressure in the exhaust system. This is called a **positive backpressure** EGR valve. At low engine speeds and light engine loads, the EGR system is not needed, and the backpressure in it is also low. Without sufficient backpressure, the EGR valve does not open even though vacuum may be present at the EGR valve.

On each exhaust stroke, the engine emits an exhaust "pulse." Each pulse represents a positive pressure. Behind each pulse is a small area of low pressure. Some EGR valves react to this low pressure area by closing a small internal valve, which allows the EGR valve to be opened by vacuum. This type of EGR valve is called a **negative backpressure** EGR valve. See Figure 17-3. The following conditions must occur:

1. Vacuum must be applied to the EGR valve itself. This is usually ported vacuum on some TBI fuel-injected systems. The vacuum source is often manifold vacuum and is controlled by the computer through a solenoid valve.
2. Exhaust backpressure must be present to close an internal valve inside the EGR to allow the vacuum to move the diaphragm.

NOTE: The installation of a low restriction exhaust system could prevent the proper operation of the backpressure-controlled EGR valve.

COMPUTER-CONTROLLED EGR SYSTEMS

Many computer-controlled EGR systems have one or more solenoids controlling the EGR vacuum. The computer controls a solenoid to shut off vacuum to the EGR valve at cold engine temperatures, idle speed, and wide-open throttle operation. If two solenoids are used, one acts as an off/on control of supply vacuum, while the second solenoid vents vacuum when EGR flow is not desired or needs to be reduced. The second solenoid is used to control a vacuum air bleed, allowing atmospheric pressure in to modulate EGR flow according to vehicle operating conditions.

EGR Valve Position Sensors

Late-model, computer-controlled EGR systems use a sensor to indicate EGR operation. On-board diagnostics generation-II (OBD-II) EGR system monitors require an EGR sensor to do their job. A linear potentiometer on the top of the EGR valve stem indicates valve position for the computer. This is called an **EGR valve position (EVP)** sensor. See Figure 17-4. Some later-model Ford EGR systems, however, use a feedback signal provided by an EGR exhaust backpressure sensor which converts the exhaust backpressure to a voltage signal. This sensor is called a **pressure feedback EGR (PFE)** sensor.

FIGURE 17-4 An EGR valve position sensor on top of an EGR valve.

FIND THE ROOT CAUSE

Excessive backpressure, such as that caused by a partially clogged exhaust system, could cause the plastic sensors on the EGR valve to melt. Always check for a restricted exhaust whenever replacing a failed EGR valve sensor.

The GM-integrated electronic EGR valve uses a similar sensor. The top of the valve contains a vacuum regulator and EGR pintle-position sensor in one assembly sealed inside a non-removable plastic cover. The pintle-position sensor provides a voltage output to the PCM, which increases as the duty cycle increases, allowing the PCM to monitor valve operation. See Figure 17-5.

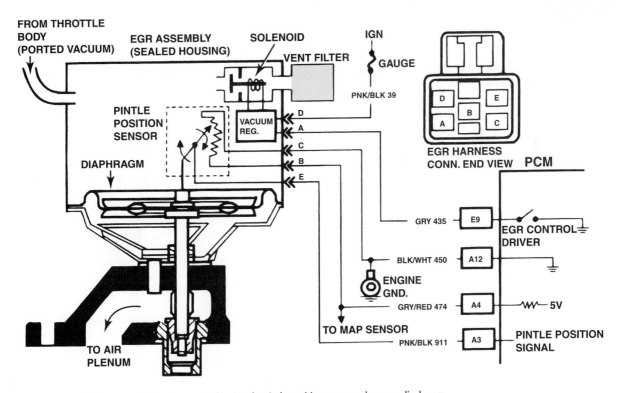

FIGURE 17-5 An integrated EGR valve system showing the pintle-position sensor and vacuum diaphragm.

Digital EGR Valves

GM introduced a completely electronic, **digital EGR** valve design on some 1990 engines. Unlike the previously mentioned vacuum-operated EGR valves, the digital EGR valve consists of three solenoids controlled by the PCM. See Figure 17-6. Each solenoid controls a different size orifice in the base—small, medium, and large. The PCM controls each solenoid ground

FIGURE 17-6 This 3,800 V-6 uses three solenoids for EGR. A scan tool can be used to turn on each solenoid to check if the valve is working and if the exhaust passages are capable of flowing enough exhaust to the intake manifold to affect engine operation when cycled.

FIGURE 17-7 A General Motors linear EGR valve.

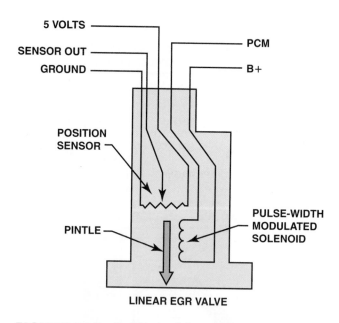

FIGURE 17-8 The EGR valve pintle is pulse-width modulated and a three-wire potentiometer provides pintle-position information back to the PCM.

individually. It can produce any of seven different flow rates, using the solenoids to open the three valves in different combinations. The digital EGR valve offers precise control, and using a swivel pintle design helps prevent carbon deposit problems.

Linear EGR

Most General Motors and many other vehicles use a **linear EGR** that contains a solenoid to precisely regulate exhaust gas flow and a feedback potentiometer that signals the computer regarding the actual position of the valve. See Figures 17-7 and 17-8.

OBD-II EGR MONITORING STRATEGIES

In 1996, the U.S. EPA began requiring OBD-II systems in all passenger cars and most light-duty trucks. These systems include emissions system monitors that alert the driver and the technician if an emissions system is malfunctioning. To be certain the EGR system is operating, the PCM runs a functional test of the system, when specific operating conditions exist. The OBD-II system tests by opening and closing the EGR valve. The PCM monitors an EGR function sensor for a change in signal voltage. If the EGR system fails, a diagnostic trouble code (DTC) is set. If the system fails two

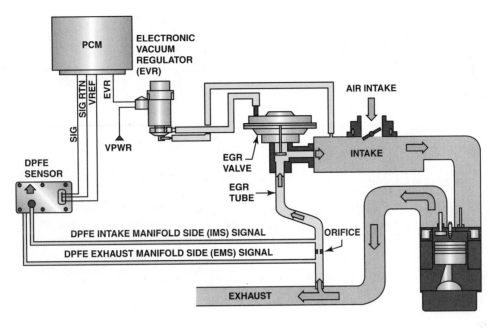

FIGURE 17-9   A DPFE sensor and related components.

consecutive times, the malfunction indicator light (MIL) is lit.

Chrysler monitors the difference in the exhaust oxygen sensor's voltage activity as the EGR valve opens and closes. Oxygen in the exhaust decreases when the EGR valve is open and increases when the EGR valve is closed. The PCM sets a DTC if the sensor signal does not change.

Depending on the vehicle application, Ford uses at least one of two types of sensors to evaluate exhaust-gas flow. The first type uses a temperature sensor mounted in the intake side of the EGR passageway. The PCM monitors the change in temperature when the EGR valve is open. When the EGR is open and exhaust is flowing, the sensor signal is changed by the heat of the exhaust. The PCM compares the change in the sensor's signal with the values in its look-up table.

The second type of Ford EGR monitor test sensor is called a **Delta Pressure Feedback EGR (DPFE) sensor.** This sensor measures the pressure differential between two sides of a metered orifice positioned just below the EGR valve's exhaust side. Pressure between the orifice and the EGR valve decreases when the EGR opens because it becomes exposed to the lower pressure in the intake. The DPFE sensor recognizes this pressure drop, compares it to the relatively higher pressure on the exhaust side of the orifice, and signals the value of the pressure difference to the PCM. See Figure 17-9. When the EGR valve is closed, the exhaust-gas pressure on both sides of the orifice is equal.

The OBD-II EGR monitor for this second system runs when programmed operating conditions (enable criteria) have been met. The monitor evaluates the pressure differential while the PCM commands the EGR valve to open. Like other systems, the monitor compares the measured value with the look-up table value. If the pressure differential falls outside the acceptable value, a DTC sets.

Many vehicle manufacturers use the manifold absolute pressure (MAP) sensor as the EGR monitor on some applications. After meeting the enable criteria (operating condition requirements), the EGR monitor is run. The PCM monitors the MAP sensor while it commands the EGR valve to open. The MAP sensor signal should change in response to the sudden change in manifold pressure or the fuel trim changes created by a change in the oxygen sensor voltage. If the signal value falls outside the acceptable value in the look-up table, a DTC sets. See Figure 17-10. If the EGR fails on two consecutive trips the PCM lights the MIL.

DPFE EGR Sensor Chart

	Pressure		Voltage
PSI	In. Hg	kPa	Volts
4.34	8.83	29.81	4.56
3.25	6.62	22.36	3.54
2.17	4.41	14.90	2.51
1.08	2.21	7.46	1.48
0	0	0	0.45

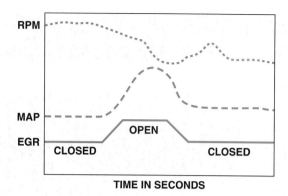

FIGURE 17-10   An OBD-II active test. The PCM opens the EGR valve and then monitors the MAP sensor and/or engine speed (RPM) to meet acceptable values.

DIAGNOSING A DEFECTIVE EGR SYSTEM

If the EGR valve is not opening or the flow of the exhaust gas is restricted, then the following symptoms are likely:

- Ping (spark knock or detonation) during acceleration or during cruise (steady-speed driving)
- Excessive oxides of nitrogen (NO_X) exhaust emissions

If the EGR valve is stuck open or partially open, then the following symptoms are likely:

- Rough idle or frequent stalling
- Poor performance/low power, especially at low engine speed

TECH TIP

WATCH OUT FOR CARBON BALLS!

Exhaust gas recirculation (EGR) valves can get stuck partially open by a chunk of carbon. The EGR valve or solenoid will test as defective. When the valve (or solenoid) is removed, small chunks or balls of carbon often fall into the exhaust manifold passage. When the replacement valve is installed, the carbon balls can be drawn into the new valve again, causing the engine to idle roughly or stall.

To help prevent this problem, start the engine with the EGR valve or solenoid removed. Any balls or chunks of carbon will be blown out of the passage by the exhaust. Stop the engine and install the replacement EGR valve or solenoid.

REAL WORLD FIX

THE BLAZER STORY

The owner of a Chevrolet Blazer equipped with a 4.3-L, V-6 engine complained that the engine would stumble and hesitate at times. Everything seemed to be functioning correctly, except that the service technician discovered a weak vacuum going to the EGR valve at idle. This vehicle was equipped with an EGR valve-control solenoid, called an **electronic vacuum regulator valve** or **EVRV** by General Motors Corporation. The computer pulses the solenoid to control the vacuum that regulates the operation of the EGR valve. The technician checked the service manual for details on how the system worked. The technician discovered that vacuum should be present at the EGR valve only when the gear selector indicates a drive gear (drive, low, reverse). Because the technician discovered the vacuum at the solenoid to be leaking, the solenoid was obviously defective and required replacement. After replacement of the solenoid (EVRV), the hesitation problem was solved.

NOTE: The technician also discovered in the service manual that blower-type exhaust hoses should not be connected to the tailpipe on any vehicle while performing an inspection of the EGR system. The vacuum created by the system could cause false EGR valve operation to occur.

The first step in almost any diagnosis is to perform a thorough visual inspection. To check for proper operation of a vacuum-operated EGR valve, follow these steps:

1. Check the vacuum diaphragm to see if it can hold vacuum.

   NOTE: Because many EGR valves require exhaust backpressure to function correctly, the engine should be running at a fast idle.

2. Apply vacuum from a hand-operated vacuum pump and check for proper operation. The valve itself should move when vacuum is applied, and the engine operation should be affected. The EGR valve should be able to hold the vacuum that was applied. If the vacuum drops off, then the valve is likely to be defective.

   If the EGR valve is able to hold vacuum, but the engine is not affected when the valve is opened, then the exhaust passage(s) must be checked for restriction. See the Tech Tip "The Snake Trick." If the EGR valve will not hold vacuum, the valve itself is likely to be defective and require replacement.

REAL WORLD FIX

I WAS ONLY TRYING TO HELP!

On a Friday, an experienced service technician found that the driveability performance problem with a Buick V-6 was a worn EGR valve. When vacuum was applied to the valve, the valve did not move at all. Additional vacuum from the hand-operated vacuum pump resulted in the valve popping all the way open. A new valve of the correct part number was not available until Monday, yet the customer wanted the vehicle back for a trip during the weekend.

To achieve acceptable driveability, the technician used a small hammer and deformed the top of the valve to limit the travel of the EGR valve stem. The technician instructed the customer to return on Monday for the proper replacement valve.

The customer did return on Monday, but now accompanied by his lawyer. The engine had developed a hole in one of the pistons. The lawyer reminded the technician and the manager that an exhaust emission control had been "modified." The result was the repair shop paid for a new engine and the technician learned to always repair the vehicle correctly or not at all.

TECH TIP

THE SNAKE TRICK

The EGR passages on many intake manifolds become clogged with carbon, which reduces the flow of exhaust and the amount of exhaust gases in the cylinders. This reduction can cause spark knock (detonation) and increased emissions of oxides of nitrogen (NO_X) (especially important in areas with enhanced exhaust emissions testing).

To quickly and easily remove carbon from exhaust passages, cut an approximately 1-foot (30-cm) length from stranded wire, such as garage door guide wire or an old speedometer cable. Flare the end and place the end of the wire into the passage. Set your drill on reverse, turn it on, and the wire will pull its way through the passage, cleaning the carbon as it goes, just like a snake in a drain pipe. Some vehicles, such as Hondas, require that plugs be drilled out to gain access to the EGR passages, as shown in Figure 17-11.

FIGURE 17-11 Removing the EGR passage plugs from the intake manifold on a Honda.

3. Connect a vacuum gauge to an intake manifold vacuum source and monitor the engine vacuum at idle (should be 17 to 21 in. Hg at sea level). Raise the speed of the engine to 2,500 RPM and note the vacuum reading (should be 17 to 21 in. Hg or higher). Activate the EGR valve using a scan tool or vacuum pump, if vacuum controlled, and observe the vacuum gauge. The results are as follows:

   - The vacuum should drop 6 to 8 in. Hg.
   - If the vacuum drops less than 6 to 8 in. Hg, the valve or the EGR passages are clogged.

EGR-Related OBD-II Diagnostic Trouble Codes

Diagnostic Trouble Code	Description	Possible Causes
P0400	Exhaust gas recirculation flow problems	- EGR valve - EGR valve hose or electrical connection - Defective PCM
P0401	Exhaust gas recirculation flow insufficient	- EGR valve - Clogged EGR ports or passages
P0402	Exhaust gas recirculation flow excessive	- Stuck-open EGR valve - Vacuum hose(s) misrouted - Electrical wiring shorted

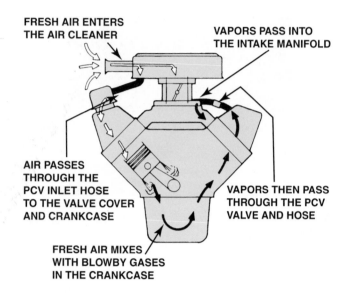

FRESH AIR ENTERS THE AIR CLEANER

VAPORS PASS INTO THE INTAKE MANIFOLD

AIR PASSES THROUGH THE PCV INLET HOSE TO THE VALVE COVER AND CRANKCASE

VAPORS THEN PASS THROUGH THE PCV VALVE AND HOSE

FRESH AIR MIXES WITH BLOWBY GASES IN THE CRANKCASE

FIGURE 17-12 A PCV system includes a hose from the air cleaner assembly so that filtered air can be drawn into the crankcase. This filtered air is then drawn by engine vacuum through the PCV valve and into the intake manifold, where the crankcase fumes are burned in the cylinder. The PCV valve controls and limits this flow of air and fumes into the engine and the valve closes in the event of a backfire to prevent flames from entering the crankcase area.

CRANKCASE VENTILATION

The problem of crankcase ventilation has existed since the beginning of the automobile, because no piston ring, new or old, can provide a perfect seal between the piston and the cylinder wall. When an engine is running, the pressure of combustion forces the piston downward. This same pressure also forces gases and unburned fuel from the combustion chamber, past the piston rings, and into the crankcase. This process of gases leaking past the rings is called **blowby,** and the gases form crankcase vapors.

These combustion by-products, particularly unburned hydrocarbons caused by blowby, must be ventilated from the crankcase. However, the crankcase cannot be vented directly to the atmosphere, because the hydrocarbon vapors add to air pollution. **Positive crankcase ventilation (PCV)** systems were developed to ventilate the crankcase and recirculate the vapors to the engine's induction system so they can be burned in the cylinders.

Closed PCV Systems

All systems use a PCV valve, calibrated orifice or separator, an air inlet filter, and connecting hoses. See Figure 17-12. An oil/vapor or oil/water separator is used in some systems

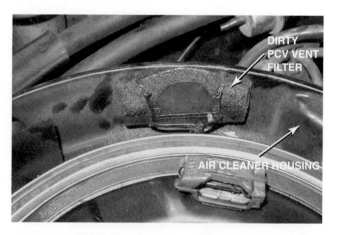

DIRTY PCV VENT FILTER

AIR CLEANER HOUSING

FIGURE 17-13 A dirty PCV vent filter inside the air cleaner housing. The air enters the crankcase through this filter and then is drawn into the engine through the PCV valve.

instead of a valve or orifice, particularly with turbocharged and fuel-injected engines. The oil/vapor separator lets oil condense and drain back into the crankcase. The oil/water separator accumulates moisture and prevents it from freezing during cold engine starts.

The air for the PCV system is drawn after the air cleaner filter, which acts as a PCV filter.

NOTE: Some older designs drew from the dirty side of the air cleaner, where a separate crankcase ventilation filter was used. See Figure 17-13.

PCV VALVES

The PCV valve in most systems is a one-way valve containing a spring-operated plunger that controls valve flow rate. See Figure 17-14. Flow rate is established for each engine and a valve for a different engine should not be substituted. The flow rate is determined by the size of the plunger and the holes inside the valve. PCV valves usually are located in the valve cover or intake manifold.

The PCV valve regulates air flow through the crankcase under all driving conditions and speeds. When manifold vacuum is high (at idle, cruising, and light-load operation), the PCV valve restricts the air flow to maintain a balanced air–fuel ratio. See Figure 17-15. It also prevents high intake manifold vacuum from pulling oil out of the crankcase and into the intake manifold. Under high speed or heavy loads, the valve opens and allows maximum air flow. See Figure 17-16. If the engine backfires, the valve will close instantly to prevent a crankcase explosion. See Figure 17-17.

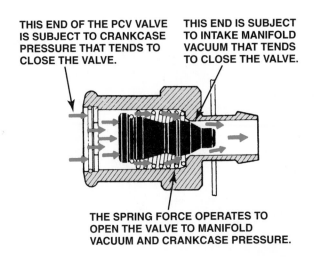

THIS END OF THE PCV VALVE IS SUBJECT TO CRANKCASE PRESSURE THAT TENDS TO CLOSE THE VALVE.

THIS END IS SUBJECT TO INTAKE MANIFOLD VACUUM THAT TENDS TO CLOSE THE VALVE.

THE SPRING FORCE OPERATES TO OPEN THE VALVE TO MANIFOLD VACUUM AND CRANKCASE PRESSURE.

FIGURE 17-14 Spring force, crankcase pressure, and intake manifold vacuum work together to regulate the flow rate through the PCV valve.

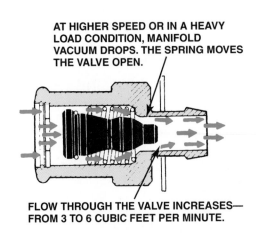

AT HIGHER SPEED OR IN A HEAVY LOAD CONDITION, MANIFOLD VACUUM DROPS. THE SPRING MOVES THE VALVE OPEN.

FLOW THROUGH THE VALVE INCREASES— FROM 3 TO 6 CUBIC FEET PER MINUTE.

FIGURE 17-16   Air flows through the PCV valve during acceleration and when the engine is under a heavy load.

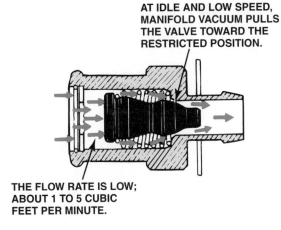

AT IDLE AND LOW SPEED, MANIFOLD VACUUM PULLS THE VALVE TOWARD THE RESTRICTED POSITION.

THE FLOW RATE IS LOW; ABOUT 1 TO 5 CUBIC FEET PER MINUTE.

FIGURE 17-15   Air flows through the PCV valve during idle, cruising, and light-load conditions.

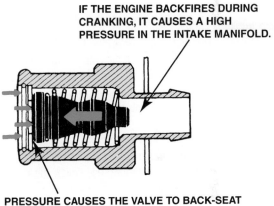

IF THE ENGINE BACKFIRES DURING CRANKING, IT CAUSES A HIGH PRESSURE IN THE INTAKE MANIFOLD.

PRESSURE CAUSES THE VALVE TO BACK-SEAT AND SEAL OFF THE INLET. THIS KEEPS THE BACKFIRE OUT OF THE CRANKCASE.

FIGURE 17-17   PCV valve operation in the event of a backfire.

ORIFICE-CONTROLLED SYSTEMS

The closed PCV system used on some 4-cylinder engines contains a calibrated orifice instead of a PCV valve. The orifice may be located in the valve cover or intake manifold, or in a hose connected between the valve cover, air cleaner, and intake manifold.

While most orifice flow control systems work the same as a PCV valve system, they may not use fresh air scavenging of the crankcase. Crankcase vapors are drawn into the intake manifold in calibrated amounts depending on manifold pressure and the orifice size. If vapor availability is low, as during idle, air is drawn in with the vapors. During off-idle operation, excess vapors are sent to the air cleaner.

At idle, PCV flow is controlled by a 0.050-inch (1.3-mm) orifice. As the engine moves off-idle, ported vacuum pulls a spring-loaded valve off of its seat, allowing PCV flow to pass through a 0.090-inch (2.3-mm) orifice.

Separator Systems

Turbocharged and many fuel-injected engines use an oil/vapor or oil/water separator and a calibrated orifice instead of a PCV valve. In the most common applications, the air intake throttle body acts as the source for crankcase ventilation vacuum, and a calibrated orifice acts as the metering device.

REAL WORLD FIX

THE WHISTLING ENGINE

An older vehicle was being diagnosed for a whistling sound whenever the engine was running, especially at idle. It was finally discovered that the breather in the valve cover was plugged and caused high vacuum in the crankcase. The engine was sucking air from what was likely the rear main seal lip, making the "whistle" noise. After replacing the breather and PCV, the noise stopped.

POSITIVE CRANKCASE VENTILATION (PCV) SYSTEM DIAGNOSIS

When intake air flows freely, the PCV system functions properly, as long as the PCV valve or orifice is not clogged. Modern engine design includes the air and vapor flow as a calibrated part of the air–fuel mixture. In fact, some engines receive as much as 30% of their idle air through the PCV system. For this reason, a flow problem in the PCV system results in driveability problems.

A blocked or plugged PCV system is a major cause of high oil consumption, and contributes to many oil leaks. Before expensive engine repairs are attempted, check the condition of the PCV system. See Figure 17-18.

PCV System Performance Check

A properly operating positive crankcase ventilation system should be able to draw vapors from the crankcase and into the intake manifold. If the pipes, hoses, and PCV valve itself are not restricted, vacuum is applied to the crankcase. A slight vacuum is created in the crankcase (usually less than 1 in. Hg if measured at the dipstick) and is also applied to other areas of the engine. Oil drainback holes provide a path for oil to drain back into the oil pan. These holes also allow crankcase vacuum to be applied under the rocker covers and in the valley area of most V-type engines. There are several methods that can be used to test a PCV system.

The Rattle Test

The rattle test is performed by simply removing the PCV valve and shaking it in your hand. See Figure 17-19.

- If the PCV valve does *not* rattle, it is definitely defective and must be replaced.

FIGURE 17-18   A visual inspection found this deteriorated PCV vacuum hose.

TECH TIP

CHECK FOR OIL LEAKS WITH THE ENGINE OFF

The owner of an older vehicle equipped with a V-6 engine complained to his technician that he smelled burning oil, but only *after* shutting off the engine. The technician found that the rocker cover gaskets were leaking. But why did the owner only notice the smell of hot oil when the engine was shut off? Because of the positive crankcase ventilation (PCV) system, engine vacuum tends to draw oil away from gasket surfaces. But when the engine stops, engine vacuum disappears and the oil remaining in the upper regions of the engine will tend to flow down and out through any opening. Therefore, a good technician should check an engine for oil leaks not only with the engine running but also shortly after shutdown.

- If the PCV valve *does* rattle, it does not necessarily mean that the PCV valve is good. All PCV valves contain springs that can become weaker with age and heating and cooling cycles. Replace any PCV valve with the *exact* replacement according to vehicle manufacturers' recommended intervals (usually every 3 years or 36,000 miles, or 60,000 km).

The 3 × 5 Card Test

Remove the oil-fill cap (where oil is added to the engine) and start the engine. See Figure 17-20.

FIGURE 17-19   A typical PCV valve. A defective or clogged PCV valve or hose can cause a rough idle or stalling problem. Because the air flow through the PCV valve accounts for about 20% of the air needed by the engine at idle, use of the incorrect valve for an application could have a severe effect on idle quality.

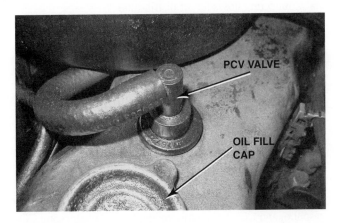

FIGURE 17-20   A typical PCV valve installed in a rubber grommet in the valve cover.

NOTE: Use care on some overhead camshaft engines. With the engine running, oil may be sprayed from the open oil-fill opening.

Hold a 3 × 5 card over the opening (a dollar bill or any other piece of paper can be used for this test).

- If the PCV system, including the valve and hoses, is functioning correctly, the card should be held down on the oil-fill opening by the slight vacuum inside the crankcase.
- If the card will not stay, carefully inspect the PCV valve, hose(s), and manifold vacuum port for carbon buildup (restriction). Clean or replace as necessary.

NOTE: On some 4-cylinder engines, the 3 × 5 card may vibrate on the oil-fill opening when the engine is running at idle speed. This is normal because of the time intervals between intake strokes on a 4-cylinder engine.

FIGURE 17-21   A water manometer being used to check for a slight vacuum when testing at the oil dipstick tube.

The Snap-Back Test

The proper operation of the PCV valve can be checked by placing a finger over the inlet hole in the valve when the engine is running and removing the finger rapidly. Repeat several times. The valve should "snap back." If the valve does not snap back, replace the valve.

Crankcase Vacuum Test

Sometimes the PCV system can be checked by testing for a weak vacuum at the oil dipstick tube using an inches-of-water manometer or gauge as follows:

Step 1   Remove the oil-fill cap and cover the opening.
Step 2   Remove the oil level indicator (dipstick).
Step 3   Connect a water manometer or gauge to the dipstick tube.
Step 4   Start the engine and observe the gauge at idle and at 2500 RPM. See Figure 17-21.

The gauge should show some vacuum, especially at 2500 RPM. If not, carefully inspect the PCV system for blockages or other faults.

PCV MONITOR

Starting with 2004 and newer vehicles, all vehicles must be checked for proper operation of the PCV system. The PCV monitor will fail if the PCM detects an opening between the crankcase and the PCV valve or between the PCV valve and the intake manifold.

PCV-Related Diagnostic Trouble Code

Diagnostic Trouble Code	Description	Possible Causes
P1480	PCV solenoid circuit fault	• Defective PCV solenoid • Loose or corroded electrical connection • Loose defective vacuum hoses/connections

AIR PUMP SYSTEM

An air pump provides the air necessary for the oxidizing process inside the catalytic converter. See Figure 17-22.

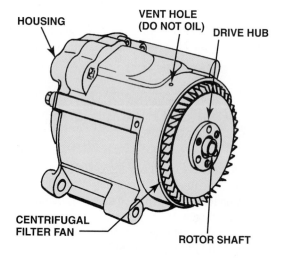

HOUSING **VENT HOLE (DO NOT OIL)** **DRIVE HUB** **CENTRIFUGAL FILTER FAN** **ROTOR SHAFT**

FIGURE 17-22   A typical belt-driven air pump. Air enters through the revolving fins. These fins act as a moving air filter because dirt is heavier than air, and therefore the dirt in the air is deflected off the fins at the same time the air is drawn into the pump.

NOTE: This system is commonly called **AIR**, meaning **air injection reaction.** Therefore, an AIR pump does pump air.

The AIR pump, sometimes referred to as a **smog pump** or **thermactor pump,** is mounted at the front of the engine and driven by a belt from the crankshaft pulley. It pulls fresh air in through an external filter and pumps the air under slight pressure to each exhaust port through connecting hoses or a manifold.

- A belt-driven pump with inlet air filter (older models); or,
- An electronic air pump (newer models)
- One or more air distribution manifolds and nozzles
- One or more exhaust check valves
- Connecting hoses for air distribution
- Air management valves and solenoids on all newer applications

With the introduction of NO_x reduction converters (also called dual-bed, three-way converters, or TWC), the output of the AIR pump is sent to the center of the converter where the extra air can help oxidize HC and CO into H_2O and CO_2.

The computer controls the air flow from the pump by switching on and off various solenoid valves. When the engine is cold, the air pump output is directed to the exhaust manifold to help provide enough oxygen to convert HC (unburned gasoline) and CO (carbon monoxide) to H_2O (water) and CO_2 (carbon dioxide). When the engine becomes warm and is operating in closed loop, the computer operates the air valves so as to direct the air pump output to the catalytic converter. When the vacuum rapidly increases above the normal idle level, as during rapid deceleration, the computer diverts the air pump output to the air cleaner assembly to silence the air. Diverting the air to the air cleaner prevents exhaust backfire during deceleration. See Figure 17-23.

AIR DISTRIBUTION MANIFOLDS AND NOZZLES

The air-injection system sends air from the pump to a nozzle installed near each exhaust port in the cylinder head. This provides equal air injection for the exhaust from each cylinder and makes it available at a point in the system where exhaust gases are the hottest.

Air is delivered to the exhaust system in one of two ways:

- An external air manifold, or manifolds, distributes the air through injection tubes with stainless steel nozzles. The

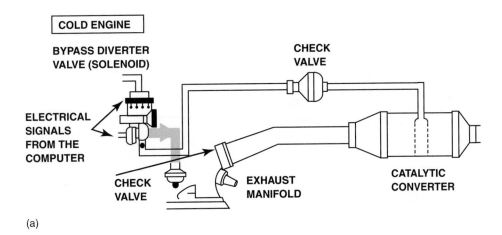

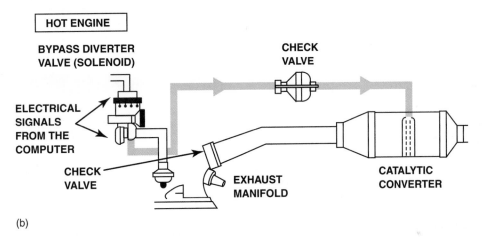

FIGURE 17-23   (a) When the engine is cold and before the oxygen sensor is hot enough to reach closed loop, the air flow is directed to the exhaust manifold(s) through one-way check valve(s). These valves keep exhaust gases from entering the switching solenoids and the air pump itself. (b) When the engine achieves closed loop, the air flows through the pump, is directed to the catalytic converter, and then moves through a check valve.

nozzles are threaded into the cylinder heads or exhaust manifolds close to each exhaust valve. This method is used primarily with smaller engines.

- An internal air manifold distributes the air to the exhaust ports near each exhaust valve through passages cast in the cylinder head or the exhaust manifold. This method is used mainly with larger engines.

Three basic types of air pumps are the belt-driven air pump, the pulse air-driven air pump, and the electric motor-driven air pump.

Exhaust Check Valves

All air-injection systems use one or more one-way check valves to protect the air pump and other components from reverse exhaust flow. A **check valve** contains a spring-type metallic disc or reed that closes the air line under exhaust backpressure. Check

valves are located between the air manifold and the diverter valve. See Figure 17-24. If exhaust pressure exceeds injection pressure, or if the air pump fails, the check valve spring closes the valve to prevent reverse exhaust flow. See Figure 17-25.

All air pump systems use one-way check valves to allow air to flow into the exhaust manifold and to prevent the hot exhaust from flowing into the valves on the air pump itself.

NOTE: These check valves commonly fail, resulting in excessive exhaust emissions (CO especially). When the check valve fails, hot exhaust can travel up to and destroy the switching valve(s) and air pump itself.

Belt-Driven Air Pumps

The belt-driven air pump uses a centrifugal filter just behind the drive pulley. As the pump rotates, underhood air is drawn

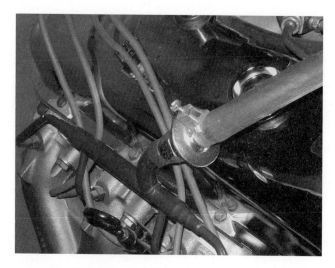

FIGURE 17-24 An AIR exhaust check valve between the rubber air hose and the metal discharge tubes.

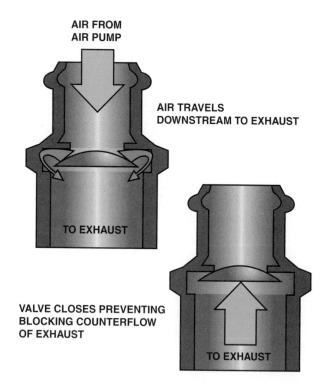

FIGURE 17-25 Exhaust check valves in the AIR system allow air to flow in only one direction.

into the pump and slightly compressed. See Figure 17-26. The air is then directed to:

- The exhaust manifold when the engine is cold to help oxidize CO and HC into carbon dioxide (CO_2) and water vapor (H_2O).

FIGURE 17-26 A typical belt-driven air pump used on an older model Chevrolet Corvette.

- The catalytic converter on many models to help provide the extra oxygen needed for the efficient conversion of CO and HC into CO_2 and H_2O.
- The air cleaner during deceleration or wide-open throttle (WOT) engine operation. See Figure 17-27.

Electric Motor-Driven Air Pumps

This style of pump is generally used only during cold engine operation and is computer controlled. The air injection reaction (AIR) system helps reduce hydrocarbon (HC) and carbon monoxide (CO). It also helps to warm up the three-way catalytic converters quickly on engine start-up so conversion of exhaust gases may occur sooner.

The AIR pump and solenoid is controlled by the PCM. The PCM turns on the AIR pump by providing the ground to complete the circuit which energizes the AIR pump solenoid relay. When air to the exhaust ports is desired, the PCM energizes the relay in order to turn on the solenoid and the AIR pump.

The PCM turns on the AIR pump during start-up any time the engine coolant temperature is above 32°F (0°C). A typical electric AIR pump operates for a maximum of 240 seconds, or until the system enters closed-loop operation. The AIR system is disabled under the following conditions:

- The PCM recognizes a problem and sets a diagnostic trouble code.
- The AIR pump has been on for 240 seconds.

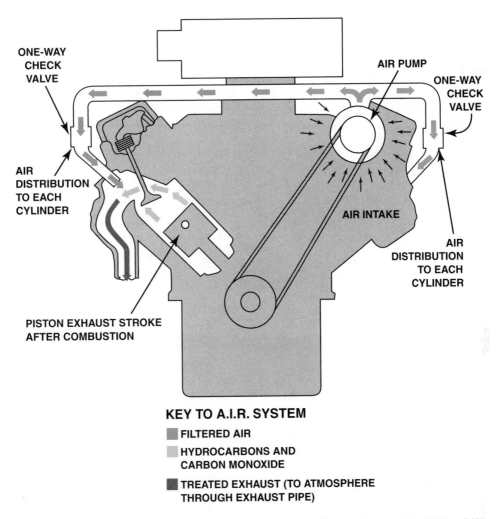

FIGURE 17-27   The air pump supplies air to the exhaust port of each cylinder. Unburned HCs are oxidized into CO_2 and H_2O, and CO is converted to CO_2.

- The engine speed is more than 2825 RPM.
- The manifold absolute pressure (MAP) is less than 6 in. Hg/ 20 kPa.
- Warm up three-way catalytic converters over temperature detected.
- The short- and long-term fuel trim are not in their normal ranges.
- Power enrichment is detected.

If no air (oxygen) enters the exhaust stream at the exhaust ports, the HC and CO emission levels will be higher than normal.

Air flowing to the exhaust ports at all times could increase temperature of the three-way catalytic converter.

The diagnostic trouble codes P0410 and/or P0418 set if there is a malfunction in the following components:

- The AIR pump
- The AIR solenoid
- The AIR pump solenoid relay

- Leaking hoses or pipes
- Leaking check valves
- The circuits going to the AIR pump and the AIR pump solenoid relay

The AIR pump is an electric type pump that requires no periodic maintenance. To check the operation of the AIR pump, the engine should be at normal operating temperature in neutral at idle. Using a scan tool, enable the AIR pump system and watch the heated oxygen sensor (HO2S) voltages for both bank 1 and bank 2 HO2S. The HO2S voltages for both sensors should remain under 350 mV because air is being directed to the exhaust ports. If the HO2S voltages remain low during this test, the AIR pump, solenoid, and shutoff valve are operating satisfactorily. If the HO2S voltage does not remain low when the AIR pump is enabled, inspect for the following:

- Voltage at the AIR pump when energized
- A seized AIR pump

FIGURE 17-28 Cutaway of a pulse air-driven air device used on many older engines to deliver air to the exhaust port through the use of the exhaust pulses acting on a series of one-way check valves. Air from the air cleaner assembly moves through the system and into the exhaust port where the additional air helps reduce HC and CO exhaust emissions.

- The hoses, vacuum lines, pipes, and all connections for leaks and proper routing
- Air flow going to the exhaust ports
- AIR pump for proper mounting
- Hoses and pipes for deterioration or holes

If a leak is suspected on the pressure side of the system, or if a hose or pipe has been disconnected on the pressure side, the connections should be checked for leaks with a soapy water solution. With the AIR pump running, bubbles form if a leak exists.

The check valves should be inspected whenever the hose is disconnected or whenever check valve failure is suspected. An AIR pump that had become inoperative and had shown indications of having exhaust gases in the outlet port would indicate check valve failure.

Pulse Air-Driven Devices

The pulse air-driven air pump uses the exhaust system pulses to draw in the compressed air. See Figure 17-28. Pulse air or aspirator valves are similar in design to exhaust check valves. Each valve contains a spring-loaded diaphragm or reed valve and is connected by tubing to the exhaust port of each cylinder or the exhaust manifold. Each time an exhaust valve closes, there is a period when exhaust manifold pressure drops below atmospheric pressure. During these low-pressure (slight vacuum) pulses, the pulse valve opens to admit fresh air to the exhaust. When the exhaust valve opens and exhaust pressure rises above atmospheric pressure, the pulse air valve acts as a

check valve and closes. As a result, air "injection" or more correctly, ingestion, occurs without the need for a power-consuming air pump.

Pulse air injection works best at low engine speeds when extra air is needed most by the catalytic converter. At high engine speeds, the vacuum pulses occur too rapidly for the valve to follow, and the internal spring simply keeps the valve closed. Pulse air valves must be connected upstream in the exhaust system where negative pressure pulses are strongest. This means that pulse air cannot be switched downstream for use in the converter or between oxidation and reduction catalysts.

AIR PUMP SYSTEM DIAGNOSIS

The air pump system should be inspected if an exhaust emissions test failure occurs. In severe cases, the exhaust will enter the air cleaner assembly, resulting in a horribly running engine because the extra exhaust displaces the oxygen needed for proper combustion. With the engine running, check for normal operation:

Engine Operation	Normal Operation of a Typical Air Injection Reaction (AIR) Pump System
Cold engine (open-loop operation)	Air is diverted to the exhaust manifold(s) or cylinder head
Warm engine (closed-loop operation)	Air is diverted to the catalytic converter
Deceleration	Air is diverted to the air cleaner assembly
Wide-open throttle	Air is diverted to the air cleaner assembly

Visual Inspection

Carefully inspect all air injection reaction (AIR) system hoses and pipes. Any pipes that have holes and leak air or exhaust require replacement. The check valve(s) should be checked when a pump has become inoperative. Exhaust gases could have gotten past the check valve and damaged the pump. Check the drive belt on an engine-driven pump for wear and proper tension.

Four-Gas Exhaust Analysis

An AIR system can be easily tested using an exhaust gas analyzer. Follow these steps:

1. Start the engine and allow it to run until normal operating temperature is achieved.
2. Connect the analyzer probe to the tailpipe and observe the exhaust readings for hydrocarbons (HC) and carbon monoxide (CO).
3. Using the appropriate pinch-off pliers, shut off the air flow from the AIR system. Observe the HC and CO readings. If the AIR system is working correctly, the HC and CO should increase when the AIR system is shut off.
4. Record the O_2 reading with the AIR system still inoperative. Unclamp the pliers and watch the O_2 readings. If the system is functioning correctly, the O_2 level should increase by 1% to 4%.

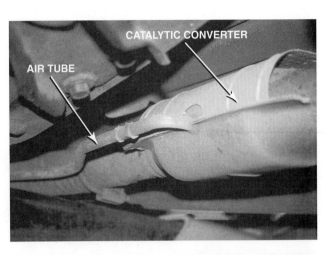

FIGURE 17-29 Typical catalytic converter. The small tube into the side of the converter comes from the air pump. The additional air from the air pump helps oxidize the exhaust into harmless H_2O and CO_2.

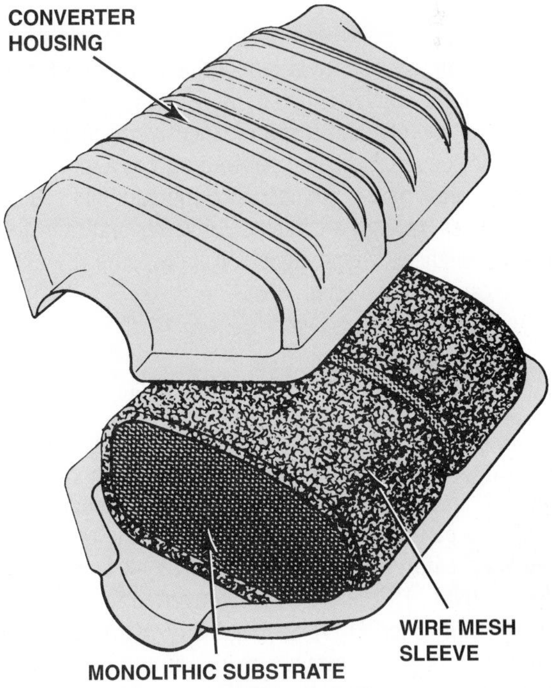

Air-Related Diagnostic Trouble Code

Diagnostic Trouble Code	Description	Possible Causes
P1485	AIR solenoid circuit fault	▪ Defective AIR solenoid ▪ Loose or corroded electrical connections ▪ Loose, missing, or defective rubber hose(s)

CATALYTIC CONVERTERS

A **catalytic converter** is an aftertreatment device used to reduce exhaust emissions outside of the engine. This device is installed in the exhaust system between the exhaust manifold and the muffler, and usually is positioned beneath the passenger compartment. See Figure 17-29. The location of the converter is important, since as much of the exhaust heat as possible must be retained for effective operation. The nearer it is to the engine, the better.

CERAMIC MONOLITH CATALYTIC CONVERTER

Most catalytic converters are constructed of a ceramic material in a honeycomb shape with square openings for the exhaust gases. There are approximately 400 openings per square

FIGURE 17-30 A typical catalytic converter with a monolithic substrate.

inch (62 per sq. cm) and the wall thickness is about 0.006 in. (1.5 mm). The substrate is then coated with a porous aluminum material called the **washcoat,** which makes the surface rough. The catalytic materials are then applied on top of the washcoat. The substrate is contained within a round or oval shell made by welding together two stamped pieces of aluminum or stainless steel. See Figure 17-30.

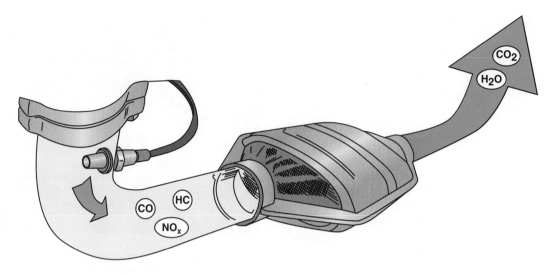

FIGURE 17-31 The three-way catalytic converter first separates the NO_x into nitrogen and oxygen and then converts the HC and CO into harmless water (H_2O) and carbon dioxide (CO_2).

The ceramic substrate in monolithic converters is not restrictive, but the converter breaks more easily when subject to shock or severe jolts and is more expensive to manufacture. Monolithic converters can be serviced only as a unit.

An exhaust pipe is connected to the manifold or header to carry gases through a catalytic converter and then to the muffler or silencer. V-type engines usually route the exhaust into one catalytic converter.

Catalytic Converter Operation

The converter contains small amounts of **rhodium, palladium,** and **platinum.** These elements act as catalysts. A **catalyst** is an element that starts a chemical reaction without becoming a part of, or being consumed in, the process. In a **three-way catalytic converter (TWC)** all three exhaust emissions (NO_x, HC, and CO) are converted to carbon dioxide (CO_2) and water (H_2O). See Figure 17-31. As the exhaust gas passes through the catalyst, oxides of nitrogen (NO_x) are chemically reduced (that is, nitrogen and oxygen are separated) in the first section of the catalytic converter. In the second section of the catalytic converter, most of the hydrocarbons and carbon monoxide remaining in the exhaust gas are oxidized to form harmless carbon dioxide (CO_2) and water vapor (H_2O). An air-injection system or pulse air system is used on some engines to supply additional air that may be needed in the oxidation process. See Figure 17-32.

NOTE: A two-way converter used in most vehicles from 1975 to 1980 only contained the oxidation portion.

FIGURE 17-32 A cutaway of a three-way catalytic converter showing the air tube in the center of the reducing and oxidizing section of the converter. Note the small holes in the tube to distribute air from the AIR pump to the oxidizing rear section of the converter.

Since the early 1990s, many converters also contain cerium, an element that can store oxygen. The purpose of the cerium is to provide oxygen to the oxidation bed of the converter when the exhaust is rich and lacks enough oxygen for proper oxidation. When the exhaust is lean, the cerium absorbs the extra oxygen. For most efficient operation, the converter should have a 14.7:1 air–fuel ratio exhaust but can use a mixture that varies slightly.

- A rich exhaust is required for reduction—stripping the oxygen (O_2) from the nitrogen in NO_x
- A lean exhaust is required to provide the oxygen necessary to oxidize HC and CO (combining oxygen with HC and CO to form H_2O and CO_2)

If the catalytic converter is not functioning correctly, check to see that the air–fuel mixture being supplied to the engine is correct and that the ignition system is free of defects.

Converter Light-Off

The catalytic converter does not work when cold and it must be heated to its **light-off** temperature of close to 500°F (260°C) before it starts working at 50% effectiveness. When fully effective, the converter reaches a temperature range of 900° to 1,600°F (482° to 871°C). In spite of the intense heat, however, catalytic reactions do not generate a flame associated with a simple burning reaction. Because of the extreme heat (almost as hot as combustion chamber temperatures), a converter remains hot long after the engine is shut off. Most vehicles use a series of heat shields to protect the passenger compartment and other parts of the chassis from excessive heat. Vehicles have been known to start fires because of the hot converter causing tall grass or dry leaves beneath the just-parked vehicle to ignite, especially if the engine is idling.

Converter Usage

A catalytic converter must be located as close as possible to the exhaust manifold to work effectively. The farther back the converter is positioned in the exhaust system, the more gases cool before they reach the converter. Since positioning in the exhaust system affects the oxidation process, cars that use only an oxidation converter generally locate it underneath the front of the passenger compartment.

Some vehicles have used a small, quick heating oxidation converter called a **preconverter, pup,** or **mini-converter** that connects directly to the exhaust manifold outlet. These have a small catalyst surface area close to the engine that heats up rapidly to start the oxidation process more quickly during cold engine warm-up. For this reason, they were often called **light-off converters,** or **LOC.** The oxidation reaction started in the LOC is completed by the larger main converter under the passenger compartment.

OBD-II CATALYTIC CONVERTER PERFORMANCE

With OBD-II equipped vehicles, catalytic converter performance is monitored by **heated oxygen sensor (HO2S),** both before and after the converter. See Figure 17-33. The converters used on these vehicles have what is known as **OSC** or **oxygen storage capacity.** OSC is due mostly to the cerium coating in the catalyst rather than the precious metals used. When the TWC is operating as it should, the post-converter HO2S is far less active than the preconverter sensor. The converter stores, then releases, the oxygen during its normal reduction and oxidation of the exhaust gases, smoothing out the variations in O2 being released.

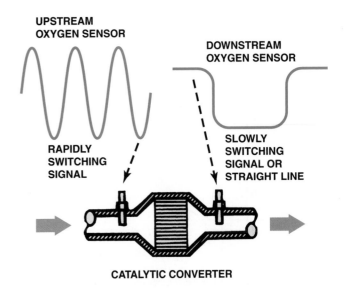

FIGURE 17-33   The OBD-II catalytic converter monitor compares the signals of the upstream and downstream HO2S to determine converter efficiency.

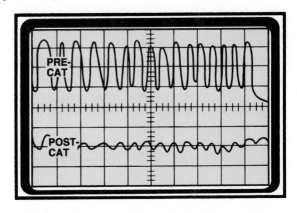

FIGURE 17-34   The waveform of an HO2S downstream from a properly functioning converter shows little, if any, activity.

Where a cycling sensor voltage output is expected before the converter, because of the converter action, the post-converter HO2S should read a steady signal without much fluctuation. See Figure 17-34. With the rapid light-off and more efficient converters used today, the air pump needs to supply only secondary air during the first few minutes of cold-engine operation.

CONVERTER-DAMAGING CONDITIONS

Since converters have no moving parts, they require no periodic service. Under federal law, catalyst effectiveness is warranted for 80,000 miles or 8 years.

The three main causes of premature converter failure are:

- **Contamination.** Substances that can destroy the converter include exhaust that contains excess engine oil,

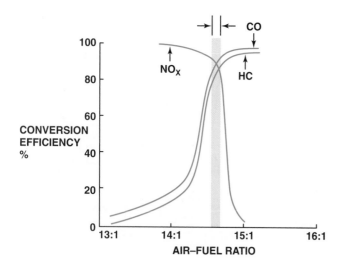

FIGURE 17-35 The highest catalytic converter efficiency occurs when the air–fuel mixture is about 14.7:1.

antifreeze, sulfur (from poor fuel), and various other chemical substances.

- **Excessive temperatures.** Although a converter operates a high temperature, it can be destroyed by excessive temperatures. This most often occurs either when too much unburned fuel enters the converter, or with excessively lean mixtures. Excessive temperatures may be caused by long idling periods on some vehicles, since more heat develops at those times than when driving at normal highway speeds. Severe high temperatures can cause the converter to melt down, leading to the internal parts breaking apart and either clogging the converter or moving downstream to plug the muffler. In either case, the restricted exhaust flow severely reduces engine power.

- **Improper air–fuel mixtures.** Rich mixtures or raw fuel in the exhaust can be caused by engine misfiring, or an excessively rich air–fuel mixture resulting from a defective coolant temp sensor or defective fuel injectors. Lean mixtures are commonly caused by intake manifold leaks. See Figure 17-35. When either of these circumstances occurs, the converter can become a catalytic furnace, causing the previously described damage.

To avoid excessive catalyst temperatures and the possibility of fuel vapors reaching the converter, follow these rules:

1. Do not try to start the engine by pushing the vehicle. Use jumper cables or a jump box to start the engine.
2. Do not crank an engine for more than 40 seconds when it is flooded or firing intermittently.
3. Do not turn off the ignition switch when the vehicle is in motion.

FIGURE 17-36 This catalytic converter blew up when gasoline from the excessively rich-running engine ignited. Obviously, raw gasoline was trapped inside and all it needed was a spark. No further diagnosis of this converter is necessary. However, the fuel and ignition systems would need to be tested and repaired before operating the engine to prevent a reoccurrence.

4. Do not disconnect a spark plug wire for more than 30 seconds.
5. Repair engine problems such as dieseling, misfiring, or stumbling as soon as possible.

DIAGNOSING CATALYTIC CONVERTERS

The Tap Test

The simple **tap test** involves tapping (not pounding) on the catalytic converter using a rubber mallet. If the substrate inside the converter is broken, the converter will rattle when hit. If the converter rattles, a replacement converter is required. See Figure 17-36.

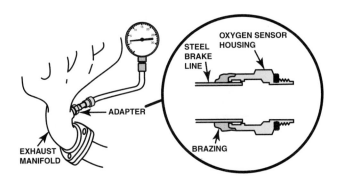

FIGURE 17-37   A backpressure tool can be easily made by attaching a short section of brake line to the shell of an old oxygen sensor. Braze or epoxy the tube to the shell.

Testing Backpressure with a Vacuum Gauge

A vacuum gauge can be used to measure manifold vacuum at a high idle (2000 to 2500 RPM). If the exhaust system is restricted, pressure increases in the exhaust system. This pressure is called **backpressure.** Manifold vacuum will drop gradually if the engine is kept at a constant speed if the exhaust is restricted.

The reason the vacuum will drop is that all the exhaust leaving the engine at the higher engine speed cannot get through the restriction. After a short time (within 1 minute), the exhaust tends to "pile up" above the restriction and eventually remains in the cylinder of the engine at the end of the exhaust stroke. Therefore, at the beginning of the intake stroke, when the piston traveling downward should be lowering the pressure (raising the vacuum) in the intake manifold, the extra exhaust in the cylinder *lowers* the normal vacuum. If the exhaust restriction is severe enough, the vehicle can become undriveable because cylinder filling cannot occur except at idle.

Testing Backpressure with a Pressure Gauge

Exhaust system backpressure can be measured directly by installing a pressure gauge in an exhaust opening. This can be accomplished in one of the following ways:

1. To test an oxygen sensor, remove the inside of an old, discarded oxygen sensor and thread in an adapter to convert it to a vacuum or pressure gauge.

NOTE: An adapter can be easily made by inserting a metal tube or pipe. A short section of brake line works great. The pipe can be brazed to the oxygen sensor housing or it can be glued with epoxy. An 18-millimeter compression gauge adapter can also be adapted to fit into the oxygen sensor opening. See Figure 17-37.

2. To test an exhaust gas recirculation (EGR) valve, remove the EGR valve and fabricate a plate.
3. To test an air injection reaction (AIR) check valve, remove the check valve from the exhaust tubes leading to the exhaust manifold. Use a rubber cone with a tube inside to seal against the exhaust tube. Connect the tube to a pressure gauge.

At idle the maximum backpressure should be less than 1.5 PSI (10 kPa), and it should be less than 2.5 PSI (15 kPa) at 2500 RPM.

Testing a Catalytic Converter for Temperature Rise

A properly working catalytic converter should be able to reduce NO_x exhaust emissions into nitrogen (N) and oxygen (O_2) and oxidize unburned hydrocarbon (HC) and carbon monoxide (CO) into harmless carbon dioxide (CO_2) and water vapor (H_2O). During these chemical processes, the catalytic converter should increase in temperature at least 10% if the converter is working properly. To test the converter, operate the engine at 2500 RPM for at least 2 minutes to fully warm up the converter. Measure the inlet and the outlet temperatures using an **infrared pyrometer** as shown in Figure 17-38.

NOTE: If the engine is extremely efficient, the converter may not have any excessive unburned hydrocarbons or carbon monoxide to convert! In this case, a spark plug wire could be grounded out using a vacuum hose and a test light to create some unburned hydrocarbon in the exhaust. Do not ground out a cylinder for longer than 10 seconds or the excessive amount of unburned hydrocarbon could overheat and damage the converter.

Catalytic Converter Efficiency Tests

The efficiency of a catalytic converter can be determined using an exhaust gas analyzer.

Oxygen level test.   With the engine warm and in closed loop, check the oxygen (O_2) and carbon monoxide (CO) levels.

- If O_2 is zero, go to the snap-throttle test.
- If O_2 is greater than zero, check the CO level.
- If CO is greater than zero, the converter is *not* functioning correctly.

Snap-throttle test.   With the engine warm and in closed loop snap the throttle to wide open (WOT) in park or neutral and observe the oxygen reading.

- O_2 reading should not exceed 1.2%; if it does, the converter is *not* working.

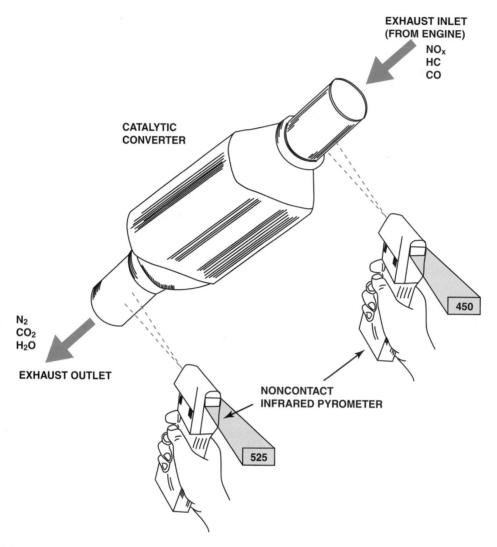

FIGURE 17-38 The temperature of the outlet should be at least 10% hotter than the temperature of the inlet. This converter is very efficient. The inlet temperature is 450°F. Ten percent of 450° is 45° (45° + 450° = 495°). In other words, the outlet temperature should be at least 495°F for the converter to be considered okay. In this case, the outlet temperature of 525°F is more than the minimum 10% increase in temperature. If the converter is not working at all, the inlet temperature will be hotter than the outlet temperature.

- If the O_2 rises to 1.2%, the converter may have low efficiency.
- If the O_2% remains below 1.2%, then the converter is okay.

OBD-II CATALYTIC CONVERTER MONITOR

The catalytic converter monitor of OBD II uses an upstream and downstream HO2S to test catalyst efficiency. When the engine combusts a lean air–fuel mixture, higher amounts of oxygen flow through the exhaust into the converter. The catalyst materials absorb this oxygen for the oxidation process, thereby removing it from the exhaust stream. If a converter cannot absorb enough oxygen, oxidation does not occur. Engineers established a correlation between the amount of oxygen absorbed and converter efficiency.

The OBD-II system monitors how much oxygen the catalyst retains. A voltage waveform from the downstream HO2S of a good catalyst should have little or no activity. A voltage waveform from the downstream HO2S of a degraded catalyst shows a lot of activity. In other words, the closer the activity of the downstream HO2S matches that of the upstream HO2S, the greater the degree of converter degradation. In operation, the OBD-II monitor compares activity between the two exhaust oxygen sensors.

CATALYTIC CONVERTER REPLACEMENT GUIDELINES

Because a catalytic converter is a major exhaust gas emission control device, the Environmental Protection Agency (EPA) has strict guidelines for its replacement, including:

- If a converter is replaced on a vehicle with less than 80,000 miles/8 years, depending on the year of the vehicle, an original equipment catalytic converter *must* be used as a replacement.
- The replacement converter must be of the same design as the original. If the original had an air pump fitting, so must the replacement.
- The old converter must be kept for possible inspection by the authorities for 60 days.
- A form must be completed and signed by both the vehicle owner and a representative from the service facility. This form must state the cause of the converter failure and must remain on file for 2 years.

Catalytic Converter-Related Diagnostic Trouble Code

Diagnostic Trouble Code	Description	Possible Causes
P0422	Catalytic converter efficiency failure	1. Engine mechanical fault 2. Exhaust leaks 3. Fuel contaminants, such as engine oil, coolant, or sulfur

TECH TIP

AFTERMARKET CATALYTIC CONVERTERS

Some replacement aftermarket (non-factory) catalytic converters do not contain the same amount of cerium as the original part. **Cerium** is the element that is used in catalytic converters to store oxygen. As a result of the lack of cerium, the correlation between the oxygen storage and the conversion efficiency may be affected enough to set a false diagnostic trouble code (P0422).

NOTE: If an aftermarket converter is being installed, be sure that the distance between the rear of the catalyst block is the same distance from the rear oxygen sensor as the factory converter to be insured of proper operation. Always follow the instructions that come with the replacement converter.

TECH TIP

CATALYTIC CONVERTERS ARE MURDERED

Catalytic converters start a chemical reaction but do not enter into the chemical reaction. Therefore, catalytic converters do not wear out and they do not die of old age. If a catalytic converter is found to be defective (nonfunctioning or clogged), look for the *root* cause. Remember this:

"Catalytic converters do not commit suicide—they're murdered."

Items that should be checked when a defective catalytic converter is discovered include all components of the ignition and fuel systems. Excessive unburned fuel can cause the catalytic converter to overheat and fail. The oxygen sensor must be working and fluctuating from 0.5 to 5 Hz (times per second) to provide the necessary air–fuel mixture variations for maximum catalytic converter efficiency.

SUMMARY

1. Recirculating 6% to 10% inert exhaust gases back into the intake system reduces peak temperature inside the combustion chamber and reduces NO_X exhaust emissions.

2. EGR is usually not needed at idle, at wide-open throttle, or when the engine is cold.

3. Many EGR systems use a feedback potentiometer to signal the PCM the position of the EGR valve pintle.

4. OBD II requires that the flow rate be tested and then is achieved by opening the EGR valve and observing the reaction of the MAP sensor.

5. Positive crankcase ventilation (PCV) systems use a valve or a fixed orifice to transfer and control the fumes from the crankcase back into the intake system.

6. A PCV valve regulates the flow of fumes depending on engine vacuum and seals the crankcase vent in the event of a backfire.

7. As much as 30% of the air needed by the engine at idle speed flows through the PCV system.

8. The AIR system forces air at low pressure into the exhaust to reduce CO and HC exhaust emissions.

9. A catalytic converter is an aftertreatment device that reduces exhaust emissions outside of the engine. A catalyst is an element that starts a chemical reaction but is not consumed in the process.

10. The catalyst material used in a catalytic converter includes rhodium, palladium, and platinum.

11. The OBD-II system monitor compares the relative activity of a rear oxygen sensor to the pre-catalytic oxygen sensor to determine catalytic converter efficiency.

REVIEW QUESTIONS

1. How does the use of exhaust gas recirculation NO_X exhaust emission?

2. How does the DPFE sensor work?

3. What exhaust emissions does the PCV valve and AIR system control?

4. How does a catalytic converter reduce NO_X to nitrogen and oxygen?

5. How does the computer monitor catalytic converter performance?

CHAPTER QUIZ

1. Two technicians are discussing clogged EGR passages. Technician A says clogged EGR passages can cause excessive NO_X exhaust emission. Technician B says that clogged EGR passages can cause the engine to ping (spark knock or detonation). Which technician is correct?

   a. Technician A only
   b. Technician B only
   c. Both Technicians A and B
   d. Neither Technician A nor B

2. An EGR valve that is partially stuck open would *most likely* cause what condition?

   a. Rough idle/stalling
   b. Excessive NO_X exhaust emissions
   c. Ping (spark knock or detonation)
   d. Missing at highway speed

3. How much air flows through the PCV system when the engine is at idle speed?

   a. 1% to 3%
   b. 5% to 10%
   c. 10% to 20%
   d. Up to 30%

4. Technician A says that if a PCV valve rattles, then it is okay and does not need to be replaced. Technician B says that if a PCV valve does not rattle, it should be replaced. Which technician is correct?

   a. Technician A only
   b. Technician B only
   c. Both Technicians A and B
   d. Neither Technician A nor B

5. The switching valves on the AIR pump have failed several times. Technician A says that a defective exhaust check valve could be the cause. Technician B says that a restricted exhaust system could be the cause. Which technician is correct?

   a. Technician A only

   b. Technician B only

   c. Both Technicians A and B

   d. Neither Technician A nor B

6. Two technicians are discussing testing a catalytic converter. Technician A says that a vacuum gauge can be used and observed to see if the vacuum drops with the engine at idle for 30 seconds. Technician B says that a pressure gauge can be used to check for backpressure. Which technician is correct?

   a. Technician A only

   b. Technician B only

   c. Both Technicians A and B

   d. Neither Technician A nor B

7. At about what temperature does oxygen combine with the nitrogen in the air to form NO_X?

   a. 500°F (260°C)

   b. 750°F (400°C)

   c. 1,500°F (815°C)

   d. 2,500°F (1,370°C)

8. A P0401 is being discussed. Technician A says that a stuck-closed EGR valve could be the cause. Technician B says that clogged EGR ports could be the cause. Which technician is correct?

   a. Technician A only

   b. Technician B only

   c. Both Technicians A and B

   d. Neither Technician A nor B

9. Two technicians are discussing P1480 DTC. Technician A says that a defective PCV solenoid could be the cause. Technician B says that a corroded electrical connection on the solenoid could be the cause. Which technician is correct?

   a. Technician A only

   b. Technician B only

   c. Both Technicians A and B

   d. Neither Technician A nor B

10. Two technicians are discussing P0422 DTC. Technician A says that the engine may have mechanical faults. Technician B says that the vehicle may have exhaust leaks. Which technician is correct?

   a. Technician A only

   b. Technician B only

   c. Both Technicians A and B

   d. Neither Technician A nor B

CHAPTER 18

INTAKE AND EXHAUST SYSTEMS

OBJECTIVES

After studying Chapter 18, the reader will be able to:

1. Prepare for ASE Engine Performance (A8) certification test content area "C" (Air Induction and Exhaust Systems Diagnosis and Repair).
2. Discuss the purpose and function of intake manifolds.
3. Explain the differences between throttle fuel-injection manifolds and port fuel-injection manifolds.
4. Describe the operation of the exhaust gas recirculation system in the intake manifold.
5. List the materials used in exhaust manifolds and exhaust systems.

KEY TERMS

Annealing (p. 319)
Exhaust Gas Recirculation (EGR) (p. 317)
Hangers (p. 321)

Helmholtz Resonator (p. 315)
Micron (p. 313)
Plenum (p. 318)

AIR INTAKE FILTRATION

Gasoline must be mixed with air to form a combustible mixture. Air movement into an engine occurs due to low pressure (vacuum) being created in the engine. See Figure 18-1.

Like gasoline, air contains dirt and other materials which cannot be allowed to reach the engine. Just as fuel filters are used to clean impurities from gasoline, an air cleaner and filter are used to remove contaminants from the air. The three main jobs of the air cleaner and filter are to:

- Clean the air before it is mixed with fuel
- Silence intake noise
- Act as a flame arrester in case of a backfire

The automotive engine uses about 9,000 gallons (34,069 liters) of air for every gallon of gasoline burned at an air–fuel ratio of 14.7 to 1. Without proper filtering of the air before intake, dust and dirt in the air seriously damage engine parts and shorten engine life.

While abrasive particles can cause wear any place inside the engine where two surfaces move against each other, they first attack piston rings and cylinder walls. Contained in the blowby gases, they pass by the piston rings and into the crankcase. From the crankcase, the particles circulate throughout the engine in the oil. Large amounts of abrasive particles in the oil can damage other moving engine parts.

The filter that cleans the intake air is in a two-piece air cleaner housing made either of stamped steel or composite materials. The air cleaner housing is located on top of the throttle-body injection (TBI) unit or is positioned to one side of the engine. See Figure 18-2.

Filter Replacement

Manufacturers recommend cleaning or replacing the air filter element at periodic intervals, usually listed in terms of distance driven or months of service. The distance and time intervals are based on so-called normal driving. More frequent air filter replacement is necessary when the vehicle is driven under dusty, dirty, or other severe conditions.

It is best to replace a filter element before it becomes too dirty to be effective. A dirty air filter passes contaminants that cause engine wear.

Air Filter Elements

The paper air filter element is the most common type of filter. It is made of a chemically treated paper stock that contains tiny passages in the fibers. These passages form an indirect path for the airflow to follow. The airflow passes through several fiber surfaces, each of which traps microscopic particles of dust, dirt, and carbon. Most air filters are capable of trapping dirt and other particles larger than 10 to 25 microns in size. One **micron** is equal to 0.000039 in.

NOTE: A person can only see objects that are 40 microns or larger in size. A human hair is about 50 microns in diameter.

NOTE: Do not attempt to clean a paper element filter by rapping it on a sharp object to dislodge the dirt, or blowing compressed air through the filter. This tends to clog the paper pores and further reduce the airflow capability of the filter.

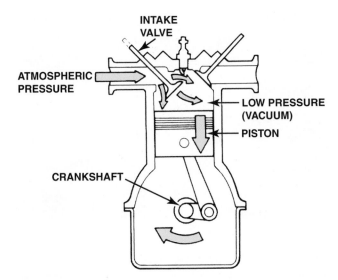

FIGURE 18-1 Downward movement of the piston lowers the air pressure inside the combustion chamber. The pressure differential between the atmosphere and the inside of the engine forces air into the engine.

FIGURE 18-2 Dust and dirt in the air are trapped in the air filter so they do not enter the engine.

FIGURE 18-3 Most air filter housings are located on the side of the engine compartment and use flexible rubber hose to direct the airflow into the throttle body of the engine.

Remotely Mounted Air Filters and Ducts

Air cleaner and duct design depend on a number of factors such as the size, shape, and location of other engine compartment components, as well as the vehicle body structure.

Port fuel-injection systems generally use a horizontally mounted throttle body. Some systems also have a mass airflow (MAF) sensor between the throttle body and the air cleaner. See Figure 18-3. Because placing the air cleaner housing next to the throttle body would cause engine and vehicle design problems, it is more efficient to use this remote air cleaner placement.

Turbocharged engines present a similar problem. The air cleaner connects to the air inlet elbow at the turbocharger. However, the tremendous heat generated by the turbocharger makes it impractical to place the air cleaner housing too close to the turbocharger. For better protection, the MAF sensor is installed between the turbocharger and the air cleaner in some vehicles. Remote air cleaners are connected to the turbocharger air inlet elbow or fuel-injection throttle body by composite ducting, which is usually retained by clamps. The ducting used may be rigid or flexible, but all connections must be airtight.

ENGINE AIR TEMPERATURE REQUIREMENTS

Some form of thermostatic control has been used on vehicles equipped with a throttle-body fuel injection to control intake air temperature for improved driveability. In a throttle-body fuel injection system, the fuel and air are combined above the throttle plate and must travel through the intake manifold

before reaching the cylinders. Air temperature control is needed under these conditions to help keep the gas and air mixture combined.

TECH TIP

ALWAYS CHECK THE AIR FILTER

Always inspect the air filter and the air intake system carefully during routine service. Debris or objects deposited by animals can cause a restriction to the airflow and can reduce engine performance. See Figure 18-4.

(a)

(b)

FIGURE 18-4 (a) Note the discovery as the air filter housing was opened during service on a Pontiac Bonneville. The nuts were obviously deposited by squirrels (or some other animal). (b) Not only was the housing filled with nuts, but also this air filter was extremely dirty, indicating that this vehicle had not been serviced for a long time.

FREQUENTLY ASKED QUESTION

WHAT DOES THIS TUBE DO?

What is the purpose of the odd-shaped tube attached to the inlet duct between the air filter and the throttle body, as seen in Figure 18-5?

The tube shape is designed to dampen out certain resonant frequencies that can occur at certain engine speeds. The length and shape of this tube are designed to absorb shock waves that are created in the air intake system and to provide a reservoir for the air that will then be released into the airstream during cycles of lower pressure. This resonance tube is often called a **Helmholtz resonator,** named for the discoverer of the relationship between shape and value of frequency Herman L. F. von Helmholtz (1821–1894) of the University of Hönizsberg in East Prussia. The overall effect of these resonance tubes is to reduce the noise of the air entering the engine.

FIGURE 18-5 A resonance tube, called a Helmholtz resonator, is used on the intake duct between the air filter and the throttle body to reduce air intake noise during engine acceleration.

Heat radiating from the exhaust manifold is retained by the heat stove and sent to the air cleaner inlet to provide heated air to the throttle body.

An air control valve or damper permits the air intake of:

- Heated air from the heat stove
- Cooler air from the snorkel or cold-air duct
- A combination of both

While the air control valve generally is located in the air cleaner snorkel, it may be in the air intake housing or ducting of remote air cleaners. Most fuel-injection systems do not use temperature control.

THROTTLE-BODY INJECTION INTAKE MANIFOLDS

The *intake manifold* is also called the *inlet manifold*. Smooth operation can only occur when each combustion chamber produces the same pressure as every other chamber in the engine. For this to be achieved, each cylinder must receive a charge exactly like the charge going into the other cylinders in quality and quantity. The charges must have the same physical properties and the same air–fuel mixture.

A throttle-body fuel injector forces finely divided droplets of liquid fuel into the incoming air to form a combustible air–fuel mixture. See Figure 18-6 for an example of a typical throttle-body injection (TBI) unit. These droplets start to evaporate as soon as they leave the throttle-body injector nozzles. *The droplets stay in the charge as long as the charge flows at high velocities.* At maximum horsepower, these velocities may reach 300 feet per second. Separation of the droplets from the charge as it passes through the manifold occurs when the velocity drops below 50 feet per second. Intake charge velocities at idle speeds are often below this value. When separation occurs—at low engine speeds—extra fuel must be supplied to the charge in order to have a combustible mixture reach the combustion chamber.

FIGURE 18-6 A throttle-body injection (TBI) unit used on a GM V-6 engine.

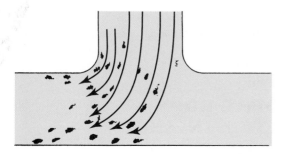

FIGURE 18-7 Heavy fuel droplets separate as they flow around an abrupt bend in an intake manifold.

TECH TIP

CHECK THE INTAKE IF THERE IS AN EXHAUST NOISE

Because many V-type engines equipped with a throttle-body injection and/or EGR valve use a crossover exhaust passage, a leak around this passage will create an exhaust leak and noise. Always check for evidence of an exhaust leak around the intake manifold whenever diagnosing an exhaust sound.

Manifold sizes represent a compromise. They must have a cross-section large enough to allow charge flow for maximum power. The cross-section must be small enough that the flow velocities of the charge will be high enough to keep the fuel droplets in suspension. This is required so that equal mixtures reach each cylinder. Manifold cross-sectional size is one reason why engines designed especially for racing will not run at low engine speeds. Racing manifolds must be large enough to reach maximum horsepower. This size, however, allows the charge to move slowly, and the fuel will separate from the charge at low engine speeds. Fuel separation leads to poor accelerator response. See Figure 18-7. Standard passenger vehicle engines are primarily designed for economy during light-load, partial-throttle operation. Their manifolds, therefore, have a much smaller cross-sectional area than do those of racing engines. This small size will help keep flow velocities of the charge high throughout the normal operating speed range of the engine.

PORT FUEL-INJECTION INTAKE MANIFOLDS

The size and shape of port fuel-injected engine intake manifolds can be optimized because the only thing in the manifold

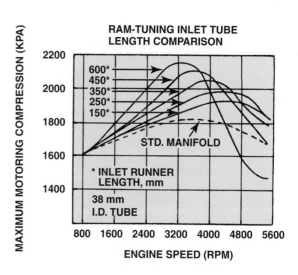

FIGURE 18-8 The graph shows the effect of sonic tuning of the intake manifold runners. The longer runners increase the torque peak and move it to a lower RPM. The 600-mm-long intake runner is about 24 inches long.

is air. The fuel injection is located in the intake manifold about 3 to 4 inches (70 to 100 mm) from the intake valve. Therefore, the runner length and shape are designed for tuning only. There is no need to keep an air–fuel mixture homogenized throughout its trip from the TBI unit to the intake valve. Typically, long runners build low-RPM torque while shorter runners provide maximum high-RPM power. See Figures 18-8 and 18-9. Some engines with four valve heads utilize a dual or variable intake runner design. At lower engine speeds, long intake runners provide low-speed torque. At higher engine speeds, shorter intake runners are opened by means of a computer-controlled valve to increase high-speed power.

VARIABLE INTAKES

Many intake manifolds are designed to provide both short runners, best for higher engine speed power, and longer runners, best for lower engine speed torque. The valve(s) that control the flow of air through the passages of the intake manifold are computer controlled. See Figure 18-10.

PLASTIC INTAKE MANIFOLDS

Most thermoplastic intake manifolds are molded from fiberglass-reinforced nylon. The plastic manifolds can be cast or injection molded. Some manifolds are molded in two parts and bonded together. Plastic intake manifolds are lighter than aluminum manifolds and can better insulate engine heat from the fuel injectors.

Plastic intake manifolds have smoother interior surfaces than do other types of manifolds, resulting in greater airflow. See Figure 18-11.

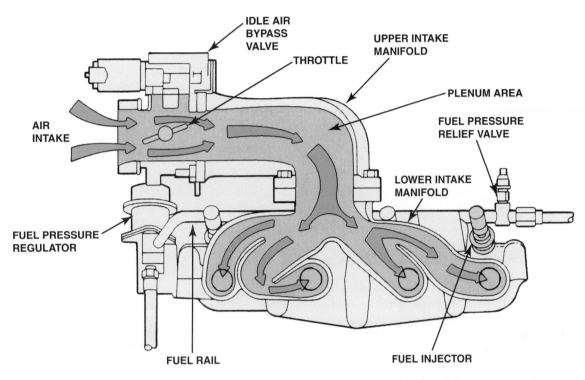

IDLE AIR
BYPASS
VALVE

THROTTLE

UPPER INTAKE
MANIFOLD

PLENUM AREA

AIR
INTAKE

FUEL PRESSURE
RELIEF VALVE

LOWER INTAKE
MANIFOLD

FUEL PRESSURE
REGULATOR

FUEL RAIL

FUEL INJECTOR

FIGURE 18-9   Airflow through the large diameter upper intake manifold is distributed to smaller diameter individual runners in the lower manifold in this two-piece manifold design.

FIGURE 18-10   The air flowing into the engine can be directed through long or short runners for best performance and fuel economy.

FIGURE 18-11   Many plastic intake manifolds are constructed using many parts glued together to form complex passages for airflow into the engine.

EXHAUST GAS RECIRCULATION PASSAGES

To reduce the emission of oxides of nitrogen (NO_x), engines have been equipped with **exhaust gas recirculation (EGR)** valves. From 1973 until recently, they were used on almost all vehicles. Because of the efficiency of computer-controlled fuel injection, some newer engines do not require an EGR system to meet emission standards. Some engines use intake and exhaust valve overlap as a means of trapping some exhaust in the cylinder as an alternative to using an EGR valve.

The EGR valve opens at speeds above idle on a warm engine. When open, the valve allows a small portion of the exhaust gas (5% to 10%) to enter the intake manifold. Here,

FIGURE 18-12 The exhaust gas recirculation system is more efficient at controlling NO$_x$ emissions if the exhaust gases are cooled. A long metal tube between the exhaust manifold and the intake manifold allows the exhaust gases to cool before entering the engine.

the exhaust gas mixes with and takes the place of some of the intake charge. This leaves less room for the intake charge to enter the combustion chamber. The recirculated exhaust gas is inert and does *not* enter into the combustion process. The result is a lower peak combustion temperature. As the combustion temperature is lowered, the production of oxides of nitrogen is also reduced.

The EGR system has some means of interconnecting the exhaust and intake manifolds. The interconnecting passage is controlled by the EGR valve. On V-type engines, the intake manifold crossover is used as a source of exhaust gas for the EGR system. A cast passage connects the exhaust crossover to the EGR valve. On inline-type engines, an external tube is generally used to carry exhaust gas to the EGR valve. The exhaust gases are more effective in reducing oxides of nitrogen (NO$_X$) emissions if the exhaust is cooled before being drawn into the cylinders. This tube is often designed to be long so that the exhaust gas is cooled before it enters the EGR valve. Figure 18-12 shows a typical long EGR tube.

UPPER AND LOWER INTAKE MANIFOLDS

Many intake manifolds are constructed in two parts.

- A lower section, usually called the **plenum,** attaches to the cylinder heads and includes passages from the intake ports.
- An upper manifold connects to the lower unit and includes the long passages needed to help provide the ram effect that helps the engine deliver maximum torque at low engine speeds. The throttle body attaches to the upper intake.

The use of a two-part intake manifold allows for easier manufacturing as well as assembly, but can create additional locations for leaks. If the lower intake manifold gasket leaks, not only could a vacuum leak occur affecting the operation of the engine, but a coolant leak or an oil leak can also occur. A leak at the gasket(s) of the upper intake manifold usually results in a vacuum (air) leak only.

EXHAUST MANIFOLD DESIGN

The exhaust manifold is designed to collect high-temperature spent gases from the head exhaust ports. See Figure 18-13. The hot gases are sent to an exhaust pipe, then to a catalytic converter, to the muffler, to a resonator, and on to the tailpipe, where they are vented to the atmosphere. This must be done with the least-possible amount of restriction or backpressure while keeping the exhaust noise at a minimum.

Exhaust gas temperature will vary according to the power produced by the engine. The manifold must be designed to operate at both engine idle and continuous full power. Under full-power conditions, the exhaust manifold will become red-hot, causing a great deal of expansion.

NOTE: The temperature of an exhaust manifold can exceed 1-500°F (815°C).

At idle, the exhaust manifold is just warm, causing little expansion. After casting, the manifold may be annealed.

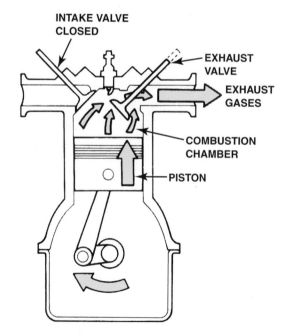

FIGURE 18-13 The exhaust gases are pushed out of the cylinder by the piston on the exhaust stroke.

Annealing is a heat-treating process that takes out the brittle hardening of the casting to reduce the chance of cracking from the temperature changes. During vehicle operation, manifold temperatures usually reach the high-temperature extremes. Most exhaust manifolds are made from cast iron to withstand extreme and rapid temperature changes. The manifold is bolted to the head in a way that will allow expansion and contraction. In some cases, hollow-headed bolts are used to maintain a gas-tight seal while still allowing normal expansion and contraction.

The exhaust manifold is designed to allow the free flow of exhaust gas. Some manifolds use internal cast-rib deflectors or dividers to guide the exhaust gases toward the outlet as smoothly as possible.

Some exhaust manifolds are designed to go above the spark plug, whereas others are designed to go below. The spark plug and carefully routed ignition wires are usually shielded from the exhaust heat with sheet-metal deflectors. Many exhaust manifolds have heat shields as seen in Figure 18-14.

Exhaust systems are especially designed for the engine-chassis combination. The exhaust system length, pipe size, and silencer are designed, where possible, to make use of the tuning effect of the gas column resonating within the exhaust system. Tuning occurs when the exhaust pulses from the cylinders are emptied into the manifold between the pulses of other cylinders. See Figure 18-15.

? FREQUENTLY ASKED QUESTION

? HOW CAN A CRACKED EXHAUST MANIFOLD AFFECT ENGINE PERFORMANCE?

A crack in an exhaust manifold will not only allow exhaust gases to escape and cause noise but the crack can also allow air to enter the exhaust manifold. See Figure 18-16.

Exhaust flows from the cylinders as individual puffs or pressure pulses. Behind each of these pressure pulses, a low pressure (below atmospheric pressure) is created. Outside air at atmospheric pressure is then drawn into the exhaust manifold through the crack. This outside air contains 21% oxygen and is measured by the oxygen sensor (O2S). The air passing the O2S signals the engine computer that the engine is operating too lean (excess oxygen) and the computer, not knowing that the lean indicator is false, adds additional fuel to the engine. The result is that the engine will be operating richer (more fuel than normal) and spark plugs could become fouled causing poor engine operation.

FIGURE 18-14 This exhaust manifold has a heat shield to help retain the heat and help reduce exhaust emissions.

FIGURE 18-15 Many exhaust manifolds are constructed of pressed steel and are free flowing to improve engine performance.

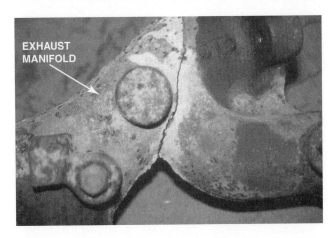

EXHAUST MANIFOLD

FIGURE 18-16 A crack in an exhaust manifold is often not this visible. A crack in the exhaust manifold upstream of the oxygen sensor can fool the sensor and affect engine operation.

EXHAUST MANIFOLD GASKETS

Exhaust heat will expand the manifold more than it will expand the head. It causes the exhaust manifold to slide on the sealing surface of the head. The heat also causes thermal stress. When the manifold is removed from the engine for service, the stress is relieved and this may cause the manifold to warp slightly. Exhaust manifold gaskets are included in gasket sets to seal slightly warped exhaust manifolds. These gaskets *should* be used, even if the engine did not originally use exhaust manifold gaskets. When a perforated core exhaust manifold gasket has facing on one side only, put the facing side against the head and put the manifold against the perforated metal core. The manifold can slide on the metal of the gasket just as it slid on the sealing surface of the head.

Gaskets are used on new engines with tubing- or header-type exhaust manifolds. The gaskets often include heat shields to keep exhaust heat from the spark plugs and spark plug cables. They may have several layers of steel for high-temperature sealing. The layers are spot-welded together. Some are embossed where special sealing is needed. See Figure 18-17.

Many new engines do not use gaskets with cast exhaust manifolds. The flat surface of the new cast-iron exhaust manifold fits tightly against the flat surface of the new head.

MUFFLERS

When the exhaust valve opens, it rapidly releases high-pressure gas. This sends a strong air pressure wave through the atmosphere, which produces a sound we call an explosion. It is the same sound produced when the high-pressure gases from burned gunpowder are released from a gun. In an engine, the pulses are released one after another. The explosions come so fast that they blend together in a steady roar.

FIGURE 18-17 Typical exhaust manifold gaskets. Note how they are laminated to allow the exhaust manifold to expand and contract due to heating and cooling.

TECH TIP

THE CORRECT TOOLS SAVE TIME

When cast-iron exhaust manifolds are removed, the stresses built up in the manifolds often cause the manifolds to twist or bend. This distortion even occurs when the exhaust manifolds have been allowed to cool before removal. Attempting to reinstall distorted exhaust manifolds is often a time-consuming and frustrating exercise.

However, special spreading jacks can be used to force the manifold back into position so that the fasteners can be lined up with the cylinder head. See Figure 18-18.

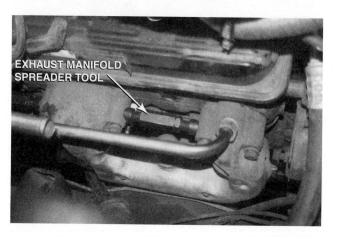

EXHAUST MANIFOLD SPREADER TOOL

FIGURE 18-18 An exhaust manifold spreader tool is a tool that is absolutely necessary to use when reinstalling exhaust manifolds. When they are removed from the engine, they tend to warp slightly even though the engine is allowed to cool before being removed. The spreader tool allows the technician to line up the bolt holes without doing any harm to the manifold.

Sound is air vibration. When the vibrations are large, the sound is loud. The muffler catches the large bursts of high-pressure exhaust gas from the cylinder, smoothing out the pressure pulses and allowing them to be released at an even and constant rate. It does this through the use of perforated tubes within the muffler chamber. The smooth-flowing gases are released to the tailpipe. In this way, the muffler silences engine exhaust noise. Sometimes resonators are used in the exhaust system and the catalytic converter also acts as a muffler. They provide additional expansion space at critical points in the exhaust system to smooth out the exhaust gas flow. See Figure 18-19.

Most mufflers have a larger inlet diameter than outlet diameter. As the exhaust enters the muffler, it expands and cools. The cooler exhaust is more dense and occupies less volume. The diameter of the outlet of the muffler and the diameter of the tailpipe can be reduced with no decrease in efficiency.

The tailpipe carries the exhaust gases from the muffler to the air, away from the vehicle. In most cases, the tailpipe exit is at the rear of the vehicle, below the rear bumper. In some cases, the exhaust is released at the side of the vehicle, just ahead of or just behind the rear wheel.

FIGURE 18-19 Exhaust gases expand and cool as they travel through the passages in the muffler.

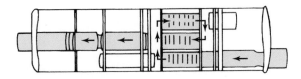

FREQUENTLY ASKED QUESTION

WHY IS THERE A HOLE IN MY MUFFLER?

Many mufflers are equipped with a small hole in the lower rear part to drain accumulated water. About 1 gallon of water is produced in the form of steam for each gallon of gasoline burned. The water vapor often condenses on the cooler surfaces of the exhaust system unless the vehicle has been driven long enough to fully warm the muffler above the boiling point of water (212°F [100°C]). See Figure 18-20.

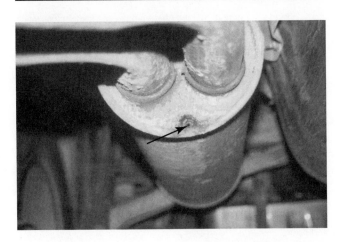

FIGURE 18-20   A hole in the muffler allows condensed water to escape.

The muffler and tailpipe are supported with brackets called **hangers.** The hangers are made of rubberized fabric with metal ends that hold the muffler and tailpipe in position so that they do not touch any metal part. This helps to isolate the exhaust noise from the rest of the vehicle.

TECH TIP

MORE AIRFLOW = MORE POWER

One of the most popular high-performance modifications is to replace the factory exhaust system with a low-restriction design and to replace the original air filter and air filter housing with a low-restriction unit as shown in Figure 18-21.

The installation of an aftermarket air filter not only increases power, but also increases air induction noise, which many drivers prefer. The aftermarket filter housing, however, may not be able to effectively prevent water from being drawn into the engine if the vehicle is traveling through deep water.

Almost every modification that increases performance has a negative effect on some other part of the vehicle, or else the manufacturer would include the change at the factory.

FIGURE 18-21   A high-performance aftermarket air filter often can increase airflow into the engine for more power.

SUMMARY

1. All air entering an engine must be filtered.
2. Engines that use throttle-body injection units are equipped with intake manifolds that keep the airflow speed through the manifold at 50 to 300 feet per second.
3. Most intake manifolds have an EGR valve that regulates the amount of recirculated exhaust that enters the engine to reduce NO_x emissions.
4. Exhaust manifolds can be made from cast iron or stainless steel.
5. The exhaust system also contains a catalytic converter, exhaust pipes, and muffler. The entire exhaust system is supported by rubber hangers that isolate the noise and vibration of the exhaust from the rest of the vehicle.

REVIEW QUESTIONS

1. Why is it necessary to have intake charge velocities of about 50 feet per second?
2. Why can fuel-injected engines use larger (and longer) intake manifolds and still operate at low engine speed?
3. What is a tuned runner in an intake manifold?
4. How does a muffler quiet exhaust noise?

CHAPTER QUIZ

1. Intake charge velocity has to be _____ to prevent fuel droplet separation.
   a. 25 feet per second
   b. 50 feet per second
   c. 100 feet per second
   d. 300 feet per second

2. The intake manifold of a port fuel-injected engine _____.
   a. Uses a dual heat riser
   b. Contains a leaner air–fuel mixture than does the intake manifold of a TBI system
   c. Contains only fuel (gasoline)
   d. Contains only air

3. Why are the EGR gases cooled before entering the engine on some engines?
   a. Cool exhaust gas is more effective at controlling NO_x emissions
   b. To help prevent the exhaust from slowing down
   c. To prevent damage to the intake valve
   d. To prevent heating the air–fuel mixture in the cylinder

4. A heated air intake system is usually necessary for proper cold-engine drive ability on _____.
   a. Port fuel-injection systems
   b. Throttle-body fuel-injection systems
   c. Both a port-injected and throttle-body injected engine
   d. Any fuel-injected engine

5. Air filters can remove particles and dirt as small as _____.
   a. 5 to 10 microns
   b. 10 to 25 microns
   c. 30 to 40 microns
   d. 40 to 50 microns

6. Why do many port fuel-injected engines use long intake manifold runners?
   a. To reduce exhaust emissions
   b. To heat the incoming air
   c. To increase high-RPM power
   d. To increase low-RPM torque

7. Exhaust passages are included in some intake manifolds. Technician A says that the exhaust passages are used for exhaust gas recirculation (EGR) systems. Technician B says that the exhaust heat is used to warm the intake charge on some engines equipped with a throttle-body-type fuel-injection system. Which technician is correct?
   a. Technician A only
   b. Technician B only
   c. Both Technicians A and B
   d. Neither Technician A nor B

8. The lower portion of a two-part intake manifold is often called the _____.
   a. Housing
   b. Lower part
   c. Plenum
   d. Vacuum chamber

9. Technician A says that a cracked exhaust manifold can affect engine operation. Technician B says that a leaking lower intake manifold gasket could cause a vacuum leak. Which technician is correct?
   a. Technician A only
   b. Technician B only
   c. Both Technicians A and B
   d. Neither Technician A nor B

10. Technician A says that some intake manifolds are plastic. Technician B says that some intake manifolds are constructed in two parts or sections: upper and lower. Which technician is correct?
   a. Technician A only
   b. Technician B only
   c. Both Technicians A and B
   d. Neither Technician A nor B

CHAPTER 19

TURBOCHARGING AND SUPERCHARGING

OBJECTIVES

After studying Chapter 19, the reader will be able to:

1. Prepare for ASE Engine Performance (A8) certification test content area "C" (Fuel, Air Induction, and Exhaust Systems Diagnosis and Repair).

2. Explain the difference between a turbocharger and a supercharger.

3. Describe how the boost levels are controlled.

4. Discuss maintenance procedures for turbochargers and superchargers.

KEY TERMS

Bar (p. 326)
Boost (p. 326)
Bypass Valve (p. 328)
Compressor Bypass Valve (CBV) (p. 332)
Dry System (p. 334)
Dump Valve (p. 332)
Intercooler (p. 330)
Naturally (normally) Aspirated (p. 326)
Nitrous Oxide (p. 333)
Positive Displacement (p. 327)

Power Adder (p. 333)
Relief Valve (p. 332)
Roots-Type Supercharger (p. 327)
Supercharger (p. 326)
Turbo Lag (p. 330)
Turbocharger (p. 328)
Vent Valve (p. 332)
Volumetric Efficiency (p. 325)
Wastegate (p. 331)
Wet System (p. 334)

AIRFLOW REQUIREMENTS

Naturally aspirated engines with throttle bodies rely on atmospheric pressure to push an air–fuel mixture into the combustion chamber vacuum created by the downstroke of a piston. The mixture is then compressed before ignition to increase the force of the burning, expanding gases. The greater the mixture compression, the greater the power resulting from combustion.

All gasoline automobile engines share certain air–fuel requirements. For example, a four-stroke engine can take in only so much air, and how much fuel it consumes depends on how much air it takes in. Engineers calculate engine airflow requirements using these three factors:

- Engine displacement
- Engine revolutions per minute (RPM)
- Volumetric efficiency

Volumetric Efficiency

Volumetric efficiency is a comparison of the actual volume of air–fuel mixture drawn into an engine to the theoretical maximum volume that could be drawn in. Volumetric efficiency is expressed as a percentage, and changes with engine speed. For example, an engine might have 75% volumetric efficiency at 1000 RPM. The same engine might be rated at 85% at 2000 RPM and 60% at 3000 RPM.

If the engine takes in the airflow volume slowly, a cylinder might fill to capacity. It takes a definite amount of time for the airflow to pass through all the curves of the intake manifold and valve port. Therefore, volumetric efficiency decreases as engine speed increases. At high speed, it may drop to as low as 50%.

The average street engine never reaches 100% volumetric efficiency. With a street engine, the volumetric efficiency is about 75% at maximum speed, or 80% at the torque peak. A high-performance street engine is about 85% efficient, or a bit more efficient at peak torque. A race engine usually has 95% or better volumetric efficiency. These figures apply only to naturally aspirated engines, however, and turbocharged and supercharged engines easily achieve more than 100% volumetric efficiency. Many vehicles are equipped with a supercharger or a turbocharger to increase power. See Figures 19-1 and 19-2.

Engine Compression

Higher compression increases the thermal efficiency of the engine because it raises compression temperatures, resulting in hotter, more complete combustion. However, a higher compression can cause an increase in NO_X emissions and would require the use of high-octane gasoline with effective anti-knock additives.

FIGURE 19-1   A supercharger on a Ford V-8.

FIGURE 19-2   A turbocharger on a Toyota engine.

SUPERCHARGING PRINCIPLES

The amount of force an air–fuel charge produces when it is ignited is largely a function of the charge density. Density is the mass of a substance in a given amount of space. See Figure 19-3.

The greater the density of an air–fuel charge forced into a cylinder, the greater the force it produces when ignited, and the greater the engine power.

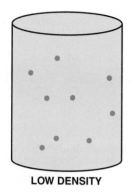
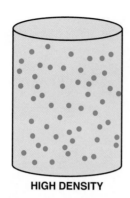

LOW DENSITY   **HIGH DENSITY**

FIGURE 19-3   The more air and fuel that can be packed in a cylinder, the greater the density of the air–fuel charge.

An engine that uses atmospheric pressure for intake is called a **naturally (normally) aspirated** engine. A better way to increase air density in the cylinder is to use a pump.

When air is pumped into the cylinder, the combustion chamber receives an increase of air pressure known as **boost** and is measured in pounds per square inch (PSI), atmospheres (ATM), or **bar.** While boost pressure increases air density, friction heats air in motion and causes an increase in temperature. This increase in temperature works in the opposite direction, decreasing air density. Because of these and other variables, an increase in pressure does not always result in greater air density.

Another way to achieve an increase in mixture compression is called **supercharging.** This method uses a pump to pack a denser air–fuel charge into the cylinders. Since the density of the air–fuel charge is greater, so is its weight— and power is directly related to the weight of an air–fuel charge consumed within a given time period. The result is similar to that of a high-compression ratio, but the effect can be controlled during idle and deceleration to avoid high emissions.

Air is drawn into a naturally aspirated engine by atmospheric pressure forcing it into the low-pressure area of the intake manifold. The low pressure or vacuum in the manifold results from the reciprocating motion of the pistons. When a piston moves downward during its intake stroke, it creates an empty space, or vacuum, in the cylinder. Although atmospheric pressure pushes air to fill up as much of this empty space as possible, it has a difficult path to travel. The air must pass through the air filter, the throttle body, the manifold, and the intake port before entering the cylinder. Bends and restrictions in this pathway limit the amount of air reaching the cylinder before the intake valve closes; therefore, the volumetric efficiency is less than 100%.

Pumping air into the intake system under pressure forces it through the bends and restrictions at a greater speed than it would travel under normal atmospheric pressure, allowing more air to enter the intake port before it closes. By increasing the airflow into the intake, more fuel can be mixed with the air while still maintaining the same air–fuel ratio. The denser the air–fuel charge entering the engine during its intake stroke, the greater the potential energy released during combustion. In addition to the increased power resulting from combustion, there are several other advantages of supercharging an engine including:

- It increases the air–fuel charge density to provide high-compression pressure when power is required, but allows the engine to run on lower pressures when additional power is not required.
- The pumped air pushes the remaining exhaust from the combustion chamber during intake and exhaust valve overlap.
- The forced airflow and removal of hot exhaust gases lowers the temperature of the cylinder head, pistons, and valves, and helps extend the life of the engine.

A supercharger pressurizes air to greater than atmospheric pressure. The pressurization above atmospheric pressure, or boost, can be measured in the same way as atmospheric pressure. Atmospheric pressure drops as altitude increases, but boost pressure remains the same. If a supercharger develops 12 PSI (83 kPa) boost at sea level, it will develop the same amount at a 5,000-foot altitude because boost pressure is measured inside the intake manifold. See Figure 19-4.

Boost and Compression Ratios

Boost increases the amount of air drawn into the cylinder during the intake stroke. This extra air causes the effective compression ratio to be greater than the mechanical compression ratio designed into the engine. The higher the boost pressure, the greater the compression ratio. See the following table for an example of how much the effective compression ratio is increased compared to the boost pressure.

SUPERCHARGERS

A supercharger is an engine-driven air pump that supplies more than the normal amount of air into the intake manifold and boosts engine torque and power. A supercharger provides an instantaneous increase in power without the delay or lag often associated with turbochargers. However, a supercharger, because it is driven by the engine, does require horsepower to operate and is not as efficient as a turbocharger.

In basic concept, a supercharger is nothing more than an air pump mechanically driven by the engine itself. Gears, shafts, chains, or belts from the crankshaft can be used to turn the pump. This means that the air pump or supercharger pumps air in direct relation to engine speed.

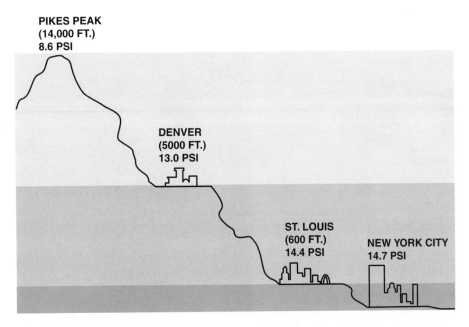

PIKES PEAK
(14,000 FT.)
8.6 PSI

DENVER
(5000 FT.)
13.0 PSI

ST. LOUIS
(600 FT.)
14.4 PSI

NEW YORK CITY
14.7 PSI

FIGURE 19-4 Atmospheric pressure decreases with increases in altitude.

Final Compression Ratio Chart at Various Boost Levels
Blower Boost (PSI)

Comp Ratio	2	4	6	8	10	12	14	16	18	20
6.5	7.4	8.3	9.2	10	10.9	11.8	12.7	13.6	14.5	15.3
7	8	8.9	9.9	10.8	11.8	12.7	13.6	14.5	15.3	16.2
7.5	8.5	9.5	10.6	11.6	12.6	13.6	14.6	15.7	16.7	17.8
8	9.1	10.2	11.3	12.4	13.4	14.5	15.6	16.7	17.8	18.9
8.5	9.7	10.8	12	13.1	14.3	15.4	16.6	17.8	18.9	19.8
9	10.2	11.4	12.7	13.9	15.1	16.3	17.6	18.8	20	21.2
9.5	10.8	12.1	13.4	14.7	16	17.3	18.5	19.8	21.1	22.4
10	11.4	12.7	14.1	15.4	16.8	18.2	19.5	20.9	22.2	23.6

There are two general types of superchargers:

- **Roots-type supercharger.** Named for Philander and Francis Roots, two brothers from Connersville, Indiana, who patented the design in 1860 as a type of water pump to be used in mines. Later it was used to move air and is used today on two-stroke cycle Detroit diesel engines and other supercharged engines. The **roots-type supercharger** is called a **positive displacement** design because all of the air that enters is forced through the unit. Examples of a roots-type supercharger include the GMC 6-71 (used originally on GMC diesel engines that had six cylinders each with 71 cu. in.) and Eaton used on supercharged 3800 V-6 General Motors engines. See Figure 19-5.

- **Centrifugal supercharger.** A centrifugal supercharger is similar to a turbocharger but is mechanically driven by the engine instead of being powered by the hot exhaust gases. A centrifugal supercharger is not a positive displacement pump and all of the air that enters is not forced through the unit. Air enters a centrifugal supercharger housing in the center and exits at the outer edges of the compressor wheels at a much higher speed due to centrifugal force. The speed of the blades has to be higher than engine speed

LOBE

FIGURE 19-5 A roots-type supercharger uses two lobes to force the air around the outside of the housing into the intake manifold.

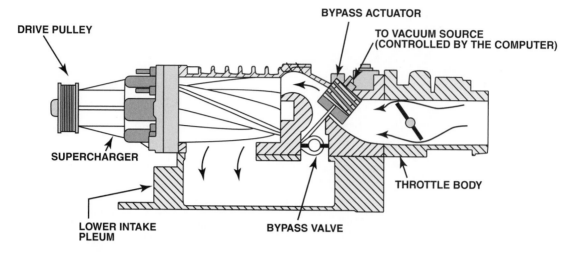

FIGURE 19-6 The bypass actuator opens the bypass valve to control boost pressure.

so a smaller pulley is used on the supercharger and the crankshaft overdrives the impeller through an internal gear box achieving about seven times the speed of the engine. Examples of centrifugal superchargers include Vortech and Paxton.

Supercharger Boost Control

Many factory-installed superchargers are equipped with a **bypass valve** that allows intake air to flow directly into the intake manifold bypassing the supercharger. The computer controls the bypass valve actuator. See Figure 19-6.

The airflow is directed around the supercharger whenever any of the following conditions occur:

- The boost pressure, as measured by the MAP sensor, indicates that the intake manifold pressure is reaching the predetermined boost level.
- During deceleration.
- Whenever reverse gear is selected.

Supercharger Service

Superchargers are usually lubricated with synthetic engine oil inside the unit. This oil level should be checked and replaced as specified by the vehicle or supercharger manufacturer. The drive belt should also be inspected and replaced as necessary.

TURBOCHARGERS

The major disadvantage of a supercharger is its reliance on engine power to drive the unit. In some installations, as much as 20% of the engine's power is used by a mechanical supercharger. However, by connecting a centrifugal supercharger to

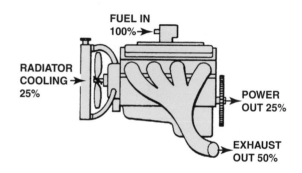

FIGURE 19-7 A turbocharger uses some of the heat energy that would normally be wasted.

a turbine drive wheel and installing it in the exhaust path, the lost engine horsepower is regained to perform other work and the combustion heat energy lost in the engine exhaust (as much as 40% to 50%) can be harnessed to do useful work. This is the concept of a **turbocharger.**

The turbocharger's main advantage over a mechanically driven supercharger is that the turbocharger does not drain power from the engine. In a naturally aspirated engine, about half of the heat energy contained in the fuel goes out the exhaust system. See Figure 19-7. Another 25% is lost through radiator cooling. Only about 25% is actually converted to mechanical power. A mechanically driven pump uses some of this mechanical output, but a turbocharger gets its energy from the exhaust gases, converting more of the fuel's heat energy into mechanical energy.

A turbocharger turbine looks much like a typical centrifugal pump used for supercharging. See Figure 19-8. Hot exhaust gases flow from the combustion chamber to the turbine wheel. The gases are heated and expanded as they leave the engine. It is not the speed of force of the exhaust gases that forces the turbine wheel to turn, as is commonly

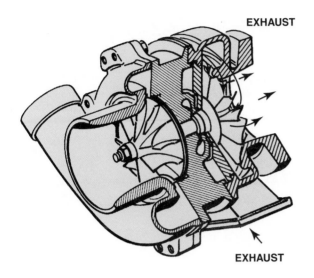

FIGURE 19-8 A turbine wheel is turned by the expanding exhaust gases.

FIGURE 19-9 The exhaust drives the turbine wheel on the left, which is connected to the impeller wheel on the right through a shaft. The bushings that support the shaft are lubricated with engine oil under pressure.

thought, but the expansion of hot gases against the turbine wheel's blades.

Turbocharger Design and Operation

A turbocharger consists of two chambers connected by a center housing. The two chambers contain a turbine wheel and a compressor wheel connected by a shaft which passes through the center housing.

To take full advantage of the exhaust heat which provides the rotating force, a turbocharger must be positioned as close as possible to the exhaust manifold. This allows the hot exhaust to pass directly into the unit with a minimum of heat loss. As exhaust gas enters the turbocharger, it rotates the turbine blades. The turbine wheel and compressor wheel are on the same shaft so that they turn at the same speed. Rotation of the compressor wheel draws air in through a central inlet and centrifugal force pumps it through an outlet at the edge of the housing. A pair of bearings in the center housing support the turbine and compressor wheel shaft, and are lubricated by engine oil. See Figure 19-9.

Both the turbine and compressor wheels must operate with extremely close clearances to minimize possible leakage around their blades. Any leakage around the turbine blades causes a dissipation of the heat energy required for compressor rotation. Leakage around the compressor blades prevents the turbocharger from developing its full boost pressure.

When the engine is started and runs at low speed, both exhaust heat and pressure are low and the turbine runs at a low speed (approximately 1000 RPM). Because the compressor does not turn fast enough to develop boost pressure, air simply passes through it and the engine works like any naturally

aspirated engine. As the engine runs faster or load increases, both exhaust heat and flow increases, causing the turbine and compressor wheels to rotate faster. Since there is no brake and very little rotating resistance on the turbocharger shaft, the turbine and compressor wheels accelerate as the exhaust heat energy increases. When an engine is running at full power, the typical turbocharger rotates at speeds between 100,000 and 150,000 RPM.

Engine deceleration from full power to idle requires only a second or two because of its internal friction, pumping resistance, and drivetrain load. The turbocharger, however, has no such load on its shaft, and is already turning many times faster than the engine at top speed. As a result, it can take as much as a minute or more after the engine has returned to idle speed before the turbocharger also has returned to idle. If the engine is decelerated to idle and then shut off immediately, engine lubrication stops flowing to the center housing bearings while the turbocharger is still spinning at thousands of RPM. The oil in the center housing is then subjected to extreme heat and can gradually "coke" or oxidize. The coked oil can clog passages and will reduce the life of the turbocharger.

The high rotating speeds and extremely close clearances of the turbine and compressor wheels in their housings require equally critical bearing clearances. The bearings must keep radial clearances of 0.003 to 0.006 inch (0.08 to 0.15 mm). Axial clearance (end play) must be maintained at 0.001 to 0.003 inch (0.025 to 0.08 mm). If properly maintained, the turbocharger also is a trouble-free device. However, to prevent problems, the following conditions must be met:

- The turbocharger bearings must be constantly lubricated with clean engine oil—turbocharged engines should have regular oil changes at half the time or mileage intervals specified for nonturbocharged engines.

- Dirt particles and other contamination must be kept out of the intake and exhaust housings.
- Whenever a basic engine bearing (crankshaft or camshaft) has been damaged, the turbocharger must be flushed with clean engine oil after the bearing has been replaced.
- If the turbocharger is damaged, the engine oil must be drained and flushed and the oil filter replaced as part of the repair procedure.

Late-model turbochargers all have liquid-cooled center bearings to prevent heat damage. In a liquid-cooled turbocharger, engine coolant is circulated through passages cast in the center housing to draw off the excess heat. This allows the bearings to run cooler and minimize the probability of oil coking when the engine is shut down.

Turbocharger Size and Response Time

A time lag occurs between an increase in engine speed and the increase in the speed of the turbocharger. This delay between acceleration and turbo boost is called **turbo lag.** Like any material, moving exhaust gas has inertia. Inertia also is present in the turbine and compressor wheels, as well as the intake airflow. Unlike a supercharger, the turbocharger cannot supply an adequate amount of boost at low speed.

Turbocharger response time is directly related to the size of the turbine and compressor wheels. Small wheels accelerate rapidly; large wheels accelerate slowly. While small wheels would seem to have an advantage over larger ones, they may not have enough airflow capacity for an engine. To minimize turbo lag, the intake and exhaust breathing capacities of an engine must be matched to the exhaust and intake airflow capabilities of the turbocharger.

BOOST CONTROL

Both supercharged and turbocharged systems are designed to provide a pressure greater than atmospheric pressure in the intake manifold. This increased pressure forces additional amounts of air into the combustion chamber over what would normally be forced in by atmospheric pressure. This increased charge increases engine power. The amount of "boost" (or pressure in the intake manifold) is measured in pounds per square inch (PSI), in inches of mercury (in. Hg), in bars, or in atmospheres. The following values will vary due to altitude and weather conditions (barometric pressure).

1 atmosphere = 14.7 PSI
1 atmosphere = 29.50 in. Hg
1 atmosphere = 1.0 bar
1 bar = 14.7 PSI

FIGURE 19-10 The unit on top of this Subaru that looks like a radiator is the intercooler, which cools the air after it has been compressed by the turbocharger.

The higher the level of boost (pressure), the greater the horsepower potential. However, other factors must be considered when increasing boost pressure:

1. As boost pressure increases, the temperature of the air also increases.
2. As the temperature of the air increases, combustion temperatures also increase, which increases the possibility of detonation.
3. Power can be increased by cooling the compressed air after it leaves the turbocharger. *The power can be increased about 1% per 10°F by which the air is cooled.* A typical cooling device is called an **intercooler** and is similar to a radiator, wherein outside air can pass through, cooling the pressurized heated air. See Figure 19-10. Some intercoolers use engine coolant to cool the hot compressed air that flows from the turbocharger to the intake.
4. As boost pressure increases, combustion temperature and pressures increase, which, if not limited, can do severe engine damage. The maximum exhaust gas temperature must be 1,550°F (840°C). Higher temperatures decrease the durability of the turbocharger *and* the engine.

Wastegate

A turbocharger uses exhaust gases to increase boost, which causes the engine to make more exhaust gases, which in turn increases the boost from the turbocharger. To prevent overboost

TECH TIP

BOOST IS THE RESULT OF RESTRICTION

The boost pressure of a turbocharger (or supercharger) is commonly measured in pounds per square inch. If a cylinder head is restricted because of small valves and ports, the turbocharger will quickly provide boost. Boost results when the air being forced into the cylinder heads cannot flow into the cylinders fast enough and "piles up" in the intake manifold, increasing boost pressure. If an engine had large valves and ports, the turbocharger could provide a much greater *amount* of air into the engine at the same boost pressure as an identical engine with smaller valves and ports. Therefore, by increasing the size of the valves, a turbocharged or supercharged engine will be capable of producing much greater power.

and severe engine damage, most turbocharger systems use a wastegate. A **wastegate** is a valve similar to a door that can open and close. The wastegate is a bypass valve at the exhaust inlet to the turbine. It allows all of the exhaust into the turbine, or it can route part of the exhaust past the turbine to the exhaust system. If the valve is closed, all of the exhaust travels to the turbocharger. When a predetermined amount of boost pressure develops in the intake manifold, the wastegate valve is opened. As the valve opens, most of the exhaust flows directly out the exhaust system, bypassing the turbocharger. With less exhaust flowing across the vanes of the turbocharger, the turbocharger decreases in speed and boost pressure is reduced. When the boost pressure drops, the wastegate valve closes to direct the exhaust over the turbocharger vanes and again allow the boost pressure to rise. Wastegate operation is a continuous process to control boost pressure.

The wastegate is the pressure control valve of a turbocharger system. The wastegate is usually controlled by the onboard computer through a boost control solenoid. See Figure 19-11.

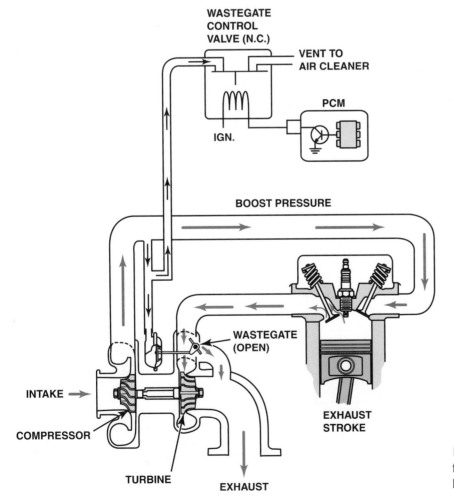

FIGURE 19-11 A wastegate is used on the first-generation Duramax diesel to control maximum boost pressure.

Relief Valves

A wastegate controls the exhaust side of the turbocharger. A relief valve controls the intake side. A **relief valve** vents pressurized air from the connecting pipe between the outlet of the turbocharger and the throttle whenever the throttle is closed during boost, such as during shifts. If the pressure is not released, the turbocharger turbine wheel will slow down, creating a lag when the throttle is opened again after a shift has been completed. There are two basic types of relief valves including:

- **Compressor bypass valve** or **CBV** This type of relief valve routes the pressurized air to the inlet side of the turbocharger for reuse and is quiet during operation.
- Blow-off valve or BOV This is also called a **dump valve** or **vent valve** and features an adjustable spring design that keeps the valve closed until a sudden release of the throttle. The resulting pressure increase opens the valve and vents the pressurized air directly into the atmosphere. This type of relief valve is noisy in operation and creates a whooshing sound when the valve opens. See Figure 19-12.

TURBOCHARGER FAILURES

When turbochargers fail to function correctly, a drop in power is noticed. To restore proper operation, the turbocharger must

TECH TIP

IF ONE IS GOOD, TWO ARE BETTER

A turbocharger uses the exhaust from the engine to spin a turbine, which is connected to an impeller inside a turbocharger. This impeller then forces air into the engine under pressure higher than is normally achieved without a turbocharger. The more air that can be forced into an engine, the greater the power potential. A V-type engine has two exhaust manifolds and so two small turbochargers can be used to help force greater quantities of air into an engine, as shown in Figure 19-13.

be rebuilt, repaired, or replaced. It is not possible to simply remove the turbocharger, seal any openings, and still maintain decent driveability. Bearing failure is a common cause of turbocharger failure, and replacement bearings are usually only available to rebuilders. Another common turbocharger problem is excessive and continuous oil consumption resulting

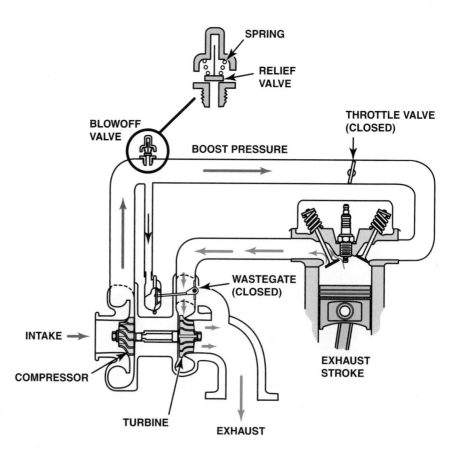

FIGURE 19-12 A blow-off valve is used in some turbocharged systems to relieve boost pressure during deceleration.

FIGURE 19-13   A dual turbocharger system installed on a small block Chevrolet V-8 engine.

in blue exhaust smoke. Turbochargers use small rings similar to piston rings on the shaft to prevent exhaust (combustion gases) from entering the central bearing. Because there are no seals to keep oil in, excessive oil consumption is usually caused by:

1. A plugged positive crankcase ventilation (PCV) system resulting in excessive crankcase pressures forcing oil into the air inlet. This failure is not related to the turbocharger, but the turbocharger is often blamed.
2. A clogged air filter, which causes a low-pressure area in the inlet, which can draw oil past the turbo shaft rings and into the intake manifold.
3. A clogged oil return (drain) line from the turbocharger to the oil pan (sump), which can cause the engine oil pressure to force oil past the turbocharger's shaft rings and into the intake *and* exhaust manifolds. Obviously, oil being forced into both the intake and exhaust would create lots of smoke.

NITROUS OXIDE (N_2O)

Principles

Nitrous oxide is a colorless and nonflammable gas. Nitrous oxide was discovered by a British chemist, Joseph Priestly (1733–1804), who also discovered oxygen. He found that nitrous oxide caused a person to be light-headed when it was breathed and soon became known as *laughing gas*. Nitrous oxide was used in dentistry during tooth extraction to reduce the pain or at least make the patient forget what occurred.

Nitrous oxide has two nitrogen atoms and one oxide atom. About 36% of the molecule weight is oxygen. Nitrous

oxide is a manufactured gas because, even though both nitrogen and oxygen are present in our atmosphere, they are not combined into one molecule and require heat and a catalyst to be combined.

Engine Power Adder

A **power adder** is a device or system added to an engine such as a supercharger, turbocharger, or nitrous oxide to increase power. When nitrous oxide is injected into an engine along with gasoline, engine power is increased. The addition of N_2O supplies the needed oxygen for the extra fuel. By itself, N_2O does not burn, but rather provides the oxygen for additional fuel that is supplied along with the N_2O to produce more power.

NOTE: Nitrous oxide was used as a power adder in World War II on some fighter aircraft. Having several hundred more horsepower for a short time saved many lives.

Pressure and Temperature

It requires about 11 pounds of pressure per degree Fahrenheit to condense nitrous oxide gas into liquid nitrous oxide. For example, at 70°F it requires a pressure of about 770 PSI to condense N_2O into a liquid. To change N_2O from a liquid under pressure to a gas, all that is needed is to lower its pressure below the pressure it takes to cause it to become a liquid.

The temperature also affects the pressure of N_2O. See the following chart.

Temperature (°F/°C)	Pressure (PSI/kPa)
−30°F/−34°C	67 PSI/468 kpa
−20°F/−29°C	203 PSI/1,400 kpa
−10°F/−23°C	240 PSI/1,655 kpa
0°F/−18°C	283 PSI/1,950 kpa
10°F/−12°C	335 PSI/2,310 kpa
20°F/−7°C	387 PSI/2,668 kpa
30°F/−1°C	460 PSI/3,172 kpa
40°F/4°C	520 PSI/3,585 kpa
50°F/10°C	590 PSI/4,068 kpa
60°F/16°C	675 PSI/4,654 kpa
70°F/21°C	760 PSI/5,240 kpa
80°F/27°C	865 PSI/5,964 kpa
90°F/32°C	985 PSI/6,792 kpa
100°F/38°C	1,120 PSI/7,722 kpa

Nitrous oxide is stored in a pressurized storage container and installed at an angle so the pickup tube is in the liquid. The

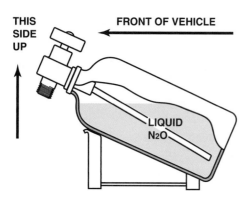

FIGURE 19-14 Nitrous bottles have to be mounted at an angle to ensure that the pickup tube is in the liquid N₂O.

front of the discharge end of the storage bottle should be toward the front of the vehicle. See Figure 19-14.

Wet and Dry Systems

There are two different types of N_2O system that depend on whether additional fuel (gasoline) is supplied at the same time as when the nitrous oxide is squirted. If additional fuel is also injected, this type of system is called a **wet system.** A wet system is identified as having both a red and a blue nozzle with the red flowing gasoline and the blue flowing nitrous oxide. In a system such as an engine using port fuel injection, only nitrous oxide needs to be injected because the PCM can be commanded to provide more fuel when the N_2O is being sprayed. As a result, the intake manifold contains only air and the injected gaseous N_2O, which is called a **dry system.**

Engine Changes Needed for N₂O

If nitrous oxide is going to be used to increase horsepower more than 50 hp, the engine must be designed and built to withstand the greater heat and pressure that will occur in the combustion chambers. For example, the following items should be considered if adding a turbocharger, supercharger, or nitrous oxide system:

- Forged pistons are best able to withstand the pressure and temperature when using nitrous oxide or an other power adder.
- Cylinder-to-wall clearance should be increased. Due to the greater amount of heat created by the extra fuel and N_2O injection, the piston temperature will be increased. While using forged pistons will help, most experts recommend using increased cylinder-to-wall clearance. Check the instructions from the nitrous oxide supplier for details and other suggested changes.

FIGURE 19-15 An electrical heating mat is installed on the bottle of nitrous oxide to increase the pressure of the gas inside.

TECH TIP

INCREASE BOTTLE PRESSURE

To increase the pressure of the nitrous oxide in a bottle, an electrical warming blanket can be used as seen in Figure 19-15. The higher the temperature, the higher the pressure and the greater amount of flow of N_2O that will occur when energized.

CAUTION: The use of a nitrous oxide injection system can cause catastrophic engine damage. Always follow the instructions that come with the kit and be sure that all of the internal engine parts meet the standard specified to help avoid severe engine damage.

System Installation and Calibration

Nitrous oxide systems are usually purchased as a kit with all of the needed components included. The kit also includes one or more sizes of nozzle(s), which are calibrated to control the flow of nitrous oxide into the intake manifold. Installation of a nitrous oxide kit also includes the installation of an on/off switch and a switch on or near the throttle, which is used to activate the system only at the wide-open throttle (WOT) position.

SUMMARY

1. Volumetric efficiency is a comparison of the actual volume of air–fuel mixture drawn into the engine to the theoretical maximum volume that can be drawn into the cylinder.

2. A supercharger operates from the engine by a drive belt and, while it does consume some engine power, it forces a greater amount of air into the cylinders for even more power.

3. A turbocharger uses the normally wasted heat energy of the exhaust to turn an impeller at high speed. The impeller is linked to a turbine wheel on the same shaft and is used to force air into the engine.

4. There are two types of superchargers: roots-type and centrifugal.

5. A bypass valve is used to control the boost pressure on most factory-installed superchargers.

6. An intercooler is used on many turbocharged and some supercharged engines to reduce the temperature of air entering the engine for increased power.

7. A wastegate is used on most turbocharger systems to limit and control boost pressures, as well as a relief valve, to keep the speed of the turbine wheel from slowing down during engine deceleration.

8. Nitrous oxide injection can be used as a power adder, but only with extreme caution.

REVIEW QUESTIONS

1. What are the reasons why supercharging increases engine power?

2. How does the bypass valve work on a supercharged engine?

3. What are the advantages and disadvantages of supercharging?

4. What are the advantages and disadvantages of turbocharging?

5. What turbocharger control valves are needed for proper engine operation?

CHAPTER QUIZ

1. Boost pressure is generally measured in _____.
   a. in. Hg
   b. PSI
   c. in. H_2O
   d. in. lb

2. Two types of superchargers include _____.
   a. Rotary and reciprocating
   b. Roots-type and centrifugal
   c. Double and single acting
   d. Turbine and piston

3. Which valve is used on a factory supercharger to limit boost?
   a. A bypass valve
   b. A wastegate
   c. A blow-off valve
   d. An air valve

4. How are most superchargers lubricated?
   a. By engine oil under pressure through lines from the engine
   b. By an internal oil reservoir
   c. By greased bearings
   d. No lubrication is needed because the incoming air cools the supercharger

5. How are most turbochargers lubricated?
   a. By engine oil under pressure through lines from the engine
   b. By an internal oil reservoir
   c. By greased bearings
   d. No lubrication is needed because the incoming air cools the supercharger

6. Two technicians are discussing the term "turbo lag." Technician A says that it refers to the delay between when the exhaust leaves the cylinder and when it contacts the turbine blades of the turbocharger. Technician B says that it refers to the delay in boost pressure that occurs when the throttle is first opened. Which technician is correct?

   a. Technician A only

   b. Technician B only

   c. Both Technicians A and B

   d. Neither Technician A nor B

7. What is the purpose of an intercooler?

   a. To reduce the temperature of the air entering the engine

   b. To cool the turbocharger

   c. To cool the engine oil on a turbocharged engine

   d. To cool the exhaust before it enters the turbocharger

8. Which type of relief valve used on a turbocharged engine is noisy?

   a. A bypass valve

   b. A BOV

   c. A dump valve

   d. Both b and c

9. Technician A says that a stuck-open wastegate can cause the engine to burn oil. Technician B says that a clogged PCV system can cause the engine to burn oil. Which technician is correct?

   a. Technician A only

   b. Technician B only

   c. Both Technicians A and B

   d. Neither Technician A nor B

10. What service operation is *most* important on engines equipped with a turbocharger?

    a. Replacing the air filter regularly

    b. Replacing the fuel filter regularly

    c. Regular oil changes

    d. Regular exhaust system maintenance

ENGINE CONDITION DIAGNOSIS

OBJECTIVES

After studying Chapter 20, the reader will be able to:

1. Prepare for ASE Engine Performance (A8) certification test content area "A"(General Engine Diagnosis).
2. List the visual checks to determine engine condition.
3. Discuss engine noise and its relation to engine condition.
4. Describe how to perform a dry and a wet compression test.
5. Explain how to perform a cylinder leakage test.
6. Discuss how to measure the amount of timing chain slack.
7. Describe how an oil sample analysis can be used to determine engine condition.

KEY TERMS

Backpressure (p. 350)
Compression Test (p. 342)
Cranking Vacuum Test (p. 347)
Cylinder Leakage Test (p. 345)
Dynamic Compression Test (p. 345)
Idle Vacuum Test (p. 347)
Inches of Mercury (in. Hg) (p. 347)

Paper Test (p. 343)
Power Balance Test (p. 346)
Restricted Exhaust (p. 349)
Running Compression Test (p. 345)
Vacuum Test (p. 347)
Wet Compression Test (p. 344)

If there is an engine operation problem, then the cause could be any one of many items, including the engine itself. The condition of the engine should be tested anytime the operation of the engine is not satisfactory.

TYPICAL ENGINE-RELATED COMPLAINTS

Many driveability problems are *not* caused by engine mechanical problems. A thorough inspection and testing of the ignition and fuel systems should be performed before testing for mechanical engine problems.

Typical engine mechanical-related complaints include the following:

- Excessive oil consumption
- Engine misfiring
- Loss of power
- Smoke from the engine or exhaust
- Engine noise

ENGINE SMOKE DIAGNOSIS

The color of engine exhaust smoke can indicate what engine problem might exist.

Typical Exhaust Smoke Color	Possible Causes
Blue	Blue exhaust indicates that the engine is burning oil. Oil is getting into the combustion chamber either past the piston rings or past the valve stem seals. Blue smoke only after start-up is usually due to defective valve stem seals. See Figure 20-1.
Black	Black exhaust smoke is due to excessive fuel being burned in the combustion chamber. Typical causes include a defective or misadjusted throttle body, leaking fuel injector, or excessive fuel-pump pressure.
White (steam)	White smoke or steam from the exhaust is normal during cold weather and represents condensed steam. Every engine creates about 1 gallon of water for each gallon of gasoline burned. If the steam from the exhaust is excessive, then water (coolant) is getting into the combustion chamber. Typical causes include a defective cylinder head gasket, a cracked cylinder head, or in severe cases a cracked block. See Figure 20-2.

NOTE: White smoke can also be created when automatic transmission fluid (ATF) is burned. A common source of ATF getting into the engine is through a defective vacuum modulator valve on the automatic transmission.

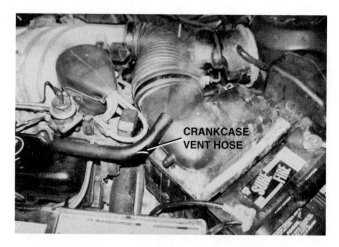

FIGURE 20-1 Blowby gases coming out of the crankcase vent hose. Excessive amounts of combustion gases flow past the piston rings and into the crankcase.

FIGURE 20-2 White steam is usually an indication of a blown (defective) cylinder head gasket that allows engine coolant to flow into the combustion chamber where it is turned to steam.

THE DRIVER IS YOUR BEST RESOURCE

The driver of the vehicle knows a lot about the vehicle and how it is driven. *Before* diagnosis is started, always ask the following questions:

- When did the problem first occur?
- Under what conditions does it occur?
  1. Cold or hot?
  2. Acceleration, cruise, or deceleration?
  3. How far was it driven?

After the nature and scope of the problem are determined, the complaint should be verified before further diagnostic tests are performed.

VISUAL CHECKS

The first and most important "test" that can be performed is a careful visual inspection.

Oil Level and Condition

The first area for visual inspection is oil level and condition.

1. Oil level—oil should be to the proper level
2. Oil condition
   a. Using a match or lighter, try to light the oil on the dipstick; if the oil flames up, gasoline is present in the engine oil.
   b. Drip some of the engine oil from the dipstick onto the hot exhaust manifold. If the oil bubbles or boils, there is coolant (water) in the oil.
   c. Check for grittiness by rubbing the oil between your fingers.

Coolant Level and Condition

Most mechanical engine problems are caused by overheating. The proper operation of the cooling system is critical to the life of any engine.

NOTE: Check the coolant level in the radiator only if the radiator is cool. If the radiator is hot and the radiator cap is removed, the drop in pressure above the coolant will cause the coolant to boil immediately and can cause severe burns when the coolant explosively expands upward and outward from the radiator opening.

1. The coolant level in the coolant recovery container should be within the limits indicated on the overflow bottle. If this level is too low or the coolant recovery container is empty, then check the level of coolant in the radiator (only when cool) and also check the operation of the pressure cap.
2. The coolant should be checked with a hydrometer for boiling and freezing temperature. This test indicates if the concentration of the antifreeze is sufficient for proper protection.
3. Pressure test the cooling system and look for leakage. Coolant leakage can often be seen around hoses or cooling system components because it will often cause:
   a. A grayish white stain
   b. A rusty color stain
   c. Dye stains from antifreeze (greenish or yellowish depending on the type of coolant)
4. Check for cool areas of the radiator indicating clogged sections.
5. Check operation and condition of the fan clutch, fan, and coolant pump drive belt.

TECH TIP

WHAT'S LEAKING?

The color of the leaks observed under a vehicle can help the technician determine and correct the cause. Some leaks, such as condensate (water) from the air-conditioning system, are normal, whereas a brake fluid leak is very dangerous. The following are colors of common leaks:

Sooty black	Engine oil
Yellow, green, blue, or orange	Antifreeze (coolant)
Red	Automatic transmission fluid
Murky brown	Brake or power steering fluid or very neglected antifreeze (coolant)
Clear	Air-conditioning condensate (water) (normal)

Oil Leaks

Oil leaks can lead to severe engine damage if the resulting low oil level is not corrected. Besides causing an oily mess where the vehicle is parked, the oil leak can cause blue smoke to occur under the hood as leaking oil drips on the exhaust system. *Finding the location of the oil leak can often be difficult.* See Figures 20-3 and 20-4. To help find the source of oil leaks follow these steps:

Step 1   Clean the engine or area around the suspected oil leak. Use a high-powered hot-water spray to wash the engine. While the engine is running, spray the entire engine and the engine compartment. Avoid letting the water come into direct contact with the air inlet and ignition distributor or ignition coil(s).

NOTE: If the engine starts to run rough or stalls when the engine gets wet, then the secondary ignition wires (spark plug wires) or distributor cap may be defective or have weak insulation. Be certain to wipe all wires and the distributor cap dry with a soft, dry cloth if the engine stalls.

An alternative method is to spray a degreaser on the engine, then start and run the engine until warm. Engine heat helps the degreaser penetrate the grease and dirt. Use a water hose to rinse off the engine and engine compartment.

Step 2   If the oil leak is not visible or oil seems to be coming from "everywhere," use a white talcum powder. The leaking oil will show as a dark area on the white powder. See the Tech Tip, "The Foot Powder Spray Trick."

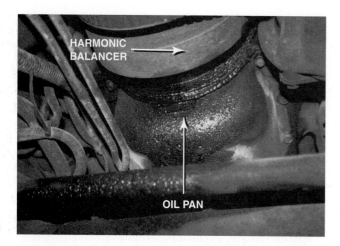

FIGURE 20-3 What looks like an oil pan gasket leak can be a rocker cover gasket leak. Always look up and look for the highest place you see oil leaking; that should be repaired first.

FIGURE 20-4 The transmission and flex plate (flywheel) were removed to check the exact location of this oil leak. The rear main seal and/or the oil pan gasket could be the cause of this leak.

Step 3 Fluorescent dye can be added to the engine oil. Add about 1/2 oz (15 cc) of dye per 5 quarts of engine oil. Start the engine and allow it to run about 10 minutes to thoroughly mix the dye throughout the engine. A black light can then be shown around every suspected oil leak location. The black light will easily show all oil leak locations because the dye will show as a bright yellow/green area. See Figure 20-5.

FIGURE 20-5 Using a black light to spot leaks after adding dye to the oil.

TECH TIP

THE FOOT POWDER SPRAY TRICK

The source of an oil or other fluid leak is often difficult to determine. A quick and easy method that works is the following. First, clean the entire area. This can best be done by using a commercially available degreaser to spray the entire area. Let it soak to loosen all accumulated oil and greasy dirt. Clean off the degreaser with a water hose. Let the area dry. Start the engine, and using spray foot powder or other aerosol powder product, spray the entire area. The leak will turn the white powder dark. The exact location of any leak can be quickly located.

NOTE: Most oil leaks appear at the bottom of the engine due to gravity. Look for the highest, most forward location for the source of the leak.

NOTE: Fluorescent dye works best with clean oil.

ENGINE NOISE DIAGNOSIS

An engine knocking noise is often difficult to diagnose. Several items that can cause a deep engine knock include:

- **Valves clicking.** This can happen because of lack of oil to the lifters. This noise is most noticeable at idle when the oil pressure is the lowest.

- **Torque converter.** The attaching bolts or nuts may be loose on the flex plate. This noise is most noticeable at idle or when there is no load on the engine.
- **Cracked flex plate.** The noise of a cracked flex plate is often mistaken for a rod- or main-bearing noise.
- **Loose or defective drive belts or tensioners.** If an accessory drive belt is loose or defective, the flopping noise often sounds similar to a bearing knock. See Figure 20-6.
- **Piston pin knock.** This knocking noise is usually not affected by load on the cylinder. If the clearance is too great, a double knock noise is heard when the engine idles. If all cylinders are grounded out one at a time and the noise does not change, a defective piston pin could be the cause.
- **Piston slap.** A piston slap is usually caused by an undersized or improperly shaped piston or oversized cylinder bore. A piston slap is most noticeable when the engine is cold and tends to decrease or stop making noise as the piston expands during engine operation.
- **Timing chain noise.** An excessively loose timing chain can cause a severe knocking noise when the chain hits the timing chain cover. This noise can often sound like a rod-bearing knock.
- **Rod-bearing noise.** The noise from a defective rod bearing is usually load sensitive and changes in intensity as the load on the engine increases and decreases. A rod-bearing failure can often be detected by grounding out the spark plugs one cylinder at a time. If the knocking noise decreases or is eliminated when a particular cylinder is grounded (disabled), then the grounded cylinder is the one from which the noise is originating.
- **Main-bearing knock.** A main-bearing knock often cannot be isolated to a particular cylinder. The sound can vary in intensity and may disappear at times depending on engine load.

FIGURE 20-6   An accessory belt tensioner. Most tensioners have a mark that indicates normal operating location. If the belt has stretched, this indicator mark will be outside of the normal range. Anything wrong with the belt or tensioner can cause noise.

Typical Noises	Possible Causes
Clicking noise—like the clicking of a ballpoint pen	1. Loose spark plug 2. Loose accessory mount (for air-conditioning compressor, alternator, power steering pump, etc.) 3. Loose rocker arm 4. Worn rocker arm pedestal 5. Fuel pump (broken mechanical fuel pump return spring) 6. Worn camshaft 7. Exhaust leak. (See Figure 20-7.)
Clacking noise—like tapping on metal	1. Worn piston pin 2. Broken piston 3. Excessive valve clearance 4. Timing chain hitting cover
Knock—like knocking on a door	1. Rod bearing(s) 2. Main bearing(s) 3. Thrust bearing(s) 4. Loose torque converter 5. Cracked flex plate (drive plate)
Rattle—like a baby rattle	1. Manifold heat control valve 2. Broken harmonic balancer 3. Loose accessory mounts 4. Loose accessory drive belt or tensioner
Clatter—like rolling marbles	1. Rod bearings 2. Piston pin 3. Loose timing chain
Whine—like an electric motor running	1. Alternator bearing 2. Drive belt 3. Power steering 4. Belt noise (accessory or timing)
Clunk—like a door closing	1. Engine mount 2. Drive axle shaft U-joint or constant velocity (CV) joint

TECH TIP

ENGINE NOISE AND COST

A light ticking noise often heard at one-half engine speed and associated with valve train noise is a less serious problem than many deep-sounding knocking noises. Generally, the deeper the sound of the engine noise, the more the owner will have to pay for repairs. A light "tick tick tick," though often not cheap, is usually far less expensive than a deep "knock knock knock" from the engine.

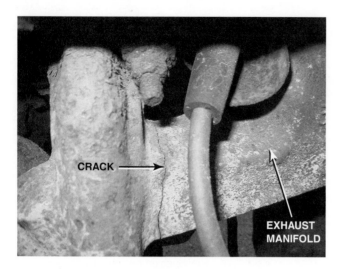

FIGURE 20-7 A cracked exhaust manifold on a Ford V-8.

Regardless of the type of loud knocking noise, after the external causes of the knocking noise have been eliminated, the engine should be disassembled and carefully inspected to determine the exact cause.

OIL PRESSURE TESTING

Proper oil pressure is very important for the operation of any engine. *Low oil pressure can cause engine wear, and engine wear can cause low oil pressure.*

If main thrust or rod bearings are worn, oil pressure is reduced because of leakage of the oil around the bearings. Oil pressure testing is usually performed with the following steps:

Step 1   Operate the engine until normal operating temperature is achieved.

Step 2   With the engine off, remove the oil pressure sending unit or sender, usually located near the oil filter. Thread an oil pressure gauge into the threaded hole. See Figure 20-8.

> **NOTE:** An oil pressure gauge can be made from another gauge, such as an old air-conditioning gauge and a flexible brake hose. The threads are often the same as those used for the oil pressure sending unit.

Step 3   Start the engine and observe the gauge. Record the oil pressure at idle and at 2500 RPM. Most vehicle manufacturers recommend a minimum oil pressure of 10 PSI per 1000 RPM. Therefore, at 2500 RPM, the oil pressure should be at least 25 PSI. Always compare your test results with the manufacturer's recommended oil pressure. Besides engine bearing wear, other possible causes for low oil pressure include:

- Low oil level
- Diluted oil
- Stuck oil pressure relief valve

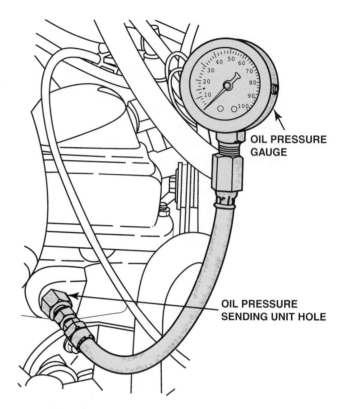

FIGURE 20-8 To measure engine oil pressure, remove the oil pressure sending (sender) unit usually located near the oil filter. Screw the pressure gauge into the oil pressure sending unit hole.

OIL PRESSURE WARNING LAMP

The red oil pressure warning lamp in the dash usually lights when the oil pressure is less than 4 to 7 PSI, depending on vehicle and engine. The oil light should not be on during driving. If the oil warning lamp is on, stop the engine immediately. Always confirm oil pressure with a reliable mechanical gauge before performing engine repairs. The sending unit or circuit may be defective.

COMPRESSION TEST

An engine **compression test** is one of the fundamental engine diagnostic tests that can be performed. For smooth engine operation, all cylinders must have equal compression. An engine can lose compression by leakage of air through one or more of only three routes:

- Intake or exhaust valve
- Piston rings (or piston, if there is a hole)
- Cylinder head gasket

TECH TIP

USE THE KISS TEST METHOD

Engine testing is done to find the cause of an engine problem. All the simple things should be tested first. Just remember KISS—"keep it simple, stupid." A loose alternator belt or loose bolts on a torque converter can sound just like a lifter or rod bearing. A loose spark plug can make the engine perform as if it had a burned valve. Some simple items that can cause serious problems include the following:

Oil Burning

- Low oil level
- Clogged PCV valve or system, causing blowby and oil to be blown into the air cleaner
- Clogged drainback passages in the cylinder head
- Dirty oil that has not been changed for a long time (Change the oil and drive for about 1,000 miles (1,600 kilometers) and change the oil and filter again.)

Noises

- Carbon on top of the piston(s) can sound like a bad rod bearing (often called a carbon knock)
- Loose torque-to-flex plate bolts (or nuts), causing a loud knocking noise

NOTE: Often this problem will cause noise only at idle; the noise tends to disappear during driving or when the engine is under load.

- A loose and/or defective drive belt, which may cause a rod- or main-bearing knocking noise (A loose or broken mount for the generator [alternator], power steering pump, or air-conditioning compressor can also cause a knocking noise.)

For best results, the engine should be warmed to normal operating temperature before testing. An accurate compression test should be performed as follows:

Step 1   Remove all spark plugs. This allows the engine to be cranked to an even speed. Be sure to label all spark plug wires.

CAUTION: Disable the ignition system by disconnecting the primary leads from the ignition coil or module or by grounding the coil wire after removing it from the center of the distributor cap. Also disable the fuel-injection system to prevent the squirting of fuel into the cylinder.

TECH TIP

THE PAPER TEST

A soundly running engine should produce even and steady exhaust at the tailpipe. You can test this with the **paper test.** Hold a piece of paper or a "3 × 5" card (even a dollar bill works) within 1 inch (2.5 centimeters) of the tailpipe with the engine running at idle. See Figure 20-9.

The paper should blow out evenly without "puffing." If the paper is drawn *toward* the tailpipe at times, the exhaust valves in one or more cylinders could be burned. Other reasons why the paper might be sucked toward the tailpipe include the following:

1. The engine could be misfiring because of a lean condition that could occur normally when the engine is cold.
2. Pulsing of the paper toward the tailpipe could also be caused by a hole in the exhaust system. If exhaust escapes through a hole in the exhaust system, air could be drawn in during the intervals between the exhaust puffs from the tailpipe to the hole in the exhaust, causing the paper to be drawn toward the tailpipe.
3. Ignition fault causing misfire.

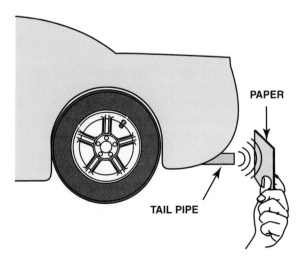

FIGURE 20-9   The paper test involves holding a piece of paper near the tailpipe of an idling engine. A good engine should produce even, outward puffs of exhaust. If the paper is sucked in toward the tailpipe, a burned valve is a possibility.

FIGURE 20-10   A two-piece compression gauge set. The threaded hose is screwed into the spark plug hole after removing the spark plug. The gauge part is then snapped onto the end of the hose.

Step 2   Block open the throttle. This permits the maximum amount of air to be drawn into the engine. This step also ensures consistent compression test results.

Step 3   Thread a compression gauge into one spark plug hole and crank the engine. See Figure 20-10.

Continue cranking the engine through *four* compression strokes. Each compression stroke makes a puffing sound.

NOTE: Note the reading on the compression gauge after the first puff. This reading should be at least one-half the final reading. For example, if the final, highest reading is 150 PSI, then the reading after the first puff should be higher than 75 PSI. A low first-puff reading indicates possible weak piston rings. Release the pressure on the gauge and repeat for the other cylinders.

Step 4   Record the highest readings and compare the results. Most vehicle manufacturers specify the minimum compression reading and the maximum allowable variation among cylinders. Most manufacturers specify a maximum difference of 20% between the highest reading and the lowest reading. For example:

If the high reading is	150 PSI
Subtract 20%	−30 PSI
Lowest allowable compression is	120 PSI

NOTE: To make the math quick and easy, think of 10% of 150, which is 15 (move the decimal point to the left one place). Now double it: 15 × 2 = 30. This represents 20%.

NOTE: During cranking, the oil pump cannot maintain normal oil pressure. Extended engine cranking, such as that which occurs during a compression test, can cause hydraulic lifters to collapse. When the engine starts, loud valve clicking noises may be heard. This should be considered normal after performing a compression test, and the noise should stop after the vehicle has been driven a short distance.

TECH TIP

THE HOSE TRICK

Installing spark plugs can be made easier by using a rubber hose on the end of the spark plug. The hose can be a vacuum hose, fuel line, or even an old spark plug wire end. See Figure 20-11.

The hose makes it easy to start the threads of the spark plug into the cylinder head. After starting the threads, continue to thread the spark plug for several turns. Using the hose eliminates the chance of cross-threading the plug. This is especially important when installing spark plugs in aluminum cylinder heads.

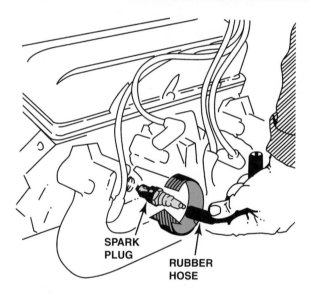

SPARK PLUG

RUBBER HOSE

FIGURE 20-11   Use a vacuum or fuel line hose over the spark plug to install it without danger of cross-threading the cylinder head.

WET COMPRESSION TEST

If the compression test reading indicates low compression on one or more cylinders, add three squirts of oil to the cylinder and retest. This is called a **wet compression test,** when oil is used to help seal around the piston rings.

CAUTION: Do not use more oil than three squirts from a hand-operated oil squirt can. Too much oil can cause a hydrostatic lock, which can damage or break pistons or connecting rods or even crack a cylinder head.

Perform the compression test again and observe the results. If the first-puff readings greatly improve and the readings are

FIGURE 20-12 Badly burned exhaust valve. A compression test could have detected a problem, and a cylinder leakage test (leak-down test) could have been used to determine the exact problem.

much higher than without the oil, the cause of the low compression is worn or defective piston rings. If the compression readings increase only slightly (or not at all), then the cause of the low compression is usually defective valves. See Figure 20-12.

NOTE: During both the dry and wet compression tests, be sure that the battery and starting system are capable of cranking the engine at normal cranking speed.

RUNNING (DYNAMIC) COMPRESSION TEST

A compression test is commonly used to help determine engine condition and is usually performed with the engine cranking.

What is the RPM of a cranking engine? An engine idles at about 600 to 900 RPM, and the starter motor obviously cannot crank the engine as fast as the engine idles. Most manufacturers' specifications require the engine to crank at 80 to 250 cranking RPM. Therefore, a check of the engine's compression at cranking speed determines the condition of an engine that does not run at such low speeds.

But what should be the compression of a running engine? Some would think that the compression would be substantially higher, because the valve overlap of the cam is more effective at higher engine speeds, which would tend to increase the compression.

A **running compression test,** also called a **dynamic compression test,** is a compression test done with the engine running rather than during engine cranking as is done in a regular compression test.

Actually, the compression pressure of a running engine is much *lower* than cranking compression pressure. This results from the volumetric efficiency. The engine is revolving faster, and therefore, there is less *time* for air to enter the combustion chamber. With less air to compress, the compression pressure is lower. Typically, the higher the engine RPM, the lower the running compression. For most engines, the value ranges are as follows:

- Compression during cranking: 125 to 160 PSI
- Compression at idle: 60 to 90 PSI
- Compression at 2000 RPM: 30 to 60 PSI

As with cranking compression, the running compression of all cylinders should be equal. Therefore, a problem is not likely to be detected by single compression values, but by *variations* in running compression values among the cylinders. Broken valve springs, worn valve guides, bent pushrods, and worn cam lobes are some items that would be indicated by a low running compression test reading on one or more cylinders.

Performing a Running Compression Test

To perform a running compression test, remove just one spark plug at a time. With one spark plug removed from the engine, use a jumper wire to *ground* the spark plug wire to a good engine ground. This prevents possible ignition coil damage. Start the engine, push the pressure release on the gauge, and read the compression. Increase the engine speed to about 2000 RPM and push the pressure release on the gauge again. Read the gauge. Stop the engine, reattach the spark plug wire, and repeat the test for each of the remaining cylinders. Just like the cranking compression test, the running compression test can inform a technician of the *relative* compression of all the cylinders.

CYLINDER LEAKAGE TEST

One of the best tests that can be used to determine engine condition is the **cylinder leakage test.** This test involves injecting air under pressure into the cylinders one at a time. The amount and location of any escaping air helps the technician determine the condition of the engine. The air is injected into the cylinder through a cylinder leakage gauge into the spark plug hole. See Figure 20-13. To perform the cylinder leakage test, take the following steps:

Step 1   For best results, the engine should be at normal operating temperature (upper radiator hose hot and pressurized).

Step 2   The cylinder being tested must be at top dead center (TDC) of the compression stroke. See Figure 20-14.

FIGURE 20-13   A typical handheld cylinder leakage tester.

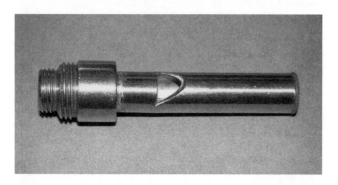

FIGURE 20-14   A whistle stop used to find top dead center. Remove the spark plug and install the whistle stop, then rotate the engine by hand. When the whistle stops making a sound, the piston is at the top.

NOTE: The greatest amount of wear occurs at the top of the cylinder because of the heat generated near the top of the cylinders. The piston ring flex also adds to the wear at the top of the cylinder.

Step 3   Calibrate the cylinder leakage unit as per manufacturer's instructions.

Step 4   Inject air into the cylinders one at a time, rotating the engine as necessitated by firing order to test each cylinder at TDC on the compression stroke.

Step 5   Evaluate the results:

Less than 10% leakage: good
Less than 20% leakage: acceptable
Less than 30% leakage: poor
More than 30% leakage: definite problem

NOTE: If leakage seems unacceptably high, repeat the test, being certain that it is being performed correctly and that the cylinder being tested is at TDC on the compression stroke.

6. Check the source of air leakage.
    a. If air is heard escaping from the oil filler cap, the *piston rings* are worn or broken.
    b. If air is observed bubbling out of the radiator, there is a possible blown *head gasket* or cracked *cylinder head.*
    c. If air is heard coming from the throttle body or air inlet on fuel injection-equipped engines, there is a defective *intake valve(s).*
    d. If air is heard coming from the tailpipe, there is a defective *exhaust valve(s).*

CYLINDER POWER BALANCE TEST

Most large engine analyzers and scan tools have a cylinder power balance feature. The purpose of a cylinder **power balance test** is to determine if all cylinders are contributing power equally. It determines this by shorting out one cylinder at a time. If the engine speed (RPM) does not drop as much for one cylinder as for other cylinders of the same engine, then the shorted cylinder must be weaker than the other cylinders. For example:

Cylinder #3 is the weak cylinder.

Cylinder Number	RPM Drop When Ignition Is Shorted
1	75
2	70
3	15
4	65
5	75
6	70

NOTE: Most automotive test equipment uses automatic means for testing cylinder balance. Be certain to correctly identify the offending cylinder. Cylinder #3 as identified by the equipment may be the third cylinder in the firing order instead of the actual cylinder #3.

POWER BALANCE TEST PROCEDURE

When point-type ignition was used on all vehicles, the common method for determining which, if any, cylinder was weak was to remove a spark plug wire from one spark plug at a time while watching a tachometer and a vacuum gauge. This method is not recommended on any vehicle with any type of electronic ignition. If any of the spark plug wires are removed from a spark plug with the engine running, the ignition coil tries to supply increasing levels of voltage attempting to jump the increasing gap as the plug wires are removed. This high voltage could easily track the ignition coil, damage the ignition module, or both.

The acceptable method of canceling cylinders, which will work on all types of ignition systems, including distributorless, is to *ground* the secondary current for each cylinder. See Figure 20-15. The cylinder with the least RPM drop is the cylinder not producing its share of power.

VACUUM TESTS

Vacuum is pressure below atmospheric pressure and is measured in **inches** (or millimeters) **of mercury (Hg).** An engine in good mechanical condition will run with high manifold vacuum. Manifold vacuum is developed by the pistons as they move down on the intake stroke to draw the charge from the throttle body and intake manifold. Air to refill the manifold comes past the throttle plate into the manifold. Vacuum will increase anytime the engine turns faster or has better cylinder sealing while the throttle plate remains in a fixed position. Manifold vacuum will decrease when the engine turns more slowly or when the cylinders no longer do an efficient job of pumping. **Vacuum tests** include testing the engine for **cranking vacuum, idle vacuum,** and vacuum at 2500 RPM.

Cranking Vacuum Test

Measuring the amount of manifold vacuum during cranking is a quick and easy test to determine if the piston rings and valves are properly sealing. (For accurate results, the engine should be warm and the throttle closed.) To perform the cranking vacuum test, take the following steps:

Step 1   Disable the ignition or fuel injection.
Step 2   Connect the vacuum gauge to a manifold vacuum source.
Step 3   Crank the engine while observing the vacuum gauge.

Cranking vacuum should be higher than 2.5 inches of mercury. (Normal cranking vacuum is 3 to 6 inches Hg.) If it is lower than 2.5 inches Hg, then the following could be the cause:

- Too slow a cranking speed
- Worn piston rings
- Leaking valves
- Excessive amounts of air bypassing the throttle plate (This could give a false low vacuum reading. Common sources include a throttle plate partially open or a high-performance camshaft with excessive overlap.)

Idle Vacuum Test

An engine in proper condition should idle with a steady vacuum between 17 and 21 inches Hg. See Figure 20-16.

NOTE: Engine vacuum readings vary with altitude. A reduction of 1 inch Hg per 1,000 feet (300 meters) of altitude should be subtracted from the expected values if testing a vehicle above 1,000 feet (300 meters).

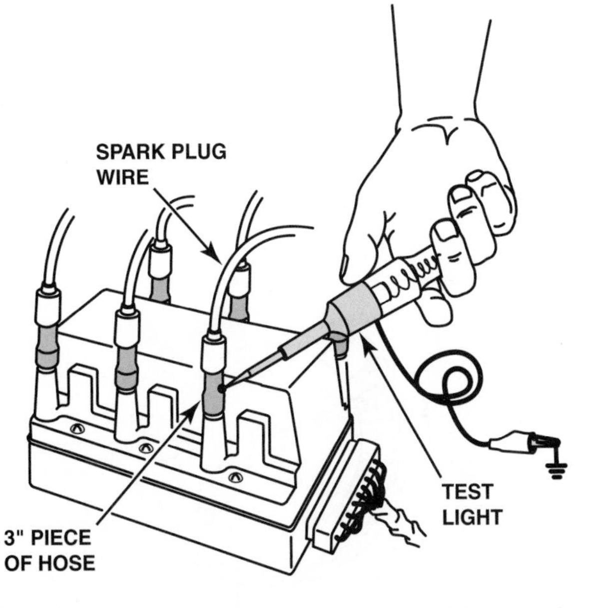

SPARK PLUG WIRE

3" PIECE OF HOSE

TEST LIGHT

FIGURE 20-15   Using a vacuum hose and a test light to ground one cylinder at a time on a distributorless ignition system. This works on all types of ignition systems and provides a method for grounding out one cylinder at a time without fear of damaging any component.

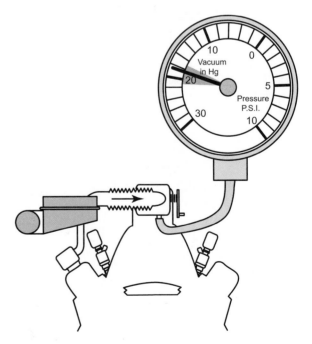

FIGURE 20-16   An engine in good mechanical condition should produce 17 to 21 in. Hg of vacuum at idle at sea level.

Low and Steady Vacuum

If the vacuum is lower than normal, yet the gauge reading is steady, the most common causes include:

- Retarded ignition timing
- Retarded cam timing (check timing chain for excessive slack or timing belt for proper installation)

See Figure 20-17.

Fluctuating Vacuum

If the needle drops, then returns to a normal reading, then drops again, and again returns, this indicates a sticking valve. A common cause of sticking valves is lack of lubrication of the valve stems. See Figures 20-18 through 20-26. If the vacuum gauge fluctuates above and below a center point, burned valves or weak valve springs may be indicated. If the fluctuation is slow and steady, unequal fuel mixture could be the cause.

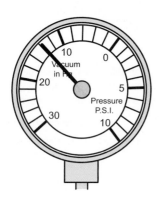

FIGURE 20-17 A steady but low reading could indicate retarded valve or ignition timing.

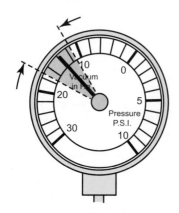

FIGURE 20-18 A gauge reading with the needle fluctuating 3 to 9 in. Hg below normal often indicates a vacuum leak in the intake system.

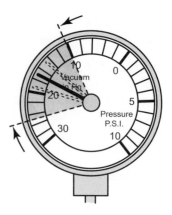

FIGURE 20-19 A leaking head gasket can cause the needle to vibrate as it moves through a range from below to above normal.

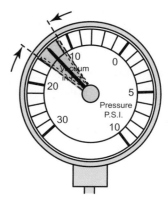

FIGURE 20-20 An oscillating needle 1 or 2 in. Hg below normal could indicate an incorrect air–fuel mixture (either too rich or too lean).

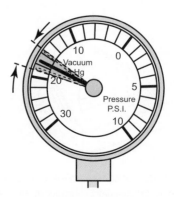

FIGURE 20-21 A rapidly vibrating needle at idle that becomes steady as engine speed is increased indicates worn valve guides.

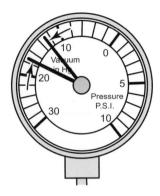

FIGURE 20-22   If the needle drops 1 or 2 in. Hg from the normal reading, one of the engine valves is burned or not seating properly.

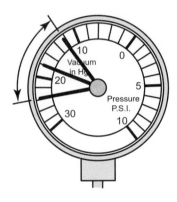

FIGURE 20-23   Weak valve springs will produce a normal reading at idle, but as engine speed increases, the needle will fluctuate rapidly between 12 and 24 in. Hg.

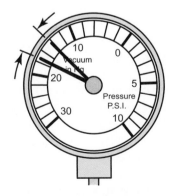

FIGURE 20-24   A steady needle reading that drops 2 or 3 in. Hg when the engine speed is increased slightly above idle indicates that the ignition timing is retarded.

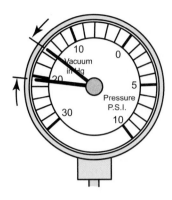

FIGURE 20-25   A steady needle reading that rises 2 or 3 in. Hg when the engine speed is increased slightly above idle indicates that the ignition timing is advanced.

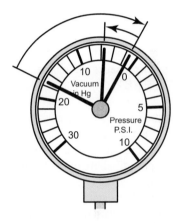

FIGURE 20-26   A needle that drops to near zero when the engine is accelerated rapidly and then rises slightly to a reading below normal indicates an exhaust restriction.

NOTE: A common trick that some technicians use is to squirt some automatic transmission fluid (ATF) down the throttle body or into the air inlet of a warm engine. Often the idle quality improves and normal vacuum gauge readings are restored. The use of ATF does create excessive exhaust smoke for a short time, but it should not harm oxygen sensors or catalytic converters.

EXHAUST RESTRICTION TEST

If the exhaust system is restricted, the engine will be low on power, yet smooth. Common causes of **restricted exhaust** include the following:

- Clogged catalytic converter. Always check the ignition and fuel-injection systems for faults that could cause excessive amounts of unburned fuel to be exhausted. Excessive unburned fuel can overheat the catalytic converter and cause the beads or structure of the converter to fuse together, creating the restriction. A defective fuel delivery system could also cause excessive unburned fuel to be dumped into the converter.

- **Clogged or restricted muffler.** This can cause low power. Often a defective catalytic converter will shed particles that can clog a muffler. Broken internal baffles can also restrict exhaust flow.
- **Damaged or defective piping.** This can reduce the power of any engine. Some exhaust pipe is constructed with double walls, and the inside pipe can collapse and form a restriction that is not visible on the outside of the exhaust pipe.

TESTING BACKPRESSURE WITH A VACUUM GAUGE

A vacuum gauge can be used to measure manifold vacuum at a high idle (2000 to 2500 RPM). If the exhaust system is restricted, pressure increases in the exhaust system. This pressure is called **backpressure.** Manifold vacuum will drop gradually if the engine is kept at a constant speed if the exhaust is restricted.

The reason the vacuum will drop is that all exhaust leaving the engine at the higher engine speed cannot get through the restriction. After a short time (within 1 minute), the exhaust tends to "pile up" above the restriction and eventually remains in the cylinder of the engine at the end of the exhaust stroke. Therefore, at the beginning of the intake stroke, when the piston traveling downward should be lowering the pressure (raising the vacuum) in the intake manifold, the extra exhaust in the cylinder *lowers* the normal vacuum. If the exhaust restriction is severe enough, the vehicle can become undriveable because cylinder filling cannot occur except at idle.

TESTING BACKPRESSURE WITH A PRESSURE GAUGE

Exhaust system backpressure can be measured directly by installing a pressure gauge into an exhaust opening. This can be accomplished in one of the following ways:

- **With an oxygen sensor.** Use a backpressure gauge and adapter or remove the inside of an old, discarded oxygen sensor and thread in an adapter to convert to a vacuum or pressure gauge.

NOTE: An adapter can be easily made by inserting a metal tube or pipe. A short section of brake line works great. The pipe can be brazed to the oxygen sensor housing or it can be glued in with epoxy. An 18-millimeter compression gauge adapter can also be adapted to fit into the oxygen sensor opening. See Figure 20-27.

FIGURE 20-27 A technician-made adapter used to test exhaust system backpressure. The upstream oxygen sensor is removed and the adaptor is threaded into the opening in the exhaust and then a pressure gauge to connected to the hose fitting so that backpressure can be measured.

- **With the exhaust gas recirculation (EGR) valve.** Remove the EGR valve and fabricate a plate to connect to a pressure gauge.
- **With the air-injection reaction (AIR) check valve.** Remove the check valve from the exhaust tubes leading down to the exhaust manifold. Use a rubber cone with a tube inside to seal against the exhaust tube. Connect the tube to a pressure gauge.

At idle, the maximum backpressure should be less than 1.5 PSI (10 kPa), and it should be less than 2.5 PSI (15 kPa) at 2500 RPM.

DIAGNOSING HEAD GASKET FAILURE

Several items can be used to help diagnose a head gasket failure:

- **Exhaust gas analyzer.** With the radiator cap removed, place the probe from the exhaust analyzer above the radiator filler neck. If the HC reading increases, the exhaust (unburned hydrocarbons) is getting into the coolant from the combustion chamber.
- **Chemical test.** A chemical tester using blue liquid is also available. The liquid turns yellow if combustion gases are present in the coolant. See Figure 20-28.
- **Bubbles in the coolant.** Remove the coolant pump belt to prevent pump operation. Remove the radiator cap and start the engine. If bubbles appear in the coolant before it begins to boil, a defective head gasket or cracked cylinder head is indicated.
- **Excessive exhaust steam.** If excessive water or steam is observed coming from the tailpipe, this means that coolant is getting into the combustion chamber from a defective head gasket or a cracked head. If there is leakage

FIGURE 20-28 A tester that uses a blue liquid to check for exhaust gases in the exhaust, which would indicate a head gasket leak problem.

between cylinders, the engine usually misfires and a power balancer test and/or compression test can be used to confirm the problem.

If any of the preceding indicators of head gasket failure occur, remove the cylinder head(s) and check all of the following:

1. Head gasket
2. Sealing surfaces—for warpage
3. Castings—for cracks

NOTE: A leaking thermal vacuum valve can cause symptoms similar to those of a defective head gasket. Most thermal vacuum valves thread into a coolant passage, and they often leak only after they get hot.

DASH WARNING LIGHTS

Most vehicles are equipped with several dash warning lights often called "telltale" or "idiot" lights. These lights are often the only warning a driver receives that there may be engine problems. A summary of typical dash warning lights and their meanings follows.

Oil (Engine) Light

The red oil light indicates that the engine oil pressure is too low (usually lights when oil pressure is 4 to 7 PSI [20 to 50 kPa]). Normal oil pressure should be 10 to 60 PSI (70 to 400 kPa) or 10 PSI per 1000 engine RPM.

When this light comes on, the driver should shut off the engine immediately and check the oil level and condition for

possible dilution with gasoline caused by a fuel system fault. If the oil level is okay, then there is a possible serious engine problem or a possible defective oil pressure sending (sender) unit. The automotive technician should always check the oil pressure using a reliable mechanical oil pressure gauge if low oil pressure is suspected.

NOTE: Some automobile manufacturers combine the dash warning lights for oil pressure and coolant temperature into one light, usually labeled "engine." Therefore, when the engine light comes on, the technician should check for possible coolant temperature and/or oil pressure problems.

Coolant Temperature Light

Most vehicles are equipped with a coolant temperature gauge or dash warning light. The warning light may be labeled "coolant," "hot," or "temperature." If the coolant temperature warning light comes on during driving, this usually indicates that the coolant temperature is above a safe level, or above about 250°F (120°C). Normal coolant temperature should be about 200° to 220°F (90° to 105°C).

If the coolant temperature light comes on during driving, the following steps should be followed to prevent possible engine damage:

1. Turn off the air conditioning and turn on the heater. The heater will help get rid of some of the heat in the cooling system.
2. Raise the engine speed in neutral or park to increase the circulation of coolant through the radiator.
3. If possible, turn the engine off and allow it to cool (this may take over an hour).
4. Do not continue driving with the coolant temperature light on (or the gauge reading in the red warning section or above 260°F) or serious engine damage may result.

NOTE: If the engine does not feel or smell hot, it is possible that the problem is a faulty coolant temperature sensor or gauge.

TECH TIP

MISFIRE DIAGNOSIS

If a misfire goes away with propane added to the air inlet, suspect a lean injector.

COMPRESSION TEST Step-by-Step

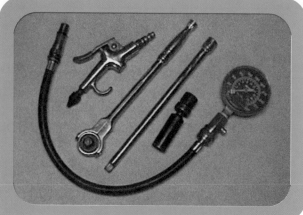

STEP 1 The tools needed to perform a compression test include a compression gauge, an air nozzle, and the socket ratchets and extensions that may be necessary to remove the spark plugs from the engine.

STEP 2 To prevent ignition and fuel-injection operation while the engine is being cranked, remove both the fuel-injection fuse and the ignition fuse.

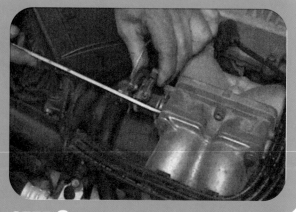

STEP 3 Block open the throttle (and choke, if the engine is equipped with a carburetor). Here a screwdriver is being used to wedge the throttle linkage open.

STEP 4 Before removing the spark plugs, use an air nozzle to blow away any dirt that may be around the spark plug.

STEP 5 Remove all of the spark plugs. Be sure to mark the spark plug wires so that they can be reinstalled onto the correct spark plugs after the compression test.

STEP 6 Select the proper adapter for the compression gauge. The threads on the adapter should match those on the spark plug.

COMPRESSION TEST   continued

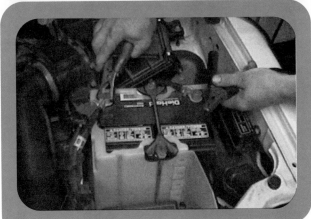

STEP 7 If necessary, connect a battery charger to the battery before starting the compression test. It is important that consistent cranking speed be available for each cylinder being tested.

STEP 8 If the first puff reading is low and the reading gradually increases with each puff, weak or worn piston rings may be indicated.

STEP 9 After the engine has been cranked for four "puffs," stop cranking the engine and observe the compression gauge.

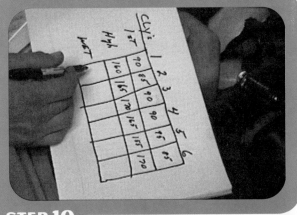

STEP 10 Record the first puff and this final reading for each cylinder. The final readings should all be within 20% of each other.

STEP 11 If a cylinder(s) is lower than most of the others, use an oil can and squirt two squirts of engine oil into the cylinder and repeat the compression test. This is called performing a wet compression test.

STEP 12 If the gauge reading is now much higher than the first test results, then the cause of the low compression is due to worn or defective piston rings. The oil in the cylinder temporarily seals the rings which causes the higher reading.

SUMMARY

1. The first step in diagnosing engine condition is to perform a thorough visual inspection, including a check of oil and coolant levels and condition.
2. Oil leaks can be found by using a white powder or a fluorescent dye and a black light.
3. Many engine-related problems make a characteristic noise.
4. A compression test can be used to test the condition of valves and piston rings.
5. A cylinder leakage test fills the cylinder with compressed air, and the gauge indicates the percentage of leakage.
6. A cylinder balance test indicates whether all cylinders are working okay.
7. Testing engine vacuum is another procedure that can help the service technician determine engine condition.

REVIEW QUESTIONS

1. Describe the visual checks that should be performed on an engine if a mechanical malfunction is suspected.
2. List three simple items that could cause engine noises.
3. Describe how to perform a compression test and how to determine what is wrong with an engine based on a compression test result.
4. Describe the cylinder leakage test.
5. Describe how a vacuum gauge would indicate if the valves were sticking in their guides.
6. Describe the test procedure for determining if the exhaust system is restricted (clogged) using a vacuum gauge.

CHAPTER QUIZ

1. Technician A says that the paper test could detect a burned valve. Technician B says that a grayish white stain on the engine could be a coolant leak. Which technician is correct?
   a. Technician A only
   b. Technician B only
   c. Both Technicians A and B
   d. Neither Technician A nor B
2. Two technicians are discussing oil leaks. Technician A says that an oil leak can be found using a fluorescent dye in the oil with a black light to check for leaks. Technician B says that a white spray powder can be used to locate oil leaks. Which technician is correct?
   a. Technician A only
   b. Technician B only
   c. Both Technicians A and B
   d. Neither Technician A nor B
3. Which of the following is the *least likely* to cause an engine noise?
   a. Carbon on the pistons
   b. Cracked exhaust manifold
   c. Loose accessory drive belt
   d. Vacuum leak
4. Normal vacuum at idle (sea level) should be:
   a. 21 in. Hg. or higher
   b. 10–12 in. Hg.
   c. 14–16 in. Hg.
   d. 17–21 in. Hg.

5. A smoothly operating engine depends on _____.

   a. High compression on most cylinders

   b. Equal compression between cylinders

   c. Cylinder compression levels above 100 PSI (700 kPa) and within 70 PSI (500 kPa) of each other

   d. Compression levels below 100 PSI (700 kPa) on most cylinders

6. A good reading for a cylinder leakage test would be _____.

   a. Within 20% between cylinders

   b. All cylinders below 20% leakage

   c. All cylinders above 20% leakage

   d. All cylinders above 70% leakage and within 7% of each other

7. Technician A says that during a power balance test, the cylinder that causes the biggest RPM drop is the weak cylinder. Technician B says that if one spark plug wire is grounded out and the engine speed does not drop, a weak or dead cylinder is indicated. Which technician is correct?

   a. Technician A only

   b. Technician B only

   c. Both Technicians A and B

   d. Neither Technician A nor B

8. *Cranking* vacuum should be _____.

   a. 2.5 inches Hg or higher

   b. Over 25 inches Hg

   c. 17 to 21 inches Hg

   d. 6 to 16 inches Hg

9. An engine that has retarded valve timing due to a stretched timing chain or a timing belt incorrectly installed will show _____ on a vacuum gauge.

   a. Lower than normal and varying

   b. Higher than normal

   c. Fluctuating

   d. Lower than normal and stready

10. The low oil pressure warning light usually comes on _____.

   a. Whenever an oil change is required

   b. Whenever oil pressure drops dangerously low (4 to 7 PSI)

   c. Whenever the oil filter bypass valve opens

   d. Whenever the oil filter antidrainback valve opens

CHAPTER 21

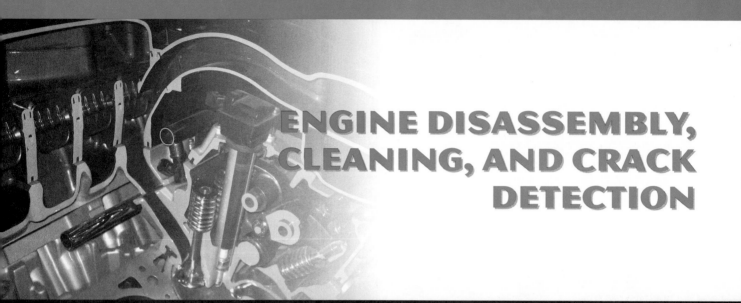

ENGINE DISASSEMBLY, CLEANING, AND CRACK DETECTION

OBJECTIVES

After studying Chapter 21, the reader will be able to:

1. Prepare for ASE Engine Repair (A1) certification test content area "A" (General Engine Diagnosis).
2. Describe how to remove an engine from a vehicle.
3. Discuss how to remove cylinder heads without causing warpage.
4. List the steps necessary to remove a piston from a cylinder.

5. Explain how to remove a valve from a cylinder head.
6. List the types of engine cleaning methods.
7. List the various methods that can be used to check engine parts for cracks.
8. Describe crack-repair procedures.

KEY TERMS

The decision to repair an engine should be based on all the information about the engine that is available to the service technician. In some cases, the engine might not be worth repairing. It is the responsibility of the technician to discuss the advantages and disadvantages of the different repair options with the customer.

ENGINE REMOVAL

The engine exterior and the engine compartment should be cleaned before work is begun. A clean engine is easier to work on and the cleaning not only helps to keep dirt out of the engine but also minimizes accidental damage from slipping tools. The battery ground cable is disconnected to avoid the chance of electrical shorts. An even better procedure is to remove the battery from the vehicle.

NOTE: Most technicians lightly scribe around the hood hinges prior to removal to make aligning the hood easier during reinstallation.

Working on the top of the engine is made easier if the hood is removed. With fender covers in place, the hood is loosened from the hinges. With a person on each side of the hood to support it, the hood is lifted off as the bolts that hold the hood are removed. The hood is usually stored on fender covers placed on the top of the vehicle, where it is least likely to be damaged.

The coolant is drained from the radiator and the engine block to minimize the chance of coolant getting into the cylinders when the head is removed. The exhaust manifold is disconnected.

NOTE: On some engines, it is easier to remove the exhaust pipe from the manifold. On others, it is easier to separate the exhaust manifold from the head and leave the manifold attached to the exhaust pipe.

On *V*-type engines, the intake manifold must be removed before the heads can be taken off. In most cases, a number of wires, accessories, hoses, and tubing must be removed before the manifold head can be removed. If the technician is not familiar with the engine, it is a good practice to put tape on each of the items removed, marked with the proper location of each item so that all items can be easily replaced during engine assembly.

All coolant hoses are removed, and the transmission oil cooler lines are disconnected from the radiator. The radiator mounting bolts are removed, and the radiator is lifted from the engine compartment. This gets the radiator out of the way so that it will not be damaged while you are working on the engine. This is a good time to have the radiator cleaned, while it is out of the chassis.

TECH TIP

A PICTURE IS WORTH A THOUSAND WORDS

Take pictures of the engine being serviced with a digital, or video camera. These pictures will be worth their weight in gold when it comes time to reassemble or reinstall the engine. It is very difficult for anyone to remember the *exact* location of every bracket, wire, and hose. Referring back to the photos of the engine before work was started will help you restore the vehicle to like-new condition.

The air-conditioning compressor can usually be separated from the engine, leaving all air-conditioning hoses securely connected to the compressor and lines. The compressor can be fastened to the side of the engine compartment, where it will not interfere with engine removal. If it is necessary to disconnect the air-conditioning lines, use a refrigerant recovery system to prevent loss of refrigerant to the atmosphere. All open air-conditioning lines should be securely plugged immediately after they are disconnected to keep dirt and moisture out of the system. They should remain plugged until immediately prior to reassembly.

There are two ways to remove the engine:

- The engine can be lifted out of the chassis with the transmission/transaxle attached.
- The transmission/transaxle can be disconnected from the engine and left in the chassis.

Under the vehicle, the drive shaft (propeller shaft) or half shafts are removed and the exhaust pipes disconnected. In some installations, it may be necessary to loosen the steering linkage idler arm to give clearance. The transmission controls, speedometer cable wiring, and clutch linkages are disconnected and tagged.

A sling, either a chain or lift cable, is attached to the engine.

NOTE: For the best results, use the factory-installed lifting hooks that are attached to the engine. These hooks were used in the assembly plant to install the engine and are usually in the best location to remove the engine.

A hoist is attached to the sling and snugged to take most of the weight. This leaves the engine resting on the mounts. (Most engines use three mounts, one on each side and one at the back

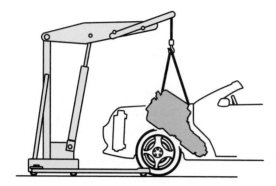

FIGURE 21-1 An engine must be tipped as it is pulled from the chassis.

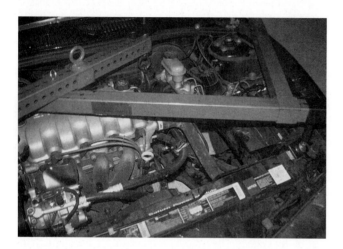

FIGURE 21-2 When removing just the engine from a front-wheel-drive vehicle, the transaxle must be supported. Shown here is a typical fixture that can be used to hold the engine if the transaxle is removed or to hold the transaxle if the engine is removed.

of the transmission or at the front of the engine.) The rear cross-member is removed, and on rear-wheel-drive vehicles, the transmission is lowered. The hoist is tightened to lift the engine. The engine will have to nose up as it is removed, and the front of the engine must come almost straight up as the transmission slides from under the floor pan, as illustrated in Figure 21-1. The engine and transmission are hoisted free of the automobile, swung clear, and lowered onto an open floor area.

NOTE: The engine is lowered and removed from underneath on many front-drive vehicles. See Figures 21-2 and 21-3.

ENGINE DISASSEMBLY

The following disassembly procedure applies primarily to pushrod engines. The procedure will have to be modified somewhat when working on overhead cam engines. Engines should be cold before disassembly to minimize the chance of warpage.

RACK AND PINION STEERING GEAR

CRADLE

FIGURE 21-3 The entire cradle, which included the engine, transaxle, and steering gear, was removed and placed onto a stand. The rear cylinder head has been removed to check for the root cause of a coolant leak.

TECH TIP

USE THE PROPER DISASSEMBLY PROCEDURE

When an engine is operated, it builds up internal stresses. Even cast-iron parts such as cylinder heads can warp if the proper disassembly procedure is not followed. To disassemble any engine without causing harm, just remember these two important points:

- Disassemble parts from an engine only after it has been allowed to sit for several hours. All engines should be disassembled when the engine is at room temperature.
- Always loosen retaining bolts/nuts in the reverse order of assembly. Most vehicle manufacturers recommend tightening bolts from the center of the component such as a cylinder head toward the outside (ends). Therefore, to disassemble the engine, the outside (outer) bolts should be loosened first, followed by bolts closer to the center.

Taking these steps will help reduce the possibility of warpage occurring when the parts are removed.

Remove the manifold hold-down cap screws and nuts, and lift off the manifold.

With the manifold off of the V-type engine, loosen the rocker arms, and remove the pushrods. The usual practice is

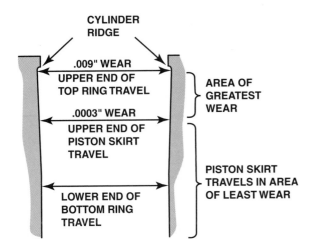

FIGURE 21-4   Most of the cylinder wear is on the top inch just below the cylinder ridge. This wear is due to the heat and combustion pressures that occur when the piston is near the top of the cylinder.

FIGURE 21-5   These connecting rods were numbered from the factory.

to leave the lifters in place when doing only a valve job. Remove the head cap screws and lift the head from the block deck.

CHECKING CYLINDER BORE

At this point, the cylinder taper and out-of-round of the cylinder bore should be checked just below the ridge and just above the piston when it is at the bottom of the stroke, as shown on the cutaway cylinder in Figure 21-4. These measurements will indicate how much cylinder-wall work is required. If the cylinders are worn beyond the specified limits, they will have to be rebored to return them to a satisfactory condition.

REMOVING THE OIL PAN

To remove the oil pan, turn the engine upside down. This will be the first opportunity to see the working parts in the bottom end of the engine. Deposits are again a good indication of the condition of the engine and the care it has had. Heavy sludge indicates infrequent oil changes; hard carbon indicates overheating. The oil pump pickup screen should be checked to see how much plugging exists. The connecting rods and caps and main bearing caps should be checked to make sure that they are *numbered*; if not, they should be numbered with number stamps or a punch so that they can be reassembled in exactly the same position. See Figures 21-5 and 21-6.

FIGURE 21-6   If the rods and mains are not marked, it is wise to use a punch to make identifying marks *before* disassembly of the engine.

REMOVING THE CYLINDER RIDGE

The ridge above the top ring must be removed before the piston and connecting rod assembly is removed. Cylinder wear leaves an upper ridge and removing it is necessary to avoid catching a ring on the ridge and breaking the piston. Failure to remove the ridge is likely to cause the second piston land to break when the engine is run after reassembly with new rings, as pictured in Figure 21-7. The ridge is removed with a cutting tool that is fed into the metal ridge. One type of ridge reamer is shown in Figure 21-8. A guide on the tool prevents accidental cutting below the ridge. The reaming job should be done carefully with frequent checks of the work so that no more material than necessary is removed.

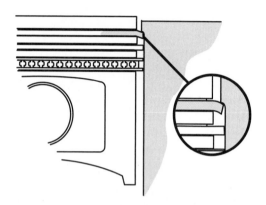

FIGURE 21-7 If the ridge at the top of a cylinder is not removed, the top piston ring could break the second piston ring land when the piston is pushed out of the cylinder during disassembly, or the second piston ring land could break when the engine is first run after reassembly with new rings.

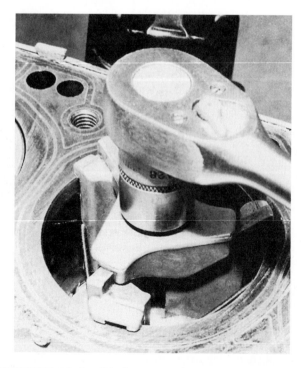

FIGURE 21-8 Ridge being removed with one type of ridge reamer before the piston assemblies are removed from the engine.

REMOVING THE PISTONS

Rotate the engine until the piston that is to be removed is at top dead center (TDC). Remove connecting rod nuts from the rod so that the rod cap with its bearing half can be taken out. Fit the rod bolts with protectors to keep the bolt threads from damaging the crankshaft journals, and remove the piston and rod assemblies.

REMOVING THE HARMONIC BALANCER

The next step in disassembly is to remove the coolant pump and the crankshaft **vibration damper** (also called a **harmonic balancer**). First, the bolt and washer that hold the damper are removed. The damper itself should be removed only with a threaded puller similar to the one in Figure 21-9. If a hook-type puller is used around the edge of the damper, it may pull the damper ring from the hub. If this happens, the damper assembly will have to be replaced with a new assembly.

REMOVING THE TIMING CHAIN AND CAMSHAFT

With the damper assembly off, the timing cover can be removed, exposing the timing gear or timing chain. Examine these parts for excessive wear and looseness. A worn timing chain on a high-mileage engine is shown in Figure 21-10. Bolted cam sprockets can be removed to free the timing chain. If camshaft thrust plate retaining screws are used, it will be necessary to remove them.

FIGURE 21-9 Puller being used to pull the vibration damper from the crankshaft.

The camshaft can be removed at this time, or it can be removed after the crankshaft is out. It must be carefully eased from the engine to avoid damaging the cam bearings or cam lobes. This is done most easily with the front of the engine pointing up. Bearing surfaces are soft and scratch easily, and the cam lobes are hard and chip easily.

REMOVING THE MAIN BEARING AND CRANKSHAFT

The main bearing caps should be checked for position markings before they are removed. They have been machined in place and will not fit perfectly in any other location. See Figure 21-11. After marking, they can be removed to free the crankshaft. When the crankshaft is removed, the main bearing caps and bearings are reinstalled on the block to reduce the chance of damage to the caps.

REMOVE AND DISASSEMBLE THE CYLINDER HEAD

Remove the cylinder head retaining bolts by loosening them from the outside toward the center to help prevent the possibility of warpage of the head. Remove the cylinder head(s) and check the head gasket for signs of failure. See Figure 21-12.

After the heads are removed and placed on the bench, the valves are removed. A C-type valve spring compressor, similar to the one in Figure 21-13, is used to free the **valve locks** or **keepers.** The valve spring compressor is air powered in production shops where valve jobs are done on a

FIGURE 21-10   Worn timing chain on a high-mileage engine. Notice that the timing chain could "jump a tooth" at the bottom of the smaller crankshaft gear where the chain is in contact with fewer teeth. Notice also that the technician placed all of the bolts back in the block after removal of the part. This procedure helps protect against lost or damaged bolts and nuts.

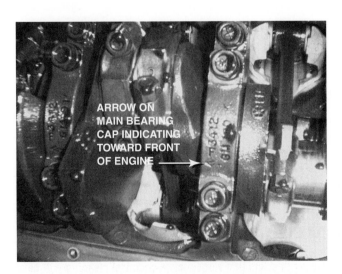

FIGURE 21-11   Most engines such as this Chevrolet V-8 with 4-bolt main bearing caps have arrows marked on the bearing caps which should point to the front of the engine.

FIGURE 21-12   This defective cylinder head gasket was discovered as soon as the head was removed. This cylinder head will require machining or replacement.

FIGURE 21-13 A valve spring compressor being used to remove the valve keepers (locks).

FIGURE 21-14 After removing this intake valve, it became obvious why this engine had been running so poorly.

FIGURE 21-15 A torch is used to heat gallery plugs. Paraffin wax is then applied and allowed to flow around the threads. This procedure results in easier removal of the plugs and other threaded fasteners that cannot otherwise be loosened.

TECH TIP

THE WAX TRICK

Before the engine block can be thoroughly cleaned, all oil gallery plugs must be removed. A popular trick of the trade for plug removal involves heating the plug (not the surrounding metal) with an oxyacetylene torch. The heat tends to expand the plug and make it tighter in the block. Do not overheat.

As the plug is cooling, touch the plug with paraffin wax (beeswax or candle wax may be used). See Figure 21-15. The wax will be drawn down around the threads of the plug by capillary attraction as the plug cools and contracts. After being allowed to cool, the plug is easily removed.

MECHANICAL CLEANING

Heavy deposits that remain after chemical cleaning will have to be removed by mechanical cleaning. Mechanical cleaning involves scraping, brushing, and abrasive blasting. It should, therefore, be done very carefully on soft metals.

regular basis. Mechanical valve spring compressors are used where valve work is done only occasionally. After the valve lock is removed, the compressor is released to free the valve retainer and spring. The spring assemblies are lifted from the head together with any spacers used under them. The parts should be removed in order to aid in diagnosing the exact cause of any malfunction that shows up. The valve tip edge and lock area should be lightly filed to remove any burrs *before* sliding the valve from the head. Burrs will scratch the valve guide.

When all valves have been removed following this procedure for each one, the valve springs, retainers, locks, guides, and seats should be given another visual examination. See Figure 21-14.

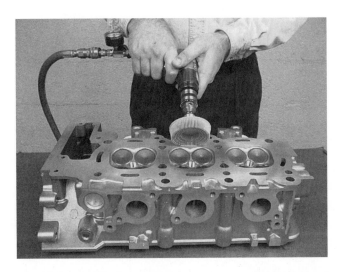

FIGURE 21-16   An air-powered grinder attached to a bristle pad being used to clean the gasket surface of a cylinder head. The color of the bristles indicates the grit number. The white is the finest and should be used on aluminum. Yellow is coarse and can be used on aluminum. Green is designed for cast-iron parts only. This type of cleaning pad should not be used on the engine block where the grit could get into the engine oil and cause harm when the engine is started and run after the repair.

The scraper most frequently used is a **putty knife** or a plastic card. The broad blade of the putty knife helps avoid scratching the surface as it is used to clean the parts. A rotary disc can be used on disassembled parts that will be thoroughly cleaned to remove the fine abrasive that is part of the plastic bristles. See Figure 21-16.

CAUTION: Do not use a steel wire brush on aluminum parts! Steel is harder than aluminum and will remove some of the aluminum from the surface during cleaning.

CHEMICAL CLEANERS

Cleaning chemicals applied to engine parts will mix with and dissolve deposits. The chemicals loosen the deposits so that they can be brushed or rinsed from the surface. A deposit is said to be **soluble** when it can be dissolved with a chemical or solvent.

Most chemical cleaners used for cleaning carbon-type deposits are strong soaps called **caustic materials.** A **pH** value, measured on a scale from 1 to 14, indicates the amount of chemical activity in the soap. The term *pH* is from the French *pouvoir hydrogine*, meaning "hydrogen power." Pure water is neutral; on the pH scale, water is pH 7. Caustic materials have pH numbers from 8 through 14. The higher the number, the stronger the caustic action will be. **Acid materials** have pH

numbers from 1 through 6. The lower the number, the stronger the acid action will be. Caustic materials and acid materials neutralize each other. This is what happens when baking soda (a caustic) is used to clean the outside of the battery (an acid surface). The caustic baking soda neutralizes any sulfuric acid that has been spilled or splashed on the outside of the battery.

CAUTION: Whenever working with chemicals, you must use eye protection.

SOLVENT-BASED CLEANING

Chemical cleaning can involve a spray washer or a soak in a cold or hot tank. The cleaning solution is usually solvent based, with a medium pH rating of between 10 and 12. Most chemical solutions also contain silicates to protect the metal (aluminum) against corrosion.

Strong caustics do an excellent job on cast-iron items but are often too corrosive for aluminum parts. Aluminum cleaners include mineral spirit solvents as well as alkaline detergents.

CAUTION: When cleaning aluminum cylinder heads, blocks, or other engine components, make sure that the chemicals used are "aluminum safe." Many chemicals that are not aluminum safe may turn the aluminum metal black. Try to explain that to a customer!

WATER-BASED CHEMICAL CLEANING

Because of environmental concerns, most chemical cleaning is now performed using water-based solutions (called **aqueous-based**). Most aqueous-based chemicals are silicate based and are mixed with water. Aqueous-based solutions can be sprayed on or used in a tank for soaking parts. Aluminum heads and blocks usually require overnight soaking in a solution kept at about 190°F (90°C). For best results, the cleaning solution should be agitated.

SPRAY WASHING

A spray washer directs streams of liquid through numerous high-pressure nozzles to dislodge dirt and grime on an engine surface. The force of the liquid hitting the surface, combined with the chemical action of the cleaning solution, produces a clean surface. Spray washing is typically performed in an enclosed washer (like a dishwasher), where parts are rotated on a washer turntable. See Figure 21-17.

Spray washing is faster than soaking. A typical washer cycle is less than 30 minutes per load, compared to eight or

FIGURE 21-17   A pressure jet washer is similar to a large industrial-sized dishwasher. The part(s) is then rinsed with water to remove chemicals or debris that may remain on the part while it is still in the tank.

more hours for soaking. Most spray washers use an aqueous-based cleaning solution heated to 160° to 180°F (70° to 80°C) with foam suppressants. High-volume remanufacturers use industrial dishwashing machines to clean the disassembled engines' component parts.

STEAM CLEANING

Steam cleaners are a special class of sprayers. Steam vapor is mixed with high-pressure water and sprayed on the parts. The heat of the steam and the propellant force of the high-pressure water combine to do the cleaning. Steam cleaning must be used with extreme care. Usually, a caustic cleaner is added to the steam and water to aid in the cleaning. This mixture is so active that it will damage and even remove paint, so painted surfaces must be protected from the spray. Engines are often steam cleaned before they are removed from the chassis.

THERMAL CLEANING

Thermal cleaning uses heat to vaporize and char dirt into a dry, powdery ash. Thermal cleaning is best suited for cleaning cast iron, where temperatures as high as 800°F (425°C) are used, whereas aluminum should not be heated to over 600°F (315°C).

The major advantages of thermal cleaning include the following:

1. This process cleans the inside as well as the outside of the casting or part.
2. The waste generated is nonhazardous and is easy to dispose of. However, the heat in the oven usually discolors the metal, leaving it looking dull.

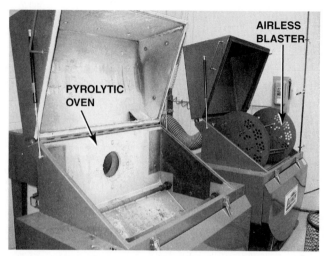

(a)

(b)

FIGURE 21-18   (a) A pyrolytic (high temperature) oven cleans by baking the engine parts. After the parts have been cleaned, they are then placed into an airless blaster. This unit uses a paddle to scoop stainless steel shot from a reservoir and forces it against the engine part. The parts must be free of grease and oil to function correctly. (b) Stainless steel shot used in an airless blaster.

A **pyrolytic** (high-temperature) oven cleans engine parts by decomposing dirt, grease, and gaskets with heat in a manner similar to that of a self-cleaning oven. This method of engine part cleaning is becoming the most popular because there is no hazardous waste associated with it. Labor costs are also reduced because the operator does not need to be present during the actual cleaning operation. See Figure 21-18.

COLD TANK CLEANING

The cold soak tank is used to remove grease and carbon. The disassembled parts are placed in the tank so that they are *completely* covered with the chemical cleaning solution. After a soaking period, the parts are removed and rinsed until the milky appearance of the emulsion is gone. The parts are then dried with compressed air. The clean, dry parts are then usually given a very light coating of clean oil to prevent rusting. Carburetor cleaner, purchased with a basket in a bucket, is one of the most common types of cold soak agents in the automotive shop. Usually, there will be a layer of water over the chemical to prevent evaporation of the chemical. This water layer is called a **hydroseal.**

Parts washers are often used in place of soaking tanks. This equipment can move parts back and forth through the cleaning solution or pumps the cleaning solution over the parts. This movement, called **agitation,** keeps fresh cleaning solution moving past the soil to help it loosen. The parts washer is usually equipped with a safety cover held open by a low-temperature **fusible link.** If a fire occurs, the fusible link will melt and the cover will drop closed to snuff the fire out.

HOT TANK CLEANING

The hot soak tank is used for cleaning heavy organic deposits and rust from iron and steel parts. The caustic cleaning solution used in the hot soak tank is heated to near 200°F (93°C) for rapid cleaning action. The solution must be inhibited when aluminum is to be cleaned. After the deposits have been loosened, the parts are removed from the tank and rinsed with hot water or steam cleaned, which dries them rapidly. They must then be given a light coating of oil to prevent rusting.

NOTE: Fogging oil from a spray can does an excellent job of coating metal parts to keep them from rusting.

VAPOR CLEANING

Vapor cleaning is popular in some automotive service shops. The parts to be cleaned are suspended in hot vapors above a perchloroethylene solution. The vapors of the solution loosen the soil from the metal so that it can be blown, wiped, or rinsed from the surface.

ULTRASONIC CLEANING

Ultrasonic cleaning is used to clean small parts that must be absolutely clean; for example, hydraulic lifters and diesel injectors. The disassembled parts are placed in a tank of cleaning solution which is then vibrated at ultrasonic speeds to loosen all the soil from the parts. The soil goes into the solution or falls to the bottom of the tank.

VIBRATORY CLEANING

The vibratory method of cleaning is best suited for small parts. Parts are loaded into a vibrating bin with small, odd-shaped ceramic or steel pieces, called media, with a cleaning solution of mineral spirits or water-based detergents that usually contain a lubricant additive to help the media pieces slide around more freely. The movement of the vibrating solution and the scrubbing action of the media do an excellent job of cleaning metal.

BLASTERS

Cleaning cast-iron or aluminum engine parts with solvents or heat usually requires another operation to achieve a uniform surface finish. Blasting the parts with steel, cast-iron, aluminum, or stainless-steel shot or glass beads is a simple way to achieve a matte or satin surface finish on the engine parts. To keep the shot or beads from sticking to the parts, they must be dry, without a trace of oil or grease, prior to blasting. This means that blasting is the second cleaning method, after the part has been precleaned in a tank, spray washer, or oven. Some blasting is done automatically in an airless shot-blasting machine. Another method is to hard-blast parts in a sealed cabinet. See Figure 21-19.

CAUTION: Glass beads often remain in internal passages of engine parts, where they can come loose and travel through the cylinders when the engine is started. Among other places, these small, but destructive, beads can easily be trapped under the oil baffles of rocker covers and in oil pans and piston-ring grooves. To help prevent the glass beads from sticking, make sure that the parts being cleaned are free of grease and dirt and completely *dry*.

FIGURE 21-19 Small engine parts can be blasted clean in a sealed cabinet.

VISUAL INSPECTION

After the parts have been thoroughly cleaned, they should be re-examined for defects. A magnifying glass is helpful in finding defects. Critical parts of a performance engine should be checked for cracks using specialized magnetic or penetration inspection equipment. Internal parts such as pistons, connecting rods, and crankshafts that have cracks should be replaced. Cracks in the block and heads, however, can often be repaired, and these repair procedures are described in a later section.

MAGNETIC CRACK INSPECTION

Checking for cracks using a magnetic field is commonly called Magnafluxing, a brand name. Cracks in engine blocks, cylinder heads, crankshafts, and other engine components are sometimes difficult to find during a normal visual inspection, which is why all remanufacturers and most engine builders use a crack detection procedure on all critical engine parts.

Magnetic flux testing is the method most often used on steel and iron components. A metal engine part (such as a cast-iron cylinder head) is connected to a large electromagnet. Magnetic lines of force are easily conducted through the iron part and concentrate on the edges of a crack. A fine iron powder is then applied to the part being tested, and the powder will be attracted to the strong magnetic concentration around the crack. See Figures 21-20 through 21-22.

DYE-PENETRANT TESTING

Dye-penetrant testing is usually used on pistons and other parts constructed of aluminum or other nonmagnetic material. A dark-red penetrating chemical is first sprayed on the component being tested. After cleaning, a white powder is sprayed over the

test area. If a crack is present, the red dye will stain the white powder. Even though this method will also work on iron and steel (magnetic) parts, it is usually used only on nonmagnetic parts because magnetic methods do not work on these parts.

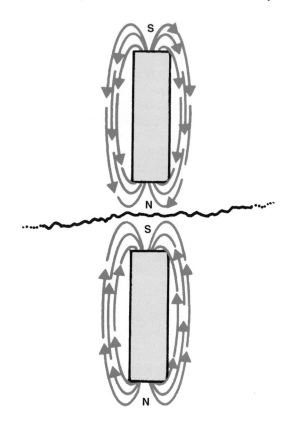

FIGURE 21-21 If the lines of force are interrupted by a break (crack) in the casting, two magnetic fields are created and the powder will lodge in the crack.

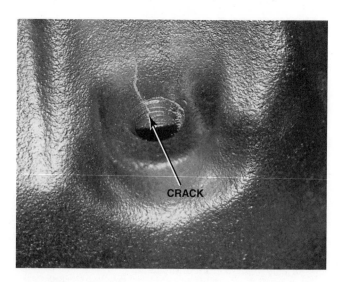

FIGURE 21-22 This crack in a vintage Ford 289, V-8 block was likely caused by the technician using excessive force trying to remove the plug from the block. The technician should have used heat and wax, not only to make the job easier, but also to prevent damaging the block.

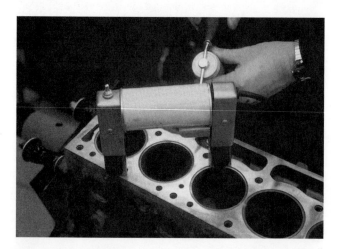

FIGURE 21-20 The top deck surface of a block being tested using magnetic crack inspection equipment.

FLUORESCENT-PENETRANT TESTING

To be seen, fluorescent penetrant requires a black light. It can be used on iron, steel, or aluminum parts. Cracks show up as bright lines when viewed with a black light. The method is commonly called **Zyglo,** a trademark of the Magnaflux Corporation.

PRESSURE TESTING

Cylinder heads and blocks are often pressure tested with air and checked for leaks. All coolant passages are blocked with rubber plugs or gaskets, and compressed air is applied to the water jacket(s). The head or block is then lowered into water, where air bubbles indicate a leak. For more accurate results, the water should be heated because the hot water expands the casting by about the same amount as an operating engine would. An alternative method involves running heated water with a dye through the cylinder or block. Any leaks revealed by the dyed water indicate a crack. See Figures 21-23 and 21-24.

CRACK REPAIR

Cracks in the engine block can cause coolant to flow into the oil or oil into the coolant. A cracked block can also cause coolant to leak externally from a crack that goes through to a coolant passage. Cracks in the head will allow coolant to leak into the engine, or they will allow combustion gases to leak into the coolant. Cracks across the valve seat cause hot spots on the valve, which will burn the valve face. A head with a crack will either have to be replaced or the crack will have to be repaired. Two common methods of crack repair are welding and plugging.

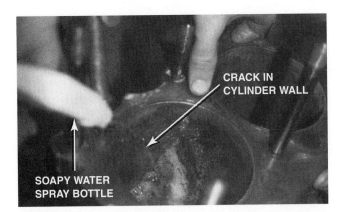

FIGURE 21-23   To make sure that the mark observed in the cylinder wall was a crack, compressed air was forced into the water jacket while soapy water was sprayed on the cylinder wall. Bubbles confirmed that the mark was indeed a crack.

NOTE: A hole can be drilled at each end of the crack to keep it from extending further, a step sometimes called **stop drilling.** Cracks that do not cross oil passages, bolt holes, or seal surfaces can sometimes be left alone if stopped.

CRACK-WELDING CAST IRON

It takes a great deal of skill to weld cast iron. The cast iron does not puddle or flow as steel does when it is heated. Heavy cast parts, such as the head and block, conduct heat away from the weld so fast that it is difficult to get the part hot enough to melt the iron for welding. When it does melt, a crack will often develop next to the edge of the weld bead. Welding can be done satisfactorily when the entire cast part is heated red hot.

A new technique involves flame welding using a special torch. See Figure 21-25.

FIGURE 21-24   A cylinder head is under water and being pressure tested using compressed air. Note that the air bubbles indicate a crack.

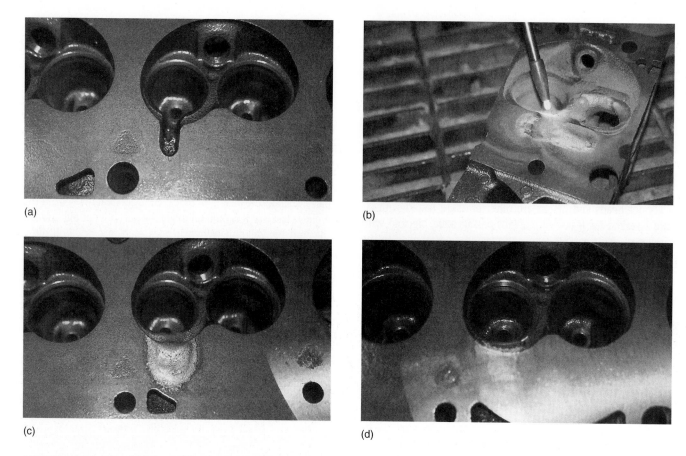

FIGURE 21-25 (a) Before welding, the crack is ground out using a carbide grinder. (b) Here the technician is practicing using the special cast-iron welding torch before welding the cracked cylinder head. (c) The finished welded crack before final machining. (d) The finished cylinder head after the crack has been repaired using welding.

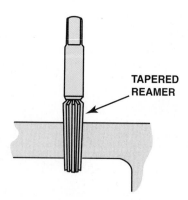

FIGURE 21-26 Reaming a hole for a tapered plug.

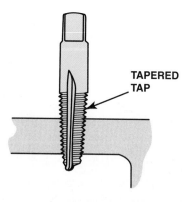

FIGURE 21-27 Tapping a tapered hole for a plug.

CRACK-WELDING ALUMINUM

Cracks in aluminum can be welded using a Heli-arc® or similar welder that is specially designed to weld aluminum. The crack should be cut or burned out before welding begins. The old valve-seat insert should be removed if the crack is in or near the combustion chamber.

CRACK PLUGGING

In the process of crack plugging, a crack is closed using interlocking tapered plugs. This procedure can be performed to repair cracks in both aluminum and cast-iron engine components. The ends of the crack are center punched and drilled with the proper size of tap drill for the plugs. The hole is reamed with a tapered reamer (Figure 21-26) and is then tapped to give full threads (Figure 21-27). The plug is coated with sealer; then

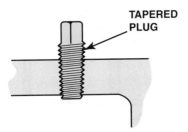

FIGURE 21-28   Screwing a tapered plug in the hole.

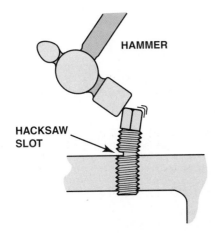

FIGURE 21-29   Cutting the plug with a hacksaw.

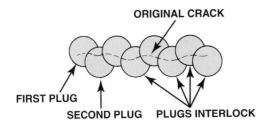

FIGURE 21-30   Interlocking plugs.

(a)

(b)

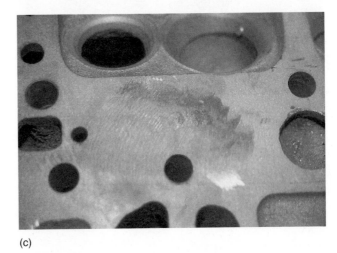

(c)

FIGURE 21-31   (a) A hole is drilled and tapped for the plugs. (b) The plugs are installed. (c) After final machining, the cylinder head can be returned to useful service.

it is tightened into the hole (Figure 21-28), sawed about one-fourth of the way through, and broken off. The saw slot controls the breaking point (Figure 21-29). If the plug should break below the surface, it will have to be drilled out and a new plug installed. The plug should go to the full depth or thickness of the cast metal. After the first plug is installed on each end, a new hole is drilled with the tap drill so that it cuts into the edge of the first plug. This new hole is reamed and tapped, and a plug is inserted as before. The plug should fit about one-fourth of the way into the first plug to lock it into place (Figure 21-30). Interlocking plugs are placed along the entire crack, alternating slightly from side to side. The exposed ends of the plugs are peened over with a hammer to help secure them in place. The surface of the plugs is then ground or filed down nearly to the gasket surface. In the combustion chamber and at the ports,

the plugs are ground down to the original surface using a hand grinder. The gasket surface of the head must be resurfaced after the crack has been repaired. See Figure 21-31 for an example of a cylinder head repair using plugs.

ENGINE REMOVAL Step-by-Step

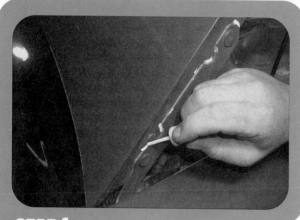

STEP 1 Before beginning work on removing the engine, mark and remove the hood and place it in a safe location.

STEP 2 For safety, remove the negative battery cable to avoid any possible electrical problems from occurring.

STEP 3 Drain the coolant and dispose of properly.

STEP 4 Disconnect all cooling system and heater hoses and remove the radiator.

STEP 5 Remove the accessory drive belt(s) and set the generator (alternator), power steering pump, and air-conditioning compressor aside.

STEP 6 Remove the air intake system including the air filter housing as needed.

ENGINE REMOVAL continued

STEP 7 Remove the electrical connector from all sensors and label.

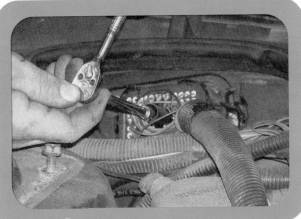

STEP 8 Disconnect the engine wiring harness connector at the bulkhead.

STEP 9 Safely hoist the vehicle and disconnect the exhaust system from the exhaust manifolds.

STEP 10 Mark and then remove the fasteners connecting the flex plate to the torque converter.

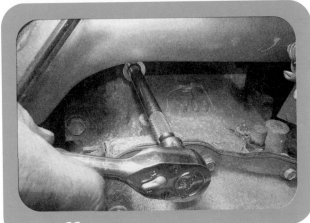

STEP 11 Lower the vehicle and remove the engine mount bolts and transaxle bell housing fasteners.

STEP 12 Secure the lifting chain to the engine hooks and carefully remove the engine from the vehicle.

SUMMARY

1. The factory-installed lifting hooks should be used when hoisting an engine.
2. Engine component parts should only be removed when the engine is cold. Also, the torque table should always be followed backward, starting with the highest-number head bolt and working toward the lowest-number. This procedure helps prevent warpage.
3. The ridge at the top of the cylinder should be removed before removing the piston(s) from the cylinder.
4. The connecting rod and main bearing caps should be marked before removing to ensure that they can be reinstalled in the exact same location when the engine is reassembled.
5. The tip of the valve stem should be filed before removing valves from the cylinder head to help prevent damage to the valve guide.
6. Mechanical cleaning with scrapers or wire brushes is used to remove deposits.
7. Steel wire brushes should never be used to clean aluminum parts.
8. Most chemical cleaners are strong soaps called caustic materials.
9. Always use aluminum-safe chemicals when cleaning aluminum parts or components.
10. Thermal cleaning is done in a pyrolytic oven in temperatures as high as 800°F (425°C) to turn grease and dirt into harmless ash deposits.
11. Blasters use metal shot or glass beads to clean parts. All of the metal shot or glass beads must be cleaned from the part so as not to cause engine problems.
12. All parts should be checked for cracks using magnetic, dye-penetrant, fluorescent-penetrant, or pressure testing methods.
13. Cracks can be repaired by welding or by plugging.

REVIEW QUESTIONS

1. When should the factory-installed lifting hooks be used?
2. State two reasons for the removal of the ridge at the top of the cylinder.
3. Explain why the burrs must be removed from valves before removing the valves from the cylinder head.
4. Describe five methods that could be used to clean engines or engine parts.
5. Explain magnetic crack inspection, dye-penetrant testing, and fluorescent-penetrant testing methods and where each can be used.

CHAPTER QUIZ

1. Technician A says that the intake and exhaust manifolds have to be removed before removing the engine from the vehicle. Technician B says that it is often easier to remove the engine from underneath rather than remove the engine from the top of the vehicle. Which technician is correct?
   a. Technician A only
   b. Technician B only
   c. Both Technicians A and B
   d. Neither Technician A nor B

2. Lifting hooks are often installed at the factory because _____.
   a. They make removing the engine easier for the technician
   b. They are used to install the engine at the factory
   c. They are part of the engine and should not be removed
   d. They make servicing the top of the engine easier for the technician

3. The ridge at the top of the cylinder _____.
   a. Is caused by wear at the top of the cylinder by the rings
   b. Represents a failure of the top piston ring to correctly seal against the cylinder wall
   c. Should not be removed before removing pistons except when reboring the cylinders
   d. Means that a crankshaft with an incorrect stroke was installed in the engine

4. Before the timing chain can be inspected and removed, the following component(s) must be removed:
   a. Rocker cover (valve cover)
   b. Vibration damper
   c. Cylinder head(s)
   d. Intake manifold (V-type engines only)

5. Before the valves are removed from the cylinder head, what operations need to be completed?
   a. Remove valve locks (keepers)
   b. Remove cylinder head(s) from the engine
   c. Remove burrs from the stem of the valve(s)
   d. All of the above

6. Cleaning chemicals are usually either a caustic material or an acid material. Which of the following statements is true?
   a. Both caustics and acids have a pH of 7 if rated according to distilled water.
   b. An acid is lower than 7 and a caustic is higher than 7 on the pH scale.
   c. An acid is higher than 7 and a caustic is lower than 7 on the pH scale.
   d. Pure water is a 1 and a strong acid is a 14 on the pH scale.

7. Many cleaning methods involve chemicals that are hazardous to use and expensive to dispose of after use. The least hazardous method is generally considered to be the _____.
   a. Pyrolytic oven
   b. Hot vapor tank
   c. Hot soak tank
   d. Cold soak tank

8. Magnetic crack inspection _____.
   a. Uses a red dye to detect cracks in aluminum
   b. Uses a black light to detect cracks in iron parts
   c. Uses a fine iron powder to detect cracks in iron parts
   d. Uses a magnet to remove cracks from iron parts

9. Technician A says that engine parts should be cleaned before a thorough test can be done to detect cracks. Technician B says that pressure testing can be used to find cracks in blocks or cylinder heads. Which technician is correct?
   a. Technician A only
   b. Technician B only
   c. Both Technicians A and B
   d. Neither Technician A nor B

10. Plugging can be used to repair cracks _____.
    a. In cast-iron cylinder heads
    b. In aluminum cylinder heads
    c. In both cast-iron and aluminum cylinder heads
    d. Only in cast-iron blocks

CHAPTER 22

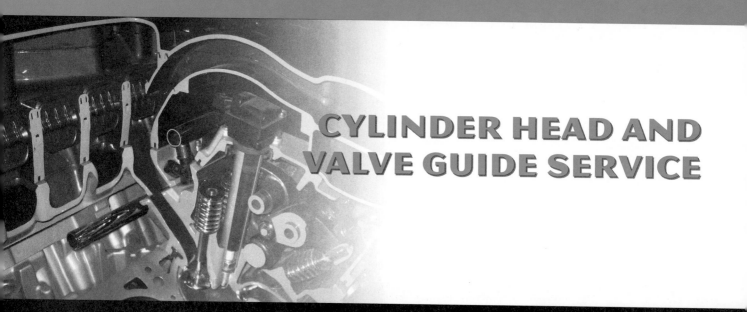

CYLINDER HEAD AND VALVE GUIDE SERVICE

OBJECTIVES

After studying Chapter 22, the reader will be able to:

1. Prepare for Engine Repair (A1) ASE certification test content area "B" (Cylinder Head and Valve Train Diagnosis and Repair).

2. Identify combustion chamber types.

3. Explain the operation of a stratified charge combustion chamber.

4. List the steps necessary to recondition a cylinder head.

5. Describe how to inspect and measure valve guides.

6. Discuss valve guide repair options.

KEY TERMS

Cylinder heads are the most frequently serviced engine components. The highest temperatures and pressures in the entire engine are located in the combustion chamber. Its valves must open and close thousands of times each time the engine is operated.

CYLINDER HEADS

Cylinder heads support the valves and valve train as well as passages for the flow of intake and exhaust gases. In an overhead camshaft design engine, the cylinder head also supports all of the valve train components including the camshaft, rocker arms, or followers, as well as the intake and exhaust valves and valve guides. See Figure 22-1.

Most cylinder designs incorporate the following design factors to achieve fast burning of the air–fuel mixture and to reduce exhaust emissions. These factors include:

- **Squish area**—This is an area of the combustion chamber where the piston nearly contacts the cylinder. When the piston is moving upward toward the cylinder head, the air–fuel mixture is rapidly pushed out of the squish area, causing turbulence. Turbulence helps mix the air and fuel, ensuring a more uniform and complete combustion. See Figure 22-2.
- **Quench area**—The squish area can also be the quench area where the air–fuel mixture is cooled by the cylinder head, thereby helping to reduce detonation caused by the auto ignition of the end gases in the combustion chamber.

- **Spark plug placement**—The best spark plug placement is the center of the combustion chamber. See Figure 22-3. The closer to the center, the shorter the flames travel to all edges of the combustion chamber, which also reduces abnormal combustion (ping or spark knock). While it is best to have the spark plug in the center, some combustion chamber designs do not allow this due to valve size, combustion chamber design, and valve placement. See Figure 22-4 for an example of a two spark plug combustion chamber used in a hemispherical (Hemi) cylinder head design.
- **Surface-to-volume ratio**—The surface-to-volume ratio is an important design consideration for combustion chambers. A typical surface-to-volume ratio is 7.5:1, which means the surface area of the combustion chamber divided by the volume is 7.5. If the ratio is too high, there is a lot of surface area where fuel can adhere, causing an increase in unburned hydrocarbon (HC) emissions. The cool cylinder head causes some of the air–fuel mixture to condense, causing a layer of liquid fuel on the surfaces of the combustion chamber. This layer of

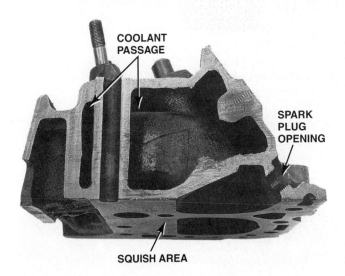

FIGURE 22-2 A wedge-shaped combustion chamber showing the squish area where the air–fuel mixture is squeezed, causing turbulence that pushes the mixture toward the spark plug.

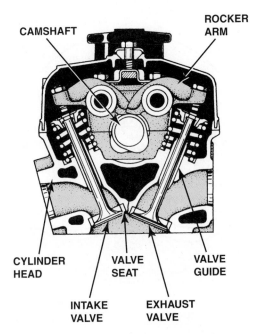

FIGURE 22-1 The seats and guides for the valves are in the cylinder head as well as the camshaft and the entire valve train if it is an overhead camshaft design.

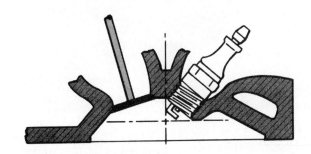

FIGURE 22-3 Locating the spark plug in the center of the combustion chamber reduces the distance the flame front must travel.

condensed fuel will not burn because it is not surrounded by oxygen needed for combustion. As a result, this unburned fuel is pushed out of the cylinder by the piston on the exhaust stroke.

FREQUENTLY ASKED QUESTION

WHAT IS CARBON KNOCK?

Carbon knock was a common occurrence in older engines that were equipped with carburetors and had high compression ratios. As carburetors aged, the mixture would tend to be richer-than-normal due to a leaking needle and seat, as well as a fuel-saturated float. This richer mixture would often cause carbon deposits to form in the combustion chamber. During light load conditions when the spark advance was greatest, a spark knock would occur, caused by a combination of the high compression ratio and the carbon deposits. This knocking was often very loud and sounded like a rod bearing noise. Many engines were disassembled in the belief that the cause of the knocking sound was a bearing, only to discover that the bearings were OK.

Carbon knock can still occur in newer engines, especially if there is a fault in the fuel system that would allow a much richer-than-normal air–fuel mixture, causing excessive carbon deposits to form in the combustion chamber. Often a decarbonization using chemicals will correct the knocking.

FIGURE 22-4 The combustion chamber of the 5.7 liter Chrysler Hemi cylinder head showing the two spark plugs used to ensure rapid burn for best power and economy with the lowest possible exhaust emissions.

- **Valve shrouding**—Shrouding means that the valve is kept close to the walls of the combustion chamber to help increase mixture turbulence. See Figure 22-5. While shrouding the intake valve can help swirl and increase turbulence, it also reduces the flow into the engine at higher engine speeds.

- **Cross flow valve placement**—Valve placement in the cylinder head is an important factor in breather efficiency. By placing the intake and the exhaust valves on the opposite sides of the combustion chamber, an easy path from the intake port through the combustion chamber to the exhaust port is provided. This is called a **cross flow head** design. See Figure 22-6.

TECH TIP

UNSHROUD THE INTAKE VALVE FOR MORE POWER

If an engine is being rebuilt for high performance, most experts recommend that the shrouded section around the intake valve be removed, thereby increasing the airflow and, therefore, the power that the engine can achieve, especially at higher engine speeds. This process is often called **unshrouding**.

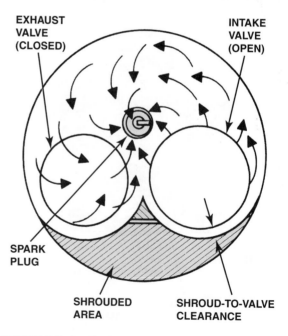

FIGURE 22-5 The shrouded area around the intake valve causes the intake mixture to swirl as it enters the combustion chamber.

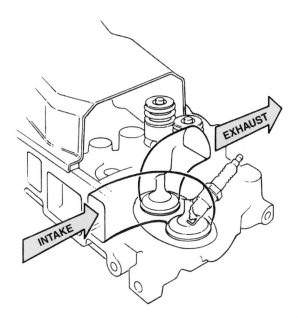

FIGURE 22-6 A typical cross flow cylinder head design where the flow into and out of the combustion chamber is from opposite sides of the cylinder head.

Combustion chambers can be cast or machined depending on the design and are referred to as polyspherical, hemi-wedge, kidney-shaped, or pentroof designs, depending on the shape.

MULTIPLE-VALVE COMBUSTION CHAMBER

The power that any engine produces is directly related to the amount of air–fuel mixture that is ignited in the cylinder. Increasing cylinder displacement is a common method of increasing engine power. Turbocharging and supercharging also increase engine power, but these increase engine cost as well.

Adding more than two valves per cylinder permits more gas to flow into and out of the engine with greater velocity without excessive valve duration. **Valve duration** is the number of degrees by which the crankshaft rotates when the valve is off the valve seat. Increased valve duration increases valve overlap. The valve overlap occurs when both valves are off their seats at the end of the exhaust stroke and at the beginning of the intake stroke. At lower engine speeds, the gases can move back and forth between the open valves. Therefore, the greater valve duration hurts low engine speed performance and driveability, but it allows for more air–fuel mixture to enter the engine for better high-speed power.

The maximum amount of gas moving through the opening area of a valve depends on the distance around the valve and the degree to which it lifts open. See Figure 22-7. The normal opening lift is about 25% of the valve head diameter. For example, if the intake valve is 2.00 inches in diameter, the normal

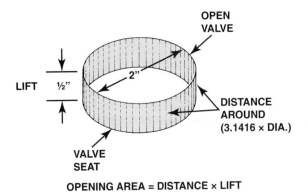

FIGURE 22-7 Method for measuring the valve opening space.

amount of lift off the seat (not cam lobe height) is 25% of 2.00 inches or 1/2 (0.500) inch. However, the amount of air–fuel mixture that can enter a cylinder depends on the total area around the valve and not just the amount of lift. The distance around a valve is calculated by the equation pi × D (3.1416 × valve diameter). See Figure 22-8.

More total area under the valve is possible when two smaller valves are used rather than one larger valve at the same valve lift. The smaller valves allow smooth low-speed operation (because of increased velocity of the mixture as it enters the cylinder as a result of smaller intake ports). Good high-speed performance is also possible because of the increased valve area and lighter-weight valves. See Figure 22-9.

When four valves are used, either the combustion chamber has a pentroof design, with each pair of valves in line (Figure 22-10), or it is hemispherical, with each valve on its own axis. Four valves on the pentroof design will be operated with dual overhead camshafts or with single overhead

TECH TIP

HORSEPOWER IS AIRFLOW

To get more power from an engine, more air needs to be drawn into the combustion chamber. One way to achieve more airflow is to increase the valve and port size of the cylinder heads along with a change in camshaft lift and duration to match the cylinder heads. One popular, but expensive, method is to replace the stock cylinder heads with high-performance cast-iron or aluminum cylinder heads such as shown in Figure 22-11 on page 379. Some vehicle manufacturers such as Audi go to a great deal of expense to design high-flow rate cylinder heads by installing five valve cylinder heads on some of their high-performance engines. See Figure 22-12 on page 379.

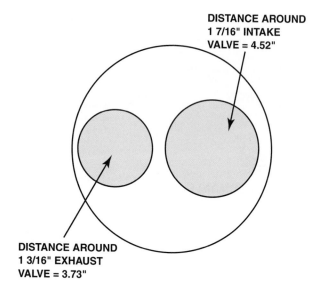

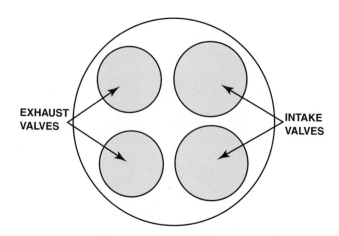

FIGURE 22-9 Typical four-valve head. The total area of opening of two small intake valves and two smaller exhaust valves is greater than the area of a two-valve head using much larger valves. The smaller valves also permit the use of smaller intake runners for better low-speed engine response.

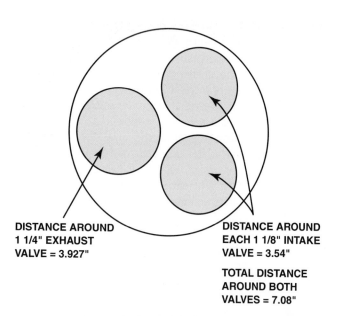

FIGURE 22-8 Comparing the valve opening areas between a two- and three-valve combustion chamber when the valves are open.

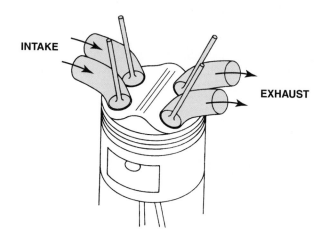

FIGURE 22-10 Four valves in a pentroof combustion chamber.

camshafts and rocker arms. When four valves are used, it is possible to place the spark plug at the center of the combustion chamber. This is the best spark plug location for fast-burning combustion.

INTAKE AND EXHAUST PORTS

The part of the intake or exhaust system passage that is cast in the cylinder head is called a **port.** Ports lead from the manifolds to the valves. The most desirable port shape is not always possible because of space requirements in the head. Space is

required for the head bolt bosses, valve guides, cooling passages, and pushrod openings. Inline engines may have both intake and exhaust ports located on the same side of the engine. Often, two cylinders share the same port because of the restricted space available. Shared ports are called **Siamese ports.** See Figure 22-13. Each cylinder uses the port at a different time. Larger ports and better breathing are possible in engines that have the intake port on one side of the head and the exhaust port on the opposite side. Sometimes a restricting hump within a port may actually increase the airflow capacity of the port. See Figure 22-14. It does this by redirecting the flow to an area of the port that is large enough to handle the flow. Modifications in the field, such as **porting** or **relieving,** would result in restricting the flow of such a carefully designed port.

The intake port in a cylinder head designed for use with a carburetor or throttle-body-type fuel injection is relatively long,

(a)

(b)

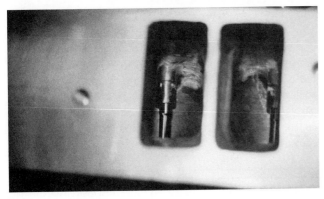

(c)

FIGURE 22-11 (a) A high-performance aftermarket aluminum cylinder head. (b) The valves are larger than the stock cast-iron cylinder head. (c) The ports are also straighter and larger than the stock cast-iron cylinder heads, requiring that a special intake manifold be used with these aluminum heads.

whereas the exhaust port is short. The long intake port wall is heated by coolant flowing through the head. The heat aids in vaporizing the fuel in the intake charge. The exhaust port is short so that the least amount of exhaust heat is transferred to the engine coolant. On engines designed for use with port fuel injection, the cylinder head ports are designed to help promote swirl in the combustion chamber, as shown in Figure 22-15.

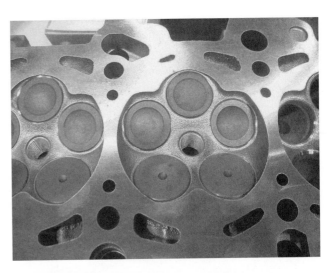

FIGURE 22-12 An Audi five-valve cylinder head, which uses three intake valves and two exhaust valves.

FIGURE 22-13 Close-up view of a Siamese exhaust port.

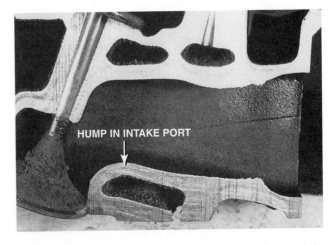

HUMP IN INTAKE PORT

FIGURE 22-14 A hump in the intake port that actually increases the airflow capacity of the port.

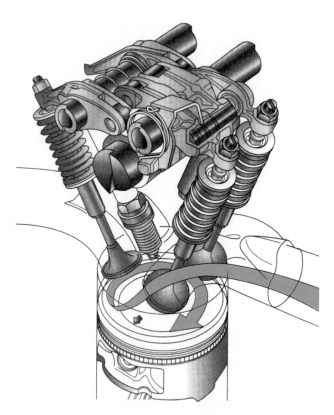

FIGURE 22-15   The intake manifold design and combustion chamber design both work together to cause the air–fuel mixture to swirl as it enters the combustion chamber.

FIGURE 22-16   The top cylinder head is stock and the bottom cylinder head has been ported using two different methods. The first inch from the gasket surface has been ground using a grinder to make the opening in the cylinder head match the intake manifold. The rest of the port between the valve and the gasket surfaces has been enlarged using acid. This acid treatment is a common "trick" used to increase the flow characteristics of a stock class cylinder head. The acid treatment gives the same rough cast-like surface as a completely stock cylinder head.

CYLINDER HEAD COOLANT PASSAGES

The engine is designed so that coolant will flow from the coolest portion of the engine to the warmest portion. The water pump takes the coolant from the radiator. The coolant is pumped into the block, where it is directed all around the cylinders. The coolant then flows upward through the gasket to the cooling passages cast into the cylinder head. The heated coolant is collected at a common point and returned to the radiator to be cooled and recycled.

NOTE: Reversed-flow cooling systems, such as that used on the Chevrolet LT1 V-8, send the coolant from the radiator to the cylinder heads first. This results in a cooler cylinder head and allows for more spark advance without engine-damaging detonation.

Typical coolant passages in a head are shown in Figure 22-17.

There are relatively large holes in the gasket surface of the head leading to the head cooling passages. The large holes are necessary to support the cooling passage core through these openings while the head is being cast. After casting, the core is broken up and removed through these same openings. Core support openings to the outside of the engine are closed with expansion plugs or soft plugs. These plugs are often mistakenly called freeze plugs. The openings between the head

TECH TIP

SNEAKY ACID PORTING

Some classifications of motor sports racing forbid any porting (enlarging) of the cylinder head ports.

If the cylinder head is ported using a grinder, the surface is smooth and does not resemble the as-cut appearance of a stock cylinder head, so some racers use acid to enlarge the ports of cast-iron cylinder heads. The appearance after the acid treatment is the same rough casting look of a completely stock cylinder head. See Figure 22-16. It just goes to show that the old saying may be right: "There are two types of racers—cheaters and losers."

and the block are usually too large for the correct coolant flow. When the openings are too large, the head gasket performs an important coolant flow function. Special-size holes are made in the gasket. These holes correct the coolant flow rate at each opening. Therefore, it is important that the head gasket be installed correctly for proper engine cooling. A head gasket with special-size holes to cover the head openings is shown in Figure 22-18.

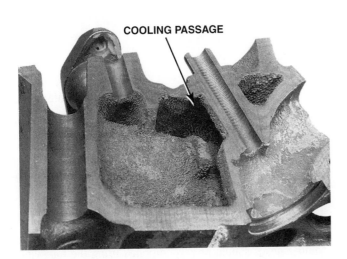

FIGURE 22-17   Coolant passages can be seen in this section of a cylinder head.

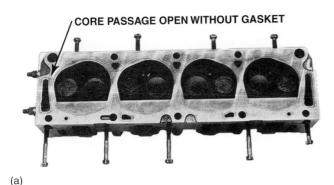

(a)

(b)

FIGURE 22-18   Coolant flow control. (a) Head core passages open without a gasket. (b) Gasket covering the left-hand core passage opening.

Carefully located openings, or deflectors, may be designed into the head. They direct the coolant toward a portion of the head where localized heat must be removed. Usually, this is in the area of the exhaust valve. Some of the deflectors are cast in the cooling passages.

LUBRICATING OVERHEAD VALVES

Lubricating oil is delivered to the overhead valve mechanism, either through the valve pushrods or through drilled passages in the head and block casting. There are special openings in the head gasket to allow the oil to pass between the block and head without leaking. After the oil passes through the valve mechanisms, it returns to the oil pan through oil return passages. Some engines have drilled oil return holes, but most engines have large cast holes that allow the oil to return freely to the engine oil pan. The cast holes are large and do not easily become plugged.

NOTE: Many aluminum cylinder heads have smaller-than-normal drain-back holes. If an engine has excessive oil consumption, check the drain holes before removing the engine.

REMOVING THE OVERHEAD CAMSHAFT

The overhead camshaft will have either one-piece bearings in a solid bearing support or split bearings and a bearing cap. When one-piece bearings are used, the valve springs will have to be compressed with a fixture or the finger follower will have to be removed before the camshaft can be pulled out endwise. When bearing caps are used, they should be loosened alternately so that bending loads are not placed on either the cam or bearing caps. See Figures 22-19 and 22-20.

DISASSEMBLY OF THE CYLINDER HEAD

As discussed in Chapter 21, the cylinder head should be disassembled, cleaned, and checked for cracks or damage before performing any service work. See Figure 22-21. Many aluminum cylinder heads, especially those with overhead camshafts and multiple valves, require special valve spring compressors. Cleaning an aluminum head should only be done with tools and procedures that will not harm the cylinder head or gasket surface. Use a wooden or plastic scraper to remove old gaskets (never use a metal scraper to avoid nicking or damaging aluminum cylinder head surfaces).

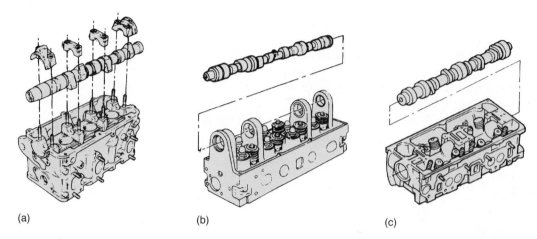

FIGURE 22-19 Overhead camshafts may be held in place with (a) bearing caps, (b) supported by towers, or (c) fitted into bearing bores machined directly into the head.

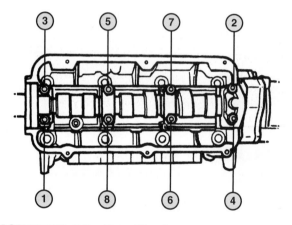

FIGURE 22-20 Always follow the specified loosening sequence to prevent valve spring tension from bending the camshaft.

FIGURE 22-21 A valve spring compressor being used to compress the valve springs so the valve locks (keepers) can be removed and the valve removed from the cylinder head.

CYLINDER HEAD RECONDITIONING SEQUENCE

Although not all cylinder heads require all service operations, cylinder heads should be reconditioned using the following sequence.

1. Disassemble and thoroughly clean the heads (see Chapter 21).
2. Check for cracks and repair as necessary (see Chapter 21).
3. Check the surface that contacts the engine block and machine, if necessary.
4. Check valve guides and replace or service, as necessary.
5. Grind valves and reinstall them in the cylinder head with new valve stem seals (see Chapter 17).

CYLINDER HEAD RESURFACING

All valve train components that are to be reused must be kept together. As wear occurs, parts become worn together. Pushrods can be kept labeled if stuck through a cardboard box, as shown in Figure 22-22. Be sure to keep the top part of the pushrod at the top. Intake and exhaust valve springs are different and must be kept with the correct valve.

The surface must be thoroughly cleaned and inspected as follows:

Step 1   After removing the old gasket material, use a file and draw it across the surface of the head to remove any small burrs. See Figure 22-23.

FIGURE 22-22   Individual parts become worn together; therefore, cardboard is a crude but effective material to use to keep all valve train parts together and labeled exactly as they came from the engine.

FIGURE 22-23   After scraping the gasket surface with a scraper, use a file and draw across the surface. When a file is drawn across the head sideways, little (if any) material is removed, but burrs and other surface imperfections are removed or highlighted.

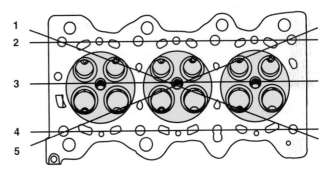

FIGURE 22-24   Cylinder heads should be checked in five planes for warpage, distortion, bend, or twist.

NOTE: The cylinder head surface that mates with the top deck of the block is often called the **fire deck.**

The head should not vary by over 0.002 inch (0.05 millimeter) in any 6-inch (15-centimeter) length, or by more than 0.004 inch overall. Always check the manufacturer's recommended specifications.

NOTE: Always check the cylinder head thickness and specifications to be sure that material can be safely removed from the surface. Some manufacturers do not recommend *any* machining, but rather require cylinder head replacement if cylinder head surface flatness is not within specifications.

? FREQUENTLY ASKED QUESTION

WHAT IS A SEASONED ENGINE?

A new engine is machined and assembled within a few hours after the heads and block are cast from melted iron. Newly cast parts have internal stresses within the metal. The stress results from the different thickness of the metal sections in the head. Forces from combustion in the engine, plus continued heating and cooling, gradually relieve these stresses. By the time the engine has accumulated 20,000 to 30,000 miles (32,000 to 48,000 kilometers), the stresses have been completely relieved. This is why some engine rebuilders prefer to work with used heads and blocks that are stress relieved. Used engines are often called **seasoned** because of the reduced stress and movement these components have as compared with new parts. The head will usually have some warpage when the engine is disassembled.

ALUMINUM CYLINDER HEAD STRAIGHTENING

Aluminum expands at about twice the rate of cast iron when heated. Aluminum cylinder heads used on cast-iron blocks

Step 2   The head should be checked in five planes, as shown in Figure 22-24. Checking the cylinder head gasket surface in five planes checks the head for **warpage, distortion, bend,** and **twist.**

These defects are determined by trying to slide a 0.004-inch (0.10-millimeter) feeler gauge under a straightedge held against the head surface.

can warp and/or crack if they are overheated. The expanding cylinder head first hits the head bolts. Further expansion of the head causes the head to expand upward and bow in the center. If a warped (bowed) cylinder head is resurfaced, the stresses of expansion are still present, and if the cylinder head uses an overhead camshaft, further problems exist. With a D-shape cylinder head (see Figure 22-25), the camshaft centerline bearing supports must also be restored. To restore the straightness of the cam-bearing bore (sometimes called the **cam tunnel**), align boring and/or honing may be necessary.

The best approach to restore a warped aluminum cylinder head (especially an overhead camshaft head) is to relieve the stress that has caused the warpage *and* to straighten the head before machining.

Step 1   Determine the amount of warpage with a straightedge and thickness (feeler) gauge. Cut shim stock (thin strips of metal) to one-half of the amount of the warpage. Place shims of this thickness under each end of the head.

Step 2   Tighten the center of the cylinder head down on a strong, flat base. A 2-inch-thick piece of steel that is 8 inches wide by 20 inches long makes a good support for the gasket surface of the cylinder head (use antiseize compound on the bolt thread to help in bolt removal).

Step 3   Place the head and base in an oven for 5 hours at 500°F (260°C). Turn the oven off and leave the assembly in the oven.

NOTE: If the temperature is too high, the valve seat inserts may fall out of the head! At 500°F, a typical valve seat will still be held into the aluminum head with a 0.002-inch interference fit based on calculations of thermal expansion of the aluminum head and steel insert.

Allow the head to cool in the oven for 4 or 5 hours to relieve any stress in the aluminum from the heating process. For best results, the cooling process should be allowed to occur overnight. Several cylinder heads can be "cooked" together.

FIGURE 22-25 Warped overhead camshaft cylinder head. If the gasket surface is machined to be flat, the camshaft bearings will still not be in proper alignment. The solution is to straighten the cylinder head or to align bore the cam tunnel.

If the cylinder head is still warped, the heating and cooling process can be repeated. After the head is straightened and the stress relieved, the gasket surface (fire deck) can be machined in the usual manner. To prevent possible camshaft bore misalignment problems, do not machine more than 0.010 to 0.015 inch (0.25 to 0.38 millimeter) from the head gasket surface.

RESURFACING METHODS

Two common resurfacing methods are used: milling and grinding. A **milling** type of resurfacer uses metal-cutting tool bits fastened in a disk. The disk is the rotating work head of the mill. This can be seen in Figure 22-26. The surface **grinder** type uses a large-diameter abrasive wheel. Both types of resurfacing can be done with table-type and with precision-type surfacers. With a table-type surfacer, the head or block is passed over the cutting head that extends slightly above a worktable. The abrasive wheel is dressed before grinding begins. The wheel head is adjusted to just touch the surface. At this point, the feed is calibrated to zero. This is necessary so that the operator knows exactly the size of the cut being made. Light cuts are taken. The abrasive wheel cuts are limited to 0.005 inch (0.015 millimeter). The abrasive wheel surface should be wire brushed after each five passes, and the wheel should be redressed after grinding each 0.100 inch (2.50 millimeters). The mill-type cutting wheel can remove up to 0.030 inch (0.075 millimeter) on each pass. A special mill-cutting tool or a dull grinding wheel is used when aluminum heads are being resurfaced.

NOTE: Resurfacing the cylinder head changes the compression ratio of the engine by about 1/10 point per 0.010 inch of removed material. For example, the compression ratio would be increased from 9.0:1 to 9.2:1 if 0.020 inch were removed from a typical cylinder head.

SURFACE FINISH

The surface finish of a reconditioned part is as important as the size of the part. Surface finish is measured in units called **microinches** (abbreviated **μ in**). The symbol in front of the inch abbreviation is the Greek letter *mu.* One microinch equals 0.000001 inch [0.025 micrometer (μ m)]. The finish classification in microinches gives the distance between the highest peak and the deepest valley. The usual method of expressing surface finish is by the **arithmetic average roughness height (RA),** that is, the average of the distances of all peaks and valleys from the mean (average) line. Surface finish is measured using a machine with a diamond stylus. See Figures 22-27 and 22-28.

Another classification of surface finish, which is becoming obsolete, is called the **root-mean-square (RMS).** The

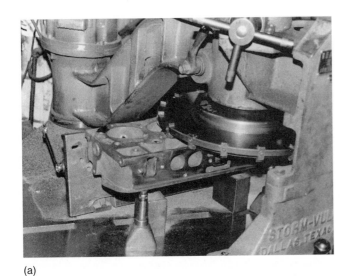

(a)

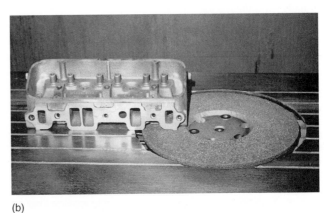

(b)

FIGURE 22-26   (a) Milling-type resurfacer machining the gasket surface of a cylinder head. (b) Grinder-type resurfacer.

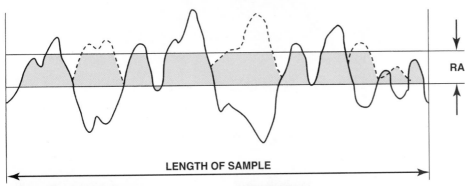

FIGURE 22-27   A graph showing a typical rough surface as would be viewed through a magnifying glass. RA is an abbreviation indicating the average height of all peaks and valleys.

FIGURE 22-28   A commercially available surface finish comparator is often used to judge the surface finish without the expense of an expensive electronic tester.

RMS is a slightly higher number and can be obtained by multiplying RA × 1.11.

Typical surface finish roughness recommendations for cast-iron and aluminum cylinder heads and blocks include the following:

Cast Iron

Maximum:	110 RA (125 RMS) (Rough surfaces can limit gasket movement and conformity.)
Minimum:	30 RA (33 RMS) (Smoother surfaces increase the tendency of the gasket to flow and *reduce* gasket sealing ability.)
Recommended range:	60 to 100 RA (65 to 110 RMS)

Aluminum

Maximum:	60 RA (65 RMS)
Minimum:	30 RA (33 RMS)
Recommended range:	50 to 60 RA (55 to 65 RMS)

The rougher the surface is, the higher the microinch finish measurement will be.

Typical preferred microinch finish standards for other engine components include the following:

Crank and rod journal: 10 to 14 RA (12 to 15 RMS)
Honed cylinder: 18 to 32 RA (20 to 35 RMS)
Connecting rod big end: 45 to 72 RA (50 to 80 RMS)

CORRECTING INTAKE MANIFOLD ALIGNMENT

The intake manifold of a V-type engine may no longer fit correctly after the gasket surfaces of the heads are ground. The ports and the assembly bolt holes may no longer match. The intake manifold surface must be resurfaced to remove enough metal to rematch the ports and bolt holes. The amount of metal that must be removed depends on the angle between the head gasket surface and the intake manifold gasket surface. Figure 22-29 shows how this is calculated. Automotive machine shops doing head resurfacing have tables that specify the exact amount of metal to be removed. It is usually necessary to remove some metal from both the front and the back gasket surface of closed-type intake manifolds used on V-type engines. This is necessary to provide a good gasket seal that will prevent oil leakage from the lifter valley.

CAUTION: Do not remove any more material than is necessary to restore a flat cylinder head-to-block surface. Some manufacturers limit *total* material that can be removed from the block deck and cylinder head to 0.008 inch (0.2 millimeter). Removal of material from the cylinder head of an overhead camshaft engine shortens the distance between the camshaft and the crankshaft. This causes the valve timing to be *retarded* unless a special copper spacer shim is placed between the block deck and the gasket to restore proper crankshaft-to-camshaft centerline dimension.

(a)

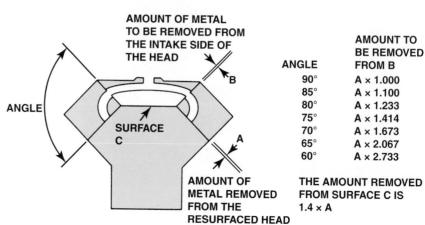

ANGLE	AMOUNT TO BE REMOVED FROM B
90°	A × 1.000
85°	A × 1.100
80°	A × 1.233
75°	A × 1.414
70°	A × 1.673
65°	A × 2.067
60°	A × 2.733

THE AMOUNT REMOVED FROM SURFACE C IS 1.4 × A

AMOUNT OF METAL TO BE REMOVED FROM THE INTAKE SIDE OF THE HEAD — B

ANGLE

SURFACE C

A

AMOUNT OF METAL REMOVED FROM THE RESURFACED HEAD

FIGURE 22-29 (a) Measuring the angle between the intake manifold and the head gasket surface. (b) The material that must be removed for a good manifold fit.

(b)

VALVE GUIDES

The valve guide supports the valve stem so that the valve face will remain perfectly centered, or **concentric,** with the valve seat. The valve guide is generally **integral** with the head casting in cast-iron heads for better heat transfer and for lower manufacturing costs. **Valve guides** and **valve seat inserts** are always used in aluminum heads. See Figure 22-30.

No matter how good the valves or seats are, they cannot operate properly if the valve guide is not accurate. In use, the valve operating mechanism pushes the valve tip sideways. This is the major cause of valve stem and guide wear. The valve normally rotates a little each time it is opened to keep wear even all around the stem. The valve guide, however, always has the wear in the same place. This causes both the top and bottom ends of the guide to wear until the guide has bell-mouth shapes at both ends. See Figure 22-31.

VALVE STEM-TO-GUIDE CLEARANCE

Engine manufacturers usually recommend the following valve stem-to-valve guide clearances.

- Intake valve: 0.001 to 0.003 inch (0.025 to 0.076 millimeter)
- Exhaust valve: 0.002 to 0.004 inch (0.05 to 0.10 millimeter)

Be sure to check the exact specifications for the engine being serviced. The exhaust valve clearance is greater than the intake valve clearance because the exhaust valve runs hotter and therefore expands more than the intake valve.

Excessive valve stem-to-guide clearance can cause excessive oil consumption. The intake valve guide is exposed to manifold vacuum that can draw oil from the top of the cylinder head down into the combustion chamber. In this situation, valves can also run hotter than usual because much of the heat in the valve is transferred to the cylinder head through the valve guide.

NOTE: A human hair is about 0.002 inch (0.05 millimeter) in diameter. Therefore, the typical clearance between a valve stem and the valve guide is only the thickness of a human hair.

TECH TIP

THE POTATO CHIP PROBLEM

Most cylinder heads are warped or twisted in the shape of a typical potato chip (high at the ends and dipped in the center). After a cylinder head is ground, the surface *should* be perfectly flat. A common problem involves grinding the cylinder head in both directions while it is being held on the table that moves to the left and right. Most grinders are angled by about 4 degrees. The lower part of the stone should be the cutting edge. If grinding occurs along the angled part of the stone, then too much heat is generated. This heat warps the head (or block) upward in the middle. The stone then removes this material, and the end result is a slight (about 0.0015 inch) depression in the center of the finished surface. To help prevent this from happening, always feed the grinder in the forward direction only (especially during removal of the last 0.003 inch of material).

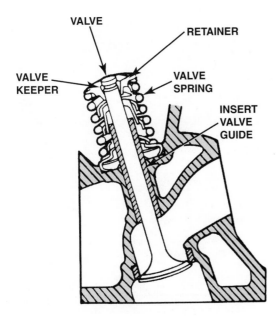

FIGURE 22-30 Insert valve guides are removable tubes driven into the head. Integral valve guides are part of the head casting.

FIGURE 22-31 Valve guides often wear to a bell-mouth shape to both ends due to the forces exerted on the valve by the valve train components.

MEASURING VALVE GUIDES FOR WEAR

Valves should be measured for stem wear before valve guides are measured. The valve guide is measured in the middle with a small-hole gauge. The gauge size is checked with a micrometer. The guide is then checked at each end. This is shown using a cut-away valve guide in Figure 22-32. The expanded part of the ball should be placed crosswise to the engine where the greatest amount of valve guide wear exists. The dimension of the valve stem diameter is subtracted from the dimension of the valve guide diameter. If the clearance exceeds the specified clearance, then the valve guide will have to be reconditioned.

Valve stem-to-guide clearance can also be checked using a dial indicator (gauge) to measure the amount of movement of the valve when lifted off the valve seat. See Figure 22-33. The valve stem should also be measured as shown in Figure 22-34.

OVERSIZE STEM VALVES

Most domestic automobile manufacturers that have integral valve guides in their engines recommend reaming worn valve guides and installing new valves with **oversize (OS) stems.** When a valve guide is worn, the valve stem is also likely to be worn. In this case, new valves are required. If new valves are used, they can just as well have oversize stems as standard stems. Typically, available sizes include 0.003, 0.005, 0.015, and 0.030 inch OS. The valve guide is reamed or honed to the correct size to fit the oversize stem of the new valve. Figure 22-35 shows a reamer in a valve guide. The resulting clearance of the valve stem in the guide is the same as the original clearance. The oil clearance and the heat transfer properties of the original valve and guide are not changed when new valves with oversize stems are installed.

(a)

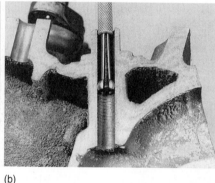
(b)

(c)

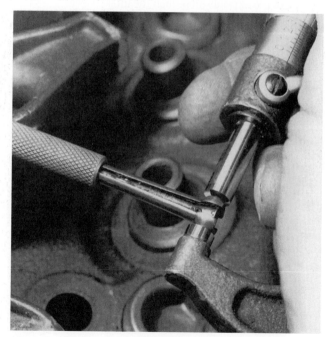
(d)

FIGURE 22-32 (a), (b), and (c) A cutaway head is used to show how a small-hole gauge is used to measure the taper and wear of a valve guide. (d) After it is adjusted to the valve guide size, the small-hole gauge is measured with an outside micrometer.

TECH TIP

TIGHT IS NOT ALWAYS RIGHT

Many engine manufacturers specify a valve stem-to-valve guide clearance of 0.001 to 0.003 inch (0.025 to 0.076 millimeter). However, some vehicles, especially those equipped with aluminum cylinder heads, may specify a much greater clearance. For example, many Chrysler 2.2-liter and 2.5-liter engines have a specified valve stem-to-valve guide clearance of 0.003 to 0.005 inch (0.076 to 0.127 millimeter). This amount of clearance feels loose to those technicians accustomed to normal valve stem clearance specifications. While this large amount of clearance may seem excessive, remember that the valve stem increases in diameter as the engine warms up. Therefore, the *operating* clearance is smaller than the clearance measured at room temperature. Always double-check factory specifications before replacing a valve guide for excessive wear.

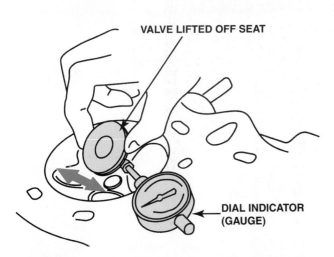

FIGURE 22-33   Measuring valve guide-to-stem clearance with a dial indicator while rocking the stem in the direction of normal thrust. The reading on the dial indicator should be compared with specifications, because it does not give the guide-to-stem clearance directly. The usual conversion factor is to record the reading on the dial indicator and divide by 2 to obtain the valve guide clearance. The valve is usually lifted off its seat to its maximum operating lift.

NOTE: Many remanufacturers of cylinder heads use oversize valve stems to simplify production.

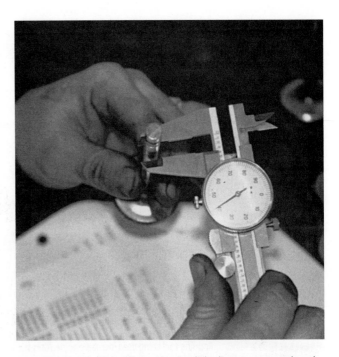

FIGURE 22-34   Using a vernier dial caliper to measure the valve stem diameter of a valve. Subtract the diameter of the valve stem from the inside diameter of the valve guide to determine the valve guide clearance.

FIGURE 22-35   Reaming a valve guide to be oversize. This permits the use of new valves with oversize stem diameters. Many remanufacturers use this method to save the money and time involved in replacing or knurling valve guides and grinding old valves.

VALVE GUIDE KNURLING

In the process known as **valve guide knurling,** a tool is rotated as it is driven into the guide. The tool *displaces* the metal to reduce the hole diameter of the guide. Knurling is ideally suited to engines with integral valve guides (guides that are part of the cylinder head and are nonremovable). It is recommended that knurling not be used to correct wear exceeding

FIGURE 22-36   Knurling tool being used in a valve guide. After the knurling tool displaces the metal inside the guide, a reamer is run through the guide to produce a restored, serviceable valve guide.

0.006 inch (0.15 millimeter). In the displacing process, the knurling tool pushes a small tapered wheel or dull threading tool into the wall of the guide hole. This makes a groove in the wall of the guide without removing any metal, as pictured in Figures 22-36 and 22-37. The metal piles up along the edge of the groove just as dirt would pile up along the edge of a tire track as the tire rolled through soft dirt. (The dirt would be displaced from under the wheel to form a small ridge alongside the tire track.)

The knurling tool is driven by an electric drill and an attached speed reducer that slows the rotating speed of the knurling tool. The reamers that accompany the knurling set will ream just enough to provide the correct valve stem clearance for commercial reconditioning standards. The valve guides are honed to size in the precision shop when precise fits are desired. Clearances of knurled valve guides are usually one-half of the new valve guide clearances. Such small clearance can be used because knurling leaves so many small oil rings down the length of the guide for lubrication.

VALVE GUIDE REPLACEMENT

When an engine is designed with replaceable valve guides, their replacement is always recommended when the valve assembly is being reconditioned. The original valve guide height should be measured before the guide is removed so that the new guide can be properly positioned.

After the valve guide height is measured, the worn guide is pressed from the head with a properly fitting *driver.* Figure 22-38 shows how the driver is used to remove and

FIGURE 22-37   Sectional view of a knurled valve guide.

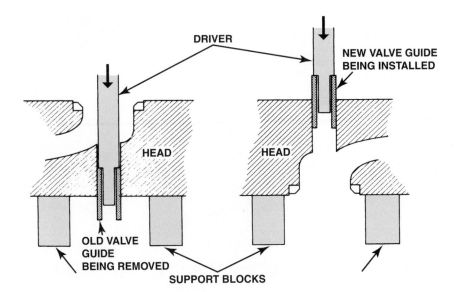

FIGURE 22-38 Valve guide replacement procedure.

TECH TIP

RIGHT SIDE UP

When replacing valve guides, it is important that the recommended procedures be followed. Most manufacturers specify that replaceable guides be driven from the combustion chamber side toward the rocker arm side. For example, big block Chevrolet V-8 heads (396, 402, 427, and 454 cubic inches) have a 0.004-inch (0.05-millimeter) taper (small end toward the combustion chamber).

Other manufacturers, however, may recommend driving the old guide from the rocker arm side to prevent any carbon buildup on the guide from damaging the guide bore. Always consult the manufacturer's recommended procedures before attempting to replace a valve guide.

replace valve guides. The driver has a stem to fit the guide opening and a shoulder that pushes on the end of the guide. If the guide has a flange, care should be taken to make sure that the guide is pushed out from the correct end, usually from the port side and toward the rocker arm side. The new guide is pressed into the guide bore using the same driver. Make sure that the guide is pressed to the correct depth. After the guides are replaced, they are reamed or honed to the proper inside diameter.

Replacement valve guides can also be installed to repair worn integral guides. Both **cast-iron** and **bronze guides** are

available. See Figure 22-39. Three common valve guide sizes are as follows:

5/16 or 0.313 inches
11/32 or 0.343 inches
3/8 or 0.375 inches

VALVE GUIDE INSERTS

When the integral valve guide is badly worn, it can be reconditioned using an insert. This repair method is usually preferred in heavy-duty and high-speed engines. Two types of guide inserts are commonly used for guide repair: a **thin-walled bronze alloy sleeve bushing** and a **spiral bronze alloy bushing.** The thin-walled bronze sleeve bushings are also called **bronze guide liners.** The valve guide rebuilding kit used to install each of these bushings includes all of the reamers, installing sleeves, broaches, burnishing tools, and cutoff tools that are needed to install and properly size the bushings.

The valve guide must be bored to a large enough size to accept the thin-walled insert sleeve. The boring tool is held in alignment by a rugged fixture. One type is shown in Figure 22-40 on page 393. Depending on the make of the equipment, the boring fixture is aligned with the valve guide hole, the valve seat, or the head gasket surface. First, the boring fixture is properly aligned. The guide is then bored, making a hole somewhat smaller than the insert sleeve that will be used. The bored hole is reamed to make a precise smooth hole that is still slightly smaller than the insert sleeve. The insert sleeve is installed with a press fit that holds it in the guide. The press fit also helps to maintain normal heat transfer from the valve to the head. The thin-walled insert sleeve is held in an installing sleeve. A driver is used to press the insert from the installing sleeve into the

(a)

(b)

HAMMER

INSTALLATION
TOOL

REPLACEMENT
VALVE GUIDE

(c)

FIGURE 22-39 (a) Drilling out old valve guide in preparation for replacing the guide. (b) Reaming the hole after drilling. (c) Replacement guide being driven into the cylinder head.

guide. A broach is then pressed through the insert sleeve to firmly seat it in the guide. The broach is designed to put a knurl in the guide to aid in lubrication. The insert sleeve is then trimmed to the valve guide length. Finally, the insert sleeve is reamed or honed to provide the required valve stem clearance. A very close clearance of 0.0005 inch (one-half of one thousandth of an inch) (0.013 millimeter) is usually used with the bronze thin-walled insert sleeve. See Figure 22-41.

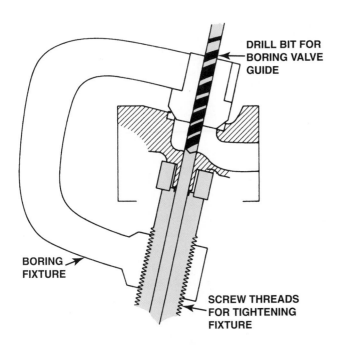

FIGURE 22-40 Type of fixture required to bore the valve guide to be oversize to accept a thin-walled insert sleeve.

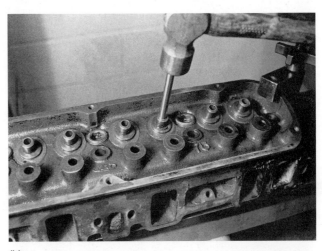

(b)

(c)

(a)

(d)

FIGURE 22-41 (a) The valve guide thin-walled insert being pushed into the valve guide from the installing sleeve. (b) Burnishing a thin-walled bronze liner. (c) Reaming a bronze guide liner (thin-walled bronze sleeve). (d) Finished installation. Bronze guides wear many times longer than cast-iron guides.

SPIRAL BRONZE INSERT BUSHINGS

The spiral bronze alloy insert bushing is screwed into a thread that is put in the valve guide. The tap used to put cut threads in the valve guide has a long pilot ahead of the thread-cutting portion of the tap. This aids in restoring the original guide alignment. The long pilot is placed in the guide from the valve seat end. A power driver is attached to the end of the pilot that extends from the spring end of the valve guide. The threads are cut in the guide from the seat end toward the spring end as the power driver turns the tap, pulling it toward the driver. The tap is stopped before it comes out of the guide, and the power driver is removed. The thread is carefully completed by hand to avoid breaking either the end of the guide or the tap. An installed spiral bronze insert bushing can be seen in Figure 22-42.

The spiral bronze bushing is tightened on an inserting tool. This holds it securely in the wound-up position so that it can be screwed into the spring end of the guide. It is screwed in until the bottom of the bushing is flush with the seat end of the guide. The holding tool is removed, and the bushing material is trimmed to one coil *above* the spring end of the guide. The end of the bushing is temporarily secured with a plastic serrated bushing retainer and a worm gear clamp. This holds the bushing in place as a broach is driven through the bushing to firmly seat it in the threads. The bushing is reamed or honed to size before the temporary bushing retainer is removed. The final step is to trim the end of the bushing with a special cut-off tool that is included in the bushing installation tool set. This type of spiral bronze bushing can be removed by using a pick

FIGURE 22-42   Installed spiral bronze insert bushing.

to free the end of the bushing. It can then be stripped out and a new bushing inserted in the original threads in the guide hole. New threads do not have to be put in the guide. The spiral bushing design has natural spiral grooves to hold oil for lubrication. The valve stem clearances are the same as those used for knurling and for the thin-walled insert (about one-half of the standard recommended clearance).

INSTALLING REPLACEMENT VALVE GUIDES   Step-by-Step

STEP 1 The first step when replacing valve guides is to square the cylinder head and secure it on the holding fixture.

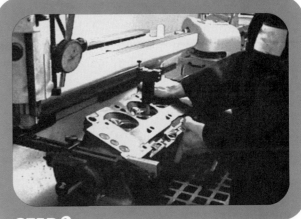

STEP 2 After the cylinder head has been installed, level the head using a bubble level inserted in the valve guide.

STEP 3 The first step is to drill and ream out the original integral valve guide. Here a combination drill and reamer is doing this in one operation and should be performed dry without using any lubricant.

STEP 4 A close-up view of the drill/reamer used to prepare the valve guide before installing the thin-wall bronze guides.

STEP 5 Before installing the thin-wall bronze guide, lubricate the guides with bronze guide lubricant.

STEP 6 Here the edge of a tapered punch is being used to taper the opening to the guide slightly so that the bronze thin-wall guide can be easily inserted.

(continued)

INSTALLING REPLACEMENT VALVE GUIDES continued

STEP 7   Installing the thin-wall bronze guide insert.

STEP 8   Using an installer to force the thin-wall bronze guide fully into the guide from the combustion chamber side of the head.

STEP 9   The thin-wall bronze guide insert is longer than the guide and protrudes out of the top of the original guide.

STEP 10   The top of the thin-wall bronze guide insert is then trimmed to the same level as the original integral guide.

SUMMARY

1. The most commonly used combustion chamber types include hemispherical, wedge, and pentroof.
2. Coolant and lubricating openings and passages are located throughout most cylinder heads.
3. Cylinder head reconditioning should start with cleaning and repairing, if needed, followed by resurfacing of valves and, finally, grinding of valves and seats.
4. Cylinder head resurfacing machines include grinders and milling machines.
5. Valve guides should be checked for wear using a ball gauge or a dial indicator. Typical valve stem-to-guide clearance is 0.001 to 0.003 inch for intake valves and 0.002 to 0.004 inch for exhaust valves.
6. Valve guide repair options include use of oversize stem valves, replacement valve guides, valve guide inserts, and knurling of the original valve guide.

REVIEW QUESTIONS

1. What are the advantages of a hemispherical combustion chamber?
2. What are the advantages of a wedge combustion chamber?
3. What is meant by the term *cross flow head?*
4. What is a Siamese port?
5. What is the recommended cylinder head reconditioning sequence?
6. What are the advantages of using four valves per cylinder?

CHAPTER QUIZ

1. The reason why cylinder heads with four valves flow more air than two-valve heads is because _____.
   a. They have a greater open area
   b. Use a higher lift camshaft
   c. Increases the velocity of the air
   d. Use a camshaft with a greater duration

2. Two technicians are discussing a Hemi engine. Technician A says that Hemi means an engine with a hemispherical-shaped combustion chamber. Technician B says that all Hemi engines use four valves per cylinder. Which technician is correct?
   a. Technician A only
   b. Technician B only
   c. Both Technician A and B
   d. Neither Technician A nor B

3. Technician A says that Audi five valve engines use three intake valves and two exhaust valves. Technician B says that the engines use two intake valves and three exhaust valves. Which technician is correct?
   a. Technician A only
   b. Technician B only
   c. Both Technician A and B
   d. Neither Technician A nor B

4. The gasket surface of a cylinder head, as measured with a straightedge, should have a maximum variation of _____.
   a. 0.002 inch in any 6-inch length or 0.004 inch overall
   b. 0.001 inch in any 6-inch length or 0.004 inch overall
   c. 0.020 inch in any 10-inch length or 0.020 inch overall
   d. 0.004 inch in any 10-inch length or 0.008 inch overall

5. A warped aluminum cylinder head can be restored to useful service by _____.
   a. Grinding the gasket surface and then align honing the camshaft bore
   b. Heating it in an oven at 500°F with shims under each end, allowing it to cool, and then machining it
   c. Heating it to 500°F for 5 hours and cooling it rapidly before final machining
   d. Machining the gasket surface to one-half of the warped amount and then heating the head in an oven and allowing it to cool slowly

6. Most vehicle manufacturers recommend repairing integral guides using _____.
   a. OS stem valves
   b. Knurling
   c. Replacement valve guides
   d. Valve guide inserts

7. Typical valve stem-to-valve guide clearance is _____.
   a. 0.030 to 0.045 inch (0.8 to 1.0 millimeter)
   b. 0.015 to 0.020 inch (0.4 to 0.5 millimeter)
   c. 0.005 to 0.010 inch (0.13 to 0.25 millimeter)
   d. 0.001 to 0.004 inch (0.03 to 0.05 millimeter)

8. What other engine component may have to be machined if the cylinder heads are machined on a V-type engine?
   a. Exhaust manifold
   b. Intake manifold
   c. Block deck
   d. Distributor mount (if the vehicle is so equipped)

9. Which operation should be performed first?
   a. Resurfacing the head
   b. Installing replacement guides

10. Which statement is true about surface finish?
   a. Cast-iron surfaces should be smoother than aluminum surfaces.
   b. The rougher the surface, the higher the microinch finish measurement.
   c. The smoother the surface, the higher the microinch finish measurement.
   d. A cylinder head should be a lot smoother than a crankshaft journal.

VALVE AND SEAT SERVICE

OBJECTIVES

After studying Chapter 23, the reader will be able to:

1. Prepare for Engine Repair (A1) ASE certification test content area "B" (Cylinder Head and Valve Train Diagnosis and Repair).
2. Discuss various engine valve types and materials.
3. Describe how to test valve springs.
4. Explain the purpose, function, and operation of valve rotators.
5. List the steps necessary to reface a valve.
6. Describe how to grind valve seats.
7. Discuss how to measure and correct installed height and valve stem height.

KEY TERMS

Valves need to be reconditioned more often than any other engine part.

INTAKE AND EXHAUST VALVES

Automotive engine valves are of a **poppet valve** design. The valve is opened by means of a valve train that is operated by a cam. The cam is timed to the piston position and crankshaft cycle. The valve is closed by one or more springs.

Typical valves are shown in Figure 23-1. Intake valves control the inlet of cool, low-pressure induction charges. Exhaust valves handle hot, high-pressure exhaust gases. This means that exhaust valves are exposed to more severe operating conditions. They are, therefore, made from much higher-quality materials than the intake valves. This makes them more expensive.

The guide is centered over the **valve seat** so that the **valve face** and seat make a gas-tight fit. The face and seat will have an angle of 30 degrees or 45 degrees. These are the nominal angles. Actual service angles might be a degree or two different from these. Most engines use a nominal 45-degree valve and seat angle. A **valve spring** holds the valve against the seat. The valve **keepers** (also called **locks**) secure the spring **retainer** to the stem of the valve. For valve removal, it is necessary to compress the spring and remove the valve keeper. Then the spring, valve seals, and valve can be removed from the head. A typical valve assembly is shown in Figure 23-2.

VALVE SIZE RELATIONSHIPS

Extensive testing has shown that a normal relationship exists between the different dimensions of valves. Engines with cylinder bores that measure from 3 to 8 inches (80 to 200 millimeters) will have intake valves that measure approximately 45% of the bore size. The exhaust valve size is approximately 38% of the cylinder bore size. The intake valve must be larger than the exhaust valve to handle the same mass of gas. The larger intake valve controls low-velocity, low-density gases. The exhaust valve, however, controls high-velocity, high-pressure, denser gases. These gases can be handled by a smaller valve. Exhaust valve heads are, therefore, approximately 85% of the size of intake valve heads. See Figure 23-3. For satisfactory operation, valve head diameter is nearly 115% of the valve port diameter. The valve must be large enough to close over the port. The extent to which the valve opens, called **valve lift,** is close to 25% of the valve diameter.

VALVE DESIGN

Poppet valve heads may be of various designs, from a **rigid valve** to an **elastic valve,** as shown in Figure 23-4. The rigid valve is strong, holds its shape, and conducts heat readily.

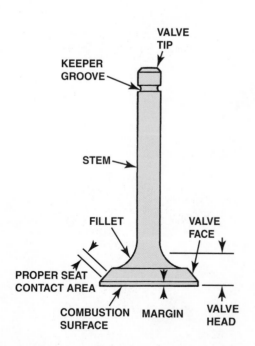

FIGURE 23-1   Identification of the parts of a valve.

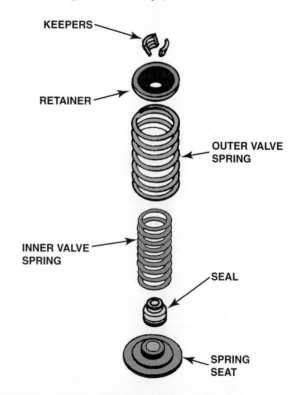

FIGURE 23-2   Typical valve spring and related components. Dual-valve springs are used to reduce valve train vibrations and a spring seat is used to protect aluminum heads.

It also causes less valve recession. Unfortunately, it is more likely to leak and burn than other valve head types. The elastic valve, however, is able to conform to valve seat shape. This allows it to seal easily, but it runs hot and the flexing to conform may cause it to break. A popular shape is one with a small cup in the top of the valve head. It offers a reasonable weight, good strength, and good heat transfer at a slight cost penalty. Elastic valve heads are more likely to be found on intake valves, and rigid, valve heads are found on exhaust valves.

FIGURE 23-3 The intake valve is larger than the exhaust valve because the intake charge is being drawn into the combustion chamber at a low speed due to differences in pressure between atmospheric pressure and the pressure (vacuum) inside the cylinder. The exhaust is actually pushed out by the piston and, therefore, the size of the valve does not need to be as large, leaving more room in the cylinder head for the larger intake valve.

VALVE MATERIALS

Alloys used in exhaust valve materials are largely of chromium for oxidation resistance, with small amounts of nickel, manganese, and nitrogen added. Heat-treating is used whenever it is necessary to produce special valve properties. Some exhaust valves are manufactured from two different materials when a

TECH TIP

HOT ENGINE + COLD WEATHER = TROUBLE

Serious valve damage can occur if cold air reaches hot exhaust valves soon after the engine is turned off. An engine equipped with exhaust headers and/or straight-through mufflers can allow cold air a direct path to the hot exhaust valve. The exhaust valve can warp and/or crack as a result of rapid cooling. This can easily occur during cold windy weather when the wind can blow cold outside air directly up the exhaust system. Using reverse-flow mufflers with tailpipes and a catalytic converter reduces the possibilities of this occurring.

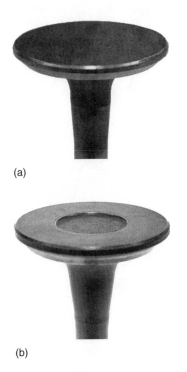

(a)

(b)

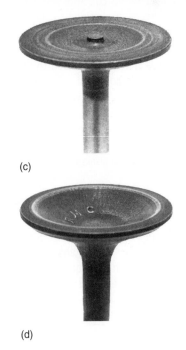

(c)

(d)

FIGURE 23-4   Valve head types, from rigid (a) to elastic (d).

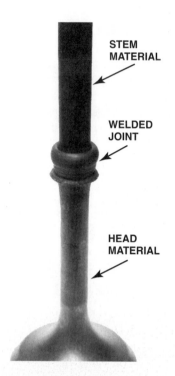

FIGURE 23-5 Inertia welded valve stem and head before machining.

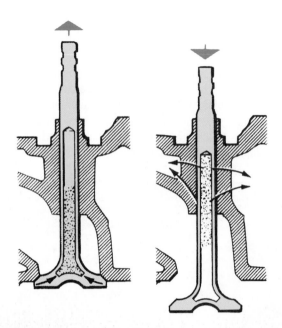

FIGURE 23-6 A sodium-filled valve uses a hollow stem, which is partially filled with metallic sodium that is a liquid when hot, to conduct heat away from the head of the valve.

one-piece design cannot meet the desired hardness and corrosion resistance specifications. The joint cannot be seen after valves have been used. The valve heads are made from special alloys that can operate at high temperatures, have physical strength, resist lead oxide corrosion, and have indentation resistance. These heads are welded to stems that have good wear resistance properties. Figure 23-5 shows an inertia welded valve before final machining. In severe applications, facing alloys such as stellite are welded to the valve face and valve tip. **Stellite** is an alloy of nickel, chromium, and tungsten that is nonmagnetic. The valve is aluminized where corrosion may be a problem. Aluminized valve facing reduces valve recession when unleaded gasoline is used. Aluminum oxide forms to separate the valve steel from the cast-iron seat to keep the face metal from sticking.

SODIUM-FILLED VALVES

Some heavy-duty applications use hollow stem exhaust valves that are partially filled with metallic sodium. An unfilled hollow valve stem is shown in Figure 23-6. The sodium in the valve becomes a liquid at operating temperatures. As it splashes back and forth in the valve stem, the sodium transfers heat from the valve head to the valve stem. The heat goes through the valve guide into the coolant. In general, a one-piece valve design using properly selected materials will provide satisfactory service for automotive engines.

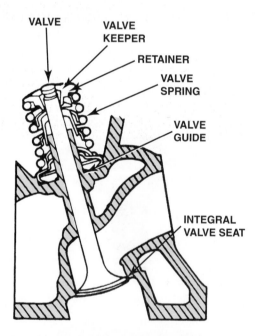

FIGURE 23-7 Integral valve seats are machined directly into the cast-iron cylinder head and are induction hardened to prevent wear.

VALVE SEATS

The valve face closes against a valve seat to seal the combustion chamber. The seat is generally formed as part of the cast-iron head of automotive engines, and is called an **integral seat.** See Figure 23-7. The seats are usually induction hardened so that unleaded gasoline can be used. This minimizes

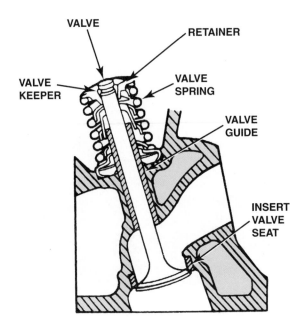

FIGURE 23-8   Insert valve seats are a separate part that is interference-fitted to a counter bore in the cylinder head.

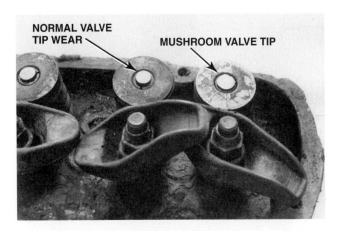

FIGURE 23-9   A mushroomed valve tip may indicate other valve train damage, such as excessive valve clearance (lash).

FIGURE 23-10   Badly burned exhaust valve.

valve recession as the engine operates. Valve recession is the wearing away of the seat, so that the valve seats further into the head. Insert seats are used in applications for which corrosion and wear resistance are critical. Insert seats and guides are always required in aluminum heads. See Figure 23-8. It should be noted that the exhaust valve seat runs as much as 180°F (100°C) *cooler* in aluminum heads than in cast-iron heads. Insert seats are also used as a salvage measure in the reconditioning of integral automotive engine valve seats that have been badly damaged.

VALVE INSPECTION

Careful inspection of the cylinder and valves can often reveal the root cause of failure. Excessive valve lash (clearance) can cause the top of the valve to be pounded until it becomes mushroomed, as shown in Figure 23-9. Valve face burning (Figures 23-10 and 23-11) and valve face **guttering** (Figure 23-12) result from poor seating that allows the high-temperature and high-pressure combustion gases to leak between the valve and seat. Poor seating results from too small a valve lash, hard carbon deposits, valve stem deposits, excessive valve stem-to-guide clearances, or out-of-square valve guide and seat. A valve lash that is too small can result from improper valve lash adjustments on solid lifter engines. It can also result from misadjustments on a valve train using hydraulic lifters. The clearance will also be reduced as a result of valve head cupping or valve face and seat wear. Figure 23-13 shows typical intake valve and seat wear.

Hard carbon deposits are loosened from the combustion chamber. Sometimes, these flaking deposits stick between the

FIGURE 23-11   Valve face burning.

FIGURE 23-12 Valve face guttering.

FIGURE 23-14 Valve face peening.

FIGURE 23-13 Typical intake valve seat wear. Also notice the excessive deposits on the valve. These deposits not only reduce the amount of air and fuel flow into the engine, but can also cause hesitation by absorbing fuel instead of allowing the fuel into the combustion chamber.

valve face and seat to hold the valve slightly off its seat. This reduces valve cooling through the seat and allows some of the combustion gases to escape. Continued pounding on hard carbon particles gives the valve face a **peened** appearance, pictured in Figure 23-14.

Fuel and oil on the hot valve will break down to become hard carbon and varnish deposits that build up on the valve stem. Heavy valve stem deposits are shown in Figure 23-15. These deposits cause the valve to stick in the guide so that the valve does not completely close on the seat and therefore cause the valve face to burn. This is one of the most common causes of valve face burning.

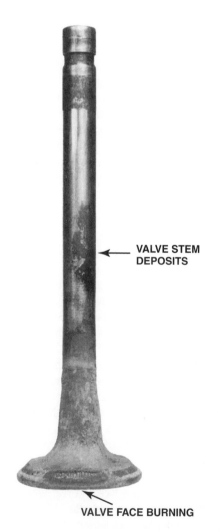

VALVE STEM DEPOSITS

VALVE FACE BURNING

FIGURE 23-15 Valve stem with heavy deposits and valve face burning.

FIGURE 23-16   Intake valve with heavy deposits.

FIGURE 23-18   Badly guttered valve face.

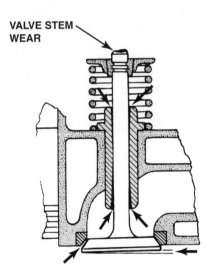

FIGURE 23-17   Excessive wear of the valve stem or guide can cause the valve to seat in a cocked position.

If there is a large clearance between the valve stem and guide or faulty valve stem seals, too much oil will go down the stem. This will increase deposits, as shown on the intake valve in Figure 23-16. In addition, a large valve guide clearance will allow the valve to cock or lean sideways, especially with the effect of the rocker arm action. Continued cocking keeps the valve from seating properly and causes it to leak, burning the valve face. See Figure 23-17.

Sometimes, the cylinder head will warp slightly as the head is tightened to the block deck during assembly. In other cases, heating and cooling will cause warpage. When head warpage causes valve guide and seat misalignment, the valve cannot seat properly and it will leak, burning the valve face.

Excessive Temperatures

High valve temperature occurs when the valve does not seat properly; however, it can occur regardless. Cooling system passages in the head may be partially blocked by faulty casting or by deposits built up from the coolant. A corroded head gasket will change the coolant flow. This can cause overheating when the coolant is allowed to flow to the wrong places. Extremely high temperatures are also produced by preignition and by detonation. These are forms of abnormal combustion. Both of these produce a very rapid increase in temperature that can cause uneven heating. The rapid increase in temperature will give a **thermal shock** to the valve. A thermal shock is a sudden change in temperature. The shock will often cause radial cracks in the valve. The cracks will allow the combustion gases to escape and gutter the valve face. A badly guttered valve face is shown in Figure 23-18. If the radial cracks intersect, a pie-shaped piece will break away from the valve head. A thermal shock can also result from rapid cycling of the engine from full throttle to closed throttle and back again. Valves with hard metal facings have special problems. Excess heat causes the base metal to expand more than the hoop of the hard face metal. The hard face metal hoop is stressed until it cracks. The crack allows gases to gutter the base metal, as shown in Figure 23-19.

High engine speeds require high gas velocities. The high-velocity exhaust gases hit on the valve stem and tend to erode or wear away the metal mechanically. The gases are also corrosive, so the valve stem will tend to corrode. Corrosion removes the metal chemically. The corrosion rate doubles for each 25°F (14°C) increase in temperature. Erosion and corrosion of the valve stem cause **necking,** which weakens the stem and leads to breakage. Necking is shown in Figure 23-20.

FIGURE 23-19   Hoop stress cracks in a valve head.

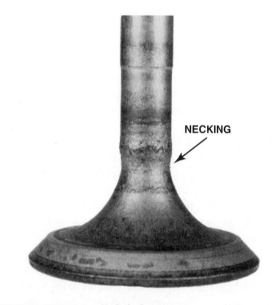

FIGURE 23-20   Necked valve stem.

FIGURE 23-21   Valve head broken from the stem.

FIGURE 23-22   Broken piston caused by a valve breaking from the stem.

Misaligned Valve Seats

When the valve-to-seat alignment is improper, the valve head must twist to seat each time the valve closes. If twisting or bending becomes excessive, it fatigues the stem, and the valve head will break from the stem. An example of this can be seen in Figure 23-21. The break appears as lines arching around a starting point. The head of the valve usually damages the piston when it gets trapped between the piston and the cylinder head.

High-Velocity Seating

High-velocity seating is indicated by excessive valve face wear, valve seat recession, and impact failure. It can be caused by excessive lash in mechanical lifters and by collapsed hydraulic lifters. Lash allows the valve to hit the seat without the effects of the cam ramp to ease the valve onto its seat. Excessive lash may also be caused by wear of parts, such as the cam, lifter base, pushrod ends, rocker arm pivot, and valve tip. Weak or broken valve springs allow the valves to float away from the cam lobes so that the valves are uncontrolled as they hit the seat. The normal tendency of hydraulic lifters is to pump up under valve float conditions, which reduces valve impact damage.

Impact breakage may occur under the valve head or at the valve keeper grooves. The break lines radiate from the starting point. Impact breakage may also cause the valve head to fall into the combustion chamber. In most cases, it will ruin the piston before the engine can be stopped, as pictured in Figures 23-22 and 23-23.

FIGURE 23-23 Everything in the valve train has to be working correctly or an engine can be destroyed. The valve in this engine separated from the retainer at high engine speed, turned around in the cylinder, and punctured the piston.

High Mileage

Excessive wear of the valve stem (Figure 23-24), guide, face, and seat is the result of high mileage. The affected valves usually have a great buildup of deposits. The valves will, however, still be seating, and they will show no sign of cracking or burning.

When the valve stems do not have enough lubricant, they **scuff.** In scuffing, the valve stem temporarily welds to the guide when the valve is closed. The weld breaks as the valve is forced to open. Welded metal tears from the guide and sticks to the valve stem. An example of valve stem scuffing is shown in Figure 23-25. The metal knobs on the valve stem scratch the valve guide as it operates. This also scuffs the valve guide. In a short time, the valve will stick in the guide and not close. This will stop combustion in that cylinder. Both the valve and valve guide will have to be replaced.

Often, valve tips become damaged. This damage can be seen before the valves are removed from the head. Some valve tip problems are caused by rapid rotation as the valve is being

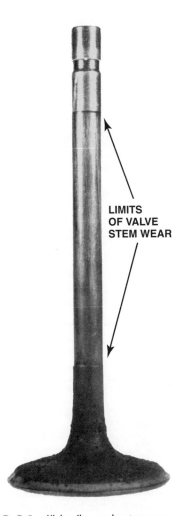

LIMITS
OF VALVE
STEM WEAR

FIGURE 23-24 High-mileage valve stem wear.

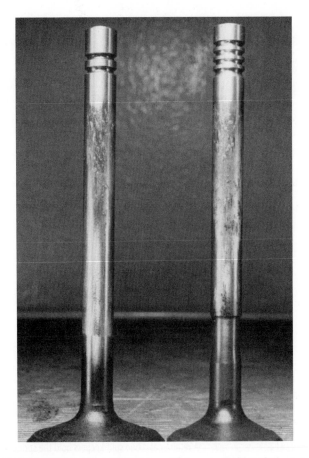

FIGURE 23-25 Valve stems scuffed as a result of loss of valve train lubrication.

opened. This causes circles on the valve tip. Still other valves do not rotate at all. These valves wear in the direction of the rocker arm or finger follower movement. Examples of excessive valve tip wear can be seen in Figure 23-26.

VALVE SPRINGS

A valve spring holds the valve against the seat when the valve is not being opened. One end of the valve spring is seated against the head. The other end of the spring is attached under compression to the valve stem through a valve spring retainer and a valve spring keeper (lock), as shown in Figure 23-27.

Valves usually have a single inexpensive valve spring. The springs are generally made of chromium vanadium alloy steel. When one spring cannot control the valve, other devices are added. Variable-rate springs add spring force when the valve is in its open position. This is accomplished by using closely spaced coils on the cylinder head end of the spring. The closely spaced coils also tend to dampen vibrations that may exist in an equally wound coil spring. The damper helps to reduce

valve seat wear. Some valve springs use a flat coiled damper inside the spring. This eliminates spring surge and adds some valve spring tension. The normal valve spring winds up as it is compressed. This causes a small but important turning motion as the valve closes on the seat. The turning motion helps to keep the wear even around the valve face. Figure 23-28 illustrates typical valve springs.

Multiple valve springs are used where large lifts are required and a single spring does not have enough strength to control the valve. Multiple valve springs generally have their coils wound in opposite directions. This is done to control valve spring surge and to prevent excessive valve rotation. **Valve spring surge** is the tendency of a valve spring to vibrate.

VALVE SPRING INSPECTION

Valve springs close the valves after they have been opened by the cam. They must close squarely to form a tight seal and to prevent valve stem and guide wear. It is necessary, therefore, that the springs be square and have the proper amount of closing force. The valve springs are checked for squareness by rotating them on a flat surface with a square held against the side. They should be within 1/16 inch or 1.6 millimeters of being square, as shown in Figure 23-30. Only the springs that

FIGURE 23-26   Excessive valve tip wear.

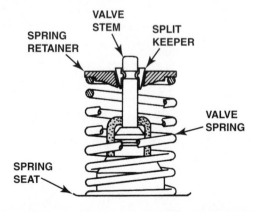

FIGURE 23-27   A retainer and two split keepers hold the spring in place on the valve. A spring seat is used on aluminum heads. Otherwise, the spring seat is a machined area in the head.

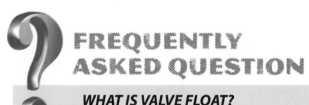

FREQUENTLY ASKED QUESTION

WHAT IS VALVE FLOAT?

Valve float occurs when the valve continues to stay open after the camshaft lobe has moved from under the lifter. This happens when the inertia of the valve train overcomes the valve spring tension at high engine speeds. See Figure 23-29.

FIGURE 23-28   Valve spring types (*left to right*): coil spring with equally spaced coils; spring with damper inside spring coil; closely spaced spring with a damper; taper wound coil spring.

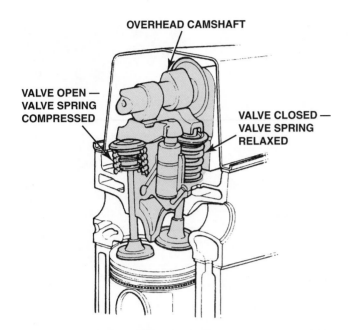

OVERHEAD CAMSHAFT

VALVE OPEN —
VALVE SPRING
COMPRESSED

VALVE CLOSED —
VALVE SPRING
RELAXED

FIGURE 23-29 Valve springs maintain tension in the valve train when the valve is open to prevent valve float, but must not exert so much tension that the cam lobes and lifters begin to wear.

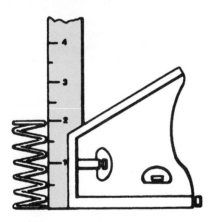

FIGURE 23-30 Determine the squareness of a valve spring with a square on a flat surface. The spring should be replaced if more than 1/16 inch (1.6 mm) is measured between the top of the spring and the square.

FIGURE 23-31 Out-of-square valve spring. This spring should not be tested further, but should be replaced. A distorted valve spring exerts side loads on the valve, which often causes excessive valve guide wear.

are square should be checked to determine their compressed force. See Figure 23-31. Out-of-square springs will have to be replaced. The surge damper should be *removed* from the valve spring when the spring force is being checked. A valve spring scale is used to measure the valve spring force. One popular type, shown in Figure 23-32, measures the spring force directly. Another type uses a torque wrench on a lever system to measure the valve spring force. Valve springs are checked for the following:

1. Free height (without being compressed) [should be within 1/16 (0.060) inch]
2. Pressure with valve closed and height as per specifications
3. Pressure with valve open and height as per specifications

Most specifications allow for variations of plus or minus 10% from the published figures.

FIGURE 23-32 One popular type of valve spring tester used to measure the compressed force of valve springs. Specifications usually include (1) free height (height without being compressed), (2) pressure at installed height *with valve closed,* and (3) pressure *with valve open* the maximum amount and height to specifications.

(a)

(b)

FIGURE 23-33   Valve split lock types (a) and stem grooves (b).

VALVE KEEPERS

A valve keeper (lock) is used on the end of the valve stem to retain the spring. The inside surface of the split keeper uses a variety of grooves or beads. The design depends on the holding requirements. The outside of the split keeper fits into a cone-shaped seat in the center of the valve spring retainer (see Figure 23-33).

VALVE ROTATORS

Some retainers have built-in devices called valve rotators. They cause the valve to rotate in a controlled manner as it is opened. The purposes and functions of valve rotators include the following:

- Help prevent carbon buildup from forming
- Reduce hot spots on the valves by constantly turning them
- Help to even out the wear on the valve face and seat
- Improve valve guide lubrication

FIGURE 23-34   Notice that there is no gap between the keepers on this Chrysler 4.7 L, V-8. As a result, the valve is free to rotate because the retainer applies a force holding the keepers in place but not tight against the stem of the valve.

The two types of valve rotators are free and positive.

- Free rotators—The free rotators simply take the pressure off the valve to allow engine vibration to rotate the valve. See Figure 23-34.
- Positive rotators—The opening of the valve forces the valve to rotate. One type of positive rotator uses small steel balls and slight ramps. Each ball moves down its ramp to turn the rotor sections as the valve opens. A second type uses a coil spring. The spring lies down as the valve opens. This action turns the rotator body in relation to the collar. Valve rotors are only used when it is desirable to increase the valve service life, because rotors cost more than plain retainers. See Figures 23-35 and 23-36.

VALVE RECONDITIONING PROCEDURE

Valve reconditioning is usually performed using the following sequence:

Step 1   The valve stem is lightly ground and chamfered. This step helps to ensure that the valve will rest in the

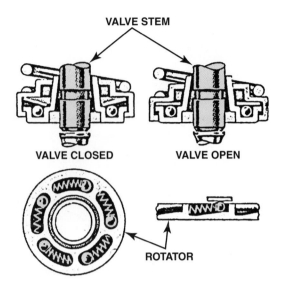

FIGURE 23-35 A ball-type positive valve rotator turns the valve slightly every time the valve opens.

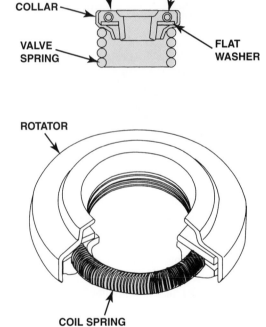

FIGURE 23-36 A coil spring-type positive valve rotator turns the valve when it is open by returning to its original shape and size as the valve is being closed.

collet (holder of the valve stem during valve grinding) of the valve grinder correctly. This process is often called **truing** the valve tip.

Step 2   The face of the valve is ground using a valve grinder.

Step 3   The valve seat is ground in the head. (The seat must be matched to the valve that will be used in that position.)

Step 4   Installed height and valve stem height are checked and corrected as necessary.

TECH TIP

GRINDING THE VALVES FOR MORE POWER

A normal "valve job" includes grinding the face of the valve to clean up any pits and grinding the valve stems to restore the proper stem height. However, a little more airflow in and out of the cylinder head can be accomplished by performing two more simple grinding operations.

- Use the valve grinder and adjust to 30 degrees (for a 45-degree valve) and grind a transition between the valve face and the valve stem area of the valve. While this step may reduce some desirable swirling of the air–fuel mixture at lower engine speeds, it also helps increase cylinder filling, especially at times when the valve is not fully open.

- Chamfer or round the head of the valve between the top of the valve and the margin on the side. By rounding this surface, additional airflow into the cylinder is achieved. See Figure 23-37.

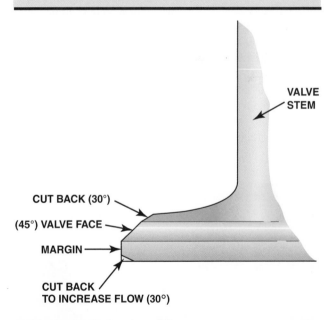

FIGURE 23-37 After grinding the 45-degree face angle, additional airflow into the engine can be accomplished by grinding a transition between the face angle and the stem, as well as angling or rounding the transition between the margin and the top of the valve.

Step 5   After a thorough cleaning, the cylinder head should be assembled with new valve stem seals installed.

The rest of the chapter discusses valve face and seat reconditioning and cylinder head reassembly.

VALVE FACE GRINDING

Each valve grinder operates somewhat differently. The operation manual that comes with the grinder should be followed for lubrication, adjustment, and specific operating procedures. The general procedures given in the following paragraphs apply to all valve grinding equipment.

CAUTION: Safety glasses should *always* be worn for valve and seat reconditioning work. During grinding operations, fine hot chips fly from the grinding stones.

The face of the valve is ground on a **valve grinder.**

NOTE: Many valve grinders use the end of the valve to center the valve while grinding. If the tip of the valve is not square with the stem, the face of the valve may be ground improperly.

See Figure 23-38. After grinding the tip, set the grinder head at the **valve face angle** as specified by the vehicle manufacturer (Figure 23-39). The grinding stone is **dressed** with a special diamond tool to remove any roughness from the stone surface (Figure 23-40). The valve stem is clamped in the work head as close to the fillet under the valve head as possible to prevent vibrations. The work head motor is turned on to rotate the valve. The wheel head motor is turned on to rotate the grinding wheel. The coolant flow is adjusted to flush the material away, but not so much that it splashes (Figure 23-41). The rotating grinding wheel is fed slowly to the rotating valve face. Light grinding is done as the valve is moved back and forth across the grinding wheel face. The valve is never moved off

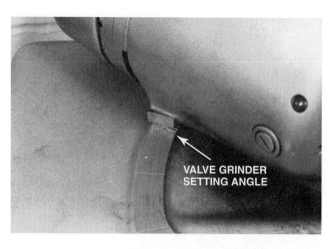

FIGURE 23-39   Valve grinder set to the recommended angle to refinish a valve face. In this case, the angle is set to 44 degrees to provide a 1-degree interference angle between the valve face and the 45-degree valve seat angle.

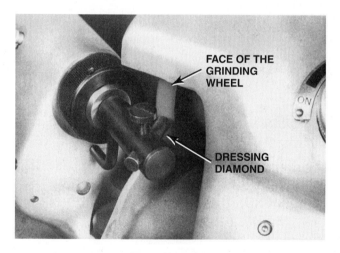

FIGURE 23-40   Dressing the face of the grinding wheel with a diamond dressing tool. This operation helps ensure a good-quality valve face finish.

the edge of the grinding wheel. It is ground only enough to clean the face (Figure 23-42). The margin of the exhaust valve should be over 0.030 inch (0.8 millimeter) when grinding is complete (Figure 23-43).

NOTE: To help visualize a 0.030-inch margin, note that this dimension is about 1/32 inch or the thickness of an American dime.

Intake valves can usually perform satisfactorily with a margin less than 0.030 inch. Always check the engine manufacturer's specifications for the cylinder being serviced. Aluminized valves will lose their corrosion resistance properties when ground. For satisfactory service, aluminized valves must be replaced if they require refacing. Figure 23-44 shows the refacing of a valve using a lathe.

FIGURE 23-38   Valve in a fixture to grind the valve tip.

FIGURE 23-41   Grinding the face of a valve. Note the use of cutting oil to lubricate and cool the grinding operation.

(a)

(b)

FIGURE 23-42   (a) Finished valve face after grinding. Do not remove any more material than is necessary. (b) A valve that is bent. Notice how the grinding stone only removed material from about one-half of the valve face. This valve should be replaced.

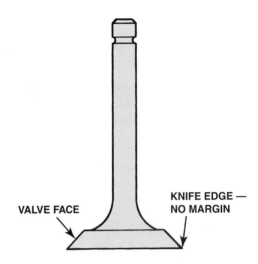

FIGURE 23-43   Never use a valve that has been ground to a sharp edge. This weakens the valve and increases the chance for burning the valve.

FIGURE 23-44   Refacing a valve on a lathe using a special silicon carbide tool bit. The valve face is smoother than it would have been if the valve had been refaced with a stone.

VALVE SEAT RECONDITIONING

The valve seats are reconditioned after the head has been resurfaced and the valve guides have been resized. The final valve seat width and position are checked with the valve that is to be used on the seat being reconditioned.

Valve seats will have a normal seat angle of either 45 degrees or 30 degrees. Narrow 45-degree valve seats will crush carbon deposits to prevent buildup of deposits on the seat. The valve will therefore close tightly on the seat. While the valve is closed on the seat, the valve heat will transfer to the seat and cylinder head. The 30-degree valve seat is more likely to burn than a 45-degree

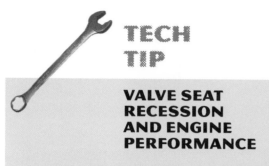

TECH TIP

VALVE SEAT RECESSION AND ENGINE PERFORMANCE

If unleaded fuel is used in an engine without hardened valve seats, valve seat recession is likely to occur in time. Without removing the cylinder heads, how can a technician identify valve seat recession?

As the valve seat wears up into the cylinder head, the valve itself also seats higher in the head. As this wear occurs, the valve lash *decreases.* If hydraulic lifters are used on the engine, this wear will go undetected until the reduction in valve clearance finally removes all clearance (bottoms out) in the lifter. When this occurs, the valve does not seat fully, and compression, power, and fuel economy are drastically reduced. With the valve not closing completely, the valve cannot release its heat and will burn or begin to melt. If the valve burns, the engine will miss and not idle smoothly.

If solid lifters are used on the engine, the decrease in valve clearance will first show up as a rough idle only when the engine is hot. As the valve seat recedes farther into the head, low power, rough idle, poor performance, and lower fuel economy will be noticed sooner than if the engine were equipped with hydraulic lifters.

To summarize, refer to the following symptoms as valve seat recession occurs.

1. Valve lash (clearance) decreases (valves are *not* noisy).
2. The engine idles roughly when hot as a result of reduced valve clearance.
3. Missing occurs, and the engine exhibits low power and poor fuel economy, along with a rough idle, as the valve seat recedes farther into the head.
4. As valves burn, the engine continues to run poorly; the symptoms include difficulty in starting (hot and cold engine), backfiring, and low engine power.

NOTE: If valve lash is adjustable, valve burning can be prevented by adjusting the valve lash regularly. Remember, as the seat recedes, the valve itself recedes, which decreases the valve clearance. Many technicians do not think to adjust valves unless they are noisy. If, during the valve adjustment procedure, a *decrease* in valve lash is noticed, then valve seat recession could be occurring.

seat because some deposits can build up to keep the valve from seating properly. The 30-degree valve seat will, however, allow more gas flow than a 45-degree valve seat when both are opened to the same amount of lift. See Figure 23-45. This is especially true with valve lifts of less than 1/4 inch (6 millimeters). The 30-degree valve seat is also less likely to have valve seat recession than is a 45-degree seat. Generally, when 30-degree valve seats are used, they are used on the cooler-operating intake valves rather than on hot exhaust valves.

The valve seats are only resurfaced enough to remove all pits and grooves and to correct any seat runout. As metal is removed from the seat, the seat is lowered into the head (Figure 23-46). This causes the valve to be located farther into the head when it is closed on the seat. The result of this is that the valve tip extends out farther from the valve guide. The valve being low in the head also tends to restrict the amount of valve opening. This will reduce the flow of gases through the opened valve. The reduced flow of gases, in turn, will reduce the maximum power the engine can produce.

Ideally, the valve face and valve seat should have exactly the same angle. This is impossible, especially on exhaust valves, because the valve head becomes much hotter than the seat and so the valve expands more than the seat. This expansion causes the hot valve to contact the seat in a different place on the valve than it did when it was cold.

Interference Angle

As a result of its shape, the valve does not expand evenly when heated. This uneven expansion also affects the way in which the hot valve contacts the seat. In valve and valve seat reconditioning, the valve is often ground with a face angle 1 degree less than the seat angle to compensate for the change in hot seating. This is illustrated in Figure 23-47. The angle between the valve face and seat is called an **interference angle**. It makes a positive seal at the combustion chamber edge of the seat when the engine is first started after a valve job. As the engine operates, the valve will peen itself on the seat. In a short time, it will make a matched seal. After a few thousand miles, the valve will have formed its own seat. The interference angle has another benefit. The valve and seat are reconditioned with different machines. Each machine must have its angle set before it is used for reconditioning. It is nearly impossible to set the exact same angles on both valve and seat reconditioning machines. Making an interference angle will ensure that any slight angle difference favors a tight seal at the combustion chamber edge of the valve seat when the valve servicing has been completed.

Valve Seat Width

As the valve seats are resurfaced, their widths increase. The resurfaced seats must be narrowed to make the seat width

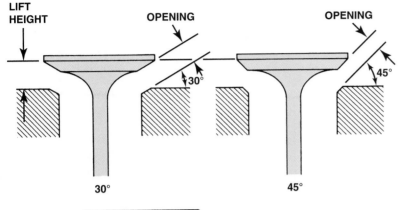

OPENING

OPENING

30°

45°

30°   45°

FIGURE 23-45   Relationship of the valve seating angles to the opening size with the same amount of valve lift. Note that the 30-degree valve angle results in more flow past the valve than is seen with a 45-degree valve.

REGROUND VALVE
SEAT IS LOWERED
INTO THE HEAD

VALVE GUIDE

VALVE TIP EXTENDS
FARTHER OUT OF
THE VALVE GUIDE

FIGURE 23-46   The valve seat is lowered into the cylinder head when ground. This places the valve tip farther from the valve guide toward the rocker arm side of the cylinder head.

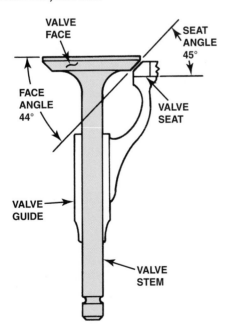

VALVE
FACE

SEAT
ANGLE
45°

FACE
ANGLE
44°

VALVE
SEAT

VALVE
GUIDE

VALVE
STEM

FIGURE 23-47   Some vehicle manufacturers recommend that the valve face be resurfaced at a 44-degree angle and the valve seat at a 45-degree angle. This 1 degree difference is known as the interference angle.

correct and to position the seat properly on the valve face. The normal automotive seat is from 1/16 to 3/32 inch (1.5 to 2.5 millimeters) wide. There should be at least 1/32 inch (0.8 millimeter) of the ground valve face extending above the seat. This is called **overhang.** The fit of a typical reconditioned valve and seat is shown in Figure 23-48. Some manufacturers recommend having the valve seat contact the middle of the valve

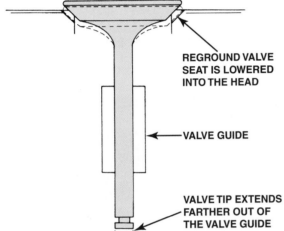

FREQUENTLY ASKED QUESTION

WHAT IS A THREE-ANGLE VALVE JOB?

A three-angle valve job means that the valve seats are ground three times.

- The first angle is the angle of the valve seat specified by the vehicle manufacturer, usually 45°. See Figure 23-49.
- The second angle uses a 60-degree stone or cutter to remove material right below the valve seat to increase flow in or out of the combustion chamber. This angle is called the **throating angle.** See Figure 23-50.
- The third angle uses a 30-degree stone or cutter and is used to smooth the transition between the valve seat and the cylinder head again to increase flow in or out of the combustion chamber. This angle is called the **topping angle.** See Figure 23-51.

The three stones or cutters can be used in combination to create the desired seat width and where it contacts the face of the valve. The 60-degree throating stone will rise and narrow the seat. The 45-degree stone will widen the seat and the 30-degree stone will lower and narrow the seat. See Figure 23-52.

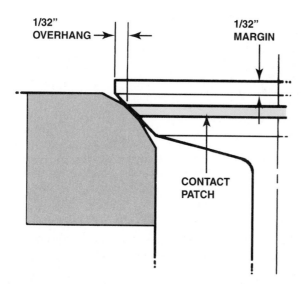

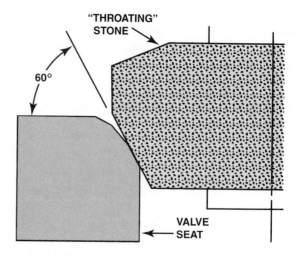

FIGURE 23-48 The seat must contact evenly around the valve face. For good service life, both the margin and the overhang should be at least 1/32 inch (0.8 mm).

FIGURE 23-50 Grinding a 60-degree angle removes metal from the bottom to raise and narrow the valve seat.

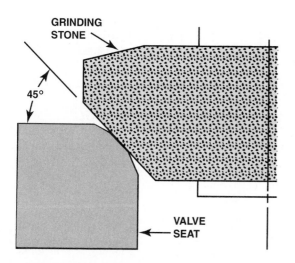

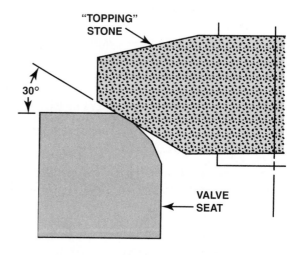

FIGURE 23-49 Grinding a 45-degree angle creates the valve seat in the combustion chamber.

FIGURE 23-51 Grinding a 30-degree angle removes metal from the top to lower and narrow the valve seat.

face. In all cases, the valve seat width and the contact with the valve face should comply with the manufacturer's specifications.

VALVE GUIDE PILOTS

Valve seat reconditioning equipment uses a pilot in the valve guide to align the stone holder or cutter. Two types of pilots are used: tapered and expandable. Examples of these are pictured in Figure 23-53. **Tapered pilots** locate themselves in the least worn section of the guide. They are made in standard sizes and in oversize increments of 0.001 inch, usually up to 0.004 inch oversize. The largest pilot that will fit into the

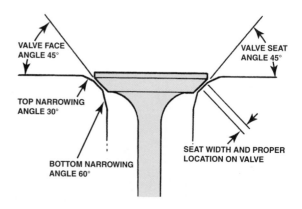

FIGURE 23-52 A typical three-angle valve job using 30-, 45-, and 60-degree stones or cutters.

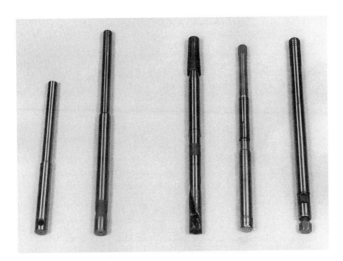

FIGURE 23-53   The two pilots on the left are of a solid tapered type. The three pilots on the right are adjustable (expandable) types.

guide is used for valve seat reconditioning. This type of pilot restores the seat to be as close to the original position as possible when used with worn valve guides.

Two types of **expandable pilots** are used with seating equipment. One type expands in the center of the guide to fit like a tapered pilot. Another expands to contact the ends of the guide where there has been the greatest wear. The valve itself will align in the same way as the pilot.

NOTE: If the guide is not reconditioned, the valve will match the seat when an expandable pilot is used.

The pilot and guide should be thoroughly cleaned. A guide cleaner, as shown in Figures 23-54 and 23-55, that is rotated by a drill motor does a good job of cleaning the guide. The pilot is placed in the guide to act as an aligned support or pilot for the seat reconditioning tools. An expandable pilot is shown in a cutaway valve guide in Figure 23-56.

VALVE SEAT GRINDING STONES

Three basic types of grinding stones are used. All are used dry. A **roughing stone** is used to rapidly remove large amounts of seat metal. This would be necessary on a badly pitted seat or when installing new valve seat inserts. The roughing stone is sometimes called a seat **forming stone.** After the seat forming stone is used, a **finishing stone** is used to put the proper finish on the seat. The finishing stone is also used to recondition cast-iron seats that are only slightly worn. **Hard seat stones** are used on hard stellite exhaust seat inserts.

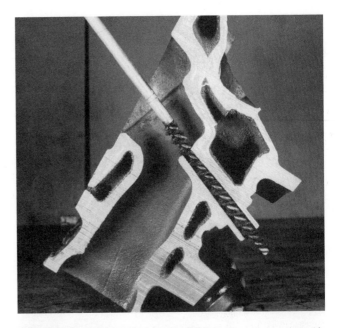

FIGURE 23-54   Sectioned head showing how a brush valve guide cleaner is used.

FIGURE 23-55   Using a valve guide brush with an electric drill. This cleaning of the valve guides is very important for proper valve seat reconditioning.

NOTE: Stellite is a nonmagnetic hard alloy used for valve seats in heavy-duty applications.

The stone diameter and face angle must be correct. The diameter of the stone must be larger than the valve head, but it must be small enough that it does not contact the edge of the combustion chamber. The angle of the grinding surface of the stone must be correct for the seat. When an interference angle is used with reground valves, it is common practice to use a seat with the standard seat angle. The interference

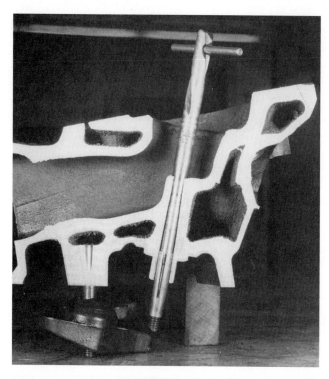

FIGURE 23-56   Expandable pilot shown in the valve guide of a sectioned head to illustrate how the pilot fits.

FIGURE 23-57   Tip of a diamond dressing tool.

angle is ground on the valve face. In some cases, such as with an aluminized valve, the valve has the standard angle and the seat is ground to give the interference angle. The required seat angle must be determined *before* the seat grinding stone is dressed.

DRESSING THE GRINDING STONE

The selected grinding stone is installed on the stone holder. A drop of oil is placed on the spindle of the dressing fixture, and the assembly is placed on the spindle. The dressing tool diamond (Figure 23-57) is adjusted so that it extends 3/8 inch or less from its support. The valve seat angle is adjusted on the fixture. The driver for the seating tool is placed in the top of the stone holder. This assembly is shown in Figure 23-58. The holder and grinding stone assembly is rotated with the driver. The diamond is adjusted so that it just touches the stone face. The diamond dressing tool is moved slowly across the face of the spinning stone, taking a very light cut. Dressing the stone in this way will give it a clean, sharp cutting surface. It is necessary to redress the stone each time a stone is placed on a holder, at the beginning of each valve job, and any time the stone is not cutting smoothly and cleanly while grinding valve seats.

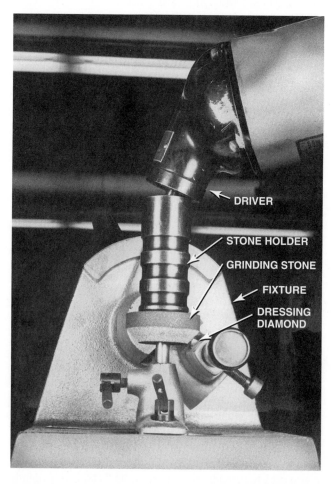

FIGURE 23-58   Typical assembly for dressing a valve seat grinding stone.

FIGURE 23-60   Finished valve seat shown on a cutaway head.

0.002 inch (0.05 millimeter) before the seat is finished. See Figure 23-61. The dial gauge measurement of the valve seat is very important. The maximum acceptable variation is 0.002 inch. This reading gives the **total indicator runout (TIR)** of the valve seat.

NARROWING THE VALVE SEAT

The valve seat becomes wider as it is ground. It is therefore necessary to narrow the seat so that it will contact the valve properly. The seat is **topped** with a grinding stone dressed to 15 degrees less than the seat angle. Topping lowers the top edge of the seat. The amount of topping required can best be checked by measuring the maximum valve face diameter using dividers. The dividers are then adjusted to a setting 1/16-inch smaller to give the minimum valve face overhang. The seat is measured and then topped with short grinding bursts, as required, to equal the diameter set on the dividers. The seat width is then measured. If it is too wide, the seat must be **throated** with a stone with a 60-degree angle. This removes metal from the port side of the seat, raising the lower edge of the seat. Generally accepted seat widths are as follows:

- For intake valves: 1/16 inch or 0.0625 inch (about the thickness of a nickel) (1.5 millimeters)
- For exhaust valves: 3/32 inch or 0.0938 inch (about the thickness of a dime and a nickel together) (2.4 millimeters)

The completed seat must be checked with the valve that is to be used on the seat. This can be done by marking across the valve face at four or five places with a felt-tip marker. The valve is then inserted in the guide so that the valve face contacts the seat. The valve is rotated 20 to 30 degrees and then removed. The location of the seat contact on the valve is observed where the felt-tip marking has been rubbed off from

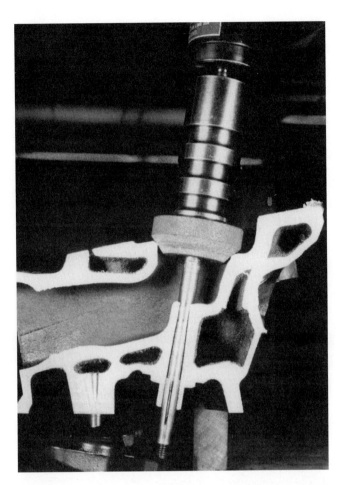

FIGURE 23-59   Typical setup for grinding a valve seat shown on a cutaway head.

VALVE SEAT GRINDING

It is a good practice to clean each valve seat before grinding. This keeps the soil from filling the grinding stone. The pilot is then placed in the valve guide. A drop of oil is placed on the end of the pilot to lubricate the holder. The holder, with the dressed grinding stone, is placed over the pilot. The driver should be supported so that no driver weight is on the holder. This allows the stone abrasive and the metal chips to fly out from between the stone and seat to give fast, smooth grinding. Grinding is done in short bursts, allowing the seating stone to rotate for approximately 10 turns. See Figure 23-59. The holder and stone should be lifted from the seat between each grinding burst to check the condition of the seat. The finished seat should be bright and smooth across the entire surface, with no pits or roughness remaining (Figure 23-60).

Some of the induction hardness from the exhaust valve seat will sometimes extend over into the intake seat. It may be necessary to apply a slight pressure on the driver toward the hardened spot to form a concentric seat. The seat is checked with a dial gauge to make sure that it is concentric within

FIGURE 23-61 Typical dial indicator-type of micrometer for measuring valve seat concentricity.

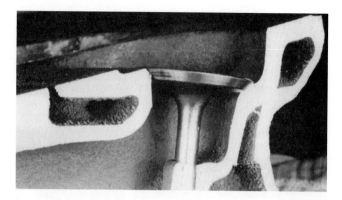

FIGURE 23-62 On this cutaway head, the location of the valve seat is shown where the ink from the felt-tip pen has transferred from the seat to the valve face. Prussian blue can also be used instead of a felt-tip marker.

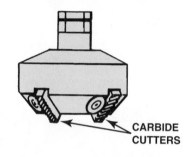

CARBIDE CUTTERS

FIGURE 23-63 A cutter is used to remove metal and form the valve seat angles.

the valve. Valve seating can be seen in Figure 23-62. Valve seat grinding is complete when each of the valve seats has been properly ground, topped, and throated.

To summarize:

- Using a 30-degree topping stone (for a 45-degree seat) *lowers* the upper outer edge and narrows the seat.
- Using a 60-degree throating stone *raises* the lower inner edge and narrows the seat.
- Using a 45-degree stone *widens* the seat.

VALVE SEAT CUTTERS

Some automotive service technicians prefer to use valve seat cutters rather than valve seat grinders. See Figure 23-63. The valve seats can be reconditioned to commercial standards in much less time when using the cutters rather than the grinders. A number of cutting blades are secured at the correct seat angle in the cutting head of this valve seat reconditioning tool. The cutter angle usually includes the interference angle so that new valves with standard valve face angles can be used

without grinding the new valve face. The cutters do not require dressing as stones do. The cutting head assembly is placed on a pilot in the same way that the grinding stone holder is used. The cutter is rotated by hand or by using a special speed reduction motor. Only metal chips are produced. The finished seat is checked for concentricity and fit against the valve face using the felt-tip marker method previously described.

CAUTION: A cutter should only be rotated clockwise. If a cutter is rotated counterclockwise, damage to the cutting surfaces ruins the cutter.

VALVE SEAT TESTING

After the valves have been refaced and the guides and valve seats have been resurfaced, the valves should be inspected for proper sealing and to make certain that the valve seat is concentric with the valve face. Several methods that are often used to check valve face-to-seat concentricity and valve seating include the following:

1. Vacuum testing can be done by applying vacuum to the intake and/or exhaust port using a tight rubber seal and

a vacuum pump. A good valve face-to-seat seal is indicated by the maintaining of at least 28 inches Hg of vacuum. This method also tests for leakage around the valve guides. Put some engine oil around the guides; if vacuum increases, valve guides may have excessive clearance.

2. The ports or chamber can be filled with mineral spirits or some other suitable fluid. A good seal should not leak fluid for at least 45 seconds.

3. Valve seating can be checked by applying air pressure to the combustion chamber and checking for air leakage past the valve seat. See Figure 23-64.

VALVE SEAT REPLACEMENT

Valve seats need to be replaced if they are cracked or if they are burned or eroded too much to be reseated. A badly eroded valve seat is shown in Figure 23-65. It may not be possible to determine whether a valve seat needs to be replaced before an attempt is made to recondition the valve seat. Valve seat replacement is accomplished by using a pilot in the valve guide. This means that the valve guide must be reconditioned *before* the seat can be replaced. Damaged **insert valve seats** are removed and the old seat counter bore is cleaned to accept a new oversize seat insert. Damaged integral valve seats must be counter bored to make a place for the new insert seat.

The old insert seat is removed by one of several methods. A small pry bar can be used to snap the seat from the counter bore. It is sometimes easier to do this if the old seat is drilled to weaken it. Be careful not to drill into the head material. Sometimes, an expandable hook-type puller is used to remove the seat insert. See the Tech Tip, "The MIG Welder Seat Removal Trick." The seat counter bore must be cleaned before the new, oversize seat is installed. The replacement inserts have a 0.002- to 0.003-inch

(0.05- to 0.07-millimeter) interference fit in the counter bore. The counter bores are cleaned and properly sized, using the same equipment described in the following paragraph for installing replacement seats in place of faulty integral valve seats.

Cracked or badly burned integral valve seats can often be replaced to salvage the head. All head cracks are repaired *before* the old integral seat is removed. The replacement seat is selected first. It must have the correct inside and outside diameters and it must have the correct thickness. Manufacturers of replacement valve seats supply tables that specify the

TECH TIP

THE MIG WELDER SEAT REMOVAL TRICK

A quick and easy method to remove insert valve seats is to use a **metal inert gas (MIG)** welder, also called a **gas metal arc welding (GMAW)** welder. After the valve has been removed, use the MIG welder and lay a welding bead around the seat area of the insert. As the welder cools, it shrinks and allows the insert to be easily removed from the cylinder head.

FIGURE 23-64 Testing for leakage past the valves by injecting compressed air into the combustion chamber through the spark plug hole. To prevent leakage at the head gasket surface, the cylinder head is placed on a foam rubber pad.

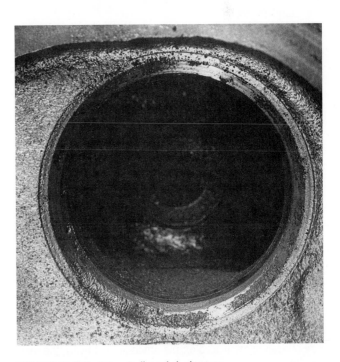

FIGURE 23-65 Badly eroded valve seat.

FIGURE 23-66 Insert valve seats are rings of metal driven into the head.

proper seat insert to be used. See Figure 23-66. If an insert is being replaced, the new insert must be of the same type of material as the original insert or better. Insert exhaust valve seats operate at temperatures that are 100° to 150°F (56° to 83°C) hotter than those of integral seats up to 900°F (480°C). Upgraded valve and valve seat materials are required to give the same service life as that of the original seats. Removable valve seats are available in different materials including:

- Cast iron
- Stainless steel
- Nickel cobalt
- Powdered metal (PM)

A counter bore cutting tool is selected that will cut the correct diameter for the outside of the insert. The diameter of the bore is smaller than the outside diameter of the seat insert. The cutting tool is positioned securely in the tool holder so that it will cut the counter bore at the correct diameter. The tool holder is attached to the size of pilot that fits the valve guide. The tool holder feed mechanism is screwed together so that it has enough threads to properly feed the cutter into the head. This assembly is placed in the valve guide so that the cutting tool rests on the seat that is to be removed.

The new insert is placed between the support fixture and the stop ring. The stop ring is adjusted against the new insert so that cutting will stop when the counter bore reaches the depth of the new insert. See Figure 23-67. The boring tool is turned by hand or with a reduction gear motor drive. It cuts until the stop ring reaches the fixture. See Figure 23-68. The support fixture and the tool holder are removed. The pilot and the correct size of adapter are placed on the driving tool. Ideally, the seats should be cooled with dry ice to cause them to shrink. Each

FIGURE 23-67 Adjusting the cutting tool stop ring with the new valve insert as a guide.

insert should be left in the dry ice until it is to be installed. This will allow it to be installed with little chance of metal being sheared from the counter bore. Sheared chips could become jammed under the insert, keeping it from seating properly. The chilled seat is placed on the counter bore. The driver with a pilot is then quickly placed in the valve guide so that the seat will be driven squarely into the counter bore. The driver is hit with a heavy hammer to seat the insert, as shown in Figure 23-69. Heavy blows are used to start the insert, and lighter blows are used as the seat reaches the bottom of the counter bore. It serves no purpose to hit the driver after the insert is seated in the bottom of the counter bore. The installed valve seat insert is peened in place by running a peening tool around the metal on the outside of the seat. The peened metal is slightly displaced over the edge of the insert to help hold it in place. A fully installed seat insert is shown in Figure 23-70 on page 424. Seats are formed on the replacement inserts using the same procedures described for reconditioning valve seats.

FIGURE 23-68   Seat cutting tool boring out the old eroded valve seat.

(a)

OUTSIDE DIAMETER (IN.)	INSERT DEPTH (IN.)	INTERFERENCE FIT (IN.)
0 – 1	0 – $\frac{1}{4}$	0.001 – 0.003
1 – 2	$\frac{1}{4} - \frac{3}{8}$	0.002 – 0.004
2 – 3	$\frac{3}{8} - \frac{9}{16}$	0.003 – 0.005
3 – 4	$\frac{9}{16} - 1$	0.004 – 0.006

(b)

FIGURE 23-69   (a) Seating the new chilled insert in the counter bore by hitting the driver with a heavy hammer. (b) Interference fit for valve inserts (hard cast or wrought inserts).

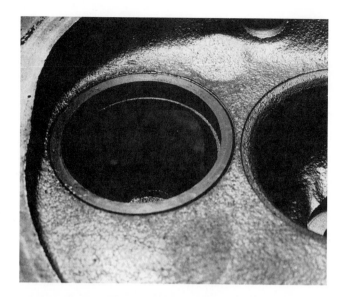

FIGURE 23-70   Fully installed valve seat insert.

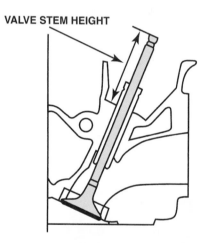

FIGURE 23-71   Valve stem height is measured from the spring seat to the tip of the valve after the valve seat and valve face have been refinished. If the valve stem height is too high, up to 0.020 inch can be ground from the tips of most valves.

VALVE STEM HEIGHT

Valve stem height is a different measurement from installed height. See Figure 23-71. Valve stem height is important to maintain for all engines, but especially for overhead camshaft engines. When the valve seat and the valve face are ground, the valve stem extends deeper into the combustion chamber and extends higher or further into the cylinder head.

The valve is put in the head, and the length of the tip is measured. The tip is ground to shorten the valve stem length to compensate for the valve face and seat grinding. The valve will not close if the valve tip extends too far from the valve guide on engines that have hydraulic lifters and nonadjustable rocker arms. If the valve is too long, the tip may be ground by

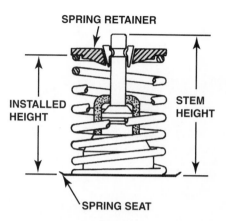

FIGURE 23-72   Measure the distance from the spring seat to the bottom of the retainer to find the installed height.

as much as 0.020 inch (0.50 millimeter) to reduce its length. If more grinding is required, the valve must be replaced. If it is too short, the valve face or seat may be reground, within limits, to allow the valve to seat deeper. Where excessive valve face and seat grinding has been done, shims can be placed under the rocker shaft on some engines as a repair to provide correct hydraulic lifter plunger centering. These shims must have the required lubrication holes to allow oil to enter the shaft.

CHECKING INSTALLED HEIGHT

When the valves and/or valve seats have been machined, the valve projects farther than before on the rocker arm side of the head. (The valve face is slightly recessed into the combustion chamber side of the head.) The valve spring tension is, therefore, reduced because the spring is not as compressed as it was originally. To restore original valve spring tension, special valve spring spacers, inserts, or shims are installed under the valve springs. These shims are usually called **valve spring inserts (VSI).** Valve spring inserts are generally available in three different thicknesses:

- 0.015 inch (0.38 millimeter)—Used for balancing valve spring pressure.
- 0.030 inch (0.75 millimeter)—Generally used for new springs on cylinder heads that have had the valve seats ground and valves refaced.
- 0.060 inch (1.5 millimeter)—Necessary to bring assembled height to specifications. (These thicker inserts may be required if the seats have been resurfaced more than one time.)

Step 1   To determine the exact thickness of insert to install, measure the valve spring height (as installed in the head). See Figure 23-72.

Step 2   If the installed height is greater than specifications, select the insert (shim) that brings the installed height to within specifications. See Figure 23-73.

VALVE STEM SEALS

Leakage past the valve guides is a major oil consumption problem in any overhead valve (or overhead cam) engine. A high vacuum exists in the intake port, as shown in Figure 23-74.

Most engine manufacturers use valve stem seals on the exhaust valve, because a weak vacuum in the exhaust port area can draw oil into the exhaust stream, as illustrated in Figure 23-75.

Valve stem seals are used on overhead valve engines to control the amount of oil used to lubricate the valve stem as it moves in the guide. The stem and guide will scuff if they do not have enough oil. Too much oil will cause excessive oil consumption and will cause heavy carbon deposits to build up on the spark plug nose and on the fillet of the valves.

(a)

(b)

FIGURE 23-73   (a) Valve spring inserts (VSI) (also called shims) are installed between the cylinder head and valve spring to restore the valve to its proper installed height. (b) The serrations of the valve spring insert should face toward the cylinder head. The purpose of the serrations is to allow air to flow between the insert and the head to help keep the spring cooler.

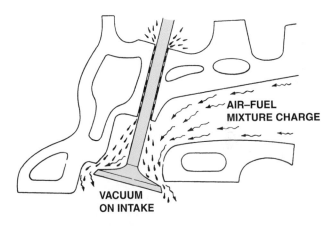

FIGURE 23-74   Engine vacuum can draw oil past the valve guides and into the combustion chamber. The use of valve stem seals limits the amount of oil that is drawn into the engine. If the seals are defective, excessive blue (oil) smoke is most often observed during engine start-up.

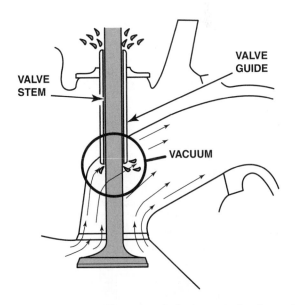

FIGURE 23-75   Engine oil can also be drawn past the exhaust valve guide because of a small vacuum created by the flow of exhaust gases. Any oil drawn past the guide would simply be forced out through the exhaust system and not enter the engine. Some engine manufacturers do not use valve stem seals on the exhaust valves.

TYPES OF VALVE STEM SEALS

- The **umbrella valve stem seal** holds tightly on the valve stem and moves up and down with the valve. Any oil that spills off the rocker arms is deflected out over the valve guide, much as water is deflected over an umbrella. See Figure 23-76. As a result, umbrella valve stem seals are often called **deflector valve stem seals.**
- **Positive valve stem seals** hold tightly around the valve guide, and the valve stem moves through the seal. The seal wipes the excess oil from the valve stem. See Figure 23-77.
- **O-ring valve stem seal** used on Chevrolet engines keeps oil from leaking between the valve stem and valve spring retainer. The oil is deflected over the retainer and shield. See Figure 23-78. The assembly controls oil like an umbrella-type oil seal. Both types of valve stem seals allow only the

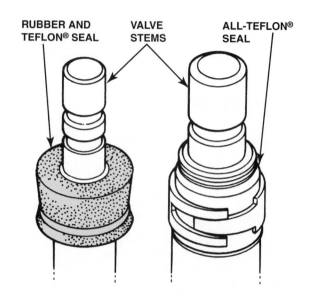

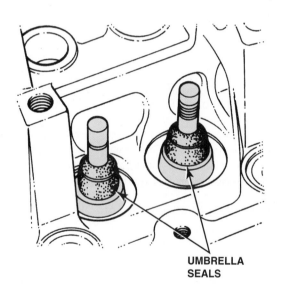

UMBRELLA SEALS

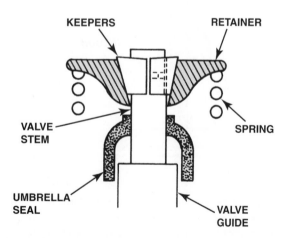

FIGURE 23-76 Umbrella seals install over the valve stems and cover the guide.

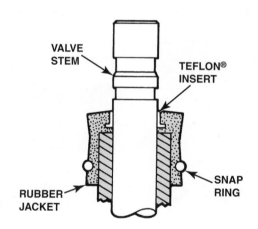

FIGURE 23-77 Positive valve stem seals are the most effective type.

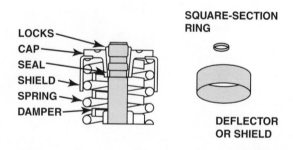

FIGURE 23-78 A small square cut O-ring is installed under the retainer in a groove in the valve under the groove(s) used for the keepers (locks).

correct amount of oil to reach the valve guide to lubricate the valve stem. The rest of the oil flows back to the oil pan.

Valve Seal Materials

Valve stem seals are made from many different types of materials. They may be made from nylon or Teflon®, but most valve stem seals are made from synthetic rubber. Three types of synthetic rubbers are in common use:

- Nitrile (Nitril)
- Polyacrylate
- Viton

Nitrile is the oldest valve stem seal material. It has a low cost and a low useful temperature. Engine temperatures have increased with increased emission controls and improved efficiencies, which made it necessary to use premium polyacrylate, even with its higher cost. In many cases, it is being retrofit to the older engines because it will last much longer than Nitrile. Diesel engines and engines used for racing, heavy trucks, and trailer towing, along with turbocharging, operate at still higher temperatures. These engines may require expensive Viton valve stem seals that operate at higher temperatures. See Figure 23-79.

It is interesting to note that an automotive service technician cannot tell the difference between these synthetic rubber valve stem seals if they have come out of the same mold for the same engine. Often suppliers that package gasket sets for sale at a low price will include low-temperature Nitrile, even when the engine needs higher-temperature polyacrylate. Your best chance of getting the correct valve stem seal material for an engine is to purchase gaskets and seals packaged by a major brand gasket company.

INSTALLING THE VALVES

The cylinder head can be assembled after the head is thoroughly cleaned with soap and water to wash away any remaining grit and metal shavings from the valve grinding operation. Valves are assembled in the head, one at a time. The valve guide and stem are given a liberal coating of engine oil, and the valve is installed in its guide. Umbrella and positive

FIGURE 23-79 Poor-quality umbrella-type valve stem seal after several months of use. Note how heat has softened this seal and destroyed its sealing ability.

TECH TIP

"CC" THE HEADS FOR BEST PERFORMANCE

For best engine performance and smooth operation, all cylinders should have the same compression. To accurately measure the volume of the combustion chamber, a graduated burette is used with mineral spirits (or automatic transmission fluid) to measure the exact volume of the chamber in cubic centimeters (cc). See Figure 23-80.

FIGURE 23-80 Setup needed to measure the combustion chamber volume in cubic centimeters (cc).

valve stem seals are installed. Push umbrella seals down until they touch the valve guide. Use a plastic sleeve over the tip of the valve when installing positive seals. Make sure that the positive seal is fully seated on the valve guide and that it is square. See Figure 23-81. Hold the valve against the seat as the valve spring seat or insert, valve spring, valve seals, and retainer are placed over the valve stem. One end of the valve spring compressor pushes on the retainer to compress the spring. See Figure 23-82. The O-ring type of valve stem seal is installed in the lower groove. The valve keepers are installed while the valve spring is compressed. See Figure 23-83.

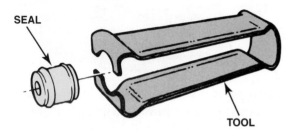

FIGURE 23-81   Use a seal installation tool to push positive-type valve stem seals onto the guides.

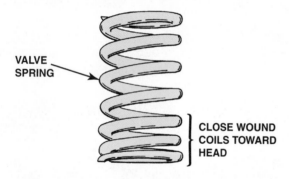

FIGURE 23-82   The tightly coiled end of a variable pitch spring should be installed toward the cylinder head.

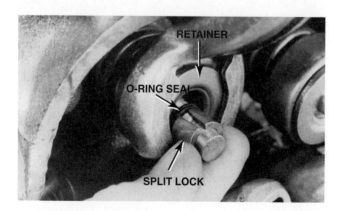

FIGURE 23-83   Proper installation of a typical Chevrolet O-ring valve stem seal and valve locks.

Release the valve spring compressor slowly and carefully while making sure that the valve keepers seat properly between the valve stem grooves and the retainer. See Figure 23-84. Each valve is assembled in the same manner. Attach the hose from a vacuum pump to the top of the assembled valve.

(a)

(b)

(c)

FIGURE 23-84   (a) Air-operated valve spring compressor being used to install valves. If the compressor compresses the valve spring too much, the O-ring valve stem seal may be knocked out of location when the compressor is released. (b) Putting grease on the split locks (keepers) helps to retain them when releasing pressure on the valve spring compressor to help prevent improper seating. (c) Valve after installation. Note the grease on the valve. The grease should be wiped off to prevent the possibility of certain greases clogging oil filters after the engine starts.

(a)

(b)

FIGURE 23-85   (a) A hand-operated vacuum pump is used to check the O-ring valve stem seals on this Chevrolet V-8 cylinder head. (b) A close-up showing the sealing cup over the retainer.

A vacuum will hold if the O-ring type of valve stem seal is correctly installed, as shown in Figure 23-85.

FLOW TESTING CYLINDER HEADS

Many specialty engines are tested for the amount of air that can flow through the ports and valves of the engine. A flow bench is used to measure the amount of air [measured in cubic feet per minute (cfm)] that can flow through the valves at various valve openings.

After completion of the valve job and any port or combustion chamber work, weak valve springs are installed temporarily. See Figure 23-86. Modeling clay is then temporarily applied around the ports to improve flow characteristics around the port area where the intake manifold would normally direct the flow into the port. See Figure 23-87.

Various thicknesses of metal spacers are placed between the cylinder head holding fixture and the valve stem. See Figure 23-88. Typical thicknesses used are 0.100 through 0.700 inch in 0.100-inch increments. The results are recorded on a work sheet. See Figure 23-89.

FIGURE 23-86   Cylinder head setup for flow testing. Note the weak valve springs that are strong enough to keep the valves shut, yet weak enough to permit the flow bench operator to vary the intake valve opening amount.

CYLINDER HEAD FLOW VERSUS HORSEPOWER

Most comprehensive engine machine shops have the equipment to measure the airflow through cylinder head ports and valves. After the airflow through the open intake valve has

FIGURE 23-87 Modeling clay is installed around the port to duplicate the flow improvement characteristics of an intake manifold.

0.100" THICK SPACER (OPENS VALVE OFF SEAT)

TEST VALVE SPRINGS

FIGURE 23-88 By varying the thickness of the metal spacers, the flow bench operator can measure the airflow through the intake and exhaust ports and valves at various valve lifts.

PRESSURE DROP _____ 28" _____   NAME _____ TEST INFO _____

APPLICATION _____ DART II IRON S.B/K. _____

_____ IN = 2.055 _____ EX = 1.600 _____

3 ANGLE   GRIND ONLY

VALVE LIFT (in.)

	CYL. #	COMMENTS	R 0.100		R 0.200		R 0.300		R 0.400		R 0.500		R 0.600		R 0.700	
	IN		3	57.5	3	93.8	4	63.5	4	73.6	4	74.8	4	76.5	4	77.5
		CFM		88		144		189		219		223		228		231
	IN															
		CFM														
	IN															
		CFM														
A I R	IN															
		CFM														
F L O W	EX		2	60.5	3	58.5	3	70.0	3	76.0	3	80.2	3	82.0	3	83.2
		CFM		54		95		113		123		130		133		135
	EX															
		CFM														
	EX															
		CFM														
	EX															
		CFM														

FIGURE 23-89 A typical flow bench worksheet. Note that the cylinder head was tested up to 0.700 inch of lift.

been determined, a formula can be used to estimate horse-power. The following formula has proven to be a fairly accurate estimate of horsepower when compared with dynamometer testing after the engine is built.

NOTE: The first part of the formula is used to convert airflow measurement from a basis of being tested at 28 inches of water to that of being tested at 20 inches of water.

Horsepower per cylinder = Airflow at 28 inches of water
$$\times \ 0.598 \times 0.43$$

For example, for a V-8 that measures 231 cfm of airflow at 28 inches of water:

Horsepower = 231 × 0.598 = 138 cfm at 20 inches of
water × 0.43 = 59.4 hp per cylinder × 8 = 475 hp

CAUTION: Even though this formula has proven to be fairly accurate, there are too many variables in the design of any engine besides the airflow through the head for this formula to be accurate under all conditions.

TECH TIP

DO NOT SIMPLY BOLT ON NEW CYLINDER HEADS

New assembled cylinder heads, whether aluminum or cast iron, are a popular engine buildup option. However, experience has shown that metal shavings and casting sand are often found inside the passages.

Before bolting on these "ready to install" heads, disassemble them and clean all passages. Often machine shavings are found under the valves. If this debris were to get into the engine, the results would be extreme wear or damage to the pistons, rings, block, and bearings. This cleaning may take several hours, but how much is your engine worth?

INSTALLING A NEW VALVE SEAT Step-by-Step

STEP 1 After the valve guide has been replaced or checked for being within specification, insert a pilot into the valve guide.

STEP 2 Level the bubble on the pilot by moving the cylinder head, which is clamped to a seat/guide machine.

STEP 3 Select the proper guide for the application. Consult guide manufacturer's literature for recommendations.

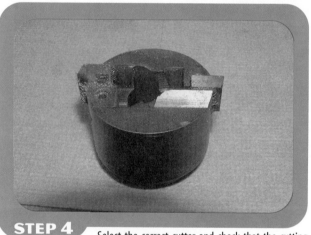

STEP 4 Select the correct cutter and check that the cutting bits are sharp.

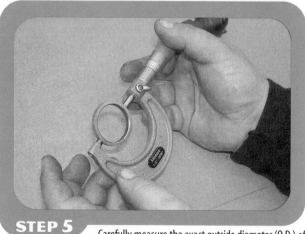

STEP 5 Carefully measure the exact outside diameter (O.D.) of the valve seat.

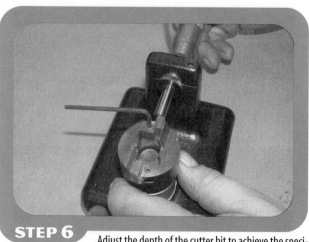

STEP 6 Adjust the depth of the cutter bit to achieve the specified interference fit for the valve seat.

INSTALLING A NEW VALVE SEAT   continued

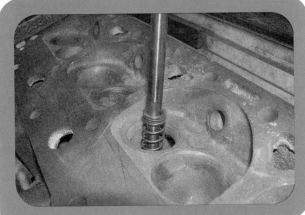

STEP 7   Install the pilot into the valve guide to support the seat cutter.

STEP 8   Install the seat cutter onto the pilot.

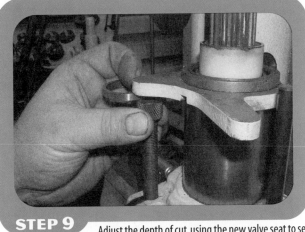

STEP 9   Adjust the depth of cut, using the new valve seat to set it to the same depth as the thickness of the seat.

STEP 10   With the cylinder head still firmly attached to the seat and guide machine, start the cutter motor and cut the head until it reaches the stop.

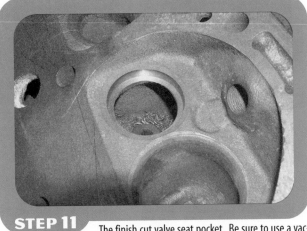

STEP 11   The finish cut valve seat pocket. Be sure to use a vacuum to remove all of the metal shavings from the cutting operation.

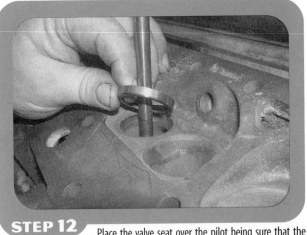

STEP 12   Place the valve seat over the pilot being sure that the chamfer is facing toward the head as shown.

(continued)

INSTALLING A NEW VALVE SEAT   continued

STEP 13   Install the correct size driver onto the valve seat.

STEP 14   Using the air hammer or press, press the valve seat into the valve pocket.

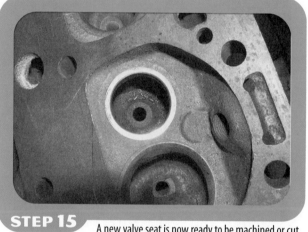

STEP 15   A new valve seat is now ready to be machined or cut.

SUMMARY

1. The exhaust valve is about 85% of the size of the intake valve.
2. Valve springs should be kept with the valve at the time of disassembly and tested for squareness and proper spring force.
3. Free and positive are two types of valve rotators.
4. Valve grinding should start with truing the valve tip; then the face should be refinished. A pilot is placed into the valve guide to position the stone or cutter correctly for resurfacing the valve seat.
5. The installed height should be checked and corrected with valve spring inserts, if needed.
6. Valve stem height should be checked and the top of the valve ground, if necessary.
7. After a thorough cleaning, the cylinder head should be assembled using new valve stem seals.

REVIEW QUESTIONS

1. Why is valve guide reconditioning the first cylinder head servicing operation?
2. When is the valve tip ground? How do you know how much to remove from the tip?
3. What is an interference angle between the valve and the seat?
4. Describe the difference between cutting and grinding valve seats.
5. How is a valve seat insert installed?
6. How are the correct valve spring inserts (shims) selected and why are they used?

CHAPTER QUIZ

1. In a normally operating engine, intake and exhaust valves are opened by a cam and closed by the _____.
   a. Rocker arms or cam follower
   b. Valve spring
   c. Lifters (tappets)
   c. Valve guide and/or pushrod

2. If an interference angle is machined on a valve or seat, this angle is usually _____.
   a. 1 degree
   b. 0.005 degree
   c. 1 to 3 degrees
   d. 0.5 to 0.75 degree

3. Never remove more material from the tip of a valve than _____.
   a. 0.001 inch
   b. 0.002 inch
   c. 0.020 inch
   d. 0.050 inch

4. A valve should be discarded if the margin is less than _____ after refacing.
   a. 0.001 inch
   b. 0.006 inch
   c. 0.025 inch
   d. 0.060 inch

5. A valve seat should be concentric to the valve guide to a maximum TIR of _____.
   a. 0.006 inch
   b. 0.004 inch
   c. 0.002 inch
   d. 0.00015 inch

6. To lower and narrow a valve seat that has been cut at a 45-degree angle, use a cutter or stone of what angle?
   a. 60 degrees
   b. 45 degrees
   c. 30 degrees
   d. 15 degrees

7. Valve spring inserts (shims) are designed to _____.
   a. Increase installed height of the valve
   b. Decrease installed height of the valve
   c. Adjust the correct installed height
   d. Decrease valve spring pressure to compensate for decreased installed height

8. The proper relationship between intake and exhaust valve diameter is _____.
   a. Intake valve size is 85% of exhaust valve size
   b. Exhaust valve size is 85% of intake valve size
   c. Exhaust valve size is 38% of intake valve size
   d. Intake valve size is 45% of exhaust valve size

9. Dampers (damper springs) are used inside some valve springs to _____.
   a. Prevent valve spring surge
   b. Keep the valve spring attached to the valve
   c. Decrease valve spring pressure
   d. Retain valve stem seals

10. Umbrella-type valve stem seals _____.
    a. Fit tightly onto the valve guide
    b. Fit on the valve face to prevent combustion leaks
    c. Fit tightly onto the valve stem
    d. Lock under the valve retainer

CAMSHAFTS AND VALVE TRAINS

OBJECTIVES

After studying Chapter 24, the reader will be able to:

1. Prepare for the Engine Repair (A1) ASE certification test content area "B" (Cylinder Head and Valve Train Diagnosis and Repair).

2. Describe how the camshaft and valve train function.
3. Discuss valve train noise and its causes.
4. Explain how to degree a camshaft.
5. Explain how a hydraulic lifter works.

KEY TERMS

Aerated (p. 472)
Asymmetrical (p. 448)
Bucket (p. 452)
Cam Chucking (p. 446)
Cam Follower (p. 452)
Cam-in-Block (p. 438)
Camshaft Bearings (p. 438)
Camshaft Duration (p. 453)
Camshaft Overlap (p. 454)
Composite Camshaft (p. 441)
Contour (p. 438)
Exhaust Valve Cam Phaser (EVCP) (p. 463)
Finger Follower (p. 452)
Flat-Link Type (p. 444)
Freewheeling (p. 445)

Hydraulic Lash Adjusters (HLA) (p. 452)
Hydraulic Valve Lifter (p. 467)
Intake Centerline (p. 459)
Intake Lobe Centerline Method (p. 458)
Lift (p. 447)
Lifter Preload (p. 469)
Lobe Centers (p. 454)
Lobe Displacement Angle (LDA) (p. 454)
Lobe Separation (p. 454)
Lobe Spread (p. 454)
Morse Type (p. 444)
Oil Control Valve (OCV) (p. 461)
Overhead Camshaft (OHC) (p. 438)
Overhead Valve (OHV) (p. 439)
Pump-Up (p. 469)

Ramp (p. 467)
Seat Duration (p. 458)
Silent Chain Type (p. 444)
Solid Valve Lifter (p. 467)
Symmetrical (p. 448)
Thrust Plate (p. 446)
Total Indicator Runout (TIR) (p. 456)
Valve Float (p. 469)
Valve Lash (p. 467)
Variable Valve Timing (VVT) (p. 462)
Variable Valve Timing and Lift Electronic Control (VTEC) (p. 466)
Zinc Dithiophosphate (ZDP) (p. 456)

CAMSHAFT PURPOSE AND FUNCTION

The camshaft is driven by timing gears, chains, or belts located at the front of the engine. The gear or sprocket on the camshaft has twice as many teeth, or notches, as the one on the crankshaft. This results in two crankshaft turns for each turn of the camshaft. *The camshaft turns at one-half the crankshaft speed in all four-stroke-cycle engines.*

The camshaft's major function is to operate the valve train. Cam shape or **contour** is the major factor in determining the operating characteristics of the engine. The lobes on the camshaft open the valves against the pressure of the valve springs. The camshaft lobe changes rotary motion (camshaft) to linear motion (valves).

Cam lobe shape has more control over engine performance characteristics than any other single engine part. Engines identical in every way except cam lobe shape may have completely different operating characteristics and performance. Two cam shapes for a small-block Chevrolet V-8 are shown in Figure 24-1.

The camshaft may also operate the following:

- Mechanical fuel pump
- Oil pump
- Distributor

See Figure 24-2.

CAMSHAFT LOCATION

Pushrod engines have the cam located in the block. See Figure 24-3.

This design is called the **cam-in-block** design. The camshaft is supported in the block by **camshaft bearings** and

driven by the crankshaft with a gear or sprocket and chain drive. Overhead camshafts are either belt or chain driven from the crankshaft and are located in the cylinder head(s). This arrangement is called **overhead camshaft (OHC)** design.

CAMSHAFT PROBLEM DIAGNOSIS

A camshaft with a partially worn lobe is often difficult to diagnose. Sometimes a valve "tick, tick, tick" noise is heard if the

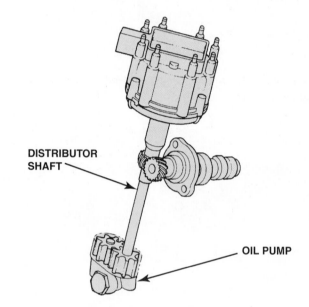

DISTRIBUTOR SHAFT

OIL PUMP

FIGURE 24-2 The camshaft often is used to drive the oil pump and distributor, if equipped.

FIGURE 24-1 Shape of two small-block Chevrolet V-8 cam lobes. A standard cam is on the left and a high-performance cam is on the right.

FIGURE 24-3 The camshaft rides on bearings inside the engine block above the crankshaft on a typical cam-in-block engine.

FIGURE 24-4 The camshaft on an overhead camshaft design engine can be easily inspected for wear or damage by removing the valve cover.

TECH TIP

THE ROTATING PUSHROD TEST

To quickly and easily test whether the camshaft is okay, observe if the pushrods are rotating when the engine is running. This test will work on any overhead valve pushrod engine that uses flat-bottom lifters. Due to the slight angle on the cam lobe and lifter offset, the lifter (and pushrod) should rotate whenever the engine is running. To check, simply remove the rocker arm cover and observe the pushrods when the engine is running. If one or more pushrods are *not* rotating, this camshaft and/or the lifter for that particular valve is worn and needs to be replaced.

cam lobe is worn. The ticking noise can be intermittent, which makes it harder to determine the cause. If the engine has an overhead camshaft (OHC), it is usually relatively easy to remove the cam cover and make a visual inspection of all cam lobes and the rest of the valve train. See Figure 24-4.

In an **overhead valve (OHV)** engine, the camshaft is in the block, where easy visual inspection is not possible. See Figure 24-5.

CAMSHAFT REMOVAL

If the engine is of an overhead valve design, the camshaft is usually located in the block above the crankshaft. The timing chain and gears (if the vehicle is so equipped) should be

(a)

(b)

FIGURE 24-5 (a) Here is what can happen if a roller lifter breaks loose from its retainer. The customer complained of "a little noise from the engine." (b) All engines equipped with roller lifters have some type of retainer for keeping the lifters from rotating.

removed after the timing chain (gear) cover is removed. Loosen the rocker arms (or rocker arm shaft) and remove the pushrods.

NOTE: Be sure to keep the pushrods and rocker arms together if they are to be reused.

Remove or lift up the lifters before carefully removing the camshaft. See the Tech Tip, "The Tube Trick."

CAMSHAFT DESIGN

The camshaft is a one-piece casting with lobes, bearing journals, drive flanges, and accessory gear blanks. The accessory drive gear is finished with a gear cutter. The lobes and journals

TECH TIP

THE TUBE TRICK

Valve lifters are often difficult to remove because the ends of the lifters become mushroomed (enlarged) where they have contacted the camshaft. Varnish buildup can also prevent the lifters from being removed. Try this method:

Step 1 Raise the lifters upward as far away from the camshaft as possible.

Step 2 Slide in a thin plastic or cardboard tube with slots in place of the camshaft. See Figure 24-6.

Step 3 Push the lifters downward into the tube. Use a long magnet to retrieve the lifters from the end of the tube.

This trick will work on almost every engine that has the camshaft in the block. If the tube is made from plastic, it has to be thin plastic to allow it to flex slightly. The length of the lifters is greater than the diameter of the cam bearings. Therefore, the lifter has to be pushed downward into the tube slightly to allow the lifter room to fall over into the tube.

FIGURE 24-6 Instead of prying old lifters up and out of the engine block, use a plastic (or cardboard) tube in place of the camshaft and push the lifters down. Then use a magnet to pull the old lifters out of the tube.

TECH TIP

HOT LIFTER IN 10 MINUTES?

A technician working in a new-vehicle dealership discovered a noisy (defective) valve lifter on a Chevrolet small-block V-8. Another technician questioned how long it would take to replace the lifter and was told, "Less than an hour"! (The factory flat-rate was much longer than one hour.) Ten minutes later the repair technician handed the questioning technician a hot lifter that had been removed from the engine. The lifter was removed by the following steps:

1. The valve cover was removed.
2. The rocker arm and pushrod for the affected valve were removed.
3. The distributor was removed.
4. A strong magnet was fed through the distributor opening into the valley area of the engine. (If the valve lifter is not mushroomed or does not have varnish deposits, the defective lifter can be lifted up and out of the engine; remember, the technician was working on a new vehicle.)
5. A replacement lifter was attached to the magnet and fed down the distributor hole and over the lifter bore.
6. The pushrod was used to help guide the lifter into the lifter bore.

After the lifter preload was adjusted and the valve cover was replaced, the vehicle was returned to the customer in less than one hour.

bearings on some engines are progressively smaller from the front journal to the rear. Other engines use the same size of camshaft bearing on all the journals.

Most older automotive camshafts were used with flat or convex-faced lifters and made from hardened alloy cast iron. The cast iron resists wear and provides the required strength. The very hardness of the camshaft causes it to be susceptible to chipping as the result of edge loading or careless handling.

Cast-iron camshafts have about the same hardness throughout. If reground, they should be recoated with a phosphate coating.

Steel camshafts are usually SAE 4160 or 4180 steel and are usually induction hardened. Induction hardening involves heating the camshaft to cherry red in an electric field (heating occurs by electrical induction). The heated camshaft is then

are ground to the proper shape. The remaining portion of the camshaft surface is not machined. See Figure 24-7.

On pushrod engines, camshaft bearing journals must be larger than the cam lobe so that the camshaft can be installed in the engine through the cam bearings. Some overhead cam engines have bearing caps on the cam bearings. These cams can have large cam lobes with small bearing journals. Cam

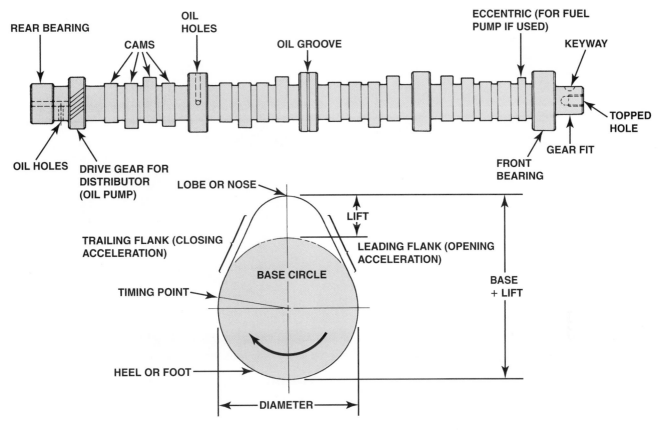

FIGURE 24-7   Cam and camshaft terms (nomenclature).

FIGURE 24-8   Worn camshaft with two lobes worn to the point of being almost round.

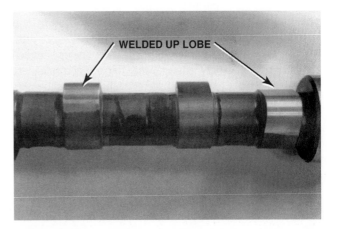

FIGURE 24-9   Worn camshaft that has been restored by welding the lobes and regrinding the original contour.

NOTE: Rockwell is a type of hardness test, and the *c* represents the scale used. The higher the number, the harder the surface. The abbreviation *Rc60*, therefore, indicates Rockwell hardness of 60 as measured on the "c" scale.

---

dropped into oil. The rapid cooling hardens the surface. Camshafts can also be hardened by using the following:

- **Liquid nitriding.** Hardens to 0.001 to 0.0015 inch of thickness
- **Gas nitriding.** Hardens to 0.004 to 0.006 inch of thickness

Typical camshaft hardness should be 42 to 60 on the Rockwell "c" scale. If this outer hardness wears off, the lobes of the camshaft are easily worn until they are almost completely rounded, as shown in Figures 24-8 and 24-9.

COMPOSITE CAMSHAFTS

A **composite camshaft** uses a lightweight tubular shaft with hardened steel lobes press-fitted over the shaft. See Figure 24-10.

FIGURE 24-10 A composite camshaft is lighter in weight than a conventional camshaft made from cast iron.

The actual production of these camshafts involves placing the lobes over the tube shaft in the correct position. A steel ball is then drawn through the hollow steel tube, expanding the tube and securely locking the cam lobes in position.

CAMSHAFT LUBRICATION

Some engines transfer lubrication oil from the main oil gallery to the crankshaft around the camshaft journal or around the outside of the camshaft bearing. Cam bearing clearance is critical in these engines. If the clearance is too great, oil will leak out and the crankshaft bearings will not get enough oil. Other engines use drilled holes in the camshaft bearing journals to meter lubricating oil to the overhead rocker arm. Oil goes to the rocker arm each time the holes line up between the bearing oil gallery passage and the outlet passage to the rocker arm. Camshaft oil metering holes are shown in Figures 24-11 and 24-12.

FUEL-PUMP ECCENTRICS

An eccentric cam lobe for the mechanical fuel pump is often cast as part of the camshaft. A mechanical engine-driven fuel pump is used on older engines equipped with a carburetor. The fuel pump is operated by this eccentric with a long pump arm or pushrod. Some engines use a steel cup type of eccentric that is bolted to the front of the cam drive gear. This allows a damaged fuel-pump eccentric to be replaced without replacing an entire camshaft. Typical fuel-pump eccentrics are identified on a number of camshafts pictured in Figure 24-13.

CAMSHAFT DRIVES

The camshaft is driven by the crankshaft through gears, sprockets and chains, or sprockets and timing belts. Timing chains

FIGURE 24-11 Hole through a camshaft bearing journal. The hole meters oil to a rocker shaft when it lines up with oil passages in the cam bearings.

FIGURE 24-12 Damaged camshaft bearing support. This overhead camshaft engine overheated because of an electric cooling fan circuit failure. The cylinder head warped upward in the center, causing a binding of the camshaft in the bearing.

are not as wide as timing belts, so engines with timing chains can be shorter. Timing chains often have tensioners (dampers) pressing on the unloaded side of the chain. The tensioner pad is a Nylatron™ molding that is filled with molybdenum disulfide to give it low friction. The tensioner is held against the chain by either a spring or hydraulic oil pressure as shown in Figure 24-14.

The gears or sprockets are keyed to their shafts so that they can be installed in only one position. The gears and sprockets are then indexed together by marks on the gear teeth or chain links. When the crankshaft and camshaft timing marks are properly lined up, the cam lobes are indexed to the crankshaft throws of each cylinder so that the valves will open and close correctly in relation to the piston position.

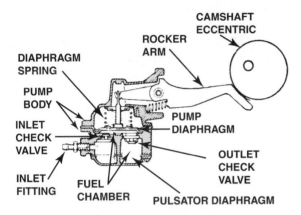

FIGURE 24-13 One part of the camshaft used on older model vehicles includes an eccentric that is used to operate the mechanical fuel pump.

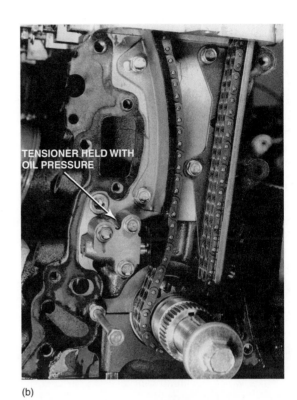

(b)

(a)

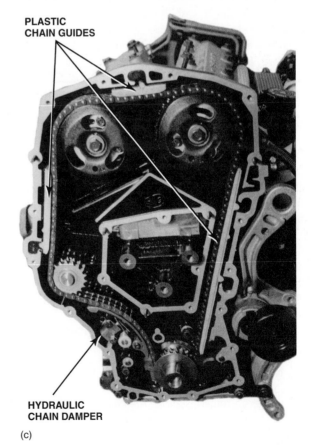

(c)

FIGURE 24-14   (a) A spring-loaded timing chain tensioner (also called a damper). (b) Most overhead camshaft engines use a hydraulic tensioner. (c) Hydraulic tensioners use engine oil pressure to keep tension on the chain. A ratchet mechanism in the tensioner maintains some tension on the chain when the engine is shut off and oil pressure is zero. This design helps reduce noise when the engine starts and before oil pressure is again applied to the tensioner.

TECH TIP

CHECK THE CAMSHAFT AND THEN THE FUEL PUMP

Many mechanical fuel pumps operate off of a separate lobe on the camshaft. If this fuel-pump lobe becomes worn, the stroke of the fuel pump is reduced and the amount of fuel being supplied to the engine is reduced. The engine may experience a lack of power or cut out and miss under load. The problem can also be intermittent, depending on other factors. A worn fuel-pump cam lobe is often found on Ford 240- and 300-cubic-inch inline 6-cylinder engines. Some Ford Escort engines experience a worn fuel-pump *pushrod* and behave similarly to an engine with a worn fuel-pump cam lobe.

If a worn fuel-pump cam lobe is suspected, perform a fuel-pump capacity (volume) test. If the pump does not pump at least 1/2 pint in 15 seconds (1 pint in 30 seconds), then remove the pump and inspect for excessive cam lobe wear or fuel-pump pushrod wear before replacing the fuel pump.

CAMSHAFT CHAIN DRIVES

The crankshaft gear or sprocket that drives the camshaft is usually made of sintered iron. When gears are used on the camshaft, the teeth must be made from a soft material to reduce noise. Usually, the whole gear is made of aluminum or fiber. When a chain and sprocket are used, the camshaft sprocket may be made of iron or it may have an aluminum hub with nylon teeth for noise reduction. Two types of timing chains are used.

1. **Silent chain type** (also known as a **flat-link type,** or **Morse type** for its original manufacturer). This type operates quietly but tends to stretch with use. See Figures 24-15 through 24-17.

    NOTE: When the timing chain stretches, the valve timing will be retarded and the engine will lack low-speed power. In some instances, the chain can wear through the timing chain cover and create an oil leak.

2. **Roller chain type.** This type is noisier but operates with less friction and stretches less than the silent type of chain.

FIGURE 24-15   Two types of sprockets that can be used on the same engine. A cast-iron sprocket is on the left, and an aluminum nylon sprocket is on the right.

FIGURE 24-16   Close-up view of two types of timing chains. A silent chain is on the left, and a roller chain is on the right.

FIGURE 24-17   Excessively worn timing gear and chain.

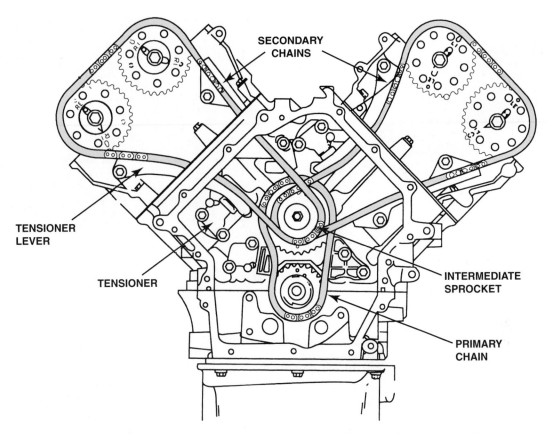

FIGURE 24-18   Typical dual-overhead camshaft V-type engine that uses one primary timing chain and two secondary chains.

Some four-cam engines use a two-stage camshaft drive system:

- Primary: From crankshaft to camshaft
- Secondary: From one camshaft to another

See Figure 24-18.

CAMSHAFT BELT DRIVES

Many overhead camshaft engines use a timing belt rather than a chain. Cam-driven belts are made from rubber and fabric and are usually reinforced with fiberglass or Kevlar®. The belt sprocket teeth are square-cut or cogged. The belt sprockets are usually made from aluminum. Drive belts and sprockets reduce weight compared to a chain drive and require no lubrication with reduced noise. However, the belt requires periodic replacement, usually every 60,000 miles (100,000 kilometers). See Figures 24-19 and 24-20.

Unless the engine is **freewheeling,** the piston can hit the valves if the belt breaks. See Figure 24-21.

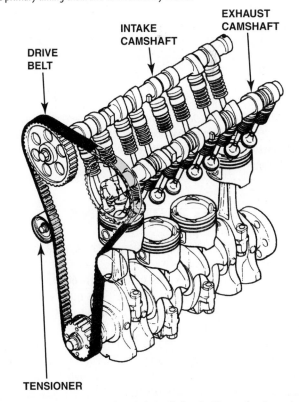

FIGURE 24-19   A typical 4-cylinder double overhead camshaft (DOHC) engine, which uses a belt drive from the camshaft.

FIGURE 24-20 Notice the teeth missing from this timing belt. This belt broke at 88,000 miles because the owner failed to replace it at the recommended interval of 60,000 miles.

FREEWHEELING ENGINE DESIGN

NO VALVE/PISTON INTERFERENCE

INTERFERENCE ENGINE DESIGN

VALVE/PISTON COLLISION

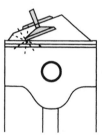

FIGURE 24-21 Many engines are of the interference design. If the timing belt (or chain) breaks, the piston still moves up and down in the cylinder while the valves remain stationary. With a freewheeling design, nothing is damaged, but in an interference engine, the valves are often bent.

FIGURE 24-22 Thrust plate controlling the camshaft end thrust on an overhead camshaft engine.

FIGURE 24-23 Typical thrust plate between the cam gear and a flange on the camshaft. Note the hole in the fiber composition gear to provide access to the thrust plate bolts.

CAMSHAFT MOVEMENT

As the camshaft lobe pushes the lifter upward against the valve spring force, a backward twisting force is developed on the camshaft. After the lobe goes past its high point, the lifter moves down the backside of the lobe. This makes a forward twisting force. This action produces an alternating torsion force forward, then backward, at each cam lobe. This alternating torsion force is multiplied by the number of cam lobes on the shaft. The camshaft must have sufficient strength to minimize torsion twist and also be tough enough to minimize fatigue from the alternating torsion forces.

Cam chucking is the movement of the camshaft *lengthwise in the engine during operation.* Each camshaft must have some means to control the shaft end thrust. Two methods are in common usage. One method is to use a **thrust plate** between the camshaft drive gear or sprocket and a flange on the camshaft. See Figures 24-22 and 24-23. This thrust plate is attached to the engine block with cap screws. In a few camshafts, a button, spring, or retainer that contacts the timing cover limits forward motion of the camshaft.

LIFTER ROTATION

Valve trains that use flat-bottom lifters use a spherical (curved) lifter face that slides against the cam lobe. This produces a surface on the lifter face that is slightly convex, by about 0.002 inch. The lifter also contacts the lobe at a point that is slightly off center. This produces a small turning force on the lifter to cause some lifter rotation for even wear. In operation, there is a wide line of contact between the lifter and the high point of the cam lobe. See Figure 24-24.

These are the highest loads that are produced in an engine. This surface is the most critical lubrication point in an engine.

CAMSHAFT LIFT

The **lift** of the cam is usually expressed in decimal inches and represents the distance that the valve is lifted off the valve seat. See Figures 24-25 and 24-26.

The higher the lift, the more air and fuel that can theoretically enter the engine. The more air and fuel burned in an engine, the greater the power potential of the engine. The amount of lift of a camshaft is often different for the

TECH TIP

ROLLER LIFTER CAM WEAR

After any engine equipped with roller lifters is run for a short time, it will wear a path on the camshaft. The path traveled by the roller over the cam causes the area to have a mirrorlike appearance. The area on both sides of this shiny path retains the dull finish of the original camshaft.

This wear pattern is often mistakenly assumed to be abnormal, and as a result, the camshaft and lifters are sometimes needlessly replaced. To avoid replacing good parts or not replacing worn parts, always carefully measure all engine parts.

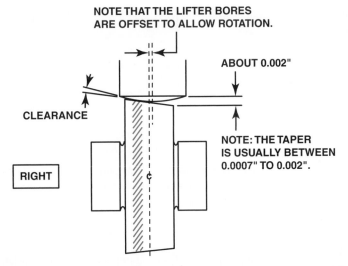

NOTE THAT THE LIFTER BORES ARE OFFSET TO ALLOW ROTATION.

ABOUT 0.002"

CLEARANCE

RIGHT

NOTE: THE TAPER IS USUALLY BETWEEN 0.0007" TO 0.002".

MOST LATE MODEL AUTOMOTIVE CAMS ARE TAPERED TO PROVIDE LIFTER ROTATION. THE LIFTERS HAVE A SPHERICAL GRIND SO THAT THEY DO NOT RIDE ON THE EDGE OF THE CAM LOBE. THIS CONTACT SPREADS THE LOAD OF THE VALVE TRAIN AGAINST MORE OF THE LOBE FACE.

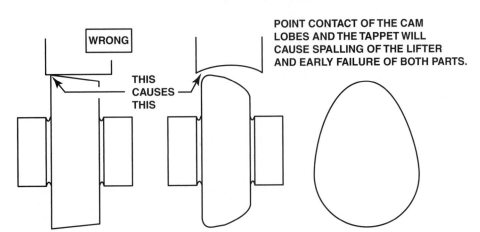

WRONG

POINT CONTACT OF THE CAM LOBES AND THE TAPPET WILL CAUSE SPALLING OF THE LIFTER AND EARLY FAILURE OF BOTH PARTS.

THIS CAUSES THIS

FIGURE 24-24 New lifters should always be used with a new camshaft. If worn lifters are used on a new camshaft, edge wear on the cam lobes will quickly wear the camshaft.

TECH TIP

BEST TO WARN THE CUSTOMER

A technician replaced a timing chain and gears on a Chevrolet V-8. The repair was accomplished correctly, yet after starting, the engine burned an excessive amount of oil. Before the timing chain replacement, oil consumption was minimal. The replacement timing chain restored proper operation of the engine and increased engine vacuum. Increased vacuum can draw oil from the crankcase past worn piston rings and through worn valve guides during the intake stroke. Similar increased oil consumption problems occur if a valve regrind is performed on a high-mileage engine with worn piston rings and/or cylinders.

To satisfy the owner of the vehicle, the technician had to disassemble and refinish the cylinders and replace the piston rings. Therefore, all technicians should warn customers that increased oil usage may result from almost any repair to a high-mileage engine.

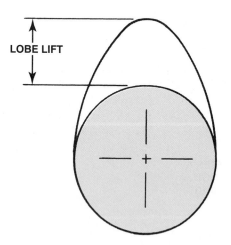

FIGURE 24-25 Lobe lift is the amount the cam lobe lifts the lifter.

intake and exhaust valves. If the specifications vary, the camshaft is called **asymmetrical.** If the lift is the same, the cam is called **symmetrical.** However, when the amount of lift increases, so do the forces on the camshaft and the rest of the valve train. Generally, a camshaft with a lift of over 0.500 inch (1.3 centimeters) is unsuitable for street operation except for use in engines that are over 400 cubic inches (6.0 liters).

The lift specifications at the valve face assume the use of the stock rocker arm ratio. If nonstock rocker arms with a

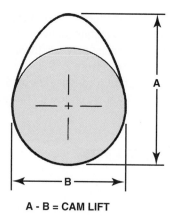

A - B = CAM LIFT

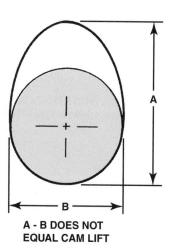

A - B DOES NOT EQUAL CAM LIFT

FIGURE 24-26 Some cam lobes provide lift for more than 180 degrees of camshaft rotation, so it is not possible to get an accurate base circle measurement using a micrometer.

higher ratio are installed (for example, 1.6:1 rockers replacing the stock 1.5:1 rocker arms), the lift at the valve is increased. Also, because the rocker arm rotation covers a greater distance at the pivot of the rocker arm, the rocker arm can hit the edge of the valve retainer.

ROCKER ARMS

A rocker arm reverses the upward movement of the pushrod to produce a downward movement on the tip of the valve. Engine designers make good use of the rocker arm. It is designed to reduce the travel of the cam follower or lifter and pushrod while maintaining the required valve lift. This is done by using a rocker arm ratio of 1.5:1, as shown in Figure 24-27.

For a given amount of lift on the pushrod, the valve will open to 1.5 times the pushrod lift distance. This ratio allows the camshaft to be small, so the engine can be smaller. It also results in lower lobe-to-lifter rubbing speeds.

CAUTION: Using rocker arms with a higher ratio than stock can also cause the valve spring to compress too much and actually bind. Valve spring bind (coil bind) occurs when the valve spring is compressed to the point where there is no clearance in the spring. (It is completely compressed.) When coil bind occurs in a running engine, bent pushrods, broken rocker arms, or other valve train damage can result. See Figure 24-28.

REAL WORLD FIX

THE NOISY CAMSHAFT

The owner of an overhead cam 4-cylinder engine complained of a noisy engine. After taking the vehicle to several technicians and getting high estimates to replace the camshaft and followers, the owner tried to find a less expensive solution. Finally, another technician replaced the serpentine drive belt on the front of the engine and "cured" the "camshaft" noise for a fraction of the previous estimates.

Remember, accessory drive belts can often make noises similar to valve or bad bearing types of noises. Many engines have been disassembled and/or overhauled because of a noise that was later determined to be from one of the following:

- Loose or defective accessory drive belt(s)
- Loose torque converter-to-flex plate (drive plate) bolts (nuts)
- Defective mechanical fuel pump

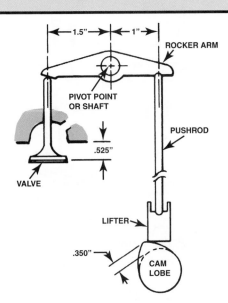

FIGURE 24-27   A rocker arm showing a 1.5:1 ratio. The distance from the pivot to the pushrod seat is shorter than the distance from the pivot to the valve stem.

Rocker arms may be cast, forged, or stamped. Forged rocker arms are the strongest, but they require expensive manufacturing operations. Rocker arms may have bushings or bearings installed to reduce friction and increase durability. Cast rocker arms cost less to make and do not usually use bushings, but they do require several machining operations. They are not as strong as forged rocker arms but are satisfactory for passenger vehicle service.

Shaft-Mounted Rocker Arms

On some overhead valve and most single overhead camshaft engines, the rocker arms are mounted on a shaft that runs the full length of the cylinder head. See Figures 24-29 and 24-30.

Because the shaft provides a strong and stable platform for the rocker arms, shaft-mounted rocker arms work well, especially at high engine speeds. While shaft-mounted rocker arms resist flex and accurately transmit the cam profile to the valve, they do add weight and cost to the engine.

While most overhead camshaft engines and some overhead valve (OHV) engines that use rocker arm shafts do use an adjustable rocker arm, most OHV engines have no provision for adjustment. Shaft-mounted rocker arms are lubricated through oil passages that travel from the block through the head and into the shaft, and then to the rocker arms.

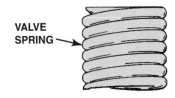

FIGURE 24-28   If the space between the coils is not adequate, coil bind occurs.

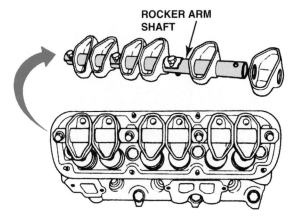

FIGURE 24-29   Typical rocker arm shaft design on an overhead valve engine.

Stud-Mounted Rocker Arms

Stud-mounted rockers are only found on overhead valve (OHV) engines and each rocker arm is attached to a stud that is pressed or threaded into the cylinder head. A ball on top of the rocker arm provides the bearing surface as the rocker arm pivots and is held in place and adjusted for valve clearance by a nut. While this design looks less stable than a shaft-mounted rocker, this design has proved to be reliable and is inexpensive to manufacture. Some engines use pushrod guide plates fastened to the head. See Figures 24-31 and 24-32. The rocker arms are lubricated through hollow pushrods.

Pedestal-Mounted Rocker Arms

Pedestal-mounted rocker arms are similar to stud-mounted rocker arms but do not use a stud and are used only in overhead valve engines. Two rocker arms are attached to and pivot on a pedestal attached to the cylinder head with one or two bolts. The rocker arms are usually stamped steel, which is lightweight and not adjustable. See Figures 24-33 and 24-34. The rocker arms are lubricated through hollow pushrods.

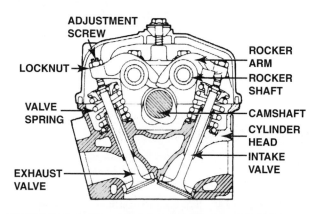

FIGURE 24-30 A typical single overhead camshaft (SOHC) engine with shaft-mounted rocker arms, which ride directly on the camshaft.

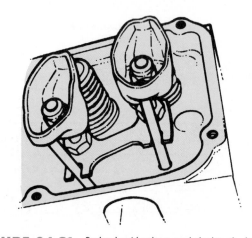

FIGURE 24-31 Pushrod guide plates are bolted to the head and help stabilize the valve train, especially at high engine speeds.

PUSHRODS

Pushrods transfer the lifting motion of the valve train from the cam lobe and lifters to the rocker arms. See Figure 24-35.

Pushrods are designed to be as light as possible and still maintain their strength. They may be either solid or hollow. If they are to be used as passages for oil to lubricate rocker arms, they *must* be hollow. Pushrods use a convex ball on the lower end that seats in the lifter. The rocker arm end is also a convex ball, unless there is an adjustment screw in the pushrod end of the rocker arm. In this case, the rocker arm end of the pushrod has a concave socket. It mates with the convex ball on the adjustment screw in the rocker arm. Pushrod end types are shown in Figure 24-36.

All pushrods should be rolled on a flat surface to check for straightness. See Figure 24-37.

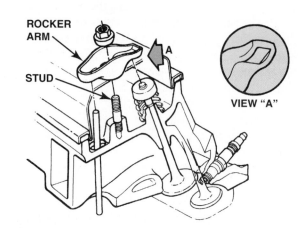

FIGURE 24-32 A typical stud-mounted rocker arm.

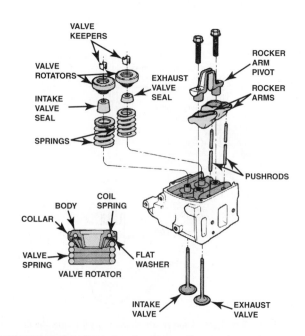

FIGURE 24-33 A pedestal-type rocker arm design that uses two bolts for each rocker arm pivot and is not adjustable.

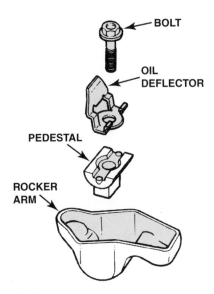

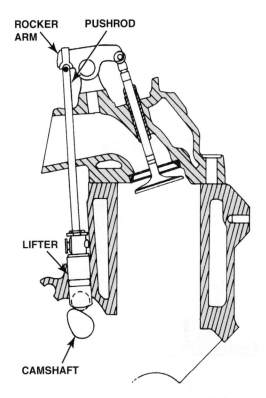

FIGURE 24-34 A pedestal-type rocker arm design that used one bolt for each rocker arm and is not adjustable. If valve lash needs to be adjusted, different length pushrod(s) must be used.

FIGURE 24-35 Overhead valve engines are also known as pushrod engines because of the long pushrod that extends from the lifter to the rocker arm.

TECH TIP

ROCKER ARM SHAFTS CAN CAUSE STICKING VALVES

As oil oxidizes, it forms a varnish. Varnish buildup is particularly common on hot upper portions of the engine, such as rocker arm shafts. The varnish restricts clean oil from getting into and lubricating the rocker arms. The cam lobe can easily *force* the valves open, but the valve springs often do not exert enough force to fully close the valves. The result is an engine miss, which may be intermittent. Worn valve guides and/or weak valve springs can also cause occasional rough idle, uneven running, or missing.

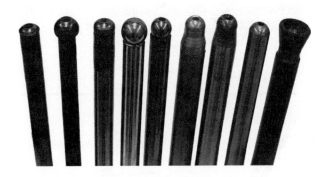

FIGURE 24-36 Types of pushrod ends.

The tolerance in the valve train allows for some machining of engine parts without the need to change pushrod length. However, if one or more of the following changes have been made to an engine, a different pushrod length may be necessary:

- Block deck height machined
- Cylinder head deck height machined
- Camshaft base circle size reduced
- Valve length increased
- Lifter design changed

FIGURE 24-37 It was easy to see that these pushrods needed to be replaced because they became bent when the timing chain broke.

OVERHEAD CAMSHAFT VALVE TRAINS

Overhead camshaft engines use several methods for opening the valves.

TECH TIP

HOLLOW PUSHROD DIRT

Many engine rebuilders and remanufacturers do not reuse old hollow pushrods. Dirt, carbon, and other debris are difficult to thoroughly clean from inside a hollow pushrod. When an engine is run with used pushrods, the trapped particles can be dislodged and ruin new bearings and other new engine parts.

TECH TIP

THE SCRATCH TEST

All pushrods used with guide plates *must* be hardened on the sides and on the tips. To easily determine if a pushrod is hardened, simply use a sharp pocketknife to scrape the wall of the pushrod. A heat-treated pushrod will not scratch. See Figure 24-38.

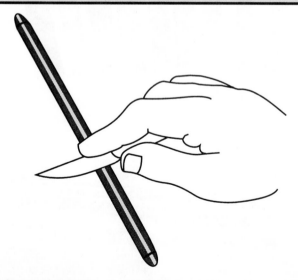

FIGURE 24-38 Hardened pushrods should be used in any engine that uses pushrod guides (plates). To determine if the pushrod is hardened, simply try to scratch the side of the pushrod with a pocketknife.

1. One type opens the valves directly with a **bucket.** See Figure 24-39.
2. The second type uses a **cam follower,** also called a **finger follower,** that provides an opening ratio similar to that of a rocker arm. See Figure 24-40. Finger followers open the valves by approximately 1 1/2 times the cam lift. The pivot point of the finger follower may have a mechanical adjustment or it may have an automatic hydraulic adjustment.
3. A third type moves the rocker arm directly through a hydraulic lifter. See Figure 24-41.
4. In the fourth design, some newer engines have the hydraulic adjustment in the rocker arm and are commonly called **hydraulic lash adjusters (HLA).** See Figure 24-42.

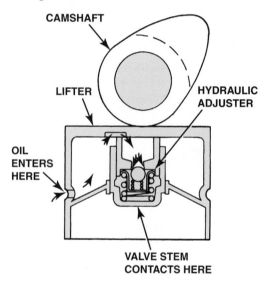

FIGURE 24-39 Hydraulic lifters may be built into bucket-type lifters on some overhead camshaft engines.

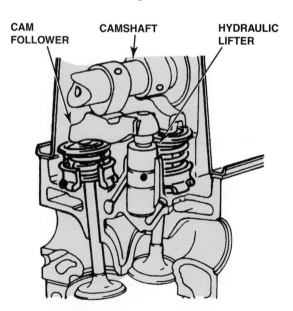

FIGURE 24-40 The use of cam followers allow the use of hydraulic lifters with an overhead camshaft design.

FIGURE 24-41 The overhead cam operates the rocker arm through a hydraulic lifter.

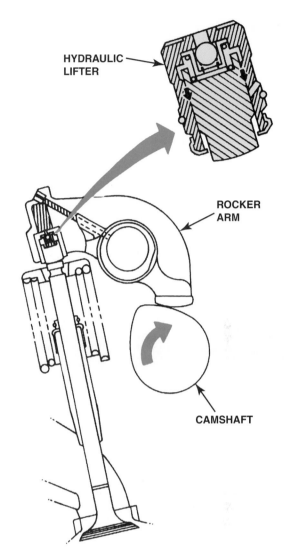

FIGURE 24-42 Hydraulic lifters (hydraulic lash adjusters) may be built into rocker arms on some overhead camshaft engines.

CAMSHAFT SPECIFICATIONS

Camshaft duration is the number of degrees of crankshaft rotation for which the valve is lifted off the seat. The specifications for duration can be different for the intake valves and the exhaust valves. If the durations of the intake and exhaust valves are different from each other, the cam is called asymmetrical. The specification for duration can be expressed by several different methods, which must be considered when comparing one cam with another. The three most commonly used methods are as follows:

1. **Duration of valve opening at zero lash (clearance).** If a hydraulic lifter is used, the lash is zero. If a solid lifter is used, this method of expression refers to the duration of the opening of the valve after the specified clearance (lash) has been closed.
2. **Duration at 0.050-inch lifter (tappet) lift.** Because this specification method eliminates all valve lash clearances and compensates for lifter (tappet) styles, it is the preferred method to use when comparing one camshaft with another. Another method used to specify duration of some factory camshafts is to specify crankshaft duration at 0.010-inch lifter lift. The important point to remember is that the technician must be sure to use

equivalent specification methods when comparing or selecting camshafts.

NOTE: Fractions of a degree are commonly expressed in units called minutes ('). **Sixty minutes equal one degree.** For example, 45' = 3/4 degree, 30' = 1/2 degree, and 15' = 1/4 degree.

3. **SAE camshaft specifications.** The valve timing and valve overlap are expressed in the number of degrees of crankshaft rotation for which the valves are off their seats. SAE's recommended practice is to measure all valve events at 0.006-inch (0.15-millimeter) valve lift. This method differs from the usual method used by vehicle or camshaft manufacturers. Whenever comparing valve timing events, be certain that the exact same methods are used on all camshafts being compared.

Valve Overlap

Another camshaft specification is the number of degrees of overlap. **Camshaft overlap** is the number of degrees of crankshaft rotation between the exhaust and intake strokes for which both valves are off their seats.

- A lower amount of overlap results in smoother idle and low-engine speed operation, but it also means that a lower amount of power is available at higher engine speeds.
- A greater valve overlap causes rougher engine idle, with decreased power at low speeds, but it also means that high-speed power is improved.

For example: A camshaft with 50 degrees (or less) of overlap may be used in an engine in which low-speed torque and smooth idle qualities are desired. Engines used with overdrive automatic transmissions benefit from the low-speed torque and fuel economy benefits of a small-overlap cam. A camshaft with 100 degrees of overlap is more suitable for use with a manual transmission, with which high-RPM power is desired. An engine equipped with a camshaft with over 100 degrees of overlap tends to idle roughly and exhibit poorer low-engine speed response and lowered fuel economy. See Figure 24-43.

The valve overlap is the number of degrees for which both valves are open near TDC. In the previous example, the intake valve starts to open at 19 degrees. The exhaust valve is also open during this upward movement of the piston on the exhaust stroke. The exhaust valve is open until 22 degrees ATDC.

To determine overlap, total the number of degrees for which the intake valve is open BTDC (19 degrees) and the number of degrees for which the exhaust valve is open ATDC (22 degrees):

$$\text{Valve overlap} = 19° + 22° = 41°$$

Lobe Centers

Another camshaft specification that creates some confusion is the angle of the centerlines of the intake and exhaust lobes. This separation between the centerlines of the intake and exhaust lobes is called **lobe center, lobe separation, lobe displacement angle (LDA),** or **lobe spread** and is measured in degrees. See Figure 24-44.

Two camshafts with identical lift and duration can vary greatly in operation because of variation in the angle between the lobe centerlines.

1. The smaller the angle between the lobe centerlines, the greater the amount of overlap. For example, 108 degrees is a narrower lobe center angle.
2. The larger the angle between the lobe centerlines, the less the amount of overlap. For example, 114 degrees is a wider lobe center angle.

NOTE: Some engines that are equipped with dual overhead camshafts and four valves per cylinder use a different camshaft profile for each of the intake and exhaust valves. For example, one intake valve for each cylinder could have a cam profile designed for maximum low-speed torque. The other intake valve for each cylinder could be designed for higher-engine-speed power. This results in an engine that is able to produce a high torque over a broad engine speed range.

To find the degree of separation between intake and exhaust lobes of a cam, use the following formula:

$$(\text{Intake duration} + \text{Exhaust duration})/4 - \text{Overlap}/2 = \\ \text{Number of degrees of separation}$$

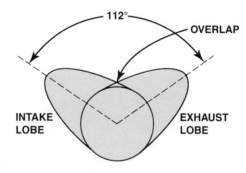

FIGURE 24-44   As the lobe center angle decreases, the overlap increases, with no other changes in the lobe profile lift and duration.

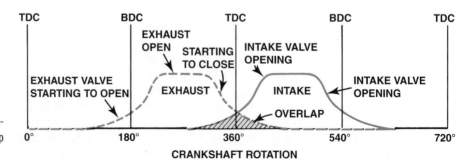

FIGURE 24-43 Graphic representation of a typical camshaft showing the relationship between the intake and exhaust valves.

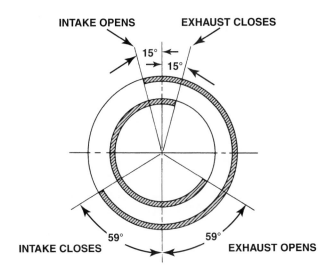

FIGURE 24-45 Typical cam timing diagram.

See Figure 24-45 for a typical camshaft valve timing diagram.

The lobe separation angle can be determined by transferring the intake and exhaust duration and overlap into the formula as follows:

$$\text{Intake duration} = 15° + 59° + 180° = 254°$$
$$\text{Exhaust duration} = 59° + 15° + 180° = 254°$$
$$\text{Overlap} = 15° + 15° = 30°$$
$$(254° + 254°)/4 - 30°/2 = 508°/4 - 30°/2$$
$$= 127° - 15° = 112°$$

CAM TIMING SPECIFICATIONS

Cam timing specifications are stated in terms of the angle of the crankshaft in relation to top dead center (TDC) or bottom dead center (BDC) when the valves open and close.

Intake Valve

The intake valves should open slightly before the piston reaches TDC and starts down on the intake stroke. This ensures that the valve is fully open when the piston travels downward on the intake stroke. The flow through a partially open valve (especially a valve ground at 45 degrees instead of 30 degrees) is greatly reduced as compared with that when the valve is in its fully open position. The intake valve closes after the piston reaches BDC because the air–fuel mixture has inertia, or the tendency of matter to remain in motion. Even after the piston stops traveling downward on the intake stroke and starts upward on the compression stroke, the inertia of the air–fuel mixture can still be used to draw in additional charge.

Typical intake valve specifications are to open at 19 degrees before top dead center (BTDC) and close at 46 degrees after bottom dead center (ABDC).

Exhaust Valve

The exhaust valve opens while the piston is traveling down on the power stroke, before the piston starts up on the exhaust stroke. Opening the exhaust valve before the piston starts up on the exhaust stroke ensures that the combustion pressure is released and the exhaust valve is mostly open when the piston does start up. The exhaust valve does not close until after the piston has traveled past TDC and is starting down on the intake stroke. Because of inertia of the exhaust, some of the burned gases continue to flow out the exhaust valve after the piston is past TDC. This can leave a partial vacuum in the combustion chamber to start pulling in the fresh charge.

Typical exhaust valve specifications are to open at 49 degrees before bottom dead center (BBDC) and close at 22 degrees after top dead center (ATDC).

Cam Timing Chart

During the four strokes of a four-stroke-cycle gasoline engine, the crankshaft revolves 720 degrees (it makes two complete revolutions [$2 \times 360° = 720°$]). Camshaft specifications are given in crankshaft degrees. In the example in Figure 24-46, the intake valve starts to open at 39 degrees BTDC, remains open through the entire 180 degrees of the intake stroke, and does not close until 71 degrees ATDC. Therefore, the duration of the intake valve is 39 degrees + 180 degrees + 71 degrees, or 290 degrees.

The exhaust valve of the example camshaft opens at 78 degrees BBDC and closes at 47 degrees ATDC. When the exhaust valve specifications are added to the intake valve specifications in the diagram, the overlap period is easily observed. The overlap in the example is 39 degrees + 47 degrees, or

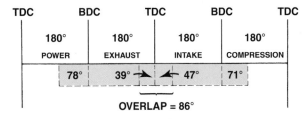

FIGURE 24-46 Typical high-performance camshaft specifications on a straight-line graph. Intake valve duration = 39° + 180° + 71° = 290°. Exhaust valve duration = 78° + 180° + 47° = 305°. Because intake and exhaust valve specifications are different, the camshaft grind is called asymmetrical.

86 degrees. The duration of the exhaust valve opening is 78 degrees + 180 degrees + 47 degrees, or 305 degrees. Because the specifications of this camshaft indicate close to and over 300 degrees of duration, this camshaft should only be used where power is more important than fuel economy.

The usual method of drawing a camshaft timing diagram is in a circle illustrating two revolutions (720 degrees) of the crankshaft. See Figure 24-47 for an example of a typical camshaft timing diagram for a camshaft with the same specifications as the one illustrated in Figure 24-46.

MEASURING AND REGRINDING CAMSHAFTS

All camshafts should be checked for straightness by placing them on a V block and measuring the cam bearings for runout by using a dial indicator. The maximum **total indicator runout (TIR)** should be less than 0.002 inch (0.05 millimeter). See Figure 24-48.

Worn camshafts can be restored to original lift and duration by one of two methods:

1. If the camshaft is not excessively worn (less than 0.030 inch), the lobes can be reground by decreasing the diameter of the base circle, restoring the original lift and duration. See Figures 24-49 and 24-50.
2. If the cam lobe wear is excessive, the lobes can be welded and reground back to their original specifications.

NOTE: According to major engine remanufacturers, only about 35% of camshafts can be reground. Therefore, about two-thirds of the camshafts received in engine cores are excessively worn and must be replaced.

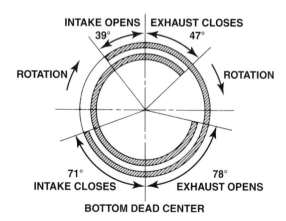

INTAKE OPENS | **EXHAUST CLOSES**
39° | 47°

ROTATION | **ROTATION**

71° | 78°
INTAKE CLOSES | **EXHAUST OPENS**

BOTTOM DEAD CENTER

THIS VALVE TIMING DIAGRAM SHOWS TWO REVOLUTIONS (720°) OF THE CRANKSHAFT

FIGURE 24-47 Typical camshaft valve timing diagram with the same specifications as those shown in Figure 24-46.

INSTALLING THE CAMSHAFT

When the camshaft is installed, the lobes must be coated with a special lubricant that contains molydisulfide. This special lube helps to ensure proper initial lubrication to the critical cam lobe sections of the camshaft. Many manufacturers recommend multiviscosity engine oil such as SAE 5W-30 or SAE 10W-30. Some camshaft manufacturers recommend using straight SAE 30 or SAE 40 engine oil and not a multiviscosity oil for the first oil fill. Some manufacturers also recommend the use of an antiwear additive such as **zinc dithiophosphate (ZDP).** See Figure 24-51.

NOTE: Most camshafts are coated at the factory with a polycrystalline-structure chemical treatment. This coating is typically manganese phosphate and gives the camshaft a dull black appearance. The purpose of this treatment is to absorb and hold oil to help ensure lubrication during the break-in period. Under a microscope, this surface treatment looks like the surface of a golf ball.

DIAL INDICATOR

CAM BEARING JOURNAL

FIGURE 24-48 A camshaft being checked for total indicator runout as it is being rotated on V blocks using a dial indicator.

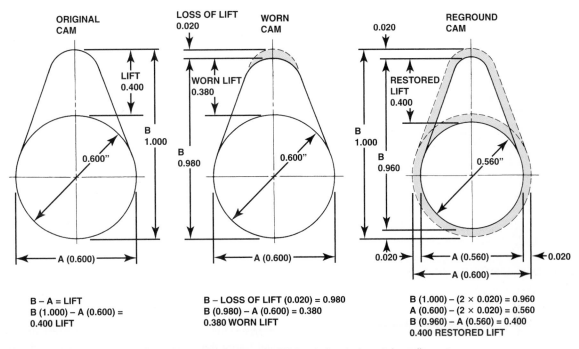

B – A = LIFT
B (1.000) – A (0.600) =
0.400 LIFT

B – LOSS OF LIFT (0.020) = 0.980
B (0.980) – A (0.600) = 0.380
0.380 WORN LIFT

B (1.000) – (2 × 0.020) = 0.960
A (0.600) – (2 × 0.020) = 0.560
B (0.960) – A (0.560) = 0.400
0.400 RESTORED LIFT

FIGURE 24-49   A worn camshaft lobe can be restored to its original lift by grinding the base circle smaller.

FIGURE 24-50   A camshaft being ground on a camshaft grinding machine.

FIGURE 24-51   Special lubricant such as this one from General Motors is required to be used on the lobes of the camshaft and the bottom of the flat-bottomed lifters.

A flat-bottom lifter camshaft must be broken in by maintaining engine speed above 1500 RPM for the first 10 minutes of engine operation. If the engine speed is decreased to idle (about 600 RPM), the lifter (tappet) will be in contact with and exerting force *on* the lobe of the cam for a longer period of time than occurs at higher engine speeds. The pressure and volume of oil supplied to the camshaft area are also increased at the higher engine speeds. Therefore, to ensure long camshaft and lifter life, make certain that the engine will start quickly after reassembly to prevent long cranking periods and subsequent low engine speeds after a new camshaft and lifters have

been installed. Whenever repairing an engine, follow these rules regarding the camshaft and lifters:

NOTE: When installing a roller lifter camshaft, no break-in is necessary.

1. When installing a new camshaft, always install new valve lifters (tappets).

TECH TIP

TOO BIG = TOO BAD

A common mistake of beginning engine builders is to install a camshaft with too much duration for the size of the engine. This extended duration of valve opening results in a rough idle and low manifold vacuum, which causes carburetor metering problems and lack of low-speed power.

For example, a hydraulic cam with a duration greater than 225 degrees at 0.050-inch lift for a 350-cubic-inch engine will usually not be suitable for street driving. **Seat duration** is the number of degrees of crankshaft rotation that the valve is off the seat.

2. When installing new lifters, if the original cam is not excessively worn and if the pushrods all rotate with the original camshaft, the camshaft may be reused.

NOTE: Some manufacturers recommend that a new camshaft always be installed when replacing valve lifters.

3. *Never* use a hydraulic camshaft with solid lifters or hydraulic lifters with a solid lifter camshaft.
4. New flat-bottom lifters will be more compatible if the bottom part of the lifter that contacts the cam is polished with #600 grit sandpaper.

NOTE: Many molydisulfide greases can start to clog oil filters within 20 minutes after starting the engine. Most engine rebuilders recommend changing the oil and filter after one-half hour of running time.

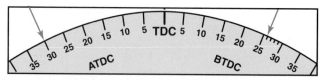

FIGURE 24-52 Degree wheel indicating where the piston stopped near top dead center. By splitting the difference between the two readings, the true TDC (28 degrees) can be located on the degree wheel.

DEGREEING THE CAMSHAFT

The purpose of degreeing the camshaft in the engine is to locate the valve action exactly as the camshaft manufacturers intended. The method most often recommended by camshaft manufacturers is the **intake lobe centerline method.** This method determines the exact centerline of the intake lobe and compares it to the specifications supplied with the replacement camshaft. On an overhead valve engine, the camshaft is usually degreed after the crankshaft, piston, and camshaft are installed and before the cylinder heads are installed. To determine the centerline of the intake lobe, follow these steps using a degree wheel mounted on the crankshaft:

Step 1   Locate the exact top dead center. Install a degree wheel and bring the cylinder #1 piston close to TDC. Install a piston stop. (A piston stop is any object attached to the block that can act as a solid mechanical stop to prevent the piston from reaching the top of the cylinder.) Turn the engine clockwise until the piston *gently* hits the stop.

CAUTION: Do not use the starter motor to rotate the engine. Use a special wrench on the flywheel or the front of the crankshaft.

Record the reading on the degree wheel, and then turn the engine in the opposite direction until it stops again and record that number. Figure 24-52 indicates a reading of 30 degrees ATDC and 26 degrees BTDC. Add the two readings together and divide by two (30° + 26° = 56° ÷ 2 = 28°). Move the degree

Common Usage	Seat Duration	Lift	Duration at 0.050 Inch	Characteristics
Street	246°–254°	0.400	192°–199°	Smooth idle, power idle to 4500 RPM
Street	262°	0.432	207°	Broad power range, smooth idle, power idle to 4800 RPM
Street	266°	0.441	211°	Good idle for 350-cubic-inch engines, power idle to 5200 RPM
Street/drag strip	272°	0.454	217°	Lope idle, power idle to 5500 RPM
Street/racetrack	290°	0.500	239°	Shaky idle, power idle to 5500–6500 RPM

wheel until it is 28 degrees and the engine has stopped rotating in either direction. Now TDC on the degree wheel is exactly at top dead center.

Step 2   Remove the piston stop and place a dial indicator on an intake valve lifter. To accurately locate the point of maximum lift (intake lobe centerline), rotate the engine until the lifter drops 0.050 inch on

each side of the maximum lift point. Mark the degree wheel at these points on either side of the maximum lift point. Now count the degrees between these two points and mark the halfway point. This halfway point represents the **intake centerline.** This point is often located between 100 degrees and 110 degrees. See Figure 24-53.

(a)

(b)

(c)

FIGURE 24-53   (a) Photo showing the setup required to degree a camshaft. (b) Close-up of the pointer and the degree wheel. (c) The dial indicator used to find exact top dead center.

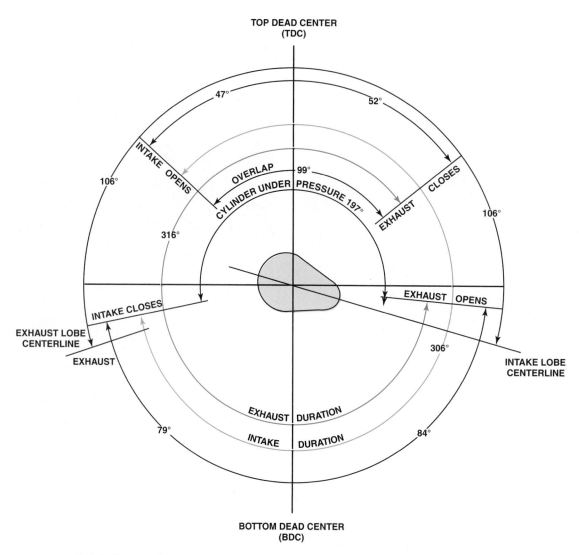

FIGURE 24-54 Typical valve timing diagram showing the intake lobe centerline at 106 degrees ATDC.

Step 3 Now that both TDC and intake centerline have been marked, compare the actual intake centerline with the specification. For example, if the actual intake centerline is 106 degrees and the camshaft specification indicates 106 degrees, then the camshaft is installed *straight up*. See Figure 24-54. If the actual reading is 104 degrees, the camshaft is advanced by 2 degrees. If the actual reading is 108 degrees, the camshaft is retarded by 2 degrees.

Advanced Cam Timing

If the camshaft is slightly ahead of the crankshaft, the camshaft is called *advanced*. An advanced camshaft (maximum of 4 degrees) results in more low-speed torque with a slight decrease in high-speed power. Some aftermarket camshaft manufacturers design about a 4-degree advance into their timing gears or camshaft. This permits the use of a camshaft with more lift and duration, yet still provides the smooth idle and low-speed responses of a milder camshaft.

Retarded Cam Timing

If the camshaft is slightly behind the crankshaft, the camshaft is called *retarded*. A retarded camshaft (maximum of 4 degrees) results in more high-speed power at the expense of low-speed torque.

If the measured values are different from specifications, special offset pins or keys are available to relocate the cam gear by the proper amount. Some manufacturers can provide adjustable cam timing sprockets for overhead cam engines.

TECH TIP

VALVE-TO-PISTON CLEARANCE VERSUS CAM TIMING

If the cam timing is *advanced* (relative to the crankshaft), the intake valve-to-piston clearance is *reduced*. If the cam timing is *retarded*, the exhaust valve-to-piston clearance is *reduced*.

This is true because the intake valve lags behind the motion of the piston on the intake stroke, whereas the piston "chases" the exhaust valve on the exhaust stroke. See Figure 24-55.

FIGURE 24-55 Modeling clay was used to determine valve-to-piston clearance. Most manufacturers recommend a minimum of 0.070 inch (1.8 millimeters). The clay is cut with a knife and the thickness of the clay is measured to determine the static (engine not running) clearance. The clearance decreases as the speed of the engine increases because of valve timing variations connecting rod stretch.

VARIABLE VALVE TIMING

Conventional camshafts are permanently synchronized to the crankshaft so that they operate the valves at a specific point in each combustion cycle. In an engine, the intake valve opens slightly before the piston reaches the top of the cylinder and closes about 60 degrees after the piston reaches the bottom of the stroke on every cycle, regardless of the engine speed or load.

Variable-cam timing allows the valves to be operated at different points in the combustion cycle, to improve performance. See the chart.

There are three basic types of variable valve timing used on General Motors vehicles:

1. Exhaust camshaft variable action only on overhead camshaft engines, such as the inline 4.2-liter 4200 used in Trailblazers.
2. Intake and exhaust camshaft variable action on both camshafts used in many General Motors engines.
3. Overhead valve, cam-in-block engines use variable valve timing by changing the relationship of the camshaft to the crankshaft.

The camshaft position actuator **oil control valve (OCV)** directs oil from the oil feed in the head to the appropriate camshaft position actuator oil passages. There is one OCV for each camshaft position actuator. The OCV is sealed and mounted to the front cover. The ported end of the OCV is inserted into the cylinder head with a sliding fit. A filter screen protects each OCV oil port from any contamination in the oil supply.

The camshaft position actuator is mounted to the front end of the camshaft and the timing notch in the nose of the camshaft aligns with the dowel pin in the camshaft position actuator to ensure proper cam timing and camshaft position actuator oil hole alignment. See Figure 24-56.

OHV Variable Timing

The 3900 is the first GM overhead valve (OHV) engine to utilize variable valve timing (VVT) and active fuel management (displacement on demand—DOD). Engine size was increased

Driving Condition	Change in Camshaft Position	Objective	Result
Idle	No change	Minimize valve overlap	*Stabilize idle speed*
Light engine load	Retard valve timing	Decrease valve overlap	*Stable engine output*
Medium engine load	Advance valve timing	Increase valve overlap	*Better fuel economy with lower emissions*
Low to medium RPM with heavy load	Advance valve timing	Advance intake valve closing	*Improve low to midrange torque*
High RPM with heavy load	Retard valve timing	Retard intake valve closing	Improve engine output

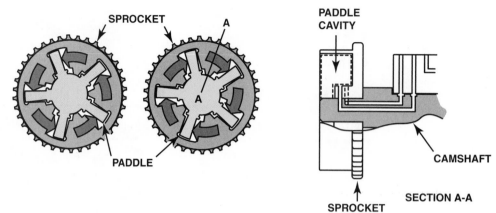

FIGURE 24-56 Camshaft rotation during advance and retard.

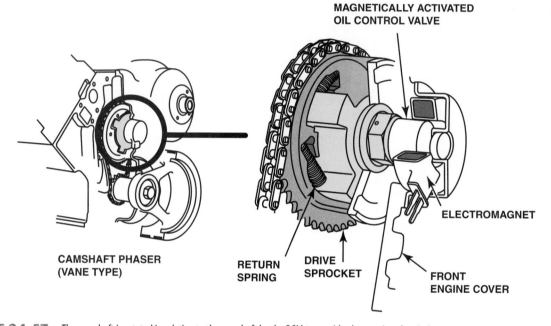

FIGURE 24-57 The camshaft is rotated in relation to the camshaft by the PCM to provide changes in valve timing.

400 cc because the larger displacement was needed to obtain good performance in the three-cylinder mode.

The variable valve timing system uses electronically controlled, hydraulic gear-driven cam phaser that can alter the relationship of the camshaft from 15 degrees retard to 25 degrees advance (40 degrees overall) relative to the crankshaft. By using **variable valve timing (VVT),** GM engineers were able to eliminate the EGR valve. The VVT also works in conjunction with an active manifold that gives the engine a broader torque curve.

A valve in the intake manifold creates a longer path for intake air at low speeds, improving combustion efficiency and torque output. At higher speed the valve opens creating a shorter air path for maximum power production.

The LZ4 3500 is an OHV engine based on the 3.9 L V-6. It was introduced for the 2006 model year in the Chevrolet Impala and Monte Carlo. It includes continuously variable cam timing (fixed overlap). See Figure 24-57.

Varying the exhaust and/or the intake camshaft position allows for reduced exhaust emissions and improved performance. See the chart.

Camshaft Phasing Changed	Improves
Exhaust cam phasing	*Reduces exhaust emissions*
Exhaust cam phasing	*Increases fuel economy (reduced pumping losses)*
Intake cam phasing	*Increases low-speed torque*
Intake cam phasing	*Increases high-speed power*

By varying the exhaust cam phasing, vehicle manufacturers are able to meet newer NO_X reduction standards and eliminate the exhaust gas recirculation (EGR) valve. By using exhaust cam phasing, the PCM can close the exhaust valves sooner than usual, thereby trapping some exhaust gases in the combustion chamber. General Motors uses one or two actuators that allow the camshaft piston to change by up to 50 degrees in relation to the crankshaft position.

There are two types of cam phasing devices used on General Motors engines:

- Spline phaser—used on overhead camshaft (OHC) engines
- Vane phaser—used on overhead camshaft (OHC) and overhead valve (OHV) cam-in-block engines

Spline Phaser System

The spline phaser system is also called the **exhaust valve cam phaser (EVCP)** and consists of the following components:

- Engine control module (ECM)
- Four-way pulse-width-modulated (PWM) control valve
- Cam phaser assembly
- Camshaft position (CMP) sensor

See Figure 24-58.

Spline Phaser System Operation

On the 4200 inline 6-cylinder engine used in the Chevrolet Trailblazer, the pulse-width-modulated (PWM) control valve is located on the front passenger side of the cylinder head. Oil pressure is regulated by the control valve and then directed to the ports in the cylinder head leading to the camshaft and cam phaser position. The cam phaser is located on the exhaust cams and is part of the exhaust cam sprocket. When the ECM commands an increase in oil pressure, the piston is moved inside the cam phaser and rides along the helical splines, which compresses the coil spring. This movement causes the cam phaser gear and the camshaft to move in an opposite direction, thereby retarding the cam timing. See Figure 24-59.

TECH TIP

CHECK THE SCREEN ON THE CONTROL VALVE IF THERE ARE PROBLEMS

If a NO_X emission failure at a state inspection occurs or a diagnostic trouble code is set related to the cam timing, remove the control valve and check for a clogged oil screen. A lack of regular oil changes can cause the screen to become clogged, thereby preventing proper operation. A rough idle is a common complaint because the spring may not be able to return the camshaft to the idle position after a long highway trip.

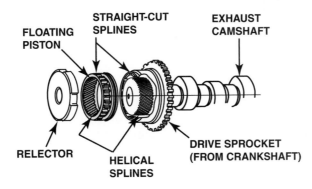

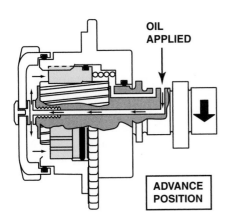

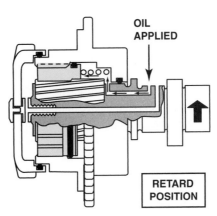

FIGURE 24-58 Spline cam phaser assembly.

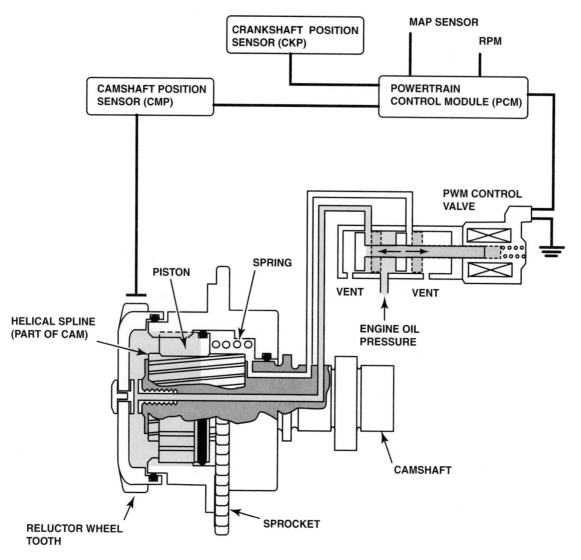

FIGURE 24-59   A spline phaser.

NOTE: A unique cam-within-a-cam is used on the 2008 + Viper V-10 OHV engine. This design allows the exhaust lobes to be moved by up to 36° to improve idle quality and reduction of exhaust emissions.

Vane Phaser System on an Overhead Camshaft Engine

The vane phaser system used on overhead camshaft (OHC) engines uses a camshaft piston (CMP) sensor on each camshaft. Each camshaft has its own actuator and its own oil control valve (OCV). Instead of using a piston along a helical spline, the vane phaser uses a rotor with four vanes, which is connected to the end of the camshaft. The rotor is located inside the stator, which is bolted to the cam sprocket. The stator and rotor are not connected. Oil pressure is controlled on both sides of the vanes of the rotor, which creates a hydraulic link between the two parts. The oil control valve varies the balance of pressure on either side of the vanes and thereby controls the position of the camshaft. A return spring is used under the reluctor of the phaser to help return it to the home or zero degrees position. See Figure 24-60.

Magnetically Controlled Vane Phaser

A magnetically controlled vane phaser is controlled by the ECM by using a 12-volt pulse-width-modulated (PWM) signal to an electromagnet, which operates the oil control valve (OCV). A magnetically controlled vane phaser is used on many General Motors double overhead camshaft engines on both the intake and exhaust camshaft. The OCV directs pressurized engine oil to either advance or retard chambers of the camshaft actuator to change the camshaft position in relation to the crankshaft position. See Figure 24-61.

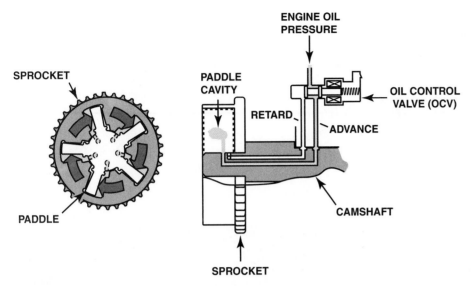

FIGURE 24-60 A vane phaser is used to move the camshaft using changes of oil pressure from the oil control valve.

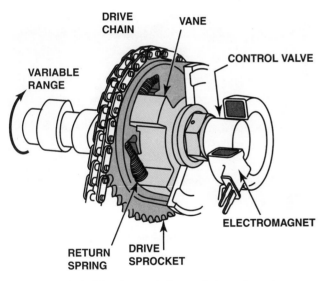

FIGURE 24-61 A magnetically controlled vane phaser.

The following occurs when the pulse width is changed:

- **0% pulse width**—The oil is directed to the advance chamber of the exhaust camshaft actuator and the retard chamber of the intake camshaft actuator.

- **100% pulse width**—The oil is directed to the retard chamber of the exhaust camshaft actuator and the advance chamber of the intake camshaft actuator.

The cam phasing is continuously variable with a range from 40 degrees for the intake camshaft and 50 degrees for the exhaust camshaft. The ECM uses the following sensors to determine the best position of the camshaft for maximum power and lowest possible exhaust emissions.

- Engine speed (RPM)
- MAP sensor

- Crankshaft position (CKP)
- Camshaft position (CMP)
- Barometric pressure (BARO)

Cam-in-Block Engine Cam Phaser

Overhead valve engines that use a cam-in-block design use a magnetically controlled cam phaser to vary the camshaft in relation to the crankshaft. This type of phaser is not capable of changing the duration of valve opening or valve lift.

Inside the camshaft actuator is a rotor with vanes that are attached to the camshaft. Oil pressure is supplied to the vanes, which causes the camshaft to rotate in relation to the crankshaft. The camshaft actuator solenoid valve directs the flow of oil to either the advance or retard side vanes of the actuator. See Figure 24-62.

The ECM sends a pulse-width-modulated (PWM) signal to the camshaft actuator magnet. The movement of the pintle is used to direct oil flow to the actuator. The higher the duty cycle, the greater the movement in the valve position and change in camshaft timing.

NOTE: When oil pressure drops to zero when the engine stops, a spring-loaded locking pin is used to keep the camshaft locked to prevent noise at engine start. When the engine starts, oil pressure releases the locking pin.

VARIABLE VALVE TIMING AND LIFT

Many engines use variable valve timing in an effort to improve high-speed performance without the disadvantages of a

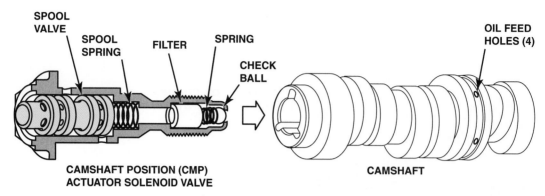

FIGURE 24-62   A camshaft position actuator used in a cam-in-block engine.

high-performance camshaft at idle and low speeds. There are two basic systems including:

- Variable camshafts such as the system used by Honda/Acura called **Variable Valve Timing and Lift Electronic Control** or **VTEC.** This system uses two different camshafts for low and high RPM. When the engine is operating at idle and speeds below about 4000 RPM, the valves are opened by camshafts that are optimized by maximum torque and fuel economy. When engine speed reaches a predetermined speed, depending on the exact make and model, the computer turns on a solenoid, which opens a spool valve. When the spool valve opens, engine oil pressure pushes against pins that lock the three intake rocker arms together. With the rocker arms lashed, the valves must follow the profile of the high RPM cam lobe in the center. This process of switching from the low-speed camshaft profile to the high-speed profile takes about 100 milliseconds (0.1 sec). See Figures 24-63 and 24-64.
- Variable camshaft timing is used on many engines including General Motors 4-, 5-, and 6-cylinder engines, as well as engines from BMW, Chrysler, and Nissan. On a system that controls the intake camshaft only, the camshaft timing is advanced at low engine speed, closing the intake valves earlier to improve low RPM torque. At high engine speeds, the camshaft is retarded by using engine oil pressure against a helical gear to rotate the camshaft. When the camshaft is retarded, the intake valve closing is delayed, improving cylinder filling at higher engine speeds. See Figure 24-65. Variable cam timing can be used to control exhaust cam timing only. Engines that use this system, such as the 4.2-liter GM in-line 6-cylinder engines, can eliminate the exhaust gas recirculation (EGR) valve because the computer can close the exhaust valve sooner than normal, trapping some exhaust gases in the combustion chamber and therefore eliminating the need for an EGR valve. Some engines use variable camshaft timing on both intake and exhaust cylinder cams.

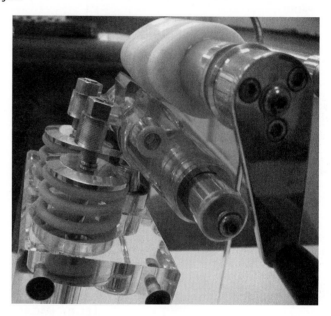

FIGURE 23-63   A plastic mock-up of a Honda VTEC system that uses two different camshaft profiles; one for low-speed engine operation and the other for high speed.

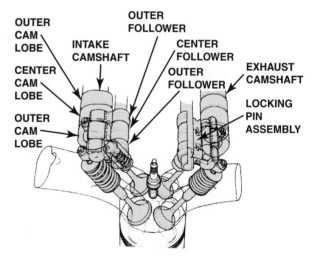

FIGURE 24-64   Engine oil pressure is used to switch cam lobes on this VTEC system.

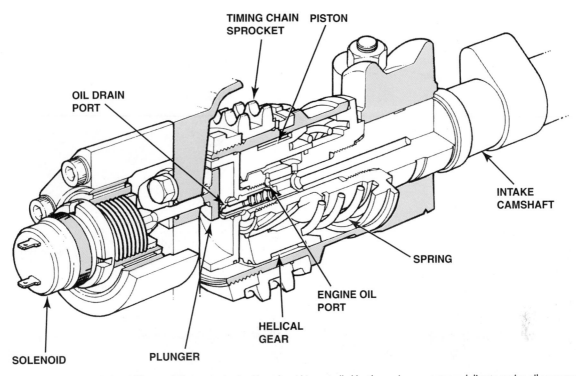

FIGURE 24-65   A typical variable cam timing control valve. The solenoid is controlled by the engine computer and directs engine oil pressure to move a helical gear, which rotates the camshaft relative to the timing chain sprocket.

LIFTERS OR TAPPETS

Valve lifters or tappets follow the contour or shape of the camshaft lobe. This arrangement changes the cam motion to a reciprocating motion in the valve train. Most older-style lifters have a relatively flat surface that slides on the cam.

Most lifters, however, are designed with a roller to follow the cam contour. Roller lifters are used primarily in production engines to reduce valve train friction (by up to 8%). This friction reduction can increase fuel economy and help to offset the greater manufacturing cost. All roller lifters must use a retainer to prevent lifter rotation. The retainer ensures that the roller is kept in line with the cam. If the retainer broke, the roller lifter could turn, destroying both the lifter and the camshaft. See Figures 24-66 and 24-67.

Valve train clearance is also called **valve lash.** Valve train clearance must not be excessive, or it will cause noise or result in premature failure. Two methods are commonly used to make the necessary valve clearance adjustments. One involves a **solid valve lifter** with a mechanical adjustment, and the other involves a lifter with an automatic hydraulic adjustment built into the lifter body called a **hydraulic valve lifter.**

SOLID LIFTERS

Overhead valve engines with mechanical lifters have an adjustment screw at the pushrod end of the rocker arm or an

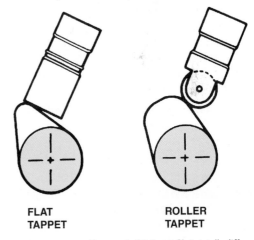

FIGURE 24-66   The camshaft lobe profile is totally different for an engine that uses a roller lifter compared to a flat-bottom lifter.

adjustment nut at the ball pivot. Adjustable pushrods are available for some specific applications.

Valve trains using solid lifters must run with some clearance to ensure positive valve closure, regardless of the engine temperature. This clearance is matched by a gradual rise in the cam contour called a **ramp.** (Hydraulic lifter camshafts do not have this ramp.) The ramp will take up the clearance before the valve begins to open. The camshaft lobe also has a closing ramp to ensure quiet operation.

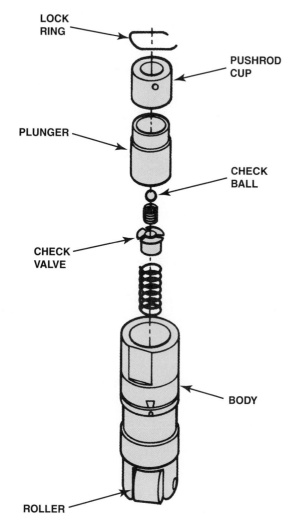

FIGURE 24-67   Many engines use hydraulic roller lifters to reduce frictional losses and improve fuel economy.

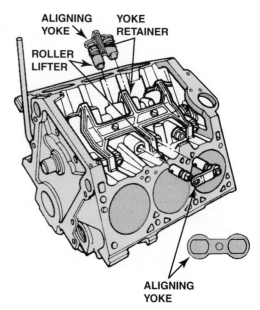

FIGURE 24-68   Roller lifters must be used with a part that keeps the lifters from rotating as they move up and in the lifter bore.

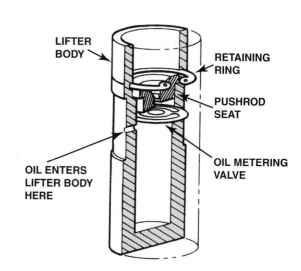

FIGURE 24-69   A cutaway of a flat-bottom solid lifter. Because this type of lifter contains a retaining ring and oil holes, it is sometimes confused with a hydraulic lifter that also contains additional parts. The holes in this lifter are designed to supply oil to the rocker arms through a hollow pushrod.

A lifter is solid in the sense that it transfers motion directly from the cam to the pushrod or valve. Its physical construction is that of a lightweight cylinder, either hollow or with a small-diameter center section and full-diameter ends. In some types that transfer oil through the pushrod, the external appearance is the same as for hydraulic lifters. See Figure 24-68.

HYDRAULIC LIFTERS

A hydraulic lifter consists primarily of a hollow cylinder body enclosing a closely fit hollow plunger, a check valve, and a pushrod cup. Lifters that feed oil up through the pushrod have a metering disk or restrictor valve located under the pushrod cup. Engine oil under pressure is fed through an engine passage to the exterior lifter body. An undercut portion allows the oil under pressure to surround the lifter body. Oil

under pressure goes through holes in the undercut section into the center of the plunger. From there, it goes down through the check valve to a clearance space between the bottom of the plunger and the interior bottom of the lifter body. It fills this space with oil at engine pressure. Slight leakage allowance is designed into the lifter so that the air can bleed out and the lifter can leak down if it should become overfilled. The operating principle of a hydraulic lifter is shown in Figures 24-69 through 24-71.

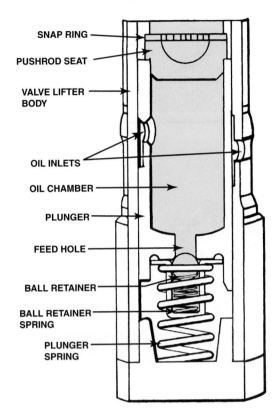

SNAP RING

PUSHROD SEAT

VALVE LIFTER BODY

OIL INLETS

OIL CHAMBER

PLUNGER

FEED HOLE

BALL RETAINER

BALL RETAINER SPRING

PLUNGER SPRING

FIGURE 24-70 Cutaway of a typical flat-bottom hydraulic valve lifter.

The pushrod fits into a cup in the top, open end of the lifter plunger. Holes in the pushrod cup, pushrod end, and hollow pushrod allow oil to transfer from the lifter piston center, past a metering disk or restrictor valve, and up through the pushrod to the rocker arm. Oil leaving the rocker arm lubricates the rocker arm assembly.

As the cam starts to push the lifter against the valve train, the oil below the lifter plunger is squeezed and tries to return to the lifter plunger center. A lifter check valve, either ball or disk type, traps the oil below the lifter plunger. This hydraulically locks the operating length of the lifter. The hydraulic lifter then opens the engine valve as would a solid lifter. When the lifter returns to the base circle of the cam, engine oil pressure again works to replace any oil that may have leaked out of the lifter.

The hydraulic lifter's job is to take up all clearance in the valve train. Occasionally, engines are run at excessive speeds. This tends to throw the valve open, causing **valve float.** During valve float, clearance exists in the valve train. The hydraulic lifter will take up this clearance as it is designed to do. When this occurs, it will keep the valve from closing on the seat. This is called **pump-up.** Pump-up will not occur when the engine is operated in the speed range for which it is designed.

FREQUENTLY ASKED QUESTION

HOW DOES CYLINDER DEACTIVATION WORK?

Some engines are designed to be operated on four of eight or three of six cylinders during low load conditions to improve fuel economy.

The power train computer monitors engine speed, coolant temperature, throttle position, and load and determines when to deactivate cylinders. The key to this process is the use of two-stage hydraulic valve lifters. In normal operation, the inner and outer lifter sleeves are held together by a pin and operate as an assembly. When the computer determines that the cylinder can be deactivated, oil pressure is delivered to a passage, which depresses the pin and allows the outer portion of the lifter to follow the contour of the cam while the inner portion remains stationary, keeping the valve closed. The electronic operation is achieved through the use of lifter oil manifold containing solenoids to control the oil flow, which is used to activate or deactivate the cylinders. General Motors used to call this system Displacement on Demand (DOD), but now calls it Active Fuel Management. Chrysler calls this system Multiple Displacement System (MDS). See Figures 24-72 and 24-73 on pages 470–471.

LIFTER PRELOAD

Lifter preload is actually the distance between the pushrod seat inside the lifter and the snap ring of the lifter when the lifter is resting on the base circle (or heel) of the cam and the valve is closed. This distance should be about 0.020 to 0.045 inch. On engines with adjustable rocker arms, this distance or preload is determined by turning the rocker arm adjusting nut one-quarter to one full turn after zero lash (clearance) is determined. See Figure 24-74 on page 471.

Tightening this adjusting nut further can cause the pushrod to bottom out in the lifter. If the engine is rotated with the pushrod bottomed out, bent valves, as well as bent or damaged pushrods, rocker arms, or rocker arm studs can result.

Engines that have been rebuilt or repaired and that do not use adjustable rocker arms are particularly at risk for damage. If any of the following operations have been performed, lifter preload *must* be determined:

- Regrinding the camshaft (reduces base circle dimensions)
- Milling or resurfacing cylinder heads

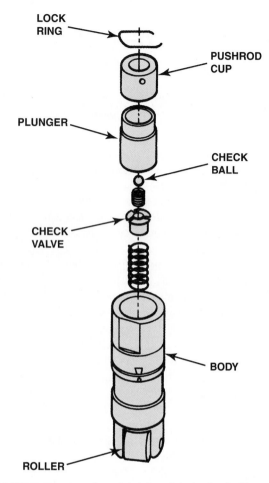

FIGURE 24-71 An exploded view of a hydraulic roller lifter.

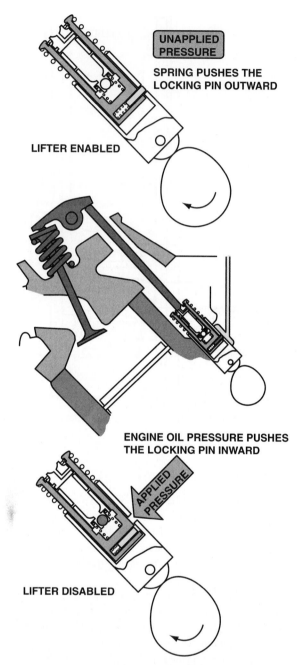

FIGURE 24-72 Oil pressure applied to the locking pin causes the inside of the lifter to freely move inside the outer shell of the lifter, thereby keeping the valve closed.

- Milling or resurfacing block deck
- Grinding valves and/or facing valve stems
- Changing to a head gasket thinner or thicker than the original

Most lifters can accept a total variation in the entire valve train of about 0.080 to 0.180 inch. To determine lifter preload, rotate the engine until the valve being tested is resting on the base circle of the cam. For example, with the valve cover off and rotating the engine in the normal operating direction, watch the exhaust valve start to open. This means that the intake valve for that cylinder is resting on the base circle (heel) of the cam. Apply pressure down on the lifter. Wait several minutes for the lifter to bleed down. Measure the distance between rocker arm and valve stem. If the proper clearance is not obtained (generally between 0.020 and 0.045 inch), the following may need to be done to get the proper clearance:

1. Install longer or shorter pushrods. Manufacturers produce pushrods in various lengths. Some are available in lengths up to 0.100 inch longer or shorter than stock.

2. Install adjustable pushrods or rocker arms, if possible.
3. Shim or grind rocker stands or shafts.

NOTE: Shim rocker arm supports to three-fifths of the measurement removed from the cylinder head (1.5:1 rocker ratio). For example, if 0.030 inch is removed from a cylinder head, shim the rocker arm to 0.030 inch times 3/5, or 0.018 inch.

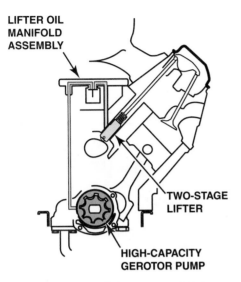

FIGURE 24-73 Active fuel management includes many different components and changes to the oiling system, which makes routine oil changes even more important on engines equipped with this system.

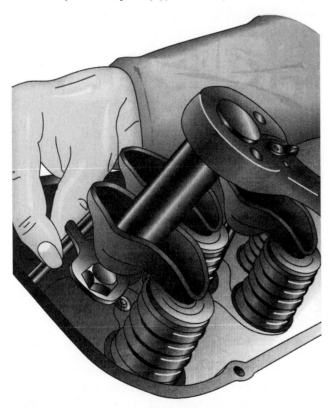

FIGURE 24-74 Operating principle of hydraulic lifters.

DETERMINING LIFTER PRELOAD

The process of adjusting valves that use hydraulic valve lifters involves making certain that the lifter has the specified preload.

A properly adjusted valve train should position the lifter in the center of its travel dimension.

The procedure for a valve train with *adjustable* rocker arms is as follows:

1. Rotate the engine clockwise as viewed from the nonprincipal or belt end (normal direction of rotation) until the exhaust lifter starts to move up.
2. Adjust the intake valve to zero lash (no preload) and then one-half turn more.
3. Rotate the engine until the intake valve is almost completely closed. Adjust the exhaust valve to zero lash and then one-half turn more.
4. Continue with this procedure for each cylinder until all the valves are correctly adjusted.

If the valve train uses *nonadjustable* rocker arms, the lifter preload must still be determined. The lifter preload *must* be measured if any or all of the following procedures have been performed on the engine:

- Head(s) milled
- Block decked
- Valves ground
- Any other machining operation that could change the valve train measurement

Shorter (or longer) replacement pushrods may be required to produce the correct lifter preload. Some engine manufacturers recommend using thin metal shims under the rocker arm supports if needed.

CAUTION: If shims are used under the rocker arm supports, be sure that the shim has the required oil holes.

DETERMINING PROPER LIFTER TRAVEL

To determine if shimming or use of replacement pushrods of different lengths is required, use the following procedure:

1. With the valve cover removed, rotate the engine until the valve lifter being tested is resting on the base circle of the camshaft.
2. Depress the pushrod into the lifter with steady pressure. This should cause the lifter to bleed down until the pushrod bottoms out in the lifter bore.
3. Measure clearance (lash) between the rocker arm tip and the stem of the valve. This measurement varies according to manufacturer and engine design, but it usually ranges from 0.020 to 0.080 inch. See Figure 24-75. Always consult exact manufacturer's specifications before taking any corrective measures.

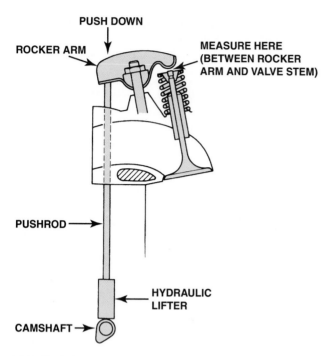

FIGURE 24-75 Procedure for determining proper lifter travel.

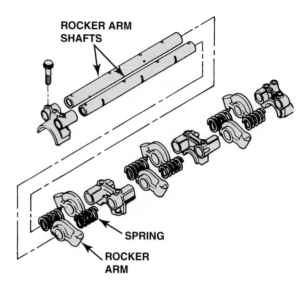

FIGURE 24-76 Shaft-mounted rocker arms are held in position by an assortment of springs, spacers, and washers which should be removed so that the entire shaft can be inspected for wear.

If the measurement is not within acceptable range, select the proper length pushrods to achieve the proper lifter travel dimension and preload.

NOTE: Some engines use several different pushrod lengths depending on the exact build date! Block casting numbers may be the same, but the engines may require different internal parts. Check with the manufacturer's specifications in the factory service manual for proper interchangeable parts.

VALVE NOISE DIAGNOSIS

Valve lifters are often noisy, especially at engine start-up. When the engine is off, some valves are open. The valve spring pressure forces the inner plunger to leak down (oil is forced out of the lifter). Therefore, many vehicle manufacturers consider valve ticking at one-half engine speed after start-up to be normal, especially if the engine is quiet after 10 to 30 seconds. Be sure that the engine is equipped with the correct oil filter, and that the filter has an internal check valve. If in doubt, use an original-equipment oil filter. If all of the valves are noisy, check the oil level. If low, the oil may have been **aerated** (air mixed with the oil), which would prevent proper operation of the hydraulic lifter. Low oil pressure can also cause all valves to be noisy. The oil level being too high can also cause noisy valve lifters. The connecting rods create foam as they rotate through the oil. This foam can travel through the oiling systems to the lifters. The foam in the lifters prevents normal operation and allows the valves to make noise.

If the valves are abnormally noisy, remove the valve arm cover and use a stethoscope to determine which valves or valve train parts may be causing the noise. Check for all of the following items:

- Worn camshaft lobe
- Dirty, stuck, or worn lifters
- Worn rocker arm (if the vehicle is so equipped)
- Worn rocker arm shaft (See Figure 24-76.)
- Worn or bent pushrods (if the vehicle is so equipped)
- Broken or weak valve springs
- Sticking or warped valves

MECHANICAL LIFTER SERVICE

Mechanical lifters, like hydraulic lifters, should be replaced if the camshaft is replaced. If the lifters are to be reused, they *must* be kept in order and reinstalled in the exact positions in which they were originally used in the engine. All lifters should be cleaned and carefully inspected. If the base of the lifter is dished (concave), the lifter should be replaced. As with any lifter, new or used, the bore clearance should be checked.

NOTE: Regrinding of valve lifter bases is generally not recommended because the hardened areas of the lifter can be ground through.

HYDRAULIC LIFTER SERVICE

Hydraulic lifter service begins with a thorough visual inspection. Compare the lifter wear with the corresponding lobe on the camshaft. *All lifters should be replaced during a major engine overhaul or a camshaft replacement.*

Vehicle manufacturers usually recommend that, because of their high cost, hydraulic roller lifters be checked for wear, disassembled, and cleaned rather than being replaced. Any other hydraulic lifter that is to be reused should also be disassembled and cleaned using the following steps:

Step 1   Select a clean work area and tray for the disassembled parts. See Figure 24-77.

Step 2   Disassemble the lifters and keep all parts in order.

Step 3   Clean all parts and reassemble. Always use a lint-less cloth because lint can affect lifter operation.

Step 4   Test leak-down rate using a leak-down tester and special-viscosity fluid. See Figure 24-78.

a. Measure the time required for the fluid to pass between the inner and outer body of the lifter.

b. The time it takes for the lifter to collapse under a given weight should be longer than 10 seconds and less than 90 seconds.

c. Check service information for the exact leak-down time for your vehicle. The average time for leak-down is 20 to 40 seconds.

HYDRAULIC VALVE LIFTER INSTALLATION

Most vehicle manufacturers recommend installing lifters *without* filling or pumping the lifter full of oil. If the lifter is filled with oil during engine start-up, the lifter may not be able to bleed down quickly enough and the valves may be kept open. Not only will the engine not operate correctly with the valves held open, but the piston could hit the open valves, causing serious engine damage. Most manufacturers usually specify that the lifter be lubricated. Roller hydraulic lifters can be lubricated with engine oil, whereas flat lifters require that engine assembly lube or extreme pressure (EP) grease be applied to the base.

BLEEDING HYDRAULIC LIFTERS

Air trapped inside a hydraulic valve lifter can be easily bled by simply operating the engine at a fast idle (2500 RPM). Normal oil flow through the lifters will allow all of the air inside the lifter to be bled out.

NOTE: Some engines, such as many Nissan overhead camshaft engines, *must* have the air removed from the lifter before installation. This is accomplished by submerging the lifter in a container of engine oil and using a straightened paper clip to depress the oil passage check ball.

Consult a service manual if in doubt about the bleeding procedure for the vehicle being serviced. See Figure 24-79 for an example of the special tool needed to bleed out the air on hydraulic lash adjusters (HLA) used on a Chrysler 3.2/3.5 L, V-6 overhead camshaft.

VALVE TRAIN LUBRICATION

The lifters in an overhead valve (OHV) engine are lubricated through oil passages drilled through the block. The engine oil then flows through the lifter, and up through the hollow pushrod where the oil flows over the rocker arms to lubricate and cool the valve and valve spring.

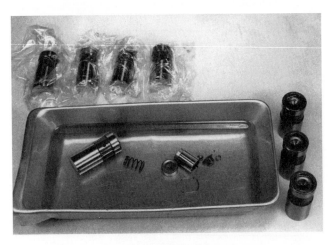

FIGURE 24-77 Cleaning a disassembled hydraulic lifter (tappet) in clean petroleum solvent. After cleaning and reassembly, all hydraulic lifters should be checked for proper leak-down rate using a special fluid and tester.

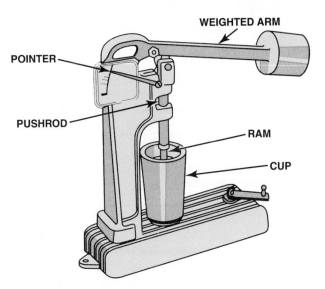

FIGURE 24-78 Typical hydraulic lifter leak-down tester.

FIGURE 24-79 A special tool with a small needlelike probe is used to bleed air from the hydraulic lash adjuster (HLA).

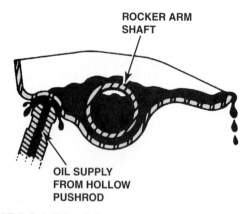

FIGURE 24-80 Hollow pushrods supply oil to pushrod ends, rocker arms, and shafts. Oil then drips from the rocker arm onto the valve springs and returns to the oil pan through oil drain holes in the cylinder head.

NOTE: The Chrysler 5.7-liter Hemi engine is opposite because the oil is first sent to the rocker arm through passages in the block and head and then down through the hollow pushrod to the lifters.

See Figure 24-80.

Other engine designs supply engine oil to the rocker arms and valves through passages in the block and head. See Figure 24-81.

TECH TIP

TWO CHOICES IF USING FLAT-BOTTOM LIFTERS

An old or rebuilt engine that uses flat-bottom lifters must use one of two lubricants:

1. Oils that contain at least 0.15% or 1,500 PPM of zinc in the form of ZDDP. Oils that contain this much zinc are designed for off-road use only and in a vehicle that does not have a catalytic converter, such as racing oils. If the vehicle is equipped with a catalytic converter, replace the camshaft and lifters to roller-type so that newer oils with lower levels of zinc can be used.

2. Use a newer oil and an additive such as:
   a. GM engine oil supplement (EOS)
   b. Comp Cams® camshaft break-in oil additive, Part #159
   c. Crane Cams® Moly Paste, Part #99002-1
   d. Crane Cams® Super Lube oil additive, Part #99003-1
   e. Lumati Assembly lube, Part #99010
   f. Mell-Lube camshaft tube oil additive, Part #M-10012

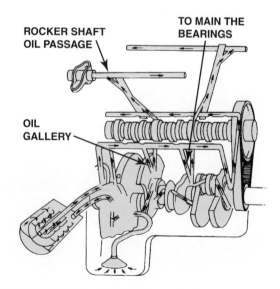

FIGURE 24-81 Oil galleries (passages) often supply oil to the rocker shafts.

FREQUENTLY ASKED QUESTION

WHAT IS A FLAT HEAD ENGINE?

Most early engines had the valves placed in the block operated by the cam-in-block camshaft. This type of engine design is called a flat head because the cylinder head is flat and does not contain any coolant passages or ports. In 1932, Ford introduced the first low-cost V-8 engine using the flat head or side valve design. This engine was used in early hot rods and even into the 1960s after overhead valve (OHV) design engines were becoming more popular and powerful. Old-timers used to have a common expression about their Ford flat-head V-8s that said.

"Flat heads forever" and "Real engines do not have valve covers."

See Figure 24-82.

FREQUENTLY ASKED QUESTION

WHEN WAS THE FIRST CHRYSLER HEMI?

The original Chrysler Hemi engine that used a combustion chamber with a hemispherical shape was offered as an option in 1951. The original engine design was over-square with a bore (3.81 in.) longer than the stroke (3.63 in.) for a total displacement of 331 cu. in. See Figure 24-83.

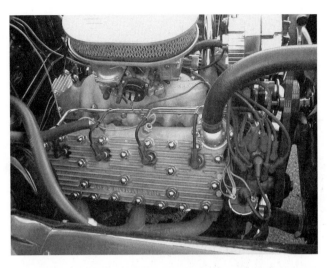

FIGURE 24-82   A flat-head Ford V-8 engine. Note that the exhaust manifold has only three exhaust ports. The center two cylinders shared one port.

FIGURE 24-83   A cutaway of an early Chrysler Hemi showing the valves and hemispherical combustion chamber.

SUMMARY

1. The camshaft rotates at one-half the crankshaft speed.
2. The pushrods should be rotating while the engine is running if the camshaft and lifters are okay.
3. On overhead valve engines, the camshaft is usually placed in the block above the crankshaft. The lobes of the camshaft are usually lubricated by splash lubrication.
4. Silent chains are quieter than roller chains but tend to stretch with use.
5. The lift of a cam is usually expressed in decimal inches and represents the distance that the valve is lifted off the valve seat.
6. In many engines, camshaft lift is transferred to the tip of the valve stem to open the valve by the use of a rocker arm or follower.
7. Pushrods transfer camshaft motion upward from the camshaft to the rocker arm.

8. Camshaft duration is the number of degrees of crankshaft rotation for which the valve is lifted off the seat.

9. Valve overlap is the number of crankshaft degrees for which both valves are open.

10. Camshafts should be installed according to the manufacturer's recommended procedures. Flat lifter camshafts should be thoroughly lubricated with extreme pressure lubricant.

11. If a new camshaft is installed, new lifters should also be installed.

REVIEW QUESTIONS

1. Explain why the lift and duration and lobe-center dimension of the camshaft determine the power characteristics of the engine.

2. Explain lobe centerline.

3. Describe the operation of a hydraulic lifter.

4. Describe how to adjust hydraulic lifters.

CHAPTER QUIZ

1. The camshaft makes _____ for every revolution of the crankshaft.
   a. One-quarter revolution
   b. One-half revolution
   c. One revolution
   d. Two revolutions

2. Flat-bottom valve lifters rotate during operation because of the _____ of the camshaft.
   a. Taper of the lobe
   b. Thrust plate
   c. Chain tensioner
   d. Bearings

3. If lift and duration remain constant and the lobe center angle decreases _____.
   a. The valve overlap decreases
   b. The effective lift increases
   c. The effective duration increases
   d. The valve overlap increases

4. Which timing chain type is also called a "silent chain"?
   a. Roller
   b. Morse
   c. Flat link
   d. Both b and c

5. Two technicians are discussing variable valve timing. Technician A says that changing the exhaust valve timing helps reduce exhaust emissions. Technician B says that changing the intake valve timing helps increase low-speed torque. Which technician is correct?
   a. Technician A only
   b. Technician B only
   c. Both Technicians A and B
   d. Neither Technician A nor B

6. Many technicians always use new pushrods because _____.
   a. It is less expensive to buy than clean
   b. All of the dirt cannot be cleaned out from the hollow center
   c. Pushrods wear at both ends
   d. Pushrods shrink in length if removed from an engine

7. A DOHC V-6 has how many camshafts?
   a. 4
   b. 3
   c. 2
   d. 1

8. The intake valve opens at 39° BTDC and closes at 71° ABDC. The exhaust valve opens at 78° BBDC and closes at 47° ATDC. Which answer is correct?
   a. Intake valve duration is 110°
   b. Exhaust valve duration is 125°
   c. Overlap is 86°
   d. Both a and b

9. Hydraulic valve lifters can make a ticking noise when the engine is running if _____.
   a. The valve lash is too close
   b. The valve lash is too loose
   c. The lobe centerline is over 110°
   d. Both a and c

10. Hydraulic lifters or hydraulic lash adjusters (HLA) may not bleed down properly and cause an engine miss if _____.
    a. The engine oil is one quart low
    b. The wrong API-rated engine oil is used
    c. The wrong SAE-rated engine oil is used
    d. Both a and b

CHAPTER 25

PISTONS, RINGS, AND CONNECTING RODS

OBJECTIVES

After studying Chapter 25, the reader will be able to:

1. Prepare for Engine Repair (A1) ASE certification test content area "C"(Engine Block Diagnosis and Repair).

2. Describe the purpose and function of pistons, rings, and connecting rods.

3. Explain how pistons and rods are constructed and what to look for during an inspection.

4. Discuss connecting rod reconditioning procedures.

5. Explain how piston rings operate and how to install them on a piston.

KEY TERMS

All engine power is developed by burning fuel in the presence of air in the combustion chamber. Heat from the combustion causes the burned gas to increase in pressure. The force of this pressure is converted into useful work through the piston, connecting rod, and crankshaft.

PURPOSE AND FUNCTION OF PISTONS, RINGS, AND CONNECTING RODS

The **piston** forms a movable bottom to the combustion chamber. It is attached to the connecting rod with a **piston pin** or **wrist pin.** See Figure 25-1. The piston pin is allowed to have a rocking movement because of a swivel joint at the piston end of the connecting rod. The connecting rod is connected to a part of the crankshaft called a **crank throw, crankpin,** or **connecting rod bearing journal.** This provides another swivel joint. The center of the crank throw is the amount by which the large end of the connecting rod is offset from the crankshaft main bearing centerline. This dimension of the crankshaft determines the stroke of the engine.

NOTE: The stroke is the distance from the center of the main bearing journal to the center of the connecting rod journal times two.

    Piston rings seal the small space between the piston and cylinder wall, keeping the pressure above the piston. When the pressure builds up in the combustion chamber, it pushes on the piston. The piston, in turn, pushes on the piston pin and upper end of the connecting rod. The lower end of the connecting rod pushes on the crank throw. This provides the force to turn the crankshaft. As the crankshaft turns, it develops inertia. *Inertia is the force that causes the crankshaft to continue rotating.* This action will bring the piston back to its original position, where it will be ready for the next power stroke. While the engine is running, the combustion cycle keeps repeating as the piston reciprocates (moves up and down) and the crankshaft rotates.

PISTON AND ROD REMOVAL

After the oil pan and cylinder head(s) have been removed, the piston and rod can be removed by the following steps:

Step 1   The rod and caps should be checked for markings that identify their location. *If the rod and caps are not marked, they should be marked before disassembly.* If number stamps are not available, punch marks, as shown in Figure 25-2, can be used.

CAUTION: Powdered metal connecting rods should only be marked with a permanent marker to avoid damage to the rod. See Figure 25-3.

Step 2   The crankshaft is turned until the piston is at the bottom of its stroke. This places the connecting rod nuts or cap screws where they are easily accessible. They are removed, and the rod cap is taken off. This may require light tapping on the connecting rod bolts with a soft-faced hammer.

Step 3   Protectors should be placed over the rod bolt threads to protect the threads and the surface of the crankshaft journal. The piston and rod assembly is pushed out, with care being taken to avoid hitting the bottom edge of the cylinder with the rod.

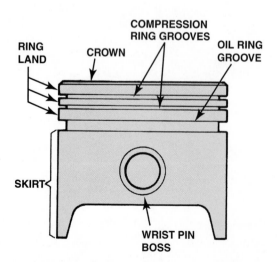

FIGURE 25-1 All pistons share these parts in common.

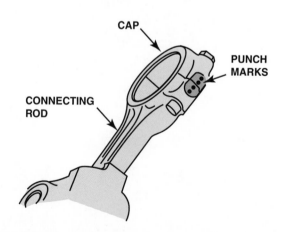

FIGURE 25-2 Punch marks on connecting rod and rod cap to identify their location in the engine. The cap and rod were machined together and must remain together.

FIGURE 25-3 Powdered metal connecting rods can be identified by their smooth appearance.

The rod caps should be reattached to the rod after the assembly has been removed from the cylinder. The rod caps are not interchangeable between rods. The assembly must be handled carefully. It should be placed on a parts stand so that the piston and rod do not strike each other. The aluminum piston can be easily scratched or nicked.

The rings are carefully removed from the piston to avoid damage to either the piston or the ring. The best way to remove them is to use a **piston ring expanding tool.**

PISTON DESIGN

When the engine is running, the piston starts at the top of the cylinder. As it moves downward, it accelerates until it reaches a maximum velocity slightly before it is halfway down. The piston comes to a stop at the bottom of the cylinder at 180 degrees of crankshaft rotation. During the next 180 degrees of crankshaft rotation, the piston moves upward. It accelerates to reach a maximum velocity slightly above the halfway point and then comes to a stop at the top of the stroke. Thus, the piston starts, accelerates, and stops twice in each crankshaft revolution.

NOTE: A typical piston in an engine at 4000 RPM accelerates from 0 to 60 miles per hour (97 kilometers per hour) in about 0.004 second (4 milliseconds) as it descends about halfway down the cylinder.

This reciprocating action of the piston produces large **inertia forces.** Inertia is the force that causes a part that is stopped to stay stopped or a part that is in motion to stay in motion. The lighter the piston can be made, the less inertia force that is developed. Less inertia will allow higher engine operating speeds. For this reason, pistons are made to be as light as possible while still having the strength that is needed.

The piston operates with its head exposed to the hot combustion gases, whereas the skirt contacts the relatively cool cylinder wall. This results in a temperature difference of about 275°F (147°C) between the top and bottom of the piston.

TECH TIP

PISTON WEIGHT IS IMPORTANT!

All pistons in an engine should weigh the same to help ensure a balanced engine. Piston weight becomes a factor when changing pistons. Most aluminum pistons range in weight from 10 to 30 ounces (280 to 850 grams) (1 oz = 28.35 grams). *A typical paper clip weighs 1 gram.* If the cylinder has been bored, larger replacement pistons are obviously required. If the replacement pistons weigh more, this puts additional inertia loads on the rod bearings. Therefore, to help prevent rod bearing failure on an overhauled engine, the replacement pistons should not weigh more than the original pistons.

CAUTION: Some less-expensive replacement cast pistons or high-performance forged pistons are much heavier than the stock pistons, even in the stock bore size. This means that the crankshaft may need heavy metal added to the counterweights of the crankshaft for the engine to be balanced.

For the same reason, if one piston is being replaced, all pistons should be replaced or at least checked and corrected to ensure the same weight.

PISTON HEADS

Because the piston head forms a portion of the combustion chamber, its shape is very important to the combustion process. Generally, low-cost, low-performance engines have **flat-top pistons.** Some of these flat-top pistons come so close to the cylinder head that **recesses** are cut in the piston top for valve clearance. Pistons used in high-powered engines may have raised domes or **pop-ups** on the piston heads. These are used to increase the compression ratio. Pistons used in other engines may be provided with a depression or a **dish.** The varying depths of the dish provide different compression ratios required by different engine models. Several piston head shapes are shown in Figure 25-4.

FIGURE 25-4   Piston head shapes: (a) flat (b) recessed, (c and d) pop-up, and (e and f) dished.

NOTE: Newer engines do not use valve reliefs because this requires that the thickness of the top of the piston be increased to provide the necessary strength. The thicker the top of the piston, the lower down from the top of the top piston ring. To reduce unburned hydrocarbon (HC) exhaust emissions, engineers attempt to place the top piston ring as close to the top of the piston as possible to prevent the unburned fuel from being trapped (and not burned) between the top of the piston and the top of the top piston ring.

Recesses machined or cast into the tops of the pistons for valve clearance are commonly called **eyebrows, valve reliefs,** or **valve pockets.** The depth of the eyebrows has a major effect on the compression ratio and is necessary to provide clearance for the valves if the timing belt of an overhead camshaft engine should break. Without the eyebrows, the pistons could hit the valves near TDC if the valves are not operating (closing) because of nonrotation of the camshaft. If an engine is designed not to have the pistons hitting the valves, the engine is called freewheeling.

CAM GROUND PISTONS

Aluminum pistons expand when they get hot. A method of expansion control was devised using a **cam ground** piston skirt. With this design, the piston thrust surfaces closely fit the cylinder, and the piston pin boss diameter is fitted loosely. As the cam ground piston is heated, it expands along the piston pin so that it becomes nearly round at its normal operating temperatures. A cam ground piston skirt is illustrated in Figure 25-5. See Figure 25-6 for an example of how to measure the diameter of a piston.

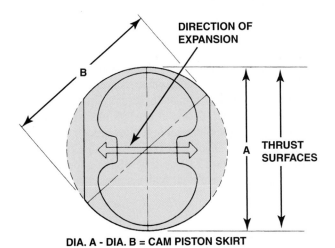

FIGURE 25-5   Piston cam shape. The largest diameter is across the thrust surfaces and perpendicular to the piston pin (lettered A).

PISTON FINISH

The finish on pistons varies with the manufacturer, but they all are designed to help reduce scuffing. Scuffing is a condition where the metal of the piston actually contacts the cylinder wall. When the piston stops at the top of the cylinder, welds or transfer of metal from one part to the other can take place. Scuffing can be reduced by coating the piston skirts with tin 0.0005 inch (0.0125 mm) thick or a moly graphite coating. See Figure 25-7.

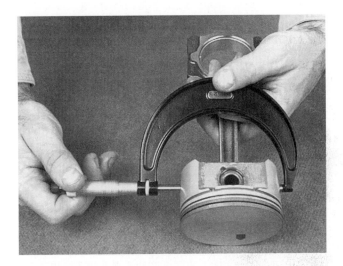

FIGURE 25-6   A piston diameter is measured across the thrust surfaces.

FIGURE 25-7   A moly graphite coating on the skirt of this piston from a General Motors 3800 V-6 engine helps prevent piston scuffing when the engine is cold.

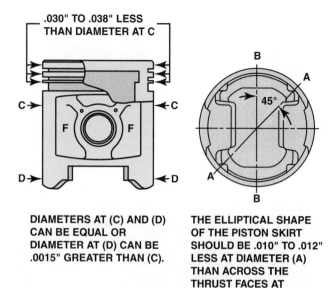

DIAMETERS AT (C) AND (D) CAN BE EQUAL OR DIAMETER AT (D) CAN BE .0015" GREATER THAN (C).

THE ELLIPTICAL SHAPE OF THE PISTON SKIRT SHOULD BE .010" TO .012" LESS AT DIAMETER (A) THAN ACROSS THE THRUST FACES AT DIAMETER (B). MEASUREMENT IS MADE 1/8" BELOW LOWER RING GROOVE.

FIGURE 25-8   Piston skirt cam shape.

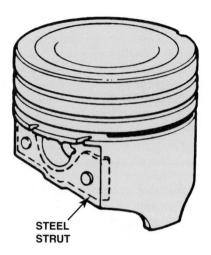

FIGURE 25-9   Steel struts cast inside pistons help control expansion.

PISTON HEAD SIZE

The top or head of the piston is smaller in diameter than the rest of the piston. The top of the piston is exposed to the most heat and therefore tends to expand more than the rest of the piston. See Figure 25-8. Most pistons have horizontal separation **slots** that act as **heat dams.** These slots reduce heat transfer from the hot piston head to the lower skirt. This, in turn, keeps the skirt temperature lower so that there will be less skirt expansion. Because the slot is placed in the oil ring groove, it can be used for oil drainback and expansion control.

PISTON STRUT INSERTS

A major development in expansion control occurred when the piston aluminum was cast around two stiff steel **struts.** The struts are not chemically bonded to the aluminum, nor do they add any strength to the piston. There is only a mechanical bond between the steel and aluminum. The bimetallic action of this strut in the aluminum forces the piston to bow outward along the piston pin. This keeps the piston skirt thrust surfaces from expanding more than the cast-iron cylinder in which the piston operates. Pistons with steel strut inserts allow good piston-to-cylinder wall clearance at normal temperatures. At the same time, they allow the cold operating clearance to be as small as 0.0005 inch (one-half thousandth of an inch) (0.0127 millimeter). This small clearance will prevent cold piston slap and noise. A typical piston expansion control strut is visible in Figure 25-9.

With newer engines, the number and thickness of the piston rings have decreased and the cast-aluminum piston skirt has been reduced to a minimum by using an open-type **slipper skirt.** Examples of the slipper skirt piston are shown in Figure 25-10.

HYPEREUTECTIC PISTONS

A standard cast-aluminum piston contains about 9% to 12% silicon and is called a eutectic piston. To add strength, the silicon content is increased to about 16%, and the resulting piston is called a **hypereutectic** piston. Other advantages of a hypereutectic piston are its 25% weight reduction and lower expansion rate. The disadvantage of hypereutectic pistons is their higher cost, because they are more difficult to cast and machine.

Hypereutectic pistons are commonly used in the aftermarket and as original equipment in many turbocharged and supercharged engines.

FORGED PISTONS

High-performance engines need pistons with added strength. Forged pistons have a dense grain structure and are very strong. Forged pistons are often used in turbocharged or supercharged engines. Because forged pistons are less porous than cast pistons, they conduct heat more quickly. Forged pistons generally run about 20% cooler than cast pistons. See Figure 25-11. Figure 25-12 on page 484 is a forged heavy-duty truck aluminum piston, which shows the grain of the aluminum.

PISTON PINS

Piston pins are used to attach the piston to the connecting rod. Piston pins are also known as **gudgeon pins** (a British term).

(a)

(b)

FIGURE 25-10 Two sectional views of a slipper-skirt-type piston that uses a steel expansion strut.

The piston pin transfers the force produced by combustion chamber pressures and piston inertia to the connecting rod. The piston pin is made from high-quality steel in the shape of a tube to make it both strong and light. Sometimes, the interior hole of the piston pin is tapered, so it is large at the ends and small in the middle of the pin. This gives the pin strength that is proportional to the location of the load placed on it. A double-taper hole such as this is more expensive to manufacture, so it is used only where its weight advantage merits the extra cost. See Figure 25-13.

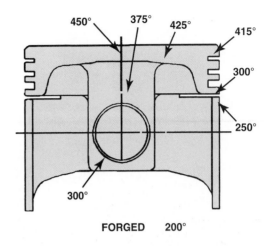

FORGED 200°

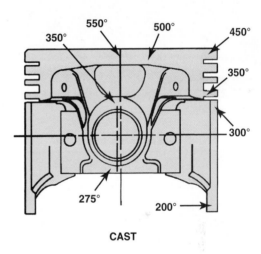

CAST

FIGURE 25-11 The critical crown temperature can be 100°F (38°C) cooler on a forged piston compared to a cast piston.

Piston Pin Offset

The piston pin holes are not centered in the piston. They are located toward the **major thrust surface,** approximately 0.062 inch (1.57 millimeters) from the piston centerline, as shown in Figure 25-14.

Pin offset is designed to reduce piston slap and the noise that can result as the large end of the connecting rod crosses over top dead center.

The minor thrust side of the piston head has a greater area than does the major side. This is caused by the pin offset. As the piston moves up in the cylinder on the compression stroke, it rides against the minor thrust surface. When compression pressure becomes high enough, the greater head area on the minor side causes the piston to cock slightly in the cylinder. This keeps the *top* of the minor thrust surface on the cylinder. It forces the *bottom* of the major thrust surface to contact the cylinder wall. As the piston approaches top center,

FIGURE 25-12 Grain flow lines can be seen in this forged aluminum piston with a trunk skirt.

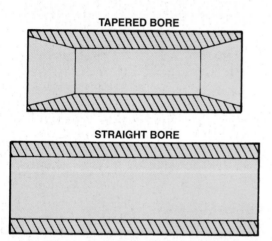

FIGURE 25-13 Most piston pins are hollow to reduce weight and have a straight bore. Some pins have a tapered bore to reinforce the pin.

both thrust surfaces are in contact with the cylinder wall. When the crankshaft crosses over top center, the force on the connecting rod moves the entire piston toward the major thrust surface. The lower portion of the major thrust surface has already been in contact with the cylinder wall. The rest of the piston skirt slips into full contact just after the crossover point, thereby controlling piston slap. This action is illustrated in Figure 25-15.

Offsetting the piston toward the minor thrust surface would provide a better mechanical advantage. It also would cause less piston-to-cylinder friction. For these reasons, the offset is often placed toward the minor thrust surface in racing

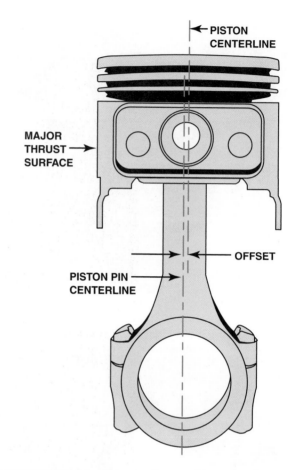

FIGURE 25-14 Piston pin offset toward the major thrust surface.

engines. Noise and durability are not as important in racing engines as is maximum performance.

NOTE: Not all piston pins are offset. In fact, many engines operate without the offset to help reduce friction and improve power and fuel economy.

Piston Pin Fit

The finish and size of piston pins are closely controlled. Piston pins have a smooth mirrorlike finish. Their size is held to tens of thousandths of an inch so that exact fits can be maintained. If the piston pin is loose in the piston or in the connecting rod, it will make a sound while the engine is running. This is often described as a **double-knock.** The noise is created when the piston stops at top dead center and occurs again as it starts to move downward, creating a double-knock sound, which is also described as a rattling sound. If the piston pin is too tight in the piston, it will restrict piston expansion along the pin diameter. This will lead to piston scuffing. Normal piston pin clearances range from 0.0005 to 0.0007 inch (0.0126 to 0.0180 millimeter).

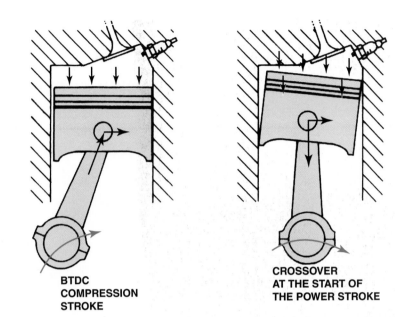

BTDC COMPRESSION STROKE

CROSSOVER AT THE START OF THE POWER STROKE

ATDC POWER STROKE

FIGURE 25-15 Engine rotation and rod angle during the power stroke causes the piston to press harder against one side of the cylinder, which is called the major thrust surface.

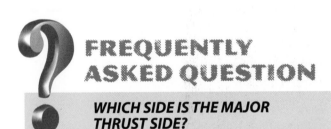

FREQUENTLY ASKED QUESTION

WHICH SIDE IS THE MAJOR THRUST SIDE?

The thrust side is the side the rod points to when the piston is on the power stroke. Any V-block engine (V-6 or V-8) that rotates clockwise is viewed from the front of the engine—the left bank piston thrust side faces the inside (center) of the engine. The right bank piston thrust side faces the outside of the block. This rule is called the **left-hand rule** and states:

- Stand at the rear of the engine and point toward the front of the engine.
- Raise your thumb straight up, indicating the top of the engine.
- Point your middle finger toward the right. This represents the major thrust side of the piston.

Always assemble the connecting rods onto the rods so that the notch or "F" on the piston is pointing toward the front of the engine and the oil squirt hole on the connecting rod is pointing toward the major thrust side with your left hand.

PISTON PIN RETAINING METHODS

Full Floating

It is necessary to retain or hold piston pins so that they stay centered in the piston. If piston pins are not retained, they will move endwise and groove the cylinder wall. The piston pin may be **full floating,** with some type of stop located at each end.

Full-floating piston pins in automotive engines are retained by **lock rings** located in grooves in the piston pin hole at the ends of the piston pin. See Figure 25-16. Some engines use aluminum or plastic plugs in both ends of the piston pin. These plugs touch the cylinder wall without scoring, to hold the piston pin centered in the piston.

Interference Fit

The modern method of retaining the piston pin in the connecting rod is to make the connecting rod hole slightly smaller than the piston pin. The pin is installed by heating the rod to expand the hole or by pressing the pin into the rod. This retaining method will securely hold the pin. See Figure 25-17. This press or shrink fit is called an **interference fit.** Care must be taken to have the correct hole sizes, and the pin must be centered in the connecting rod. The interference fit method is the least expensive to use. It is, therefore, used in the majority of engines.

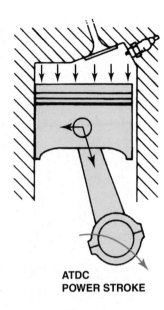

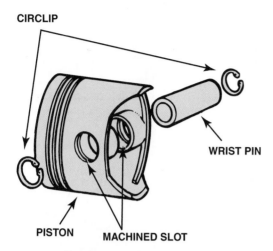

FIGURE 25-16   Circlips hold full-floating piston pins in place.

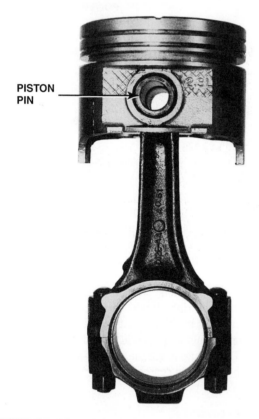

FIGURE 25-17   Interference fit type of piston pin.

PISTON RING GROOVES

Piston ring **grooves** are located between the piston head and skirt. The width of the grooves, the width of the **lands** between the ring grooves, and the number of rings are major factors in determining minimum piston height. The outside diameter of the lands is about 0.020 to 0.040 inch (0.5 to 1.0 millimeter) smaller than the **skirt** diameter.

REAL WORLD FIX

BIG PROBLEM, NO NOISE

Sometimes the piston pin can "walk"off the center of the piston and score the cylinder wall. This scoring is often not noticed because this type of wear does not create noise. Because the piston pin is below the piston rings, little combustion pressure is lost past the rings until the groove worn by the piston pin has worn the piston rings.

Troubleshooting the exact cause of the increased oil consumption is difficult because the damage done to the oil control rings by the groove usually affects only one cylinder.

Often, compression tests indicate good compression because the cylinder seals, especially at the top. More than one technician has been surprised to see the cylinder gouged by a piston pin when the cylinder head has been removed for service. In such a case, the cost of the engine repair immediately increases far beyond that of normal cylinder head service.

PISTON RINGS

Piston rings serve several major functions in engines.

- They form a sliding combustion chamber seal that prevents the high-pressure combustion gases from leaking past the piston.
- They keep engine oil from getting into the combustion chamber.
- The rings transfer some of the piston heat to the cylinder wall, where it is removed from the engine through the cooling system. See Figure 25-18.

Piston rings are classified into two types: two **compression rings,** located toward the top of the piston, and one **oil control ring,** located below the compression rings. See Figure 25-19.

NOTE: Some engines, such as the Honda high-fuel-economy engines, use pistons with only two rings: one compression ring and one oil control ring.

The first piston rings were made with a simple rectangular cross-section. This cross-section was modified with tapers, chamfers, counterbores, slots, rails, and expanders. Piston ring materials have also changed from plain cast iron to materials such as pearlitic and nodular iron, as well as steel. **Ductile iron,** which is very flexible and can be twisted without breaking, is also used as a piston ring material in some automotive engines.

COMPRESSION RINGS

A compression ring is designed to form a seal between the moving piston and the cylinder wall. This is necessary to get maximum power from the combustion pressure. At the same time, the compression ring must keep friction at a minimum. This is made possible by providing only enough static or built-in mechanical tension to hold the ring in contact with the cylinder wall during the intake stroke. Combustion chamber pressure during the compression, power, and exhaust strokes is applied to the top and back of the ring. This pressure will add the force on the ring that is required to seal the combustion chamber during these strokes. Figure 25-20 illustrates how the combustion chamber pressure adds force to the ring.

The space in the ring groove above the ring is called the **side clearance** and the space behind the ring is called the **back clearance.** See Figure 25-21.

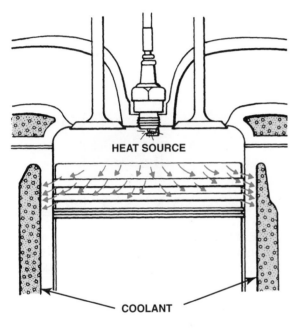

FIGURE 25-18   The rings conduct heat from the piston to the cylinder wall.

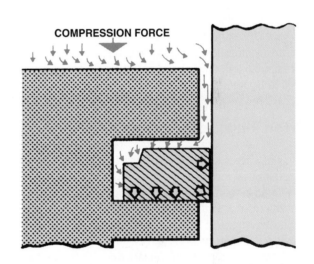

FIGURE 25-20   Combustion chamber pressure forces the ring against the cylinder wall and the bottom of the ring groove, effectively sealing the cylinder.

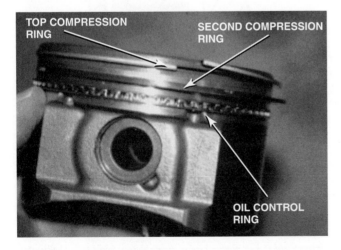

FIGURE 25-19   Most pistons use two compression rings and one oil control ring.

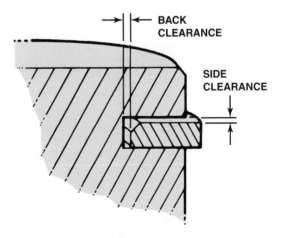

FIGURE 25-21   The side and back clearances must be correct for the compression rings to seal properly.

Ring Gap

The piston **ring gap** will allow some leakage past the top compression ring. This leakage is useful in providing pressure on the second ring to develop a dynamic sealing force. The amount of piston ring gap is critical. Too much gap will allow excessive **blowby.** Blowby is the leakage of combustion gases past the rings. Blowby will blow oil from the cylinder wall. This oil loss is followed by piston ring scuffing. Too little gap, however, will allow the piston ring ends to butt when the engine is hot. Ring end butting increases the mechanical force against the cylinder wall, causing excessive wear and possible engine failure.

A butt-type piston ring gap is the most common type used in automotive engines. Some low-speed industrial engines and some diesel engines use a more expensive tapered or seal-cut ring gap. These gaps are necessary to reduce losses of the high-pressure combustion gases. At low speeds, the gases have more time to leak through the gap. Typical ring gaps are illustrated in Figure 25-22.

Piston Ring Cross-Sections

As engine speeds have increased, inertia forces on the piston rings have also increased. As a result, engine manufacturers have found it desirable to reduce inertia forces on the rings by reducing their weight. This has been done by narrowing the piston ring from 1/4 inch (6 millimeters) to as little as 1/16 inch (1.6 millimeters).

A **taper face ring** will contact the cylinder wall at the lower edge of the piston ring. See Figure 25-23. When either a chamfer or counterbore relief is made on the *upper inside* corner of the piston ring, the ring cross-section is unbalanced. This will cause the ring to twist in the groove in a positive direction. **Positive twist** will give the same wall contact as the taper-faced ring. It will also provide a line contact seal on the bottom side of the groove. Sometimes, twist and a taper face are used on the same compression ring.

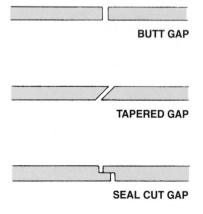

FIGURE 25-22 Typical ring gaps.

Some second rings are notched on the *outer lower* corner. This, too, provides a positive ring twist. The sharp lower outer corner becomes a scraper that helps in oil control, but this type of ring has less compression control than the preceding types.

By chamfering the ring's *lower inner* corner, a **reverse twist** is produced. This seals the lower outer section of the ring and piston ring groove, thus improving oil control. Reverse twist rings require a greater taper face or barrel face to maintain the desired ring face-to-cylinder wall contact. See Figure 25-24.

Another style of positive twist ring has a counterbore at the lower outside edge. See Figure 25-25. This ring is called a **scraper ring** because it does a good job of oil control and is usually recommended for use at the second compression ring.

Some rings replace the outer ring taper with a barrel face. The barrel is 0.0003 inch per 0.100 inch (0.0076 millimeter

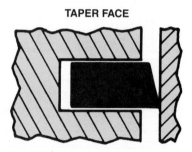

FIGURE 25-23 The taper face ring provides good oil control by scraping the cylinder wall. This style of ring must be installed right side up or the ring will not seal and oil will be drawn into the combustion chamber.

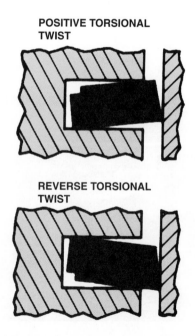

FIGURE 25-24 Torsional twist rings provide better compression sealing and oil control than regular taper face rings.

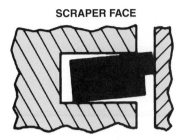

FIGURE 25-25   Scraper rings improve oil control.

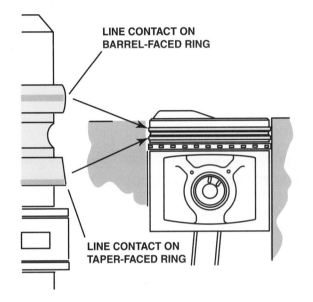

FIGURE 25-26   The piston rings are slightly used, so only the line contact shows. The upper, barrel-faced ring has line contact in the center. The second, taper-faced ring has line contact along the lower edge of the ring.

per 0.254 millimeter) of piston ring width. Barrel faces are found on rectangular rings and on torsionally twisted rings. See Figure 25-26.

Chromium Piston Rings

A chromium facing on cast-iron rings greatly increases piston ring life, especially where abrasive materials are present in the air. During manufacture, the chromium-plated ring is slightly chamfered at the outer corners. About 0.0004 inch (0.010 millimeter) of chrome is then plated on the ring face. Chromium-faced rings are then prelapped or honed before they are packaged and shipped to the customer. The finished chromium facing is shown in a sectional view in Figure 25-27.

Molybdenum Piston Rings

Early in the 1960s, molybdenum piston ring faces were introduced. These rings proved to have good service life, especially

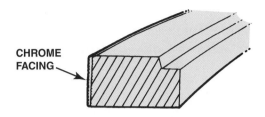

FIGURE 25-27   The chrome facing on this compression ring is about 0.004-inch (0.10-mm) thick.

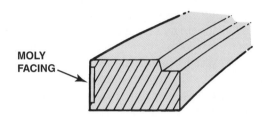

FIGURE 25-28   The moly facing on this compression ring is about 0.005-inch (0.13-mm) thick.

under scuffing conditions. The plasma method is a spray method used to deposit molybdenum on cast iron to produce a long-wearing and low-friction piston ring. The plasma method involves an electric arc plasma (ionized gas) that generates an extremely high temperature to melt the molybdenum and spray-deposit a molten powder of it onto a piston ring. Therefore, plasma rings are molybdenum (moly) rings that have the moly coating applied by the plasma method. Most molybdenum-faced piston rings have a groove that is 0.004- to 0.008-inch (0.1- to 0.2-millimeter) deep cut into the ring face. This groove is filled with molybdenum, using a metallic (or plasma) spray method, so that there is a cast-iron edge above and below the molybdenum. This edge may be chamfered in some applications. A sectional view of a molybdenum-faced ring is shown in Figure 25-28.

Molybdenum-faced piston rings will survive under high-temperature and scuffing conditions better than chromium-faced rings. Under abrasive wear conditions, chromium-faced rings will have a better service life. There is little measurable difference between these two facing materials with respect to blowby, oil control, break-in, and horsepower. Piston rings with either of these two types of facings are far better than plain cast-iron rings with phosphorus coatings. A molybdenum-faced ring, when used, will be found in the top groove, and a plain cast-iron or chromium-faced ring will be found in the second groove.

Moly-Chrome-Carbide Rings

Rings with moly-chrome-carbide coating are also used in some original equipment (OE) and replacement applications. The coating has properties that include the hardness of the chrome and carbide combined with the heat resistance of molybdenum. Ceramic-coated rings are also being used where additional heat resistance is needed, such as in some heavy-duty, turbocharged, or supercharged engines.

Oil Control Rings

The scraping action of the oil control ring allows oil to return through the ring and openings in the piston. Figure 25-29 shows how the scraping action of the oil control ring can be used to lubricate the piston pin. Steel spring expanders were placed in the ring groove behind the ring to improve static radial tension. They forced the ring to conform to the cylinder wall. Many expander designs are used. On the three-piece ring, a spacer-expander lies between the top and bottom rails. The spacer-expander keeps the rails separated and pushes them out against the cylinder wall. See Figure 25-30.

FIGURE 25-29   The oil scraped from the cylinder walls by the oil control ring is directed to lubricate the piston pin in this design.

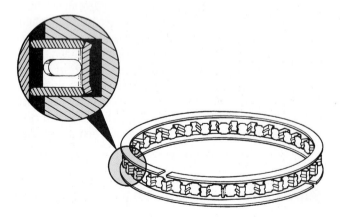

FIGURE 25-30   This typical three-piece oil control ring uses a hump-type stainless steel spacer-expander. The expander separates the two steel rails and presses them against the cylinder wall.

PISTON SERVICE

The pistons are removed from the rods using a special fixture shown in Figure 25-31. After cleaning, the skirts of the used industrial pistons should be resized, and a spacer is placed in the top of the upper ring grooves.

As the piston goes rapidly up and down in the cylinder, it tosses the rings to the top and to the bottom of the ring grooves. The pounding of each ring in its groove gradually increases the piston ring side clearance. Material is worn from both the ring and the groove. See Figure 25-32. Replace the piston if the ring groove is larger than factory specifications.

CONNECTING RODS

The connecting rod transfers the force and reciprocating motion of the piston to the crankshaft. The small end of the connecting rod reciprocates with the piston. The large end rotates with the crankpin. See Figure 25-32. These dynamic motions make it desirable to keep the connecting rod as light as possible while still having a rigid beam section. See Figure 25-33.

Connecting rods are manufactured by casting, forging, and powdered (sintered) metal processes.

Cast Connecting Rods

Casting materials and processes have been improved so that they are used in most vehicle engines with high production standards. Cast connecting rods can be identified by their

FIGURE 25-31   A press used to remove the connecting rod from the piston.

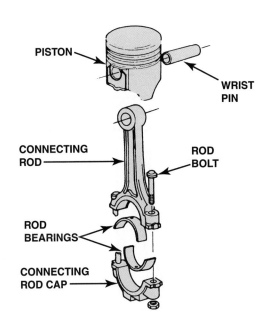

FIGURE 25-32   The connecting rod is the most highly stressed part of any engine because combustion pressure tries to compress it and piston inertia tries to pull it apart.

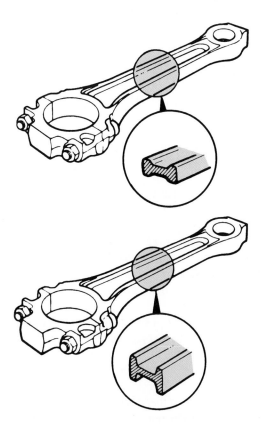

FIGURE 25-33   Even though different rods may have different cross-sections, most are I-beam shaped.

narrow parting line. A typical rough connecting rod casting is shown in Figure 25-34.

Forged Connecting Rods

Forged connecting rods have been used for years. They are generally used in heavy-duty and high-performance engines. Generally, the forging method produces lighter weight and stronger, but more expensive, connecting rods. Forged connecting rods can be identified by their *wide parting line.* Many high-performance connecting rods use a bronze bushing in the small end of the rod as shown in Figure 25-35.

FIGURE 25-34   Rough casting for a connecting rod.

FIGURE 25-35   This high-performance connecting rod uses a bronze bushing in the small end of the rod and oil hole to allow oil to reach the full-floating piston pin.

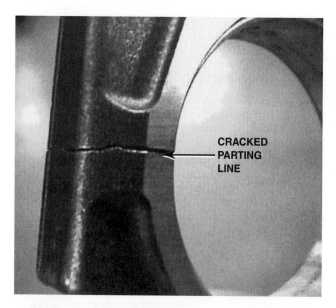

FIGURE 25-36 Powdered metal connecting rods feature a fractured parting line at the big end of the rod.

Powdered Metal Connecting Rods

Most new production engines, such as the General Motors Northstar and Chrysler Hemi, use powdered metal (PM) rods.

Powdered metal connecting rods have many advantages over conventional cast or forged rods including precise weight control. Each rod is created using a measured amount of material so that rod balancing, and therefore engine balancing, is now achieved without extra weighting and machining operations.

Powdered metal connecting rods start as powdered metal, which includes iron, copper, carbon, and other alloying agents. This powder is then placed in a die and compacted (forged) under a pressure of 30 to 50 tons per square inch. After the part is shaped in the die, it is taken through a sintering operation where the part is heated, without melting, to about 2,000°F. During the sintering process, the ingredients are transformed into metallurgical bonds, giving the part strength. Machining is very limited and includes boring the small and big ends and drilling the holes for the rod bearing cap retaining bolts. The big end is then fractured using a large press. The uneven parting line helps ensure a perfect match when the pieces are assembled. See Figure 25-36.

CONNECTING ROD DESIGN

The big end of the connecting rod must be a perfect circle. Therefore, the rod caps must not be interchanged. Assembly bolt holes are closely reamed in both the cap and connecting

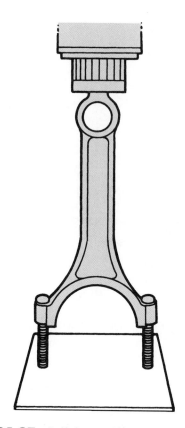

FIGURE 25-37 Rod bolts are quickly removed by using a press.

rod to ensure alignment. The connecting rod bolts have **piloting surfaces** that closely fit these reamed holes. The fit of the connecting rod bolts is so tight that a press must be used to remove the bolts when they are to be replaced, as shown in Figure 25-37.

In some engines, offset connecting rods provide the most economical distribution of main bearing space and crankshaft cheek clearance.

Connecting rods are made with **balancing bosses (pads)** so that their weight can be adjusted to specifications. Some have balancing bosses only on the rod cap. Others also have a balancing boss above the piston. Some manufacturers put balancing bosses on the side of the rod, near the center of gravity of the connecting rod. Typical balancing bosses can be seen in Figure 25-38. Balancing is done on automatic balancing machines as the final machining operation before the rod is installed in an engine.

Most connecting rods have a **spit hole** that bleeds some of the oil from the connecting rod journal. See Figure 25-39. On inline engines, oil is thrown up from the spit hole into the cylinder in which the rod is located. On V-type engines, it is often thrown into a cylinder in the opposite bank. The oil that is spit from the rod is aimed so that it will splash into the interior of the piston. This helps to lubricate the piston pin. A hole similar to the spit holes may be used. It is called a **bleed hole.** Its only purpose is to control the oil flow through the bearing.

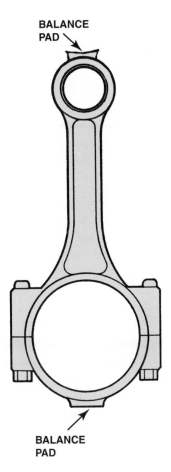

FIGURE 25-38   Some rods have balance pads on each end of the connecting rod.

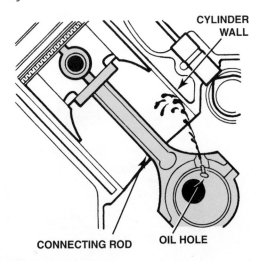

FIGURE 25-39   Some connecting rods have spit holes to help lubricate the cylinder walls or piston pins.

ROD TWIST

During connecting rod reconditioning, the rod should be checked for twist. See Figure 25-40. In other words, the

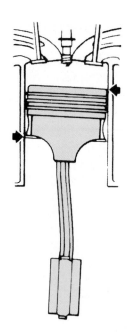

FIGURE 25-40   If the rod is twisted, it will cause diagonal-type wear on the piston skirt.

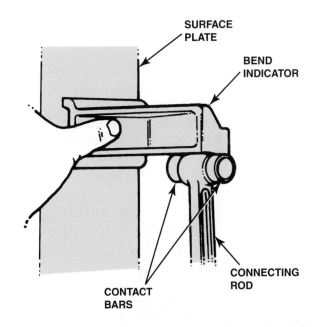

FIGURE 25-41   A rod alignment fixture being used to check a connecting rod to see if it is bent or twisted.

hole at the small end and the hole at the big end of the connecting rod should be parallel. No more than 0.002-inch (0.05-millimeter) twist is acceptable. See Figure 25-41 for the fixture used to check connecting rods for twist. If measured rod twist is excessive, some specialty shops can remove the twist by bending the rod cold. Both cast and forged rods can be straightened. However, many engine builders replace the connecting rod if it is twisted.

CONNECTING ROD SERVICE

As an engine operates, the forces go through the large end of the connecting rod. This causes the crankshaft end opening of the rod (eye) to gradually deform. See Figure 25-42. The large eye of the connecting rod is resized during precision engine service.

Step 1   The parting surfaces of the rod and cap are smoothed to remove all high spots before resizing. A couple of thousandths of an inch of metal is removed from the rod cap parting surface. This is done using the same grinder that is used to remove a slight amount of metal from the parting surface of main bearing caps. The amount removed from the rod and rodcap only reduces the bore size 0.003 to 0.006 inch (0.08 to 0.15 millimeter).

> **NOTE:** Powdered metal connecting rods cannot be reconditioned using this method. Most manufacturers recommend replacing worn powdered metal connecting rods.

Step 2   The cap is installed on the rod, and the nuts or cap screws are properly torqued. The hole is then bored or honed to be perfectly round and of the size and finish required to give the correct connecting rod bearing crush. Figure 25-43 shows the setup for resizing the rod on a typical hone used in engine reconditioning.

Even though material is being removed at the big end of the rod, the compression ratio is changed very little. The inside of the bore at the big end should have a 60- to 90-microinch finish for proper bearing contact and heat transfer.

PISTON AND ROD ASSEMBLY

To assemble the piston and rod, the piston pin is put in one side of the piston. The small end of the connecting rod should be checked for proper size. The small eye of the connecting rod is heated before the pin is installed. See Figure 25-44. This causes the rod eye to expand so that the pin can be pushed into place with little force. The pin must be rapidly pushed into the correct center position. There is only one chance to get it in the right place because the rod will quickly seize on the pin as the rod eye is cooled by the pin.

Full-floating piston pins operate in a bushing in the small eye of the connecting rod. The bushing can be replaced. The bushing and the piston are honed to the same diameter. This allows the piston pin to slide freely through both. The full-floating piston pin is held in place with a lock ring at each end of the piston pin. The lock ring expands into a small groove in the pin hole of the piston.

> **NOTE:** The lock rings should always be replaced with new rings.

Care must be taken to ensure that the pistons and rods are in the correct cylinder. They must face in the correct direction. There is usually a **notch** on the piston head indicating the *front*. Using this will correctly position the piston pin offset toward the right side of the engine. The connecting rod **identification marks** on pushrod inline engines are normally placed on the camshaft side.

> **NOTE:** The camshaft side of an inline OHV engine is also the oil filter side of most engines.

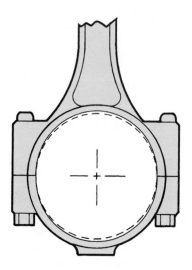

FIGURE 25-42   Rod bearing bores normally stretch from the top to the bottom, with most wear concentrated on the cap.

FIGURE 25-43   Resizing the big end of the connection rod with a hone. To help ensure a more accurate and straighter job, hone two connecting rods at a time.

(a)

(b)

FIGURE 25-44   (a) Flame-type connecting rod heater, the type most often used by remanufacturers because of the rapid heating. The rod should not be heated to more than 700°F (370°C). (If the rod turns blue, it is too hot.) (b) An operator removing the heated connecting rod and preparing to install it on the piston. Note the fixture used to hold the piston pin, and the dial indicator (gauge) used to ensure proper positioning.

The notch and numbers on a piston and rod assembly can be seen in Figure 25-45. On V-type engines, the connecting rod cylinder identification marks are on the side of the rods that can be seen from the bottom of the engine when the piston and rod assemblies are installed in the engine. The service manual should be checked for any special piston and rod assembly instructions.

PISTON RING SERVICE

Each piston ring, one at a time, should be placed backward in the groove in which it is to be run. Its side clearance in the groove should be checked with a feeler gauge, as shown in

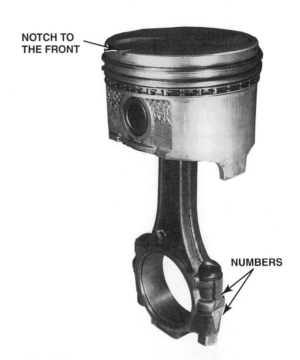

FIGURE 25-45   Position of the notch at the front of the piston, and the connecting rod numbers.

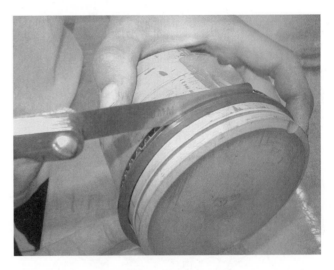

FIGURE 25-46   The side clearance of the piston ring is checked with a thickness (feeler) gauge.

Figure 25-46. If a ring is tight at any spot, check for deposits or burrs in the ring groove. Each piston ring, one at a time, is then placed in the cylinder in which it is to operate.

After the block and cylinder bores have been reconditioned, invert the piston and push each ring into the lower quarter of the cylinder; then measure the ring gap. See Figure 25-47. It should be approximately 0.004 inch for each inch of bore diameter (0.004 millimeter for each centimeter of bore diameter). If necessary, use a file or hand-operated piston ring grinder to achieve the necessary ring gap. See Figure 25-48.

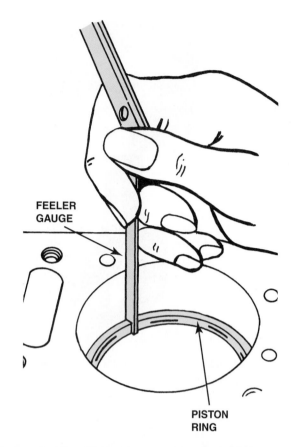

FEELER GAUGE

PISTON RING

FIGURE 25-47   The ring gap is measured with a feeler gauge.

The oil rings are installed first. The expander-spacer of the oil ring is placed in the lower ring groove. One oil ring rail is carefully placed above the expander-spacer by winding it into the groove. The other rail is placed below the expander-spacer. The ring should be rotated in the groove to ensure that the expander-spacer ends have not overlapped. If they have, the ring must be removed and reassembled correctly.

Installing the compression rings requires the use of a piston ring expander tool that will only open the ring gap enough to slip the ring on the piston. See Figure 25-49. Be careful to install the ring with the correct side up. The top of the compression ring is marked with a dot, the letter *T*, or the word *top*. See Figure 25-50. After the rings are installed, they should be rotated in the groove to ensure that they move freely, and checked to ensure that they will go fully into the groove so that the ring face is flush with the surface of the piston ring lands. Usually, the rings are placed on all pistons before any pistons are installed in the cylinders.

FIGURE 25-49   A typical ring expander being used to install a piston ring.

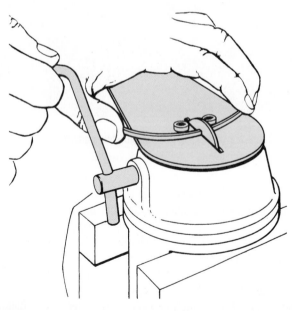

FIGURE 25-48   A hand-operated piston ring end gap grinder being used to increase the end gap of a piston ring in order to bring it to within factory specifications before installation on the piston.

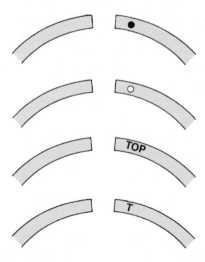

FIGURE 25-50   Identification marks used to indicate the side of the piston ring to be placed toward the head.

SUMMARY

1. The connecting rods should be marked before disassembly.

2. Pistons are cam ground so that when operating temperature is reached, the piston will have expanded enough across the piston pin area to become round.

3. Replacement pistons should weigh the same as the original pistons to maintain proper engine balance.

4. Some engines use an offset piston pin to help reduce piston slap when the engine is cold.

5. Piston rings usually include two compression rings at the top of the piston and an oil control ring below the compression rings.

6. If the ring end gap is excessive, blowby gases can travel past the rings and into the crankcase.

7. Many piston rings are made of coated cast iron to provide proper sealing.

8. If the connecting rod is twisted, diagonal wear will be noticed on the piston skirt.

9. Powdered metal connecting rods are usually broken at the big end parting line. Because of this rough junction, powdered metal connecting rods cannot be reconditioned—they must be replaced if damaged or worn.

10. The piston and the connecting rod must be correctly assembled according to identifying notches or marks.

REVIEW QUESTIONS

1. Describe the procedure for correctly removing the piston and rod assembly from the engine.

2. What methods are used to control piston heat expansion?

3. Why are some piston skirts tin plated?

4. Describe the effect of the piston pin offset as it controls piston slap.

5. Why is it important to keep the connecting rod cap with the rod on which it was originally used, and to install it in the correct way?

6. What causes the piston ring groove clearance to widen in service?

7. Describe how connecting rods are reconditioned.

8. How is the piston pin installed in the piston and rod assembly?

CHAPTER QUIZ

1. Connecting rod caps should be marked (if they were not marked at the factory) before the piston and connecting rod assembly is removed from the engine _____.
   a. Because they are balanced together
   b. Because they are machined together
   c. To make certain that the heavier rod is matched to the heavier piston
   d. To make certain that the lighter rod is matched to the lighter piston

2. Many aluminum piston skirts are plated with _____.
   a. Tin
   b. Lead
   c. Antimony
   d. Terneplate

3. A hypereutectic piston has _____.
   a. A higher weight than a eutectic piston
   b. A higher silicon content
   c. A higher tin content
   d. A higher nickel content

4. The purpose of casting steel struts into an aluminum piston is to _____.
   a. Provide increased strength
   b. Provide increased weight at the top part of the piston where it is needed for stability
   c. Provide increased heat transfer from the piston head to the piston pin
   d. Control thermal expansion

5. Full-floating piston pins are retained by _____.
   a. Lock rings
   b. A drilled hole with roll pin
   c. An interference fit between rod and piston pin
   d. An interference fit between piston and piston pin

6. The space behind the ring is called _____.
   a. side clearance
   b. forward clearance
   c. back clearance
   d. piston ring clearance

7. A misaligned connecting rod causes what type of engine wear?
   a. Cylinder taper
   b. Barrel-shaped cylinders
   c. Ridge wear
   d. Angle wear on the piston skirt

8. Side clearance is a measure taken between the _____ and the _____.
   a. Piston (side skirt); cylinder wall
   b. Piston pin; piston pin retainer (clip)
   c. Piston ring; piston ring groove
   d. Compression ring; oil control ring

9. Piston ring gap should only be measured _____.
   a. After all cylinder work has been performed
   b. After installing the piston in the cylinder
   c. After installing the rings on the piston
   d. Both a and c

10. Which type of connecting rod needs to be heated to be installed?
    a. forged
    b. interference fit
    c. floating
    d. PM rods

CHAPTER **26**

ENGINE BLOCKS

OBJECTIVES

After studying Chapter 26, the reader will be able to:

1. Prepare for Engine Repair (A1) ASE certification test content area "C" (Engine Block Diagnosis and Repair).
2. Describe the types of engine blocks and how they are manufactured.

3. List the machining operations required on most engine blocks.
4. List the steps necessary to prepare an engine block for assembly.

KEY TERMS

ENGINE BLOCKS

The engine block, which is the supporting structure for the entire engine, is made from gray cast iron or from cast or die-cast aluminum alloy. The gray color is a result of the 3% carbon in the form of graphite in the cast iron. The liquid cast iron is poured into a mold. The carbon in the cast iron allows for easy machining, often without coolant. The graphite in the cast iron also has lubricating properties. Newer blocks use thinner walls to reduce weight. Cast iron is strong for its weight and usually is magnetic. All other engine parts are mounted on or in the block. This large casting supports the crankshaft and camshaft and holds all the parts in alignment. Blocks are often of the **monoblock** design, which means that the cylinder, water jacket, main bearing supports (saddles), and oil passages are all cast as one structure for strength and quietness. Large-diameter holes in the block casting form the cylinders to guide the pistons. The cylinder holes are called **bores** because they are made by a machining process called boring. Combustion pressure loads are carried from the head to the crankshaft bearings through the block structure. The block has webs, walls, and drilled passages to contain the coolant and lubricating oil and to keep them separated from each other. See Figure 26-1.

Mounting pads or lugs on the block transfer the engine torque reaction to the vehicle frame through attached engine mounts. A large mounting surface at the rear of the engine block is used for fastening a bell housing or transmission.

The cylinder head(s) attaches to the block. The attaching joints are sealed so that they do not leak. Gaskets are used in the joints to take up differences that are created by machining irregularities and that result from different pressures and temperatures.

Block Manufacturing

Cast-iron cylinder block casting technology continues to be improved. The trend is to make blocks with larger cores, using fewer individual pieces. Oil-sand cores are forms that shape the internal openings and passages in the engine block. Before casting, the cores are supported within a core box. The core box also has a liner to shape the outside of the block. Special alloy cast iron is poured into the box. It flows between the cores and the core box liner. As the cast iron cools, the core breaks up. When the cast iron has hardened, it is removed from the core box, and the pieces of sand core are removed through the openings in the block by vigorously shaking the casting. These openings in the block are plugged with **core plugs.** Core plugs are also called **freeze plugs** or **frost plugs.** Although the name seems to mean that the plugs would be pushed outward if the coolant in the passages were to freeze, they seldom work this way. See Figure 26-2.

One way to keep the engine weight as low as possible is to make the block with minimum wall thickness. The cast iron used with thin-wall casting techniques has higher nickel content and is harder than the cast iron previously used. Engine designers have used foundry techniques to make engines lightweight by making the cast-iron block walls and bulkheads only as heavy as necessary to support their required loads.

Aluminum Blocks

Aluminum is used for some cylinder blocks and is nonmagnetic and lightweight. See Figure 26-3 for an example of a core used to sand-cast an aluminum block.

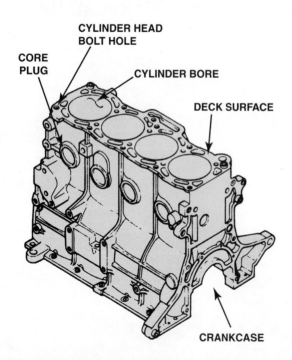

FIGURE 26-1 The cylinder block usually extends from the oil pan rails at the bottom to the deck surface at the top.

FIGURE 26-2 An expansion plug is used to block the opening in the cylinder head or block the holes where the core sand was removed after the part was cast.

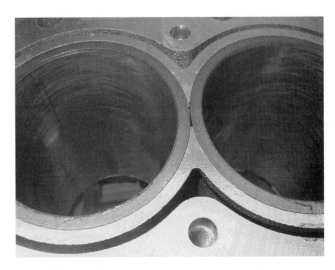

FIGURE 26-4 Cast-iron dry sleeves are used in aluminum blocks to provide a hard surface for the rings.

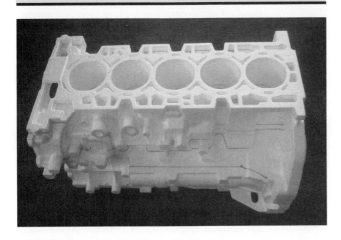

FIGURE 26-3 A Styrofoam casting mold used to make the five cylinder engine blocks for the Chevrolet Colorado and the Hummer H3. The brown lines are glue used to hold the various parts together. Sand is packed around the mold and molten aluminum is poured into the sand, which instantly vaporizes the Styrofoam. The aluminum then flows and fills the area of the mold.

Aluminum blocks may have one of several different types of cylinder walls:

- Cast-aluminum blocks may have steel cylinder liners (Saturn, Northstar, and Ford modular V-8s and V-6s). The cast-iron cylinder sleeves are either cast into the aluminum block during manufacturing or pressed into the aluminum block. These sleeves are not in contact with the coolant passages and are called **dry cylinder sleeves.** See Figure 26-4.
- Another aluminum block design has the block die-cast from silicon-aluminum alloy with no cylinder liners. Pistons with zinc-copper-hard iron coatings are used in these aluminum bores (some Porsche engines).

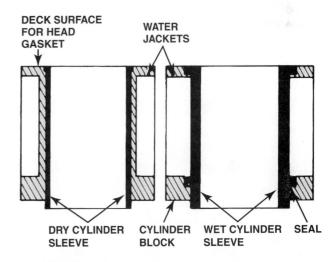

FIGURE 26-5 A dry sleeve is supported by the surrounding cylinder block. A wet sleeve must be thicker to be able to withstand combustion pressures without total support from the block.

- Some engines have die-cast aluminum blocks with replaceable cast-iron cylinder sleeves. The sleeves are sealed at the block deck and at their base. Coolant flows around the cylinder sleeve, so this type of sleeve is called a **wet cylinder sleeve** (Cadillac 4.1, 4.5, and 4.9 L V-8 engines). See Figure 26-5.

Cast-iron main bearing caps are used with aluminum blocks to give the required strength.

Bedplate Design Blocks

A **bedplate** is a structural member that attaches to the bottom of the block and supports the crankshaft. Under the bedplate

FREQUENTLY ASKED QUESTION

WHAT ARE FRM-LINED CYLINDERS?

Fiber reinforced matrix (FRM) is used to strengthen cylinder walls in some Honda/Acura engines. FRM is a ceramic material similar to that used to construct the insulators of spark plugs. The lightweight material has excellent wear resistance and good heat transfer properties making it ideal for use as a cylinder material. FRM inserts are placed in the mold and the engine block is cast over them. The inserts are rough and can easily adhere to the engine block. The inserts are then bored and honed to form the finished cylinders. FRM blocks were first used in a production engine on the Honda S2000 and are also used on the turbocharged Acura RDX sport utility vehicle.

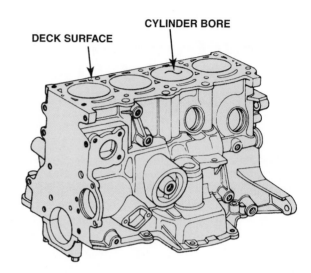

FIGURE 26-7 The deck is the machined top surface of the block. Note all of the passages and holes that are part of the typical block.

displacement and other information, such as year of manufacture. Sometimes changes are made to the mold, yet the casting number is not changed. Most often the casting number is the best piece of identifying information that the service technician can use.

Block Deck

The cylinder head is fastened to the top surface of the block. This surface is called the **block deck.** The deck has a smooth surface to seal *against* the head gasket. Bolt holes are positioned around the cylinders to form an even holding pattern. Four, five, or six head bolts are used around each cylinder in automobile engines. These bolt holes go into reinforced areas within the block that carry the combustion pressure load to the main bearing bulkheads. Additional holes in the block are used to transfer coolant and oil, as seen in Figure 26-7.

Cooling Passages

Cylinders are surrounded by cooling passages. These coolant passages around the cylinders are often called the **cooling jacket.** In most skirtless cylinder designs, the cooling passages extend nearly to the bottom of the cylinder. In extended skirt cylinder designs, the cooling passages are limited to the upper portion of the cylinder.

Some engines are built with *Siamese cylinder bores* where the cylinder walls are cast together without a water jacket (passage) between the cylinders. While this design improves the strength of the block and adds stability to the cylinder bores, it can reduce the cooling around the cylinders.

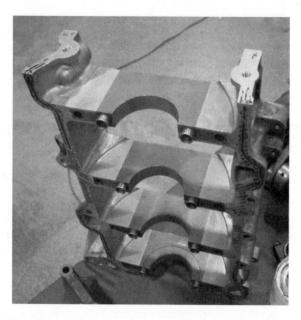

FIGURE 26-6 A bedplate is a structural part of the engine that is attached between the block and the oil pan and supports the crankshaft.

is the oil pan, which in most cases is also part of the structure and support for the block assembly. See Figure 26-6.

Casting Numbers

Whenever an engine part such as a block is cast, a number is put into the mold to identify the casting. These casting numbers can be used to check dimensions such as the cubic inch

FIGURE 26-8 Cutaway of a Chevrolet V-8 block showing all of the internal passages.

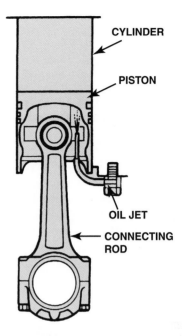

FIGURE 26-9 Oil jets are often used in some turbocharged, and many diesel, engines to cool the pistons.

FREQUENTLY ASKED QUESTION

WHAT IS AN OIL JET?

Some turbocharged gasoline engines and many diesel engines have an oil jet that directs a shot of oil directly to the underside of the piston crown. See Figure 26-9.

The spray of oil not only lubricates, but helps reduce piston temperatures. Combustion chamber temperatures are always higher in turbocharged and diesel engines.

Figure 26-8 is a typical V-8 engine cutaway that shows the coolant jackets and some of the lubrication holes.

Lubricating Passages

An engine block has many oil holes that carry lubricating oil to the required locations. During manufacture, all oil holes, called the **oil gallery,** are drilled from outside the block. When a curved passage is needed, intersecting drilled holes are used. In some engines, plugs are placed in the oil holes to direct oil to another point before it comes back to the original hole, on the opposite side of the plug. After oil holes are drilled, the unneeded open ends may be capped by pipe plugs, steel balls, or cup-type soft plugs, often called **oil gallery plugs.** These end plugs in the oil passages can be a source of oil leakage in operating engines. See Figure 26-10.

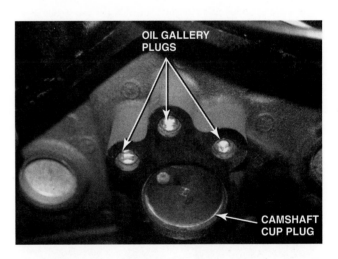

FIGURE 26-10 Typical oil gallery plugs on the rear of a Chevrolet small-block V-8 engine.

Main Bearing Caps

The main bearing caps are cast or manufactured from sintered or billeted materials, separately from the block. They are machined and then installed on the block for a final bore finishing operation. With caps installed, the main bearing bores and cam bearing bores are machined to the correct size and alignment. On some engines, these bores are honed to a very fine finish and exact size. Main bearing caps are not interchangeable or reversible, because they are individually finished in place. Main bearing caps may have cast numbers

TECH TIP

WHAT DOES LHD MEAN?

The abbreviation LHD means *left-hand dipstick,* which is commonly used by rebuilders and remanufacturers in their literature in describing Chevrolet small-block V-8 engines. Before about 1980, most small-block Chevrolet V-8s used an oil dipstick pad on the left side (driver's side) of the engine block. Starting in about 1980, when oxygen sensors were first used on this engine, the dipstick was relocated to the right side of the block.

Therefore, to be assured of ordering or delivering the correct engine, knowing the dipstick location is critical. An LHD block cannot be used with the exhaust manifold setup that includes the oxygen sensor without major refitting or the installing of a different style of oil pan that includes a provision for an oil dipstick. Engine blocks with the dipstick pad cast on the right side are, therefore, coded as right-hand dipstick (RHD) engines.

NOTE: Some blocks cast around the year 1980 are cast with both right- and left-hand oil dipstick pads, but only one is drilled for the dipstick tube. See Figure 26-11.

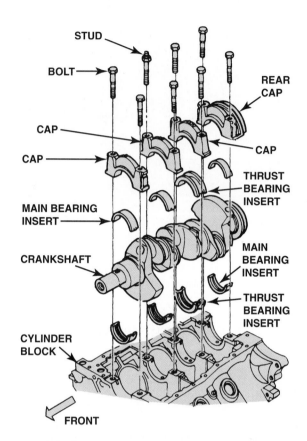

FIGURE 26-12 Two-bolt main bearing caps provide adequate bottom end strength for most engines.

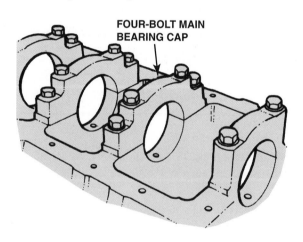

FIGURE 26-13 High-performance and truck engines often use four-bolt main bearing caps for greater durability.

FIGURE 26-11 Small-block Chevrolet block. Note the left-hand dipstick hole and a pad cast for a right-hand dipstick.

indicating their position on the block. If not, they should be marked.

Standard production engines usually use two bolts to hold the main bearing cap in place. See Figure 26-12.

Heavy-duty and high-performance engines often use additional main bearing support bolts. A four-bolt, and even six-bolt, main cap can be of a cross-bolted design in a deep skirt block or of a parallel design in a shallow skirt block. See Figures 26-13 and 26-14. Expansion force of the combustion chamber gases will try to push the head off the top and the crankshaft off the bottom of the block. The engine is held

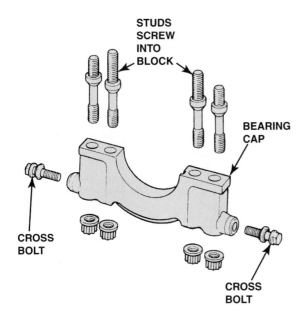

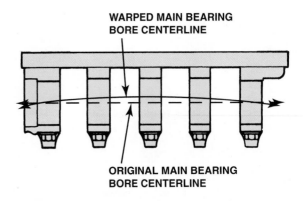

FIGURE 26-15   The main bearing bores of a warped block usually bend into a bowed shape. The greatest distortion is in the center bores.

FIGURE 26-14   Some engines add to the strength of a four-bolt main bearing cap by also using cross bolts through the bolt on the sides of the main bearing caps.

together with the head bolts and main bearing cap bolts screwed into bolt bosses and ribs in the block. The extra bolts on the main bearing cap help to support the crankshaft when there are high combustion pressures and mechanical loads, especially during high-engine speed operation.

ENGINE BLOCK SERVICE

The engine block is the foundation of the engine. All parts of the block must be of the correct size and they must be aligned. The parts must also have the proper finishes if the engine is to function dependably for a normal service life. Blueprinting is the reconditioning of all the critical surfaces and dimensions so that the block is actually like new.

After a thorough cleaning, the block should be inspected for cracks or other flaws before machine work begins. If the block is in serviceable condition, the block should be prepared in the following sequence:

Operation 1	Align boring or honing main bearing saddles and caps
Operation 2	Machining the block deck surface parallel to the crankshaft
Operation 3	Cylinder boring and honing

Main Bearing Housing Bore Alignment

The main bearing journals of a straight crankshaft are in alignment. If the main bearing housing bores in the block are not

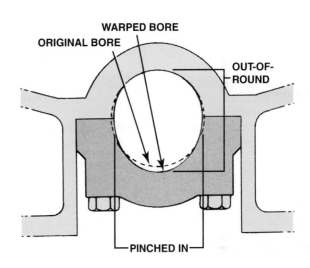

FIGURE 26-16   When the main bearing caps bow downward, they also pinch in at the parting line.

in alignment, the crankshaft will bend as it rotates. This will lead to premature bearing failure and it could lead to a broken crankshaft. The original stress in the block casting is gradually relieved as the block is used. Some slight warpage may occur as the stress is relieved. In addition, the continued pounding caused by combustion will usually cause some stretch in the main bearing caps. See Figure 26-15.

The main bearing bores gradually bow from the cylinder head and elongate vertically. This means that the bearing bore becomes smaller at the centerline as the block distorts, pinching the bore inward at the sides. See Figure 26-16.

The first step in determining the condition of the main bearing bores is to determine if the bore alignment in the block is straight. These bores are called the **saddles.** A precision ground straightedge and a feeler gauge are used to determine the amount of warpage. The amount of variation along the entire length of the block should not exceed 0.0015 inch (0.038 mm).

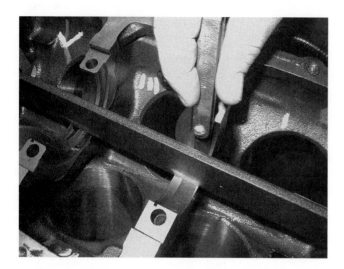

FIGURE 26-17 The main bearing bores can be checked using a precision straightedge and a feeler gauge.

CAUTION: When performing this measurement, be sure that the block is resting on a flat surface. If the engine is mounted to an engine stand, the weight of the block on the unsupported end can cause an error in the measurement of the main bearing bores and saddle alignment.

If the block saddles exceed one-and-a-half thousandth of an inch distortion, then align honing is required to restore the block. If the block saddles are straight, the bores should be measured to be sure that the bearing caps are not distorted. The bearing caps should be installed and the retaining bolts tightened to the specified torque before measuring the main bearing bores.

Using a telescoping gauge, measure each bore in at least two directions. Check the service information for the specified main bearing bore diameter. The bearing bore should vary by more than one-half of a thousandth of an inch or 0.0005 inch (0.0127 mm). See Figure 26-17.

A dial bore gauge is often used to measure the main bearing bore. Set up the dial bore gauge in the fixture with the necessary extensions to achieve the nominal main bearing bore diameter. Check the service information for the specified main bearing bore diameter and determine the exact middle of the range.

Machining the Deck Surface of the Block

An engine should have the same combustion chamber size in each cylinder. For this to occur, each piston must come up an equal distance from the block deck. The connecting rods are attached to the rod bearing journals of the crankshaft. Pistons are attached to the connecting rods. As the crankshaft rotates,

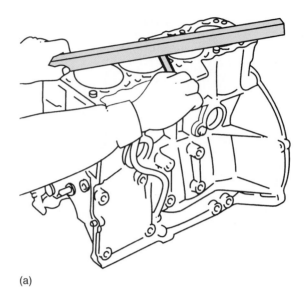

(a)

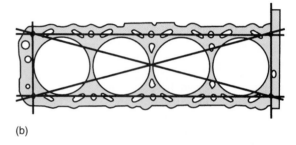

(b)

FIGURE 26-18 (a) Checking the flatness of the block deck surface using a straightedge and a feeler gauge. (b) To be sure that the top of the block is flat, check the block in six locations as shown.

the pistons come to the top of the stroke. When all parts are sized equally, all the pistons will come up to the same level. This can only happen if the block deck is parallel to the main bearing bores. See Figure 26-18.

The block deck must be resurfaced in a surfacing machine that can control the amount of metal removed when it is necessary to match the size of the combustion chambers. This procedure is called **decking the block.** The block is set up on a bar located in the main bearing saddles, or set up on the oil pan rails of the block. The bar is parallel to the direction of cutting head movement. The block is leveled sideways, and then the deck is resurfaced in the same manner as the head is resurfaced. Figure 26-19 shows a block deck being resurfaced by grinding.

The surface finish should be 60 to 100 Ra (65 to 110 RMS) for cast iron and 50 to 60 Ra (55 to 65 RMS) for aluminum block decks to be assured of a proper head gasket surface. The surface finish is determined by the type of grinding stone used, as well as the speed and coolant used in the finishing operation.

FIGURE 26-19   Grinding the deck surface of the block.

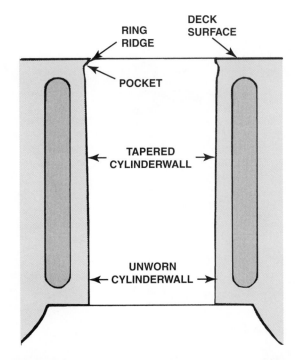

FIGURE 26-20   Cylinders wear in a taper, with most of the wear occurring at the top of the cylinder where the greatest amount of heat is created. The ridge is formed because this very top part of the cylinder is not worn by the rings.

Cylinder Boring

Cylinders should be measured across the engine (perpendicular to the crankshaft), where the greatest wear occurs. Most wear will be found just below the ridge, and the least amount of wear will occur below the lowest ring travel. See Figure 26-20. The cylinder should be checked for out-of-round and taper. See Figure 26-21.

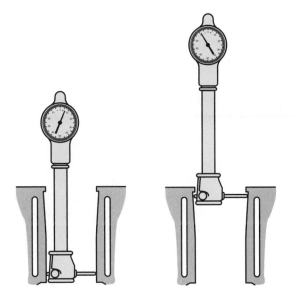

FIGURE 26-21   Using a dial bore gauge to measure the bore diameter at the top just below the ridge and at the bottom below the ring travel. Take the measurements in line with the crankshaft and then repeat the measurements at right angles to the centerline of the block in each cylinder.

Most cylinders are serviceable if:

- Maximum of 0.003 inch (0.076 millimeter) out-of-round
- No more than 0.005 inch (0.127 millimeter) taper
- Have no deep scratches in the cylinder wall

NOTE: Always check the specifications for the engine being surfaced. For example, the General Motors 5.7 L, LS-1, V-8 has a maximum out-of-round of only 0.0003 (3/10 of one thousandths of an inch). Normally this specification is about three times that dimension or about 0.001 inch.

The most effective way to correct excessive cylinder out-of-round, taper, or scoring is to *rebore* the cylinder. The rebored cylinder requires the use of a new, oversize piston.

The maximum bore oversize is determined by two things: the cylinder wall thickness and the size of the available oversize pistons. If in doubt as to the amount of overbore that is possible without causing structural weakness, an ultrasonic test should be performed on the block to determine the thickness of the cylinder walls. All cylinders should be tested. Variation in cylinder wall thickness occurs because of core shifting (moving) during the casting of the block. For best results, cylinders should be rebored to the smallest size possible.

NOTE: The pistons that will be used should always be in hand *before* the cylinders are rebored. The cylinders are then bored and honed to match the exact size of the pistons.

FREQUENTLY ASKED QUESTION

HOW DO I DETERMINE WHAT OVERSIZE BORE IS NEEDED?

An easy way to calculate oversize piston size is to determine the amount of taper, double it, and add 0.010 inch (Taper $\times$ 2 + 0.010 in. = OS piston). Common oversize measurements include 0.020 inch, 0.030 inch, 0.040 inch, and 0.060 inch. Use caution when boring for an oversize measurement larger than 0.030 inch.

The cylinder must be perpendicular to the crankshaft for normal bearing and piston life. If the block deck has been aligned with the crankshaft, it can be used to align the cylinders. Portable cylinder boring bars are clamped to the block deck. Heavy-duty production boring machines support the block on the main bearing bores.

Main bearing caps should be torqued in place when cylinders are being rebored. In precision boring, a torque plate is also bolted on in place of the cylinder head while boring cylinders. In this way, distortion is kept to a minimum. The general procedure used for reboring cylinders is to set the boring bar up so that it is perpendicular to the crankshaft. It must be located over the center of the cylinder. The cylinder center is found by installing centering pins in the bar. The bar is lowered so that the centering pins are located near the bottom of the cylinder, where the least wear has occurred. This locates the boring bar over the original cylinder center. Once the boring bar is centered, the boring machine is clamped in place to hold it securely. This will allow the cylinder to be rebored on the original centerline, regardless of the amount of cylinder wear. A sharp, properly ground cutting tool is installed and adjusted to the desired dimension. Rough cuts remove a great deal of metal on each pass of the cutting tool. The rough cut is followed by a fine cut that produces a much smoother and more accurate finish. Different-shaped tool bits are used for rough and finish boring. The last cut is made to produce a diameter that is at least 0.002 inch (0.05 millimeter) smaller than the required diameter. See Figure 26-22.

Sleeving the Cylinder

Sometimes, cylinders have a gouge so deep that it will not clean up when the cylinder is rebored to the maximum size. This could happen if the piston pin moved endways and rubbed on the cylinder wall. Cylinder blocks with deep gouges can be salvaged by **sleeving** the cylinder. This is done by boring the cylinder to a dimension that is greatly oversize to almost match the outside diameter of the cylinder sleeve. The

FIGURE 26-22 A cylinder boring machine is to enlarge cylinder bore diameter so a replacement oversize piston can be used to restore a worn engine to useful service or to increase the displacement of the engine in an attempt to increase power output.

FIGURE 26-23 A dry cylinder sleeve can also be installed in a cast-iron block to repair a worn or cracked cylinder.

sleeve is pressed into the rebored block, then the center of the sleeve is bored to the diameter required by the piston. The cylinder can be sized to use a standard-size piston when it is sleeved. See Figure 26-23.

Cylinder Honing

It is important to have the proper surface finish on the cylinder wall for the rings to seat against. Some ring manufacturers

FIGURE 26-24 An assortment of ball-type deglazing hones. This type of hone does not straighten wavy cylinder walls.

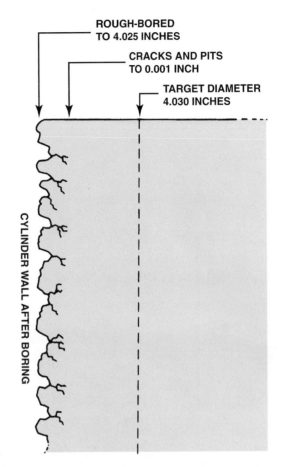

FIGURE 26-25 After boring, the cylinder surface is rough, pitted, and fractured to a depth of about 0.001 inch.

recommend breaking the hard surface glaze on the cylinder wall with a hone before installing new piston rings. Honing the cylinder removes the fractured metal that is created by boring. The cylinder wall should be honed to straighten the cylinder when the wall is wavy or scuffed. If honing is being done with the crankshaft remaining in the block, the crankshaft should be protected to keep honing chips from getting on the shaft.

Two types of hones are used for cylinder service.

- A *deglazing hone* removes the hard surface glaze remaining in the cylinder. It is a flexible hone that follows the shape of the cylinder wall, even when the wall is wavy. It cannot be used to straighten the cylinder. A brush-type (ball-type) deglazing hone is shown in Figure 26-24.

- A *sizing hone* can be used to straighten the cylinder and to provide a suitable surface for the piston rings. The cylinders must be honed a minimum of 0.002 inch (0.050 mm) after boring to cut below the rough surface and provide an adequate finish. Honing leaves a plateau surface that can support the oil film for the rings and piston skirt. This plateau surface is achieved by first using a coarse stone followed by a smooth stone to achieve the desired surface. The process of using a coarse and fine stone is called **plateau honing.** See Figure 26-25.

The honing stones are held in a rigid fixture with an expanding mechanism to control the size of the hone. The sizing hone can be used to straighten the cylinder taper by honing the lower cylinder diameter more than the upper diameter. As it rotates, the sizing hone only cuts the high spots so that cylinder out-of-round is also reduced. The cylinder wall surface finish is about the same when the cylinder is refinished with either type of hone. See Figure 26-26.

ALWAYS USE TORQUE PLATES

Torque plates are thick metal plates that are bolted to the cylinder block to duplicate the forces on the block that occur when the cylinder head is installed. Even though not all machine shops use torque plates during the boring operation, the use of torque plates during the final dimensional honing operation is very beneficial. Without torque plates, cylinders can become out-of-round (up to 0.003 inch) and distorted when the cylinder heads are installed and torqued down. Even though the use of torque plates does not eliminate all distortion, their use helps to ensure a truer cylinder dimension. See Figure 26-27.

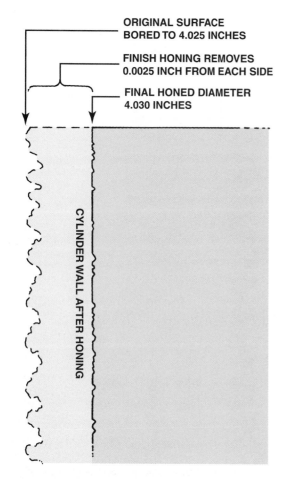

ORIGINAL SURFACE
BORED TO 4.025 INCHES

FINISH HONING REMOVES
0.0025 INCH FROM EACH SIDE

FINAL HONED DIAMETER
4.030 INCHES

CYLINDER WALL AFTER HONING

FIGURE 26-26   Honing enlarges the cylinder bore to the final size and leaves a plateau surface finish that retains oil.

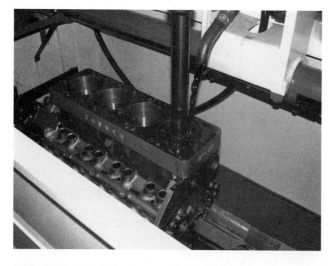

FIGURE 26-27   A torque plate being used during a cylinder honing operation. The thick piece of metal is bolted to the block and simulates the forces exerted on the block by the head bolts when the cylinder head is attached.

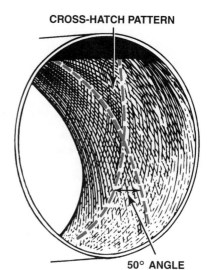

CROSS-HATCH PATTERN

50° ANGLE

FIGURE 26-28   The crosshatched pattern holds oil to keep the rings from wearing excessively, and also keeps the rings against the cylinder wall for a gas-tight fit.

TECH TIP

BORE TO SIZE, HONE FOR CLEARANCE

Many engine rebuilders and remanufacturers bore the cylinders to the exact size of the oversize pistons that are to be used. After the block is bored to a standard oversize measurement, the cylinder is honed. The rigid hone stones, along with an experienced operator, can increase the bore size by 0.001 to 0.003 inch (1 to 3 thousandths of an inch) for the typical clearance needed between the piston and the cylinder walls.

For example:

Actual piston diameter = 4.028 in.
Bore diameter = 4.028 in.
Diameter after honing = 4.030 in.
Amount removed by honing = 0.002 in.

NOTE: The minimum amount recommended to be removed by honing is 0.002 inch to remove the fractured metal in the cylinder wall caused by boring.

The hone is stroked up and down in the cylinder as it rotates. This produces a **crosshatch finish** on the cylinder wall. A typical honed cylinder is pictured in Figure 26-28. The angle of the crosshatch should be between 20 and 60 degrees.

Higher angles are produced when the hone is stroked more rapidly in the cylinder.

Cylinder Surface Finish

The size of the abrasive particles in the grinding and honing stones controls the surface finish. The size of the abrasive is called the **grit size.** The abrasive is sifted through a screen mesh to sort out the grit size. A coarse-mesh screen has few wires in each square inch, so large pieces can fall through the screen. A fine-mesh screen has many wires in each square inch so that only small pieces can fall through. The screen is used to separate the different grit sizes. The grit size is the number of wires in each square inch of the mesh. A low-numbered grit has large pieces of abrasive material; a high-numbered grit has small pieces of abrasive material. The higher the grit number, the smoother the surface finish.

Grit Sizing Chart

Grit/Sieve Size	Inches	Millimeters
12	0.063	1.600
16	0.043	1.092
20	0.037	0.939
24	0.027	0.685
30	0.022	0.558
36	0.019	0.482
46	0.014	0.355
54	0.012	0.304
60	0.010	0.254
70	0.008	0.203
80	0.0065	0.165
90	0.0057	0.144
100	0.0048	0.121
120	0.0040	0.101
150	0.0035	0.088
180	0.0030	0.076
220	0.0025	0.063
240	0.0020	0.050

A given grit size will produce the same finish as long as the cutting pressure is constant. With the same grit size, light cutting pressure produces fine finishes, and heavy cutting pressure produces rough finishes.

The surface finish should match the surface required for the type of piston rings to be used. Typical grit and surface finish standards include the following:

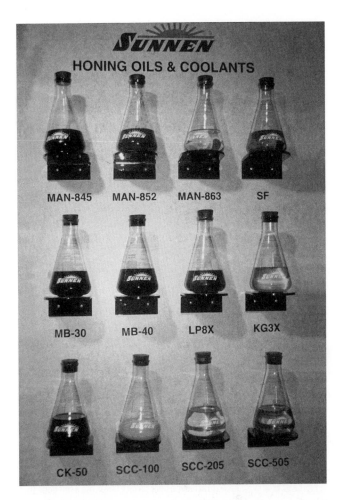

FIGURE 26-29 An assortment of the various honing oils and coolants available. Always use the correct oil or coolant as specified by the equipment manufacturer.

- Chrome—#180 grit (25 to 35 micro inches)
- Cast iron—#200 grit (20 to 30 micro inches)
- Moly—#220 grit (18 to 25 micro inches)

NOTE: The correct honing oil and/or coolant are critical to proper operation of the honing equipment and to the quality of the finished cylinders. See Figure 26-29 for the many different examples of honing oil and coolants that one equipment manufacturer has available.

The hone is placed in the cylinder. Before the drive motor is turned on, the hone is moved up and down in the cylinder to get the feel of the stroke length needed. The end of the hone should just break out of the cylinder bore on each end. The hone must *not* be pulled from the top of the cylinder while it is rotating. Also, it must not be pushed so low in the cylinder that it hits the main bearing web or crankshaft. The sizing hone is adjusted to give a solid drag at the lower end of the stroke. The hone drive motor is turned on and stroking begins immediately. Stroking continues until the sound of the drag is reduced. The hone drive motor is turned off while it is still stroking. Stroking is stopped as the rotation of the hone stops. After rotation stops, the hone is collapsed and removed from the cylinder. The cylinder is examined to check the bore size and finish of the wall. If more honing is needed, the cylinder is again coated with honing oil and the cylinder is honed again. The finished cylinder should be within 0.0005 inch (0.013 millimeter) on both out-of-round and taper measurements. See Figure 26-30.

See Figure 26-31a and b for an example of cylinder surface finish reading.

FIGURE 26-30 To achieve a finer surface finish, use a soft hone that is made from nylon bristles with impregnated abrasive. This hone is ideal for engines using low tension piston rings and provides a smooth surface that allows the rings to seal immediately.

BLOCK CLEANING AND PREPARATION FOR ASSEMBLY

After the cylinders have been honed and before the block is cleaned, use a sandpaper cone to chamfer the top edge of the cylinder. Cleaning the honed cylinder wall is an important part of the honing process. If any grit remains on the cylinder wall, it will rapidly wear the piston rings. This wear will cause premature failure of the reconditioning job. Degreasing and decarbonizing procedures will only remove the honing oil. They will *not* remove the abrasive. The *best* way to clean the honed cylinders is to scrub the cylinder wall with a brush using a mixture of *soap* or *detergent* and *water*. The block is scrubbed until it is absolutely clean. This can be determined by wiping the cylinder wall with a clean cloth. The cloth will pick up no soil when the cylinder wall is clean.

Block Detailing

Before the engine block can be assembled, a final detailed cleaning should be performed.

1. All oil passages (galleries) should be cleaned by running a long bottle-type brush through all holes in the block.
2. All tapped holes should be chamfered and cleaned with the correct size of thread chaser to remove any dirt and burrs. See Figures 26-32 and 26-33.
3. Coat the newly cleaned block with fogging oil to prevent rust. Cover the block with a large plastic bag to keep out dirt until it is time to assemble the engine.

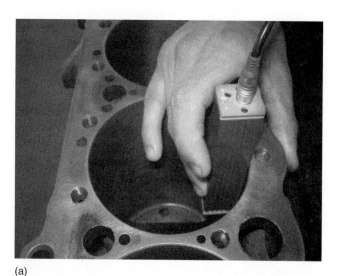

(a)

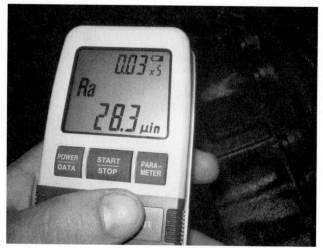

(b)

FIGURE 26-31 (a) The surface finish tool is being held against the cylinder wall. (b) The reading indicates the Ra roughness of the cylinder. More work is needed if moly piston rings are to be used.

FIGURE 26-32 Notice on this cutaway engine block that some of the head bolt holes do not extend too far into the block and dead end. Debris can accumulate at the bottom of these holes and it must be cleaned out before final assembly.

FIGURE 26-33 A thread chaser or bottoming tap should be used in all threaded holes before assembling the engine.

FIGURE 26-34 High-performance engine builders will often install bronze sleeves in the valve lifter bores.

CYLINDER MEASUREMENT AND HONING   Step-by-Step

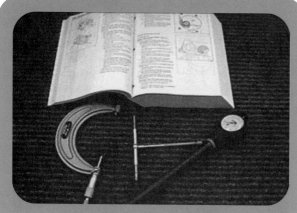

STEP 1 The tools and equipment needed to hone the cylinder include the service manual for engine block specifications and a dial bore gauge, along with a telescoping gauge and outside micrometer, to accurately measure the cylinder bore.

STEP 2 Start the honing process by carefully lowering the engine block into the cylinder hone bay. Use a nylon strap to support and hoist the block to avoid causing harm to the machined surfaces of the block that may occur if a metal chain is used.

STEP 3 Clamping the block to the holding fixture.

STEP 4 After the block has been securely attached to the holding fixture, the hone has to be adjusted for the bore diameter. The technician is gauging the shims for the honing head.

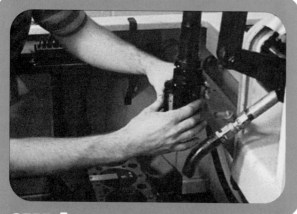

STEP 5 After gauging the honing head, the shims are installed in the honing head.

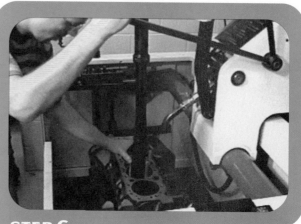

STEP 6 After the honing head has been shimmed, it is lowered into the cylinder.

CYLINDER MEASUREMENT AND HONING continued

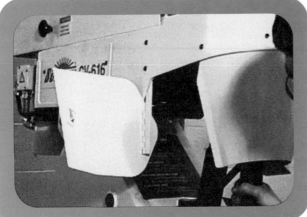

STEP 7 After installing the honing head into the cylinder, the top limit of the stroke has to be set. Notice the safety shield is open.

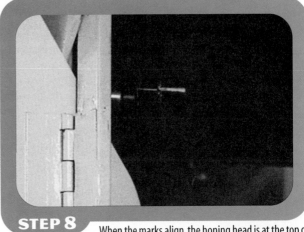

STEP 8 When the marks align, the honing head is at the top of the stroke.

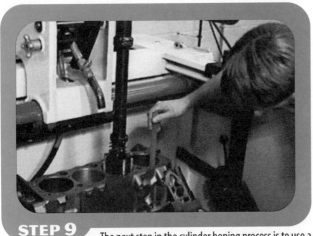

STEP 9 The next step in the cylinder honing process is to use a hook ruler to measure the length of the cylinder.

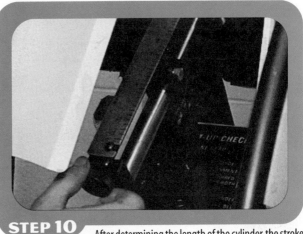

STEP 10 After determining the length of the cylinder, the stroke length is set.

STEP 11 Setting the "crown" for stock removal. This adjusts the pressure of the honing stone against the cylinder walls.

STEP 12 The honing operation is started after all adjustments and settings have been performed.

(continued)

CYLINDER MEASUREMENT AND HONING   continued

STEP 13 The crown may need adjustment for the correct honing pressure.

STEP 14 The bar graph indicates honing pressure. For a rough cut, the pressure should be set to 60% to 80% and to 20% to 40% for a finish cut.

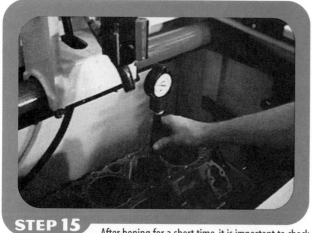

STEP 15 After honing for a short time, it is important to check the cylinder for proper dimension using a dial bore gauge.

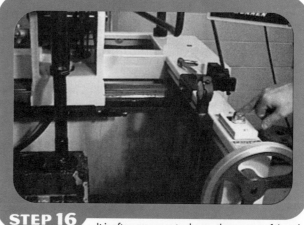

STEP 16 It is often necessary to change the amount of time the hone stays in a certain area. For example, a dwell button is pushed to achieve greater stock removal at the bottom of the cylinder.

STEP 17 The finish cylinder hone should have the characteristic 60-degree crosshatch pattern as shown.

STEP 18 Finish honing should be performed using a torque plate. Using a finish honing stone results in a round cylinder with a plateau hone surface and correct surface finish.

MAIN BEARING HOUSING BORE ALIGN HONING   Step-by-Step

STEP 1
Before align honing the main bearing bores, the main bearing caps are installed and torqued to factory specifications. A dial bore gauge is then used to determine the variation in diameter in the original housing bores.

STEP 2
The dial bore gauge is also used to check for taper and out-of-round of each bore.

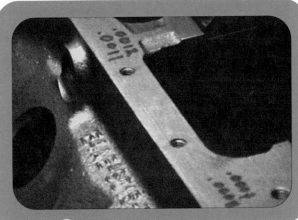

STEP 3
The machinist wrote the variation in the bore housing on the rail of the block using a felt-tip marker for easy reference.

STEP 4
After all main bearing bores have been measured and recorded, the main bearing caps are removed from the engine and placed on a cap grinder to remove material from the main bearing cap.

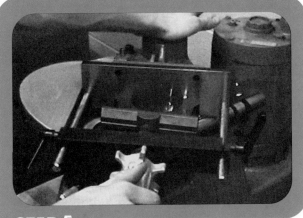

STEP 5
The cap is first placed flat and clamped tight into the vise and then the side of the cap is ground.

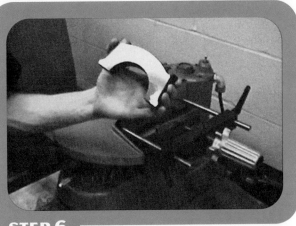

STEP 6
Grinding the side of the cap first ensures that the cap is clamped into the vise squarely.

(continued)

MAIN BEARING HOUSING BORE ALIGN HONING   continued

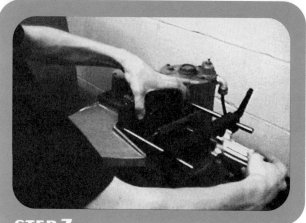

STEP 7 After the side of the bearing cap is ground, it is then placed vertically in the vise with the machined surface of the main bearing cap against the flat surface of the holding fixture.

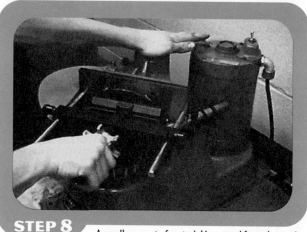

STEP 8 A small amount of material is ground from the mating surface of the main bearing cap. The amount removed should be the same for each cap.

STEP 9 The cap grinder is being adjusted for the amount of material to be removed from the main bearing cap.

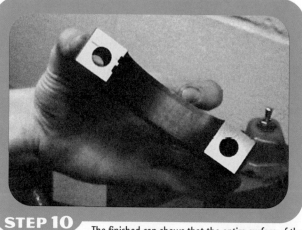

STEP 10 The finished cap shows that the entire surface of the end of the cap has been ground. This procedure is repeated for all main bearing caps.

STEP 11 Before reassembling the bearing caps onto the engine block, use a file to remove any sharp edges from the saddle area that could interfere with the proper joining of the bearing caps in the block.

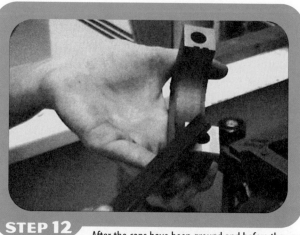

STEP 12 After the caps have been ground and before they are installed on the block, a file is used to remove any burrs from the sharp edges created by the grinding.

MAIN BEARING HOUSING BORE ALIGN HONING   continued

STEP 13 To be sure that everything is clean, all oil passages are blown out using compressed air.

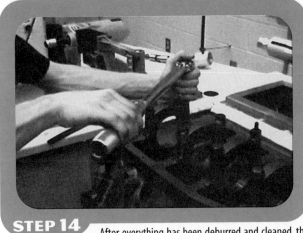

STEP 14 After everything has been deburred and cleaned, the main bearing caps are reinstalled onto the block and torqued to factory specifications.

STEP 15 The main bearing bores are again measured using a dial bore gauge to make sure that each is the same size. If necessary, a cap may have to be removed and additional material ground from the mating surface to achieve the proper diameter.

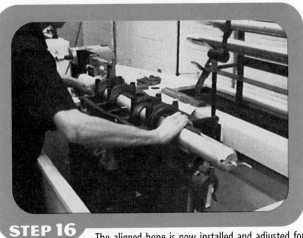

STEP 16 The aligned hone is now installed and adjusted for proper tension.

STEP 17 The main bearing bores are then honed round by using a large electric motor to drive the honing stones through the bores.

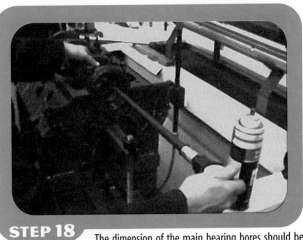

STEP 18 The dimension of the main bearing bores should be checked after performing the honing process.

DECKING A BLOCK Step-by-Step

STEP 1 Before the deck surface of the block can be machined, it has to be precisely located onto the surface mounts by aligning the main bearing bores on a 2-inch diameter ground shaft.

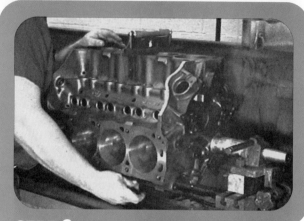

STEP 2 After attaching the main bearing caps over the pucks, the engine block is leveled by rotating the jack screw mechanism. Note the bubble level on the deck surface.

STEP 3 To determine the deck height, a depth micrometer is being used to measure the distance between the deck surface and the ground shaft.

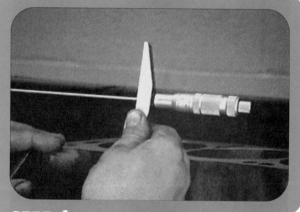

STEP 4 Because the supporting shaft is exactly 2 inches in diameter, the deck height is determined by adding 1 inch to the measurement obtained on the micrometer.

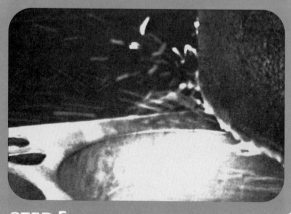

STEP 5 After the block has been securely attached, leveled, and measured, the deck surface can be ground. A typical pass across the deck surface will remove about 0.001 to 0.0015 inch.

STEP 6 It is wise to double-check the deck height especially if more than one cut is required to straighten the top of the block surface.

DECKING A BLOCK continued

STEP 7 A typical block may require 0.004 to 0.006 inches to be removed from the deck surface to eliminate any warpage or waviness.

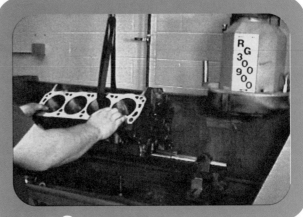

STEP 8 After both deck surfaces have been machined and checked, the block can be removed from the attachment using an engine hoist equipped with a nylon strap to prevent damaging the machined surfaces of the block.

SUMMARY

1. Engine blocks are either cast iron or aluminum.
2. Cores are used inside a mold to form water jackets and cylinder bores. After the cast iron has cooled, the block is shaken, which breaks up the cores so that they fall out of openings in the side of the block. Core plugs are used to fill the holes.
3. The block deck is the surface to which the cylinder head attaches. This surface must be flat and true for proper engine operation.
4. The cylinder should be bored and/or honed to match the size of the pistons to be used.
5. All bolt holes should be chamfered and cleaned with a thread chaser before assembly.

REVIEW QUESTIONS

1. What does "decking the block" mean?
2. What is the purpose of core plugs?
3. What is the difference between deglazing and honing a cylinder?
4. What is the best method to use to clean an engine block after honing?

CHAPTER QUIZ

1. The block deck is the _____.
   a. Bottom (pan rail) of the block
   b. Top surface of the block
   c. Valley surface of a V-type engine
   d. Area where the engine mounts are attached to the block

2. The standard measurement for surface finish is the microinch. Which of the following is correct?
   a. The rougher the surface, the higher the microinch finish measurement.
   b. The smoother the surface, the higher the microinch finish measurement.
   c. The rougher the surface, the lower the microinch finish measurement.
   d. Both b and c.

3. What surface finish is needed to be achieved if moly piston rings are going to be used?
   a. 35 to 45 micro inches
   b. 28 to 30 micro inches
   c. 18 to 25 micro inches
   d. 10 to 15 micro inches

4. Cast iron has about how much carbon content?
   a. 1%
   b. 2%
   c. 3%
   d. 4+%

5. Engine blocks can be manufactured using which method(s)?
   a. Sand-cast
   b. Sand-cast or die-cut
   c. Extruded cylinder
   d. Machined from a solid piece of metal (either cast iron or aluminum)

6. A bedplate is located between the _____ and the _____.
   a. Cylinder bores / water jacket
   b. Cylinder head / block deck
   c. Bottom of the block / oil pan
   d. Block deck / cylinder bore

7. Siamese cylinder bores are _____.
   a. Cylinders that do not have a coolant passage between them
   b. Aluminum cylinders
   c. Another name for cylinder liners
   d. Cast-iron cylinders

8. An oil jet is commonly used on which type of engine?
   a. Turbocharged/supercharged gas engines
   b. Turbocharged diesel engines
   c. Small displacement, high RPM engines
   d. Both a and b

9. An engine block should be machined in which order?
   a. Align honing, cylinder boring, block deck machining
   b. Block decking, align honing, cylinder boring
   c. Cylinder boring, align honing, block decking
   d. Align honing, block decking, cylinder boring

10. After the engine block has been machined, it should be cleaned using _____.
   a. Soap and water
   b. SAE 10W-30 oil and a shop cloth
   c. Brake cleaner sprayed to remove the cutting oil
   d. Sprayed WD-40

CHAPTER 27

CRANKSHAFTS AND BEARINGS

OBJECTIVES

After studying Chapter 27, the reader will be able to:

1. Prepare for Engine Repair (A1) ASE certification test content area "C" (Engine Block Diagnosis and Repair).

2. Describe the purpose and function of a crankshaft.
3. Explain how crankshafts are machined and polished.
4. Discuss engine bearing construction and installation procedures.

KEY TERMS

CRANKSHAFT

Purpose and Function

Power from expanding gases in the combustion chamber is delivered to the crankshaft through the piston, piston pin, and connecting rod. The connecting rods and their bearings are attached to a bearing journal on the crank throw. The crank throw is offset from the **crankshaft centerline.** The combustion force is applied to the crank throw after the crankshaft has moved past top center. This produces the turning effort or torque, which rotates the crankshaft. The crankshaft rotates on the main bearings. These bearings are split in half so that they can be assembled around the crankshaft main bearing journals. The crankshaft includes the following parts:

- Main bearing journals
- Rod bearing journals
- Crankshaft throws
- Counterweights
- Keyways
- Oil passages

See Figure 27-1.

Main Bearing Journals

The crankshaft rotates in the cylinder block on main bearings. See Figure 27-2.

The bearings support the crankshaft and allow it to rotate easily without excessive wear. The number of cylinders usually determines the number of main bearings.

- Four-cylinder engines and V-8 engines usually have five main bearings.
- Inline 6-cylinder engines usually have seven main bearings.
- V-6 engines normally have only four main bearings.

See Figure 27-3.

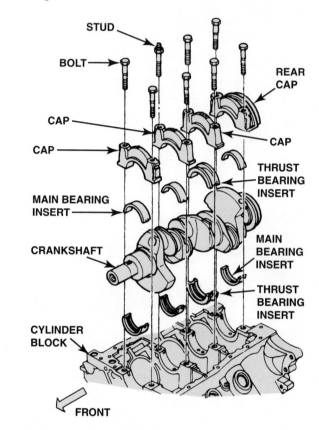

FIGURE 27-2 The crankshaft rotates on main bearings. Longitudinal (end-to-end) movement is controlled by the thrust bearing.

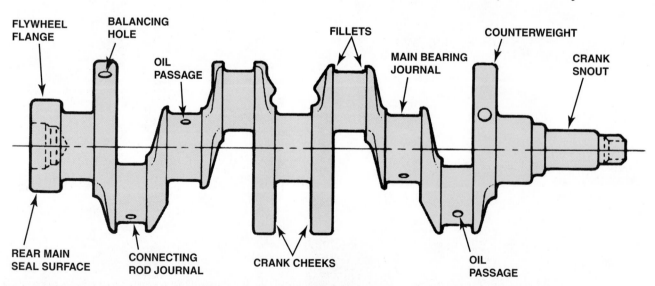

FIGURE 27-1 Typical crankshaft with main journals that are supported by main bearings in the block. Rod journals are offset from the crankshaft centerline.

The crankshaft also has to be able to absorb thrust loads from the clutch on a manual transmission vehicle or the torque converter on a vehicle equipped with an automatic transmission. Thrust loads are forces that push and pull the crankshaft forward and rearward in the engine block. A **thrust bearing** supports these loads and maintains the front-to-rear position of the crankshaft in the block. See Figure 27-4.

The thrust surface is usually located at the middle on one of the end main bearings. On most engines, the bearing insert for the main bearing is equipped with thrust bearing flanges that ride against the thrust surface.

Rod Bearing Journals

The rod bearing journals, also called **crankpins,** are offset from the centerline of the crank. Insert-type bearings fit between the big end of the connecting rod and the crankpin of the crankshaft.

The amount of offset of the rod bearing journal determines the stroke of the engine. The crankshaft with throws that measure one-half of the stroke has a direct relationship to the displacement of the engine. See Figure 27-5.

FIGURE 27-4   A ground surface on one of the crankshaft cheeks next to a main bearing supports thrust loads on the crank.

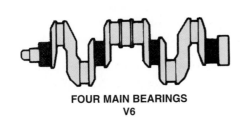

FOUR MAIN BEARINGS
V6

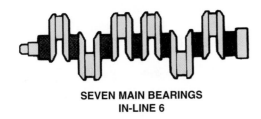

SEVEN MAIN BEARINGS
IN-LINE 6

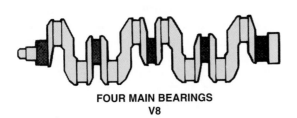

FOUR MAIN BEARINGS
V8

FIGURE 27-3   The longer the crankshaft, the more main bearing journals are needed.

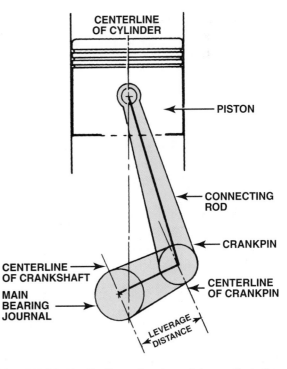

FIGURE 27-5   The distance from the crankpin centerline to the centerline of the crankshaft determines the stroke, which is the leverage available to turn the crankshaft.

Surface Finish

All crankshaft journals are ground to a very smooth finish. **Surface finish** is measured in micro-inches and the smaller the number, the smoother the surface. Where the surface finish of a machined block deck or cylinder head may range from 60 to 100 RA (roughness average), the typical specification for main and rod crankshaft journals is between 10 and 20 RA. This very smooth surface finish is achieved by polishing the crank journals after the grinding operation.

Journal Hardness

To improve wear resistance, some manufacturers harden the crankshaft journals. One method used is called **case hardening,** where only the outer portion of the surface is hardened. Case hardening involves heating the crankshaft and adding carbon to the journals where it causes the outer surface to become harder than the rest of the crankshaft. If the entire crankshaft was hardened, it would become too brittle to be able to absorb the torsional stresses of normal engine operation.

Another form of case hardening is called **nitriding.** The crankshaft is heated to about 1,000°F (540°C) in a furnace filled with ammonia gas, and then allowed to cool. The process adds nitrogen (from the ammonia) into the surface of the metal—forming hard nitrides in the surface of the crankshaft to a depth of about 0.007 inch (0.8 mm).

Another variation of this process involves heating the crankshaft in a molten cyanide salt bath. General Motors Corporation uses this process referred to by the trade name **Tuftriding.**

CRANKSHAFT CONSTRUCTION

Forged

Crankshafts used in high-production automotive engines may be either forged or cast. Forged crankshafts are stronger than the cast crankshaft, but they are more expensive. Forged crankshafts have a wide separation line, as seen in Figure 27-6.

Most high-performance forged crankshafts are made from SAE 4340 or a similar type of steel. The crankshaft is formed from a hot steel billet through the use of a series of forging dies. Each die changes the shape of the billet slightly. The crankshaft blank is finally formed with the last die. The blanks are then machined to finish the crankshaft. Forging makes a very dense, tough crankshaft with the metal's grain structure running parallel to the principal direction of stress.

FIGURE 27-6 Wide separation lines where the flashings have been removed from this forged crankshaft show that it has been twisted to index the crank throws. Most newer forged crankshafts are not twisted.

Two methods are used to forge crankshafts.

- One method is to forge the crankshaft *in place*. This is followed by straightening. The forging in place method is primarily used with forged 4- and 6-cylinder crankshafts.
- A second method is to forge the crankshaft in a *single plane*. It is then twisted in the main bearing journal to index the throws at the desired angles.

Cast Crankshafts

Casting materials and techniques have improved cast crankshaft quality so that cast crankshafts are used in most production automotive engines. Automotive crankshafts may be cast in steel, nodular iron, or malleable iron. The major advantage of the casting process is that crankshaft material and machining costs are less than they are with forging. The reason is that the crankshaft can be made close to the required shape and size, including all complicated counterweights. The only machining required on a carefully designed cast crankshaft is the grinding of bearing journal surfaces and the finishing of front and rear drive ends. Metal grain structure in the cast crankshaft is uniform and random throughout; thus, the shaft is able to handle loads from all directions. Counterweights on cast crankshafts are slightly larger than counterweights on a forged crankshaft, because the cast shaft metal is less dense

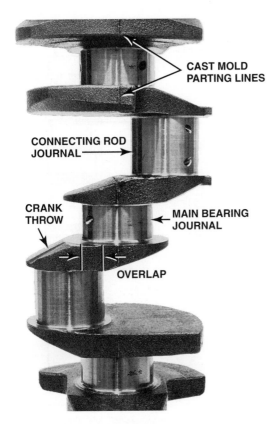

FIGURE 27-7   Cast crankshaft showing the bearing journal overlap and a straight, narrow cast mold parting line.

and therefore somewhat lighter. The narrow mold parting surface lines can be seen on the cast crankshaft pictured in Figure 27-7.

V-8 ENGINE CRANKSHAFTS

The V-8 engine has four inline cylinders in each of the two blocks that are placed at a 90-degree angle to each other. Each group of four inline cylinders is called a **bank.** The crankshaft for the V-8 engine has four throws. The connecting rods from two cylinders are connected to each throw, one from each bank. This arrangement results in a condition of being only minimally unbalanced. The V-8 engine crankshaft has two planes, so there is one throw every 90 degrees. A plane is a flat surface that cuts through the part. These planes could be seen if the crankshaft were cut lengthwise through the center of the main bearing and crankpin journals. Looking at the front of the crankshaft with the first throw at 360 degrees (up), the second throw is at 90 degrees (to the right), the third throw is at 270 degrees (to the left), and the fourth throw is at 180 degrees (down). In operation with this arrangement, one piston reaches top center at each 90 degrees of crankshaft rotation so that the engine operates smoothly with even firing at each 90 degrees of crankshaft rotation.

FOUR-CYLINDER ENGINE CRANKSHAFTS

The crankshaft used on 4-cylinder inline engines has four throws on a single plane. There is usually a main bearing journal between each throw, making it a five-main bearing crankshaft. Pistons also move as pairs in this engine. Pistons in #1 and #4 cylinders move together, and pistons #2 and #3 move together. Each piston in a pair is 360 degrees out-of-phase with the other piston in the 720-degree four-stroke cycle. With this arrangement, the 4-cylinder inline engine fires one cylinder at each 180 degrees of crankshaft rotation.

A 4-cylinder opposed engine and a 90-degree V-4 engine have crankshafts that look like that of the 4-cylinder inline engine.

FIVE-CYLINDER ENGINE CRANKSHAFTS

The inline 5-cylinder engine has a five-throw crankshaft with one throw at each 72 degrees. Six main bearings are used on this crankshaft. The piston in one cylinder reaches top center at each 144 degrees of crankshaft rotation. The throws are arranged to give a firing order of 1-2-4-5-3. Dynamic balancing has been one of the major problems with this engine design, yet the vibration was satisfactorily dampened and isolated on both the Audi and Acura 5-cylinder engines.

THREE-CYLINDER ENGINE CRANKSHAFTS

A 3-cylinder engine uses a 120-degree three-throw crankshaft with four main bearings. This engine requires a balancing shaft that turns at crankshaft speed, but in the opposite direction, to reduce the vibration to an acceptable level.

ODD-FIRING 90-DEGREE V-6 ENGINE CRANKSHAFTS

The 90-degree V-6 engine uses a three-throw crankshaft with four main bearings. The throws are 120 degrees apart. As in typical V-type engines, each crank throw has two connecting rods attached, one from each bank. This V-6 engine design does not have even-firing impulses, because the pistons, connected to the 120-degree crankpins, do not reach top center at even intervals. The engine has a firing pattern of 150°-90°-150°-90°-150°-90°, as illustrated in Figure 27-8.

This firing pattern produces unequal pulses that have to be isolated with engine mounts that have been carefully designed.

REAL WORLD FIX

THE MYSTERIOUS ENGINE VIBRATION

A Buick-built, 3.8-liter V-6 engine vibrated the whole car after a new short block had been installed. The technician who had installed the replacement engine did all of the following:

1. Checked the spark plugs
2. Checked the spark plug wires
3. Disconnected the torque converter from the flex plate (drive plate) to eliminate the possibility of a torque converter or automatic transmission pump problem
4. Removed all accessory drive belts one at a time

Yet the vibration still existed.

Another technician checked the engine mounts and found that the left (driver's side) engine mount was out of location, ripped, and cocked. The transmission mount was also defective. After the technician replaced both mounts and made certain that all mounts were properly set, the vibration was eliminated. The design and location of the engine mounts are critical to the elimination of vibration, especially on 90-degree V-6 engines.

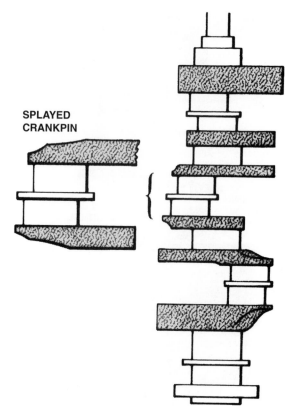

FIGURE 27-9 A splayed crankshaft design is used to create an even-firing 90-degree V-6.

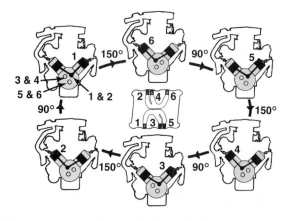

FIGURE 27-8 The firing impulses of this odd-fire V-6 are unequally spaced because two cylinders share a common crankpin.

EVEN-FIRING 90-DEGREE V-6 ENGINE CRANKSHAFTS

The crank throws for an even-firing V-6 engine are split, making separate crankpins for each cylinder. The split throw can be seen in Figure 27-9.

This angle between the crankpins on the crankshaft throws is called a **splay angle.** A flange was left between the split crankpin journals. This provides a continuous fillet or edge for

machining and grinding operations. It also provides a normal flange for the rod and bearing. This flange between the splayed crankpin journals is sometimes called a **flying web.**

SIXTY-DEGREE V-6 ENGINE CRANKSHAFTS

The 60-degree V-6 engine is similar to the even-firing 90-degree V-6 engine. The adjacent pairs of crankpins on the crankshaft used in the 60-degree V-6 engine have a splay angle of 60 degrees.

With this large 60-degree splay angle, the flange or flying web between the splayed crankpins is made heavier than on crankshafts with smaller splay angles. This is necessary to give strength to the crankshaft. The crankshaft of the 60-degree V-6 engine also uses four main bearings.

COUNTERWEIGHTS

Crankshafts are balanced by **counterweights,** which are cast or forged as part of the crankshaft. A crankshaft that has counterweights on both sides of each connecting rod journal is called **fully counterweighted.** See Figure 27-10.

A fully counterweighted crankshaft is the smoothest running and most durable design, but it is also the heaviest and most expensive to manufacture. Most vehicle manufacturers do not use fully counterweighted crankshafts in an effort to lighten the rotating mass of the engine. An engine with a light crankshaft allows the engine to accelerate quicker.

Vibration Damage

Each time combustion occurs, the force deflects the crankshaft as it transfers torque to the output shaft. This deflection occurs in two ways, to bend the shaft sideways and to twist the shaft in torsion. The crankshaft must be rigid enough to keep the deflection forces to a minimum.

FIGURE 27-10   A fully counterweighted 4-cylinder crankshaft.

FREQUENTLY ASKED QUESTION

WHAT IS AN OFFSET CRANKSHAFT?

To reduce side loads, some vehicle manufacturers offset the crankshaft from center. For example, if an engine rotates clockwise as viewed from the front, the crankshaft may be offset to the left to reduce the angle of the connecting rod during the power stroke. See Figure 27-11.

The offset usually varies from 1/16 to 1/2 inch, depending on make and model. Most gasoline engines used in hybrid gasoline/electric vehicles use an offset crankshaft.

Crankshaft deflections are directly related to the operating roughness of an engine. When back-and-forth deflections occur at the same vibration **frequency** (number of vibrations per second) as that of another engine part, the parts will vibrate together. When this happens, the parts are said to **resonate**. These vibrations may become great enough to reach the audible level, producing a thumping sound. If this type of vibration continues, the part may fail. See Figure 27-12.

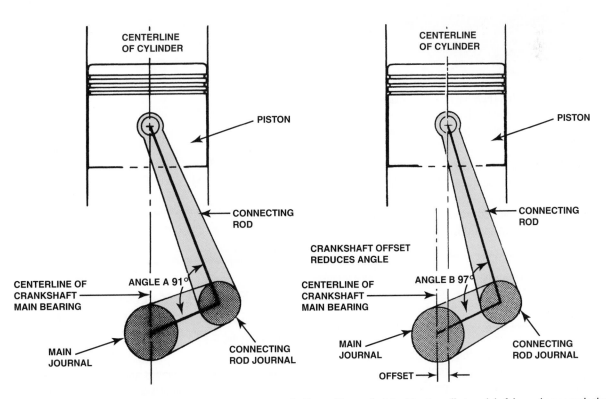

FIGURE 27-11   The crank throw is halfway down on the power stroke. The position on the left without an offset crankshaft has a sharper angle than the engine on the right with an offset crankshaft.

FIGURE 27-12   A crankshaft broken as a result of using the wrong torsional vibration damper.

FIGURE 27-13   This Chevy V-8 harmonic balancer also has a line cut into the outer ring that is used to indicate top dead center to set the ignition timing on engines that are equipped with a distributor ignition.

Harmful crankshaft twisting vibrations are dampened with a torsional vibration damper. It is also called a harmonic balancer. This damper or balancer usually consists of a cast-iron **inertia ring** mounted to a cast-iron **hub** with an **elastomer** sleeve. An example is shown in Figure 27-13.

NOTE: Push on the rubber (elastomer sleeve) of the vibration damper with your fingers or a pencil. *If the rubber does not spring back, replace the damper.*

Elastomers are actually synthetic, rubber-like materials. The inertia ring size is selected to control the **amplitude** of the crankshaft vibrations for each specific engine model. See Figure 27-14.

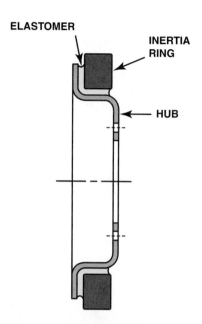

FIGURE 27-14   The hub of the harmonic balancer is attached to the front of the crankshaft. The elastomer (rubber) between the inertia ring and the center hub allows the absorption of crankshaft firing impulses.

TECH TIP

HIGH ENGINE SPEEDS REQUIRE HIGH-PERFORMANCE PARTS

Do not go racing with stock parts. The harmonic balancer shown in Figure 27-15 came apart and the resulting vibration broke the crankshaft when the owner attempted to race with his stock engine.

The owner had made some engine modifications, but he did not change the stock harmonic balancer even though the other changes allowed the engine to rev to much higher speeds than stock parts normally would permit.

EXTERNALLY AND INTERNALLY BALANCED ENGINES

Most crankshaft balancing is done during manufacture. Holes are drilled in the counterweight to lighten it to improve balance. Sometimes these holes are drilled after the crankshaft is

FIGURE 27-15 Harmonic balancer that separated at high engine speed.

FIGURE 27-16 Crankshaft sawed in half, showing drilled oil passages between the main and rod bearing journals.

installed in the engine. Some manufacturers are able to control casting quality so closely that counterweight machining for balancing is not necessary.

There are two ways engine manufacturers balance an engine:

- **Externally balanced**—Weight is added to the harmonic balancer (vibration damper) and flywheel or the flex plate.
- **Internally balanced**—All rotating parts of the engine are individually balanced, including the harmonic balancer and flywheel (flex plate).

For example, the 350-cubic-inch Chevrolet V-8 is internally balanced, whereas the 400-cubic-inch Chevrolet V-8 uses an externally balanced crankshaft. The harmonic balancer used on an externally balanced engine has additional weight.

CRANKSHAFT OILING HOLES

The crankshaft is drilled, as shown in Figure 27-16, to allow oil from the main bearing oil groove to be directed to the connecting rod bearings.

The oil on the bearings forms a hydrodynamic oil film to support bearing loads. Some of the oil may be sprayed out through a spit or bleed hole in the connecting rod. The rest of the oil leaks from the edges of the bearing. It is thrown from the bearing against the inside surfaces of the engine. Some of the oil that is thrown from the crankshaft bearings will land on the camshaft to lubricate the lobes. A part of the throw-off oil splashes on the cylinder wall to lubricate the piston and rings.

Stress tends to concentrate at oil holes drilled through the crankshaft journals. These holes are usually located where the crankshaft loads and stresses are the lowest. The edges of the oil holes are carefully chamfered to relieve as much stress concentration as possible. Chamfered oil holes are shown in Figure 27-17.

FREQUENTLY ASKED QUESTION

WHAT DOES A "CROSS-DRILLED CRANKSHAFT" MEAN?

A cross-drilled crankshaft means that there are two instead of only one oil hole leading from the main bearing journal to the rod bearing journal. Oil is supplied to the main bearing journals through oil galleries in the block. A cross-drilled crankshaft has two outlet holes for oil to reach the drilled passage that supplies oil to the rod journal. See Figure 27-18.

CRANKSHAFT INSPECTION

Shaft damage includes scored bearing journals, bends or warpage, and cracks. Damaged shafts must be reconditioned or replaced.

The crankshaft is one of the most highly stressed engine parts. *The stress on the crankshaft increases by four times every time the engine speed doubles.* Any sign of a crack is a cause to reject the crankshaft. Most cracks can be seen during a close visual inspection. Crankshafts should also be checked with Magnaflux, which will highlight tiny cracks that would lead to failure.

Bearing journal scoring is a common crankshaft defect. Scoring appears as scratches around the bearing journal surface. Generally, there is more scoring near the center of the bearing journal, as shown in Figure 27-19.

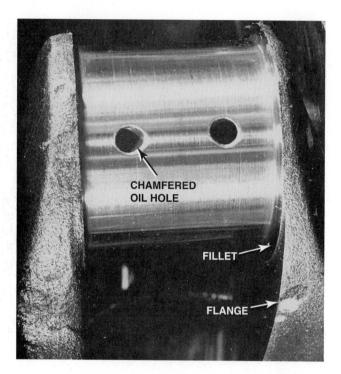

FIGURE 27-17 Typical chamfered hole in a crankshaft bearing journal.

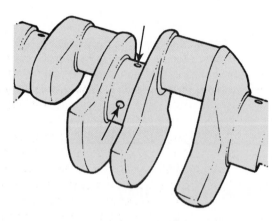

FIGURE 27-18 A cross-drilled crankshaft is used on some production engines and is a common racing modification.

Crankshaft journals should be inspected for nicks, pits, or corrosion. Roughness and slight bends in journals can be corrected by grinding the journals.

NOTE: If your fingernail catches on a groove when rubbed across a bearing journal, the journal is too rough to reuse and must be reground. Another test is to rub a copper penny across the journal. If any copper remains on the crankshaft, it must be reground.

FIGURE 27-19 Scored connecting rod bearing journal.

FIGURE 27-20 Connecting rod journal badly worn from lack of lubrication.

CRANKSHAFT GRINDING

Crankshaft journals that have excessive scoring, out-of-round, or taper should be reground. See Figure 27-20.

Crankshafts may require straightening before grinding. Both crankshaft ends are placed in rotating heads on one style of crankshaft grinder. The main bearing journals are ground on the centerline of the crankshaft. The crankshaft is then offset in the two rotating heads just enough to make the crankshaft main bearing journal centerline rotate around the centerline of the crankpin. The crankshaft will then be rotating around the crankpin centerline. The journal on the crankpin is reground in this position. The crankshaft must be repositioned for each different crankpin center.

In another type of crankshaft grinder, the crankshaft always turns on the main bearing centerline. The grinding head is programmed to move in and out as the crankshaft turns to grind the crankpin bearing journals. The setup time is reduced when this type of grinder is used. Figure 27-21 shows a crankshaft being ground.

Crankshafts are usually ground to the following undersize:

- 0.010 inch
- 0.020 inch
- 0.030 inch

The finished journal should be accurately ground to size with a smooth-surface finish. The radius of the fillet area on the sides of the journal should also be the same as the original. The journal is polished after grinding using a 320-grit polishing cloth and oil to remove the fine metal "fuzz" remaining on the journal. See Figure 27-22.

This fuzz feels smooth when the shaft turns in its direction. As the shaft turns in the opposite direction, the fuzz feels like a fine milling cutter. Polishing removes this fuzz. The crankshaft is rotated in its normal direction of rotation so that the polishing cloth can remove the fuzz. This leaves a smooth shaft with the proper surface finish. *Most crankshaft grinders grind in the direction opposite of rotation and then polish in the same direction as rotation.* The oil

hole chamfer in the journal should be smoothed so that no sharp edge remains to cut the bearing. Finally, the crankshaft oil passages are thoroughly cleaned.

The reground journals are coated with oil to keep them from rusting until they are to be cleaned for assembly.

WELDING A CRANKSHAFT

Sometimes it is desirable to salvage a crankshaft by building up a bearing journal and then grinding it to the original journal size. This is usually done by either electric arc welding or a metal spray. See Figure 27-23.

FIGURE 27-22   All crankshafts should be polished after grinding. Both the crankshaft and the polishing cloth are being revolved.

FIGURE 27-21   A crankshaft being ground.

FIGURE 27-23   An excessively worn crankshaft can be restored to useful service by welding the journals, and then machining them back to the original size.

Sometimes the journal is chrome plated. Chrome plating makes an excellent bearing surface when the chrome is well bonded. If the bonding loosens, it will cause an immediate bearing failure.

STRESS RELIEVING THE CRANKSHAFT

The greatest area of stress on a crankshaft is the fillet area. See Figure 27-24.

Stress relief is achieved by blasting the fillet area of the journals with #320 steel shot. This strengthens the fillet area and helps to prevent the development of cracks in this area. Gray duct tape is commonly used to cover the journal to prevent damage to the rest of it. Stress relief procedures are usually performed after the grinding and polishing of the crankshaft.

ENGINE BEARINGS

Engine bearings are the main supports for the major moving parts of any engine. Engine bearings are important for the following reasons:

1. The clearance between the bearings and the crankshaft is a major factor in maintaining the proper oil pressure throughout the entire engine. Most engines are designed to provide the maximum protection and lubrication to the engine bearings above all else.

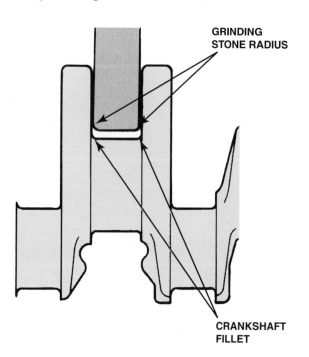

GRINDING
STONE RADIUS

CRANKSHAFT
FILLET

FIGURE 27-24 The rounded fillet area of the crankshaft is formed by the corners of the grinding stone.

TECH TIP

THE KNOCK OF A FLEX PLATE

The source of a knocking noise in an engine is often difficult to determine without disassembling the engine. Generally, a deep engine knocking noise means that serious damage has occurred to the rods or main bearings and related parts. A flex plate (drive plate) is used on automatic transmission-equipped engines to drive the torque converter and provide a ring gear for the starter motor to crank the engine. Two common flex plate-related noises and their causes are as follows:

- Torque converter attaching bolts or nuts can loosen (this is most common in 4-cylinder engines, where vibration is more severe than in 6- or 8-cylinder engines). The torque converter can then pound on the holes of the flex plate, causing a loud knocking sound. However, if there is a load on the engine, as when the transmission is in drive or while driving under load, the sound should stop. At idle in park or neutral, the noise will be loudest, because the torque converter can float and will hit the sides of the holes in the flex plate.
- If the flex plate is cracked, the resulting noise is very similar to a connecting rod or main bearing knock. The noise also seems to change at times, leading many technicians to believe that it involves a moving internal part that is lubricated, such as a rod or main bearing. The drive belts can also make a similar noise when they are loose, and belt-driven accessories can also produce similar noises.

Diagnosis should proceed as follows:

During the diagnostic procedure, the technician should disconnect one drive belt at a time (if there is more than one) and then start the engine in an attempt to isolate the noise. Noises can be transmitted throughout the entire length of the engine through the crankshaft, making the source of the noise more difficult to isolate. If the flex plate is cracked, the noise is most noticeable when there is a change in engine speed or load. To help diagnose a cracked flex plate, raise engine speed to a high idle (1500 to 2000 RPM), then turn the ignition switch off. Before the engine stops, turn the ignition back on. If a knocking noise is heard when the engine restarts, the flex plate is cracked.

2. Engine durability relies on bearing life. Bearing failure usually results in immediate engine failure.
3. Engine bearings are designed to support the operating loads of the engine and, with the lubricant, provide minimum friction. This must be achieved at all designed engine speeds. The bearings must be able to operate for long periods of time, even when small foreign particles are in the lubricant.

Most engine bearings are of the **plain** or **sleeve bearing** type. See Figure 27-25.

Most bearing halves, or shells, do not have uniform thickness. The wall thickness of most bearings is largest in the center, called the **bearing crown.** The bearing thickness then tapers to a thinner measurement at each parting line. See Figure 27-26.

The tapered wall keeps bearing clearances close at the top and bottom of the bearing, which are the more loaded areas and allow more oil flow at the sides of the bearing. Both need a constant flow of lubricating oil. In automotive engines, the lubricating system supplies oil to each bearing continuously when the engine runs. Bearings and journals *only* wear when the parts come in contact with each other or when foreign particles are present.

Oil enters the bearing through the oil holes and grooves. It spreads into a smooth wedge-shaped oil film that supports the bearing load.

Bearing Loads

It is important that the engine have large enough bearings that the bearing load is within the strength limits of the bearings. Bearing load capacity is calculated by dividing the bearing load in pounds by the projected area of the bearing. The projected area is the bearing length multiplied by the bearing diameter. The load on engine bearings is determined by developing a polar bearing load diagram that shows the amount and direction of the instantaneous bearing loads. Bearing load diagrams are shown in Figure 27-27.

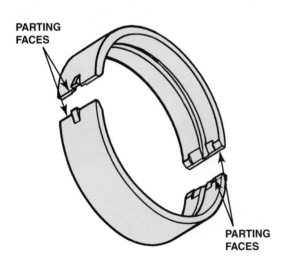

FIGURE 27-25 The two halves of a plain bearing meet at the parting faces.

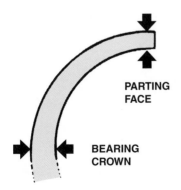

FIGURE 27-26 Bearing manufacturers refer to this bearing wall shape as a eccentric wall.

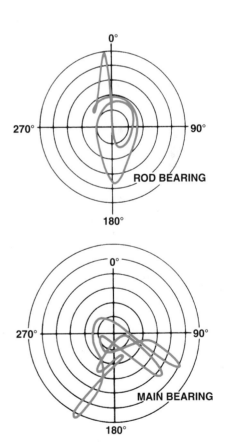

FIGURE 27-27 Typical rod and main bearing load diagrams. The circles on these polar diagrams indicate the amount of force on the bearing as it rotates. Notice that most of the forces on the connecting rod bearing are vertical (up and down), as you would expect; most of the forces on the main bearing are downward, again as expected.

The forces on the engine bearings vary with engine speed and load. On the intake stroke, the inertia force is opposed by the force of drawing in the air–fuel mixture. On the compression and power strokes, there is also an opposing force on the rod bearings. On the exhaust stroke, however, there is no opposing force to counteract the inertia force of the piston coming to a stop at TDC. The result is a higher force load on the *bottom* rod bearing due to inertia at TDC of the exhaust stroke. These forces tend to stretch the big end of the rod in the direction of rod movement.

1. As engine speed (RPM) increases, rod bearing loads decrease because of the balancing of inertia and opposing loads.
2. As engine speed (RPM) increases, the main bearing loads increase.

> **NOTE:** This helps explain why engine blocks with four-bolt main bearing supports are really only needed for high-engine speed stability.

3. Because the loads on bearings vary and affect both rod and main bearings, it is generally recommended that *all* engine bearings be replaced at one time.

Bearing Fatigue

Bearings tend to flex or bend slightly under changing loads. This is especially noticeable in reciprocating engine bearings. Bearing metals, like other metals, tend to fatigue and break after being flexed or bent a number of times. Flexing starts fatigue, which shows up as fine cracks in the bearing surface because the bearing material became **work hardened.** These cracks gradually deepen almost to the bond between the bearing metal and the backing metal. The cracks then cross over and intersect with each other, as illustrated in Figure 27-28.

In time, this will allow a piece of bearing material to fall out. The length of time before fatigue will cause failure is called the **fatigue life** of the bearing. Bearings must have a long fatigue life for normal engine service. The harder the bearing material, the longer its fatigue life. Soft bearings have a short fatigue life and low bearing load strength. They are generally

low in cost and can only be used where the bearing requirements are low. See Figures 27-29 and 27-30.

Bearing Conformability

The ability of bearing materials to creep or flow slightly to match shaft variations is called **conformability.** The bearing conforms to the shaft during the engine break-in period. In modern automobile engines, there is little need for bearing conformability or break-in, because automatic processing has achieved machining tolerances that keep the shaft very close to the designed size. See Figure 27-31.

FIGURE 27-29 Bearing material missing from the shell as a result of fatigue.

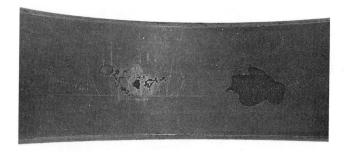

FIGURE 27-30 Bearing material missing from the bearing as a result of fatigue failure.

FIGURE 27-31 Bearing wear caused by a misaligned journal. A bent connecting rod could also cause similar bearing wear.

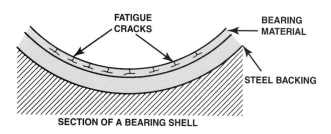

FIGURE 27-28 Shape of fatigue cracks in a bearing. If the bearing is subjected to continued high loads, the cracks expand and eventually cause the bearing material to flake off from the steel backing.

Bearing Embedability

Engine manufacturers have designed engines to produce minimum crankcase deposits. This has been done by providing them with oil filters, air filters, and closed crankcase ventilation systems that minimize contaminants. Still, some foreign particles get into the bearings. The bearings must be capable of embedding these particles into the bearing surface so that they will not score the shaft. To fully embed the particle, the bearing material gradually works across the particle, completely covering it. The bearing property that allows it to do this is called **embedability.** Embedability is illustrated in Figures 27-32 and 27-33.

Bearing Damage Resistance

Under some operating conditions, the bearing will be temporarily overloaded. This will cause the oil film to break down and allow the shaft metal to come in contact with the bearing metal. As the rotating crankshaft contacts the bearing high spots, the spots become hot from friction. The friction causes localized hot spots in the bearing material that seize or weld to the crankshaft. The crankshaft then breaks off particles of the bearing material and pulls the particles around with it, scratching or scoring the bearing surface. See Figures 27-34 and 27-35.

Bearings have a characteristic called **score resistance.** It prevents the bearing materials from seizing to the shaft during oil film breakdown.

By-products of combustion form acids in the oil. The bearings' ability to resist attack from these acids is called **corrosion resistance.** Corrosion can occur over the entire surface of the bearing. This will remove material and increase the oil clearance. It can also leach or eat into the bearing material, dissolving some of the bearing material alloys. Either type of corrosion will reduce bearing life.

BEARING CONSTRUCTION

Materials

Three materials are used for automobile engine bearings: **babbitt, copper-lead alloy,** and *aluminum.* A layer of the bearing materials 0.010 to 0.020 inch (0.25 to 0.50 millimeter) thick is applied over a low-carbon steel backing. An engine bearing is called a *bearing shell,* which is a steel backing with a surface coating of bearing material. The steel provides support needed for the shaft load. The bearing material meets the rest of the bearing operating requirements.

FIGURE 27-33 Foreign particles such as dirt embedded in the bearing material.

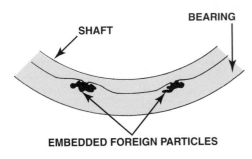

FIGURE 27-32 Bearing material covers foreign material as it embeds into the bearing.

FIGURE 27-34 Bearing material starting to leave the steel backing.

Babbitt. Babbitt is the oldest automotive bearing material. Isaac Babbitt (1799–1862) first formulated this material in 1839. An excellent bearing material, it was originally made from a combination of lead, tin, and antimony. Lead and tin are alloyed with small quantities of copper and antimony to give it the required strength. Babbitt is still used in applications in which material is required for soft shafts running under moderate loads and speeds. It will work with occasional borderline lubrication and oil starvation without failure.

Tri-Metal. Copper-lead alloy is a stronger and more expensive bearing material than babbitt. It is used for intermediate- and high-speed applications. Tin, in small quantities, is often alloyed with the copper-lead bearings. This bearing material is most easily damaged by corrosion from acid accumulation in the engine oil. Corrosion results in bearing journal wear as the bearing is eroded by the acids.

Many of the copper-lead bearings have an **overlay**, or third layer, of metal. This overlay is usually of babbitt. Babbitt-overlayed bearings have high fatigue strength, good conformity, good embedability, and good corrosion resistance. The overplated bearing is a premium bearing. It is also the most expensive because the overplating layer, from 0.0005 to 0.001 inch (0.0125 to 0.025 millimeter) thick, is put on the bearing with an **electroplating** process. The layers of bearing material on a bearing shell are illustrated in Figure 27-36.

Aluminum. Aluminum was the last of the three materials to be used for automotive bearings. Automotive bearing aluminum has small quantities of tin and silicon alloyed with it. This makes a stronger but more expensive bearing than either babbitt or copper-lead alloy.

(a)

(b)

FIGURE 27-35 Typical results of oil pressure loss: (a) extreme wear of the connecting rod journal, (b) overheating finally leading to failure of the bearing.

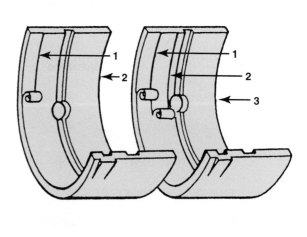

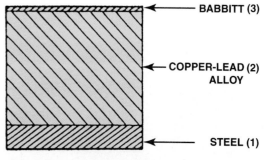

BABBITT (3)

COPPER-LEAD (2) ALLOY

STEEL (1)

FIGURE 27-36 Typical two-layer and three-layer engine bearing insert showing the relative thickness of the various materials.

Most of its bearing characteristics are equal to or better than those of babbitt and copper lead. **Aluminum bearings** are well suited to high-speed, high-load conditions and do not contain lead, which is a benefit to the environment both at the manufacturing plant and for the technician who may be exposed to the bearings.

BEARING MANUFACTURING

Modern automotive engines use **precision insert-type bearing shells,** sometimes called **half-shell bearings.** The bearing is manufactured to very close tolerance so that it will fit correctly in each application. The bearing, therefore, must be made from precisely the correct materials under closely controlled manufacturing conditions. Figure 27-37 shows the typical bearing shell types found in most engines.

Bearing Sizes

Bearings are usually available in standard (std) size, and in measurements 0.010, 0.020, and 0.030 inch *undersize.* See Figure 27-38.

Even though the bearing itself is thicker for use on a machined crankshaft, the bearing is referred to as undersize because the crankshaft journals are undersize. Factory bearings may be available in 0.0005 or 0.001 inch undersize for precision fitting of a production crankshaft.

Before purchasing bearings, be sure to use a micrometer to measure *all* main and connecting rod journals.

BEARING CLEARANCE

The bearing-to-journal clearance may be from 0.0005 to 0.0025 inch (0.025 to 0.060 millimeter), depending on the engine. Doubling the journal clearance will allow more than *four* times as much oil to flow from the edges of the bearing. The oil clearance must be large enough to allow an oil film to build up, but small enough to prevent excess oil leakage, which would cause loss of oil pressure. A large amount of oil leakage at one of the bearings would starve other bearings farther along in the oil system. This would result in the failure of the oil-starved bearings. See Figure 27-39.

BEARING SPREAD AND CRUSH

A lip or tang locates the bearing shell in the housing, as shown in Figure 27-40. The bearing design also includes bearing **spread** and **crush,** as illustrated in Figure 27-41.

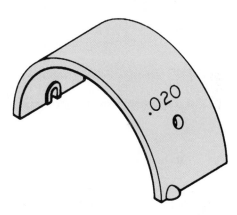

FIGURE 27-38   Bearings are often marked with an undersize dimension. This bearing is used on a crankshaft with a ground journal that is 0.020-inch smaller in diameter than the stock size.

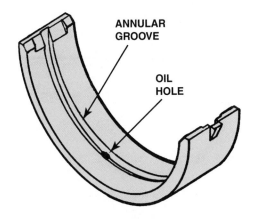

FIGURE 27-39   Many bearings are manufactured with a groove down the middle to improve the oil flow around the main journal.

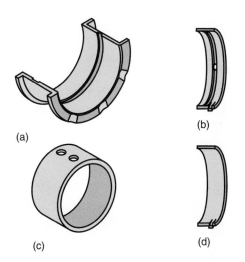

FIGURE 27-37   Typical bearing shell types found in modern engines: (a) half-shell thrust bearing, (b) upper main bearing insert, (c) full round-type camshaft bearing, (d) lower main bearing insert.

The bearing shell has a slightly larger arc than does the bearing housing. This difference is called bearing spread and it makes the shell 0.005 to 0.020 inch (0.125 to 0.500 millimeter) wider than the housing bore. Spread holds the bearing shell in the housing while the engine is being assembled. When the bearing is installed, each end of the bearing shell is slightly above the parting surface. When the bearing cap is tightened, the ends of the two bearing shells touch and are forced together. This force is called bearing crush. Crush holds the bearing in place and keeps the bearing from turning when the engine runs. Crush must exert a force of at least 12,000 PSI (82,740 kPa) at 250°F (121°C) to hold the bearing securely in place. A stress of 40,000 PSI (275,790 kPa) is considered maximum to avoid damaging the bearing or housing. See Figure 27-42.

Bearing shells that do not have enough crush may rotate with the shaft. The result is called a **spun bearing,** as pictured in Figure 27-43.

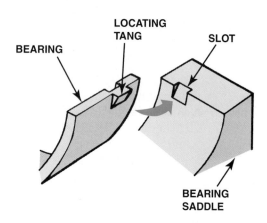

FIGURE 27-40 The tang and slot help index the bearing in the bore.

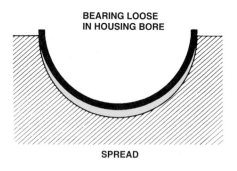

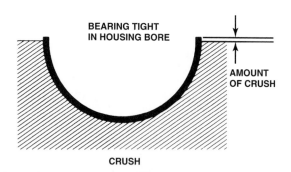

FIGURE 27-41 Bearing spread and crush.

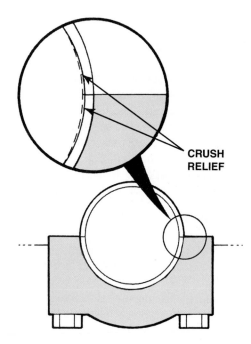

FIGURE 27-42 Bearings are thinner at the parting line faces to provide crush relief.

FIGURE 27-43 Spun bearing. The lower cap bearing has rotated under the upper rod bearing.

Replacement bearings should be of a quality as good as or better than that of the original bearings. The replacement bearings must also have the same oil holes and grooves.

CAUTION: Some bearings may have oil holes in the top shell only. If these are incorrectly installed, no oil will flow to the connecting rods or main rods, which will result in instant engine failure.

Modified engines have more demanding bearing requirements and therefore usually require a higher-quality bearing to provide satisfactory service.

CAMSHAFT BEARINGS

The camshaft in pushrod engines rotates in sleeve bearings that are pressed into bearing bores within the engine block. Overhead camshaft bearings may be either sleeve-type bushings called **full round bearings** or **split-type (half-shell) bearings,** depending on the design of the bearing supports. In pushrod engines, the cam bearings are installed in the block. See Figure 27-44.

The best rule of thumb to follow is to replace the cam bearings whenever the main bearings are replaced. The replacement cam bearings must have the correct outside diameter to fit snugly in the cam bearing bores of the block. They must have the correct oil holes and be positioned correctly. See Figure 27-45. Cam bearings must also have the proper inside diameter to fit the camshaft bearing journals.

In many engines, each cam bearing is a different size—the largest is in the front and the smallest is in the rear. The

TECH TIP

COUNT YOUR BLESSINGS AND YOUR PAN BOLTS!

Replacing cam bearings can be relatively straightforward or can involve keeping count of the number of oil pan bolts! For example, Buick-built V-6 engines use different cam bearings depending on the number of bolts used to hold the oil pan to the block.

- Fourteen bolts in the oil pan. The front bearing is special, but the rest of the bearings are the same.
- Twenty bolts in the oil pan. Bearings #1 and #4 use two oil feed holes. Bearings #2 and #3 use single oil feed holes.

cam bearing journal size must be checked and each bearing identified before assembly is begun. The location of each new cam bearing can be marked on the outside of the bearing with a felt-tip marker to help avoid mixing up bearings. Marking in this way will not affect the bearing size or damage the bearing in any way. Cam bearings should be installed "dry" (not oiled) to prevent the cam bearing from moving (spinning) after installation. If the cam bearing were oiled, the rotation of the camshaft

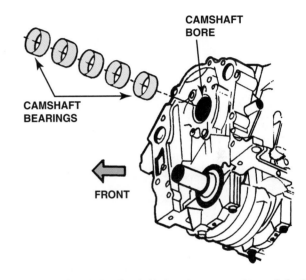

FIGURE 27-44 Cam-in-block engines support the camshaft with sleeve-type bearings.

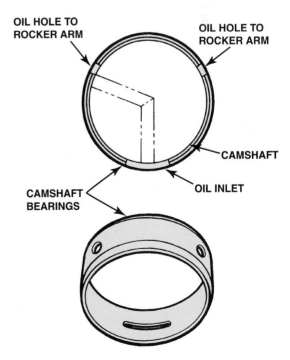

FIGURE 27-45 Camshaft bearings must be installed correctly so that oil passages are not blocked.

could cause the cam bearing to rotate and block oil holes that lubricate the camshaft.

Camshaft bearings used on overhead camshaft engines may be either full round or split depending on the engine design. See Figure 27-46.

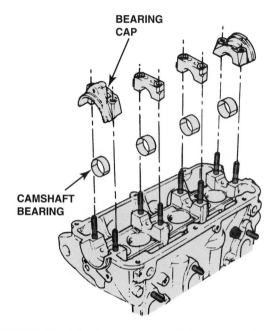

FIGURE 27-46   Some overhead camshaft engines use split bearing inserts.

DO NO HARM

All engine parts should be stored in a safe location to help avoid damage prior to being installed in an engine. All camshafts and crankshafts should be stored vertically to avoid causing bending or warpage of these parts that could cause difficulty when the engine is being assembled. See Figure 27-47 for one method of safely storing crankshafts.

FIGURE 27-47   Crankshafts should be stored vertically to prevent possible damage or warpage. This clever bench-mounted tray for crankshafts not only provides a safe place to store crankshafts but it is out-of-the-way and cannot be accidentally tipped.

CHECKING BEARING CLEARANCE WITH PLASTIGAGE Step-by-Step

STEP 1 Clean the main bearing journal and then place a strip of Plastigage material across the entire width of the journal.

STEP 2 Carefully install the main bearing cap with the bearing installed.

STEP 3 Torque the main bearing cap bolts to factory specifications.

STEP 4 Carefully remove the bearing cap and, using the package that contained the Plastigage strips, measure the width of the compressed material. The gauge is calibrated in thousanths of an inch. Repeat for each main bearing.

STEP 5 To measure rod bearing oil clearance, start by removing the rod cap.

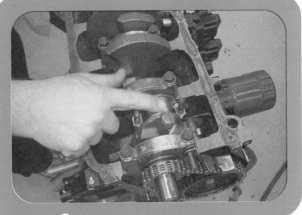

STEP 6 Clean the rod bearing journal and then place a strip of Plastigage across the entire width of the journal.

(continued)

CHECKING BEARING CLEARANCE WITH PLASTIGAGE continued

STEP 7 Torque the rod bearing cap nuts to factory specifications.

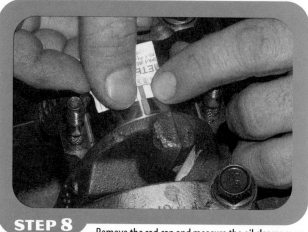

STEP 8 Remove the rod cap and measure the oil clearance using the markings on the Plastigage package. The wider the compressed gauge material, the narrower the bearing oil clearance. Repeat for all rod bearings.

SUMMARY

1. Cast crankshafts have a narrow mold parting line.
2. Even-fire 90-degree V-6 engines require that the crankshaft be splayed to allow for even firing.
3. Lubrication to the main bearings is fed through the main oil gallery in the block. Oil for the rod bearings comes from holes in the crankshaft drilled between the main journal and the rod journal.
4. A vibration damper, also known as a harmonic balancer, is used to dampen harmful twisting vibrations of the crankshaft.
5. Most engines are internally balanced. This means that the crankshafts and vibration damper are both balanced.

Other engines use the vibration damper to balance the crankshaft and are called externally balanced engines.
6. Most crankshafts can be reground to be 0.010, 0.020, or 0.030 inch undersize.
7. Most engine bearings are constructed with a steel shell for strength and are covered with a copper-lead alloy. Many bearings also have a thin overlay of babbitt.
8. Bearings should have spread and crush to keep them from spinning when the crankshaft rotates.

REVIEW QUESTIONS

1. How many degrees of crankshaft rotation are there between cylinder firings on an inline 4-cylinder engine, an inline 6-cylinder engine, and a V-8 engine?

2. List four engine bearing properties.

3. Describe bearing crush and bearing spread.

CHAPTER QUIZ

1. A forged crankshaft has _____.
   a. A wide parting line
   b. A thin parting line
   c. A parting line in one plane
   d. Both b and c

2. A typical V-8 engine crankshaft has _____ main bearings.
   a. Three
   b. Four
   c. Five
   d. Seven

3. A 4-cylinder engine fires one cylinder at every _____ degrees of crankshaft rotation.
   a. 27
   b. 180
   c. 120
   d. 90

4. A splayed crankshaft is a crankshaft that _____.
   a. Is externally balanced
   b. Is internally balanced
   c. Has offset main bearing journals
   d. Has offset rod journals

5. The thrust bearing surface is located on one of the main bearings to control thrust loads caused by _____.
   a. Lugging the engine
   b. Torque converter or clutch release forces
   c. Rapid deceleration forces
   d. Both a and c

6. If any crankshaft is ground, it must also be _____.
   a. Shot peened
   b. Chrome plated
   c. Polished
   d. Externally balanced

7. If bearing-to-journal clearance is doubled, how much oil will flow?
   a. One-half as much
   b. The same amount if the pressure is kept constant
   c. Double the amount
   d. Four times the amount

8. Typical journal-to-bearing clearance is _____.
   a. 0.00015 to 0.00018 inch
   b. 0.0005 to 0.0025 inch
   c. 0.150 to 0.250 inch
   d. 0.020 to 0.035 inch

9. A bearing shell has a slightly larger arc than the bearing housing. This difference is called _____.
   a. Bearing crush
   b. Bearing tang
   c. Bearing spread
   d. Bearing saddle

10. Bearing _____ occurs when a bearing shell is slightly above the parting surface of the bearing cap.
    a. Overlap
    b. Crush
    c. Cap lock
    d. Interference fit

ENGINE BALANCING AND BALANCE SHAFTS

OBJECTIVES

After studying Chapter 28, the reader will be able to:

1. Prepare for Engine Repair (A1) ASE certification test content area "C" (Engine Block Diagnosis and Repair).

2. Explain the causes of primary and secondary engine vibration.

3. Describe why balance shafts are used.

4. Explain what parts are rotating weight and what parts are reciprocating weight.

5. List the steps needed to balance an engine.

KEY TERMS

Dampening (p. 547)
Primary Vibration (p. 547)

Rocking Couple (p. 547)
Secondary Vibration (p. 547)

ENGINE BALANCE

Anything that rotates will vibrate. This means that an engine will vibrate during operation, although engine designers attempt to reduce the vibration as much as possible. When pistons move up and down in the cylinders they create a **primary vibration,** which is a strong low-frequency vibration.

A counterweight on the crankshaft opposite the piston/rod assembly helps reduce this vibration. An inline 4-cylinder engine has very little primary vibration because as two pistons are traveling upward in the cylinders, two are moving downward at the same time, effectively canceling out primary unbalances. See Figure 28-1.

Four-cylinder engines, however, suffer from a vibration at twice engine speed. This is called a **secondary vibration,** which is a weak high-frequency vibration caused by a slight difference in the inertia of the pistons at top dead center compared to bottom dead center. This vibration is most noticeable at high-engine speeds, especially if the engine size is greater than 2.0 liters. The larger the displacement of the engine, the larger the bore and the heavier the pistons contribute to the buzzing-type secondary vibration. See Figure 28-2.

BALANCE SHAFTS

Some engines use balance shafts to dampen normal engine vibrations. **Dampening** is reducing the vibration to an acceptable level. A balance shaft that is turning at crankshaft speed, but in the opposite direction, is used on a 3-cylinder inline engine. Weights on the ends of the balance shaft move in a direction opposite to the direction of the end piston. When the piston goes up, the weight goes down, and when the piston goes down, the weight goes up. This reduces the end-to-end rocking action on the 3-cylinder inline engine.

Another type of balance shaft system is designed to counterbalance vibrations on a 4-stroke, 4-cylinder engine. Two shafts are used, and they turn at *twice* the engine speed. One shaft turns in the same direction as the crankshaft, and the other turns in the opposite direction. The oil pump gears are used to drive the reverse-turning shaft. Counterweights on the balance shafts are positioned to oppose the natural rolling action of the engine, as well as the secondary vibrations caused by the piston and rod movements. This design is shown in Figure 28-3.

Balance shafts are commonly found on the larger-displacement (over 2.0 liter) 4-cylinder automotive engines. Mitsubishi introduced counterbalance shafts on 4-cylinder engines in 1974. Since the late 1980s, both Ford and General Motors added a balance shaft to many of their V-6 engines. These 90-degree V-6 engines use a split-crank journal to create an even-firing arrangement, but these engines suffer from forces that cause the engine to rock back and forth. This motion is called a **rocking couple** and is dampened by the use of

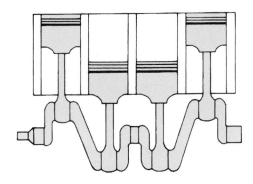

FIGURE 28-1 In a 4-cylinder engine, the two outside pistons move upward at the same time as the inner pistons move downward, which reduces primary unbalance.

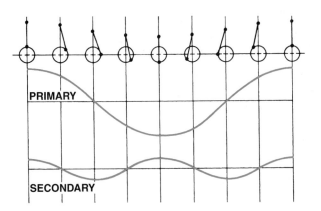

FIGURE 28-2 Primary and secondary vibrations in relation to piston position.

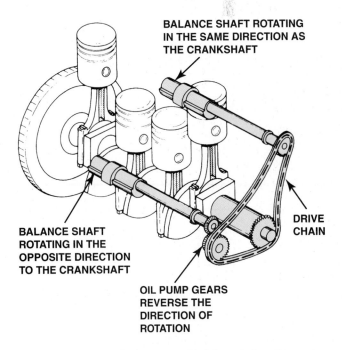

BALANCE SHAFT ROTATING IN THE SAME DIRECTION AS THE CRANKSHAFT

BALANCE SHAFT ROTATING IN THE OPPOSITE DIRECTION TO THE CRANKSHAFT

DRIVE CHAIN

OIL PUMP GEARS REVERSE THE DIRECTION OF ROTATION

FIGURE 28-3 Two counter-rotating balance shafts used to counterbalance the vibrations of a 4-cylinder engine.

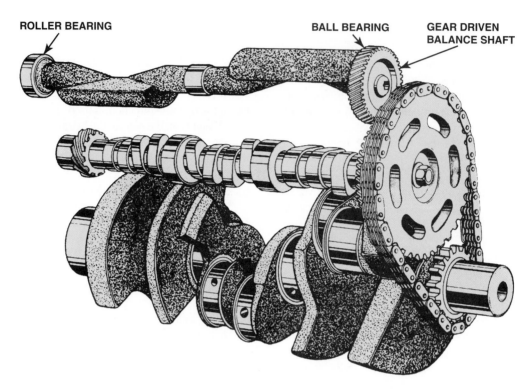

FIGURE 28-4 Many 90-degree V-6 engines use a balance shaft to reduce vibrations and effectively cancel a rocking motion (rocking couple) that causes the engine to rock front to back.

a balance shaft. Other V-6 engines that use a 60-degree V-6 engine do not create a rocking couple and, therefore, do not need a balance shaft. See Figure 28-4. The addition of balance shafts makes a big improvement in the smoothness of the engine. In V-6 engines, the improvement is most evident during idling and low-speed operation, whereas in the 4-cylinder engines, balance shafts are especially helpful at higher engine speeds.

BALANCING AN ENGINE

For any engine to operate with a minimum amount of vibration, all of the reciprocating parts must be close to the same weight. Production engines use parts that are usually within 3 grams of each other and result in a relatively smooth operating engine.

NOTE: A gram is 1/28 of an ounce or the weight of a typical small paper clip.

Custom engine builders attempt to get all reciprocating parts to 1 gram or less. The reason for such accuracy is that any unbalance is increased greatly by centrifugal force as the engine operates. The force of the unbalance increases by the square of the speed. In other words, if the engine RPM doubles, the force of any unbalance is multiplied by four. An unbalance of

1 ounce that is 1 inch from the center of rotation becomes a force of 7 ounces at 500 RPM. At 5000 RPM, this same 1 ounce of unbalance would be increased to 44 pounds.

Engine Balancing Procedure

All rotating and reciprocating parts of an engine are balanced. Before the engine can be balanced, all of the following parts are needed:

- Crankshaft
- Vibration damper (harmonic balancer)
- Flywheel or flex plate
- Pressure plate
- All bolts, lock washers, keys, and spacers needed to assemble the above parts on the crankshaft
- Connecting rods
- Pistons
- Wrist pins

To balance a V-type engine, the following additional parts are needed:

- Rod bearings
- Piston rings
- Wrist pin locks (if full-floating piston pins)

The first step is to equalize the *reciprocating mass,* includes the pistons and rods. Reciprocating weight is also called *inertia weight.* The pistons should be weighed, including the piston pin and rings, to determine the lightest. Material should be ground from the heavier pistons until they match the weight of the lightest piston. Material should be removed from the weight balancing pads.

CAUTION: Do not grind or attempt to remove weight from the piston pin. This could weaken a highly stressed part and could lead to engine failure.

Connecting rods have a big end and a small end. The big end of the rod is considered to be part of the rotating weight and the small end part of the reciprocating weight after the rod has been reconditioned. The two ends should be weighed and matched separately. See Figure 28-5.

After all of the rods have been weighed, then material should be removed from the balancing pads of the heavier rods until they match the lightest rods. See Figure 28-6.

Bob Weights

Bob weights are attached to the rod journals on V-type engines to simulate the weight of the rods and pistons. See Figure 28-7. The bob weight must equal the total of the following for each journal:

- Rotating weight
- A percentage of the reciprocating weight
- An amount for the weight of the oil trapped between the journal and the bearing The rotating weight includes the big end of the connecting rod and the connecting rod bearings.

FIGURE 28-5   Weighing the big end of a connecting rod on a scale that keeps it perfectly horizontal so that each end can be weighed separately.

NOTE: On V-8 engines, two rods share a crankpin so that the calculations for bob weight, including the weight of both big ends of the connecting rods and bearings, should be taken into consideration.

The reciprocating weight includes the small end of the rod(s) and the piston assemblies, which include the rings, pin, and locks, if equipped.

Balancing Factor

A balancing factor is a formula used to determine what percentage (usually 50%) of the reciprocating weight needs to be included in the bob weight. Most balancing machines

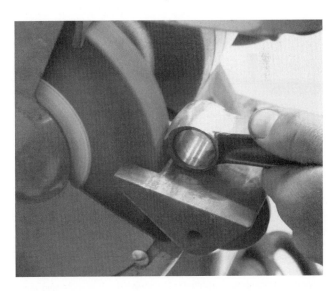

FIGURE 28-6   Removing material from the balancing pad on the small end of the rod to match it to the weight of the small end of the lightest rod being used in the engine.

FIGURE 28-7   A crankshaft with bob weights attached.

calculate the bob weight automatically after inputting all of the weight information and then display where and how much material needs to be removed to achieve proper balance. See Figure 28-8.

A drill is commonly used to remove weight from the counterweight of the crankshaft to achieve proper balance. See Figure 28-9. After the specified material has been removed, the counterweight is checked again by the balance machine. When the procedure has been completed, the *rotating assembly* is then in balance.

Sometimes weight has to be added to a crankshaft to achieve proper balance. In this case, a hole is drilled parallel to the crankshaft in a counterweight and extra heavy metal is added.

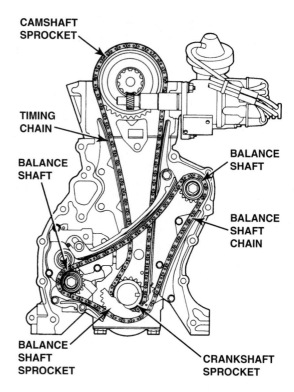

FIGURE 28-10   Worn balance shaft bearings and chains can be the cause of a noisy engine.

FIGURE 28-8   The display of a crankshaft balancer showing where weight needs to be removed to achieve a balanced assembly.

TECH TIP

NOISY ENGINE? CHECK THE CHAINS

Some 4-cylinder engines use multiple chains to drive the overhead camshafts and balance shafts. See Figure 28-10. If any one of these chains has stretched, it can cause noise as it hits the chain guide. Bearings for the balance shafts are also a common cause of engine noise.

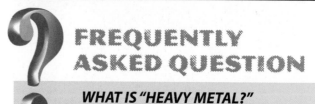

FREQUENTLY ASKED QUESTION

WHAT IS "HEAVY METAL?"

Heavy metal, also called Mallory metal, is a tungsten steel alloy that is one and half times heavier than lead. It is used to add weight to a crankshaft if needed usually on engines that have been stroked using a stroker crankshaft. The heavy metal must be installed parallel to the centerline axis of the crankshaft.

FIGURE 28-9   A drill is usually used to remove weight from the crankshaft to achieve proper balance.

ROD WEIGHING   Step-by-Step

STEP 1 The equipment needed to weigh connecting rods includes the scale and the connecting rod big-end and small-end holding fixtures.

STEP 2 Before starting, double-check that all rods have been reconditioned and that the bolts and nuts are replaced, if necessary.

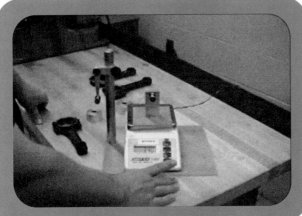

STEP 3 Start the weighing process by weighing the fixture used to hold the small end of the rod and then set the scale to zero.

STEP 4 Select the proper-size holding fixture for the big end of the rod.

STEP 5 Insert the big end of the rod into the holding fixture and place the small end on the scale.

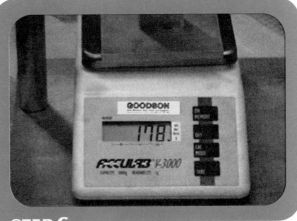

STEP 6 Read and record the weight of the small end of the rod.

(continued)

ROD WEIGHING   continued

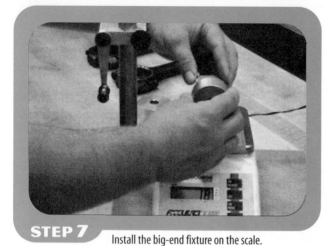

STEP 7   Install the big-end fixture on the scale.

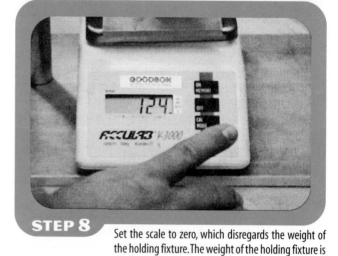

STEP 8   Set the scale to zero, which disregards the weight of the holding fixture. The weight of the holding fixture is called the tare weight.

STEP 9   Weigh the big end of the rod.

STEP 10   Record all weights from all connecting rods to be used in the engine. Compare the readings and determine where weight must be removed to make all rods weigh the same as the lightest rod in the set.

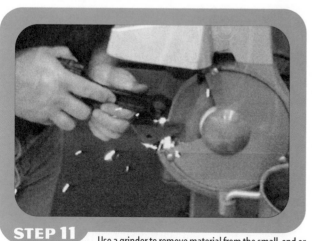

STEP 11   Use a grinder to remove material from the small-end or big-end balancing pad to achieve the proper weight.

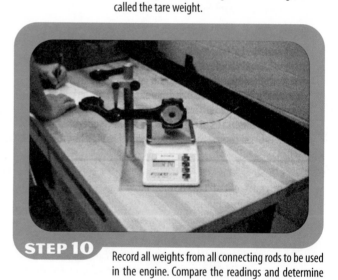

STEP 12   Remeasure the weight of the rod after grinding.

CRANKSHAFT BALANCING   Step-by-Step

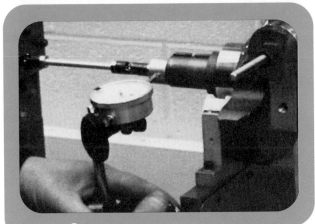

STEP 1 Before the crankshaft can be checked for balance, the crankshaft has to be installed onto the balancer and the sensor at the end adjusted to eliminate any runout.

STEP 2 The bearings on which the crankshaft rides must be properly lubricated.

STEP 3 All necessary dimensions and weights are entered into the balancer and the balancer itself does the necessary calculations.

STEP 4 After the correct bob weights have been attached to the rod bearing journals and all necessary preliminary steps have been completed, the balancer is turned on and the crankshaft is spun.

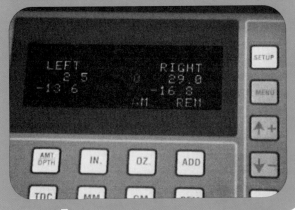

STEP 5 After the crankshaft stops spinning, the balancer displays the amount of weight (in grams) that should be removed and its location.

STEP 6 An air-powered die grinder is being used to remove a small amount of weight from the crankshaft in the location specified by the balancer.

(continued)

CRANKSHAFT BALANCING continued

STEP 7 Before spinning the crankshaft to recheck the balance, the rubbing blocks are again lubricated.

STEP 8 The crankshaft is spun again to check the balance after material has been removed.

STEP 9 A small amount of additional material is being removed using a hand grinder.

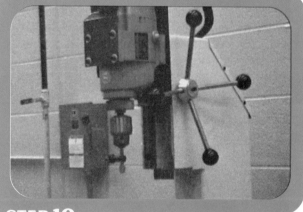

STEP 10 If more weight needs to be removed, the balancer is programmed to direct the technician as to how deep to drill into the counterweight and with which diameter drill bit.

STEP 11 This counterweight has been drilled to reduce its weight. The bigger the diameter and the deeper the hole is drilled, the more weight is removed from the crankshaft counterweight.

STEP 12 After weight has been drilled or ground from the crankshaft, the display will indicate that it is within acceptable balance tolerance.

SUMMARY

1. Primary vibration is a strong low-frequency vibration caused by the movement of the piston traveling up and down in the cylinder.

2. Secondary vibration is created by the slight differences in the inertia of the pistons between top dead center and bottom dead center.

3. Balance shafts are used to counteract vibration created in the engine.

4. Proper balancing of the engine is important for smooth operation.

5. Both rotating weight and reciprocating weight are considered during the balancing procedure.

REVIEW QUESTIONS

1. Why is a balance shaft needed on some V-6 engines?

2. What parts must be measured when measuring rotating weight?

3. What parts must be measured when measuring reciprocating weight?

4. What is done to the crankshaft to achieve a balanced rotating engine assembly?

CHAPTER QUIZ

1. What part(s) primarily causes primary vibration?
   a. Harmonic balancer
   b. Pistons
   c. Flex plate
   d. Big end of the connecting rod

2. What part(s) primarily causes secondary vibration?
   a. Harmonic balancer
   b. Pistons
   c. Flex plate
   d. Big end of the connecting rod

3. Why does a 4-cylinder engine have very little, if any, primary vibration?
   a. A 4-cylinder engine uses a splayed crankshaft.
   b. A 4-cylinder engine has two pistons traveling upward at the same time two pistons are traveling downward, thereby canceling primary vibration.
   c. Two cylinders fire at the same time, reducing the primary vibration.
   d. The bore of 4-cylinder engines is small, reducing the primary vibration.

4. A balance shaft used in a 90-degree V-6 engine is used to correct what type of force?
   a. Primary vibration
   b. Secondary vibration
   c. Rocking couple
   d. Rolling couple

5. A gram weighs about the same as a _____.
   a. Paper clip
   b. Chicken feather
   c. Penny
   d. Dime

6. Reciprocating weight is also called _____.
   a. Balance weight
   b. Bob weight
   c. Rotating weight
   d. Inertia weight

7. Connecting rods should be weighed and balanced _____.
   a. Before reconditioning
   b. After reconditioning

8. Pistons and connecting rods can be ground from what area when removing weight?

   a. Balancing pad

   b. Weight bore

   c. Sides

   d. Thrust surface(s)

9. Which of the following is not reciprocating weight?

   a. Piston

   b. Big end of a connecting rod

   c. Small end of a connecting rod

   d. Piston ring

10. How is the crankshaft usually balanced?

   a. Material is welded onto the counterweight.

   b. Pistons are replaced until a matched set is achieved.

   c. Material is drilled out of the counterweight.

   d. Heavy metal is used to increase the weight of the counterweight.

CHAPTER 29

PREPARATION FOR ASSEMBLY

OBJECTIVES

After studying Chapter 29, the reader will be able to:

1. Describe the steps that should be followed in preparation for assembly.

2. Explain clamping force.

3. Discuss the advantages of performing a trial assembly of the engine.

KEY TERMS

Clamping Force (p. 563)
Cylinder Head Cover Gasket (p. 562)
Fogging Oil (p. 561)

Fretting (p. 564)
Head Gaskets (p. 562)

DETAILS, DETAILS, DETAILS

Successful engine assembly depends on getting all of the details right. Where to start? Start when all parts have been purchased or prepared for assembly.

When starting to assemble the engine, be sure to have all of the instructions from all of the parts used.

- **Read**—Read *all* instructions. Often very important information or suggested specifications are included and may be at the end.
- **Understand**—Be sure to fully understand everything that is stated in the instructions. If unsure as to what is meant, ask a knowledgeable technician or call the company to be sure that all procedures are clearly understood. This is especially important if working on an engine that is not very common, such as the Audi/Volkswagen W-8. This engine has seven rotating shafts, including four overhead camshafts, two counterrotating balance shafts, and the crankshaft. See Figure 29-1.
- **Follow**—Be sure to follow *all* of the instructions. Do not pick the easy procedures and skip others.

SHORT BLOCK PREPARATION

The details that should be checked on the block include:

- All passages should be clean and free of rust and debris.
- All cups and plugs should be installed.
- The final bore dimension is correct for the piston.
- The surface finish of the cylinder bore matches with the specified finish required for the piston rings that are going to be used.

- All sharp edges and burrs have been removed. See Figure 29-2.
- The main bearing bore (saddle) is straight and inline.
- The lifter bores have been honed and checked for proper dimension.

Surface Finish

The surface finish is important for the proper sealing of any gasket.

- Surface too rough—If the surface finish is too rough, the gasket will not be able to seal the deep grooves in the surface.
- Surface too smooth—If the surface finish is too smooth, the gasket can move out of proper location, causing leakage.

Surface finish is measured in microinches, usually abbreviated by using the Greek letter *mu* (μ) and the abbreviation for inches together (μin.).

- The higher the μin. finish, the rougher the surface.
- The lower the μin. finish, the smoother the surface. The specification for surface finish is usually specified in roughness average or Ra.

Engine Part Material	Gasket Material	Acceptable Surface Finish (Ra)
Cast iron/cast iron	Composite	60 to 80 μin.
Aluminum/cast iron	Composite	20 to 30 μin.
Aluminum/cast iron	Rubber-coated multilayered steel	20 to 30 μin.

Check the instruction sheet that comes with the gasket for the specified surface finish.

FIGURE 29-1 A uniquely designed W-8 engine installed in some Audi and Volkswagen vehicles. Rebuilding the engine would require detailed service information to be sure that all steps are taken to ensure proper assembly.

FIGURE 29-2 Deburring all sharp edges is an important step that has to be done to achieve proper engine assembly.

Checking Surfaces Before Assembly

All surfaces of an engine should be clean and straight and have the specified surface finish and flatness. Flatness is a measure of how much the surface varies in any 6-inch span. An industry standard maximum limit for flatness is usually 0.002 inch. If the surface is not flat, the gaskets will not be able to seal properly.

Preparing for Installation of Cylinder Head Studs

Similar to using studs for the main bearing caps, studs for cylinder heads are recommended for all high-performance applications. However, studs should not be used on a street-driven vehicle engine because the studs would prevent the cylinder heads from being removed unless the engine is first removed from the vehicle. Most vehicles do not have enough room under the hood to allow the cylinder heads to be moved upward far enough for removal.

Similar to main bearing caps, studs do provide for more accurate and consistent torque loading and clamping force. For example, when a bolt is used to attach a cylinder head, it is being twisted and pulled at the same time. In comparison, a stud is only being stretched. Also, a stud uses a fine thread for the retaining nut and this allows for more precise torque readings.

Preparing for Installation of Main Cap Studs

Purpose of Studs. For high-performance use, most experts recommend the use of studs instead of bolts. Studs are

TECH TIP

BE AWARE OF BMW ENGINE PROCEDURES

If rebuilding a BMW engine, check service information carefully because most require that threaded inserts be installed in all head bolt threads. Performing this operation can increase the cost and time needed. Always follow all recommended service procedures on the engine being serviced.

FIGURE 29-3 Main bearing studs installed on a V-8 block.

able to obtain more accurate torque values because studs do not twist during tightening like bolts. See Figure 29-3.

The use of studs for the main bearing saddles helps main cap alignment because the torque applied is more consistent and there is less chance of the bearing cap moving during the tightening operation.

Preparing Threaded Holes

Step 1   All threads in the block should be thoroughly cleaned. Use a thread chaser and not a tap as a tap could cut and remove metal. A chaser will restore the threads without removing metal.

Step 2   Use a calibrated torque wrench. Torque applied by a torque wrench can change over time due to temperature changes and how it is stored.

TECH TIP

CREEP UP ON THE TORQUE VALUE

Do not jerk or rapidly rotate a torque wrench. For best results and more even torque, slowly apply force to the torque wrench until it reaches the preset value or the designated torque. Jerking or rapidly moving the torque wrench will often cause the torque to be uneven and not accurate.

Step 3   Screw the studs into the block *finger-tight only*. Do not tighten a stud more than finger-tight. A nut should not be used to double nut a stud to keep it in position.

NOTE: The tightening torque in the installation instructions is for the *nut* and not the stud itself.

In most cases, a thread locker such as Loctite 242 can be used on the threads of the stud being inserted into the block to make the installation of the stud more permanent.

CAUTION: If a thread locker is used, be sure to immediately install the main bearing caps before the compound cures to help avoid misalignment.

CYLINDER HEAD PREPARATION

The details that should be checked on the cylinder head(s) include:

- The surface finish of the fire deck is as specified for the head gasket type to be used.
- All valves should be checked for leakage by pouring mineral spirits into the intake and exhaust ports and looking for leakage past the valves.
- All valve springs should be checked for even spring pressure and installed height.
- Check for proper pushrod length. If the cylinder head(s) has been machined and/or the block deck machined, the pushrods may be too long. If the pushrods are too long, the rocker arm geometry will not be correct. One problem that can occur with incorrect rocker arm geometry is spring bind, which can cause severe engine damage.
- If replacement rocker arms are used, be sure that the geometry and total lift will be okay.

REAL WORLD FIX

VALVE SPRINGS CAN VARY

A technician was building a small-block Chevrolet V-8 engine at home and was doing the final detailed checks and found that many of the valve springs did not have the same tension. Using a borrowed valve spring tester, the technician visited a local parts store and measured all of the valve springs that the store had in stock. The technician selected and purchased the 16 that were within specification and were also within a very narrow range of tension. While having all valve springs equal may or may not affect engine operation, the technician was pleased that all of the valve springs were equal.

FIGURE 29-4   A trial assembly showed that some grinding of the block will be needed to provide clearance for the counterweight of the crankshaft. Also, notice that the engine has been equipped with studs for the four-bolt main bearing caps.

TRIAL ASSEMBLY

Short Block

Before performing final engine assembly, the wise technician checks that all parts will fit and work. This is especially important if using a different crankshaft that changes the stroke. See Figure 29-4 for an example of a 400-cu. in. Chevrolet crankshaft being fitted to a 350-cu. in. Chevrolet engine.

Valve Train

Another place where a trial fit is needed is in the valve train. Some timing chain mechanisms require more space than the stock component so some machining may be needed.

If the rocker arms have been upgraded to roller rockers, these should be installed and checked that the tip of the roller rests at the center of the valve stem. See Figure 29-5.

If there is a problem, further investigation will be needed because the pushrods may be too long due to machining of the block deck and/or cylinder head. Rotate the engine and check for proper clearance throughout the entire opening and closing of the valves. Use a feeler gauge between the coils of the valve spring to check for coil bind. If coil bind occurs, a different camshaft should be used.

FIGURE 29-6   Fogging oil is used to cover bare metal parts to prevent corrosion when the engine is being stored.

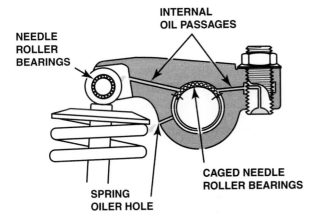

FIGURE 29-5   A typical high-performance aftermarket rocker arm that is equipped with needle roller bearings at the valve stem end and caged needle bearings at the pivot shaft end to reduce friction, which increases engine horsepower and improves fuel economy.

TECH TIP

FOGGING OIL AND ASSEMBLY FLUID

When assembling an engine, the parts should be coated with a light oil film to keep them from rusting. This type of oil is commonly referred to as **fogging oil** and is available in spray cans. See Figure 29-6.

During engine assembly, the internal parts should be lubricated. While engine oil or grease could be used, most experts recommend the use of a specific lubricant designed for engine assembly. This lubricant is designed to remain on the parts and not drip or run and is called assembly lube. See Figure 29-7.

FIGURE 29-7   Engine assembly lube is recommended to be used on engine parts during assembly.

TECH TIP

KEEP THE ENGINE COVERED

Using a large plastic trash bag is an excellent way to keep the engine clean when storing it between work sessions. See Figure 29-8.

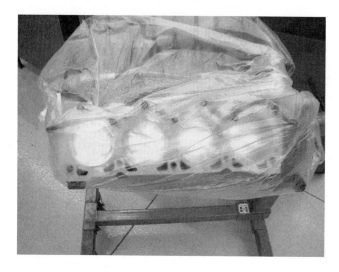

FIGURE 29-8 Placing a plastic trash bag over the engine and tying it shut is an excellent way to keep the engine clean.

CHECK THE ANGLE BETWEEN HEADS

During the trial assembly, use a gauge to check that the heads are at the correct angle to ensure proper intake manifold gasket sealing. See Figure 29-9.

PAINTING THE ENGINE

While most technicians wait until the engine has been assembled, started, and tested before painting, others prefer to paint each component or assembly individually. If components are being painted before assembly, be sure to keep the paint off of the mating surfaces. Only use paint that can withstand the temperature of an operating engine.

GASKETS AND CLAMPING FORCE

Purpose and Function

A gasket is a device used to fill a space or gap between two objects to prevent leakage from occurring either from the inside outward or outside inward. In an engine, gaskets are used between the cylinder head and engine block, which are called *head gaskets.* A gasket is also used between the valve cover and the cylinder head. These gaskets are called *valve cover gaskets, cylinder head cover gaskets,* or *rocker arm cover gaskets,* depending on the make and model of engine. Other gaskets are used between the intake and exhaust manifolds and the cylinder head(s) as well as on the oil pan and front covers of the engine.

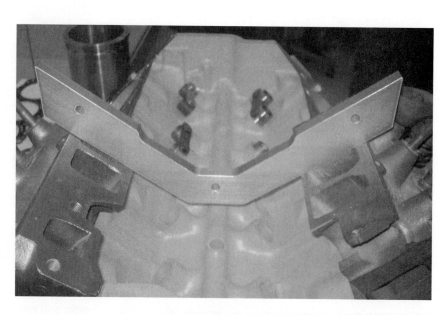

FIGURE 29-9 An angle gauge being used to check the angle between the cylinder heads on this small-block Chevrolet V-8 engine.

Types of Gaskets

Gaskets are made from a variety of materials and construction types based mainly on the need. Gaskets can be made from sheet or solid materials, such as paper, rubber, cork, felt, or fiberglass and combined with other materials, if necessary, such as neoprene and plastic. Some newer-style gaskets combine two or more gaskets into one easy-to-use unit. Consider using one of these gaskets to eliminate gaps and thereby reduce the chance of leakage. See Figure 29-10.

Clamping Force

Clamping force is the amount of force exerted on a gasket. The clamping force is not the same as the torque applied to the fastener. When tightening a bolt or nut, about 80% of the applied torque is used to overcome friction between the threads. Therefore, it is very important that the threads be clean and lubricated with the proper (specified) lubricant.

Fastener Consideration

Because most of the torque applied to a fastener is absorbed by friction, it is extremely important that the following steps be performed:

Step 1   Clean the threads of all fasteners before using.
Step 2   Check service information for the specified thread lubricant. Many vehicle manufacturers recommend the use of 30 weight engine oil (SAE 30).

CAUTION: SAE 5W-30 or SAE 10W-30 is not the same as SAE 30 engine oil. A multiviscosity oil such as SAE 5W-30 is actually SAE 5 oil with additives to provide the protection of a SAE 30 oil when it gets hot. Always use the exact oil specified by the vehicle manufacturer.

If using aftermarket bolts or studs, such as ARP (American Racing Products®), use the lubricant the company specifies

FREQUENTLY ASKED QUESTION

WHY DO BOTH HEAD GASKETS HAVE "FRONT" MARKED?

A common question asked by beginning technicians or students is how to install head gaskets on a V-6 engine that is mounted transversely (sideways) in the vehicle. The technician usually notices that "front" is marked on one gasket and therefore installs that gasket on the block on top of the forward facing cylinder bank. Then, the other gasket is picked up and the technician notices that "front" is also marked on this gasket. How could both be marked front? There must be some mistake. The mistake is in the terminology used. In the case of head gaskets, the "front" means toward the accessory belt end of the engine and *not* on the cylinder bank toward the front of the vehicle.

TECH TIP

ALWAYS "EXERCISE" NEW BOLTS

New bolts and studs are manufactured by rolling the threads and heat treating. Due to this operation, the threads usually have some rough areas, which affect the clamping force on the gasket. Many engine building experts recommend that all new bolts be installed in the engine using a new or used gasket and torqued to specifications at least five times, except for torque-to-yield bolts. This process burnishes the ramps of the threads and makes the fastener provide a more even clamping force. The bolts should be torqued and removed and then torqued again, using the recommended lubricant.

FIGURE 29-10   An oil pan gasket assembly which includes the windage tray is an aftermarket part that can be used to simplify assembly.

TECH TIP

RUBBER OR CONTACT CEMENT

One of the reasons why gaskets fail is due to being moved during installation. Some gaskets, such as cork or rubber valve cover gaskets or oil pan gaskets, can be held onto the cover using a rubber or contact cement.

To use a rubber or contact cement, perform the following steps:

Step 1 Apply a thin layer to one side of the gasket and to the cover where the gasket will be placed.

Step 2 Allow the surfaces to air-dry until touch free.

Step 3 Carefully place the gaskets onto the cover being sure to align all of the holes.

CAUTION: Do not attempt to remove the gasket and reposition it. The glue is strong and the gasket will be damaged if removed. If the gasket has been incorrectly installed, remove all of the gasket, clean the gasket surface, and repeat the installation using a new gasket.

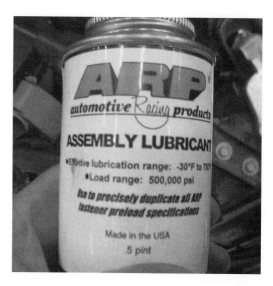

FIGURE 29-11 Special lubricant is specified when using ARP fasteners. This lubricant reduces the friction of the threads and therefore a lower-than-factory-specified torque specification is mandated when using the special lubricant.

FIGURE 29-12 This intake manifold gasket was damaged due to fretting. Newer designs allow for more movement between the intake manifold and the cylinder head.

and the torque they recommend. Do not use ARP lubricant and the factory torque specifications or the fasteners will be greatly overtightened. The same applies if using thread sealant to the threads of fasteners being installed in wet holes (holes that extend into the cooling passages). See Figure 29-11.

Gasket Failures

Gaskets can fail to seal properly, but the root cause is often a severe condition. For example, a head gasket can fail due to detonation (spark knock or ping), which causes extreme pressure to be exerted on the armor of the head gasket, causing it to deform. Improper installation such as incorrect torquing sequence can cause gasket failure.

Fretting is a condition that can destroy intake manifold gaskets and is caused by the unequal expansion and contraction of two different engine materials. For example, if the intake manifold is constructed of aluminum and the cylinder heads are cast iron, the intake manifold will expand more than the cylinder heads. This causes a shearing effect, which can destroy the gasket. See Figure 29-12. Therefore, before assembling an engine, check for newer gasket designs that are often different from the type originally used in the engine.

SUMMARY

1. Gaskets are used to fill a space or gap between two objects to prevent leakage from occurring.
2. There are many types of gaskets including cylinder head cover gaskets, valve cover gaskets, and timing cover gaskets.
3. The clamping force which keeps the gaskets compressed is achieved by torquing the fastener to a specified torque and/or angle.
4. Rubber or contact cement is used to hold a gasket in place.
5. Sealers are used to help gaskets seal.

REVIEW QUESTIONS

1. What is the purpose of a gasket?
2. Why is clamping force different from bolt torque?
3. What is the difference between a bolt and a stud?

CHAPTER QUIZ

1. About how much of the turning torque applied to a head bolt is lost to friction?
   a. 20%
   b. 40%
   c. 60%
   d. 80%

2. Service information states that SAE 30 engine oil should be used on the threads of the head bolts before installation and torquing. Technician A says that SAE 5W-30 will work. Technician B says that SAE 10W-30 will work. Which technician is correct?
   a. Technician A only
   b. Technician B only
   c. Both Technicians A and B
   d. Neither Technician A nor B

3. Technician A says that the torque applied to the head bolts is the same as the clamping force on the gasket. Technician B says that the clamping force is the force actually applied to the surfaces of the gasket. Which technician is correct?
   a. Technician A only
   b. Technician B only
   c. Both Technicians A and B
   d. Neither Technician A nor B

4. A coating that is used to keep an engine from rusting during assembly is called _____?
   a. Engine oil
   b. Assembly lube
   c. Flogging oil
   d. Penetrating oil

5. Head gasket installation is being discussed. Technician A says that the surface finish of the cylinder head or block deck is very important for proper sealing to occur. Technician B says that if "front" is marked on a head gasket, the mark should be installed near the accessory belt end of the engine. Which technician is correct?
   a. Technician A only
   b. Technician B only
   c. Both Technicians A and B
   d. Neither Technician A nor B

6. Technician A says that studs should be installed finger tight. Technician B says that thread locker must be used if installing studs. Which technician is correct?
   a. Technician A only
   b. Technician B only
   c. Both Technicians A and B
   d. Neither Technician A nor B

7. What can be used to check that the heads are at the proper angle for the intake manifold?
   a. A metal rule
   b. An angle gauge
   c. A tape measure
   d. A dial indicator

8. What should be used to check for coil bind?
   a. dial indicator
   b. feeler gauge
   c. micrometer
   d. angle gauge

9. If a stoker crankshaft is being installed, what additional work may be required?

   a. The crankshaft may have to be shortened to fit the block

   b. The crankshaft main bearing journals will need to reground

   c. The block may need to be ground for clearance

   d. Both a and b

10. The movement of engine parts that are constructed from two different materials, such as aluminum and cast iron, is called _____.

    a. Cracking

    b. Fretting

    c. Shearing

    d. Stretching

CHAPTER 30

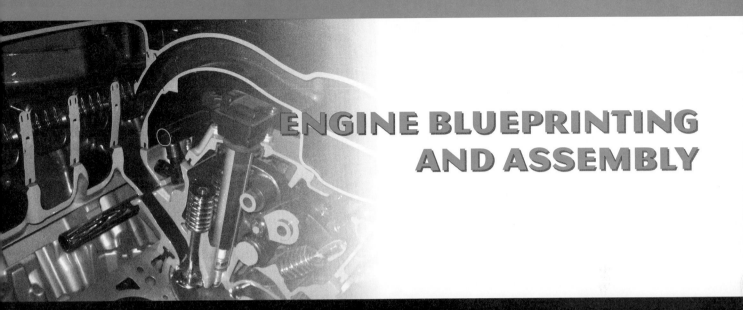

ENGINE BLUEPRINTING AND ASSEMBLY

OBJECTIVES

After studying Chapter 30, the reader will be able to:

1. Prepare for Engine Repair (A1) ASE certification test content area "C" (Engine Block Diagnosis and Repair).

2. List the steps for assembling an engine.

3. Describe how to measure bearing oil clearance using plastic gauging material.

4. Explain how to check for crankshaft end play and connecting rod side clearance.

5. Discuss how to fit pistons to individual cylinder bores.

6. Describe how to test for proper oil pressure before starting the engine.

KEY TERMS

All parts are attached to the engine block. The block, therefore, must be prepared before assembly can begin. The key to proper assembly of any engine is cleanliness. The work area and the workbench space must be clean to prevent dirt or other engine-damaging particles from being picked up and causing possible serious engine damage.

BLUEPRINTING

The term *blueprinting* means that all of the components of an engine have been carefully measured and checked that they match the specifications listed by the manufacturer. The engine manufacturer builds a new engine to the dimensions and tolerances specified on the blueprint, which is the engineering drawing of the parts and assembly. Therefore, to "blueprint" an engine is to make sure that all component parts and dimensions are within the range specified by the engine manufacturer.

BLOCK PREPARATION

All surfaces of the block should also be checked for damage resulting from the machining processes. Items that should be done before assembly begins include the following:

1. The block, including the oil gallery passages, should be thoroughly cleaned. See Figures 30-1 and 30-2.
2. All threaded bolt holes should be chamfered.
3. All threaded holes should be cleaned with a tap. See Figure 30-3.

INSTALLING CUPS AND PLUGS

Oil gallery plugs should be installed using sealant on the threads. Core holes left in the external block wall are machined

FIGURE 30-2 All oil galleries should be cleaned using soap (detergent) and water using a long oil gallery cleaning brush.

FIGURE 30-3 All threaded holes should be cleaned using a thread chaser or a bottoming tap.

FIGURE 30-1 The best way to clean cylinders is to use soap (detergent) and water and thoroughly clean using a large washing brush. This method floats the machining particles out of the block and washes them away.

and sealed with soft core plugs or expansion plugs (also called freeze plugs or **welsh plugs).**

CAUTION: Avoid using Teflon tape on the threads of oil gallery plugs. The tape is often cut by the threads, and thin strips of the tape are then free to flow through the oil galleries where the tape can cause a clog, thereby limiting lubricating engine oil to important parts of the engine.

Soft plugs are of two designs:

- **Convex type.** The core hole is counter bored with a shoulder. The convex soft plug is placed in the counter bore, convex side out. It is driven in and upset with a fitted seating tool. This causes the edge of the soft plug to enlarge to hold it in place. Figure 30-4 shows an installed convex soft plug. A convex plug should be driven in until it reaches the counter bore of the core plug hole.

- **Cup type.** This most common type fits into a smooth, straight hole. The outer edge of the cup is slightly bell mouthed. The bell mouth causes it to tighten when it is driven into the hole to the correct depth with a seating tool. An installed cup-type soft plug is shown in Figure 30-5. A cup plug is installed about 0.020 to 0.050 inch (0.5 to 1.3 millimeters) below the surface of the block, using sealant to prevent leaks. See Figure 30-6.

INSTALLING CAM BEARINGS

A cam bearing installing tool is required to insert the new cam bearing without damaging the bearing. A number of tool manufacturers design and sell cam bearing installing tools. Their common feature is a shoulder on a bushing that fits inside the cam bearing, with a means of keeping the bearing aligned as it is installed. Figure 30-7 shows a camshaft bearing on the removing and installing tool. The bearing is placed on the bushing of the tool and rotated to properly align the oil hole. The

FIGURE 30-5 This engine uses many cup plugs to block off coolant and oil passages as well as a large plug over the end of the camshaft bore.

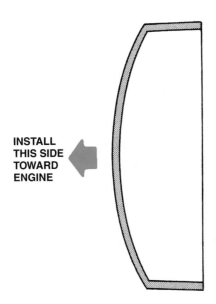

FIGURE 30-4 Convex plugs have a deep tapered flange. The flange should be coated with water-resistant sealer before being driven into the block.

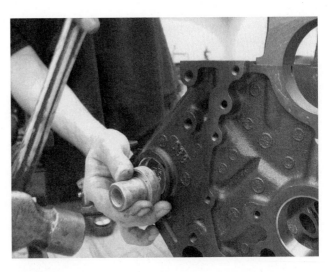

FIGURE 30-6 Sealer should be used on the cup plug before being driven into the block.

bearing is then forced into the bearing bore of the block by either a pulling screw or a slide hammer. A pulling screw type of tool is illustrated in Figure 30-8. The installed bearing must be checked to make sure that it has the correct depth and that the oil hole is indexed with the oil passage in the block. No additional service is required on cam bearings that have been properly installed. The opening at the back of the camshaft is closed with an expansion plug.

CAUSES OF PREMATURE BEARING FAILURE

According to a major manufacturer of engine bearings, the major causes of premature (shortly after installation) bearing failure include the following:

FIGURE 30-7 Cam bearing tool being used to remove a used cam bearing.

Dirt (45%)
Misassembly (13%)
Misalignment (13%)
Lack of lubrication (11%)
Overloading or lugging (10%)
Corrosion (4%)
Other (4%)

Many cases of premature bearing failure may result from a combination of several of these items. Therefore, to help prevent bearing failure, *keep everything as clean as possible.*

MEASURING MAIN BEARING CLEARANCE

The engine is assembled from the inside out. Checks are made during assembly to ensure correct fits and proper assembly of the parts.

The main bearings are properly fit before the crankshaft is lubricated or turned. The oil clearance of both main and connecting rod bearings is set by selectively fitting the bearings. In this way, the oil clearance can be adjusted to within 0.0005 inch of the desired clearance.

CAUTION: Avoid touching bearings with bare hands. The oils on your fingers can start corrosion of the bearing materials. Always wear protective cloth or rubber gloves to avoid the possibility of damage to the bearing surface.

Bearings are usually made in 0.010, 0.020, and 0.030 inch undersize for use on reground journals. See Figure 30-9 for a typical main bearing set.

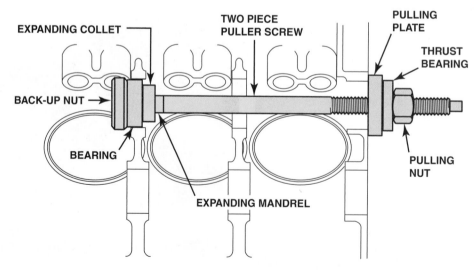

FIGURE 30-8 Screw-type puller being used to install a new cam bearing. Most cam bearings are crush fit. The full, round bearing is forced into the cam bearing bore. Cam bearing are installed "dry" without any lubrication.

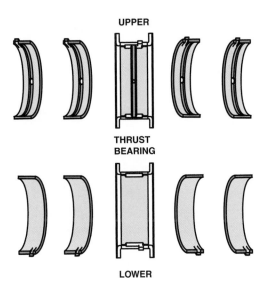

FIGURE 30-10   Crankshaft being carefully lowered into place.

FIGURE 30-9   Typical main bearing set. Note that the upper halves are grooved for better oil flow and the lower halves are plain for better load support. This bearing set uses the center main bearing for thrust control.

The crankshaft bearing journals should be measured with a micrometer to select the required bearing size. Remember that each of the main bearing caps will only fit one location and the caps must be positioned correctly. The correct-size bearings should be placed in the block and cap, making sure that the bearing tang locks into its slot. The upper main bearing has an oil feed hole. Carefully rest the clean crankshaft in the block on the upper main bearings. Lower it squarely, as shown in Figure 30-10, so that it does not damage the thrust bearing. Place a strip of Plastigage (gauging plastic) on each main bearing journal. Install the main bearing caps and tighten the bolts to specifications. Remove each cap and check the width of the Plastigage with the markings on the gauge envelope, as shown in Figure 30-11. This will indicate the oil clearance. If the shaft is out-of-round, the oil clearance should be checked at the point that has the *least* oil clearance.

CORRECTING BEARING CLEARANCE

The oil clearance can be reduced by 0.001 inch by replacing both bearing shells with bearing shells that are 0.001 inch undersize. The clearance can be reduced by 0.0005 inch by replacing only one of the bearing shells with a bearing shell that is 0.001 inch smaller. This smaller bearing shell should be placed in the engine-block side of the bearing (the upper shell). Oil clearance can be adjusted accurately using this procedure. Never mismatch the bearing shells by more than a 0.001 inch difference in size. Oil clearances normally run from 0.0005 to 0.002 inch.

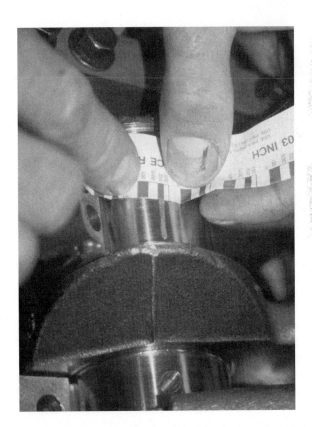

FIGURE 30-11   Checking the width of the plastic gauging strip to determine the oil clearance of the main bearing. An alternate method of determining oil clearance includes careful measurement of the crankshaft journal and bearings after they are installed and the main housing bore caps are torqued to specifications.

The crankshaft is removed once the correct oil clearance has been established. The rear oil seal is installed in the block and cap; then the crankshaft journals are lubricated with assembly lubricant.

TECH TIP

"ONE TO THREE"

When engine technicians are talking about clearances and specifications, the unit of measure most often used is thousandths of an inch (0.001 inch). Therefore, a clearance expressed as "one to three" would actually be a clearance of 0.001 to 0.003 inch. The same applies to parts of a thousandth of an inch. For example, a specification of 0.0005 to 0.0015 inch would be spoken of as simply being "one-half to one and one-half." The unit of a thousandth of an inch is assumed, and this method of speaking reduces errors and misunderstandings.

NOTE: Most engine clearance specifications fall within one- to three-thousandths of an inch. The written specification could be a misprint; therefore, if the specification does not fall within this general range, double-check the clearance value using a different source.

LIP SEAL INSTALLATION

Seals are always used at the front and rear of the crankshaft. Overhead cam engines may also have a seal at the front end of the camshaft and at the front end of an auxiliary accessory shaft. Either a lip seal or a rope seal is used in these locations. See Figure 30-12. The rear crankshaft oil seal is installed after the main bearings have been properly fit.

The lip seal may be molded in a steel case or it may be molded around a steel stiffener. The counter bore or guide that supports the seal must be thoroughly clean. In most cases, the back of the lip seal is dry when it is installed. Occasionally, a manufacturer will recommend the use of sealants behind the seal. The engine service manual should be consulted for specific sealing instructions. The lip of the seal should be well lubricated before the shaft and cap are installed. See Figures 30-13 and 30-14.

CAUTION: Teflon seals should not be lubricated. This type of seal should be installed dry. When the engine is first started, some of the Teflon transfers to the crankshaft so a Teflon-to-Teflon surface is created. Even touching the seal with your hands could remove some of the outer coating on the seal and could cause a leak. Carefully read, understand, and follow the installation instructions that should come with the seal.

FIGURE 30-12 Lip-type rear main bearing seal in place. The crankshaft is removed.

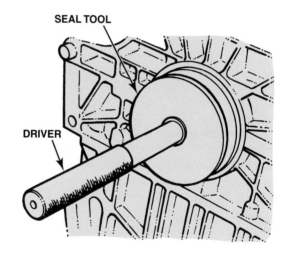

FIGURE 30-13 Always use the proper driver to install a main seal. Never pound directly on the seal.

ROPE SEAL INSTALLATION

Rope-type seals, usually called **braided fabric seals,** are sometimes used as rear crankshaft oil seals. Some engines manufactured by Buick use rope-type seals at both the front and rear of the crankshaft. Rope-type oil seals must be compressed tightly into the groove so that no oil can leak behind them. With the crankshaft removed, the upper half of the rope seal is put in a clean groove and compressed by rolling a round object against it to force it tightly into the groove. A piece of pipe, a large socket, or even a hammer handle can be used for this, as shown in Figure 30-15. When the seal is fully seated in the groove, the ends that extend above the parting surface are cut to be flush with the surface using a sharp single-edge razor blade or a sharp tool specially designed to cut the seal.

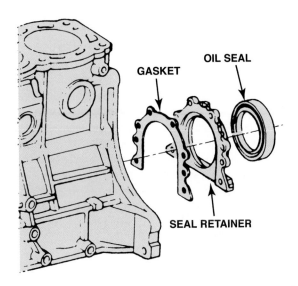

FIGURE 30-14   The rear seal for this engine mounts to a retainer plate. The retainer is then bolted to the engine block.

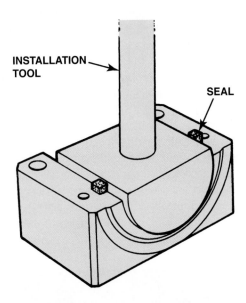

FIGURE 30-15   Use a special tool or other round object like a hammer handle to roll the seal to the bottom of the groove.

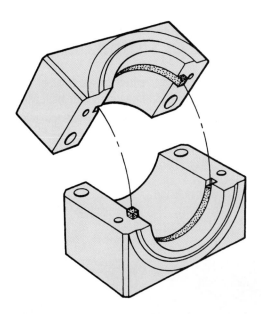

FIGURE 30-16   Many engine builders prefer to stagger the parting lines of a split seal.

FIGURE 30-17   Engine assembly lubricant is best to use because it contains additives that provide protection to engine parts during the critical original start-up phase.

The same procedures are used to install the lower half of the rope seal in the rear main bearing cap or seal retainer. See Figure 30-16.

INSTALLING THE CRANKSHAFT

The main bearing saddles, the caps, and the back of all the main bearing shells should be wiped clean; the bearing shells can then be put in place. It is important that each bearing tang line up with the slot in the bearing support.

The bearing shells must have some spread to hold them in the bearing saddles and caps during assembly. The surface of the bearings is then given a thin coating of assembly lubricant to provide initial lubrication for engine start-up. See Figure 30-17.

The crankshaft with lubricant on the journals is carefully placed in the bearings to avoid damage to the thrust bearing surfaces. The bearing caps are installed with their identification numbers correctly positioned. The caps were originally machined in place, so they can only fit correctly in their original position. The main bearing cap bolts are tightened finger-tight, and the crankshaft is rotated. It should rotate freely.

MEASURING THRUST BEARING CLEARANCE

Pry the crankshaft forward and rearward to align the cap half of the thrust bearing with the block saddle half. Most engine specifications for thrust bearing clearance (also called **crankshaft end play**) can range from 0.002 to 0.012 inch (0.02 to 0.3 millimeter). This clearance or play can be measured with a feeler gauge (Figure 30-18) or a dial indicator (Figure 30-19).

If the clearance is too great, oversize main thrust bearings may be available for the engine. Semifinished bearings may have to be purchased and machined to size to restore proper tolerance.

FIGURE 30-18   Checking crankshaft thrust bearing clearance with a feeler gauge. The technician in this photo has not yet installed the thrust bearing cap; this allows a better view of the actual movement and clearance as the crankshaft is pried back and forth.

FIGURE 30-19   A dial indicator is being used to check the crankshaft end play (also known as thrust bearing clearance). Always follow the manufacturer's recommended testing procedures.

TIGHTENING PROCEDURE FOR THE MAIN BEARING

Tighten the main bearing caps to the specified assembly torque, and in the specified sequence. Many manufacturers require that the crankshaft be pried forward or rearward during the main bearing tightening process. The crankshaft should turn freely after all main bearing cap bolts are fully torqued. See Figure 30-20. It should never require over 5 pound-feet (6.75 Newton-meters [N-m]) of torque to rotate the crankshaft. An increase in the torque needed to rotate the crankshaft is often caused by a foreign particle that was not removed during cleanup. It may be on the bearing surface, on the crankshaft journal, or between the bearing and saddle.

INSTALLING TIMING CHAINS AND GEARS

On pushrod engines, the timing gears or chain and sprocket can be installed after the crankshaft. The timing marks should be aligned according to the factory-specified marks. See Figure 30-21. When used, the replaceable fuel-pump eccentric is installed as the cam sprocket is fastened to the cam. The crankshaft should be rotated several times to see that the camshaft and timing gears or chain rotate freely. The timing mark alignment should be rechecked at this time. If the engine is equipped with a slinger ring, it should also be installed on the crankshaft, in front of the crankshaft gear.

It is assumed that the front oil seal is installed in the cover. The timing cover and gasket are placed over the timing gears and/or chain and sprockets. The attaching bolts are loosely installed to allow the damper hub to align with the cover as it

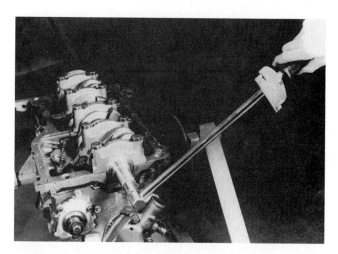

FIGURE 30-20   Measuring the crankshaft turning torque after each main bearing cap is properly tightened. An abnormal increase in torque indicates a problem that should be corrected before additional assembly.

FIGURE 30-21 Timing chain and gears can be installed after the crankshaft and camshaft have been installed. The technician is rotating the crankshaft using the harmonic balancer bolt to check for proper rotating torque and to confirm that the timing marks are aligned.

fits in the seal. The damper is installed on the crankshaft. On some engines, it is a press-fit and on others it is held with a large center bolt. After the damper is secured, the attaching bolts on the timing cover can be tightened to the specified torque.

PISTON FITTING

After thorough block cleaning, the piston-to-cylinder clearance should be checked to ensure that the piston properly fits the cylinder in which it is to operate. The fit can be checked by determining the difference in the measured size of the piston and cylinder. A **strip feeler gauge** placed between the piston and the cylinder can be used to measure the piston-to-cylinder clearance. The gauge thickness is the desired clearance measurement. Typical piston clearances range from about 0.0005 in. (1/2 thousandth of an inch) to 0.0025 in. (2 1/2 thousandths of an inch) (0.02 to 0.06 millimeter).

The cylinders and pistons, without rings, should be wiped thoroughly clean to remove any excess protective lubricant and dust that may have accumulated on the surface. The strip thickness (feeler) gauge is placed in the cylinder along the thrust side. The piston is inserted in the cylinder upside down, with the piston thrust surface against the thickness (feeler) gauge. The piston is held in the cylinder with the connecting rod as the strip gauge is withdrawn. A moderate pull (from 5 to 10 pounds) on the gauge indicates that the clearance is the same as the gauge thickness. A light pull indicates that the clearance is greater than the gauge thickness, whereas a heavy pull indicates that the clearance is smaller than the gauge thickness.

All pistons should be tested in all cylinder bores. Even though all cylinders were honed to the exact same dimension

FIGURE 30-22   A feeler gauge is used to check piston ring gap.

and all pistons were machined to the same diameter, some variation in dimensions will occur. *Each piston should be selectively fitted to each cylinder.* This procedure helps to prevent mismatched assembled components and results in a better-performing and longer-lasting engine. By checking all cylinders, the technician is also assured that the machining of the block was done correctly.

Ring End Gap

The bottom of the combustion chamber is sealed by the piston rings. They have to fit correctly in order to seal properly. Piston rings are checked both for side clearance and for gap. See Figure 30-22. Typical ring gap clearances are about 0.004 inch per inch of cylinder bore, or as follows:

Piston Diameter	Ring Gap
2 to 3 inches	0.007 to 0.018 inch
3 to 4 inches	0.010 to 0.020 inch
4 to 5 inches	0.013 to 0.023 inch

NOTE: If the gap is greater than recommended, some engine performance is lost. However, too small a gap will result in scuffing because of ring butting during operation, which forces the rings to scrape the cylinders.

If the ring gap is too large, the ring should be replaced with one having the next oversize diameter. If the ring gap is too small, the ring should be removed and filed to make the gap larger.

INSTALLING PISTON AND ROD ASSEMBLIES

Be sure to note which piston/rod assembly goes into which cylinder. Double-check the following:

1. Be sure the piston notch "front" or arrow points toward the front of the engine.
2. Be sure that the valve reliefs end up closest to the lifter valley on a V-type OHV engine.
3. Be sure that the larger valve reliefs always match the intake valve.
4. Make sure the connecting rod has been installed on the piston correctly—the chamfer on the side of the big end should face outward (toward the crank throw). See Figure 30-23.
5. Be sure the piston ring gaps are set according to the manufacturer's recommendations. See Figure 30-24.

The cylinder is wiped with a lintless cleaning cloth. It is then given a liberal coating of clean engine oil. This oil is spread over the entire cylinder wall surface by hand.

The connecting rod bearings are prepared for assembly in the same way, as are the main bearings. The piston can be dipped in a bath of clean engine oil to lubricate the piston pin as well as the piston rings. See Figure 30-25.

NOTE: Some overlapping (gapless) piston rings are installed dry, without oil. See Figure 30-26. Some manufacturers recommend oiling only the oil control ring. Always check the piston ring instruction sheet for the exact procedure.

When the piston is lifted from the oil, it is held and let drip for a few seconds. This allows the largest part of the oil to run

out of the piston and ring grooves. The **piston ring compressor** is then put on the piston to hold the rings in their grooves. See Figures 30-27 and 30-28.

The bearing cap is removed from the rod, and protectors are placed over the rod bolts. See Figure 30-29. The crankshaft is rotated so that the crankpin is at the bottom center. The upper rod bearing should be in the rod, and the piston should

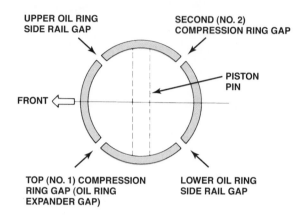

FIGURE 30-24   One method of piston ring installation showing the location of ring gaps. Always follow the manufacturer's recommended method for the location of ring gaps and for ring gap spacing.

FIGURE 30-25   Dipping the piston, with rings installed, into a container of engine oil is one method that can be used to ensure proper lubrication of pistons during installation in the engine cylinder. This method also ensures that the piston pin will be well lubricated.

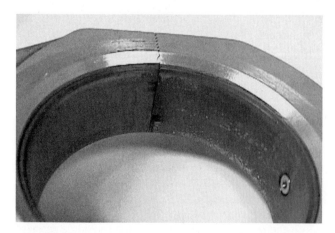

FIGURE 30-23   On V-type engines that use paired rod journals, the side of the rod with the large chamfer should face toward the crank throw (outward).

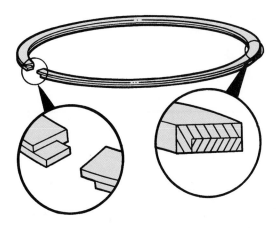

FIGURE 30-26   A gapless ring is made in two pieces that overlap.

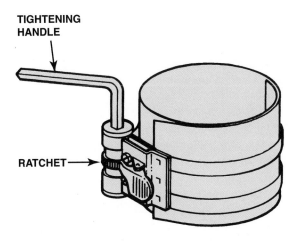

FIGURE 30-27   This style of ring compressor uses a ratchet to contract the spring band and compress the rings into their grooves.

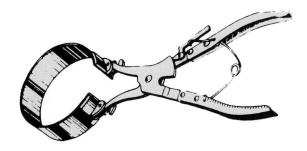

FIGURE 30-28   This plierslike tool is used to close the metal band around the piston to compress the rings. An assortment of bands are available to service different size pistons.

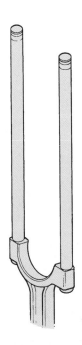

FIGURE 30-29   When threaded onto the rod bolts, these guides not only help align the rod but they also protect the threads and hold the bearing shell in place. The soft ends also will not damage the crankshaft journals.

FIGURE 30-30   Installing a piston using a ring compressor to hold the rings in the ring grooves of the piston and then using a hammer handle to drive the piston into the bore. Connecting rod bolt protectors have been installed to help prevent possible damage to the crankshafts during piston installation.

be turned so that the notch on the piston head is facing the front of the engine.

The piston and rod assembly is placed in the cylinder through the block deck. The ring compressor must be kept tightly against the block deck as the piston is pushed into the cylinder. The ring compressor holds the rings in their grooves so that they will enter the cylinder. See Figure 30-30. The piston is pushed into the cylinder until the rod bearing is fully seated on the journal.

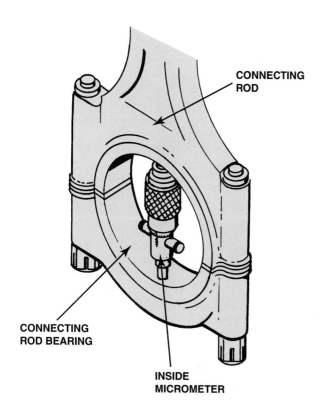

CONNECTING ROD

CONNECTING ROD BEARING

INSIDE MICROMETER

FIGURE 30-31 An inside micrometer can be used to measure the inside diameter of the big end of the connecting rod with the bearings installed. This dimension subtracted from the rod journal diameter is equal to the bearing clearance.

Connecting Rod Bearing Clearance

The rod cap, with the bearing in place, is put on the rod. There are two methods that can be used to check for proper connecting rod clearance:

- Use Plastigage following the same procedure discussed for main bearing clearance.
- Measure the assembled connecting rod big-end devices with the bearing installed and the caps torqued to specification. Subtract the diameter of the rod journal to determine the bearing clearance. See Figure 30-31.

NOTE: Be certain to check for piston-to-crankshaft counterweight clearance. Most manufacturers specify a minimum 0.060 inch (1.5 millimeters).

Connecting Rod Side Clearance

The connecting rods should be checked to make sure that they still have the correct side clearance. This is measured by

TECH TIP

TIGHTENING TIP FOR ROD BEARINGS

Even though the bearing clearances are checked, it is still a good idea to check and record the torque required to rotate the crankshaft with all piston rings dragging on the cylinder walls. Next, the retaining nuts on one bearing should be torqued; then the torque required to rotate the crankshaft should be rechecked and recorded. Follow the same procedure on all rod bearings. If tightening any one of the rod bearing caps causes a large increase in the torque required to rotate the crankshaft, immediately stop the tightening process. Determine the cause of the increased rotating torque using the same method, as used on the main bearings. Rotate the crankshaft for several revolutions to make sure that the assembly is turning freely and that there are no tight spots.

The rotating torque of the crankshaft with all connecting rod cap bolts fully torqued should be as follows:

- **four-cylinder engine**—20 pound-feet maximum (88 Newton-meters)
- **six-cylinder engine**—25 pound-feet maximum (110 Newton-meters)
- **eight-cylinder engine**—30 pound-feet maximum (132 Newton-meters)

---

fitting the correct thickness of feeler gauge between the connecting rod and the crankshaft cheek of the bearing journal. See Figure 30-32.

A dial gauge can also be set up to measure the connecting rod side clearance.

- *If the side clearance is too great*, excessive amounts of oil may escape that can cause lower-than-normal oil pressure. To correct excessive clearance:

  1. Weld and regrind or replace the crankshaft
  2. Carefully measure all connecting rods and replace those that are too thin or mismatched.

- *If the side clearance is too small*, there may not be enough room for heat expansion. To correct a side clearance that is too small:

  1. Regrind the crankshaft
  2. Replace the rods

FIGURE 30-32   The connecting rod side clearance is measured with a feeler gauge.

INSTALLING THE CAMSHAFT FOR OVERHEAD CAM ENGINES

The camshaft is usually installed on overhead cam engines before the head is fastened to the block deck. Some engines have the camshaft located directly over the valves. The cam bearings on these engines can be either one piece or split. The cam bearings and journals are lubricated before assembly. In other engine types, the camshaft bearings are split to allow the camshaft to be installed without the valves being depressed. The caps are tightened evenly to avoid bending the camshaft. The valve clearance or lash is checked with the overhead camshaft in place. Some engines use shims under a follower disk as shown in Figure 30-33. On these, the camshaft is turned so that the follower is on the base circle of the cam. The clearance of each bucket follower can then be checked with a feeler gauge. The amount of clearance is recorded and compared with the specified clearance, and then a shim of the required thickness is put in the top of the bucket followers, as shown in Figure 30-34.

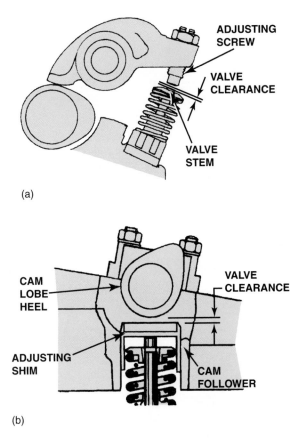

(a)

(b)

FIGURE 30-33   Valve clearance allows the metal parts to expand and maintain proper operation, both when the engine is cold or at normal operating temperature. (a) Adjustment is achieved by turning the adjusting screw. (b) Adjustment is achieved by changing the thickness of the adjusting shim.

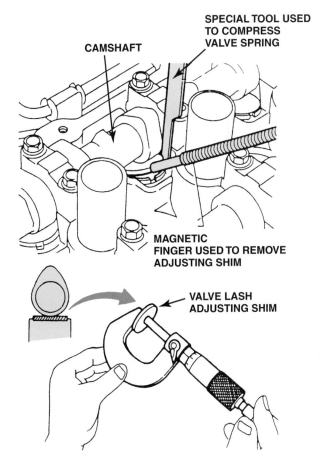

FIGURE 30-34   Some overhead camshaft engines use valve lash adjusting shims to adjust the valve lash. A special tool is usually required to compress the valve spring so that a magnet can remove the shim.

HEAD GASKETS

The head gasket is under the highest clamping loads. It must seal passages that carry coolant with antifreeze and often is required to seal a passage that carries hot engine oil. The most demanding job of the head gasket is to seal the combustion chamber. As a rule of thumb, about 75% of the head bolt clamping force is used to seal the combustion chamber. The remaining 25% seals the coolant and oil passages. See Figure 30-35.

The gasket must seal when the temperature is as low as 40° below zero and as high as 400°F (204°C). The combustion pressures can get up to 1,000 PSI (6,900 kPa) on gasoline engines.

Cylinder head bolts are tightened to a specified torque, which stretches the bolt. The combustion pressure tries to push the head upward and the piston downward on the power stroke. This puts additional stress on the head bolts and it reduces the clamping load on the head gasket just when the greatest seal is needed. On a normally aspirated engine (without turbocharging), a partial vacuum on the intake stroke tries to pull the head more tightly against the gasket. As the crankshaft rotates, the force on the head changes from pressure on the combustion stroke to vacuum on the intake stroke, then back to pressure. Newer engines have lightweight thin-wall castings. The castings are quite flexible, so that they move as the pressure in the combustion chamber changes from high pressure to vacuum. The gasket must be able to compress and recover fast enough to maintain a seal as the pressure in the combustion chamber changes back and forth between pressure and vacuum. As a result, head gaskets are made of several different materials assembled in numerous ways, depending on the engine.

NOTE: Older gasket designs often contained asbestos and required that the head bolts be retorqued after the engine had been run to operating temperature. Head gaskets today are dense and do not compress like those older-style gaskets. Therefore, most gaskets are called **no-retorque**-type gaskets, meaning the cylinder head bolts do not have to be retorqued after the engine has run. New gaskets do not contain asbestos.

Perforated Steel-Core Gaskets

A perforated steel-core gasket uses a wire-mesh core with fiber facings. Another design has rubber-fiber facings cemented to a solid steel core with an adhesive. See Figures 30-36 and 30-37. The thickness of the gasket is controlled by the thickness of the metal core. The facing is thick enough to compensate for minor warpage and surface defects.

TECH TIP

WOW—I CAN'T BELIEVE A CYLINDER CAN DEFORM THAT MUCH!

An automotive instructor used a dial bore gauge in a four-cylinder, cast-iron engine block cylinder to show students how much a block can deform. Using just one hand, the instructor was able to grasp both sides of the block and squeeze. The dial bore gauge showed that the cylinder deflected about 0.0003 in. (3/10,000 of an inch) just by squeezing the block with one hand—and that was with a cast-iron block!

After this demonstration, the students were more careful during engine assembly and always used a torque wrench on each and every fastener that was installed in or on the engine block.

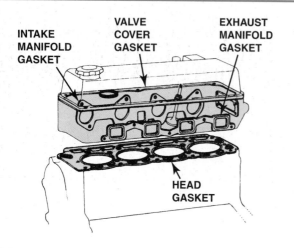

FIGURE 30-35 Gaskets help prevent leaks between two surfaces.

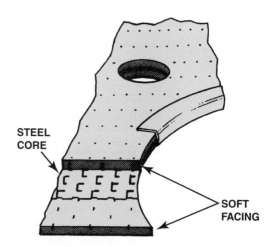

FIGURE 30-36 A typical perforated steel core head gasket with a graphite or composite facing material.

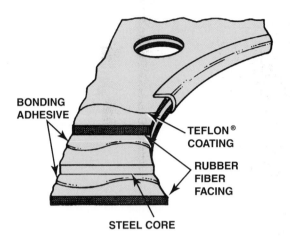

FIGURE 30-37   A solid steel core head gasket with a non-stick coating, which allows some movement between the block and the head, which is especially important on engines that use cast-iron blocks with aluminum cylinder heads.

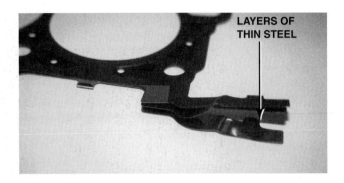

FIGURE 30-39   Multilayer steel (MLS) gaskets are used on many newer all-aluminum engines as well as engines that use a cast block with aluminum cylinder heads. This type of gasket allows the aluminum to expand without losing the sealing ability of the gasket.

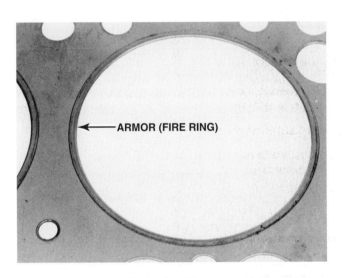

FIGURE 30-38   Head gasket with armor.

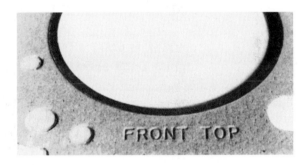

FIGURE 30-40   Typical head gasket markings.

steel gaskets also reduces the torque requirement and, therefore, reduces the stresses on the fastener and engine block.

INSTALLING THE HEAD GASKET

The block deck and head surfaces should be rechecked for any handling nicks that could cause a gasket leak. All tapped holes should be cleaned with the correct-size thread chaser. Also check the block and cylinder head surfaces for any dirt or burrs. There are usually alignment pins or dowels at the front and rear of the block deck to position the gasket and head. Care should be taken to properly position any head gasket with markings (up, top, front, and so forth). See Figure 30-40. The gasket and head are placed on the block deck. All the head bolts are loosely installed. Very often, the head bolts have different lengths. Make sure that a bolt of the correct length is put into each location.

The fiber facing is protected around the combustion chamber with a metal **armor** (also called **fire ring**). See Figure 30-38. The metal also increases the gasket thickness around the cylinder so that it uses up to 75% of the clamping force and forms a tight combustion seal.

MULTILAYERED STEEL GASKETS

Multilayered steel (MLS) is being used from the factory on many newer engine designs such as the overhead camshaft Ford V-8s. The many layers of thin steel reduce bore and overhead camshaft distortion with less clamping force loss than previous designs. See Figure 30-39. The use of multilayered

---

NOTE: The word "front" means toward the timing belt or chain end of the engine. This can be confusing for a technician working on an engine in a front-wheel-drive vehicle.

Put sealer on the threads of the assembly bolts that go into the cooling system. Put antiseize compound on bolts that hold the exhaust manifold. Lightly oil the threads of bolts that go into blind holes. See the Tech Tip, "Watch Out for Wet and Dry Holes."

NOTE: Most manufacturers recommend putting oil on the threads of bolts (not in the block holes!) during reassembly. Lubricated threads will give as much as 50% more clamping force at the same bolt torque than threads that are tightened dry.

Often, the assembly bolts have different lengths. Make sure that the correct length of bolt is put into each hole.

TECH TIP

WATCH OUT FOR WET AND DRY HOLES

Many engines, such as the small-block Chevrolet V-8, use head bolts that extend through the top deck of the block and end in a coolant passage. These bolt holes are called **wet holes.** When installing head bolts that end up in the coolant passage, use sealer on the threads of the head bolt. Some engines have head bolts that are "wet," whereas others are "dry" because they end in solid cast-iron material. Dry hole bolts do not require sealant, but they still require some oil on the threads of the bolts for lubrication. Do not put oil into a dry hole because the bolt may bottom out in the oil. The liquid oil cannot compress, so the force of the bolt being tightened is transferred to the block by hydraulic force, which can crack the block.

NOTE: Apply oil to a shop cloth and rotate the bolt in the cloth to lubricate the threads. This procedure lubricates the threads without applying too much oil.

HEAD BOLT TORQUE SEQUENCE

The torque put on the bolts is used to control the clamping force. The clamping force is correct only when the threads are clean and properly lubricated. In general, the head bolts are tightened in a specified torque sequence in three steps. By tightening the head bolts in three steps, the head gasket has time to compress and conform to the block deck and cylinder head gasket surfaces. Follow that sequence and tighten the bolts to *one-third* the specified torque. Tighten them a second time following the torque sequence to *two-thirds* the specified torque. Follow the sequence with a final tightening to the specified torque. See Figures 30-41 and 30-42.

TORQUE-TO-YIELD BOLTS

Many engines use a tightening procedure called the **torque-to-yield,** or **torque-angle,** method. The purpose of the torque-to-yield procedure is to have a more constant clamping load from bolt to bolt. This aids in head gasket sealing performance and eliminates the need for retorquing. The torque-to-yield head bolts are made with a narrow section between the head and threads. As the bolts are tightened

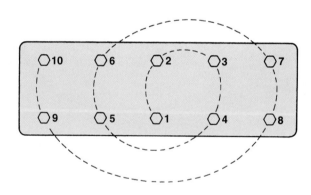

FIGURE 30-41 Typical cylinder head tightening sequence.

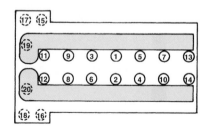

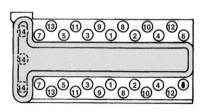

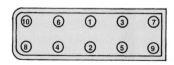

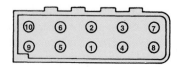

FIGURE 30-42 Examples of cylinder head bolt torquing sequences.

past their elastic limit, they yield and begin to stretch in this narrow section.

Torque-to-yield head bolts will not become any tighter once they reach this elastic limit, as you can see on the graph in Figure 30-43. The torque-angle method also decreases the differences in clamping force that can occur depending on the condition or lubrication of the threads. See Figure 30-44.

As a result, many engine manufacturers specify *new* head bolts each time the head is installed. If these bolts are reused, they are likely to break during assembly or fail prematurely as the engine runs. If there is any doubt about the head bolts, replace them.

Torque-to-yield bolts are tightened to a specific initial torque, from 18 to 50 pound-feet (25 to 68 Newton-meters).

The bolts are then tightened a specified number of degrees, following the tightening sequence. In some cases they are turned a specified number of degrees two or three times. Some specifications limit the maximum torque that can be applied to the bolt while the degree turn is being made. Torque tables in a service manual will show how much initial torque should be applied to the bolt and how many degrees the bolt should be rotated after torquing.

NOTE: The torque-turn method does not necessarily mean torque-to-yield. Some engine specifications call for a beginning torque and then a specified angle, but the fastener is not designed to yield. These head bolts can often be reused. Always follow the manufacturer's recommended procedures.

Head bolts are tightened following a sequence specified in the service manual or torque tables. In general, the tightening sequence starts at the center of the head and moves outward, alternating front to rear and side to side. The bolts are usually tightened to approximately one-half the specified torque, following the tightening sequence. They are then retorqued to the specified torque following the same tightening sequence. See Figures 30-45 and 30-46.

TIMING DRIVES FOR OVERHEAD CAM ENGINES

After the head bolts have been torqued, the cam drive can be installed on overhead cam engines. This is done by aligning the timing marks of the crankshaft and camshaft drive sprockets with their respective timing marks. The location of these marks differs between engines, but the marks can

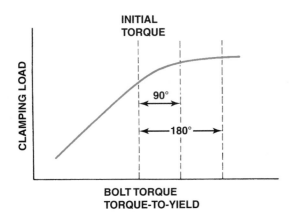

FIGURE 30-43 Due to variations in clamping force with turning force (torque) of head bolts, some engines are specifying the torque-to-yield procedure. The first step is to torque the bolts by an even amount called the initial torque. Final clamping load is achieved by turning the bolt a specified number of degrees. Bolt stretch provides the proper clamping force.

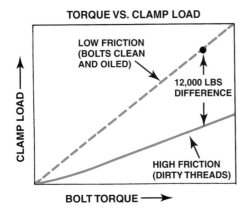
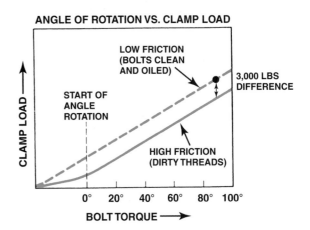

FIGURE 30-44 To ensure consistent clamp force (load), many manufacturers are recommending the torque-angle or torque-to-yield method of tightening head bolts. The torque-angle method specifies tightening fasteners to a low torque setting and then giving an additional angle of rotation. Notice that the difference in clamping force is much smaller than it would be if just a torque wrench with dirty threads were used.

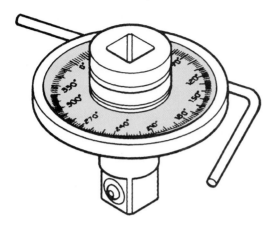

FIGURE 30-45 Torque angle can be measured using a special adaptor.

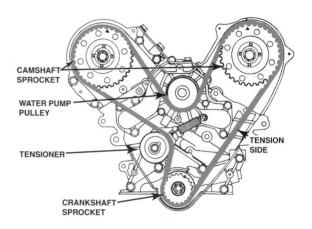

FIGURE 30-47 Both crankshafts have to be timed on this engine, and the timing belt also drives the water pump.

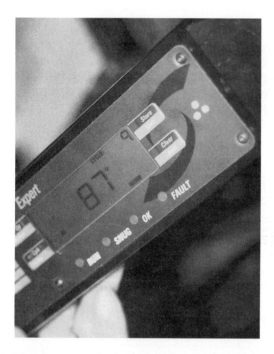

FIGURE 30-46 An electronic torque wrench showing the number of degrees of rotation. These very accurate and expensive torque wrenches can be programmed to display torque or number of degrees of rotation.

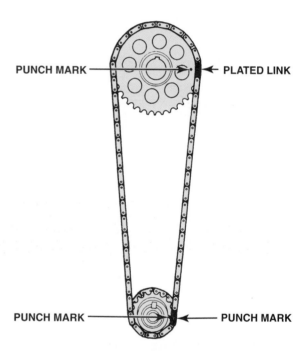

FIGURE 30-48 Some timing chains have plated links that are used to correctly position the chain on the sprockets.

NOTE: Always check the manufacturer's recommended timing chain installation procedure. Engines that use primary and secondary timing chains often require an exact detailed procedure for proper installation.

---

be identified by looking carefully at the sprockets. See Figures 30-47 and 30-48. The tightening idler may be on either or both sides of the timing belt or chain. After the camshaft drive is engaged, rotate the crankshaft through two full revolutions. On the first full revolution, you should see the exhaust valve almost close and the intake valve just starting to open when the *crankshaft* timing mark aligns. At the end of the second revolution, both valves should be closed, and all the timing marks should align on most engines. This is the position the crankshaft should have when cylinder #1 is to fire.

LIFTER AND PUSHROD INSTALLATION

The outside of the lifters and the lifter bores in the block should be cleaned and coated with assembly lubricant. The lifters are installed in the lifter bores and the pushrods put in

TECH TIP

SOAK THE TIMING CHAIN

Many experts recommend that a new timing chain be soaked in engine oil prior to engine assembly to help ensure full lubrication at engine start-up. The timing chain is one of the last places in the engine to get lubrication when the engine first starts. This procedure may even extend the life of the chain.

place. There are different-length pushrods on some engines. Make sure that the pushrods are installed in the proper location. The rocker arms are then put in place, aligning with the valves and pushrods. Rocker arm shafts should have their retaining bolts tightened a little at a time, alternating between the retaining bolts. This keeps the shaft from bending as the rocker arm pushes some of the valves open.

HYDRAULIC LIFTERS

The retaining nut on some rocker arms mounted on studs can be tightened to a specified torque. The rocker arm will be adjusted correctly at this torque when the valve tip has the correct height. Other types of rocker arms require tightening the nut to a position that will center the hydraulic lifter. The general procedure for adjusting the hydraulic lifter types is to tighten the retaining nut to the point that all the free lash is gone. See Figure 30-49. The lifter plunger starts to move down after the lash is gone. From this point, the retaining nut is tightened by a specified amount, such as three-fourths of a turn or one and one-half turns.

NOTE: This method usually results in about three threads showing above the adjusting nut on a *stock* small-block Chevrolet V-8 equipped with flat-bottom hydraulic lifters.

SOLID LIFTERS

The valve clearance or **lash** must be set on a solid lifter engine, so that the valves can positively seat. Some service manuals give an adjustment sequence to follow to set the lash. If this is not available, then the following procedure can be used on all engines requiring valve lash adjustment. The valve lash is adjusted with the valves completely closed. See Figure 30-50.

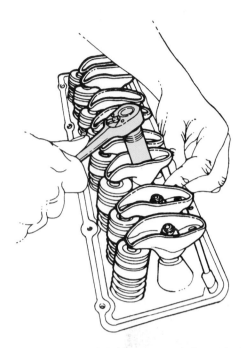

FIGURE 30-49   With the lifter resting on the base circle of the cam, zero lash is achieved by tightening the rocker arm lock nut until the pushrod no longer rotates freely.

FIGURE 30-50   Most adjustable valves use a nut to keep the adjustment from changing, so to adjust the valves the nut has to be loosened and the screw rotated until the proper valve clearance is achieved. Then the screw should be held while tightening the lock nut to keep the adjustment from changing. Double-check the valve clearance after tightening the nut.

After the valve lash on cylinder #1 is set, the crankshaft is rotated in its normal direction of rotation to the next cylinder in the firing order. This is done by turning the crankshaft 90 degrees on eight-cylinder engines, 120 degrees on even-firing six-cylinder engines, and 180 degrees on four-cylinder engines. The valves on this next cylinder are adjusted in the same manner, as were those on cylinder #1. This procedure is repeated on each cylinder *following the engine firing order* until all the valves have been adjusted.

The same valve lash adjustment sequence is used on overhead cam engines. Those engines with rocker arms or with adjustable finger follower pivots are adjusted in the same way, as are pushrod engines with rocker arms.

ASSEMBLY SEALANTS

RTV Silicone

RTV Silicone is used by most technicians in sealing engines. **RTV, or room-temperature vulcanization,** means that the silicone rubber material will cure at room temperature. It is not really the temperature that causes RTV silicone to cure, but the moisture in the air. RTV silicone cures to a tack-free state in about 45 minutes. It takes 24 hours to fully cure.

CAUTION: Some RTV silicone sealers use **acetic acid,** and the fumes from this type can be drawn through the engine through the PCV system and cause damage to oxygen sensors. Always use an **amine-type** RTV **silicone** or one that states on the package that it is safe for oxygen sensors.

RTV silicone is available in several different colors. The color identifies the special blend within a manufacturer's product line. Equal grades of silicone made by different manufacturers may have different colors. RTV silicone can be used in two ways in engine sealing:

1. It can be used as a gasket substitute between a stamped cover and a cast surface.
2. It is used to fill gaps or potential gaps. A joint between gaskets or between a gasket and a seal is a potential gap.

NOTE: RTV silicone should *never* be used around fuel because the fuel will cut through it. Silicone should not be used as a sealer on gaskets. It will squeeze out to leave a bead inside and a bead outside the flange. The inside bead might fall into the engine, plugging passages and causing engine damage. The thin film still remaining on the gasket stays uncured, just as it would be in the original tube. The uncured silicone is likely to let the gasket or seal slip out of place. See Figure 30-51.

Anaerobic Sealers

Anaerobic sealers are sealers that cure in the absence of air. They are used as thread lockers (such as Loctite), and they are used to seal rigid machined joints between cast parts. Anaerobic sealers lose their sealing ability at temperatures above

FIGURE 30-51   Improperly sealed valve cover gasket. Note the use of RTV silicone sealant on a cork-rubber gasket. The cover bolts were also overtightened, which deformed the metal cover around the bolt holes.

300°F (149°C). On production lines, the curing process is speeded up by using ultraviolet light.

When the anaerobic sealer is used on threads, air does not get to it so it hardens to form a seal to prevent the fastener from loosening. Teflon is added to some anaerobic sealers to seal fluids better. Anaerobic sealers can be used to seal machined surfaces without a gasket. The surfaces *must* be thoroughly clean to get a good seal. Special primers are recommended for use on the sealing surface to get a better bond with anaerobic sealers.

INSTALLING MANIFOLDS

The intake manifold gasket for a V-type engine may be a one-piece gasket or it may have several pieces. V-type engines with open-type manifolds have a cover over the lifter valley. The cover may be a separate part or it may be part of a one-piece intake manifold gasket. Closed-type intake manifolds on V-type engines require gasket pieces (end seals) at the front and rear of the intake manifold. See Figure 30-52. Inline engines usually have a one-piece intake manifold gasket.

The intake manifold is put in place over the gaskets. Use a contact adhesive to hold the gasket and end seal if there is a chance they might slip out of place. Just before the manifold is installed, put a spot of RTV silicone on each of the four joints between the intake manifold gasket and end seals. Install the bolts and tighten to the specified torque following the correct tightening sequence.

Only some exhaust manifolds use gaskets. The exhaust manifold operates at very high temperatures, so there is usually some expansion and contraction movement in the manifold-to-head joint. It is very important to use attachment bolts, cap screws, and clamps of the correct type and length. See Figure 30-53. They must be properly torqued to avoid both leakage and cracks.

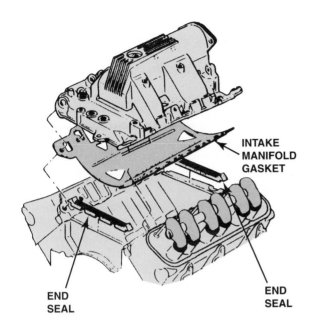

FIGURE 30-52   This intake manifold gasket includes end seals and a full shield cover for the valley to keep hot engine oil from heating the intake manifold.

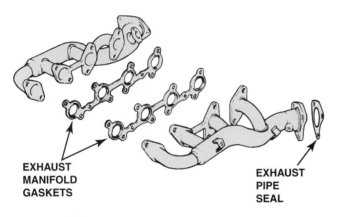

FIGURE 30-53   An exhaust manifold gasket is used on some engines and seals the exhaust manifold to the cylinder head.

NOTE: When the exhaust manifold gasket has facing on one side, put the facing toward the head and let the manifold rest against the metal side of the gasket.

COVER GASKET MATERIALS

The gasket must be *impermeable* to the fluids it is designed to seal in or out. The gasket must *conform* to the shape of the surface, and it must be *resilient*, or elastic, to maintain the sealing force as it is compressed. Gaskets work best when they are compressed about 30%.

FIGURE 30-54   *Left to right:* Cork-rubber, paper, composite, and synthetic rubber (elastomer) gaskets.

Cork Gaskets

Cork is the bark from a Mediterranean cork oak tree. It is made of very small, flexible, 14-sided, air-filled fiber cells, about 0.001 inch (0.025 millimeter) in size. The air-filled cells act like a pneumatic system. This gives resiliency to the cork gasket until the air leaks out. Because cork is mostly wood, it expands when it gets wet and shrinks when it dries. This causes cork gaskets to change in size when they are in storage and while installed in the engine. Oil gradually wicks through the organic binder of the cork, so a cork gasket often looks like it is leaking. Problems with cork gaskets led the gasket industry to develop cork cover gaskets using synthetic rubber as a binder for the cork. This type of gasket is called a **cork-rubber gasket.** These cork-rubber gaskets are easy to use, and they outlast the old cork gaskets. See Figure 30-54.

Fiber Gaskets

Some oil pans use fiber gaskets. Covers with higher clamping forces use gaskets with fibers that have greater density. For example, timing covers may have either fiber or paper gaskets.

Synthetic Rubber Gaskets

Molded, oil-resistant synthetic rubber is being used in more applications to seal covers. When it is compounded correctly, it forms a superior cover gasket. It operates at high temperatures for a longer period of time than does a cork-rubber cover gasket. See Figure 30-55.

FIGURE 30-55 Typical cast-aluminum cam (valve) cover. Note the rubber gasket in the cast groove of the cover.

Sealers

Sealers are nonhardening materials. Examples of sealer trade names include Form-A-Gasket 2, Pli-A-Seal, Tight Seal 2, Aviation Form-A-Gasket, Brush Tack, Copper Coat, Spray Tack, and High Tack. Sealers are always used to seal the threads of bolts that break into coolant passages. Sealers for sealing threads may include Teflon. Sealer is often recommended for use on shim-type head gaskets and intake manifold gaskets. These gaskets have a metal surface that does not conform to any small amounts of surface roughness on the sealing surface. The sealer fills the surface variations between the gasket and the sealing surface.

Sealer may be used as a sealing aid on paper and fiber gaskets if the gasket needs help with sealing on a scratched, corroded, or rough surface finish. The sealer may be used on one side or on both sides of the gasket.

CAUTION: Sealer should *never* be used on rubber or cork-rubber gaskets. Instead of holding the rubber gasket or seal, it will help the rubber to slip out of place because the sealer will never harden.

Antiseize Compounds

Antiseize compounds are used on fasteners in the engine that are subjected to high temperatures to prevent seizing caused by galvanic action between dissimilar metals. These compounds minimize corrosion from moisture. Exhaust manifold bolts and nuts, oxygen sensors, and spark plugs, especially those that go into aluminum heads, are kept from seizing. The antiseize compound minimizes the chance of threads being pulled or breaking as the oxygen sensor or spark plug is removed.

INSTALLING TIMING COVERS

Most timing covers are installed with a gasket, but some use RTV sealer in place of the gasket. Cast covers use anaerobic

TECH TIP

HINTS FOR GASKET USAGE

Never reuse an old gasket. A used gasket or seal has already been compressed, has lost some of its resilience, and has taken a set. If a used gasket does reseal, it will not seal as well as a new gasket or seal.

A gasket should be checked to make sure it is the correct gasket. Also check the list on the outside of the gasket set to make sure that the set has all the gaskets that may be needed *before* the package is opened.

An instruction sheet is included with most gaskets. It includes a review of the things the technician should do to prepare and install the gaskets to give the best chance of a good seal. The instruction sheet also includes special tips on how to seal spots that are difficult to seal or that require special care to seal on a particular engine.

FIGURE 30-56 1/8- to 3/16-inch (3- to 5-millimeter) bead of RTV silicone on a parting surface with silicone going around the bolt hole.

compound as a gasket substitute. A bead of RTV silicone 1/8 to 3/16 inch in diameter is put on the clean sealing surface. See Figure 30-56. Encircle the bolt holes with the sealant. Install the cover before the silicone begins to cure so that the uncured silicone bonds to both surfaces. While installing the cover, do not touch the silicone bead; otherwise, the bead might be displaced, causing a leak. Carefully press the cover into place. Do not slide the cover after it is in place. Install the assembly bolts finger-tight, and let the silicone cure for about 30 minutes; then torque the cover bolts.

FIGURE 30-57 Installing the harmonic balancer. Always follow the manufacturer's recommended procedure and torque specifications.

INSTALLING THE VIBRATION DAMPER

Vibration dampers are seated in place by one of three methods.

- The damper hub of some engines is pulled into place using the hub-attaching bolt. See Figure 30-57.
- The second method uses a special installing tool that screws into the attaching bolt hole to pull the hub into place. The tool is removed and the attaching bolt is installed and torqued.
- The last method is used on engines that have no attaching bolt. These hubs depend on a press-fit to hold the hub on the crankshaft. The hub is seated using a hammer and a special tube-type driver.

INSTALLING THE OIL PUMP

When an engine is rebuilt, the oil pump should be replaced with a new pump. This ensures positive lubrication and long pump life. Oil pump gears should be coated with assembly lubricant before the cover is put on the pump. This provides initial lubrication, and it primes the pump so that it will draw the oil from the pan when the lubrication system is first operated.

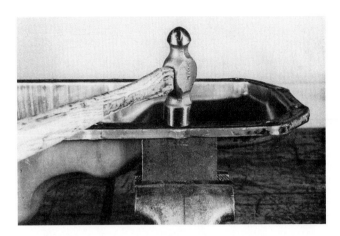

FIGURE 30-58 Using a hammer to straighten the gasket rail surface before installing a new gasket. When the retaining bolts are tightened, some distortion of sheet-metal covers occurs. If the area around the bolt holes is not straightened, leaks can occur with the new gasket.

THE OIL PAN

The oil pan should be checked and straightened as necessary. See Figure 30-58. With the oil pump in place, the oil pan gaskets are properly positioned. A spot of RTV silicone is placed at each gasket joint just before the pan is installed. The oil pan is carefully placed over the gaskets. All oil pan bolts should be started into their holes before any are tightened. The bolts should be alternately snugged up; then they should be properly torqued.

REAL WORLD FIX

THE NEW OIL PUMP THAT FAILED

A technician replaced the oil pump and screen on a V-8 with low oil pressure. After the repair, the oil pressure returned to normal for two weeks, but then the oil pressure light came on and the valve train started making noise. The vehicle owner returned to the service garage where the oil pump had been replaced. The technician removed the oil pan and pump. The screen was almost completely clogged with the RTV sealant that the technician had used to "seal" the oil pan gasket. The technician had failed to read the instructions that came with the oil pan gasket. Failure to follow directions and using too much of the wrong sealer cost the repair shop an expensive comeback repair.

TECH TIP

OIL PUMP PRECAUTIONS

The oil pump is the heart of any engine, and any failure of the oil circulation system often results in severe and major engine damage. To help prevent possible serious oil pump-related failures, many engine builders recommend the following precautions:

1. Always be sure that the oil pump pickup tube (screen) is securely attached to the oil pump to prevent the pickup tube from vibrating out of the pump.
2. Use modeling clay to check pickup screen-to-oil pan clearance. For proper operation, there should be about 1/4 inch (6 millimeters) between the oil pump pickup screen and the bottom of the oil pan.

INSTALLING THE WATER PUMP

A reconditioned, rebuilt, or new water pump should be used. Once gaskets are fitted in place, the pump is secured with assembly bolts tightened to the correct torque.

A new thermostat is usually installed at this time. It is put in place, with care being taken to place the correct side of the thermostat toward the engine. The thermostat gasket is put in place. Sealers are used on the gasket where they are required. The thermostat housing is installed, and the retaining bolts are tightened to the proper torque.

ENGINE PAINTING

Painting an engine helps prevent rust and corrosion and makes the engine look new. Standard engine paints with original colors are usually available at automotive parts stores. Engine paints should be used rather than other types of paints. Engine paints are compounded to stay on the metal as the engine temperatures change. Normal engine fluids will not remove them. These paints are usually purchased in pressure cans so that they can be sprayed from the can directly onto the engine.

All parts that should not be painted must be covered before spray painting. This can be done with old parts, such as old spark plugs and old gaskets. This can also be done by taping paper over the areas to be covered. If the intake manifold

REAL WORLD FIX

"OOPS"

After overhauling a big-block Ford V-8 engine, the technician used an electric drill to rotate the oil pump with a pressure gauge connected to the oil pressure sending unit hole. When the electric drill was turned on, oil pressure would start to increase (to about 10 PSI), then drop to zero. In addition, the oil was very aerated (full of air). Replacing the oil pump did not solve the problem. After hours of troubleshooting and disassembly, it was discovered that an oil gallery plug had been left out underneath the intake manifold. The oil pump was working correctly and pumped oil throughout the engine and out of the end of the unplugged oil gallery. It did not take long for the oil pan to empty; therefore, the oil pump began drawing in air that aerated the oil and the oil pressure dropped. Installing the gallery plug solved the problem. It was smart of the technician to check the oil pressure before starting the engine. This oversight of leaving out one gallery plug could have resulted in a ruined engine shortly after the engine was started.

NOTE: Many overhead camshaft engines use an oil passage check valve in the block near the deck. The purpose of this valve is to hold oil in the cylinder head around the camshaft and lifters when the engine is stopped. Failure to reinstall this check valve can cause the valve train to be noisy after engine start-up.

of an inline engine is to be painted, it can be painted separately. Engine assembly can continue after the paint has dried.

CHECKING FOR PROPER OIL PRESSURE

With oil in the engine and the distributor out of the engine, oil pressure should be established before the engine is started. This can be done on most engines by rotating the oil pump by hand. This ensures that oil is delivered to all parts of the engine before the engine is started. A socket speed handle makes an ideal crank for turning the oil pump. A flat-blade adapter that fits the speed handle will operate on General Motors engines. The V-type Chrysler engine requires the use of the same flat-blade adapter, but it also requires an oil pump drive. One can be made by removing the gear from an

FIGURE 30-59   Drivers used to rotate oil pumps to prelubricate all parts of the engine before installing the distributor and starting the engine.

FIGURE 30-60   The engine can be pressurized with engine oil from an aerosol can as shown or from a pressurized oil container designed for preoiling the engine.

old oil pump hex driveshaft. A 1/4-inch drive socket can be used on Ford engines. Examples of these are pictured in Figure 30-59. Engines that do not drive the oil pump with the distributor will have to be cranked with the spark plugs removed to establish oil pressure. The load on the starter and battery is reduced with the spark plugs out so that the engine will have a higher cranking speed. A pressurized oil container or an engine oil aerosol could also be used, as shown in Figure 30-60.

SETTING INITIAL IGNITION TIMING

After oil pressure is established, the distributor, if equipped, can be installed. Rotate the crankshaft in its normal direction of rotation until there is compression on cylinder #1. This can be done with the starter or by using a wrench on the damper bolt. The compression stroke can be determined by covering the opening of spark plug #1 with a finger as the crankshaft is rotated. Continue to rotate the crankshaft slowly as compression is felt, until the timing marks on the damper align with the timing indicator on the timing cover.

The angle of the distributor gear drive will cause the distributor rotor to turn a few degrees when installed. Before the distributor is installed, the shaft must be positioned to compensate for the gear angle. After installation, the rotor should be pointing to the #1 tower of the distributor cap.

The distributor position should be close enough to the basic timing position to start the engine. If the distributor hold-down clamp is slightly loose, the distributor housing can be adjusted to make the engine run smoothly after the engine has been started.

PREOILING AN ENGINE Step-by-Step

STEP 1 Whenever an engine has been disassembled and then reassembled, it is important to make sure that all internal parts are preoiled before starting the engine. Start by filling the crankcase with the specified amount of oil.

STEP 2 Attach an oil pressure gauge to the engine. On this small-block Chevrolet V-8, the oil pressure tap is located near the distributor at the top of the block.

STEP 3 To rotate the oil pump an old distributor was cut down and the shaft installed in the chuck of an electric drill.

STEP 4 Rotating the oil pump using an electric drill results in the oil pressure increasing to over 50 PSI.

STEP 5 The drill should continue being used to prime the engine with oil until oil is observed coming from the rocker arms, indicating that oil has reached the highest part of the engine.

STEP 6 An overall view of the oil pump drive adapter made from an odd distributor and the oil pressure gauge. After the engine has been primed, the distributor can be installed and the engine can be installed into the vehicle.

VALVE ADJUSTMENT Step-by-Step

STEP 1 Before starting the process of adjusting the valves, look up the specifications and exact procedures. The technician is checking this information from a computer CD-ROM-based information system.

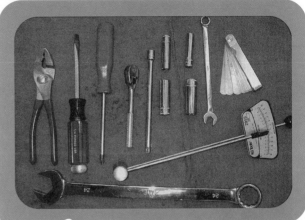

STEP 2 The tools necessary to adjust the valves on an engine with adjustable rocker arms include basic hand tools, feeler gauge, and a torque wrench.

STEP 3 An overall view of the four-cylinder engine that is due for a scheduled valve adjustment according to the vehicle manufacturer's recommendations.

STEP 4 Start the valve adjustment procedure by first disconnecting and labeling, if necessary, all vacuum lines that need to be removed to gain access to the valve cover.

STEP 5 The air intake tube is being removed from the throttle body.

STEP 6 With all vacuum lines and the intake tube removed, the valve cover can be removed after removing all retaining bolts.

(continued)

VALVE ADJUSTMENT   continued

STEP 7 Notice how clean the engine appears. This is a testament to proper maintenance and regular oil changes by the owner.

STEP 8 To help locate how far the engine is being rotated, the technician is removing the distributor cap to be able to observe the position of the rotor.

TIMING MARKS

STEP 9 The engine is rotated until the timing marks on the front of the crankshaft line up with zero degrees—top dead center (TDC)—with both valves closed on #1 cylinder.

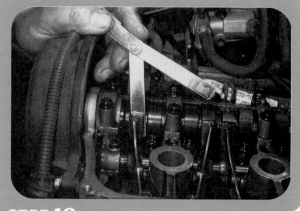

STEP 10 With the rocker arms contacting the base circle of the cam, insert a feeler gauge of the specified thickness between the camshaft and the rocker arm. There should be a slight drag on the feeler gauge.

STEP 11 If the valve clearance (lash) is not correct, loosen the retaining nut and turn the valve adjusting screw with a screwdriver to achieve the proper clearance.

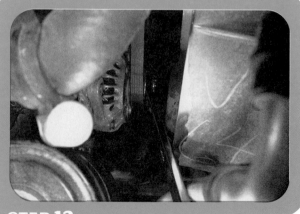

STEP 12 After adjusting the valves that are closed, rotate the engine one full rotation until the engine timing marks again align.

VALVE ADJUSTMENT   continued

STEP 13 The engine is rotated until the timing marks again align indicating that the companion cylinder will now be in position for valve clearance measurement.

STEP 14 On some engines, it is necessary to watch the direction the rotor is pointing to help determine how far to rotate the engine. Always follow the vehicle manufacturer's recommended procedure.

STEP 15 The technician is using a feeler gauge that is one-thousandth of an inch thinner and another one-thousandth of an inch thicker than the specified clearance as a double-check that the clearance is correct.

STEP 16 Adjusting a valve takes both hands—one to hold the wrench to loosen and tighten the lock nut and one to turn the adjusting screw. Always double-check the clearance after an adjustment is made.

STEP 17 After all valves have been properly measured and adjusted as necessary, start the reassembly process by replacing all gaskets and seals as specified by the vehicle manufacturer.

STEP 18 Reinstall the valve cover being careful to not pinch a wire or vacuum hose between the cover and the cylinder head.

(continued)

VALVE ADJUSTMENT continued

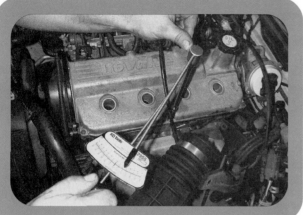

STEP 19 Use a torque wrench and torque the valve cover retaining bolts to factory specifications.

STEP 20 Reinstall the distributor cap.

STEP 21 Reinstall the spark plug wires and all brackets that were removed to gain access to the valve cover.

STEP 22 Reconnect all vacuum and air hoses and tubes. Replace with new any vacuum hoses that are brittle or swollen.

STEP 23 Be sure that the clips are properly installed. Start the engine and check for proper operation.

STEP 24 Double-check for any oil or vacuum leaks after starting the engine.

SUMMARY

1. All oil galleries must be thoroughly cleaned before engine assembly can begin.
2. All expansion cups and plugs should be installed with a sealer to prevent leaks. Avoid the use of Teflon tape on threaded plugs.
3. The cam bearings should be installed using a cam bearing installation tool.
4. Main bearings and rod bearings should be checked for proper oil clearance by precision measuring the crankshaft journals and inside diameter of bearings or by using plastic gauging material.
5. The piston and rod assembly should be installed in the cylinder after being carefully fitted for each bore.
6. Connecting rod side clearance should be checked with a feeler (thickness) gauge.
7. Double-check the flatness of the block deck and cylinder head before installing the cylinder head.
8. Torque the cylinder head bolts according to the proper sequence and procedures.
9. Many cylinder heads use the torque-to-yield method, wherein the head bolts are tightened to a specified torque and then rotated a specified number of degrees.
10. The oil pressure should be tested before installation of the engine in the vehicle.

REVIEW QUESTIONS

1. Describe the procedure for fitting pistons to a cylinder.
2. Explain how main bearings should be checked and fitted to the crankshaft.
3. How is plastic gauging material used to determine oil clearance?
4. What is the procedure for checking thrust bearing clearance?
5. How should the connecting rod side clearance be measured and corrected?
6. How is the piston and connecting rod assembly installed in the engine?
7. What procedures should be followed for installing and torquing the cylinder head?
8. Describe the torque-to-yield head bolt tightening procedure.

CHAPTER QUIZ

1. Typical piston-to-cylinder clearance is _____.
   a. 0.001 to 0.003 inch
   b. 0.010 to 0.023 inch
   c. 0.100 to 0.150 inch
   d. 0.180 to 0.230 inch
2. If the gauging plastic strip is wide after the bearings are tightened, this indicates _____.
   a. A large oil clearance
   b. An old, dried strip of plastic gauging material
   c. A small oil clearance
   d. A small side (thrust) clearance
3. The most common cause of premature bearing failure is _____.
   a. Misassembly
   b. Dirt
   c. Lack of lubrication
   d. Overloading
4. Typical thrust bearing clearance is _____.
   a. 0.001 to 0.003 inch
   b. 0.002 to 0.012 inch
   c. 0.025 to 0.035 inch
   d. 0.050 to 0.100 inch

5. Piston ring end gap can be *increased* by _____.
   a. Filing the ring to make the gap larger
   b. Installing oversize rings
   c. Sleeving the cylinder
   d. Knurling the piston

6. The cylinder head bolts should be tightened (torqued) in what general sequence?
   a. The four outside bolts first, then from the center out
   b. From the outside bolts to the inside bolts
   c. From the inside bolts to the outside bolts
   d. Starting at the front of the engine and torquing bolts from front to rear

7. The torque-angle method involves _____.
   a. Turning all bolts the same number of turns
   b. Torquing to specifications and loosening by a specified number of degrees
   c. Torquing to one-half specifications, then to three-quarter torque, then to full torque
   d. Turning bolts a specified number of degrees after initial torque

8. Turning the oil pump before starting the engine should be done _____.
   a. To lubricate engine bearings
   b. To lubricate valve train components
   c. To supply oil to the camshaft
   d. All of the above

9. Most bolt torque specifications are for _____.
   a. Clean threads only
   b. Clean and lubricated threads
   c. Dirty threads
   d. Dirty threads, but 50% can be added for clean threads

10. Cam bearings should be installed _____.
    a. Dry
    b. Oiled
    c. With at least 0.010 inch of crush
    d. Both b and c

CHAPTER 31

ENGINE INSTALLATION AND IN-VEHICLE SERVICE

OBJECTIVES

After studying Chapter 31, the reader will be able to:

1. Prepare for Engine Repair (A1) ASE certification test content area "E" (Fuel, Electrical, Ignition, and Exhaust System Inspection and Service).

2. List the steps necessary to install and start-up a rebuilt engine.

3. Discuss the importance of torquing all bolts or fasteners that connect accessories to the engine block.

4. Describe what precautions must be taken to prevent damage to the engine when it is first started.

5. Explain how to break-in a newly rebuilt engine.

6. Describe how to replace a timing belt on an overhead camshaft engine.

KEY TERMS

Lugging (p. 604)

Normal Operating Temperature (p. 603)

When installing an engine, the engine installation will have to be thoroughly checked to make sure that it is in proper condition to give the customer dependable operation for a long time.

All operating accessories have to be reinstalled on the engine. They have to be adjusted so that the engine will operate correctly.

PREINSTALLATION CHECKLIST

Before installing or starting a new or rebuilt engine in a vehicle, be sure all of the following items have been checked.

1. Battery fully charged.
2. Prelube the engine and check for proper oil pressure. See Figure 31-1.
3. Check that all of the vacuum lines are correctly installed and routed.
4. Know the ignition timing specification and procedure.
5. Check that fresh fuel is in the fuel tank.
6. Be sure that the radiator has been tested, is free from leaks, and flows correctly.
7. Check that all accessory drive belts are routed and tensioned correctly.

CAUTION: Be sure to have a fire extinguisher near when the engine is first started.

FIGURE 31-1 Prelubricating the engine is a very important step that should be performed before starting the engine. Notice that oil is flowing through the pushrods, over the rocker arms, and onto the valve springs.

MANUAL TRANSMISSION INSTALLATION

If the engine was removed with the transmission attached, the transmission should be reinstalled on the engine before other accessories are added. The flywheel is installed on the back of the crankshaft. Often, the attaching bolt holes are unevenly spaced so that the flywheel will fit in only one way to maintain engine balance. The pilot bearing or bushing in the rear of the crankshaft is usually replaced with a new one to minimize the possibility of premature failure of this part.

The clutch is installed next. Usually, a new clutch is used; at the least, a new clutch friction disk is installed. The clutch friction disk must be held in position using an alignment tool (sometimes called a dummy shaft) that is secured in the pilot bearing. This holds the disk in position while the pressure plate is being installed. Finally, the engine bell housing is put on the engine, if it was not installed before. The alignment of this type of bell housing is then checked. See Figure 31-2.

CAUTION: Perfectly round cylinders can be distorted whenever another part of the engine is bolted and torqued to the engine block. For example, it has been determined that after the cylinders are machined, the rear cylinder bore can be distorted to be as much as 0.006 inch (0.15 millimeter) out-of-round after the bell housing is bolted onto the block! To help prevent this distortion, always apply the specified torque to all fasteners going into the engine block and tighten in the recommended sequence.

The clutch release yoke should be checked for free movement. Usually, the clutch release bearing is replaced to ensure that the new bearing is securely attached to the clutch release yoke. The transmission can then be installed.

FIGURE 31-2 Bell housing alignment dowel pins are used to ensure proper alignment between the engine block and the transmission.

TECH TIP

THE HEADLESS BOLT TRICK

Sometimes parts do not seem to line up correctly. Try this tip the next time. Cut the head off of extra-long bolts that are of the same diameter and thread as those being used to retain the part, such as a transmission. See Figure 31-3. Use a hacksaw to cut a slot in this end of the guide bolts for a screwdriver slot. Install the guide bolts; then install the transmission. Use a straight-blade screwdriver to remove the guide bolts after securing the transmission with the retaining bolts.

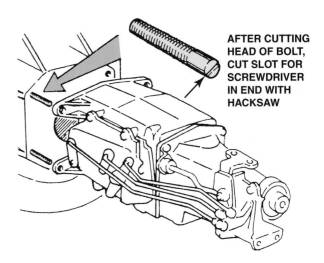

AFTER CUTTING HEAD OF BOLT, CUT SLOT FOR SCREWDRIVER IN END WITH HACKSAW

FIGURE 31-3 Headless long bolts can be used to help install a transmission to the engine.

The transmission clutch shaft must be guided straight into the clutch disk and pilot bearing. See the Tech Tip, "The Headless Bolt Trick." The transmission clutch shaft is rotated, as required, to engage in the splines of the clutch disk. The assembly bolts are secured when the transmission fully mates with the bell housing.

CAUTION: Always adjust the clutch free play *before* starting the engine to help prevent thrust bearing damage.

AUTOMATIC TRANSMISSION INSTALLATION

On engines equipped with automatic transmission, the drive plate is attached to the back of the crankshaft. Its assembly bolts are tightened to the specified torque. The bell housing is part of the transmission case on most automatic transmissions. Usually, the torque converter will be installed on the transmission before the transmission is put on the engine. See Figure 31-4. The torque converter should be rotated as it is pushed onto the transmission shafts until the splines of all shafts are engaged in the torque converter. The torque converter is held against the transmission as the transmission is fitted on the back of the engine. The transmission mounting bolts are attached finger tight. The torque converter should be rotated to make sure that there is no binding. The bell housing is secured to the block; then the torque converter is fastened to the drive plate. The engine should be rotated. Any binding should be corrected before any further assembly is done.

FIGURE 31-4 Typical automatic transmission torque converter.

STARTER

It is generally easier to install the starter before the engine is put in the chassis. The starter should be checked to make sure that the starter drive pinion does not bind on the ring gear. Shims can be installed between the starter mounting pad and the starter to adjust the pinion-to-ring gear clearance on the

GM-type mounting. The starter mounting bolts are then tightened to the specified torque.

ACCESSORIES

All belt-driven engine accessories are mounted on the front of the engine. Some engines drive all these accessories with one belt. Other engines use as many as four belts. Service information or decals under the hood should be checked to determine the specific belt routing for the accessories used on the engine being built up. On some engines it is more convenient to install the front accessories before the engine is installed; on other engines, it is easier to put the engine in the chassis before installing the front accessories.

Install new spark plugs and spark plug wires. Service information should be checked for the proper routing of the plug wires.

ENGINE INSTALLATION

A sling, either a chain or lift cable, is attached to the manifold or head bolts on the top of the engine. A hoist is attached to the sling and snugged up to take the weight and to make sure that the engine is supported and balanced properly.

NOTE: Many engines for front-wheel-drive vehicles are installed from underneath the vehicle. Often the entire drivetrain package is placed back in the vehicle while it is attached to the cradle. Always check the recommended procedure for the vehicle being serviced.

The engine must be tipped as it was during removal to let the transmission go into the engine compartment first. The transmission is worked under the floor pan on rear-wheel-drive vehicles as the engine is lowered into the engine compartment. The front engine mounts are aligned; then the rear cross-member and rear engine mount are installed. The engine mount bolts are installed, and the nuts are torqued. Then the hoist is removed. Controls are connected to the transmission under the vehicle. This is also a good time to connect the electrical cables and wires to the starter. The exhaust system is then attached to the exhaust manifolds. If any of the steering linkage was previously disconnected, it can be reattached while work is being done under the vehicle. After the engine is in place, the front engine accessories can all be installed, if they were not installed before the engine was put in the chassis. The air-conditioning compressor is reattached to the engine, with care being taken to avoid damaging the air-conditioning hoses and lines.

COOLING SYSTEM

The radiator is installed and secured in place, followed by the cooling fan and shroud. The fan and new drive belts are then installed and adjusted. New radiator hoses, including new heater hoses, should be installed. Coolant, a 50/50 mixture of antifreeze and water, is put in the cooling system after making sure that the radiator petcock is closed and the block drain plugs are in place. See Chapter 13 for proper procedures to follow to bleed trapped air from the cooling system. See Figure 31-5 for additional precautions.

FUEL AND EMISSION CONTROLS

The carburetor (if the vehicle is so equipped) should be installed with a new gasket. The fuel and vacuum hoses should be inspected carefully and replaced as required. The fuel-injection system (if the vehicle is so equipped) should be carefully inspected for damage while it is off the engine and then reinstalled, being certain to follow recommended procedures and torque settings. The fuel and air filters should be replaced. If the vacuum hoses and/or electrical wiring were not marked, refer to the engine emission decal and service manual for the proper location and routing.

NOTE: The oxygen sensor should be replaced, especially if the engine had a blown head gasket or other problem that could have caused coolant to get on the sensor.

FIGURE 31-5 Most engine rebuilders install a temperature-sensitive device on the engine. These sensors are used by the rebuilders for warranty purposes to record any occurrence of engine overheating. This small disk is glued to the engine block and will pop out if the engine overheats.

ELECTRICAL SYSTEM

Connect all wiring to the starter and generator (alternator) as required. Connect the instrument and computer sensor wires to the sensors on the engine. Double-check the condition and routing of all wiring, being certain that wires have not been pinched or broken, before installing a fully charged battery. Attach the positive cable first and then the ground cable. Check to make sure that the starter will crank the engine. Install and time the distributor; then connect the ignition cables to the spark plugs, again being sure that they are routed according to the manufacturer's recommendations.

ENGINE START

The engine installation should be given one last inspection to ensure that everything has been put together correctly before the engine is started. If the engine overhaul and installation are done properly, the engine should crank and start on its own fully charged battery without the use of a fast charger or jumper battery. As soon as the engine starts and shows oil pressure, it should be brought up to a fast idle speed and *kept there* to ensure that the engine gets proper lubrication. The fast-running oil pump develops full pressure, and the fast-turning crankshaft throws plenty of oil on the cam and cylinder walls.

NOTE: In camshaft-in-block engines, the only lubrication sent to the contact point between the camshaft lobes and the lifters (tappets) is from the splash off the crankshaft and connecting rods. At idle, engine oil does not splash enough for proper break-in lubrication of the camshaft.

FREQUENTLY ASKED QUESTION

WHAT IS BREAK-IN ENGINE OIL?

Many years ago, vehicle manufacturers used straight weight nondetergent engine oil as break-in oil. Today, the engine oil recommended for break-in (running in) is the same type of oil that is recommended for use in the engine. No special break-in oil is recommended or used by the factory in new vehicles. SAE 5W-30 or SAE 10W-30 engine oil is usually the specified viscosity recommended by most vehicle manufacturers.

After the engine has started, the following items should be checked:

1. Is the valve train quiet? Some engines will require several minutes to quiet down.
2. Record the engine vacuum. It should be 17 to 21 in. Hg at sea level.
3. Check for any gasoline, coolant, or oil leaks. Stop the engine and repair the leaks as soon as possible.
4. Check the charging system for proper operation. The charging voltage should be 13.5 to 15.0 volts.

As soon as you can tell that no serious leaks exist, and the engine is running reasonably well, the vehicle should be driven to a road having minimum traffic. Here, the vehicle should be accelerated, full throttle, from 30 to 50 miles per hour (48 to 80 kilometers per hour). Then the throttle is fully closed while the vehicle is allowed to return to 30 miles per hour (48 kilometers per hour). This sequence is repeated 10 to 12 times. The acceleration sequence puts a high load on the piston rings to properly seat them against the cylinder walls. The piston rings are the only part of the modern engine that needs to be broken in. Good ring seating is indicated by a dry coating inside the tailpipe at the completion of the ring seating drive.

The vehicle is returned to the service area, where the basic ignition timing is set and the idle speed is properly adjusted, if possible. The engine is again checked for visible fluid leaks. If the engine is dry, it is ready to be turned over to the customer.

The customer should be instructed to drive the vehicle in a normal fashion, neither babying it at slow speeds nor beating it at high speeds for the first 100 miles (160 kilometers). The oil and filter should be changed at 500 miles (800 kilometers) to remove any dirt that may have been trapped in the engine during assembly and to remove the material that has worn from the surfaces during the break-in period.

A well-designed engine that has been correctly reconditioned and assembled using the techniques described should give reliable service for many miles.

NORMAL OPERATING TEMPERATURE

Normal operating temperature is the temperature at which the upper radiator hose is hot and pressurized. Another standard method used to determine when normal operating temperature is reached is to observe the operation of the electric cooling fan, when the vehicle is so equipped. Many manufacturers define **normal operating temperature** as being reached when the cooling fan has cycled on and off at least once after the engine has been started. Some vehicle manufacturers specify that the cooling fan should cycle twice. This method also helps assure the technician that the engine is not being overheated.

HOW TO WARM UP A COLD ENGINE

The greatest amount of engine wear occurs during start-up. The oil in a cold engine is thick, and it requires several seconds to reach all the moving parts of an engine. After the engine starts, the engine should *not* be raced, but rather allowed to idle at the normal fast idle speed as provided for by the choke fast idle cam (on carburetor-equipped engines) or by the computer-controlled speed on fuel-injected engines. After the engine starts, allow the engine to idle until the oil pressure peaks. This will take from 15 seconds to about 1 full minute, depending on the outside temperature. *Do not allow the engine to idle for longer than 5 minutes.* Because an engine warms up faster under load, drive the vehicle in a normal manner until the engine is fully warm. Avoid full-throttle acceleration until the engine is completely up to normal operating temperature. This method of engine warm-up also warms the rest of the power train, including transmission and final drive component lubricants.

BREAK-IN PRECAUTIONS

Any engine overhaul represents many hours of work and a large financial investment. Precautions should be taken to protect the investment, including the following:

1. Never add cold water to the cooling system while the engine is running.
2. Never lug any engine. **Lugging** means increasing the throttle opening without increasing engine speed (RPM). Applying loads to an engine for *short periods* of time creates higher piston ring pressure against the cylinder walls and helps in the breaking-in process by helping to seat the rings.
3. Change the oil and filter at 500 miles (800 kilometers) or after 20 hours of operation.
4. Remember that the proper air–fuel ratio is important to the proper operation and long life of any engine. Any air leak (vacuum leak) could cause engine damaging detonation.
5. Be certain to use spark plugs for the proper heat range.

OIL CHANGE Step-by-Step

STEP 1 Begin the oil change process by safely hoisting the vehicle.

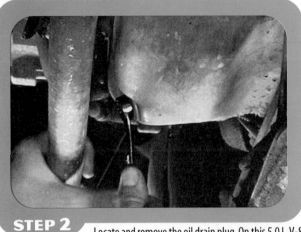

STEP 2 Locate and remove the oil drain plug. On this 5.0 L, V-8 Ford Mustang, two oil drain plugs are used. This is the front drain plug.

STEP 3 Loosen and remove the rear oil drain plug.

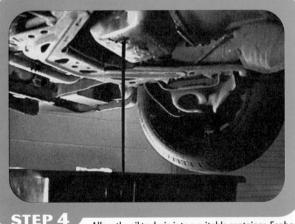

STEP 4 Allow the oil to drain into a suitable container. For best results, the oil drain should be close to the oil pan to help prevent the possibility of the oil splashing onto the floor or onto the service technician.

STEP 5 Carefully inspect the oil drain plug and gasket. Replace the gasket as needed or specified by the vehicle manufacturer (for example, Honda specifies that the aluminum seal on the drain plug be replaced at every oil change).

STEP 6 After all of the oil has been allowed to drain from the oil pan, reinstall the plug in the rear portion of the oil pan.

(continued)

OIL CHANGE continued

STEP 7 Also replace the oil drain plug in the front portion of the oil pan.

STEP 8 Using an oil filter wrench, remove the oil filter. Remember, "righty, tighty and lefty, loosy." Also be sure the oil drain pan is placed under the oil filter.

STEP 9 Check the area where the oil filter gasket seats to be sure that no part of the gasket remains that could cause an oil leak if not fully removed.

STEP 10 Also check the old oil filter to make sure the gasket has been removed with the oil filter. Also compare the replacement filter with the oil filter to double-check that the correct filter will be installed.

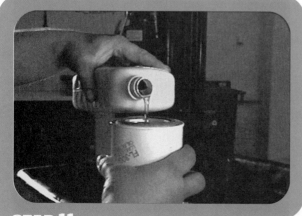

STEP 11 The wise service technician adds oil to the oil filter whenever possible. This provides faster filling of the filter during start-up and a reduced amount of the time that the engine does not have oil pressure.

STEP 12 Apply a thin layer of clean engine oil to the gasket of the new filter. This oil film will allow the rubber gasket to slide and compress as the oil filter is being rotated on the oil filter thread.

OIL CHANGE continued

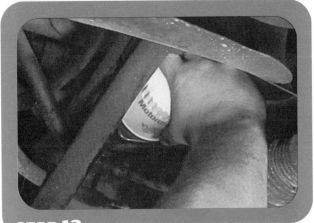

STEP 13 Install the new oil filter and tighten the recommended amount—usually 3/4 of a turn after the gasket contacts the engine.

STEP 14 Use a funnel to help avoid spills and add the specified amount of oil to the engine at the oil-filling opening. Oil capacity for passenger vehicles can vary from 3 quarts (liters) to over 7 quarts (liters).

STEP 15 Inspect and clean the oil-fill cap and reinstall it before starting the engine.

STEP 16 Start the engine and allow it to idle while watching the oil pressure gauge and/or oil pressure warning lamp.

STEP 17 The oil pressure gauge should register and the oil pressure warning lamp should go out within 15 seconds of starting the engine. If not, stop the engine and determine the cause before starting the engine again.

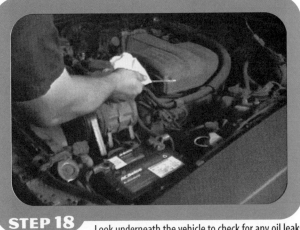

STEP 18 Look underneath the vehicle to check for any oil leaks at the oil drain plug(s) or oil filter. Pull out the oil-level dipstick and wipe it clean with a shop cloth.

(continued)

OIL CHANGE continued

STEP 19 Reinstall the oil-level dipstick to check the oil level.

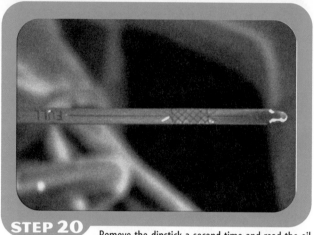

STEP 20 Remove the dipstick a second time and read the oil level. The oil level should be at the full mark as shown. If overfilled, hoist the vehicle and drain some oil out. An engine that has been overfilled with oil can be damaged because the oil can be aerated (filled with air like a milkshake) reducing the lubricating properties of the engine oil. Be sure to thoroughly wash your hands with soap and water after touching used engine oil or wear protective rubber gloves.

WATER PUMP AND TIMING BELT REPLACEMENT   Step-by-Step

STEP 1   A view of the 3.0 L, V-6 Dodge minivan that needs a new water pump because it is leaking from the weep hole.

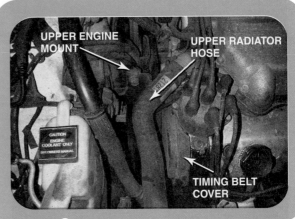

STEP 2   Because the entire front of the engine has to be disassembled, including the removal of the upper engine mount on the passenger side, the timing belt will also be replaced.

STEP 3   After draining the cooling system, the upper radiator hose and the accessory drive belt are removed.

STEP 4   The vehicle is hoisted and the right front wheel/tire assembly is removed to gain access to the front of the engine.

STEP 5   The splash shield has to be removed to gain access to the front accessory drive pulley.

STEP 6   The retaining bolts holding the accessory drive belt pulley to the harmonic balancer are removed.

(continued)

WATER PUMP AND TIMING BELT REPLACEMENT continued

STEP 7 A puller is used to remove the harmonic balancer.

STEP 8 While under the vehicle, the air-conditioning compressor bracket is removed.

STEP 9 Before removing the upper engine mount, the engine is being supported by a floor jack. Notice that a block of wood is placed between the oil pan and the jack.

STEP 10 With the engine supported from underneath, the upper engine mount is removed.

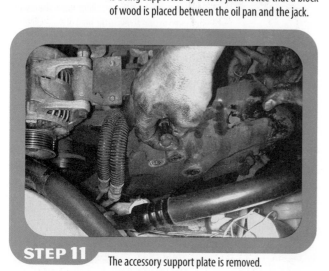

STEP 11 The accessory support plate is removed.

STEP 12 The timing belt cover(s) can now be removed.

WATER PUMP AND TIMING BELT REPLACEMENT   continued

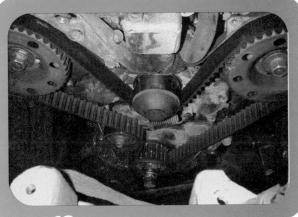

STEP 13 A view of the front of the engine with the timing belt covers removed.

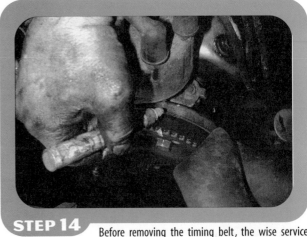

STEP 14 Before removing the timing belt, the wise service technician marks the location of the belt and pulley as a precaution to be sure that the new replacement belt will be placed back into proper time.

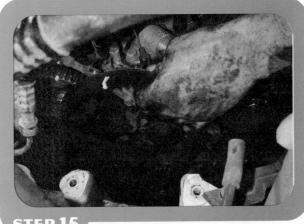

STEP 15 The spring tensioner is moved and the belt removed.

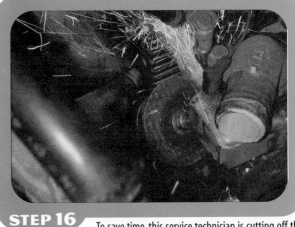

STEP 16 To save time, this service technician is cutting off the head of one bolt that holds a support bracket. This bolt cannot be removed without removing the entire intake manifold.

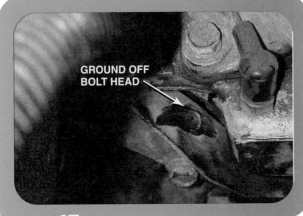

GROUND OFF
BOLT HEAD

STEP 17 With the bolt head removed, the bracket is lifted up slightly, allowing room to remove the water pump. The bracket is still retained by another bolt.

STEP 18 After the water pump retaining bolts have been removed, a screwdriver or pry bar is needed to remove the water pump. *(continued)*

WATER PUMP AND TIMING BELT REPLACEMENT continued

WATER PUMP

STEP 19 Removing the water pump from the front of the engine.

WATER PUMP TUBE

STEP 20 After the water pump is removed, the tube used to transfer coolant the length of the block is visible. The water pump slides over the seal on the end of the tube. This tube and seal are the reason why a pry bar was needed to remove the water pump.

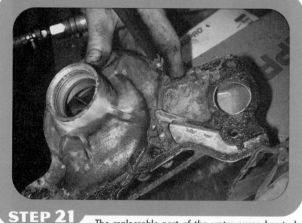

STEP 21 The replaceable part of the water pump has to be removed from the housing. There is a hidden Phillips screw on the backside that has to be removed.

STEP 22 After removing the Phillips screw on the backside, turn the water pump over and remove the rest of the retaining bolts.

STEP 23 After all retaining bolts have been removed, separate the water pump from the housing.

STEP 24 A fiber disc on an air grinder is being used to remove the old gasket material.

WATER PUMP AND TIMING BELT REPLACEMENT   continued

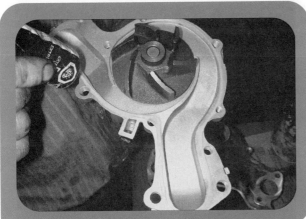

STEP 25 Gasket adhesive is being applied to the gasket surface of the replacement water pump.

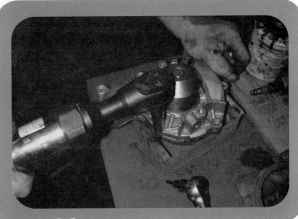

STEP 26 Assembling the new water pump onto the original water pump housing.

STEP 27 Attaching new gaskets to the outlet flanges of the water pump.

STEP 28 Before installing the water pump, the block has to be cleaned of the old gaskets.

STEP 29 A view of the front of the engine with the replacement water pump installed.

STEP 30 After the water pump is installed, the new timing belt can be installed.

(continued)

WATER PUMP AND TIMING BELT REPLACEMENT continued

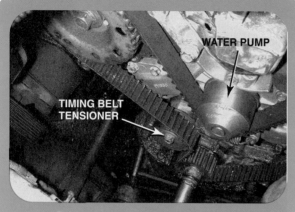

STEP 31
Notice that the timing belt drives the water pump. This is the reason why both the timing belt and the water pump are being replaced. The spring-loaded tensioner applies tension to the timing belt.

STEP 32
Before reinstalling everything, the cooling system is connected and partially filled and then pressure tested to check to make sure there are no leaks. This step is very important on this engine because of the design of the water pump fitting over the transfer tube.

STEP 33
After making sure that everything is okay with the installation of the water pump and there are no leaks, the timing belt cover and upper engine mount can be reinstalled.

STEP 34
After the engine mount has been replaced, the floor jack being used to support the engine is removed.

STEP 35
All the other brackets and hoses can now be reinstalled.

STEP 36
The vehicle is hoisted and the harmonic balancer and air-conditioning bracket is reinstalled.

WATER PUMP AND TIMING BELT REPLACEMENT continued

STEP 37 The accessory drive pulley is then installed on the harmonic balancer and the bolts torqued to factory specifications.

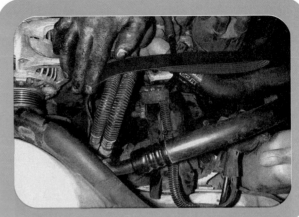

STEP 38 After the drive pulley has been installed, the accessory drive belt is installed.

STEP 39 After double-checking that everything is properly reinstalled and torqued, the splash shield can be installed.

STEP 40 Install the wheel/tire assembly and wheel cover.

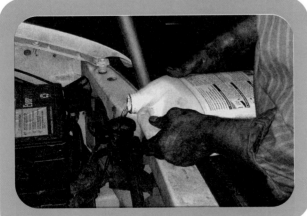

STEP 41 The vehicle is now lowered and the cooling system filled with new coolant.

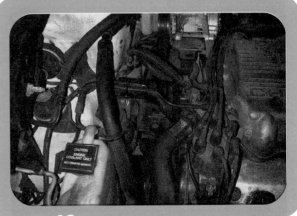

STEP 42 The repair is completed four hours after starting. The vehicle should be test driven and all connections double-checked before returning the vehicle to the customer.

SUMMARY

1. Carefully install all accessories.
2. When installing the transmission and other components on the engine block, be sure to use a torque wrench and tighten all fasteners to factory specifications.
3. Always adjust the clutch free play before starting the engine.
4. Temperature recording sensors should be installed on cylinder heads. This lets the rebuild technician know if the engine has been overheated.
5. A new oxygen sensor(s) should be installed to ensure that the engine operation is within acceptable limits. If the oxygen sensor is defective, the engine may operate too lean. A lean-operating engine runs hotter than normal.
6. Change the engine oil after 500 miles (800 kilometers) or sooner, and use SAE 5W-30 or SAE 10W-30 engine oil.

REVIEW QUESTIONS

1. How are the clutch and bell housing installed?
2. What should be done to help prevent rear cylinder distortion when the bell housing is being installed on the engine?
3. Describe the engine break-in procedure.

CHAPTER QUIZ

1. What can an engine rebuilder install that monitors if the engine has been overheated?
   a. A thermal disc
   b. A coolant leak detector
   c. An oil level gauge
   d. Either b or c

2. If the bell housing is not properly torqued to the engine block, _____.
   a. The bell housing will distort
   b. The engine block will crack
   c. The rear cylinder can be distorted (become out-of-round)
   d. The crankshaft will crack

3. Break-in engine oil is _____.
   a. Of the same viscosity and grade as that specified for normal engine operation
   b. SAE 40
   c. SAE 30
   d. SAE 20W-50

4. Normal operating temperature is reached when _____.
   a. The radiator cap releases coolant into the overflow
   b. The upper radiator hose is hot and pressurized
   c. The electric cooling fan has cycled at least once (if the vehicle is so equipped)
   d. Both b and c occur

5. Lugging an engine means _____.
   a. Wide-open throttle in low gear above 25 miles per hour
   b. That engine speed does not increase when the throttle is opened wider
   c. Starting a cold engine and allowing it to idle for longer than 5 minutes
   d. Both b and c

6. Which computer sensor should be replaced if the engine had been found to have a defective head gasket or cracked head?
   a. Throttle position sensor
   b. Oxygen sensor
   c. Manifold absolute pressure sensor
   d. Engine coolant temperature sensor

7. How should the vehicle bc driven to best break in a newly overhauled engine?
   a. At steady and low speeds
   b. At varying speeds and loads
   c. At high speeds and heavy loads
   d. A idle speed and little or no load

8. Normal operating temperature is achieved when _____?

   a. When heat comes from the heater

   b. When the cooling fan cycle

   c. When the engine exhaust gets hot

   d. When the lower radiator hose gets hot

9. Pre-lubricating the engine should be done by using the starter motor to rotate the engine until oil pressure is displayed on a gauge.

   a. True

   b. False

10. Why must an engine equipped with flat-bottom lifters be broken in at a fast idle?

    a. The camshaft in a cam-in-block engine is only lubricated by splash oil

    b. The flat-bottom lifters have to wear slightly concave in order to rotate

    c. Both a and b are correct

    d. Neither a nor b are correct

TIMING BELT REPLACEMENT GUIDE

(The number in parentheses represents a footnote at the end of the vehicle listing.)

Vehicle Manufacturer	Engine	Manufacturers' Recommended Replacement Intervals	Interference?	Engine Damage if Belt Breaks? (22)
Acura	1.6L	(1)	Yes	Yes
	1.7L, 2.5L, & 2.7L V-6	90,000 miles or 72 months	Yes	Yes
	2.2L	105,000 miles or 84 months	Yes	Yes
	1.8L, 2.5L 5-Cyl	(2)	Yes	Yes
	3.2L V-6 (Legend & 3.2TL)	(2)	Yes	Yes
	3.0L, 3.5L	(3)	Yes	Yes
	3.2L, 3.5L (SLX)	60,000 miles	Yes	Yes
Alfa Romeo	3.0L	(1)	No	No
American Motors	2.0L	(1)	No	No
Audi	Gasoline Engines	(1)	No	No
BMW	Diesel Engines	(1)	Yes	Yes
	2.5L, 2.7L	60,000 miles (4)	Yes	Yes
Chrysler	1.4L, 1.5L, 1.6L SOHC and DOHC	60,000 miles	Yes	Yes
	1.8L, 3.0L SOHC	(5)	No	No
	3.0L DOHC	(5)	Yes	Yes
	1.7L	(1)	No	No
	2.0L, 2.4L SOHC	(6)	No	No
	2.0L DOHC	(6)	Yes	Yes
	2.2L SOHC, 2.5L	90,000 miles	No	No
	2.2L DOHC	90,000 miles	Yes	Yes
	2.3L Diesel	50,000 miles	Yes	Yes
	2.4L DOHC	(7)	Yes	Yes
	2.5L V-6	(8)	No	No
	3.5L	105,000 miles	No	No

(continued)

Vehicle Manufacturer	Engine	Manufacturers' Recommended Replacement Intervals	Interference?	Engine Damage if Belt Breaks? (22)
Daewoo	1.6L, 2.0L	(1)	No	No
Daihatsu	1.0L	(9)	Yes	Yes
	1.3L	60,000 miles	Yes	Yes
Fiat	1.3L (Air Pump & Camshaft)	36,000 miles (10)	Yes	Yes
	1.5L, 2.0L	30,000 miles (10)	Yes	Yes
	1.6L	25,000 miles or 24 months (10)	Yes	Yes
	1.8L (1974–1977)	25,000 miles or 24 months (10)	Yes	Yes
	1.8L (1978)	25,000 miles (10)	Yes	Yes
Ford	1.3L, 1.6L SOHC (Ford)	60,000 miles	Yes	Yes
	1.6L SOHC (Mazda) & 1.6L DOHC, 1.8L	60,000 miles	No	No
	1.9L, 2.0L DOHC Gasoline (except Probe)	(1)	No	No
	2.0L SOHC Gasoline (except 1997 Escort/Tracer)	100,000 miles	No	No
	2.0L SOHC Gasoline (1997 Escort/Tracer)	(1)	No	No
	2.0L DOHC Gasoline (Probe) 2.5L V-6	60,000 miles	No	No
	2.2L	60,000 miles	Yes	Yes
	2.0L Diesel, 2.3L Diesel (Camshaft and Balance Shaft Belts)	(1)	Yes	Yes
	2.3L SOHC Gasoline	(1)	No	No
	3.0L & 3.2L SHO	100,000 miles	No	No
General Motors	1.0L, 1.4L, 1.6L, 1.8L Gasoline	(1)	No	No
	1.0L Diesel	(1)	Yes	Yes
	2.0L, 2.3L	(1)	No	No
	3.0L V-6	(1)	Yes	Yes
	1.5L, 2.2L Diesel	60,000 miles	Yes	Yes
	3.4L DOHC	60,000 miles	No	No
GEO	1.0L, 1.6L SOHC (Tracker)	(11)	No	No
	1.3L	100,000 miles	No	No
	1.5L	60,000 miles	Yes	Yes
	1.6L DOHC (Storm)	(1)	No	No

Vehicle Manufacturer	Engine	Manufacturers' Recommended Replacement Intervals	Interference?	Engine Damage if Belt Breaks? (22)
GEO (cont.)	1.6L SOHC & DOHC (Prizm), 1.8L DOHC, 1993 & Prior	60,000 miles	Yes	Yes
	1.6L SOHC & DOHC (Prizm)	(1)	No	No
	1.8L DOHC (Prizm) 1994 and Later	(1)	No	No
	1.8L DOHC (Storm) 1994 & Later	(1)	Yes	Yes
Honda	1.2L, 1.3L, 1.8L	(1)	Yes	Yes
	1.5L, 1.6L, 2.0L DOHC	(12)	Yes	Yes
	2.0L SOHC	(12)	No	No
	2.1L, 2.3L	90,000 miles or 72 months	Yes	Yes
	2.2L SOHC & DOHC, 2.7L	(12)	Yes	Yes
	2.6L	60,000 miles	Yes	Yes
	3.2L	60,000 miles	No	No
Hyundai	1.5L, 1.6L, 1.8L, 2.0L, 2.4L	60,000 miles	Yes	Yes
	3.0L (1995 & Prior)	60,000 miles	No	No
	1.5L, 1.6L, 1.8L, 2.0L, 2.4L	(1)	Yes	Yes
	3.0L (1996 & Later)	(1)	No	No
Infiniti	3.0L (1993 & Prior)	60,000 miles	Yes	Yes
	3.0L (1994 & Later)	105,000 miles	Yes	Yes
	3.3L	105,000 miles	Yes	Yes
Isuzu	1.5L, 1.6L DOHC, 1.8L DOHC Gasoline	60,000 miles	Yes	Yes
	1.6L SOHC	60,000 miles	No	No
	1.8L Diesel, 2.0L, 2.2L Diesel, 2.3L, 2.6L	60,000 miles	Yes	Yes
	3.2L, 3.5L	60,000 miles	Yes	Yes
Jeep	2.0L	(1)	No	No
KIA	1.6L DOHC, 1.8L DOHC, 2.0L DOHC	(13)	Yes	Yes
	1.6L SOHC, 2.0L SOHC	(13)	No	No
Lancia	1.8L	25,000 miles	Yes	Yes
Lexus	2.5 L	60,000 miles	No	No
	3.0L Inline, 3.0L V-6, 4.0L V-8	(21)	No	No

(continued)

Vehicle Manufacturer	Engine	Manufacturers' Recommended Replacement Intervals	Interference?	Engine Damage if Belt Breaks? (22)
Mazda	1.6L SOHC & DOHC, 1.8L SOHC & DOHC 4-Cyl	60,000 miles	No	No
	1.8L V-6	105,000 miles	No	No
	2.0L SOHC	60,000 miles	No	No
	2.0L DOHC, 2.2L	60,000 miles	Yes	Yes
	2.0L Diesel (Camshaft & Injection Pump)	100,000 miles	Yes	Yes
	2.3L (B2300)	(1)	No	No
	2.3L V-6, 2.5L	60,000 miles	No	No
	3.0L SOHC & DOHC	60,000 miles	Yes	Yes
Mitsubishi	1.5L, 1.6L SOHC & DOHC, 1.8L, 2.0L DOHC	(5)	Yes	Yes
	1.8L & 2.0L SOHC, 2.4L SOHC, 3.0L SOHC	(5)	No	No
	2.3L Diesel, 2.4L DOHC, & 3.0L DOHC, 3.5L	(5)	Yes	Yes
Nissan	1.5L	(1)	Yes	Yes
	1.6L SOHC, 1.7L Diesel, 2.0L, 3.0L SOHC	(14)	Yes	Yes
	1.6L DOHC, 1.8L DOHC	60,000 miles	Yes	Yes
	3.0L DOHC	(15)	Yes	Yes
	3.3L	105,000 miles	Yes	Yes
Peugeot	1.9L	(1)	No	No
	2.2L	(1)	Yes	Yes
Porsche	2.0L, 2.5L, 2.7L, 3.0L	(16)	Yes	Yes
	4.5L, 4.7L, 5.0L, 5.4L	(17)	Yes	Yes
Renault	1.7L	(1)	Yes	Yes
	2.2L	(1)	No	No
Saab	2.5L & 3.0L	(1)	Yes	Yes
Sterling	2.5L & 2.7L	(1)	Yes	Yes
Subaru	1.2L, 2.2L, 2.7L, 3.3L, 1.8L (Impreza)	60,000 miles	No	No
	1.8L (except Impreza)	52,000 miles	No	No
Suzuki	1.3L SOHC, 1.6L (8-Valve)	(18)	No	No
	1.3L DOHC, 1.6L (16-Valve)	(18)	Yes	Yes

Vehicle Manufacturer	Engine	Manufacturers' Recommended Replacement Intervals	Interference?	Engine Damage if Belt Breaks? (22)
Toyota	1.5L, 1.6L DOHC	(21)	Yes	Yes
	1.6L SOHC, 1.8L Gasoline	(21)	No	No
	1.8L Diesel, 2.2L Diesel	60,000 miles	Yes	Yes
	2.5L, 2.8L	60,000 miles	No	No
	2.0L, 2.2L Gasoline, 3.0L Inline, 3.0L V-6	(21)	No	No
	2.4L Diesel	100,000 miles	Yes	Yes
	3.4L	(1)	No	No
Volkswagen	Gasoline Engine	(1)	No	No
	Diesel Engine	(1)	Yes	Yes
Volvo	2.1L, 2.3L (B23), 2.3L 4-Cyl (B230, B230F, & B230FT)	(19)	Yes	Yes
	2.3L 4-Cyl (B234)	50,000 miles	Yes	Yes
	2.3L 5-Cyl, 2.4L 5-Cyl Gasoline	70,000 miles	Yes	Yes
	2.9L	70,000 miles	No	No
Yugo	1.1L & 1.3L	(20)	Yes	Yes

Footnotes

(1) Manufacturer does not recommend a specific maintenance interval.

(2) On 1996 and prior models, 90,000 miles or 72 months; on 1997 models, under normal conditions, 105,000 miles or 84 months (60,000 miles if the vehicle is operated at ambient temperatures under −20°F or above 110°F).

(3) Under normal conditions, 105,000 miles or 84 months (60,000 miles if the vehicle is operated at ambient temperatures under −20°F or above 110°F).

(4) When the tensioner roller has been released, regardless of belt age or condition. After replacement, a label indicating the mileage and date that service has been performed should be affixed to the cylinder head cover.

(5) On 1994 and prior models, 60,000 miles; on 1995 to 1997 California models, 60,000 miles is recommended but not required; on all 1995 to 1997 models, at 100,000 miles (if not previously replaced).

(6) 1994 and prior models, intervals of 60,000 miles; on 1995 to 1997 Breeze, Cirrus, Stratus, and Sebring Convertible models, 105,000-mile intervals are recommended but not required. On Avenger and Sebring (except convertible), Summit Wagon, and Talon California models, 60,000-mile intervals are recommended but not required. On all 1995 to 1997 Avenger, Sebring (except convertible), Summit Wagon, and Talon models, at 100,000 miles (if not previously replaced).

(7) On California models, 60,000-mile intervals are recommended but not required; on all models, replace at 100,000 miles (if not previously replaced).

(8) On Breeze, Cirrus, Stratus, and Sebring Convertible models, 105,000-mile intervals are recommended but not required; on Avenger and Sebring California models (except convertible), 60,000-mile intervals are recommended but not required; on Avenger and Sebring models (except convertible), at 100,000 miles (if not previously replaced).

(9) 60,000-mile intervals if vehicle operates under extensive idling, low-speed driving for long distances, on dusty, muddy, or rough roads.

(10) Timing belt must be replaced any time tension is relieved.

(11) On 1996 and prior models, inspect and adjust belt at 30,000 and 60,000 miles; replace timing belt at 60,000 miles. On 1996 and later models, inspect and adjust belt at 30,000- and 60,000-mile intervals; replace timing belt at 100,000 miles.

(12) On 1989 and prior models, manufacturer does not recommend a specific interval; on 1990 to 1996 models, 90,000-mile intervals or 72 months; on 1997 models, under normal conditions, at intervals of 105,000 miles or 84 months (60,000-mile intervals if operated at ambient temperatures under −20°F or above 110°F).

(13) On non-California models, 60,000-mile intervals; on California models, inspect at 60,000-mile intervals and replace at 90,000-mile intervals.

(14) On 1985 and prior models, manufacturer does not recommend a specific interval; on 1986 to 1993 models, 60,000-mile intervals; on 1994 to 1997 and later models, 105,000-mile intervals.

(15) On early 1993 and prior models, 60,000-mile intervals; on late 1993 and later models less turbo, 105,000-mile intervals; on late 1993 and later models with turbo, 60,000-mile intervals.

(continued)

(16) Under normal operation, 45,000-mile intervals; check tension at 2,000 miles, then every 15,000 miles.

(17) Under normal operation, 60,000-mile intervals; check tension at 2,000 miles, then every 15,000 miles.

(18) On 1994 and prior models, manufacturer does not recommend a specific interval; on 1995 to 1997 California models, 60,000-mile intervals are recommended but not required; on all 1995 to 1997 models, at 100,000 miles (if not previously replaced).

(19) On 1985 and prior models, 40,000-mile intervals; 1986 to 1994 and later models, 50,000-mile intervals; 1995 and later models, 100,000-mile intervals.

(20) Inspect every 15,000 miles.

(21) On 1993 and prior models, replace at 60,000-mile intervals; on 1994 and later models, manufacturer does not recommend a specific maintenance interval.

(22) Always check for engine damage that can still occur in the event of a timing belt failure even if "no" is listed.

ASE TEST CORRELATION CHART

Engine Repair (A1)

ASE Task List	Textbook Page No.
A. General Engine Diagnosis (17 questions)	
1. Verify the driver's complaint and/or road test the vehicle; determine necessary action.	339
2. Determine if the no-crank, no-start, or hard starting condition is an ignition system, cranking system, fuel system, or engine mechanical problem.	340
3. Inspect the engine assembly for fuel, oil, coolant, and other leaks; determine necessary action.	340
4. Listen to engine noises; determine necessary action.	341
5. Diagnose the cause of excessive oil consumption, coolant consumption, unusual engine exhaust color, odor, and sound; determine necessary action.	340
6. Perform engine vacuum tests; determine necessary action.	347–350
7. Perform cylinder power balance tests; determine necessary action.	343
8. Perform cylinder compression tests; determine necessary action.	342–345
9. Perform cylinder leakage tests; determine necessary action.	345–346
B. Cylinder Head and Valve Train Diagnosis and Repair (18 questions)	
1. Remove cylinder heads, disassemble, clean, and prepare for inspection according to manufacturers' procedures.	358, 381–383
2. Visually inspect cylinder heads for cracks; gasket surface areas for warpage, corrosion, and leakage; and check passage condition.	366–367
3. Inspect and test valve springs for squareness, pressure, and free height comparison; replace as necessary.	408–410
4. Inspect valve spring retainers, rotators, locks, and valve lock grooves.	426–429
5. Replace valve stem seals.	426–429
6. Inspect valve guides for wear; check valve guide height and stem-to-guide clearance; determine needed repairs.	387–389
7. Inspect valves; resurface or replace according to manufacturers' procedures.	412–414
8. Inspect and resurface valve seats according to manufacturers' procedures.	413–417
9. Check valve face-to-seat contact and valve seat concentricity (runout).	413–417
10. Check valve spring installed (assembled) height and valve stem height; service valve and spring assemblies as necessary.	424–425

(continued)

ASE Task List	Textbook Page No.
11. Inspect pushrods, rocker arms, rocker arm pivots, and shafts for wear, bending, cracks, looseness, and blocked oil passages; repair or replace as required.	448–451
12. Inspect and replace hydraulic or mechanical lifters/lash adjusters.	467–473
13. Adjust valves on engines with mechanical or hydraulic lifters.	473
14. Inspect and replace camshaft drives (includes checking gear wear and backlash, sprocket and chain wear, overhead cam drive sprockets, drive belts, belt tension, tensioners, and cam sensor components).	442–446
15. Inspect and measure camshaft journals and lobes.	447
16. Inspect and measure camshaft bore for wear, damage, out-of-round, and alignment; repair or replace according to manufacturers' specifications.	442
17. Time camshaft(s) to crankshaft.	583–584
18. Reassemble and install cylinder heads and gaskets; replace and tighten fasteners according to manufacturers' procedures.	581–583
C. Engine Block Diagnosis and Repair (18 questions)	
1. Disassemble engine block and clean and prepare components for inspection.	358–361
2. Visually inspect engine block for cracks, corrosion, passage condition, core and gallery plug holes, and surface warpage; determine necessary action.	366–367
3. Inspect and repair damaged threads where allowed; install core and gallery plugs.	38–40
4. Inspect and measure cylinder walls; remove cylinder wall ridges; hone and clean cylinder walls; determine need for further action.	359
5. Visually inspect crankshaft for surface cracks and journal damage; check oil passage condition; measure journal wear; check crankshaft sensor reluctor ring (where applicable); determine necessary action.	531
6. Inspect and measure main bearing bores and cap alignment and fit.	536–538
7. Install main bearings and crankshaft; check bearing clearances and end play; replace/retorque bolts according to manufacturers' procedures.	573–574
8. Inspect camshaft bearings for unusual wear; remove and replace camshaft bearings; install camshaft, timing chain, and gears; check end play.	569–570
9. Inspect auxiliary (balance, intermediate, idler, counterbalance, or silencer) shaft(s) and support bearings for damage and wear; determine necessary action.	547
10. Inspect, measure, service, repair, or replace pistons, piston pins, and pin bushings; identify piston and bearing wear patterns that indicate connecting rod alignment problems; determine necessary action.	490
11. Inspect connecting rods for damage, alignment, bore condition, and pin fit; determine necessary action.	493
12. Inspect, measure, and install or replace piston rings; assemble piston and connecting rod; install piston/rod assembly; check bearing clearance and sideplay; replace/retorque fasteners according to manufacturers' procedures.	495
13. Inspect, reinstall, or replace crankshaft vibration damper (harmonic balancer).	530
14. Inspect crankshaft flange and flywheel mating surfaces; inspect and replace crankshaft pilot bearing/bushing (if applicable); inspect flywheel/flexplate for cracks and wear (includes flywheel ring gear); measure flywheel runout; determine necessary action.	531

ASE Task List	Textbook Page No.
15. Inspect and replace pans, covers, gaskets, and seals.	588
16. Assemble engine parts using formed-in-place (tube-applied) sealants or gaskets.	586–587
D. Lubrication and Cooling Systems Diagnosis and Repair (9 questions)	
1. Perform oil pressure tests; determine necessary action.	342
2. Disassemble, inspect, measure, and repair oil pump (includes gears, rotors, housing, and pick-up assembly), pressure relief devices, and pump drive; replace oil filter.	220
3. Perform cooling system tests; determine necessary action.	191
4. Inspect, replace, and adjust drive belts, tensioners, and pulleys.	193, 200
5. Inspect and replace engine cooling and heater system hoses.	202
6. Inspect, test, and replace thermostat, bypass, and housing.	184
7. Inspect coolant; drain, flush, and refill cooling system with recommended coolant; bleed air as required.	187
8. Inspect and replace water pump.	194
9. Inspect, test, and replace radiator, heater core, pressure cap, and coolant recovery system.	202
10. Clean, inspect, test, and replace fan (both electrical and mechanical), fan clutch, fan shroud, air dams, and cooling related temperature sensors.	196–199
11. Inspect, test, and replace auxiliary oil coolers.	226
E. Fuel, Electrical, Ignition, and Exhaust Systems Inspection and Service (8 questions)	
1. Inspect, clean, or replace fuel and air induction system components, intake manifold, and gaskets.	586
2. Inspect, service, or replace air filters, filter housings, and intake ductwork.	313–314
3. Inspect turbocharger/supercharger; determine necessary action.	332–333
4. Test battery; charge as necessary.	237
5. Remove and replace starter.	241
6. Inspect and replace positive crankcase ventilation (PCV) system components.	296–297
7. Visually inspect and reinstall primary and secondary ignition system components; time distributor.	271–272
8. Inspect, service, and replace exhaust manifold.	586

NATEF TASK LIST

Engine Repair

For every task in Engine Repair, the following safety requirement must be strictly enforced:

Comply with personal and environmental safety practices associated with clothing; eye protection; hand tools; power equipment; proper ventilation; and the handling, storage, and disposal of chemicals/materials in accordance with local, state, and federal safety and environmental regulations.

Task	Textbook Page No.	Worktext Page No.
A. General Engine Diagnosis; Removal and Reinstallation (R & R)		
1. Complete work order to include customer information, vehicle identifying information, customer concern, related service history, cause, and correction. (P-1)	98	15
2. Identify and interpret engine concern; determine necessary action. (P-1)	338–351	16, 30, 88, 89
3. Research applicable vehicle and service information, such as internal engine operation, vehicle service history, service precautions, and technical service bulletins. (P-1)	98–105	17, 19, 20, 24, 25, 31, 42, 85, 86, 114, 124, 125, 132, 142, 149, 169
4. Locate and interpret vehicle and major component identification numbers. (P-1)	108–112	18, 22, 23, 26, 28, 29
5. Inspect engine assembly for fuel, oil, coolant, and other leaks; determine necessary action. (P-1)	339–340	90, 91, 92, 93
6. Diagnose engine noises and vibrations; determine necessary action. (P-2)	340–341	94, 95
7. Diagnose the cause of excessive oil consumption, coolant consumption, unusual engine exhaust color and odor; determine necessary action. (P-2)	338–340	96
8. Perform engine vacuum tests; determine necessary action. (P-1)	347–350	97
9. Perform cylinder power balance tests; determine necessary action. (P-2)	343	98, 99
10. Perform cylinder cranking and running compression tests; determine necessary action. (P-1)	342–345	100
11. Perform cylinder leakage tests; determine necessary action. (P-1)	345–346	101, 102
12. Remove and reinstall engine in an OBDII or newer vehicle; reconnect all attaching components and restore the vehicle to running condition. (P-2)	357–358	104, 105, 205
13. Install engine covers using gaskets, seals and sealers as required. (P-1)	588–589	170, 206

Task	Textbook Page No.	Worktext Page No.
14. Perform common fastener and thread repair, to include: remove broken bolt, restore internal and external threads, and repair internal threads with thread insert. (P-1)	38–40	4
15. Inspect, remove and replace engine mounts. (P-2)	600	106
B. Cylinder Head and Valve Train Diagnosis and Repair		
1. Remove cylinder head; inspect gasket condition; install cylinder head and gasket; tighten according to manufacturer's specifications and procedures. (P-1)	358, 381–383	115, 171
2. Clean and visually inspect a cylinder head for cracks; check gasket surface areas for warpage and surface finish; check passage condition. (P-1)	383, 366–367	116, 123, 182
3. Inspect valve springs for squareness and free height comparison; determine necessary action. (P-3)	408–410	117
4. Replace valve stem seals on an assembled engine; inspect valve spring retainers, locks/keepers, and valve lock/keeper grooves; determine necessary action. (P-3)	426–429	126
5. Inspect valve guides for wear; check valve stem-to-guide clearance; determine necessary action. (P-3)	387–389	118
6. Inspect valves and valve seats; determine necessary action. (P-3)	413–417	127, 128
7. Check valve spring assembled height and valve stem height; determine necessary action. (P-3)	424–425	129
8. Inspect pushrods, rocker arms, rocker arm pivots and shafts for wear, bending, cracks, looseness, and blocked oil passages (orifices); determine necessary action. (P-2)	448–451	133, 134
9. Inspect valve lifters; determine necessary action. (P-2)	467–473	135
10. Adjust valves (mechanical or hydraulic lifters). (P-1)	473	136
11. Inspect and replace camshaft and drive belt/chain (includes checking drive gear wear and backlash, end play, sprocket and chain wear, overhead cam drive sprocket(s), drive belt(s), belt tension, tensioners, camshaft reluctor ring/tone-wheel, and variable valve timing components). (P-1)	442–446	137, 172, 207, 208
12. Inspect and/or measure camshaft for runout, journal wear and lobe wear. (P-2)	441–448	138, 139
13. Inspect camshaft bearing surface for wear, damage, out-of-round, and alignment; determine necessary action. (P-2)	447	140
14. Establish camshaft position sensor indexing. (P-1)	583–584	141
C. Engine Block Assembly Diagnosis and Repair		
1. Disassemble engine block; clean and prepare components for inspection and reassembly. (P-1)	358–361	108
2. Inspect engine block for visible cracks, passage condition, core and gallery plug condition, and surface warpage; determine necessary action. (P-2)	366–367	150
3. Inspect and measure cylinder walls/sleeves for damage, wear, and ridges; determine necessary action. (P-2)	359	151
4. Deglaze and clean cylinder walls. (P-2)	509–511	152
5. Inspect and measure camshaft bearings for wear, damage, out-of-round, and alignment; determine necessary action. (P-3)	456	153
6. Inspect crankshaft for straightness, journal damage, keyway damage, thrust flange and sealing surface condition, and visual surface cracks; check oil passage condition; measure end play and journal wear; check crankshaft position sensor reluctor ring (where applicable); determine necessary action. (P-1)	531	161, 162, 183

Task	Textbook Page No.	Worktext Page No.
7. Inspect main and connecting rod bearings for damage and wear; determine necessary action. (P-2)	536–538	163, 173, 184
8. Identify piston and bearing wear patterns that indicate connecting rod alignment and main bearing bore problems; determine necessary action. (P-3)	493	143, 164, 185
9. Inspect and measure piston skirts and ring lands; determine necessary action. (P-2)	490	147
10. Remove and replace piston pin. (P-3)	490, 494	144
11. Determine piston-to-bore clearance. (P-2)	510	154, 174, 186
12. Inspect, measure, and install piston rings. (P-2)	495	145, 146
13. Inspect auxiliary shaft(s) (balance, intermediate, idler, counterbalance, or silencer); inspect shaft(s) and support bearings for damage and wear; determine necessary action; reinstall and time. (P-2)	547	166, 187
14. Remove, inspect or replace crankshaft vibration damper (harmonic balancer). (P-2)	530	165, 188
15. Assemble engine block. (P-1)	573–578	189, 190
D. Lubrication and Cooling Systems Diagnosis and Repair		
1. Perform oil pressure tests; determine necessary action. (P-1)	342	103
2. Inspect oil pump gears or rotors, housing, pressure relief devices, and pump drive; perform necessary action. (P-2)	220	43, 191
3. Perform cooling system pressure tests; check coolant condition; inspect and test radiator, pressure cap, coolant recovery tank, and hoses; determine necessary action. (P-1)	191	32, 33
4. Inspect, replace, and adjust drive belts, tensioners, and pulleys; check pulley and belt alignment. (P-1)	193, 200	34
5. Inspect and replace engine cooling and heater system hoses. (P-1)	202	35, 192
6. Inspect, test, and replace thermostat and gasket/seal. (P-1)	184	36, 193
7. Test coolant; drain and recover coolant; flush and refill cooling system with recommended coolant; bleed air as required. (P-1)	187	37
8. Inspect test, remove, and replace water pump. (P-2)	194	38, 194
9. Remove and replace radiator. (P-2)	203	39, 195
10. Inspect, and test fans(s) (electrical or mechanical), fan clutch, fan shroud, and air dams. (P-1)	196–199	40, 196
11. Inspect auxiliary coolers; determine necessary action. (P-3)	226	44
12. Inspect, test, and replace oil temperature and pressure switches and sensors. (P-2)	227	45
13. Perform oil and filter change. (P-1)	214	209
14. Identify causes of engine overheating. (P-1)	199	41

ENGLISH GLOSSARY

ACEA Association des Constructeurs European d'Automobiles represents most of the Western European automobile and heavy-duty truck market. The organization uses different engines for testing than those used by API and SAE, and the requirements necessary to meet the ACEA standards are different yet generally correspond with most API ratings.

Acetic acid Some RTV silicone sealers use the fumes from this acid. Use caution as this type can be drawn through the engine through the PCV system and cause damage to oxygen sensors.

Acid materials Have pH numbers from 1 through 6.

Additive package Balanced additives.

Adjustable wrench A wrench that has a movable jaw to allow it to fit many sizes of fasteners.

Aerated Air mixed with the oil.

AFV Alternative-fuel vehicle.

Agitation Keeps fresh cleaning solution moving past the soil to help loosen it.

AGST Aboveground storage tank, used to store used oil.

AIR Air injection reaction emission control system; also called secondary air injection.

Air compressor A piece of shop equipment that uses an electric motor to power an air compressor, which is stored in a pressure tank for use in the shop.

Air drill A drill driven by the elastic pressure of condensed air; a pneumatic drill.

Air ratchet An air-operated hand tool that rotates a socket.

Air-blow gun A handheld nozzle attached to a compressed air hose to apply air pressure to a component or device.

Air–fuel ratio The ratio of air to fuel in an intake charge as measured by weight.

AKI Antiknock index. The octane rating posted on a gas pump, which is the average of the RON and MON octane ratings.

Alternator Turned by the engine through an accessory drive belt. The magnetic field of the rotor generates a current in the windings of the stator by electromagnetic induction.

Ampere-hour rating An older type of battery rating.

Amplitude The difference between the highest and lowest level of a waveform.

Anhydrous ethanol Ethanol that has no water content.

Annealing Heat-treating process that takes out the brittle hardening of the casting to reduce the chance of cracking from the temperature changes.

ANSI American National Standards Institute, an organization that publishes safety standards for safety glasses and other personal protective equipment.

Antidrainback valve Prevents oil from draining out of the filter when the engine is shut off.

API American Petroleum Institute.

Aqueous-based solutions Most aqueous-based chemicals are silicate based and are mixed with water.

Armor Protects the fiber facing around the combustion chamber.

Asbestosis A health condition where asbestos causes scar tissue to form in the lungs causing shortness of breath.

ASTM American Society for Testing Materials.

Asymmetrical The amount of lift of a camshaft is often different for the intake and exhaust valves. If the specifications vary, the camshaft is called asymmetrical.

Aviation tin snips Cutters designed to cut sheet metal.

B20 A blend of 20% biodiesel with 80% petroleum diesel.

Babbitt Babbitt is the oldest automotive bearing material. Isaac Babbitt (1799–1862) first formulated this material in 1839. An excellent bearing material, it was originally made from a combination of lead, tin, and antimony.

Back flushing The use of a special gun that mixes air with water. Low-pressure air is used so that it will not damage the cooling system.

Back pressure The exhaust system's resistance to flow. Measured in pounds per square inch (PSI).

Balancing bosses Balancing pad.

Bank   Each group of four inline cylinders.

Bar   When air is pumped into the cylinder, the combustion chamber receives an increase of air pressure known as boost and is measured in pounds per square inch (PSI), atmospheres (ATM), or bar.

Barrel   A part of a micrometer, which has 40 threads per inch.

Base timing   The timing of the spark before the computer advances the timing.

BCI   Battery Council International.

Beam-type torque wrench   A type of wrench that displays the torque being applied to a fastener by the position of a deflective pointer and a scale, indicating the amount of torque.

Bearing crown   The wall thickness of most bearings is largest in the center.

Bearing splitter   A two-part steel device used between a bearing and a gear or other component, which is used to remove the bearing using a hydraulic press.

Bedplate   A structural member that attaches to the bottom of the block and supports the crankshaft.

Bench grinder   An electric motor with a grinding stone and/or wire brush attached at both ends of the armature and mounted on a bench.

Bench vise   A holding device attached to a workbench; has two jaws to hold the workpiece firmly in place.

Bin number   A United States federal rating of emissions. The lower the Bin number, the cleaner the exhaust emission.

Biodiesel   A renewable fuel manufactured from vegetable oils, animal fats, or recycled restaurant grease.

Biomass   Nonedible farm products, such as corn stalks, cereal straws, and plant wastes from industrial processes, such as sawdust and paper pulp used in making ethanol.

Bleed hole   Controls the oil flow through the bearing.

Block   The foundation of any engine. All other parts are either directly or indirectly attached to the block of an engine.

Block deck   The cylinder head is fastened to the top surface of the block.

Blowby gases   Combustion gases that leak past the piston rings into the crankcase during the compression and combustion strokes of the engine.

Bolt   A fastener consisting of a threaded pin or rod with a head at one end, designed to be inserted through holes in assembled parts and secured by a mated nut that is tightened by applying torque.

Boost   An increase in air pressure above atmospheric. Measured in pounds per square inch.

Bore   The inside diameter of the cylinder in an engine.

Boundary lubrication   When the oil film is thick enough to keep the surfaces from seizing, but can allow some contact to occur.

Box-end wrench   A wrench with a closed loop (a socket) that fits over a nut or bolt head.

Boxer   A type of engine design that is flat and has opposing cylinders. Called a boxer because the pistons on one side resemble a boxer during engine operation. Also called a pancake engine.

Braided fabric seals   Used as rear crankshaft oil seals.

Breaker bar   A long-handled socket drive tool.

Bronze guide liners   See *thin-walled bronze alloy sleeve bushing*.

BTU   British thermal unit. A measure of heat energy. One BTU of heat will raise the temperature of one pound of water one Fahrenheit degree.

Bucket   Opens overhead camshaft valve trains.

Bump cap   A hat that is plastic and hard to protect the head from bumps.

Bypass   Allows a small part of the coolant to circulate within the engine during warm-up. It is a small passage that leads from the engine side of the thermostat to the inlet side of the water pump. It allows some coolant to bypass the thermostat even when the thermostat is open.

Bypass valve   Allows intake air to flow directly into the intake manifold, bypassing the supercharger.

CAA   Clean Air Act. Federal legislation passed in 1970 that established national air quality standards.

Calendar year (CY)   A calendar year is from January 1 through December 31 each year.

Calibration codes   Codes used on many powertrain control modules.

California Air Resources Board (CARB)   A state of California agency that regulates the air quality standards for the state.

Cam chucking   The movement of the camshaft lengthwise in the engine during operation.

Cam follower   Opens overhead camshaft valve trains with a ratio similar to that of a rocker arm.

Cam ground   Once a certain temperature is reached, the piston will have expanded enough across the piston pin area to become round.

Cam-in-block   Pushrod engines have the cam located in the block.

Cam-in-block design   An engine where the crankshaft is located in the block rather than in the cylinder head.

Camshaft   A shaft with lobes that open valves when being rotated through a chain, belt, or gear from the crankshaft.

Camshaft bearings   The camshaft is supported in the block by these bearings.

Camshaft duration   The number of degrees of crankshaft rotation for which the valve is lifted off the seat.

Camshaft overlap   The number of degrees of crankshaft rotation between the exhaust and intake strokes for which both valves are off their seats.

Cap screw   A bolt that is threaded into a casting.

Capillary action   The movement of a liquid through tiny openings or small tubes.

Case hardening   Involves heating the crankshaft and adding carbon to the journals where it causes the outer surface to become harder than the rest of the crankshaft.

Casting number   An identification code cast into an engine block or other large cast part of a vehicle.

Catalyst   An element that starts a chemical reaction without becoming a part of, or being consumed in, the process.

Catalytic converter   An emission control device located in the exhaust system that changes HC and CO into harmless H_2O and CO_2. In a three-way catalyst, NO_x is also divided into harmless separate nitrogen (N_2) and oxygen (O_2).

Catalytic cracking   Breaking hydrocarbon chains using heat in the presence of a catalyst.

Caustic material   Chemical cleaners or strong soaps.

Cavitation   A process of creating a cavity or void area. Cavitation is usually used in the automotive field to describe what happens in the cooling system when water boils, creating a bubble in the system, and then cools below 212°F, which causes the bubble to collapse. When this event occurs, water rushes back into the void left by the bubble. The force of this moving water can cause noise as well as damage to cooling system parts such as water pumps.

Cellulose ethanol   Ethanol produced from biomass feedstock such as agricultural and industrial plant wastes.

Cellulosic biomass   Composed of cellulose and lignin, with smaller amounts of proteins, lipids (fats, waxes, and oils), and ash.

Centrifugal pump   A rotodynamic pump that uses a rotating impeller to increase the velocity of a fluid.

Cerium   An element that can store oxygen.

Cetane rating   A diesel fuel rating that indicates how easily the fuel can be ignited.

CFR   Code of Federal Regulations.

Cheater bar   A pipe or other object used to lengthen the handle of a ratchet or breaker bar.

Check valve   Contains a spring-type metallic disc or reed that closes the air line under exhaust backpressure.

Chisel   A sharpened tool used with a hammer to separate two pieces of an assembly.

Christmas tree clips   Plastic clips used to hold interior panels in place. The end that goes into a hole in the steel door panel is tapered and looks like a Christmas tree.

Clamping force   The amount of force exerted on a gasket.

Clicker-type torque wrench   A type of wrench that is first set to the specified torque and then it "clicks" when the set torque value has been reached.

Close end   An end of a wrench that grips all sides of the fastener.

Cloud point   The low-temperature point at which the waxes present in most diesel fuel tend to form wax crystals that clog the fuel filter.

CNG   Compressed natural gas.

Coil-by-plug   See *coil-on-plug*.

Coil-near-plug   See *coil-on-plug*.

Coil-on-plug (COP)   Uses one ignition for each spark plug.

Coil-over-plug   See *coil-on-plug*.

Cold chisel   A type of chisel used to remove rivets or to break off fasteners.

Cold-cranking amperes (CCA)   The cold cranking performance rating.

Combination wrench   A type of wrench that has an open end at one end and a closed end at the other end of the wrench.

Combustion   The rapid burning of the air–fuel mixture in the engine cylinders, creating heat and pressure.

Combustion chamber   The space left within the cylinder when the piston is at the top of its combustion chamber.

Compacted graphite iron (CGI)   A type of iron that is used for bedplates and many diesel engine blocks. It has higher strength, stiffness, and toughness than gray iron. The enhanced strength has been shown to permit reduced weight while still reducing noise vibration and harshness.

Composite camshaft   A lightweight tubular shaft with hardened steel lobes press-fitted over the shaft.

Compression ratio (CR)   The ratio of the volume in the engine cylinder with the piston at bottom dead center (BDC) to the volume at top dead center (TDC).

Compression rings   Designed to form a seal between the moving piston and the cylinder wall.

Compression test   A test that can be used to test the condition of valves and piston rings.

Compressor bypass valve   This type of relief valve routes the pressurized air to the inlet side of the turbocharger for reuse and is quiet during operation.

Concentric   Centered.

Conformability   The ability of bearing materials to creep or flow slightly to match shaft variations.

Connecting rod   A rod that transmits motion or power from one moving part to another, especially the rod connecting the crankshaft of a motor vehicle to a piston.

Connecting rod bearing journal   See *crank throw.*

Coolant recovery system   When the system cools, the pressure in the cooling system is reduced and a partial vacuum forms. This pulls the coolant from the plastic container back into the cooling system, keeping the system full.

Cooling fins   Fins that are exposed to airflow, which removes heat from the radiator and carries it away.

Copper-lead alloy   Alloy is a stronger and more expensive bearing material than babbitt. It is used for intermediate- and high-speed applications. Tin, in small quantities, is often alloyed with the copper-lead bearings.

Core plugs   A subset of the plugs on a car engine cylinder block or cylinder head. The traditional plug is a thin, domed disc of metal which fits into a machined hole in the casting and is secured by striking or pressing the center to expand the disc.

Core tubes   Made from 0.0045- to 0.012-inch (0.1- to 0.3-millimeter) sheet brass or aluminum, using the thinnest possible materials for each application. The metal is rolled into round tubes and the joints are sealed with a locking seam.

Cork-rubber gaskets   Gaskets that use synthetic rubber as a binder for the cork.

Corrosion resistance   The bearings' ability to resist attack from the acids in the oil.

Cotter key   A metal loop used to retain castle nuts by being installed through a hole. Size is measured by diameter and length (for example, 1/8" × 1 1/2"). Also called a cotter pin. Named for the Old English verb meaning "to close or fasten."

Counterweights   Used to balance the crankshaft.

Country of origin   The first number of the vehicle identification number (VIN), which identifies where the vehicle was assembled.

Cracking   A refinery process in which hydrocarbons with high boiling points are broken into hydrocarbons with low boiling points.

Crank throw   The journals of the off-center bearings of the crankshaft.

Cranking amperes (CA)   A battery rating tested at 32°F (0°C).

Cranking vacuum test   Measuring the amount of manifold vacuum during cranking is a quick and easy test to determine if the piston rings and valves are properly sealing.

Crankpin   See *crank throw.*

Crankshaft   A shaft that turns or is turned by a crank.

Crankshaft end play   Thrust bearing clearance.

Creeper   A small platform mounted on short casters designed for a service technician to lie down and maneuver under a vehicle.

Crest   The outside diameter of a bolt measured across the threads.

Cross flow head design   By placing the intake and the exhaust valves on the opposite sides of the combustion chamber, an easy path from the intake port through the combustion chamber to the exhaust port is provided.

Crowfoot socket   A type of socket that slips onto the side of the bolt or nut. Used where direct access from the top is restricted.

Crush   Occurs when the bearing cap is tightened, the ends of the two bearing shells touch and are forced together.

CTL   Coal-to-liquid.

Cycle   A complete series of events that continually repeat.

Cylinder   The chamber in which a piston of a reciprocating engine moves.

Cylinder head cover gasket   A gasket that is used between the valve cover and the cylinder head.

Cylinder leakage test   Fills the cylinder with compressed air, and the gauge indicates the percentage of leakage.

Dampening   Reducing the vibration to an acceptable level.

dB   An abbreviation for decibel, a measure of relative noise level.

Dead-blow hammer   A type of hammer that has lead shot (small pellets) inside a steel housing, which is then covered with a plastic covering. Used to apply a blunt force to an object.

Decking the block   A procedure where the block deck must be resurfaced in a surfacing machine that can control the amount of metal removed when it is necessary to match the size of the combustion chambers.

Deflector valve stem seal   See *umbrella valve stem seal.*

Detonation   A violent explosion in the combustion chamber created by uncontrolled burning of the air–fuel mixture; often causes a loud, audible knock. Also known as spark knock or ping.

DEX-COOL   Extended life coolant.

DI   Distillation index. A rating of the volatility of a fuel and how well it evaporates in cold temperatures.

Diagonal pliers   Pliers designed to cut wire and to remove cotter keys. Also called side cuts or dike pliers.

Die   A hardened steel round cutter with teeth on the inside of the center hole.

Die grinder   A handheld air-operated tool used with a grinding stone or a wire brush.

Diesel oxidation catalyst   Consists of a flow-through honeycomb-style substrate structure that is washcoated with a layer of catalyst materials, similar to those used in a gasoline engine catalytic converter.

Diesohol   Standard #2 diesel fuel combined with up to 15% ethanol.

Differential pressure sensor   Designed to remove diesel particulate matter or soot from the exhaust gas of a diesel engine.

Digital EGR   The digital EGR valve consists of three solenoids controlled by the PCM.

Direct injection   Fuel is injected directly into the cylinder.

Dish   Pistons used in other engines may be provided with a depression.

Displacement   The total volume displaced or swept by the cylinders in an internal combustion engine.

Distillation   The process of purification through evaporation and then condensation of the desired liquid.

Distillation curve   A graph that plots the temperatures at which the various fractions of a fuel evaporate.

Distributor ignition (DI)   The term specified by the Society of Automotive Engineers (SAE) for an ignition system that uses a distributor.

Double-cut file   A file that has two rows of teeth that cut at an opposite angle.

Double-knock   The noise that is created when the piston stops at top dead center and occurs again as it starts to move downward, creating a double-knock sound, which is also described as a rattling sound.

DPFE   This sensor measures the pressure differential between two sides of a metered orifice positioned just below the EGR valve's exhaust side.

Drive size   The size in fractions of an inch of the square drive for sockets.

Dry cylinder sleeve   Cast-iron dry sleeves are used in aluminum blocks to provide a hard surface for the rings.

Dry sump   The oil pan is shallow and the oil is pumped into a remote reservoir. In this reservoir, the oil is cooled and any trapped air is allowed to escape before being pumped back to the engine.

Dual overhead camshaft (DOHC)   An engine design with two camshafts above each line of cylinders—one for the exhaust valves and one for the intake valves.

Ductile iron   Very flexible material that can be twisted without breaking; also used as a piston ring material in some automotive engines.

Dump valve   Features an adjustable spring design that keeps the valve closed until a sudden release of the throttle.

Dynamic compression test   A compression test done with the engine running rather than during engine cranking as is done in a regular compression test.

E10   A fuel blend of 10% ethanol and 90% gasoline.

E85   A fuel blend of 85% ethanol and 15% gasoline.

Easy out   A tool used to extract a broken bolt.

E-diesel   Standard #2 diesel fuel combined with up to 15% ethanol. Also known as diesohol.

EGR   Exhaust gas recirculation. An emission control device to reduce NO_x (oxides of nitrogen).

Elastic valve   Type of poppet valve. The elastic valve is able to conform to valve seat shape. This allows it to seal easily, but it runs hot and the flexing to conform may cause it to break.

Elastomer   Another term for rubber.

Electromagnetic interference   Causes problems to computer signals.

Electronic control unit   Module for the EIS.

Electronic ignition (EI)   The term specified by the SAE for an ignition system that does not use a distributor.

Electronic ignition module (or igniter)   Opens and closes the primary ignition circuit by opening or closing the ground return path of the circuit.

Electronic ignition system   The system consists of a pulse generator unit in the distributor (pickup coil and reluctor).

Electroplating   A process of putting an overplating layer onto the bearing.

Embedability   The property that allows the bearing to fully embed the particle. The bearing material gradually works across the particle, completely covering it.

Embittered coolant   Coolant that has been made bitter to deter animals.

Engine stand   A floor-mounted frame usually equipped with casters on which an engine can be attached and rotated.

EPA   Environmental Protection Agency.

Ethanol (grain alcohol)   An octane enhancer added, at a rate of up to 10%, to gasoline will increase the octane rating of the fuel by 2.5 to 3.0. Ethanol is a fuel oxygenate.

Ethyl alcohol   See *ethanol*.

Ethyl tertiary butyl ether (ETBE)   An octane enhancer for gasoline. It is also a fuel oxygenate that is manufactured by reacting isobutylene with ethanol. The resulting ether is high octane and low volatility. ETBE can be added to gasoline up to a level of approximately 13%.

Ethylene glycol-based antifreeze   Antifreeze.

EVP A linear potentiometer on the top of the EGR valve stem indicates valve position for the computer.

EVRV The computer pulses the solenoid to control the vacuum that regulates the operation of the EGR valve.

Exhaust gas recirculation (EGR) The process of passing a small, measured amount of exhaust gas back into the engine to reduce combustion temperatures and formation of NO_x (oxides of nitrogen).

Exhaust valve A valve through which burned gases from a cylinder escape into the exhaust manifold.

Exhaust valve cam phaser (EVCP) Spline phaser system.

Extension A socket wrench tool used between a ratchet or breaker bar and a socket.

External combustion engine Engine combustion occurring outside the power chamber.

Eye wash station A water fountain designed to rinse the eyes with a large volume of water.

Eyebrows Recesses machined or cast into the tops of the pistons for valve clearance.

Fatigue life The length of time before fatigue will cause failure.

Feeler gauge A set of precision thickness steel blades used to measure a gap. Also called a thickness gauge.

FFV Flex-fuel vehicle. Flex-fuel vehicles are capable of running on straight gasoline or gasoline/ethanol blends.

Fiber reinforced matrix (FRM) A ceramic material similar to that used to construct the insulators of spark plugs. The lightweight material has excellent wear resistance and good heat transfer properties, making it ideal for use as a cylinder material.

File A metal smoothing tool.

Finger follower See *cam follower.*

Fire blanket A fireproof wool blanket used to cover a person who is on fire and smother the fire.

Fire deck The cylinder head surface that mates with the top deck of the block.

Fire ring See *armor.*

Firing order The order that the spark is distributed to the correct spark plug at the right time.

Fischer-Tropsch A refining process that converts coal, natural gas, or other petroleum products into synthetic motor fuels.

Fitting wrench A wrench that is used to remove the fitting holding a brake line or other line.

Flare-nut wrench A type of wrench used to remove brake lines.

Flash point The temperature at which the vapors on the surface of the fuel will ignite if exposed to an open flame.

Flat-link type See *silent chain type.*

Flat-tip screwdriver A screwdriver used to remove and insert screws that have a single slot.

Flat-top piston A type of piston found in low-cost, low-performance engines.

Flex fuel An automobile that can typically use different sources of fuel, either mixed in the same tank or with separate tanks and fuel systems for each fuel.

Floor jack A hydraulic jack mounted on casters or steel wheels and used to lift a vehicle.

Flying web The flange between the splayed crankpin journals.

Fogging oil Coats metal parts to keep them from rusting.

Forming stone See *roughing stone.*

Four-stroke cycle An internal combustion engine design where four strokes of the piston (two crankshaft revolutions) are required to complete one cycle of events. The four strokes include intake, compression, power, and exhaust.

Freeze plugs See *core plugs.*

Frequency The number of times a waveform repeats in one second, measured in hertz (Hz), frequency band.

Fretting A condition that can destroy intake manifold gaskets and is caused by the unequal expansion and contraction of two different engine materials.

Frost plugs See *core plugs.*

FTD Fischer-Tropsch diesel process. See *Fischer-Tropsch.*

Fuel compensation sensor A sensor used in flex-fuel vehicles that provides information to the PCM on the ethanol content and temperature of the fuel as it is flowing through the fuel delivery system.

Fuel composition sensor Measures both the percentage of ethanol blend and the temperature of the fuel.

Full round bearing Sleeve-type bushing.

Full-floating A type of axle assembly where the weight of the vehicle is supported by the axle housing and not on the axle itself.

Fully counterweighted A crankshaft that has counterweights on both sides of each connecting rod journal.

Fusible link A type of fuse that will melt and open the protected circuit in the event of a short circuit, which could cause excessive current flow through the fusible link. Most fusible links are actually wires that are four gauge sizes smaller than the wire of the circuits being protected.

Gallery Longitudinal header. This is a long hole drilled from the front of the block to the back. Passages drilled through the block bulkheads allow the oil to go from the main oil gallery to the main and cam bearings.

Gasoline   Refined petroleum product that is used primarily as a fuel in gasoline engines.

GAWR   Gross axle weight rating. A rating of the load capacity of a vehicle and included on placards on the vehicle and in the owner's manual.

Glow plug   A heating element that uses 12 volts from the battery and aids in the starting of a cold engine.

Grade   The strength rating of a bolt.

Grain alcohol   See *ethanol*.

Grinder   Type of resurfacer that uses a large-diameter abrasive wheel.

Grit size   The size of the abrasive particles in the grinding and honing stones controls the surface finish.

Grooves   Piston ring grooves are located between the piston head and skirt.

GTL   Gas-to-liquid. A refining process in which natural gas is converted into liquid fuel.

Gudgeon pins   A British term for pins used to attach the piston to the connecting rod.

Guttering   A result from poor seating that allows the high-temperature and high-pressure combustion gases to leak between the valve and seat.

GVWR   Gross vehicle weight rating. The total weight of the vehicle including the maximum cargo.

Hacksaw   A saw that uses a replaceable blade and is used to cut a variety of materials depending on the type of blade used.

Half-shell bearing   The bearing is manufactured to very close tolerance so that it will fit correctly in each application.

Hangers   Made of rubberized fabric with metal ends that hold the muffler and tailpipe in position so that they do not touch any metal part.

Harmonic balancer   See *vibration damper.*

Head gasket   Gasket that is used between the cylinder head and engine block.

Heat dams   Most pistons have horizontal separation slots that act as heat dams.

Heat of compression   Incoming air is compressed until its temperature reaches about 1,000°F.

Helical insert   A steel insert used to repair damaged threads.

Helicoil®   A brand name for a helical insert.

Helmholtz resonator   A resonance tube named for the discoverer of the relationship between shape and value of frequency, Herman L. F. von Helmholtz (1821–1894) of the University of Hönizsberg in East Prussia.

HEPA vacuum   High-efficiency particulate air filter vacuum, used to clean brake dust.

High energy ignition (HEI)   Uses an air-cooled, epoxy-sealed E coil.

High-pressure common rail   Newer diesel engines use a fuel delivery system referred to as a high-pressure common rail.

HO₂S   Heated oxygen sensor.

Hybrid organic additive technology (HOAT)   Coolants can be green, orange, yellow, gold, pink, red, or blue.

Hydraulic Electronic Unit Injection   The components that replace the traditional mechanical injection pump include a high-pressure oil pump and reservoir, pressure regulator for the oil, and passages in the cylinder head for flow of fuel to the injectors.

Hydraulic lash adjusters (HLA)   Some newer engines have the hydraulic adjustment in the rocker arm called HLA.

Hydraulic lifter   A valve lifter that, using simple valving and the engine's oil pressure, can adjust its length slightly, thereby maintaining zero clearance in the valve train. Hydraulic lifters reduce valve train noise and are maintenance-free.

Hydraulic press   A piece of shop equipment usually mounted on the floor, which uses a hydraulic cylinder to remove and install pressed-on components, such as bearings.

Hydrocracking   A refinery process that converts hydrocarbons with high boiling points into ones with low boiling points.

Hydrodynamic lubrication   A wedge-shaped oil film is built up between the moving block and the surface. This wedging action depends on the force applied, how fast the speed between the objects, and the thickness of the oil.

Hydroseal   A layer of water over the chemical to prevent evaporation of the chemical.

Hypereutectic   Pistons that are commonly used in the aftermarket and as original equipment in many turbocharged and supercharged engines.

Identification marks   For pushrod inline engines, they are normally placed on the camshaft side.

Idle vacuum test   An engine in proper condition should idle with a steady vacuum between 17 and 21 inches Hg.

Ignition coil   The coil creates a high-voltage spark by electromagnetic induction.

ILSAC   International Lubricant Standardization and Approval Committee. Responsible for development of the ILSAC standard for motor oil performance.

Impact wrench   An air-operated hand tool used to install and remove threaded fasteners.

Impeller   The mechanism in a water pump that rotates to produce coolant flow.

Incandescent light   A type of light that uses an incandescent rather than a fluorescent or LED light source.

Inches of mercury   Unit of measure used to measure a vacuum.

Indirect injection   Fuel is injected into a small prechamber, which is connected to the cylinder by a narrow opening.

Inert   Chemically inactive.

Inertia forces   A product of reciprocating action of the piston.

Infrared pyrometer   Measures the inlet and the outlet temperatures.

Injection pump   A diesel engine injection pump is used to increase the pressure of the diesel fuel from very low values from the lift pump to the extremely high pressures needed for injection.

Inorganic additive technology (IAT)   Conventional coolant that has been used for over 50 years. The additives used to protect against rust and corrosion include phosphate and silicates.

Intake centerline   The point that is often located between 100 degrees and 110 degrees.

Intake lobe centerline method   This method determines the exact centerline of the intake lobe and compares it to the specifications supplied with the replacement camshaft.

Integral seat   The seat is generally formed as part of the cast-iron head of automotive engines.

Intercooler   Used on many turbocharged and some super-charged engines to reduce the temperature of air entering the engine for increased power.

Interference fit   The modern method of retaining the piston pin in the connecting rod is to make the connecting rod hole slightly smaller than the piston pin. The pin is installed by heating the rod to expand the hole or by pressing the pin into the rod.

Internal combustion engine   Engine combustion occurring within the power chamber.

Jack stand   See *safety stand.*

Jam nut   A second nut used to prevent the first nut from loosening.

JASO   The Japanese Automobile Standards Organization oil standards. The JASO tests use small Japanese engines, and their ratings require more stringent valve train wear standards than other countries' oil ratings.

Julian date   The number of the day of the year. Also called JD.

Keepers   See *valve locks.*

Lands   Between the ring grooves.

Lash   Valve clearance.

LED   Light-emitting diode. A high-efficiency light source that uses very little electricity and produces very little heat.

Left-hand rule   A method of determining the direction of magnetic lines of force around a conductor. The left-hand rule is used with the electron flow theory ($-$ flowing to $+$).

Lift pump   The diesel fuel is drawn from the fuel tank by a lift pump and delivers the fuel to the injection pump.

Lifter preload   The distance between the pushrod seat inside the lifter and the snap-ring of the lifter when the lifter is resting on the base circle (or heel) of the cam and the valve is closed.

Light-off   The catalytic converter does not work when cold and it must be heated to its light-off temperature of close to 500°F (260°C) before it starts working at 50% effectiveness.

Linear EGR   Contains a solenoid to precisely regulate exhaust gas flow and a feedback potentiometer that signals the computer regarding the actual position of the valve.

Load test   One of the most accurate tests to determine the condition of any battery.

Lobe centers   Separation between the centerlines of the intake and exhaust lobes, measured in degrees.

Lobe displacement angle (LDA)   See *lobe centers.*

Lobe separation   See *lobe centers.*

Lobe spread   See *lobe centers.*

LOC   Light-off converter.

Lock rings   Retain full-floating piston pins in automotive engines.

Locking pliers   A hand tool that can be used to grasp an object and then be locked into position. Often called by a popular brand name Vise Grips®.

LPG   Liquefied petroleum gas. Another term for propane.

Lugging   Increasing the throttle opening without increasing engine speed (RPM).

M85   Internal combustion engine fuel containing 85% methanol and 15% gasoline.

Magnetic pulse   The pulse generator consists of a trigger wheel (reluctor) and a pickup coil.

Major thrust surface   The side of an engine cylinder that receives the greatest thrust or force from the piston during the power stroke.

Mechanical force   The pressure developed within the combustion chamber is applied to the head of a piston or to a turbine wheel.

Mechanical power   The output of mechanical force.

Mercury   A heavy metal.

Methanol (wood alcohol)   Typically manufactured from natural gas. Methanol content, including co-solvents, in unleaded gasoline is limited by law to 5%.

Metric bolts   Bolts manufactured and sized in the metric system of measurement.

Microbe   A microorganism that is too small to be seen by the human eye.

Micron   Unit of measure equal to 0.000039 inch.

Milling   Type of resurfacer that uses metal-cutting tool bits fastened in a disk.

Mini-converter   A small, quick heating oxidation converter.

Miscible   Capable of mixing with other oils (brands and viscosities, for example) without causing any problems such as sludge.

Model year (MY)   The year of a vehicle, which may be different from the calendar year when it is sold.

Monoblock   The cylinder, water jacket, main bearing supports (saddles), and oil passages are all cast as one structure for strength and quietness.

Morse type   See *silent chain type.*

MSDS   Material Safety Data Sheets.

MTBE   Methyl tertiary butyl ether. MTBE is an oxygenated fuel that is used as a gasoline additive to enhance its burning characteristics. It is being phased out due to groundwater contamination concerns.

MTG   Methanol-to-gasoline. A refining process in which methanol is converted into liquid gasoline.

MTHF   Methyltetrahydrofuron. A component of P-series nonpetroleum-based fuels.

Multigroove adjustable pliers   A hand tool that is capable of grasping a wide range of object sizes; also called water pump pliers or by a popular brand name of Channel Locks®.

Multilayered steel (MLS)   The many layers of thin steel reduce bore and overhead camshaft distortion with less clamping force loss than previous designs.

Mutual induction   Generation of an electric current in both coil windings.

Naturally aspirated   Refers to an internal combustion engine that is neither turbocharged nor supercharged.

Necking   Weakens the stem and leads to breakage.

Needle-nose pliers   A hand tool that is equipped with pointed jaws, which allow use in restricted areas or for small parts.

Negative Backpressure   Some EGR valves react to this low pressure area by closing a small internal valve, which allows the EGR valve to be opened by vacuum.

NGV   Natural gas vehicle.

Nitriding   The crankshaft is heated to about 1,000°F (540°C) in a furnace filled with ammonia gas, and then allowed to cool. The process adds nitrogen (from the ammonia) into the surface of the metal—forming hard nitrides in the surface of the crankshaft to a depth of about 0.007 inch (0.8 mm).

Nonprincipal end   The end of the engine that is opposite the principal end and is generally referred to as the front of the engine, where the accessory belts are used.

Normal operating temperature   When the cooling fan has cycled on and off at least once after the engine has been started. Some vehicle manufacturers specify that the cooling fan should cycle twice.

Notch   An indentation on the piston head indicating the "front."

NO$_X$ Oxides of nitrogen; when combined with HC and sunlight, form smog.

Nut splitter   A hand tool designed to break a nut that is rusted onto a bolt or stud.

Octane rating   The measurement of a gasoline's ability to resist engine knock. The higher the octane rating, the less prone the gasoline is to cause engine knock (detonation).

Offset aviation snip   A tin snip that has curved jaws allowing it to make curved cuts either left or right.

Oil control ring   Allows oil to return through the ring and openings in the piston.

Oil control valve (OCV)   Directs oil from the oil feed in the head to the appropriate camshaft position actuator oil passages.

Oil galleries   An oil pump, which is driven by the engine, forces the oil through the oil filter and then into passages in the crankshaft and block.

Opacity   The degree to which light is blocked.

Open-circuit battery voltage test   A test that is conducted with an open circuit—with no current flowing and no load applied to the battery.

Open end   The end of a wrench that is open to allow the wrench to be inserted onto a fastener from the side.

Organic   A term used to describe anything that was alive at one time.

Organic additive technology (OAT)   Antifreeze coolant that contains ethylene glycol, but does not contain silicates or phosphates. This type of coolant is usually orange in color and was first developed by Havoline (called DEX-COOL) and used in General Motors vehicles starting in 1996.

OSC   Oxygen storage capacity.

OSHA   Occupational Safety and Health Administration. OSHA is the main federal agency responsible for enforcement of workplace safety and health legislation.

Overhead camshaft (OHC)   Either belt or chain driven from the crankshaft and located in the cylinder head(s).

Overhead valve (OHV)   A type of piston engine that places the camshaft in the cylinder block (usually beside and slightly above the crankshaft in a straight engine or directly above the crankshaft in the V of a V engine) and uses pushrods or rods to actuate rocker arms above the cylinder head to actuate the valves.

Overlay   Many of the copper-lead bearings have a third layer of metal. This third layer is usually of babbitt. Babbitt-overlayed bearings have high fatigue strength, good conformity, good embedability, and good corrosion resistance.

Oxygenated fuels   Fuels such as ETBE or MTBE that contain extra oxygen molecules to promote cleaner burning. Oxygenated fuels are used as gasoline additives to reduce CO emissions.

Pal nut   See *jam nut*.

Palladium   An element that acts as a catalyst.

Pancake   A pancake engine is an internal combustion engine that has the cylinders on a horizontal plane.

Paper test   Hold a piece of paper or a "3 × 5" card (even a dollar bill works) within 1 inch (2.5 centimeters) of the tailpipe with the engine running at idle. The paper should blow out evenly without "puffing." If the paper is drawn toward the tailpipe at times, the exhaust valves in one or more cylinders could be burned.

Parallel flow system   Coolant flows into the block under pressure and then crosses the gasket to the head through main coolant passages beside each cylinder.

PASS   A word used to help remember how to use a fire extinguisher: pull pin, aim, squeeze the lever, and sweep the nozzle from side to side.

PCV   Positive crankcase ventilation.

Penetrating oil   A thin oil that is designed to penetrate through rust and provide lubrication for the threads of a fastener.

Petrodiesel   Another term for petroleum diesel, which is ordinary diesel fuel refined from crude oil.

Petroleum   Another term for crude oil. The literal meaning of petroleum is "rock oil."

PFE   Pressure feedback EGR.

pH   A measure of the acidity or alkalinity of a material. A pH of 7 is neutral, higher than 7 is alkaline, and lower than 7 is acidic.

Piloting surfaces   Closely fit reamed holes on the connecting rod bolts.

Ping   Secondary rapid burning of the last 3% to 5% of the air–fuel mixture in the combustion chamber causes a second flame front that collides with the first flame front causing a knock noise. Also called detonation or spark knock.

Piston   Forms a movable bottom to the combustion chamber.

Piston pin   Attaches the piston to the connecting rod.

Piston ring   Seals the small space between the piston and cylinder wall, keeping the pressure above the piston.

Piston ring compressor   Holds the rings in their grooves.

Piston ring expanding tool   Piston ring removal tool.

Piston stroke   A one-way piston movement between the top and bottom of the cylinder.

Pitch   The pitch of a threaded fastener refers to the number of threads per inch.

Plateau honing   Honing leaves a plateau surface that can support the oil film for the rings and piston skirt. This plateau surface is achieved by first using a coarse stone followed by a smooth stone to achieve the desired surface.

Platinum   An element that acts as a catalyst.

Plenum   A chamber, located between the throttle body and the runners of the intake manifold, used to distribute the intake charge more evenly and efficiently.

Polarity   The polarity of an ignition coil is determined by the direction of rotation of the coil windings.

Pop rivet   A type of fastener that uses a rivet gun to pull out the rivet until the end deforms, thereby creating a light clamping form.

Pop tester   A device used for checking a diesel injector nozzle for proper spray pattern.

Poppet valve   The valve is opened by means of a valve train that is operated by a cam.

Pop-ups   Raised domes.

Portable crane   A piece of shop equipment that is used to lift and move heavy pieces of equipment, such as an engine.

Positive backpressure   At low engine speeds and light engine loads, the EGR system is not needed, and the backpressure in it is also low.

Positive twist   Gives the same wall contact as the taper-faced ring.

Pour point depressants   Coat the wax crystals in the oil so that they will not stick together. The oil will then be able to flow at lower temperatures.

Power balance test   A test to determine if all cylinders are contributing power equally.

PPE   Personal protective equipment, which can include gloves, safety glasses, and other items.

PPO   Pure plant oil.

Precision insert-type bearing shells   See *half-shell bearing*.

Preconverter   See *mini-converter*.

Pressure regulator   A regulating device that maintains a specified pressure in a system.

Prevailing torque nut   A special design of nut fastener that is deformed slightly or has other properties that permit the nut to remain attached to the fastener without loosening.

Primary ignition circuit   The ignition components that regulate the current in the coil primary winding by turning it on and off.

Primary vibration   A strong low-frequency vibration when pistons move up and down in the cylinders.

Principal end   The end of the engine that the flywheel is attached to.

Propane   See *LPG*.

Pump-up   Occasionally, engines are run at excessive speeds. This tends to throw the valve open, causing valve float. During valve float, clearance exists in the valve train. The hydraulic lifter will take up this clearance as it is designed to do. When this occurs, it will keep the valve from closing on the seat, called pump-up.

Punch   A hand tool designed to be used with a hammer to drive out pins.

Pushrod   The link rod connecting the brake pedal to the master cylinder piston.

Putty knife   A scraper with a broad blade that helps to avoid scratching the surface as it is used to clean the parts.

Pyrolytic   High-temperature oven.

Quench area   See *squish area*.

Ramp   A gradual rise in the cam contour.

Ratchet   A handle used to rotate a socket, which is reversible and allows the socket to be rotated in one direction and then free movement in the opposite direction of rotation.

RCRA   Resource Conservation and Recovery Act.

Recesses   Cut in the piston top for valve clearance.

Regeneration   A process of taking the kinetic energy of a moving vehicle and converting it to electrical energy and storing it in a battery.

Reid vapor pressure (RVP)   A method of determining vapor pressure of gasoline and other petroleum products. Widely used in the petroleum industry as an indicator of the volatility of gasoline.

Relief valve   Vents pressurized air from the connecting pipe between the outlet of the turbocharger and the throttle whenever the throttle is closed during boost, such as during shifts.

Removers   Hand tools that are designed to remove broken studs, bolts, and other fasteners.

Reserve capacity   The number of minutes for which the battery can produce 25 amperes and still have a battery voltage of 1.75 volts per cell (10.5 volts for a 12-volt battery).

Resonate   Audible vibrations.

Restricted exhaust   If the exhaust system is restricted, the engine will be low on power, yet smooth.

Reverse cooling   The coolant flows from the radiator to the cylinder head(s) before flowing to the engine block.

Reverse twist   Seals the lower outer section of the ring and piston ring groove, thus improving oil control.

RFG   Reformulated gasoline.

Rhodium   An element that acts as a catalyst.

Right-to-know laws   Laws that state that employees have a right to know when the materials they use at work are hazardous.

Rigid valve   Type of poppet valve. The rigid valve is strong, holds its shape, and conducts heat readily. It also causes less valve recession. Unfortunately, it is more likely to leak and burn than other valve head types.

Ring gap   Allows some leakage past the top compression ring. This leakage is useful in providing pressure on the second ring to develop a dynamic sealing force.

Rocking couple   90-degree V-6 engines use a split-crank journal to create an even-firing arrangement. As a result, these forces cause the engine to rock back and forth.

Roots-type supercharger   Called a positive displacement design because all of the air that enters is forced through the unit.

Rotary engine   An internal-combustion engine in which power is transmitted directly to rotating components.

Roughing stone   Used to rapidly remove large amounts of seat metal. This would be necessary on a badly pitted seat or when installing new valve seat inserts.

RTV   Room-temperature vulcanization.

Running compression test   The running compression test can inform a technician of the relative compression of all the cylinders.

Saddles   Bores.

Safety stand   A metal device with an adjustable vertical support that is designed to support a vehicle after it has been raised off the ground. Also called a jack stand.

Saturation   The point at which a coil's maximum magnetic field strength is reached.

Score resistance   Prevents the bearing materials from seizing to the shaft during oil film breakdown.

Scraper ring   Usually recommended for use at the second compression ring.

Screwdriver   A hand tool designed to remove or insert screws.

Scroll A smoothly curved passage that changes the fluid flow direction with minimum loss in velocity.

Scuff The valve stem temporarily welds to the guide when the valve is closed. The weld breaks as the valve is forced to open.

Seal driver A hand tool used with a mallet or hammer to seat seals into a seal groove.

Seal puller A hand tool designed to remove seals.

Sealed lead–acid battery (SLA) Converts the released hydrogen and oxygen back into water instead of escaping as gasses.

Seat duration The number of degrees of crankshaft rotation that the valve is off the seat.

Secondary ignition circuit The components necessary to create and distribute the high voltage produced in the secondary windings of the coil.

Secondary vibration A weak high-frequency vibration caused by a slight difference in the inertia of the pistons at top dead center compared to bottom dead center.

Self-induction When current starts to flow into a coil, an opposing current is created in the windings of the coil.

Self-tapping screw A screw that has a tapered tip which allows the screw to form threads in the metal.

Series flow system Coolant flows around all the cylinders on each bank. All the coolant flows to the rear of the block, where large main coolant passages allow the coolant to flow across the gasket.

Series-parallel flow system Some engines use a combination of the series and parallel flow systems.

Service information Includes service manuals, owner's manuals, CD-ROM discs, Internet sites, or other sources where vehicle information is found.

Siamese ports Two cylinders share the same port because of the restricted space available.

Side clearance Space in the ring groove above the ring.

Silent chain type Camshaft chain drive that operates quietly but tends to stretch with use.

Silicone coupling A fan drive mounted between the drive pulley and the fan.

Single-cut file A file that has just one row of cutting teeth.

Single overhead camshaft A design in which one camshaft is placed within the cylinder head.

Skirt See *slipper skirt.*

Sleeve bearing Engine bearing.

Sleeving Cylinder blocks with deep gouges can be saved by boring the cylinder to a dimension that is greatly oversize to almost match the outside diameter of the cylinder sleeve. The sleeve is pressed into the rebored block, then the center of the sleeve is bored to the diameter required by the piston.

Slip-joint pliers A hand tool that has two positions allowing the use of two different ranges of sizes.

Slipper skirt The cast-aluminum piston skirt has been reduced to a minimum by using an open-type slipper skirt.

Slots Act as heat dams.

Small-hole gauge A handheld measuring tool that is adjustable to fit inside small holes. A micrometer is then used to measure the gauge to determine the inside diameter of the hole. Also called a split-ball gauge.

Smog pump Pulls fresh air in through an external filter and pumps the air under slight pressure to each exhaust port through connecting hoses or a manifold.

Snap ring A spring steel clip that is used to retain an object in a bore by being inserted into a groove.

Snap-ring pliers A hand tool that is designed to install or remove snap rings.

Socket A tool that fits over the head of a bolt or nut and is rotated by a ratchet or breaker bar.

Socket adapter An adapter that allows the use of one size of driver (ratchet or breaker bar) to rotate another drive size of socket.

Solid valve lifter Assists in making sure that valve train clearance is not excessive.

Soluble Dissolved with a chemical or solvent.

Solvent Usually colorless liquids that are used to remove grease and oil.

Spark knock Secondary rapid burning of the last 3% to 5% of the air–fuel mixture in the combustion chamber. Causes a second flame front that collides with the first flame front causing a knock noise. Also called detonation or ping.

Spark tester Checks spark plugs.

Specific gravity Specific gravity is the ratio of the weight of a given volume of a liquid to the weight of an equal volume of water.

Spindle The part of a micrometer that moves and contacts the object being measured.

Spiral bronze alloy bushing Guide insert for guide repair.

Spit hole Bleeds some of the oil from the connecting rod journal.

Splay angle Angle between the crankpins on the crankshaft throws.

Split-ball gauge See *small-hole gauge.*

Split-type (half-shell) bearing See *full round bearing.*

Spontaneous combustion A condition that can cause some materials, such as oily rags, to catch fire without a source of ignition.

Spread   Holds the bearing shell in the housing while the engine is being assembled.

Spun bearing   Bearing shells that do not have enough crush may rotate with the shaft.

Squish area   An area of the combustion chamber where the piston nearly contacts the cylinder.

Steam slits   See *bleed hole*.

Stellite   An alloy of nickel, chromium, and tungsten that is nonmagnetic.

Stoichiometric   An air–fuel ratio of exactly 14.7:1. At this specific rate, all the gasoline is fully oxidized by all the available oxygen.

Stone wheel   A grinding stone attached to a grinder used for cleaning, sharpening, or other similar operations.

Stop drilling   A hole drilled at each end of a crack to keep it from extending further.

Straight cut aviation snip   A tin snip that is designed with curved jaws that allow a straight cut through sheet metal.

Straightedge   A precision ground metal measuring gauge that is used to check the flatness of engine components when used with a feeler gauge.

Strip feeler gauge   Used to measure the piston-to-cylinder clearance.

Stroke   The distance the piston travels down in the cylinder.

Struts   A structural part of a suspension that includes the shock absorber.

Stud   A short rod with threads on both ends.

Stud removal tool   A hand tool used with a breaker bar or ratchet to remove what is left of a broken stud.

Stud remover   A stud removal tool grips the part of the stud above the surface and uses a cam or wedge to grip the stud as it is being rotated by a ratchet or breaker bar.

Supercharger   A gas compressor that forces more air into the combustion chamber of an internal combustion engine.

Surface finish   Measured in microinches; the smaller the number, the smoother the surface. Where the surface finish of a machined block deck or cylinder head may range from 60 to 100 RA (roughness average), the typical specification for main and rod crankshaft journals is between 10 and 20 RA.

Surface-to-volume ratio   An important design consideration for combustion chambers.

Surge tank   A reservoir mounted at the highest point in the cooling system.

SVO   Straight vegetable oil.

Switchgrass   A feedstock for ethanol production that requires very little energy or fertilizer to cultivate.

Symmetrical   The amount of lift of a camshaft is often different for the intake and exhaust valves. If the specifications are the same, the camshaft is called symmetrical.

Syn-gas   Synthesis gas generated by a reaction between coal and steam. Syn-gas is made up of mostly hydrogen and carbon monoxide and is used to make methanol. Syn-gas is also known as town gas.

Synthetic fuel   Fuels generated through synthetic processes such as Fischer-Tropsch.

TAME   Tertiary-amyl methyl ether. TAME is an oxygenating fuel and is used as a gasoline additive similar to ETBE or MTBE.

Tap   A metal cutting tool used to create threads in metal after a hole of the proper size has been drilled.

Tap test   Involves tapping (not pounding) on the catalytic converter using a rubber mallet.

Taper face ring   Contacts the cylinder wall at the lower edge of the piston ring.

Tapered pilots   Locate themselves in the least-worn section of the guide.

TDC   Top dead center.

Technical service bulletin   When a problem has a correction, the vehicle manufacturer releases a technical service bulletin (TSB), which details the repair. Also called technical service bulletin information (TSBI).

TEL   An additive that was added to gasoline in the early 1920s to reduce the tendency to knock.

Tensile strength   The maximum stress used under tension (lengthwise force) without causing failure.

Thermactor pump   See *smog pump*.

Thermal shock   A sudden change in temperature. The shock will often cause radial cracks in the valve.

Thermostatic spring   Operates a valve that allows the fan to freewheel when the radiator is cold. As the radiator warms to about 150°F (65°C), the air hitting the thermostatic spring will cause the spring to change its shape.

Thick-film integration   This system uses a smaller control module attached to the distributor and uses an air-cooled epoxy E coil.

Thickness gauge   See *feeler gauge*.

Thimble   The part of a micrometer that is rotated to move the spindle.

Thin-walled bronze alloy sleeve bushing   Guide insert for guide repair.

Threaded insert   A type of thread repair where the original threads are replaced by an insert that contains the same size threads as the original on the inside of the insert.

Throating Removes metal from the port side of the seat, raising the lower edge of the seat.

Throating angle The second angle uses a 60-degree stone or cutter to remove material right below the valve seat to increase flow in or out of the combustion chamber.

Thrust bearing Supports thrust loads and maintains the front-to-rear position of the crankshaft in the block.

Thrust plate Controls the shaft end thrust.

Tier A level of environmental regulation created by the EPA. Tier 1 is gradually being phased out in favor of stricter Tier 2 regulations.

Tin snips A hand tool used to cut sheet metal, thin cardboard, or similar material.

Topping angle The third angle uses a 30-degree stone or cutter and is used to smooth the transition between the valve seat and the cylinder head, again to increase flow in or out of the combustion chamber.

Torque angle A tightening procedure that has a more constant clamping load from bolt to bolt.

Torque-to-yield See *torque angle.*

Torque wrench A wrench that registers the amount of applied torque.

Total indicator runout (TIR) When measuring and regrinding camshafts the TIR should be less than 0.002 inch.

Transistor Electronic switch.

Trouble light A light used for close viewing of dark areas. Also called a work light.

Tube-nut wrench See *fitting wrench.*

Tuftriding A trade name that General Motors Corporation uses for the process of heating the crankshaft in a molten cyanide salt bath.

Turbo lag The delay between acceleration and turbo boost.

Turbocharger An exhaust-powered supercharger.

TWC Three-way catalytic converter, all three exhaust emissions (NO_X, HC, and CO) are converted to carbon dioxide (CO_2) and water (H_2O).

UCG Underground coal gasification.

UCO Used cooking oil.

ULSD Ultra-low-sulfur diesel. Diesel fuel with a maximum sulfur content of 15 parts per million.

Ultrasonic cleaning Parts are placed in a tank of cleaning solution which is then vibrated at ultrasonic speeds to loosen all the soil from the parts.

Umbrella valve stem seal Holds tightly on the valve stem and moves up and down with the valve. Any oil that spills off the rocker arms is deflected out over the valve guide, much as water is deflected over an umbrella.

UNC Unified national coarse.

UNF Unified national fine.

Universal joint A joint in a steering or drive shaft that allows torque to be transmitted at an angle.

Used oil Any petroleum-based or synthetic oil that has been used.

UST Underground storage tank.

Utility knife A handheld knife that uses replaceable blades.

Vacuum test A test that includes testing the engine for cranking vacuum, idle vacuum, and vacuum at 2500 RPM.

Valve duration The number of degrees by which the crankshaft rotates when the valve is off the valve seat.

Valve float Occurs when clearance exists in the valve train.

Valve guide Supports the valve stem so that the valve face will remain perfectly centered.

Valve guide knurling A tool is rotated as it is driven into the guide. The tool displaces the metal to reduce the hole diameter of the guide.

Valve keepers Secure the spring retainer to the stem of the valve.

Valve lash Valve train clearance.

Valve locks A lock for engine valves.

Valve pockets See *eyebrows.*

Valve relief See *eyebrows.*

Valve shrouding The valve is kept close to the walls of the combustion chamber to help increase mixture turbulence.

Valve spring Holds the valve against the seat.

Valve spring surge The tendency of a valve spring to vibrate.

Vapor lock Vaporized fuel, usually in the fuel line, that prevents or retards the necessary fuel delivery to the cylinders.

Variable fuel sensor See *fuel compensation sensor.*

Variable valve timing (VVT) Uses electronically controlled, hydraulic gear-driven cam phaser that can alter the relationship of the camshaft from 15 degrees retard to 25 degrees advance (40 degrees overall) relative to the crankshaft.

VECI Vehicle emissions control information. This sticker is located under the hood on all vehicles and includes emission-related information that is important to the service technician.

Vehicle identification number (VIN) Alphanumeric number identifying vehicle type, assembly plant, powertrain, and so on.

Vent valve See *dump valve.*

V-FFV Virtual flexible-fuel vehicle. This fuel system design does not use a fuel compensation sensor and instead uses the vehicle's oxygen sensor to adjust for different fuel compositions.

Vibration damper A device connected to the crankshaft of an engine to reduce torsional vibration.

Viscosity Thickness of oil as its resistance to flow.

Viscosity index An index of the change in viscosity between the cold and hot extremes.

Vise Grips® A brand name for locking pliers.

Volatility A measurement of the tendency of a liquid to change to vapor. Volatility is measured using RVP, or Reid vapor pressure.

Volumetric efficiency The ratio between the amount of air–fuel mixture that actually enters the cylinder and the amount that could enter under ideal conditions expressed in percent.

VTEC Variable valve timing and lift electronic control. A valve train control system developed by Honda Motor Company to enhance engine output and efficiency over a wide RPM range.

Wankel engine See *rotary engine*.

Washcoat A porous aluminum material.

Washers Flat or shaped pieces of round metal with a hole in the center used between a nut and a part or casting.

Wastegate A bypass valve at the exhaust inlet to the turbine.

Water pump pliers See *multigroove adjustable pliers*.

Water-fuel separator Water is heavier than diesel fuel and sinks to the bottom of the separator.

Welsh plugs Core holes left in the external block wall are machined and sealed with this type of plug.

Wet compression test When oil is used to help seal around the piston rings.

Wet cylinder sleeve Coolant flows around this type of cylinder sleeve.

Wet holes Head bolts that extend through the top deck of the block and end in a coolant passage.

Wet sump A system where oil is held in the oil pan and the oil pump drains the oil from the bottom.

WHMIS Workplace Hazardous Materials Information Systems.

Windage tray Tray that is sometimes installed in engines to eliminate the oil churning problem.

Wood alcohol See *methanol*.

Work hardened Flexing starts fatigue, which shows up as fine cracks in the bearing surface.

Work light See *trouble light*.

Wrench Any of various hand or power tools, often having fixed or adjustable jaws, used for gripping, turning, or twisting objects such as nuts, bolts, or pipes.

Wrist pin See *piston pin*.

WVO Waste vegetable oil.

WWFC World Wide Fuel Charter. A fuel quality standard developed by vehicle and engine manufacturers in 2002.

ZDDP Commonly referred to as zinc dialkyl dithiophosphate. The use of ZDDP was intended to reduce sliding friction in an engine.

Zinc dithiophosphate (ZDP) Antiwear additive.

Zyglo A method where cracks show up as bright lines when viewed with a black light.

SPANISH GLOSSARY

Abombado Los pistones utilizados en ciertos motores pueden ser provistos con una depresión.

ACEA Asociación de constructores europeos de automóviles que representa la mayoría del mercado de camiones de alto tonelaje de Europa Occidental. Esta organización utiliza motores para sus pruebas diferentes de aquellos usados por la API y la SAE, y los prerrequisitos para cumplir con los estándares de la ACEA aunque un poco diferentes, generalmente corresponden a la mayoría de los de la API.

Aceite anticorrosivo Recubre partes de metal para evitar que se oxiden.

Aceite penetrante Un aceite delgado diseñado para penetrar la corrosión y proporcionar lubricación para las ranuras de un sujetador.

Aceite usado Cualquier aceite de base petrolero o sintético que ha sido usado.

Acero multicapa (MLS) Las múltiples y delgadas capas de acero reducen el calibre y las distorsiones del árbol de levas de cabeza con menos fuerza de ajuste que los diseños anteriores.

Ácido Acético Algunos sellantes de silicona tipo RTV utilizan los humos o gases de este ácido. Utilice con precaución ya que este tipo de ácido puede meterse al motor a través del sistema PCV y puede dañar los sensores de oxígeno.

Acoplamiento de silicona Un acoplamiento de ventilador montado entre la polea de propulsión y el ventilador.

Adaptador de buje o casquillo Un instrumento utilizado para adaptar un tamaño de un propulsor de bujes o dados para ser usado con otro propulsor de bujes o dados de distinto tamaño tal como un maneral o barra rompedora.

Aditivos depresantes PPD Estos aditivos añaden una capa de cristales de cera al aceite para que estos cristales no se peguen entre ellos. De esta manera el aceite podrá fluir a temperaturas más bajas.

Agitación Mantiene la solución fresca del limpiador deslizándose sobre la tierra con la finalidad de soltarla.

AGST Siglas en inglés para depósito de almacenamiento no subterráneo, un tipo de depósito utilizado para almacenar aceite usado.

Agujero de purga Agujero que destila una pequeña cantidad de aceite del muñón del tren de varillado.

AIR Siglas en inglés de sistema de control de emisiones por reacción de inyección de aire.

Aireado Aire mezclado con aceite.

Ajuste hidráulico de huelgo (HLA por sus siglas en inglés) Algunos motores nuevos tienen el ajuste hidráulico en el brazo móvil llamado HLA.

AKI Siglas en inglés de índice antidetonante. El índice de octano fijado en una bomba de gasolina, en una estación de gasolina, que constituye un promedio entre el índice de octano RON y el índice de octano MON.

Alambre fusible (eslabón fusible) Fusible que se derrite y abre el circuito protegido en caso de que haya un corto circuito que puede resultar en un flujo de corriente excesivo a través del alambre fusible. La mayoría de los alambres fusibles en realidad son alambres cuyas entrevías tienen un cuarto del diámetro o del tamaño que el alambre de los circuitos que protegen.

Alcohol de grano *Véase* **Etanol.**

Alcohol de madera *Véase* **Metanol.**

Alcohol etílico *Véase* **Etanol.**

Aleación de cobre–plomo Esta aleación constituye un material más caro y más resistente que el babbit. Se usa en aplicaciones intermedias y de alta velocidad. El estaño, en pequeñas cantidades, a menudo se mezcla con los rodamientos de cobre–plomo.

Aletas refrigerantes Aletas de ventilación que están expuestas al flujo de aire y que se deshacen del calor del radiador y lo desplazan a otro lugar.

Alicates angulares Alicates diseñados para cortar alambre y para retirar pasadores o chavetas. También conocido como cortadoras transversales o alicates cortantes de *dike.*

Alicates de aguja Un instrumento manual que está equipado con una quijada puntiaguda, lo cual permite su utilización en áreas muy pequeñas donde hay gran restricción de movimiento o con piezas pequeñas.

Alicates o llaves bloqueantes   Un instrumento manual utilizado para sujetar un objeto y luego asegurarlo en una posición. Comúnmente conocido por el nombre de la marca popular Vise Grips®.

Alicates o llaves multiranuradas ajustables   Un instrumento manual capaz de sujetar un amplio rango de tamaños de objeto, también conocido como alicates de bomba de agua o por el nombre de la marca popular Channel Locks®.

Alternador   Un generador eléctrico que produce corriente alterna. También se llama generador de CA.

Amoladora (esmeriladora) de banco   Un motor eléctrico con un disco de grano grueso o fino y/o alambre acoplado en ambos extremos a su eje de giro y montado sobre un banco de trabajo.

Amoladora   Tipo de pulidor que utiliza una rueda abrasiva de diámetro largo.

Amortiguador de vibraciones   Un dispositivo conectado al cigüeñal de un motor para reducir la vibración torsional.

Amortiguando   Reduciendo las vibraciones a niveles aceptables.

Amperaje de arranque en frío   Valuación de la habilidad de una batería de producir un voltaje en tiempo frío.

Amplitud   La diferencia entre el pico y la parte más baja de la onda.

Ángulo de bisel   El ángulo que se encuentra entre los botones de cigüeñal y los brazos del cigüeñal.

Angulo de desplazamiento de lóbulos (LDA)   *Véase* **Centros de lóbulos.**

Ángulo de *throating*   El según ángulo usa un abrasivo o amoladora de 60 grados para sacar material justo debajo del asiento de válvula para aumentar flujo hacia adentro o hacia afuera o de la cámara de combustión.

Ángulo de torsión   Un procedimiento de apretamiento que da una carga de aprieto más constante de tornillo a tornillo.

Ángulo superior   El tercer ángulo usa un abrasivo o amoladora de 30 grados, y ayuda la transición entre asiento de válvula y la cabeza de cilindro, para aumentar el flujo a o de la cámara de combustión.

Anillo conificado frontal   Contacta la pared del cilindro al margen inferior del anillo del pistón.

Anillo de control de aceite   Permite que el aceite retorne a través del aro del pistón y otras aberturas en el pistón.

Anillo de fuego   *Véase* **Armadura.**

Anillo elástico   Forma de resorte utilizado para sujetar un objeto al interior de un agujero de taladro insertándolo en una ranura o rebaje.

Anillos de seguridad (de pistones)   Sujetan y retienen los ejes de pistón completamente flotantes al interior de un motor de automóvil.

ANSI   Siglas en inglés de Instituto Nacional Estadounidense de Estándares.

Anticongelante en base a etilenglicol (glicol de etileno)   Anticongelante.

Año calendario (AC)   Un año calendario comienza en el día primero de enero y termina el 31 de diciembre de cada año.

Año del vehículo   El año de fabricación del vehículo, el cual puede variar del año calendario cuando se vendió.

API   Siglas en inglés de Instituto Estadounidense de Petróleo.

Aplastamiento del cojinete o *crush*   Fenómeno que ocurre cuando se ajusta o aprieta un cabezal de rodamiento y los dos extremos de la carcaza del rodamiento se tocan y se unen por en una unión forzada.

Arandela   Pieza fina o plana de metal circular con un hueco por el medio, utilizado entre un perno o tuerca y una parte o plancha de metal.

Árbol de levas   Una barra cilíndrica con levas mecánicas sobresaliendo de ella que abren y cierran las válvulas de motor a medida que rota por medio de una cadena, cinturón o engranaje conectado al cigüeñal.

Árbol de leva de cadena silenciosa   Árbol de leva de cadena que opera silenciosamente pero que tiende a alargarse con el uso.

Árbol de levas de configuración OVH sencilla   Un diseño en el cual se coloca un árbol de levas dentro de la culata del cilindro.

Árbol de levas de dientes invertidos   *Véase* **Árbol de levas cadena silenciosa.**

Árbol de levas de material compuesto   Una varilla tubular ligera con levas de acero endurecido incorporadas a dicho varillaje.

Árbol de levas doble en culata   Un diseño de motor con dos árboles de leva que se ubican encima de cada línea de cilindros–una para las válvulas de agotamiento y otra para las válvulas de entrada.

Árbol de levas en culata o en cabeza   Un árbol de levas accionado por correas o cadenas desde un cigüeñal y ubicado en la culata o cabeza de los cilindros.

Árbol de levas equilibrado   Un árbol de levas que tiene contrapesos en ambos lados de los muñones del tren de varillado.

Área fría del pistón   Un área de la cámara de combustión donde el pistón casi entra en contacto con el cilindro.

Área plana de culeta de pistón   Véase **Área fría del pistón.**

Armadura   Protege la fibra que reviste el interior de la cámara de combustión.

Armazón de motor   Un marco de piso–montado usualmente equipado con casters, en el cual un motor puede ser adherido y rotado.

Aro de lubricación   Usualmente recomendable para su uso en el segundo anillo de compresión.

Aro de pistón   Sella el pequeño espacio entre el pistón y la pared del cilindro, manteniendo la presión por encima del pistón.

Aros de compresión   Diseñados para formar un sello entre el pistón en movimiento y la pared del cilindro.

Arrastre de metal   Tipo de corrosión que resulta del arrastre de una pieza pesada que gira sobre otra.

Asbestosis   Condición médica en la que el asbesto produce la formación de cicatrices en los pulmones, lo cual conduce a la falta de aliento.

Asiento integral   Este asiento está generalmente formado como parte integral del cabezal de hierro forjado de los motores de automóvil.

Asimétrico   A menudo el nivel de sustentación para la válvula de escape y de admisión es diferente. Si las especificaciones para dichas válvulas difieren de tal manera, el árbol de levas es de tipo asimétrico.

ASTM   Siglas en inglés de la Sociedad Americana para Materiales de Prueba.

Auto inducción   Cuando una corriente comienza a fluir hacia una bobina, una corriente opuesta se genera en el embobinado de la bobina.

B20   Una mezcla de un 20% de biodiésel con un 80% de petrodiésel.

Balancines   Recipiente oscilante de dos cubetas o cojinete balancín.

Balde   Jerga automovilística para referirse a la cubierta que abre los trenes de potencia de la válvula superior del árbol de levas.

Bandeja de fricción de aire   Una bandeja que a veces se instala en los motores para eliminar los problemas de agitación del aceite.

Bar   Cuando el aire es bombeado al interior del cilindro, la cámara de combustión recibe un incremento de la presión del aire conocido como sobrepresión, que se mide en libras por pulgadas cuadradas (PSI), atmósferas (ATMs), o bar.

Barra articulada (mango articulado)   Una herramienta de mango largo, para la propulsión del dado.

Barra de alargue   Una barra utilizada en una llave para incrementar el monto de torsión que se puede aplicar a un sujetador. No se recomienda.

Barrera de calor   La mayoría de los pistones tienen ranuras de separación horizontal que actúan como diques de contención del calor.

Baterías de acido del plomo (baterías SLA)   Una batería que convierte nuevamente en agua al hidrogeno y oxigeno liberados antes de que estos escapen a la atmósfera.

BCI   Siglas en inglés de Consejo Internacional de Baterías.

Biodiésel   Un combustible renovable, producido a nivel doméstico, que se obtiene mediante procesos industrializados a partir de lípidos naturales tales como los aceites vegetales, las grasas animales o la grasa de restaurante reciclada.

Biomasa   Productos agrícolas no comestibles tales como: los tallos de maíz, pajas de cereal y deshechos botánicos de procesos industriales, tales como el aserrín y la pulpa de papel utilizadas en la elaboración del etanol.

Biomasa celulósica   Compuesta principalmente de celulosa y lignina así como de proteínas, lípidos (grasas, ceras y aceites) en cantidades más pequeñas y cenizas.

Bloque   Cada una de las agrupaciones de cuatro cilindros interiores.

Bloque de motor   La base de cualquier motor. Todas las demás partes están directamente o indirectamente adheridas al bloque del motor.

Bobina del encendido   Artefacto eléctrico que consta de dos bobinas distintas de alambre; un bobinado primario y un secundario. El objetivo de un encendido es producir una corriente de alto voltaje (de entre 20.000 y 40.000 V) y amperaje suficientemente bajo (cerca de 80 mA) como para que se produzca el encendido de la chispa.

Boca abierta   El extremo de una llave que se abre para permitir que la llave encaje o se inserte de un lado a un perno, tuerca o tornillo.

Boletín de servicio técnico   Cuando el fabricante de un vehículo anuncia la corrección de una falta, publica un boletín de servicio (TSB por sus siglas en inglés), que explica en detalle la reparación necesaria. También se llama información de boletín de servicio técnico (TSBI por sus siglas in inglés).

Bolsillos de válvula   *Véase* **Muescas.**

Bomba centrífuga   Una bomba rotodinámica que utiliza un rodete para incrementar la velocidad de un líquido o fluido.

Bomba de elevación (de aceleración o de pique)   El combustible diesel es extraído del tanque de combustible por una bomba de presión para, de esta manera, hacer llegar el combustible a la bomba de inyección.

Bomba de esmog   Bombea hacia adentro el fresco a través de un filtro externo y bombea hacia afuera el aire ejerciendo una leve presión en cada puerto de salida a través de mangueras interconectadas o mediante el uso de un múltiple.

Bomba de inyección de aire   *Véase* **Bomba de esmog.**

Bomba de inyección   Una bomba de inyección de diesel es utilizada para incrementar la presión del combustible diesel desde valores muy bajos de la bomba de presión hasta la presión extremadamente alta que se necesita para la inyección de dicho combustible.

Botón de muñeca   *Véase* **Bulón o eje de pistón.**

Broca micrométrica   La parte de un micrómetro que se mueve y esta en contacto con las partes del objeto que se mide.

Bruñido   El bruñido deja una superficie aplanada que puede mantener la película de aceite para el aro y la funda del pistón. Esta superficie plana se logra primero usando una piedra abrasiva seguido de una piedra suave para obtener la superficie deseada.

BTU (*British Thermal Unit* o Unidad Térmica Británica) Una unidad de medida de calor.

Buje de camisa de aleación de bronce con paredes estrechas   Guía de inserción para reparación de guías.

Buje espiral de aleación de bronce   Guía de válvula insertadle para reparaciones.

Buje seco del cilindro   Se utilizan bujes del cilindro de hierro forjado en bloques de aluminio para proveer una superficie dura para los anillos.

Bujía de incandescencia   (bujía de encendido) Pequeño calentador eléctrico, localizado en el interior del cilindro de un motor diesel, para precalentar el aire y ayudar al arranque del motor.

Bulón o eje de pistón   Une el pistón a la varilla conector.

CAA Clean Air Act   Legislación federal adoptada en 1970 y actualizada en 1990 que introdujo e estándares de calidad de aire a nivel nacional.

Caballetes   Calibres.

Calibrador de hoja   Laminillas de metal o cuchillas de un grosor sumamente específico y con un acabado muy fino, que se utilizan para medir la holgura entre dos partes.

Calibre de agujero pequeño   Un instrumento de medición manual que se ajusta para poder caber al interior de pequeños huecos o agujeros. Entonces, se utiliza un micrómetro para medir el calibre y determinar el diámetro interno del agujero. También conocido como un calibre de micrómetro.

Calibre de hoja de huelgo   utilizado para medir el huelgo entre el pistón y el cilindro.

Calibre de micrómetro   Véase **Calibre de agujero pequeño.**

Calibre de Regla   Un calibre de precisión que mide metal molido que se utiliza para verificar la horizontalidad de los componentes de un motor cuando se usa con un calibrador de hoja.

Calibre   El diámetro interior de un cilindro en un motor.

Calificación de la hora de amperio   Una calificación de batería antigua.

Calor de compresión   El aire que ingresa es comprimido hasta que la temperatura alcanza aproximadamente los 537° C (1000° F).

Cámara de aire   Una cámara localizada entre el cuerpo de la mariposa y las varillas deslizantes del múltiple de entrada, usada para distribuir la carga de entrada de una manera más suave y eficiente.

Cámara de combustión   El espacio que queda al interior de un cilindro de motor cuando un pistón se encuentra en lo m alto de su cámara de combustión.

Candado de válvula   Un seguro para válvulas de motor.

Capacidad de arranque (CA)   Una calificación de batería que se prueba cuando el motor está en 0° centígrado.

Capacidad de reserva   El número de minutos que una batería puede producir 25 amperios y aun así mantener un voltaje de 1,75 voltios por celda (10,5 voltios para una batería de 12 voltios).

Capilaridad   El movimiento de un líquido a través de pequeños orificios o tubos.

Carrera del pistón o embolada   Movimiento del pistón de una vía entre las partes superiores e inferiores (culata y piso) del cilindro.

Cartér inferior   Una pieza estructural que se adhiere al fondo del bloque del motor y sostiene el árbol de levas.

Cascos de cojinete rotatorios   Los cascos de cojinete que no tienen suficiente están lo suficientemente aplanados o que no tiene el suficiente "crush" pueden girar descontroladamente con el varillaje.

Casquillo   Un instrumento que encaja por encima de un perno o tuerca y que es girado por un maneral o barra rompedora.

Casquillo de biela   El rodamiento es fabricado a una tolerancia muy pequeña de manera que pueda encajar correctamente en cada aplicación.

Catalizador oxigenado de diesel   Consiste en una estructura alevoal de flujo continuo que está enchapado con una capa de material catalítico similar a aquellos utilizados por los convertidores catalíticos en un motor de gasolina.

Catalizador   Un elemento que comienza una reacción química permaneciendo este elemento inalterado sin ser transformado por el proceso.

Cavitación o aspiración en Vacío   El proceso de crear una cavidad u área ahuecada. La cavitación en el área de la mecánica automovilística es un término que usualmente se usa para describir el efecto hidrodinámica que se produce cuando el agua hierve, lo cual crea una burbuja en le sistema, para posteriormente enfriarse por debajo del los 100º C lo cual hace que la burbuja implote. Cuando esto ocurre el agua vuelve inmediatamente a llenar el vacío dejado por el agua. La fuerza de este fenómeno puede causar ruido y molestias o inclusive daño a las partes del sistema de enfriamiento del coche tales como las bombas de agua.

Cementación metálica   Se refiere al recalentamiento del árbol de levas y la añadidura de moléculas de carbón a las levas de tal manera que, mediante este proceso, la superficie externa de dicho árbol de levas se endurezca mucho más que cualquier otra parte de esta pieza.

Centros de lóbulos   La separación entre las líneas centrales de los lóbulos de admisión y de escape que se mide en grados.

Cerio   Un elemento que puede almacenar oxigeno.

CFR   Siglas en inglés para el Código de Regulaciones Federales.

Chivo   Instrumento utilizado para extraer un perno quebrado.

Choque termal   Un cambio súbito en temperatura. A menudo el choque causará grietas radiales en la válvula.

Ciclo de cuatro golpes   Un diseño de motor de combustión interna, en donde cuatro golpes de pistón (dos revoluciones del cigüeñal) son requeridos para completar un ciclo de eventos. Los cuatro golpes incluyen, admisión, compresión, potencia y escape.

Ciclo de vida por fatiga de material   Número de ciclos repetitivos de tensión que se aplican en un material y que pueden resistirse antes de fallar.

Ciclo   Una serie completa de eventos continuamente recurrentes.

Cigüeñal   Un eje o varilla que gira o que es girado por medio de una biela.

Cilindro   La cámara donde un pistón de un motor reciprocante se mueve.

Cincel tipo corte frío   Un tipo de cincel utilizado para retirar remaches o romper sujetadores.

Cincel   Un instrumento afilado que se usa junto a un martillo para separar dos piezas de un ensamblaje.

Circuito de encendido primario   El componente de encendido que regula la corriente en el embobinado primario al encenderlo y apagarlo.

Circuito del encendido secundario   Componentes y conexiones eléctricos que producen y distribuyen electricidad de alto voltaje para inflamar (encender) la mezcla de combustible y aire al interior del motor.

Clips de arbolito de navidad   Jerga utilizada en el área de la mecánica automotriz para referirse a clips de plástico utilizados para sostener paneles interiores en su lugar. La cola que ingresa a través de un hueco en la puerta de acero del automóvil acaba en una punta (es puntiagudo) y se parece a un árbol de navidad.

Códigos de calibración   Códigos usados en muchos de los módulos de control del tren de fuerza.

Codo conector del cigüeñal   *Véase* **Brazo del cigüeñal.**

Codo del cigüeñal   Los codos de los rodamientos desquilibrados del cigüeñal.

Cojinete de empuje lateral   Apoya cargas de empuje y mantiene la posición delantera a trasera del cigüeñal en el bloque.

Cojinete de manguito interior   Rodamiento de motor.

Cojinetes del árbol de levas   El árbol de levas es sostenido en el bloque por estos cojinetes.

Colas   Hechas de tela engomada con terminaciones de metal que soportan el silenciador o roncador y el tubo de escape en posición de modo que no toquen ninguna parte de metal.

Colector de lubricante de cárter   Sistema donde el aceite se acumula en una bandeja de aceite y la bomba de aceite drena el aceite del fondo de dicha bandeja.

Combustibles oxigenados   Combustibles tales como el ETBE o el MTBE que contienen moléculas de oxígeno extras para promover un quemado más limpio. Los combustibles oxigenados se usan como aditivos de la gasolina para reducir las emisiones de dióxido de carbono.

Combustibles sintéticos   Combustibles creados a través de productos sintéticos tales como el proceso Fischer-Tropsch.

Combustión espontánea   Un fenómeno por el cual un incendio comienza espontáneamente en trapos llenos de aceite o grasa.

Combustión   La ignición rápida de una mezcla de aire y combustible en los cilindros del motor que genera calor y presión al interior del motor.

Compresor de aire   Una pieza de equipo mecánico que utiliza un motor eléctrico para operar un compresor de aire que se almacena al interior de un tanque de presión para su uso en el taller mecánico.

Compresor de segmentos   Mantiene los anillos en sus ranuras.

Concéntrico   Centrado.

Conducto común de alta presión   Sistema de inyección de combustible electrónicao para motor diésel en el que el combustible es aspirado directamente del depósito de combustible a un conducto común a todos los inyectores y enviado a alta presión al cilindro.

Conformabilidad   La habilidad de un material de fundición de arrastre, o sea de su alargamiento gradual y permanente con el peso de la carga, o de fluir levemente a fin de adecuarse a las variaciones del varillaje.

Contrapesos   Utilizados para equilibrar el árbol de levas.

Contrapresión   La resistencia al flujo del sistema de escape que se mide en libras por pulgada cuadrada (PSI).

Contrapresión negativa   Algunas válvulas EGR reaccionan a esta área de baja presión cerrando una pequeña válvula interna lo cual permite que la válvula EGR se habrá al vacío.

Contrapresión positiva   A velocidades bajas de motor y cargas ligeras sobre el motor, el sistema EGR no es necesario, y la presión de fondo en el mismo es también bajo.

Convertidor catalítico   Un mecanismo de control de emisiones ubicado en el sistema de escape que convierte el HC y el CO en H_2O y CO_2 inócuos. En un catalizador de tres vías, el NO_x también se divide en nitrógeno (N) y oxígeno (O).

Corona de rodamiento   El grosor de la mayoría de los rodamientos es mayor en su parte central.

Cortador helicoidal   Un instrumento de acero utilizado para reparar roscas dañadas.

Cresta   El diámetro externo de un tornillo medido de rosca a rosca.

CTL   Tecnología carbón a líquido. *Véase* **Carbón a líquido.**

Cubierta de fuego   La culata hembra del cilindro que se casa con el extremo macho del bloque.

Culata   El cabezal del cilindro está adherido a la superficie superior del bloque de cilindros o de motor.

Curva de destilación   Una gráfica que grafica las temperaturas a las cuales las se evaporan las diferentes fracciones de un combustible.

Cúter o cuchilla para moqueta   Un cuchillo manual que usa cuchillas intercambiables.

dB   Una abreviación de decibelio, una medida relativa del nivel de ruido o sonido.

Decapantes   Herramientas manuales diseñadas para retirar remaches, pernos y otros sujetadores rotos.

Demora de turbo   El retraso entre aceleración y el refuerzo de turbo.

Deposito de desagüe seco   La olla de aceite es superficial y el aceite es inyectado en un reservorio remoto. En este reservorio, el aceite es refrigerado, y cualquier aire atrapado puede escapar antes de ser inyectado de su vuelta al motor.

Desarmador o armador de sellos   Una herramienta manual utilizada en combinación con un martillo o maza para asentar los sellos en una ranura.

Desentornillador   Una herramienta manual diseñada para retirar o insertar tornillos.

Desintegración catalítica   Un proceso de refinación donde los hidrocarburos con puntos de ebullición altos se desintegran y forman hidrocarburos con puntos de ebullición bajos.

Desplazamiento (cilindrada)   El volumen total barrido en cada carrera del pistón en su movimiento dentro del cilindro al interior de un motor de combustión.

Destilación   El proceso de purificación a través de la evaporación y luego condensación del líquido deseado.

Destornillador plano   Destornillador utilizado para remover e insertar tornillos que tienen una sola ranura.

Desviación total de indicador   Cuando uno mide y remuela árboles de levas, la desviación total debe ser menos de 0,002 pulgada.

Desvío   Permite que una pequeña porción del líquido refrigerante circule al interior del motor durante su fase de enfriamiento. Es un pasaje muy estrecho que lleva del lado del motor del termóstato hacia algún.

Detonación   Una explosión violenta en la cámara de combustión creada por una incineración incontrolada de la mezcla aire–combustible; generalmente causa un golpeteo fuerte y audible. También conocido como un golpeteo o ping.

DEX-COOL   Refrigerante de larga vida.

Dialquilditiofosfatos de zinc (ZDP por sus siglas en inglés)   Aditivo anti desgaste.

Disco de esmeril   Un disco amolador adherido a una amoladora o esmeriladora que se usa para limpiar, afilar, moler, cortar u otras operaciones similares.

Disco de grano grueso o fino   Aquel disco usado para retirar grandes cantidades de metal de asiento. Este sería necesario en el caso de un asiento mal encajado o al insertar nuevos asientos de válvula.

Diseño de varillaje en bloque   Un motor donde el cigüeñal está ubicado en el bloque y no así en la culeta o cabezal.

Distancia entre roscas   El número de roscas por pulgada de un sujetador enroscado.

Divisor de rodamientos   Un dispositivo de dos partes utilizado entre un rodamiento y un engranaje u otro componente, el cual es usado para retirar el rodamiento usando una prensa hidráulica.

Duración de asiento   El número de grados de rotación del cigüeñal en que la válvula está separada de su asiento.

Duración de la rotación del cigüeñal   El número de grados de rotación del cigüeñal por los cuales la válvula está levantada del asiento.

Duración de válvula   El número de grados de rotación del cigüeñal en que la válvula está separada de su asiento.

E10   Una mezcla de combustible compuesta de un 10% de etanol y un 90% de gasolina.

E85 Una mezcla de combustible compuesta de un 85% de etanol y un 15% de gasolina.

E–diesel Diesel estándar, grado 2, que contiene hasta un 15% de etanol. También conocido como diesohol fuera de los Estados Unidos.

Eficiencia volumétrica La relación entre el volumen preciso de mezcla de aire-combustible que verdaderamente entra al cilindro y el volumen que pudiese entrar en condiciones óptimas que se expresa en un porcentaje.

EGR lineal Contiene un solenoide que regula con precisión el flujo de escape de gases y que contiene un potenciómetro de retroalimentación que informa a la computadora mediante señales en relación a la posición actual exacta de la válvula.

EGR Siglas en inglés para recirculación de los gases de escape. Un dispositivo de control de emisiones para reducir los niveles de NOx (óxidos de nitrógeno).

Eje del cigüeñal *Véase* **Codo del cigüeñal.**

Eje flotante Un tipo de ensamblaje de eje donde el peso del vehículo es sostenido por el bastidor del eje y no por el eje en sí.

Ejes de pie de biela El término que usan los ingleses en Gran Bretaña para referirse a un muñón, perno o todo eje en general utilizado para conectar el pistón al varillado.

Elastómero Un sinónimo del caucho.

Electroplastia o galvanoplastia El proceso de poner una lámina sobrepuesta que se adhiere a la superficie inicial.

Elevador de válvula solidó Facilita en la verificación de que no existe un excesivo huelgo en el tren de válvulas.

Elevador hidráulico Un elevador de válvulas que hace uso de la misma dinámica de las válvulas y de la presión del aceite para ajustar su tamaño y altura levemente a fin de mantener el suficiente huelgo y juego libre para el tren de válvulas. Los elevadores hidráulicos reducen el ruido ocasionado por los trenes de válvula y son dispositivos libres de mantenimiento.

Empujador de válvula La varilla de conexión que conecta el pedal del freno con el cilindro maestro del pistón.

Encaje de interferencia El método moderno utilizado para retener el búlon o eje de pistón en la varilla conector consiste en hacer que el agujero de la varilla conector se levemente más pequeño que el búlon o eje del pistón. El eje de pistón se instala mediante el recalentamiento de la varilla a fin de que el antedicho hueco se expanda o presionando el eje de pistón en la varilla.

Encaje de válvula La válvula se mantiene cerca a las paredes de la cámara de combustión a fin de aumentar la turbulencia de la mezcla.

Encastramientos vacíos Son encastramientos labrados en la parte superior de la válvula a fin de asegurar el huelgo de la válvula.

Encendido de alta energía (HEI por sus siglas en inglés) Usa una bombinada E, sellada por epoxia y resfriada por aire.

Enchapado o retacado Muchos de los rodamientos de cobre-plomo tienen tercer revestimiento de metal. Este revestimiento suele ser de babbit. Los rodamientos con retacado o enchapado de babbit tienen una buena resistencia a la fatiga, buen contorno, buena incrustación y una buena resistencia a la corrosión.

Endurecido por acritud La acritud comienza el proceso de fatiga de metal el cual se traduce en pequeñas ranuras y fracturas en la superficie del metal.

Enfriamiento invertido Cuando el refrigerante fluye del radiador a los cabezales de los cilindros antes de fluir hacia el bloque del motor.

Enroscado invertido Sella la sección exterior de la ranura de pistón y aro de pistón, de esta manera mejorando el control del aceite.

Enrosque positivo Proporciona el mismo contacto con la pared que el aro cónico.

Entallados de válvula *Véase* **Muescas.**

Entretuerca Un tipo de tuerca que tiene fuerza de torción; también llamada una tuerca de seguridad.

Envergadura Sostiene el casco del cojinete en la carcasa mientras se ensambla el motor.

Envergadura de los lóbulos *Véase* **Centros de lóbulos.**

EPA Siglas en inglés de Agencia de Protección Ambiental.

Equilibradora *Véase* **Amortiguador de vibraciones.**

Equipo de protección personal PPE por sus siglas en inglés. Prendas que los trabajadores llevan o utilizan a fin de protegerse de peligros en el lugar de trabajo, incluyendo los anteojos de seguridad, los guantes y los elementos de protección de la vista.

Espátula para enmasillar Espátula con una hoja flexible amplia, utilizada para aplicar y alisar masilla.

Estación de lavado de ojos Una unidad dispensadora de agua que dirige chorros de agua hacia los ojos.

Estelita Una aleación no magnética de níkel, cromo y tungsteno.

Estequiométrico Un ratio de combustible aire de exactamente 14.7:1. En esta relación o ratio especifico, toda la gasolina ha sido completamente oxidada por todo el oxigeno disponible.

Etanol (alcohol de grano) Un aditivo que sirve como mejorador de octanaje. En un ratio de hasta un 10% de etanol por gasolina el etanol aumentara el octanaje entre 2,4 a 3 veces. El etanol es un combustible oxigenado.

Etanol anhidro Etanol que no contiene agua.

Etanol celulósico   Etanol producido de cargas de alimentación de biomasa tales como residuos vegetales agrícolas e indústriales.

ETBE   Éter butil etil terciario. El ETBE es un combustible oxigenado que es utilizado como un aditivo de la gasolina para aumentar sus características inflamables.

EVCP   Sistema sincronizador de estrías.

Extensión   Barras de acero con puntales hembra y macho que se utilizan para extender el campo de acción de una matraca o mango articulado a fin de rotar una llave de cubo o dado.

Extractor de puntal   Una herramienta de extracción de puntales que aprieta firmemente parte del puntal por encima de la superficie y usa una barrena o cuña para sujetar el otro extremo del puntal mientras que un maneral se encarga de rotar el puntal.

Extremo no principal   El extremo de un motor opuesto a la terminación principal y al que generalmente se denomina como la parte frontal del motor donde se utilizan los cinturones.

Extremo principal   El extremo del motor donde se adhiere al volante.

Falda   *Véase* **Zócalo móvil.**

Fecha juliana   El número del día del año, empezando con el 1 de enero como *1,* y contando en adelante. Abreviado FJ (JD en inglés).

FFV   Siglas en inglés de vehículo *flex-fuel.* Los vehículos *flex-fuel* son capaces de funcionar con gasolina pura o mezclas de gasolina y etanol.

Filtro APEE/Filtro de aire particulado de elevada eficiencia   Tipo de filtro de aire que teóricamente puede retirar por lo menos el 99,97% de las partículas que se transportan en el aire.

Fischer-Tropsch   Un proceso de refinación mediante el cual se convierte el carbón, gas natural u otros productos del petróleo a combustibles sintéticos para motores.

Flotador de válvula   Problema mecánico que ocurre por la presencia de holgura en el tren de válvulas.

Frazada antiincendios   Una frazada de lana a prueba de incendios que se utiliza para apagar el fuego al envolverla alrededor de una víctima.

Frecuencia   El número de veces que se repite una onda en un segundo, medido en hertz (Hz), frecuencia de banda.

Fuerza de accionamiento   La cantidad de fuerza ejercida sobre una junta de estanqueidad.

Fuerza mecánica   La presión desarrollada al interior de la cámara de combustión se aplica a la culata o cabezal del pistón o a una rueda de turbina.

Fuerzas de la inercia   Un producto de la acción de reciprocidad del pistón.

Funda del cilindro mojada   El refrigerante fluye alrededor de este tipo de funda de cilindro.

Galería   Cabezal longitudinal. Este es un agujero que ha sido taladrado desde la parte frontal del bloque hacia su parte posterior. Los ductos taladrados o maquinados a través del bloque permiten que el aceite pase de la galería principal de aceite a los rodamientos y levas principales.

Galerías de aceite   Una bomba de aceite accionada por el motor que empuja el aceite a través de un filtro de aceite y después a los ductos que se encuentran al interior del cigüeñal y del bloque del motor.

Gases de escape   Gases producto de la combustión que se escurren más allá de los aros del pistón y que se introducen al cárter del cigüeñal durante los golpes de compresión y combustión del motor.

Gasolina   Producto de petróleo refinado que es utilizado principalmente como combustible en motores a gasolina.

Gata mecánica   Una gata hidráulica montada en piezas moldeadas (casters) o ruedas de acero y utilizada para levantar un vehículo.

GAWR   Siglas en inglés para peso bruto nominal por eje. Una calificación de la capacidad de carga de peso de un vehículo y que se incluye en las señalizaciones del vehículo así como en el manual de operaciones.

GLP   Gas licuado de petróleo. Otro término para el propano.

GNC   Gas natural comprimido.

Golpe   La distancia que viaja el pistón al interior del cilindro.

Golpe de la chispa   Combustión secundaria de al menos 3% a 5% de la mezcla aire combustible al interior de la cámara de combustión. Lo cual genera una llama incendiaria secundaria que se choca con la primera llama causando un.

Golpeteo   Quemado rápido secundario de los últimos 3% a 5% de la mezcla de aire–combustible en la cámara de combustión que cause un segundo frente de flama que colinda con el primer frente de flama causando un ruido de golpeteo. También llamado detonación o ping.

Golpeteo doble   El sonido que se crea cuando el pistón se detiene en TDC y que ocurre otra vez cuando comienza a moverse hacia abajo, creando un sonido de doble golpeteo, que se describe también como un sonido vibratorio.

Gorra de seguridad   Gorra que usa un técnico que protege la cabeza del daño que puede ser ocasionado por objetos sobresalientes o partes sueltas del vehículo.

Gravedad específica   La gravedad específica es el ratio de volumen de líquido al peso equivalente de volumen del agua.

Grúa portátil   Una pieza de equipo para taller mecánico utilizada para levantar y mover piezas de equipo pesadas, como un motor.

GTL   Tecnología gas a líquido o GTL por sus siglas en inglés. Un proceso de refinación mediante el cual el gas natural es convertido en líquido.

Guía de válvula   Sostiene el vástago de válvula para que la cara de la válvula permanezca perfectamente centrada.

Guía de válvula de moleteado   Una herramienta que se gira a medida que es insertada a la guía. La herramienta desplaza el metal a fin de reducir el diámetro de la guía.

Guías cónicas   Se colocan en la sección más desgastada de la guía.

Guttering   Resultado del pobre asentamiento que permite que los gases de combustión de alta temperatura y alta presión filtren entre la válvula y el asiento.

GVWR   Siglas en inglés de nivel de peso total del vehículo.

Helicoil®   Una marca para cortadores helicoidales.

Hendidura   Una indentación en la culata o cabezal del pistón que diferencia la parte delantera de la trasera.

Herramienta de extracción de puntales   Una herramienta manual que se usa en combinación con un maneral o barra rompedora para extraer lo que queda de un puntal quebrado.

Herramienta de manipulación del aro del pistón   Herramienta para retirar los aros del pistón.

Herramienta para extracción de sellos   Una herramienta manual diseñada especialmente para extraer sellos.

Hidrocraqueo   Proceso de refinamiento que convierte a los hidrocarburos con alto punto de ebullición en otros con bajo punto de ebullición.

Hierro con grafito compactado (o CGI por sus siglas en inglés)   Es un tipo de hierro utilizado en carters y muchos tipos de bloque de motor. Tiene una mayor dureza, resistencia y durabilidad que el hierro fundido gris. Esta mayor durabilidad y dureza han logrado demostrar que este tipo de hierro puede ser más ligero mientras que, al mismo tiempo, reduce su aspereza y los ruidos causados por vibraciones.

Hierro maleable   Un material muy dúctil y flexible que puede ser torcido sin quebrarse. También se utiliza para fabricar anillos de pistón en algunos modelos automovilísticos.

Hipereutéctico   Pistones que son usados comúnmente en el mercado secundario y como equipo original en muchos motores turbocargados y supercargados.

HO$_2$S   Sensor Calentado de Oxígeno.

Holgura lateral   Juego libre en la ranura del aro que se encuentra por encima del aro.

Huelgo   Juego longitudinal libre de la válvula.

Huelgo de aro de pistón   Permite que algo de presión se deslice más allá del aro de compresión. Esta fuga es útil en el sentido de que presiona a que el segundo aro desarrolle una fuerza dinámica sellante.

Huelgo de válvula   Juego libre del tren de válvulas.

Huelgo del cigüeñal   El juego libre.

ILSAC   Comité Internacional de Ratificación y Estandarización de Lubricante. Responsable por el desarrollo del estándar ILSAC para aceite de motor.

Impulsor   El mecanismo en una bomba de agua que gira para producir flujo de refrigerante.

Incrustación   Propiedad que permite al rodamiento incrustar totalmente la partícula. El material de rodamiento, trabaja gradualmente a través de la partícula, cubriéndola completamente.

Índice de cetano (cetanaje)   Medida de las características antidetonantes de un combustible diesel.

Índice de destilación   Un indicador de la volatilidad de un combustible y lo bien que se evapora en temperaturas frías.

Índice de octano   Medida de las características antidetonantes de un combustible motor. Lo más alto el número de octano, lo menos probably que el motor va a golpear (hacer golpeteos).

Inducción mutua   La generación de una corriente eléctrica a lo largo y ancho del embobinado en ambos lados.

Inerte   Químicamente inactivo.

Información de servicio automotriz   Incluye el manual de servicio, el manual de operaciones, CDs, enlaces a sitios en el Internet u otras fuentes de información acerca del vehículo.

Inserto roscado   Un tipo de reparación de roscas en que las roscas originales se reemplazan por un inserto con roscas del mismo tamaño en el interior del inserto.

Integración de filamento espeso   Este sistema usa un módulo de control pequeño, montado en el distribuidor, que usa un embobinado de epoxia E, enfriado por aire.

Intercooler   El *intercooler* es un intercambiador (radiador) aire-aire o aire-agua que se encarga de enfriar el aire comprimido por el turbocompresor de un motor de combustión interna.

Interferencia electromagnética   Causa problemas a las señales de computadora.

Inyección directa   Combustible inyectado directamente al cilindro.

Inyección indirecta   El combustible es inyectado a una pequeña antecámara que es conectada al cilindro por una apertura delgada.

Inyector de unidad electrónica hidráulica Los componentes que reemplazan la bomba de inyección mecánica tradicional, incluyen una bomba de aceite de alta presión y un depósito, un regulador de presión para el aceite, y pasajes en la cabeza del cilindro para que el combustible fluya a los inyectores.

Jam nut Segunda tuerca aplicada para inmovilizar la tuerca original.

JASO Siglas en inglés para la Organización de Estándares Automovilísticos de Aceites de Motor. Las pruebas JASO utilizan motores japoneses pequeños y sus evaluaciones requieren estándares de desgaste de tren de válvulas más exigentes que los estándares de aceite de motor de otros países.

Junta de estanqueidad superior Casquillo que es utilizado entre la cabeza del cilindro y el bloque del motor.

Junta de Recursos Atmosféricos de California (CARB por sus siglas en inglés) Una agencia del Estado de California que regula los estándares de calidad de aire para el estado de California.

Keepers *Véase* **Seguros de válvulas.**

LED Siglas en inglés para diodos fotoemisores. Una fuente de luz de alta eficiencia que utiliza muy poca electricidad y produce muy poco calor.

Leyes de derecho de saber Leyes que requieren que los negocios exhiban hojas de datos sobre la seguridad de materiales para que todos sepan cuáles materiales peligrosos se utilizan en su lugar de trabajo.

Lima Una herramienta para suavizar el metal.

Lima de corte sencillo Una lima que solamente tiene una fila de dientes cortantes.

Lima doble Una lima que tiene dos filas de dientes que cortan en ángulo opuesto.

Limpiadora ultrasónica Piezas se colocan en un tanque de solución limpiadora, que después se vibra a una velocidad ultrasónica.

Línea central de admisión El punto donde se alcanza la máxima abertura de admisión con respecto al PMS es el la línea central, generalmente de 106°. Este punto se puede cambiar al momento de instalar las levas.

Llave Cualquiera de varios tipos de herramientas manuales o neumáticas típicamente de quijadas fijas o ajustables, utilizadas para sostener, apretar y girar objetos tales como pernos, tuercas o remaches.

Llave acodada Una llave de apriete que tiene un codo que encaja sobre el cabezal de una tuerca o tornillo.

Llave combinada Un tipo de llave que tiene un extremo abierto y el otro en forma de estría.

Llave de boca ajustable Llave con una quijada móvil que le permite adaptarse a tamaños diferentes de sujetadores de tuerca.

Llave de cierre Una llave que se utiliza para retirar el ajustador de seguridad que asegura una línea de freno u otra línea o ducto similar.

Llave de impacto Una herramienta manual neumática utilizada para instalar y retirar tornillos, remaches, pernos u otros fijadores enroscados.

Llave de torsión de tipo *clicker* Un tipo de llave de torsión que inicialmente se ajusta a una torsión determinada y que posteriormente avisa, al usuario, mediante un el sonido de un clic que dicho nivel de torsión ha sido conseguido.

Llave dinamométrica Un tipo de llave de par que indica la torsión que se está aplicando a un ajustador mediante la posición de un sujetador por medio de la posición de un mano y una escala en el mango de la llave que indica la torsión aplicada.

Llave para tuercas cónicas Un tipo de llave utilizada para retirar líneas de combustible, de frenos o del aire acondicionado.

Llave poligonal de conexión perpendicular Un tipo de llave que se desliza a un lado del perno o tuerca. Se usa cuando el acceso por arriba al perno o tuerca se hace difícil.

Llave torsionométrica Una herramienta que registra la cantidad de torsión aplicada.

LOC Siglas en inglés para convertidor tipo *light-off*.

Lubricación hidrodinámica Una película de aceite con forma de cuña se forma entre el bloque movible y la superficie. Esta acción de cuña depende de la fuerza aplicada a cuan rápida es la velocidad entre los objetos y la espesura del aceite.

Lubricación limite Cuando el aceite es lo suficientemente espeso para evitar que las superficies se choquen entre si pero que puede evitar un mínimo de contacto entre ellas.

Lugging En la jerga de mecánica automotriz, *lugging* se refiere al concepto de aumentar la apertura de la mariposa sin incrementar la velocidad del motor.

Luz de trabajo *Véase* **Luz de utilidad.**

Luz de utilidad Una luz utilizada para ver en áreas oscuras. También se llama luz de trabajo.

Luz incandescente Un tipo de luz que usa una fuente de luz incandescente en lugar de fluorescente o LED.

M85 Un combustible de motor de combustión interna que contiene un 85% de metanol y un 15 % de gasolina.

Maneral (trinquete) de aire comprimido Una herramienta manual que funciona a base de aire comprimido utilizado para propulsar una llave de cubo.

Manguito   La parte de un micrómetro que se gira para mover el husillo.

Marcas de identificación   En los motores de empujadores de válvula internos, los identificadores usualmente son colocados en el lado que opera el árbol de levas.

Martillo de mazo de precisión   Un tipo de martillo que tiene plomo (en forma de perdigones pequeños) al interior de su mazo de acero el cual es posteriormente recubierto con plástico y utilizado para aplicar una fuerza bruta a un objeto.

Material cáustico   Limpiadores químicos o jabones abrasivos y fuertes.

Materiales Acídicos   tienen un número de pH que oscila entre 1 y 6.

Matriz reforzada con fibra   Un material cerámico similar al utilizado para construir las bobinas de encendido insuladores. Es un material liviano con excelente resistencia al desgaste y buenas propiedades de transferencia del calor, haciéndolo ideal para el uso como material para el cilindro.

Medidor de espesores   *Véase* **Calibrador de hoja.**

Medidor de tobera de inyección de diesel o *Pop Tester*   Un dispositivo que se usa para analizar la tobera de inyección de diesel para asegurarse que tiene un patrón de chorro aceptable.

Mercurio   Un metal pesado.

Metal Babbitt o metal blanco   El metal Babbitt es el metal para rodamientos de automovil más antiguo. Isaac Babbitt (1799–1862) creó esta aleación por primera vez en 1839. Un excelente metal para rodamientos, cuya composición original era una aleación de plomo, estaño y antimonio.

Metanol   Alcohol elaborado a base de madera que se mezcla con gasolina para producir un combustible de motores. También se llama alcohol metilo. El metanol es venenoso, así como muy corrosivo a los componentes del sistema de combustible. La ley no permite más de un 5% en una mezcla de gasolina.

MeTHF   Metil-Tetrahidrofurano, un componente de los combustibles alternativos de serie P.

Método de separación de lóbulos   La separación entre el punto de máxima abertura de admisión y máxima abertura de escape se conoce como lobe separation.

Método Reid de presión de vapor   Un método para determinar la presión del vapor de la gasolina y otros hidrocarburos. Este método es ampliamente usado en la industria petrolera como un indicador de la volatilidad de la gasolina.

Método zyglo   Un método mediante el cual se pueden ver las rajaduras como luces brillantes cuando se las ve a través de una lámpara que emite Radiación electromagnética Ultravioleta cercana, es decir a través de luz negra.

Mezcla etanol-diesel   *Véase* **E-diesel.** Combustible diesel estándar #2 combinado con hasta un 15% de etanol.

Microbio   Un microorganismo que es demasiado pequeño para ser visto por el ojo humano.

Micrón   Una unidad de medida igual a 0,000039 pulgada.

Mijo   Una planta o carga de alimentación usado en la producción de etanol que requiere muy poca energía o fertilizante para su cultivo.

Miniconvertidor   Un pequeño convertidor de oxígeno de calentamiento rápido.

Miscible   Capaz de mezclarse con otros aceites (tales como otras marcas y nivel de viscosidad) sin causar ningún problema tal como el sedimento o lodo.

Módulo de encendido electrónico   Abre y cierra un circuito de encendido primario, mediante la apertura o cierre del camino de retorno a tierra del circuito.

Moler Máquina   que corta nueva superficia en metal, usando herramientas especiales para cortar metal, fijadas en un disco.

Monobloque   El cilindro, la camisa de agua, los cojinetes principales y los ductos de aceite, están todos integrados en una estructura única para lograr así mayor fortaleza y operación más silenciosa.

Motor de combustión externa   Combustión del motor que ocurre fuera de la cámara de poder.

Motor de combustión interna   Combustión del motor que ocurre al interior de la cámara de combustión.

Motor radial   Motor de combustión interna cuyos cilindros yacen en un plano horizontal.

Motor rotativo   Un motor del tipo de combustión interna en el que el ciclo termodinámico se realiza en un mecanismo totalmente rotativo sin los elementos habituales del motor alternativo, pistón, biela y cigüeñal.

Motor tipo boxeador   Un tipo de diseño de motor que es plano y tiene cilindros oponibles. Se llama boxeador porque los pistones de un lado se asemejan a un boxeador durante la operación del motor. También llamado motor radial.

Motor Wankel   *Véase* **Motor rotativo.**

Movimiento lineal de levas   El movimiento longitudinal del árbol de levas en el motor durante su operación.

MSDS   Siglas en inglés para hojas de datos de seguridad física.

MTBE   Éter metil tertiario butílico es un líquido inflamable de olor característico desagradable. Funciona como aditivo para aumentar sus características de quemar. No se va a usar en el futuro por miedo de su contaminación de agua de tierra.

MTG   Metanol-a-gasolina, un proceso de refinación mediante el cual el metanol se convierte en gasolina líquida.

Muescas   Hendiduras maquinadas o forjadas en los cabezales de los pistones a fin de facilitar el huelgo a las válvulas.

Naturalmente aspirado   Se refiere a aquel motor de combustión interna que no es ni súpercargado ni turbocargado.

Necking   Jerga de mecánica automotriz que se refiere al fenómeno mediante el cual el varillado se debilita lo cual puede producir resquebramiento.

Nitruración   El cigüeñal es calentado a aproximadamente 540º C (1000 º F) en un horno lleno de gas de amoniaco y posteriormente enfriado. Dicho proceso añade nitrógeno (del amoniaco) al interior de la superficie del metal lo cual lleva a la formación de nitritos duros en la superficie del cigüeñal a una profundidad aproximada de 0,8 mm.

NO$_X$ óxidos de nitrógeno, los cuales cuando se combinan con el HC y la luz solar forman esmog.

Número BIN   Un rango de medición de la Agencia de Protección Ambiental que indica la "suciedad" de las emisiones de un vehiculo. Un rango Bin bajo (Vg., Bin 3) es considerado muy limpio, mientras que los números Bin más altos son indicativos de emisión más altas.

Número de identificación de vehículo (VIN por sus siglas en inglés)   Número alfanumérico que identifica el tipo, fábrica de ensamblaje y tren de fuerza entre otras cosas del vehículo.

Número de metal moldeado   Una serie de números y/o letras moldeadas en los componentes principales, tales como el bloque motor o las culatas.

Obturador de cabezal de cilindro   Un diafragma usado entre la cubierta de la válvula y la culeta o cabezal del cilindro.

Obturadores de corcho–caucho   Obturadores que utilizan caucho sintético como soldador con el corcho.

Opacidad   El grado hasta el cual la luz ha sido bloqueada.

Orden de encendido   La orden para que la chispa sea distribuida a la bobina de encendido correcta y en el momento preciso.

Orgánico   Un término que se utiliza para describir algo que alguna vez haya gozado de vida.

Orificio de purga   Controla el flujo de aceite a través del rodamiento.

OSC   Siglas en inglés para capacidad de almacenamiento de oxigeno.

OSHA   Siglas en inglés de la Administración de la Seguridad y Salud Ocupacionales, agencia gubernamental que se ocupa de la seguridad en el lugar de trabajo.

País de origen   El primer número de un número de identificación de vehículo (VIN) que identifica el lugar donde fue ensamblado el vehículo.

Paladio   Un elemento que actúa como catalizador.

Paquete de Aditivos   Aditivos balanceados.

Pareja balancín   Los motores V-6 (de seis cilindradas) utilizan un muñón del cigüeñal de una manivela seccional para generar un encendido armonizado. Como resultado de esto, estas fuerzas causan que el motor se balancee de atrás para adelante.

Pasador de chaveta   Un circuito de metal utilizado para sostener las tuercas castillo al ser instalado a través de un orificio. Su tamaño se mide por diámetro y largo (por ejemplo, 1/8 pulgada × 1 1/2 pulgada). También llamado un *perno de chaveta.* Su nombre proviene de un antiguo vocablo inglés que significaba "cerrar o asegurar".

PASS   Siglas en ingles de "Pull, Pin, Aim, Squeeze". Acrónimo utilizado para acordarse como utilizlar un extinguidor de incendios.

PCV   Siglas en inglés para ventilación positiva del cárter del cigüeñal.

Perno   Un remache o fijador enroscado que tiene una cabeza en un extremo que se usa en coordinación con una llave que está disenado para insertarse a traves de agujeros en piezas ensambladas y asegurado por un perno macho que se ajusta por medio de torsion.

Pernos de culata   Pernos de cabecera que se extienden a lo largo y ancho del bloque de cilindros y terminan en el ducto de enfriamiento.

Pernos métricos   Pernos que se fabrican y diseñan según el sistema métrico.

Petrodiesel   Otro término para el diesel de petróleo, que es el combustible diesel ordinario refinado del crudo de petróleo.

Petróleo   Otro término para el crudo de petróleo. El significado literal de petróleo es "aceite de piedra".

PFE   Retroalimentación de presión EGR.

pH   Una medida de la acidez o alcalinidad de un material. Un ph de 7 es neutral; cuando es más alto de 7 es alcalino, y cuando es más bajo de 7 es acido.

Piedra moledora   *Véase* **Disco de grano grueso o fino.**

Pirolítico   Horno de altas temperaturas.

Pirómetro infrarrojo   Mide las temperaturas de entrada y salida.

Piso de levas   una vez que el pistón llega a cierta temperatura, este se habrá expandido lo suficiente a lo largo de su eje como para volverse redondo.

Pistola de aire comprimido   Una tobera manual que está adherida a una manguera de aire comprimido y que se utiliza para aplicar aire comprimido a un componente o a un dispositivo.

Pistón   Forma un piso móvil para la cámara de combustión.

Pistón de cabezal plano   Un tipo de pistón encontrado en motores de bajo costo y bajo desempeño.

Placa de empuje   Controla el empuje del límite del eje.

Planicies   Así se denominan las áreas que yacen entre una y otra ranura de los aros de pistón.

Platino   Un elemento que actúa como catalizador.

Polaridad   La condición positiva o negativa en relación con un polo magnético, determinada en un embobinado de ignición por la dirección de movimiento del embobinado.

Potencia mecánica   El producto de la fuerza mecánica.

PPO   Siglas en inglés de aceite de planta puro.

Precarga de botador   La distancia entre el asiento del empujador de válvulas al interior del botador y el anillo elástico del botador cuando el botador está en reposo sobre la base circular del árbol de levas y la válvula está cerrada.

Preconvertidor   *Véase* **Miniconvertidor.**

Prensa hidráulica   Una pieza de equipo de taller automotriz usualmente montada en el piso, que utiliza un cilindro hidráulico para remover e instalar componentes prensados, como los rodamientos.

Prensa troqueladora o prensa punzonadora   Un instrumento manual diseñado para usarse con un martillo para sacar remaches o sujetadores.

Probador de chispa   Verifica las bobinas de encendido.

Proceso de refinación de diesel FTD   *Véase* **Fischer-Tropsch.**

Propano   *Véase* **GLP.**

Prueba de arranque de vacío   La medición o determinación de la cantidad de vacío del múltiple de admisión durante el arranque es una prueba fácil de hacer para determinar si los aros y las válvulas del pistón están adecuadamente sellados.

Prueba de capacidad de carga   Un tipo de prueba de la batería donde una carga eléctrica se aplica a la batería y se monitorea el voltaje para determinar el estado de la batería.

Prueba de compresión dinámica   Una prueba de compresión hecho con el motor en trabajo, en lugar de hacerlo cuando el motor está arrancando, como se hace regularmente en una prueba de compresión regular.

Prueba de compresión en mojado   Cuando el aceite se usa para facilitar el sellado alrededor de los aros del pistón.

Prueba de compresión   Una prueba que se usa para comprobar la condición de las válvulas y de los aros del pistón.

Prueba de equilibrio de potencia   Una prueba para determinar si todos los cilindros están contribuyendo la misma cantidad de potencia.

Prueba de golpecitos fuerte   Involucra dar golpecitos (no golpes fuertes) en el convertidor catalítico usando una maleta de goma.

Prueba de papel   Sujete un pedazo de papel o una tarjeta de 30×50 cms. (inclusive un billete de dólar funciona para estos propósitos) a una distancia de 2,5 cms. del tubo de escape, mientras el motor está funcionando en marcha mínima. El pedazo de papel debería oscilar de una manera uniforme. Si el papel tiende a ser atraído hacia el tubo de escape, las válvulas de escape en uno o más cilindros podrían estar quemadas.

Prueba de perdida de presión del cilindro   Prueba mediante la cual se llena el cilindro de aire comprimido y el medidor indica el porcentaje de perdida de presión.

Prueba de vacío de marcha mínima   Un motor en buena condición debería estar enganchado en marcha mínima con una aspiración constante entre 17 y 21 pulgadas de mercurio.

Prueba de vacío   Una prueba que consiste en probar el motor para verificar si existe un vacío al intentar arrancar el vehiculo, vacío en relación a la marcha mínima y vacío cuando se alcanzan 2,500 RPM.

Prueba de voltaje de batería de circuito abierto   Una prueba realizada con un circuito abierto sin flujo de corriente y sin carga aplicada a la batería.

Prueba operativa de compresión   La prueba de compresión puede informar a u mecánico o técnico de servicio automotriz de la compresión relativa de todos los cilindros.

Puertos siameses   Cuando dos cilindros comparten el mismo puerto debido a restricciones de espacio.

Pulgadas de mercurio   Unidad de medida utilizada para medir un vacío.

Pulido de bloque   Un procedimiento mediante el cual la culata del bloque debe ser reconstruida con una máquina troquedora que pueda controlar la cantidad de metal retirado al momento de reencajar la culata a la cámara de combustión.

Pulso magnético   El pulso generador consiste en una rueda desencadenadora (relector) y de una bobina exploradora.

Pump-up   Ocasionalmente se operan los motores a velocidades excesivas. Esto tiende a hacer que la válvula se abra de par en par, lo que ocasiona el problema de flotador de válvula. Cuando existe un problema de flotador de válvula, crece la holgura del tren de válvulas. El elevador hidráulico acortara esta holgura tal como está diseñado para hacerlo. Sin embargo, cuando esto ocurre, aquello no permitirá que la válvula se cierre en su asiento, y a este problema se lo denomina *pump–up* en la jerga automovilística.

Punta cerrada   El extremo de una llave que aprieta un perno o sujetador en todos sus extremos.

Puntal   Un aparato que transfiere la fuerza aplicada al servo a la banda de transmisión. Un puntal puede estar ubicado entre el servo o el balancín y la banda, o entre el ancla y la banda.

Puntales   Parte o pieza integral de la suspensión que incluye los amortiguadores.

Punto de inflamabilidad   Es la temperatura mínima necesaria para que un combustible desprenda vapores que, al mezclarse con el oxígeno del aire u otro oxidante capaz de arder, originan una inflamación violenta de la mezcla. Esta inflamación no suele mantenerse, por lo que se origina una llama instantánea produciéndose el fenómeno que se conoce como centelleo.

Punto de nube (punto de enturbamiento)   La temperatura en que la cera que se encuentra en la mayoría de los combustibles de tipo diésel tiende a formar cristales que enturbian el filtro de combustible.

Rampa   Una elevación gradual en el contorno de las levas.

Ranuras   Ranuras en forma de anillos en el pistón que están localizadas entre la cabeza del pistón y la falda o zócalo.

Ranuras de calefacción   Actúan como bloqueadores de calor.

Ratio de compresión (RC)   El ratio del volumen del motor de cilindro con el pistón en punto muerto inferior (BDC) al volumen en punto muerto superior (TDC).

Ratio del cigüeñal   El numero de grados de rotación del cigüeñal entre los golpes de admisión y escape cuando ambas válvulas están abiertas.

Ratio superficie volumen   Una consideración importante de diseño para las cámaras de combustión.

RCRA   Siglas en inglés para ley de conservación y recuperación de recursos naturales.

Recocido   Tratamiento térmico que elimina las superficies duras de una fundición metálica con la finalidad de reducir las potenciales fisuras que se producen en el metal con los cambios de temperatura.

Rectificado de acabado   Medible en micro pulgadas: Cuanto más suave la superficie mas pequeño el número que lo mide (número RA). Mientras que el rectificado de acabado de un bloque o culata de cilindro maquinado es de 60 a 100 RA (promedio de asperaza), las típicas especificaciones para rectificado de acabado de los muñones del varillado del cigüeñal es de 10 a 20 RA.

Refrigerante amargo   Refrigerante que se hace amargo para ahuyentar a los animales.

Regeneración   El proceso de tomar la energía cinética de un vehículo en movimiento para convertirla en energía eléctrica y almacenarla en una batería.

Regla de la mano izquierda   Un método utilizado para determinar la dirección del movimiento de las líneas magnéticas de fuerza que rodean un conductor. La regla de la mano izquierda se usa en coordinación con la teoría del flujo de electrones ($-$ fluye hacia el $+$).

Regulador de presión   Un dispositivo regulador que mantiene una presión específica en un sistema.

Relación o ratio combustible–aire   Relación de aire combustible en una carga de admisión medible en peso.

Remache tubular   Un tipo de sujetador que utiliza una remachadora para jalar hacia afuera el remache hasta que este se deforme lo suficiente para formar un sujetador.

Rendijas de vapor   *Véase* **Agujero de purga.**

Resistencia   La calificación de fuerza de una tuerca.

Resistencia a la corrosión   La habilidad de un rodamiento de resistir el ataque de la acidez en el aceite.

Resistencia al rayado   Previene que los materiales de fundición y rodamientos se adhieran por efecto del gripado al varillaje mientras la lamina de aceite se descompone.

Resistencia extensible   El estrés máximo usado bajo tensión (fuerza longitudinal) sin causar rotura.

Resonador Helmholtz   Un tubo de resonancia, llamado así por el descubridor de la relación entre forma y valor de frecuencia. Herman L. F. von Helmholtz (1821–1894) de La Universidad de Hönizsberg en el Este de Prusia.

Resonar   Vibraciones audibles.

Resorte de válvula   Mantiene la válvula asentada y asegurada en el asiento.

Resorte termostático   Maneja una válvula que permite que el ventilador marche con rueda libre cuando el radiador está frío. A medida que se calienta el radiador hasta aproximadamente 65° C (150° F), el aire que toca el resorte termostático causa que el resorte cambie su forma.

Retropurgar   El uso de una pistola de aire especial para mezclar aire con agua. Se usa aire a presión baja así que no hace daño al sistema de enfriamiento.

Revestimientos de bronce guía   *Véase* **Buje de casquillo de pared delgada de aleación de bronce.**

RFG   Siglas en inglés de gasolina reformulada.

Rodamiento de buje   Buje de camisa.

Rodamientos de casquillo de precisión.   *Véase* **Casquillo de biela.**

Rodio   Un elemento que actúa como un catalizador.

Rompetuercas   Una herramienta manual diseñada para romper una tuerca que se ha oxidado y adherido a un perno o un tornillo.

Roscadora   Una herramienta que corta metal para crear roscas interiores después de taladrar un hueco del tamaño apropiado.

Rozamiento El vástago de la válvula se adhiere temporalmente a su guía cuando se cierra la válvula. Esta unión se rompe cuando la válvula es forzada a abrirse.

RTV Siglas en inglés para vulcanización a medio ambiente.

Rueda de brida giratoria La brida que se encuentra entre las muñequillas o los muñones extendidos del cigüeñal.

Salto de resorte de válvula La tendencia que tiene un resorte de válvula a vibrar.

Saturación El punto en que el máximo nivel de fuerza de un campo magnético es alcanzado.

Seguidor de dedo *Véase* **Seguidor de leva.**

Seguidor de leva Abre los trenes de potencia de la válvula superior del árbol de levas con un ratio similar al de una mecedora.

Seguros de válvulas Aseguran el resorte del vástago de la válvula.

Sellante acuoso (sello de agua) Una lámina de agua sobre el químico para prevenir la evaporación del químico.

Sello de vástago de válvula tipo paraguas Se adhiere firmemente al vástago de válvula y se mueve hacia arriba y hacia abajo con la válvula. Cualquier aceite que se derrama de los balancines se desvía hacia afuera sobre la guía de válvula, como agua se desvía sobre un paraguas.

Sellos de fábrica retorcidos Utilizados como sellos de aceite del cigüeñal trasero.

Sensor de combustible variable *Véase* **Sensor de composición del combustible.**

Sensor de compensación del combustible Un sensor utilizado en vehículos *flex-fuel* que proporciona información del contenido de etanol al PCM y la temperatura del combustible a medida que va pasando a través del sistema de distribución del combustible.

Sensor de composición del combustible Mide ambos, el porcentaje de la mezcla de etanol y la temperatura del combustible.

Sensor de la válvula EGR Un potenciómetro lineal en la parte superior del vástago de la válvula EGR que indica la posición de la válvula en la computadora.

Sensor de presión diferencial Diseñado para remover materia particulada de diesel, o negro de humo (hollín) de los gases de escape de un motor a diesel.

Sensor DPFE Este sensor mide la presión diferencial entre dos lados de un orificio colocado justo debajo del lado de escape de la válvula EGR.

Separación de lóbulos *Véase* **Centros de lóbulos.**

Separador de combustible-agua El agua pesa más que el combustible diesel y por lo tanto se hunde al fondo del separador.

Sierra para metales Un tipo de sierra utilizada para cortar metales que utiliza una cuchilla reemplazable.

Simétrico La cantidad de elevación en relación al punto máximo de alzado de un árbol de levas a menudo difiere entre las válvulas de admisión y las de escape. Si las especificaciones son idénticas entonces al árbol de levas se lo denomina simétrico.

Sincronización de base El tiempo de encendido antes de que la computadora sincronice el avance de ignición.

Sistema de encendido con distribuidor El término especificado por la Sociedad de Ingenieros Automotrices (SAE) para un sistema de encendido que usa un distribuidor.

Sistema de encendido electrónico Es el término especificado por el SAE para un sistema de encendido que no utiliza distribuidor.

Sistema de escape restringido Si el sistema de escape es restrictivo o restringido, el motor tendrá baja potencia, pero su funcionamiento será muy suave.

Sistema de flujo en serie Sistema en el cual el refrigerante fluye alrededor de los cilindros en cada bloque de cilindros. Todo el refrigerante fluye a la parte posterior de cada bloque donde se encuentra el principal ducto de refrigeración el cual permite que dicho refrigerante fluya hacia la junta de estanqueidad.

Sistema de flujo en serie paralelo Algunos motores utilizan una combinación hibrida de sistema de flujo en serie con sistema de flujo en paralelo.

Sistema de flujo paralelo El refrigerante fluye dentro del bloque bajo presión para posteriormente cruzar la junta de estanqueidad oí el obturador hacia la culata a través del ducto de refrigerante principal que está al lado de cada cilindro.

Sistema de reciclaje del refrigerante Cuando el sistema se enfría la presión en el sistema refrigerante se reduce y dando lugar a la formación de un vació parcial en su lugar. Esto jala el refrigerante del contenedor de plástico y lo succiona d vuelta al interior del sistema refrigerante lo cual permite que el sistema este constantemente lleno.

Sistema de transferencia de flujo de culeta Cuando se colocan las válvulas de entrada y de escape en lados opuestos de la cámara de combustión se genera un camino fácil para el flujo desde el puerto de entrada al puerto de salida a través de dicha cámara de combustión.

Sistema electrónico de encendido El sistema consiste de una unidad generadora de pulso en el distribuidor (bobina exploradora y reluctor).

Sistema para la recirculación de los gases de escape (EGR) Es el proceso de pasar una pequeña, y medida cantidad de gas, de vuelta al motor para reducir las temperaturas de combustión y la formación de NOx (óxidos de nitrógeno).

Sleeving Termino que describe cuando los bloques de cilindro con gubias profundas puede ser salvado al taladrar el cilindro y rebajarlo a una dimensión mucho mayor para que de esta manera pueda casi encajar en las dimensiones de la funda del cilindro. Posteriormente, la funda es gripada al bloque reconfigurado y, entonces, el centro de la funda es taladrado para encajar las dimensiones del diámetro del pistón.

Sobrepresión Un incremento de la presión del aire por encima de la atmosférica. Medible en libras por pulgada cuadrada.

Soluble Que se disuelve con un químico o con un solvente.

Solución acuosa La mayoría de los químicos acuosos de silicatos y mezcladas con agua.

Solvente Líquido, usualmente incoloro, que se utiliza para quitar el aceite y la grasa.

Soporte de Seguridad hidráulico para automóvil Un aparato metálico que cuenta con un soporte vertical ajustable diseñado para soportar el peso de un vehículo una vez que este ha sido elevado por encima del suelo. También conocido como un Soporte para Gata.

Soporte por gato *Véase* **Soporte de seguridad para automóvil.**

Supercargador Un compresor de gas que inyecta más aire a la cámara de de combustión de un motor de combustión interna.

Superficie principal de empuje El lado de un cilindro de motor que recibe la mayor fuerza de empuje del pistón durante el golpe de poder.

Superficies piloto Asemejan agujeros con bordes sobresalientes en los pernos que conectan con el varillado.

SVO Siglas en inglés para aceite vegetal directo.

Syn gas Gas sintético creado como resultado de una reacción química entre el vapor y el carbón. El gas sintético esta principalmente compuesto de hidrogeno y monóxido de carbono y se utiliza para crear metanol. El Syn gas también es conocido como gas artificial.

Tabla de servicio Una pequeña plataforma montada sobre ruedas y diseñada para que un mecánico se recueste sobre ella a fin de deslizarse debajo de un vehículo y tener suficiente margen de maniobra.

Taladrado final Un agujero taladrado en cada extremo de una raja a fin de evitar que esta rajadura se siga propagando.

Taladro de aire comprimido Un taladro que opera con la fuerza generada por la presión elástica del aire condensado. También conocido como un taladro neumático.

Tamaño de casquillo El tamaño de los casquillos medido en fracciones de pulgadas cuadradas.

Tamaño de grano Tamaño de las partículas abrasivas de una muela abrasiva.

Tambor o escala graduada Parte de un micrómetro que tiene 40 graduaciones por pulgada.

TAME Éter metílico de amilo terciario. TAME es un combustible oxigenado y se usa como aditivo semejante a ETBE o MTBE.

Tanque de compensación Una reserva montada en el punto más alto del sistema de enfriamiento.

Tapones galeses Los agujeros dejados en las paredes exteriores del bloque de motor son maquinados y sellados con este tipo de tapón.

Tapones refrigerantes *Véase* **Tapones (sellos) del bloque del motor.**

Tapones (sellos) del bloque del motor Una subdivisión de los tapones o sellos en el bloque de cilindros o de la culata de un motor. El tapón tradicional es un disco cóncavo y delgado de metal que encaja en un hueco maquinado en la fundición y que se asegura presionando su centro para lograr la expansión del disco al interior de este hueco.

TDC Punto muerto superior del pistón.

Tecnología de aditivo orgánico (OAT por sus siglas en inglés) Refrigerante anticongelante que contiene etilenoglicol, pero que no contiene silicatos o fosfatos. Este tipo de refrigerante es, generalmente de color anaranjado y fue desarrollado inicialmente por Havoline bajo el nombre DEX-COOL, utilizado en vehículos de marca General Motors a partir de 1996.

Tecnología de aditivos inorgánica (IAT por sus siglas en inglés) Refrigerante convencional utilizado por más de 50 años. Los aditivos usados para proteger contra la oxidación y la corrosión incluyen el fosfato y el silicato.

Tecnología de aditivos orgánicos híbridos (HOAT por sus siglas en inglés) Los refrigerantes pueden ser de color verde, anaranjado, amarillo, oro, rosado, rojo o azul.

TEL Un aditivo que se agregó a la gasolina en los 1920s para reducir la tendencia de golpe de chispa.

Temperatura de operación normal Cuando el ventilador de enfriamiento ha ciclado de encendido a apagado al menos una vez después de que el motor ha sido encendido. Algunos fabricantes de vehículo especifican que el ventilador de enfriamiento debería ciclar dos veces.

Temperatura *Light-off* El convertidor catalítico no funciona cuando está frío, y por lo tanto debe calentarse hasta llegar a su temperatura *light-off*, que es un punto cerca a 260° C antes de poder comenziza trabajar por encima de un 50% de eficiencia.

Tenazas de bomba de agua *Véase* **Alicates o llaves multiranuradas ajustables.**

Tenazas de resorte Una herramienta manual que esta diseñada para instalar o retirar resortes de aro.

Tenazas tipo cobra   Un instrumento manual que tiene dos posiciones lo cual le permite el uso de dos diferentes aperturas de diverso tamaño.

Termofraccionación catalítica de las cadenas hidrocarburíficas   La desintegración de cadenas hidricarburicas utilizando el calor en presencia de un catalizador.

Throating   Un proceso de sacar metal del lado del asiento más cercano al orificio, levantando el límite más bajo del asiento.

Tier   Una categoría de regulación ambiental creado por EPA (Agencia de protección ambiental). Las regulaciones *Tier 1* se están reemplazando gradualmente con las regulaciones de *Tier 2,* que son más estrictas.

Tijeras de hojalatero   Una herramienta de mano usada para cortar metal de chapas, cartón ligero o material semejante.

Tijeras de hojalatero de aviación   Herramientas especialmente diseñadas para cortar láminas de metal.

Tijeras de hojalatero de tipo corte recto   *Véase* **Tijeras de hojalatero de aviación.**

Tijeras de hojalatero decaladas   Un tipo de par de tijeras de hojalatero que se diferencian por tener una quijada curva lo cual les permite realizar cortes transversales izquierdos o derechos.

Tipo Morse   *Véase* **Árbol de levas tipo cadena silenciosa.**

Tornillo de tope   Un nombre para un perno que se coloca en una pieza moldeada, tal como un bloque de motor.

Tornillo o tuerca auto cortante   Un tornillo que tiene un puntal puntiagudo lo cual le permite crear roscas en el metal.

Tornillos de banco   Una herramienta de sujeción adherida a un banco de trabajo que tiene dos mordaza para inmovilizar el objeto deseado firmemente en un lugar fijo.

Torque-to-yield   *Véase* **Ángulo de torsión.**

Traba de vapor   Combustible vaporizado, usualmente en las líneas de combustible, que previene o aplaza la provisión del combustible a los cilindros.

Transistor   Interruptor electrónico.

Trinquete   Un maneral usado para girar un casquillo, el cual es reversible y permite que el casquillo gire a su vez en una dirección lo cual, a su vez, libera el aparato para moverse y girar en la dirección opuesta.

Troquel amolador o esmerilador   Un instrumento de aire operado a mano que se utiliza con una piedra de molienda (o lima) o un cepillo de alambre.

Troquel cortante   Instrumento o máquina de bordes cortantes para recortar o estampar, por presión, planchas, cartones, cueros, etc. El troquelado es, por ejemplo, una de las principales operaciones en el proceso de fabricación de embalaje de cartón.

Tube-nut wrench   *Véase* **Llave de cierre.**

Tubos principales   Fabricados de láminas de bronce de 0,1 a 0,3 milímetros (0,0045–0,012 pulgada) utilizando los materiales más delgados posibles para cada aplicación. Entonces el metal es enrollado en tubos circulares y las juntas son selladas o soldadas con un fijador de cierre.

Tuerca de acompañamiento o de inmovilización   *Véase* **Jam Nut.**

Tuftriding   Un nombre registrado, utilizado por General Motors para el proceso de calentar el cigüeño en un baño de sal de cianuro.

Turbocargador   Un sobrecargador que toma su fuerza del escape.

Turbocargador o súpercargador enraizado   Es lo que se conoce como un diseño de desplazamiento positivo porque todo el aire que ingresa es forzado a pasar por la unidad.

TWC   Convertidor catalítico de triple acción que convierte todas las tres emisiones (NO_X, HC y CO) en dióxido de carbono (CO_2) y agua (H_2O).

UCG   Gasificación subterránea de carbón.

UCO   Aceite de cocinar usado.

ULSD   Combustible diesel de contenido ultra-bajo de azufre. Combustible diesel con contenido máximo de azufre de 15 partes por millón.

Un tipo   de tijeras de hojalatero que con un diseño de quijada curva para permitir un corte recto en las láminas de metal.

UNC   Rosca cruda por estándar UNC (*unified national course*).

UNF   Rosca fina por estándar UNF (*unified national fine*).

Unidad de control electrónico   Módulo para el EIS.

Unión universal   Una unión en el eje de dirección o en el eje propulsor que permite la transmisión de torsión a un ángulo.

vacío   Este actuador está controlado por el PCM y se usa para controlar el grado de vacío aplicado a un mecanismo operado a vacío.

Válvula antivaciado   Válvula que previene que el aceite se salga del filtro cuando el motor está apagado.

Válvula circular o válvula champiñón   La válvula es abierta por medio de una válvula de tren que es operada por una leva.

Válvula de cierre ajustable   Tiene un diseño de espiral ajustable que mantiene la válvula cerrada hasta que se produzca una repentina liberación de la mariposa.

Válvula de control de aceite (OCV por sus siglas en inglés)   Dirige la alimentación de aceite desde la culata o cabezal hasta la posición del varillado apropiada en los ductos de aceite del arbol de levas.

Válvula de desvío de compresión Este tipo de válvula de escape canaliza el aire presurizado a la toma de aire del turbocargador para su reutilización y opera silenciosamente.

Válvula de desvío Permite que el aire que ingresa por la toma de aire fluya directamente al múltiple de admisión sin necesidad de pasar por el súpercargador.

Válvula de escape Una válvula a través de la cual los gases quemados del cilindro de escape pasan hacia el múltiple de escape.

Válvula de escape o de alivio Ventila el aire presurizado de la tubería de conexión entre la salida del turbocargador y la mariposa cuando la mariposa está cerrada durante el aumento de la sobrepresión tal como ocurre cuando se cambia de marchas al cambiar la caja automática.

Válvula de retención o anti-retorno Contiene un disco metálico helicoidal o muelle y eje que cierra la línea de aire al experimentar contrapresión.

Válvula de ventilación *Véase* **Válvula de cierre ajustable.**

Válvula deflectora *Véase* **Sello de vástago de válvula tipo paraguas.**

Válvula elástica Es un tipo de válvula circular. La válvula elástica puede moldearse en la forma de una válvula de asiento. Esto le permite sellar fácilmente, pero trabaja produciendo mucho calor, y la flexión que realiza para adaptarse puede llevar a que se rompa.

Válvula electrónica (digital) de recirculación de gases de escape Esta válvula consiste de tres solenoides controlados por el PCM.

Válvula en culata o en cabeza Un tipo de motor de pistones que coloca el árbol de levas en el bloque de cilindros (usualmente a lado y levemente por encima del cigüeñal en un motor recto o directamente encima del cigüeñal en el ángulo que se forma en forma de V en los motores tipo V) y que utiliza empujadores de válvula o varillas para accionar los brazos mecánicos encima de la culata o cabezal de los cilindros a fine de poner en funcionamiento las válvulas.

Válvula rígida Tipo de válvula circular. La válvula rígida es una válvula fuerte que mantiene su forma y es una buena conductora del calor. También causa una menor secesión de válvula. Sin embargo, desafortunadamente, esta válvula también es más propensa a derrames y a quemarse que cualquier otro tipo de cabeza de válvula.

Válvula variable sincronizada (VVT por sus siglas en inglés) Una válvula que utiliza un sincronizador de levas que puede alterar la relación del árbol de levas con el cigüeñal desde una retardación de 15 grados hasta una retardación de 25 grados (40 grados de retardación en total).

Varilla conector Una varilla que transmite el movimiento o la potencia de una parte en movimiento a otra, en especial designa a aquella varilla conector que conecta el cigüeñal de un motor de vehiculo a un pistón.

Varillaje en bloque Los motores de empujadores de válvula tienen a las levas ubicadas al interior del bloque.

VCA Vehículos de combustibles alternativos.

VECI Siglas en inglés para información de control de emisiones de vehículos. Esta etiqueta o calcomanía se encuentra debajo del capó de todos los vehículos e incluye aquella información relativa al control de emisiones importante para el mecánico o técnico automotriz.

Vehículos bicombustibles o vehículos *flex* Un término utilizado para describir un vehículo que es capaz de moverse con pura gasolina o con una mezcla de gasolina y etanol.

V-FFV Siglas en inglés de vehículo de combustible flexible virtual. Este diseño de sistema de combustible no utiliza un sensor de compensación de combustible, a cambio de el, utiliza el sensor de oxígeno del vehículo para ajustarse a las diferentes composiciones del combustible.

VGN Vehiculo a gas natural.

VI Siglas en inglés de índice de viscosidad. Un índice del cambio en la viscosidad del aceite del motor entre extremos calientes y fríos.

Vibración primaria Una vibración fuerte de baja frecuencia que ocurre cuando los pistones se mueven de arriba para abajo al interior de los cilindros.

Vibración secundaria Una vibración débil causada por una pequeña diferencia en la inercia de los pistones en TDC en comparación al BDC.

Viscosidad Medida de qué tan fácilmente puede fluir un líquido.

Vise Grips® La marca comercial de unas tenazas o alicates bloqueantes.

Volatilidad La medida de la tendencia de un líquido a cambiar a vapor. La volatilidad se mide utilizando una unidad denominada RVP (por sus siglas en inglés) o presión de vapor Reid.

VTEC Siglas en inglés de un sistema de control en base a una serie de válvulas desarrollado por la Compañía de Motores Honda para mejorar el rendimiento y la eficiencia del motor sobre un rango amplio de RPM.

Washcoat Un material poroso de aluminio.

Wastegate Una válvula de desvío que se encuentra en la admisión de escape de la turbina.

WHMIS   Siglas en inglés para sistema de información sobre materiales peligrosos en el lugar de trabajo.

WVO   Siglas en inglés para desecho de aceite vegetal.

WWFC   Siglas en inglés de tabla mundial de combustibles. Un estándar de calidad de combustible desarrollado por los fabricantes de motores en el 2002.

ZDDP   Comúnmente llamado dialquil ditio fosfato de zinc. El uso original del ZDDP era el de reducir la fricción deslizante en los motores.

Zócalo móvil   La funda de aluminio forjado del pistón se reduce a su mínima expresión utilizando un zócalo móvil del tipo abierto.

INDEX